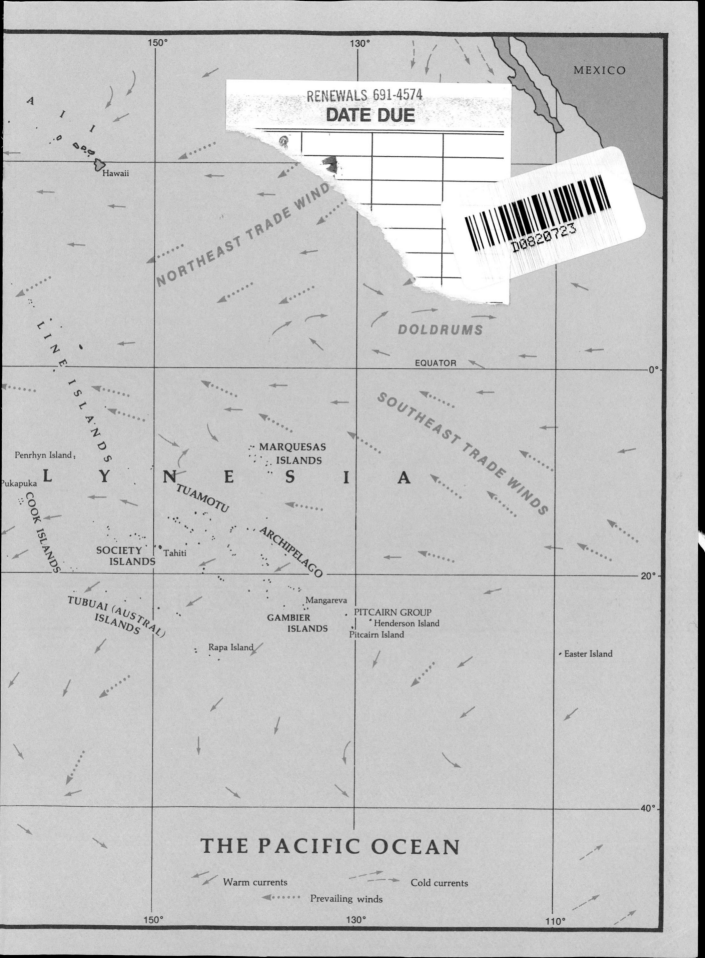

THE PACIFIC OCEAN

Warm currents · · · → Cold currents

◄····· Prevailing winds

The Prehistory of Polynesia

The Prehistory of Polynesia

JESSE D. JENNINGS, editor

HARVARD UNIVERSITY PRESS • Cambridge, Massachusetts, and London, England • 1979

Library of Congress Cataloging in Publication Data
    Main entry under title:

The Prehistory of Polynesia.

    Bibliography: p.
    Includes index.
    1. Man, Prehistoric—Polynesia. 2. Polynesians
—Origin. I. Jennings, Jesse David, 1909–
GN670.P7   996   79-1055
ISBN 0-674-70060-0

Acknowledgments

My sincere thanks must go, first and foremost, to the chapter authors. Each contributor cooperated fully by providing finished manuscripts in time to meet the deadline I proposed; each found and submitted the appropriate illustrations; each graciously and quickly complied with my requests for changes, deletions, or reductions in chapter length. Such unanimous support is rare in the life of an editor; failure to acknowledge it would be ungratefully remiss on my part.

Equally, I appreciate the unstinting, intelligent assistance in manuscript preparation I received from Edith Lamb and Talma Day through the months in which this volume took shape. And, once again, I must express my gratitude to my wife, Jane C. Jennings, who for years has been patient with my slow progress toward the completion of tasks and who has been the final reader of everything I have written, commenting on the manuscripts with critical skill.

As usual, I benefited greatly from getting better acquainted with the available data, but even more from my association with the scholars who wrote this book.

J.D.J.

Contents

Introduction

JESSE D. JENNINGS

For over two centuries the islands of the Pacific have been objects of curiosity and study because of a perennial romantic interest in the origins of their beautiful people. Thanks to radiocarbon dating and the discovery of Lapita pottery, there has been great progress in our understanding of these islands, their history, the mode of their settlement, and the close relationships among them. In addition to the changes in ideas that have come in the past decade or two because of the increasing number of young scholars at work in the area, there are hundreds of laymen who have a serious interest in the peoples of the Pacific and their history; yet there has been no organized presentation of findings. *The Prehistory of Polynesia* is an outgrowth of such diverse factors as recognized need, increasing knowledge, greater coherence of that knowledge, and the excitingly long history (3,000 years or more) of Polynesian settlement during which the islands were discovered and colonized by Southeast Asians.

My own interest in the South Pacific goes back many years; my direct contribution to the study of Polynesian prehistory consists in four seasons of research in Western Samoa. Through the years I have become acquainted with a number of students working on various aspects of Polynesian prehistory. At the invitation of the Harvard University Press, I undertook to assemble a group of scholars knowledgeable in one aspect or another of Polynesian archaeology, or in such areas as linguistics, agriculture, or physical type. I invited the individuals whose chapters follow to join me in the preparation of a book that would be written simply, as free of jargon as possible, to serve as an introductory text for undergraduate students and perhaps as a guide for use in graduate seminars. It ought also serve to introduce the lay reader to the entire field.

Readers who detect contradictory opinions from chapter to chapter should not assume that the editor has been dozing. The contradictions have been noted and left, because the contributors were explicitly asked to state *their* views.

It should be remarked that all the contributors constantly draw on historically observed ethnographic practices or customs in arriving at their conclusions. Their employment of observed data underlines a basic fact of Polynesian research: there the present is the past to a greater extent than almost anywhere else. In Polynesia the linguists, the archaeologists, and the ethnographers can still talk to, and draw data freely from, one another.

The arrangement of the chapters is entirely chronological, based on the time of the first discovery of an island chain by the founder population. Pioneer explorers called Lapita, from Southeast Island Asia (specifically off the eastern tip of New Guinea), reached both Tonga and Samoa by 1000 B.C. The first eastward movement farther into the Pacific is recorded for the Marquesas by A.D. 300. Thence went two groups, one to Easter Island by A.D. 400 and the other to Hawaii by A.D. 500. It is possible that another group went to the Societies shortly after their arrival in the Marquesas, but that thrust has not been proved. Certainly, a second movement to Tahiti (the Societies) occurred by A.D. 600 and from there to New Zealand by A.D. 800. Secondary dispersals from Tahiti to Hawaii and New Zealand after A.D. 1000 are possible but debated. These migrations are charted in Fig. I.1, from the dates established by radiocarbon assays provided by the contributors to this volume; the times, sequences, and directions of the spread of Polynesian culture over the Pacific are indicated.

The chapters of this book that summarize the archaeology of the region are arranged accordingly with the Lapita complex first; following it come Fiji, Samoa and Tonga, the Marquesas, Easter Island, Hawaii, the Societies, and, finally, New Zealand. The second cluster of chapters is a series of topical treatments in no particular order. In general, they represent new trends in archaeological research. The final chapter is a summary of the archaeological knowledge of Melanesia.

One other point should perhaps be mentioned. Pacific specialists may object to omission of some of the Polynesian outliers, small islands outside the Polynesian triangle but occupied by Polynesian populations. Most of the outliers seem to have been settled early, but both the archaeology and the language suggest origins at a major, previously settled island group. Hence these islands are not treated separately here, although scattered references to them occur in several chapters (especially Chapter 10).

In the first chapter of this volume, Bellwood provides an overview to acquaint those readers who lack previous knowledge of Oceania or of some of the geographic, ecologic, and prehistoric factors that shaped Oceanic, and hence Polynesian, prehistory. He then quickly reviews the broad outlines of the archaeological episodes that characterize the millennia before Christ. In order to do this he selects evidence from linguistics, physical types, and material and social traits, thereby touching on matters developed more fully in later chapters. He also provides some useful comparative information about Micronesia that is not included elsewhere in the book and occasionally expresses a view that differs from ideas supported by other scholars. In short, Bellwood has written a rapid indoctrination for the novice.

Chapter 2 is somewhat different from those that follow. Green provides a synthetic description of the Lapita culture,

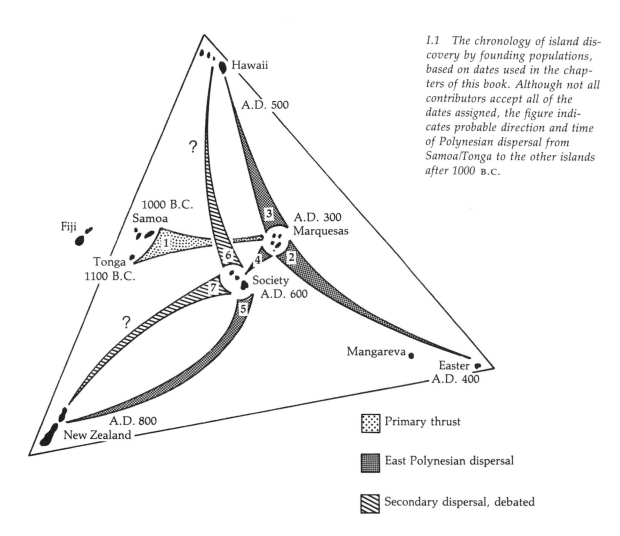

I.1 The chronology of island discovery by founding populations, based on dates used in the chapters of this book. Although not all contributors accept all of the dates assigned, the figure indicates probable direction and time of Polynesian dispersal from Samoa/Tonga to the other islands after 1000 B.C.

drawing on evidence from scores of locations across 2,500 km of ocean. His survey is more analytic than some that follow. Nonetheless, his arguments can be readily followed, and his description of Lapita is convincing because he points clearly to the gaps in the data. His chapter presents the best explanation to date of the origins of the Polynesian population and its recorded culture.

Chapter 3 describing Fiji seems, at first glance, to be a recital of what is *not* known. Research there in all fields of anthropology has been frustrating to scholars, revealing many more contradictions and discrepant findings than any location east of New Guinea. In archaeology, only just begun,

the data allow even fewer solid conclusions. Frost's account faces the situation. Thus, if he offers slimmer findings than some of the later authors, the fault lies not with him but with the state of knowledge. About all we can be sure of is that Fiji is truly a mixture of Melanesian and Polynesian elements; the problem comes in attempting to separate them into a reasonable order, a complex task not yet accomplished. What Frost has been able to present is a relative culture sequence based almost entirely on stratified ceramic material; to this control sequence he relates a series of special studies dealing with forts and other monumental remains of considerable intrinsic interest. It is evident that no well-rounded culture history, no complete culture descriptions, no reliable environmental data have been generated for the Fijian group. This condition will improve but slowly. In the meantime, we can be sure only that Fiji lies "midway from everywhere."

Chapter 4, which deals with the evidently near-contemporary Samoan/Tongan development, chronicles the transformation of Lapita into Polynesia, the two groups being regarded as the cradle of Polynesian culture. Artifacts reminiscent of Lapita, but equally presaging the Marquesan tools, are carefully described. Contradictory evidence from Tongan sites is to some extent sorted out. Although there are difficulties with the data as reported, Davidson comes up with a credible, if sometimes thin, sequence of events for these islands that are regarded as the staging area for the eastward expansion into the Pacific.

Chapter 5 is a compact account of the first of the East Polynesian cultures. The Marquesans, their islands evidently first occupied by A.D. 300 by immigrants from Samoa/Tonga, were the ancestors of all East Polynesians (see Fig. I.1). The artifacts and cultural phases observed here by Sinoto provide the comparative base for all the cultures of the other major chains and are the crucial link between West and East Polynesia. Sinoto's chapter is an extensive reworking of a previously published article listed in the bibliography to Chapter 5 as Sinoto 1970. Expanded in content, though somewhat shortened through deletion of detail, it is for practical purposes new.

Chapter 6 will surprise most readers. Few would suspect that lonely Easter Island is better understood than any other Pacific location. McCoy first reviews the history of research; next, he evaluates a series of studies by nonanthropologists, ending the survey with a careful review of Heyerdahl's romantic and widely known theories. Then he moves to a consideration of architecture, portable artifacts, and social organization, devoting several matter-of-fact pages to a description and explanation of the fabled statues. It is hard to remember, as 1,600 years of history are unveiled, that upon this tiny island (less than 400 km²) the full Polynesian story—settlement, population growth, cultural adaptation to a new environment, ecological damage, stratified society—is seen in microcosm.

In Chapter 7 Tuggle's description of Hawaiian culture at the time of white contact is based upon combined archaeological and ethnohistoric information. The sources of information about the Hawaiian past are summarized in a historical context. Two studies of regional archaeological research are presented. The origins of Hawaiian culture and changes in it that took place before outside contact are surveyed. Finally, Tuggle considers some of the processes that may have been involved in the evolution of Hawaiian culture.

From Kenneth P. Emory, the dean of Polynesianists, comes Chapter 8. Written in his eightieth year (after more than 50 years with the Bishop Museum in Honolulu), his contribution offers much more than the Society Island sequence. He draws on vast knowledge as he makes comparisons that range the entire Pacific. His chapter, though short, is one of the most stimulating in the book, especially as he differs with some of the views expressed in other chapters.

New Zealand, analyzed in Chapter 9, was the last of the major island groups to be discovered by the Polynesians. It has been the object of prehistoric study for more than a century; Davidson charts the phases of study and the rationale for each phase. The confusion that results from imperfect data, a reliance on legend, the lack of any theoretical models, and insulation from other Polynesian studies is explained. Her chapter, more or less a résumé of the unordered present state of knowledge in New Zealand despite the long period of study, also provides insights into current thought and indicates new trends in archaeological research—settlement patterns, adaptation, culture change.

Clark's Chapter 10 on language divides

readily into three sections. The first deals simply with a series of linguistic concepts that the layman needs in order to follow the evidence. Then comes the evidence that bears on the relatedness of the Polynesian languages and the significance of the relationships. Last is a review of progress in the fascinating reconstruction of the long-dead parent tongue, proto-Polynesian, possibly spoken by the Lapita themselves.

In Chapter 11 Howells analyzes the biological problems involved in tracing Polynesian origins. He succinctly summarizes present knowledge to demonstrate physical similarities of the several local Polynesian peoples. His identification of the Fijians as basically Polynesian in physical attributes will surprise readers who have been misled by the visible Fijian physical traits that resemble those of some Melanesian groups.

Although all chapters mention environmental constraints, Kirch in Chapter 12 deals directly with the matter of adaptive strategy by inspecting in detail the subsistence practices of several locations where natural resources are scant. The use of ethnographic models in the interpretation of archaeological data—ethnoarchaeology—is well exemplified.

In Chapter 13 Bellwood attempts to supply some generalizations about the few, but important, studies of settlement patterns at scattered locations over the Pacific. His conclusions are appropriately modest, reflecting the state of the art. Some of the studies were intensive ones in small areas, employing a minimum-effort/maximum-gain theory of settlement. Others were more concerned with mere distribution of human remains than with mini-max theory. Whatever the basis, Bellwood ties the studies together through the ecotonal principle—that is, the theory that preferred locations seem to lie on the boundary between two major ecological-resource zones. This principle is, of course, a variant of the more tightly applied mini-max basis. At the same time, Bellwood credits social organization as being highly relevant in a settlement's dispersal, whereas a rigorous mini-max approach would ignore social or ceremonial factors. The brevity of the chapter and the small number of samples selected result, of course, from the lack of abundant data.

For some readers Finney's Chapter 14 will be the high point of the book, as he describes one of the most exciting episodes in recent Polynesian research. Most of his chapter chronicles the building of a Hawaiian double-hull, oceangoing canoe and its epic 1976 voyage from Hawaii to Tahiti. The canoe, called the Hōkūle'a, traveled the entire distance using only Polynesian navigational techniques and skills from before the days of white contact; the result was an effective demonstration that long, open-ocean, two-way voyaging was possible with native watercraft and navigational lore before European navigational aids became available. The chapter becomes a cogent comment on the debated dispersal mode of Polynesians over the Pacific. The theory with which he closes the chapter, that changes in climate and weather patterns may have facilitated the dispersal and two-way voyaging, is one that should be testable by computer simulation.

White's Chapter 15 on Melanesia is included to provide a deeper chronological base than the treatment in Chapters 1 or 2. Some readers may prefer to consult it before reading Bellwood's overview in Chapter 1.

The Oceanic Context

CHAPTER 1

PETER S. BELLWOOD

As a distinct human population, characterized by unified origins and close ethnic homogeneity, the Polynesians were geographically the most widely spread people on earth prior to A.D. 1500. They alone settled the islands that are now called Polynesia, situated within the vast triangle formed by the Hawaiian Islands, Easter Island, and New Zealand (see Fig. I.1). With sides close to 6,500 km in length, this triangle covers almost twice the area of the continental United States, although the ratio of sea to land is in the vicinity of 70 to 1. The Polynesians began their expansion into this previously uninhabited zone soon after 1500 B.C. and had settled all major islands, including New Zealand, by A.D. 900.

The Geography of Oceania

Oceania (see Thomas 1967) comprises the three geographic areas of Melanesia, Micronesia, and Polynesia, which together contain 789 habitable island units (Douglas 1969) ranging in size from giant New Guinea at 800,000 km² to the tiniest coral atolls. Polynesia, with its 287 islands, is the largest geographic subdivision of Oceania, although its total land area of approximately 300,000 km² is much smaller than that of Melanesia. New Zealand, with 268,570 km², and the Hawaiian Islands, with 16,558, together account for about 95 percent of all Polynesian dry land.

The Pacific Ocean itself measures 20,000 km from Singapore to Panama.

While the greater part of this ocean is empty of land, a very large number of islands in tropical latitudes extend from the coasts of Southeast Asia as far as Easter Island. Beyond Easter Island lie an empty 4,000 km stretching to the South American coast. The islands of the Pacific also become smaller and more dispersed toward the east. In the far west lie the archipelagoes of the Philippines and Indonesia—large, close-set islands found for the most part on shallow shelves that extend out from the Asian continent. To the east of Indonesia lie the Melanesian islands—again large and close-set—comprising New Guinea, the Bismarck Archipelago, the Solomons, New Hebrides, New Caledonia, and Fiji. New Guinea actually forms a northerly extension of the Australian continent, having been joined to it by dry land (now the shallow Arafura Sea and Torres Straits) until the end of the last glaciation.

All these westerly archipelagoes share the presence of various volcanic and sedimentary rock types similar to those of the adjacent continents of Asia and Australia, rocks that have been subjected to comparable processes of folding and faulting. This zone is also within a belt of seismic instability that extends around the Pacific rim. Here earthquakes and explosive volcanic eruptions are frequently recorded; the famous volcano of Krakatoa lies between Java and Sumatra, and volcanoes of this explosive ash type extend as far east as Tonga and New Zealand. However, the islands of Polynesia (excluding Tonga and New Zealand) are totally different, and are generally formed of basaltic rocks extruded as lava from ancient volcanoes. Only on the island of Hawaii is there active vulcanism at present; the craters of Mauna Loa and Kilauea, although always at least gently active, do not exhibit the violent eruptions that occur so often on the Pacific rim. The Polynesian islands generally lack sedimentary rocks, other than recent alluvial deposits, and they are also much smaller and more widely separated than the islands of Melanesia. This circumstance of course made

their settlement by prehistoric voyagers far more difficult.

The best known of the Polynesian islands are the high volcanic formations (see Fig. 1.1) with their jagged profiles, deep gorge-like valleys, and cascading waterfalls. The Society, Hawaiian, and Samoa islands largely fall in this category, the Societies having the attractions of barrier reefs and gentle enclosed lagoons to add to their natural beauty. Some of the high islands lack barrier reefs; this is true of the very rugged Marquesas, as well as some of the Hawaiian Islands.

The atolls, thin strips of coral arranged like a necklace around a central lagoon, provide an extreme ecological contrast to the verdant high islands. They are the products of living coral reefs that have survived and grown since the submergence of the volcanic island to which they were originally attached. Since the resulting coral strips are raised only a few meters above sea level, these islands are extremely prone to hurricane devastation. More importantly, they lack fertile soil and surface water, so are generally poor environments for human settlement despite their well-stocked lagoons. There are quite a number of atolls in Polynesia, particularly in the northern Cook and Tuamotu islands, and they also tend to be very small in land area. The Tuamotus actually comprise 78 separate atolls, but total only 800 km² of land. Micronesia is the atoll region par excellence, and the many islands of the Carolines, Marshalls, and Gilberts are almost entirely of this form.

Between the high islands and the atolls are a number of intermediate island types, such as raised atolls or volcanic islands with raised circumferential barrier reefs. New Zealand is clearly a special case in most environmental matters (see Chapter 9). The descriptions in this chapter are concerned only with the smaller islands.

Climatically, the Polynesian islands are tropical, only Rapa and Easter Island being any distance below the Tropic of Capricorn. All have hot and fairly wet climates, with

1.1   *A view of Rarotonga, a typical Polynesian high volcanic island in the southern Cooks. Note the precipitous interior, deep valleys, and densely settled coastal strip. (Photo by author.)*

rainfall peaks generally between December and February (the southern summer). There is a belt of low rainfall in the eastern Pacific, running along the equator, but none of the major groups except the Marquesas fall in this belt. Elsewhere in Polynesia, rainfall usually exceeds 1,500 mm annually. Occasional summer hurricanes penetrate the region from the west and often cause severe devastation.

For the voyaging Polynesian, the prevailing directions of winds and currents obviously are of crucial importance. Both trend from east to west for most of the year. The trade winds blow from an easterly direction for most months, but may be replaced by occasional westerlies during the summer. Ocean currents also flow from east to west, except for a rather narrow west-east flowing countercurrent in the general vicinity of the equator. This means that a drifting canoe in Polynesia will normally move from east to west. Records of

past drift voyages, together with a more recent computer experiment (Levison et al. 1973), show this to be the case. In fact, the Polynesians would have been forced to sail close into the wind to discover many of their islands (see Chapter 14).

The Polynesian islands had little in the way of vegetable resources to support newly arrived human populations. All the major food plants and animals were introduced into Polynesia by man, with few truly indigenous plants—only some nuts, fruits, and fiber-producing plants—ever acquiring much importance. So the carbohydrate mainstays of Polynesian life—coconut, taro, yam, banana, breadfruit, and the food animals (pig, dog, and chicken)—were clearly transported intentionally by early voyagers. Marine animals were everywhere available. In New Zealand the earliest settlers were confronted also with a large edible avifauna, an unusual resource, but this was soon reduced to virtual extinction.

PETER S. BELLWOOD

Major Divisions of Oceania and Polynesia

The remainder of this chapter will utilize a number of terms connected with physical anthropology, languages, and cultural geography. Since not all readers will be familiar with these, I propose to introduce them here. In terms of physical anthropology, the peoples of Oceania fall into two major populations, the Australoids and the Mongoloids. The Australian aborigines are Australoids who have undergone very little contact with outsiders (prior to European settlement); the Melanesians are a much more varied component of the same basic race, but they have mixed to a greater extent with Southeast Asian Mongoloid populations. The Mongoloids are relative newcomers to the Pacific, and they comprise the Polynesians and the Micronesians. The Pacific Mongoloids are rather different in appearance from mainland peoples such as the Chinese and Vietnamese, and many of these differences relate to ancestral mixing with Australoid populations, especially in Melanesia.

The languages of Oceania have a slightly different geographic breakdown. The Australian languages and the Papuan languages of western Melanesia (to be described briefly below) form two unrelated groups of high antiquity; neither has close relatives elsewhere. The Polynesians and the Micronesians speak Austronesian languages related to those of Indonesia and the Philippines. However, Melanesia is a highly complex area and contains, together with the Papuan languages, a large number of diverse Austronesian languages spoken by Australoid peoples, who are physically only distantly related to the Polynesians and Micronesians.

Cultural geography in Melanesia will be dismissed for now, since it is too complex for a brief summary. In Micronesia, there are two main cultural and environmental divisions: western Micronesia (the volcanic Palau and Mariana islands) and nuclear Micronesia (the atolls of the Carolines, Marshalls, and Gilberts). These two divisions

have had different linguistic and archaeological histories, as we shall see. In Polynesia, the two main geographic divisions are the Polynesian triangle (with apexes in the Hawaiian Islands, New Zealand, and Easter Island) and outlier Polynesia, which includes a number of small islands with Polynesian-speaking inhabitants in Melanesia and the southern fringes of Micronesia. This outlier-triangle division is basically geographic, and the more meaningful cultural divisions follow rather different boundaries.

Two major cultural areas termed western Polynesia and central-marginal Polynesia were defined by Burrows in 1938. The islands within these divisions, together with a third division termed intermediate by Burrows, are shown in Fig. 1.2. Culturally, western Polynesia comprises Tonga, Samoa, the Ellice Islands (now called Tuvalu), and adjacent small islands, together with all the Polynesian outliers. Central Polynesia includes the Hawaiian, Society, southern Cook, and Austral islands with Rapa. Marginal Polynesia includes the Marquesas, Mangareva, Easter Island, and New Zealand. Today Burrows' scheme has been modified slightly, so that archaeologists consolidate the central and marginal groups as "eastern Polynesia," whereas they retain the original meaning of the term "western Polynesia."

The basic implication of this division is that the two areas have undergone rather separate sequences of development; for instance, several culture traits widely present in eastern Polynesia, such as tanged adzes, simple shell bait hooks for fishing, and human figures carved in stone or wood, are virtually absent in western Polynesia. The two regions had contrasting techniques of bark-cloth manufacture, house and temple building, and canoe construction; their kinship terminologies and religions were also unlike. These differences imply that the islands within each division apparently shared certain developments, through either common inheritance or borrowing. The classification is therefore fundamental

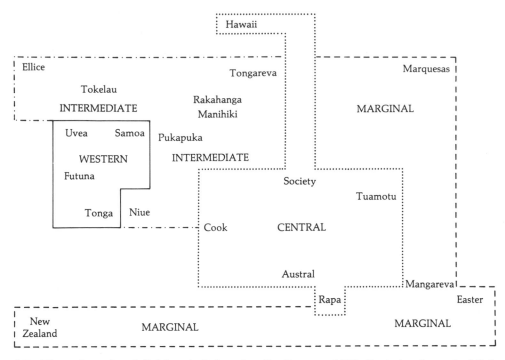

1.2 The major cultural divisions in Polynesia, after Burrows 1938. Central and marginal Polynesia today are usually grouped as eastern Polynesia. Within intermediate Polynesia Niue, Tokelau, Pukapuka, and Ellice are of western affiliation, while Rakahanga, Manihiki, and Tongareva are of eastern affiliation.

to an understanding of Polynesian cultural history.

The Peoples of Oceania

Through a large part of the 70,000 years since the beginning of the last glaciation, and until some 8,000 years ago, New Guinea and Australia were joined as one continent by the emergent Sahul Shelf and together offered an area of approximately 10 million km² for human settlement. On the other hand, at no time during the Pleistocene epoch was Indonesia ever a single land mass, owing to the persistence of numerous sea gaps to the east of the Wallace Line, which runs immediately east of Bali and Borneo. The first people to cross these gaps, possibly on rafts, were evidently *Homo sapiens* approaching the modern form. They were established in Australia by at least 40,000 years ago, and by implication in New Guinea as well. On genetic and phenotypic grounds the present indigenous populations of Australia and most of interior New Guinea may be classified as Australoids whose ancestors originally migrated into the area from Indonesia. Since the early Holocene period, New Guinea and Australia have been culturally and geographically separated by the drowning of the Sahul Shelf, and New Guinea today contains diverse populations, some of whom have attained dwarf stature in parts of the interior (the so-called Pygmies). In general, the peoples of New Guinea, and at the present time most of Melanesia, are characterized by dark skins, dark woolly hair, and varied stature. Further discussion of these traits appears in Chapter 11.

The question of just how far the Australoid populations penetrated into the Melanesian islands east of New Guinea before the expansion of the Mongoloids (that is, prior to 2000 B.C. in this area) remains unresolved. The high degree of physical and linguistic

PETER S. BELLWOOD

diversity among Melanesians suggests that they had spread as far as New Caledonia and the New Hebrides, but not to Fiji, by at least 3000 B.C. Recent evidence for an independent development of horticulture in the New Guinea highlands prior to 4000 B.C. supports this view, since horticulture implies that people have the economic means to establish viable settlements on small islands with rather impoverished natural resources as well as on large islands. If this view is correct, it implies that the populations ancestral to the Polynesians and eastern Micronesians, who were expanding through Melanesia after 2000 B.C., were obliged to coexist with resident Melanesian populations as far east as the New Hebrides. This situation, if verified, would be of considerable importance in the question of Polynesian origins. Older views (for example, those of Wurm 1967) that the Polynesians were the first settlers of the Melanesian islands east of New Guinea or the Solomons, and that they were later replaced by the expanding Melanesians, are in my view untenable, except possibly in the case of Fiji.

While most physical anthropologists would agree that the Mongoloids originated on the mainland of east Asia, there is very little evidence to date their expansion into Island Southeast Asia. The only fixed point in our chronology is their known expansion as far as Micronesia and Polynesia by 1500 B.C., and it seems reasonable to assume that they were replacing the Australoid populations of the Philippines and eastern Indonesia well prior to that date. The long period of mixing between Australoids and Mongoloids has, of course, left a clear imprint on the Polynesian physical type. In fact, individual Polynesians and Micronesians of today can be placed at various points along an Australoid-Mongoloid scale or gradient.

Genetic studies (summarized for Oceania in Simmons 1962; Kirk 1965, 1971) suggest that Australian Aborigines and highland New Guineans have retained a fairly close similarity in blood group frequencies and immunoglobulin markers. This supports a view of common ancestry, albeit a fairly ancient one. In addition, some geneticists have claimed that the Austronesian and Papuan speakers of the Markham Valley area of Papua New Guinea can be differentiated by certain marker genes (Curtain 1976); this possibility has relevance in assessing the linguistic evidence summarized below.

The genetic evidence for Polynesian origins is not presently so coherent as that for the Australoids of the western Pacific. Blood group frequencies, according to Simmons (1962), indicate some degree of similarity to the American Indians, although this situation is not altogether surprising since the Indians are basically Mongoloid peoples. It emphatically does not mean that the Polynesians came from the Americas. Indeed, recent recognition of the importance of the founder effect in human population genetics at the small-scale tribal level suggests that blood group gene frequencies alone may never give very reliable indication concerning ancient human migrations. The genetic evidence cannot be ignored, however, for it strongly suggests that Negroid or Caucasoid settlement in Oceania in prehistoric times is highly unlikely. It is equally unlikely that the Pygmies of New Guinea belong to a Negrito race of separate origin from the other inhabitants of Melanesia.

Oceanic Societies

The full prehistory of Oceania is meaningless if one ignores the ethnographic record. Of all the Oceanic peoples, the Polynesians are culturally and linguistically the most homogeneous and stem mainly from an isolate most probably located in the Tonga/Samoa islands in the late second millennium B.C. Further, Polynesian social structure is basically patrilineal and genealogically ranked, and elaborate hierarchical systems of rank and class developed in the chiefdoms of the Hawaiian, Society, and Tonga islands in particular (Sahlins 1958;

Goldman 1970). Although no Polynesian island group seems to have developed a fully centralized and unified state government in prehistoric times, many of the chiefdoms described by early European visitors clearly represented a degree of political integration greater than anywhere else in Oceania or Island Southeast Asia. It is my belief that these hereditary aristocracies developed during the period of ancestral Polynesian expansion into the western Pacific (Bellwood 1978).

Matrilineal societies, often with hereditary ranking, dominate most areas of Micronesia except Yap and the Gilberts (Mason 1968). The so-called Yapese Empire, involving a flow of tribute centered on politically dominant Yap and running through the Carolinean atolls for about 1,300 km to the east (Lessa 1950), is a phenomenon without parallel elsewhere in the Pacific. It seems to represent a political development in the atoll world of Micronesia parallel to, but different from, the chiefdoms on the larger tropical islands of Polynesia. When compared to Polynesia, the ethnic patterns in Micronesia reflect more varied origins, probably from the Philippines for the Palau and Mariana islands and from eastern Melanesia for the Carolines, Marshalls, and Gilberts. The Gilberts, in particular, have probably been in frequent contact with Polynesia also.

Melanesia, both racially and culturally, is the most diverse area of all. Hereditary ranking is present in some areas, especially Fiji, where fairly large chiefdoms may have developed in prehistoric times. But in many areas of Melanesia, especially in the west and in New Guinea, status is achieved rather than inherited. There, the "Big Man" concept developed, which merely means that political power is acquired through individual strength and qualities of leadership. The large islands of western Melanesia support complex mosaics of differing ethnic groups, mostly patrilineal in the New Guinea highlands, but with many matrilineal groups in island Melanesia. Individual trade partnerships tend to be very important, and elaborate trade networks that transcend ethnic boundaries are well-known from Papua, the New Guinea highlands, and the Solomons and Bismarcks especially. The "kula" cycle of the Massim district is perhaps the best known: it is based on a partner system, and on group voyages between neighboring islands (never around the whole system at once), when trade partners engage in exchange both of utilitarian goods and also of the nonutilitarian armshells and necklaces that travel in fixed directions around the islands and integrate the whole system. The kula cycle may be seen as a highly elaborate ritual, closely bound up with magic and considerations of personal status, which at base circulates needed goods to needy localities, but in more general terms serves a fundamental social function of high complexity.

Throughout Oceania subsistence economy (see Chapter 12) is based on the tuber and tree crops that are propagated by vegetative rather than seed methods, together with fishing in coastal areas and some pig husbandry and hunting. Pigs, dogs, and fowl were the only domesticated animals in prehistory—and not all three were always present everywhere. Cereals, domesticated herd animals, and a large number of technological innovations such as metal working, the wheel and the plow, the loom (except in the Carolines, the eastern Solomons, and the Banks Islands), and masonry dwelling construction above foundation level (except on Easter Island) were absent. The major root crops are all of Indo-Oceanic ancestry, the main ones being varieties of yams and aroids (especially taro). Tree crops include breadfruit, banana, coconut, pandanus, paper mulberry, and many others of both edible and technological value (Bellwood 1976a). The sole important Andean cultigen, the sweet potato (Yen 1974), was grown only in parts of East Polynesia (Hawaii, Marquesas, Society, Easter, and New Zealand) in prehistoric times (Dixon 1932); it was introduced by human transmission at an unknown time, possibly prior to A.D. 1000.

Over most areas of Oceania, cultivation techniques are based on shifting horticulture for tuber crops, although there were until recently quite elaborate terraced irrigation systems for taro in eastern Melanesia and parts of Polynesia, particularly in the Cook and Hawaiian islands. The Polynesians and Micronesians, with their relative concentration on wet-field cultivation and arboriculture, were able to support denser populations than were possible in most parts of Melanesia, although in parts of the New Guinea highlands drained plots on a grid pattern in swamps for sweet potato (introduced after 1521) still support populations of up to 300 persons per square kilometer in favorable areas.

The Languages of Oceania

Although there are no exact figures, it is possible that over 1,200 different languages are spoken in Oceania, a situation that reflects the high degree of cultural fragmentation in the area. Over most of New Guinea, and in scattered pockets in eastern Indonesia, the Bismarcks, and the Solomons, 700 or more languages are grouped into several different phyla and collectively designated Papuan, or non-Austronesian. The remaining languages of parts of coastal New Guinea, most of island Melanesia and Indonesia, and all of Polynesia, Micronesia, and the Philippines (together with parts of South Vietnam, Malaya, and Madagascar) belong to the Austronesian phylum.

The diversity of the Papuan languages suggests great time depth. Since New Guinea may have been settled for more than 40,000 years, the ancestry of these languages may go back to the beginning of settlement; it is possible that this time span has removed any demonstrable connection with the languages of Australia. However, recent work has tended to dispel any notion that they evolved in static isolation,

and the majority of the Papuan languages of New Guinea, apart from some large groups in the Sepik district and on the north coast of west Irian, have been compiled by Wurm (1972) in a single Trans New Guinea phylum. It seems that speakers of ancestral languages of this phylum expanded from eastern New Guinea, perhaps through the Markham Valley, into the highlands and southern districts from about 10,000 years ago. Whether this expansion began outside New Guinea is not at present clear. Papuan speakers also settled parts of island Melanesia as far east as the Santa Cruz group, but the date of this eastward movement remains unknown.

Within the 700 or 800 languages of the widespread Austronesian phylum a number of linguists recognize two major subgroups, western and eastern Austronesian (Pawley 1974; Blust 1974). Our interest here is in the eastern Austronesian subgroup, which includes all the languages of Polynesia and Melanesia (excluding, of course, the Papuan languages) and all the languages of Micronesia east of the Palau and Mariana islands (see Fig. 1.3). Within eastern Austronesian, all the languages east of the western tip of New Guinea are further classified into a major subgroup called Oceanic: these Oceanic languages total about 400, and are most diverse in the New Guinea–Bismarck area, where a time depth of over 5,000 years is indicated by glottochronological dating (described in Chapter 10). Diverse languages are present in eastern Indonesia and western New Guinea (for instance, in the border zone between the western and eastern Austronesian subgroups), and the initial Austronesian settlement of Oceania may have originated somewhere near there. Dyen (1965) has suggested that the degree of diversity in the east New Guinea-Bismarck-Solomon area indicates that this may be the area of origin for the whole of the Austronesian family, but this view is hard to reconcile with the archaeological and physical anthropological evidence, slim as it may be.

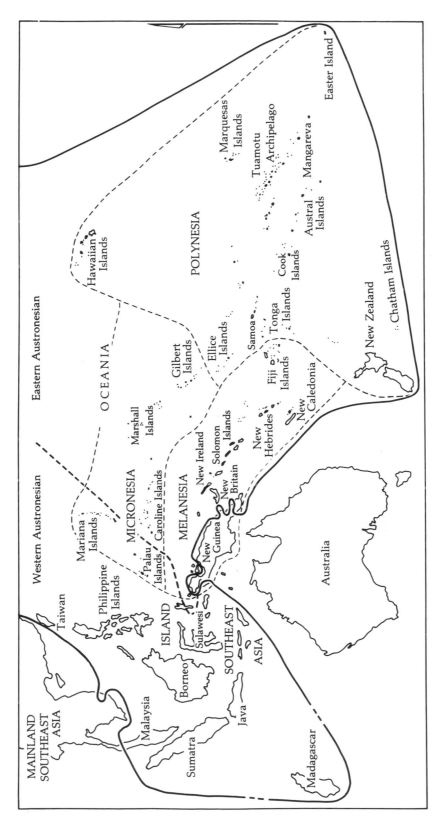

1.3 *The major Austronesian linguistic divisions.*

Other linguists have tended to attribute the diversity shown in the eastern New Guinea area to long-term borrowing from Papuan languages, the high degree of social and political fragmentation, and the extent of bilingualism in an area as ethnically diverse as western Melanesia.

The Oceanic languages of the Solomons, New Caledonia, and the southern New Hebrides are also diverse, little understood genetically, and have a glottochronological time depth of over 5,000 years. Of special importance is the probable existence of an eastern Oceanic subgroup (Pawley 1972), which includes the languages of parts of the southeastern Solomons, the central and northern New Hebrides (excluding Ambrym and Malekula), the Banks Islands, Rotuma, Fiji, all of Polynesia and the Polynesian outliers, and perhaps all of nuclear Micronesia. The formation of the proto—eastern Oceanic language or chain of languages evidently took place in eastern Melanesia (possibly in the southeastern Solomons or the New Hebrides) and its differentiation may have begun as early as 4,000 years ago. The inclusion of Polynesia together with eastern Melanesia in this subgroup is a matter of importance for any consideration of Polynesian origins. The suggestion that Polynesia was initially settled via Micronesia is not supported by the linguistic grouping.

Recent work on the fairly homogeneous languages of Polynesia suggests settlement of Tonga, Samoa, and Fiji before 1000 B.C., and formation of a proto-Polynesian language in the Tonga/Samoa area. Subsequent Polynesian linguistic splits are fairly well established:

(a) The first split at about 1000 B.C. separates Tongic (Tonga and Niue) from nuclear Polynesian (probably first located in Samoa).

(b) Nuclear Polynesian divides into Samoic (Samoa and the majority of the Polynesian outliers) and eastern Polynesian, with the first settlement of East Polynesia early in the first millennium A.D.

(c) Eastern Polynesian then splits into a Marquesic subgroup (Marquesas, Mangareva, and

Hawaii), a Tahitic subgroup (Society, Austral, and Cook islands, some Tuamotus and Maori), and Easter Island. The Easter Island language may have separated around A.D. 400, whereas the other splits belong mostly to the later first millennium A.D. (Pawley 1966; Green 1966).

In Polynesia, and to a lesser extent in eastern Melanesia, the sequence of linguistic splits is well supported by archaeology. Within nuclear Micronesia the greatest linguistic diversity seems to be in the eastern Carolines, Marshalls, and Gilberts, a hypothesis that suggests earliest settlement in this region at around 1300 B.C., perhaps from the New Hebrides (Shutler and Marck 1975; Marck 1975). In western Micronesia, the Palauan and Mariana languages probably derive from Indonesian or Philippine sources.

These inferences concerning genetic relationships among languages, derived from lexicostatistics and grammatical studies, are of crucial importance for the archaeologist. In addition, reconstruction of aspects of the vocabulary of proto-Austronesian suggests strongly that Austronesian speakers introduced horticulture (taro, yam, breadfruit, banana, and coconut), the pig, and the outrigger canoe into the Oceanic world (Pawley and Green 1973).

Oceanic Prehistory

Early Settlement in New Guinea and Western Melanesia

As we shall see in more detail in Chapter 15, no Pleistocene human fossil material is available from New Guinea. The earliest excavated Pleistocene archaeological site is at Kosipe in the Papuan highlands, where a stone industry of waisted tools and flaked "ax-adzes" has been dated to as early as 26,000 years ago—in an open site possibly associated with seasonal exploitation of pandanus. At approximately 8,000 to 10,000 years ago edge-ground and partially polished ax-adzes appear in the rock shelter of Kafiavana in the eastern highlands. Outside New Guinea the technique of edge grinding appears in Arnhem Land at about 20,000 years ago, and at Niah Cave in Sarawak by about 8,000 years ago; so New Guinea clearly was included in the early area of distribution of this important technological innovation. A number of other rock shelters in the Papua New Guinea highlands continue the cultural sequence from about 10,000 years ago and show continuity in the production of ground ax-adzes to the present. The waisted tools disappear within the last 6,000 years, although this change appears to have been very gradual and subject to fairly complex regional variation. Waisted tools of the kind under discussion appear not to be made today in New Guinea; their functions and the circumstances of their decline are obscure. An undated industry that includes flaked but unground waisted tools has been discovered near Kandrian in New Britain, and the waisting tradition may be continued in the pecked and ground waisted axes of Bougainville and Buka in the northern Solomons. The closest outside parallels for the distinctive waisted tools come from Australia and from undated Hoabinhian contexts in Southeast Asia.

These early New Guinea industries are generally associated with crude pebble tool and flake industries, in which the configuration of the cutting edge appears to have been a more important criterion in the minds of the makers than any aspect of overall shape. The recent discovery on New Ireland of a flake tool industry (White 1972) that may date to as early as 6,000 B.C. provides the first definite evidence of preceramic settlement in the islands east of New Guinea. At present, the stone tool complexes in the New Guinea highlands and adjacent areas seem to have served maintenance rather than extractive functions and cannot be related as a whole to Australia, Indonesia, or any outside area, although there are increasing signs that future analyses will establish firmer correlations.

The polished ax-adzes may indicate an increase in the tempo of forest clearance during the Holocene period, possibly as an aid to hunting or a rudimentary form of shifting horticulture. Recent evidence from the highlands of Papua New Guinea does in fact suggest that horticulture there developed independently—and earlier than any possible transference of techniques and cultigens by Austronesian speakers. Specifically, pollen analysis in the western highlands indicates clearance of vegetation (presumably by man) prior to 3000 B.C., and the pig, an animal native to Indonesia, appears to have been introduced into New Guinea about 10,000 years ago (Bulmer 1975). Tame pigs are today kept in large numbers in New Guinea and fed on cultivated products. It is unlikely that they would have been introduced into the island by populations that subsisted entirely on hunting and gathering.

Recent archaeological work in a swamp at Kuk, near Mount Hagen in the western highlands, has thrown more direct light on these developments. There a wedge of grey clay buried in the swamp is believed to represent soil erosion caused by clearance of vegetation for shifting cultivation on surrounding slopes at about 9000 B.C. (Golson 1977). By 4000 B.C. the cultivators began to move into the swamp itself, which they drained by means of long ditches up to 500 m long, 3 m deep, and 4.5 m wide. These ditches (Fig. 1.4) may have been for control of water level in the cultivation of wet-field taro, although there is no direct proof that this crop was grown. Nevertheless, New Guinea is the region where the first domestication of a number of important Oceanic crops, including taro, sugar cane, breadfruit, coconut, and a variety of banana may have occurred.

At present, the sweet potato rather than taro is the major crop in most highland areas, especially above 2,000 m, the approximate upper limit of growth for taro. The sweet potato was taken, probably by Spaniards or Portuguese, to Indonesia and the Philippines in and after the sixteenth century and evidently spread from there long before Europeans actually penetrated into New Guinea. Watson (1965) once suggested

1.4 *Cross section excavated through a drainage ditch dating from about 4000 B.C. at Kuk in the western highlands of Papua New Guinea. The ditch fill is the black material to the left of the figure. (Photo courtesy of J. Golson.)*

that the highlands were inhabited only by small patrilineal bands of hunters and gatherers prior to this time, and that the arrival of the sweet potato sparked a marked population growth and expansion of settlement. The discoveries related in the previous paragraph require that Watson's hypothesis now be modified, but it is true that New Guinea highland societies, despite their long tradition of horticulture, have retained an egalitarian form of social organization with little political integration above the community level. This circum-

stance may reflect the long tradition of hunting and gathering that they once shared with the Australian Aborigines, together with a conservative tradition reinforced by isolation.

In addition to the above evidence for horticulture, archaeologists have long attempted (so far unsuccessfully) to provide a chronology for an interesting series of stone mortars and pestles, the latter sometimes carved as schematic bird-shaped figurines such as the one shown in Fig. 1.5. They have been found especially in the Wahgi and Baiyer valleys of the highlands and more rarely in northeast New Guinea, New Britain, and the northern Solomons (see map in Pretty 1965). Bulmer (1964) has suggested convincingly that these implements were used for grinding nuts and seeds.

1.5 *Bird-headed pestle of stone, 36 cm long, from the Aikora Valley, Northern Province, of Papua New Guinea. (Photo courtesy of the Trustees of the British Museum.)*

The Austronesian Settlement of Oceania

The artifacts and sites discussed above are unlikely, on general grounds of date and distribution, to be associated with Austronesian speakers. While one cannot correlate artifacts and languages precisely in prehistory, there are good circumstantial grounds for suggesting that Austronesians were responsible for the introduction of pottery and polished stone adzes, especially those of quadrangular cross section, into Oceania. The term adz implies a single bevel, as opposed to the double bevel of an ax.

Melanesian pottery production today is generally confined to Austronesian-speaking areas (with significant exceptions such as the Sepik district of New Guinea). The main manufacturing techniques are modeling, ring building, coiling, and use of the paddle and anvil; firing is under an open bonfire, the kiln being unknown (Palmer 1972). Adzes of quadrangular or trapezoidal cross section generally become more frequent with the earliest pottery in Melanesia and dominate Austronesian prehistory in Indonesia, the Philippines, and Polynesia. In Melanesia the earlier New Guinea fashion for lenticular cross-sectioned adzes eventually dominates as far east as Fiji, but quadrangular-sectioned adzes are importantly associated with the Lapita culture described in Chapter 2. Micronesian adzes usually were made of shell; pottery was made only in western volcanic islands, although some sherds recently have been found on the island of Truk in the Carolines.

At present, the earliest archaeological evidence for pottery-using peoples in Melanesia dates back no further than 1500 B.C. The linguistic evidence noted above suggests that Austronesian speakers were settling in Melanesia from before 3000 B.C., and this circumstance presents a problem; we do not know whether these early Austronesian settlers used pottery, and we will not know until the archaeological record has been extended back in time. However, the period from 1500 B.C. to the present is now quite well documented, and it is this period that has most significance for Polynesian origins.

The earliest known settlements in the islands of eastern Melanesia, from the southeastern Solomons through to Tonga, are closely associated with the spread and development of the Lapita culture, named after the site of Lapita on the west coast of New Caledonia. Radiocarbon dates place this culture between about 1500 B.C. and A.D. 1, after which it generally disappears in Melanesia. The Lapita culture as represented in Tonga from about 1100 or 1000 B.C. is regarded as being early Polynesian, with the initial Lapita settlement of Samoa also taking place by 1000 B.C. The loss of ceramics in Polynesian culture is a product of sequential isolation—first in

18

West Polynesia, then in East Polynesian groups.

Since the sites and artifacts of the Lapita culture are described in the next chapter, I shall not go into detail here. However, Lapita pottery seems to be attributable to a mobile group of Austronesian seafarers and traders who were expanding in central and eastern Melanesia after 1500 B.C.; these people may be regarded as ancestral Polynesians, ultimately of Indonesian or Philippine origin. The degree of emphasis on dentate stamping in the decoration of Lapita pottery appears to be a localized Melanesian development, but the general Lapita combinations of dentate stamping, circle stamping, red slipping and lime infill, carinated body forms, and the absence of painting, cord marking, and tripod feet, quite clearly link it with similar and probably contemporary ceramics in the Mariana Islands, the Philippines, and Indonesia (Bellwood 1976b). There are no grounds at all for deriving the Lapita ceramic style from anywhere on the Southeast Asian mainland.

A ceramic style approximately contemporary with Lapita, with related designs but without dentate stamping, has been discovered recently on Buka Island in the northern Solomons (Specht 1972). Along the coast of the Papuan Gulf near Port Moresby and on Yule Island a red-slipped ware with dentate stamping and incised designs has been found to date back some 2,000 years. The Yule pottery is not classified as Lapita, but it may correlate with the Austronesian settlement of southern Papua (Allen 1972). However, the detailed relations of these styles to Lapita remain to be determined.

Although no published analyses of Lapita skeletal material are available, one can readily guess that the makers would be close to the Polynesian phenotype, on the grounds that the Polynesians appear to be their direct and isolated descendants. This raises the fundamental problem of why the eastern Melanesians and the Polynesians, who together form a linguistic continuum and to a lesser extent a cultural continuum,

should be physically so different. It is of course easy to overemphasize the physical differences, but it is impossible to assume that the eastern Melanesians and the Polynesians are both direct and totally isolated descendants of a single founder population. The physical differences are definite and significant; at the present time one can hypothesize that a segment of the people who made Lapita pottery formed a number of relatively endogamous seaborne trading and colonizing groups, who in most of Melanesia, with the possible exception of Fiji, coexisted with Austronesian-speaking Melanesians already in the area. Lapita pottery as such seems to disappear at about the time of Christ. It may be that in Melanesia its makers lost their distinctive lifestyle and were simply absorbed into the resident Melanesian populations, while in Polynesia the descendants of the makers of Lapita pottery lost the ceramic art altogether but retained other major aspects of the original culture as well as the physical type. We are left, of course, with the problem of where the makers of Lapita pottery came from in the first place. Ceramic features would suggest the northern region of Island Southeast Asia, and so would the physical type of the present Polynesians. But why then do the Polynesians speak languages that appear to be derived from eastern Melanesia and not in any direct way from Island Southeast Asia? One may suggest that small founder populations of Indonesian or Philippine origin adopted or borrowed from the languages of neighboring Melanesian groups (and this need only have happened once), but beyond that one is forced to conclude that the original relations between Polynesians and Melanesians are obscure, to say the least.

The foregoing paragraph may have put the cart before the horse by stating possible answers to a major problem before all the data have been considered. We have seen that the Lapita people were, on present evidence, the first potters to enter Melanesia—and they were of Polynesian rather than Melanesian ethnic affinity. Melanesian horticulturists (with or without pottery) had probably spread as far as the New Hebrides and New Caledonia well prior to Lapita times, but so far we have no direct archaeological evidence for this settlement, which stands as no more than a convenient hypothesis. Although Lapita settlement in Melanesia was relatively short-lived, the Melanesians were not slow to develop their own ceramic styles, perhaps from an initial Lapita stimulus, and Melanesian ceramic history over the past 3,000 years presents a bewildering variety. Two of the truly Melanesian ceramic styles will now be described; neither had any discernible influence in Polynesia.

In the central New Hebrides, particularly on the islands of Efate, Makura, and Tongoa, Garanger (1971) has reported pottery profusely decorated with incised and applied designs, which he calls the Mangaasi style (after a site on Efate). This ware, shown in Fig. 1.6, lacks the Lapita rim forms and dentate stamping. It was produced continuously, with stylistic changes, from the early first millennium B.C. to about A.D. 1300, at which time archaeology and surviving traditions indicate the arrival of new peoples in the central New Hebrides. These people made no pottery and are directly ancestral to the present inhabitants. In the first millennium B.C. Mangaasi pottery coexisted with Lapita; they have been found together in the Erueti site on Efate. The earliest Mangaasi ware has elaborate handle-like appendages, some of zoomorphic forms that resemble elements of the New Guinea–Bismarcks pestle and mortar complex. On Buka Island in the northern Solomons a similar incised and applied style (Sohano style) was contemporary with the Lapita-like Buka style and had replaced it by A.D. 1. It appears that Sohano, Mangaasi, and the rather later incised wares of New Caledonia and Fiji may all belong to a single important series that is different from the Lapita wares (Garanger 1972), although at the present stage of research the significance of this contrast is not clear.

Considerable complexity in later Melanesian ceramics is coming to light, but generally the inspirations for these seem to be quite localized. In New Caledonia and Fiji, Lapita is replaced by paddle-impressed wares during the first millennium B.C., but in Fiji at least these develop continuously with an incised and applied component until the period of European contact (see Chapter 3). In brief, throughout eastern Melanesia it is tempting to recognize an early Lapita ceramic series whose makers were ancestral to the Polynesians, and which was contemporary with and eventually replaced by a parallel impressed, incised, and applied series whose makers have contributed substantially to the present Melanesian culture and phenotype. The latter series, with its very simple pottery forms, does not have any close extra-Melanesian parallels, and the whole group may be ultimately of Lapita inspiration. For instance, the Lapita pottery from several sites frequently has incised and applied motifs, and paddle impression is also found on Lapita sherds in some New Caledonian sites.

Polynesia

While Melanesian prehistory is still at the basic level of establishing a time scale, prehistory in the more homogeneous and generally nonceramic area of Polynesia has been longer established and has far more to tell concerning prehistoric economics and settlement patterns. At this point it is only necessary to review the culture history, the story of which is continued from the establishment of Lapita potters in Tonga and Samoa by 1000 B.C. By the middle of the first millennium B.C. the only pottery being produced in West Polynesia was plain, and its manufacture finally died out in all areas before A.D. 300 (see Chapter 4). Pottery of late Lapita plain type has also been found on Futuna (Hoorn Islands) and on the Polynesian outliers of Anuta and Bellona in the southeastern Solomon Islands. By about A.D. 300 a few settlers had crossed at least

PETER S. BELLWOOD

1.6 *Early Mangaasi incised and relief pottery from the central New Hebrides. This style was current from about 600 B.C. to the middle of the first millennium A.D. (Photo courtesy of J. Garanger.)*

3,200 km of the Pacific Ocean from Samoa to settle the Marquesas Islands, where a few tiny sherds have been found in the very earliest levels, and possibly also the closer Society Islands, the traditional cultural center of Polynesia. Further isolation followed by dispersal from at least these two centers then took place in eastern Polynesia (see Chapters 5 and 8).

In eastern Polynesia after the middle of the first millennium A.D., following a period of isolation in the Marquesas and possibly also the Society islands, an early East Polynesian archaeological assemblage differing from but overlapping that of West Polynesia spread to all remaining parts of triangle Polynesia, including New Zealand and Easter Island. Parts of this fairly homogeneous assemblage have been recovered from early sites in the Marquesas, Hawaiian, and Society islands and in New Zea-

land. Included are one-piece fishhooks of bone or shell, two-piece trolling hooks, tanged adzes, imitation whale-tooth pendants, bone reels (except Hawaii), and open-court temples (see Chapter 13). All of these items are absent or rare in West Polynesia, or are present in different forms; for instance, West Polynesian adzes are untanged, and temples were constructed as god-houses rather than as open courts.

In the isolation that followed initial dispersal into East Polynesia, a number of significant differences developed beyond the underlying homogeneity, particularly in isolated Easter Island and in temperate New Zealand. These differences will be detailed in the following chapters.

Micronesia

The islands of Micronesia fall into two

1.7   A terraced hill with defensible crown on Babeldaob, Palau Islands. (Photo courtesy of D. Osborne.)

basic categories, which are paralleled precisely in the western and nuclear categories based on linguistics. Western Micronesia comprises the volcanic Palau and Mariana groups, settled before 1000 B.C. by peoples with pottery traditions and languages from northeastern Indonesia or the Philippines. The nuclear Micronesian islands comprise the Caroline, Marshall, and Gilbert groups, and except for Yap, Truk, Ponape, and Kusaie in the Carolines all are atolls. Attempts have been made recently to classify the nuclear Micronesian languages with the eastern Oceanic subgroup, and Marck (1975) has suggested that the region was first settled around 1300 B.C. from the northern New Hebrides. If this view is correct, then the nuclear Micronesians are indeed close cousins to the Polynesians, a view that is strongly supported by physical anthropology (Howells 1973).

To date, most archaeology has been carried out in western Micronesia. In the Palau Islands a ceramic sequence has

been postulated with guess dates back to 2000 B.C. Palau is noted for some rather remarkable terraced hills and anthropomorphic stone carvings (Osborne 1966), as shown in Fig. 1.7. On Saipan, Rota, Guam, and Pagan in the Marianas, pottery with *possible* Lapita affinities (Mariana redware) has been found in sites dating back into the second millennium B.C. At some point in the first millennium A.D., a plain ceramic style takes over in association with rectangular settings of large stone pillars (*latte*) that once formed foundations for houses (Spoehr 1957; Egami and Saito 1973; Takayama and Intoh 1976). In concept these structures (depicted in Fig. 1.8) belong to the Indonesian-Philippine area, where raised pile houses are common. Finally, on Yap, pottery that shows affinities with the later Mariana plain pottery has been recovered from early first millennium A.D. contexts, and this is followed by a local untempered and laminated ware. The origin of the famous stone money of Yap, in the

PETER S. BELLWOOD

1.8 A latte *on Tinian in the Mariana Islands, drawn on George Anson's voyage of 1740–1744. The pillars with capstones are about 4 m high.*

form of large perforated disks of calcite dripstone quarried in the Palaus, remains obscure (Gifford and Gifford 1959).

Very little archaeological work has ever been carried out in nuclear Micronesia, apart from excavation of a typical Micronesian shell assemblage of adzes, bracelets, and beads on Truk (Takayama and Seki 1973). Furthermore, Sinoto has recently found pottery on Truk, but its affinities have not yet been reported. Excavations by Davidson (1971) on the Polynesian outlier atoll of Nukuoro in the southern Carolines have established settlement from at least A.D. 1300, with an assemblage of one-piece fishhooks of basically Micronesian, rather than Polynesian, affinity. Nevertheless, these results are too limited to allow a reconstruction of nuclear Micronesian prehistory from archaeology alone, and we are forced to rely heavily on the findings of physical anthropologists and linguists.

It remains only to describe the most remarkable monument in Micronesia and perhaps in the whole Pacific; the great ceremonial complex of Nan Madol on Ponape in the Carolines. This site consists of almost 100 square or rectangular platforms

faced with basalt blocks or prisms and covers about 70 hectares. Built on a reef, the platforms are surrounded by tidal channels and protected from the sea by two massive breakwaters placed at right angles (see Hambruch 1936; Bellwood 1977; Chapter 10). The platforms support pole and thatch structures that served as dwellings for nobles and priests, and as temples; but the most magnificent structure is the walled burial enclosure called Nan Douwas (Fig. 1.9). This has four pit tombs roofed with basalt prisms, surrounded by enclosure walls up to 8.5 m high. The Nan Madol site is traditionally recent and dates to within the last few centuries; similar monuments survive on the island of Kusaie.

Conclusions

The following are the principal conclusions to be drawn from the above (see Bellwood 1975):

(a) New Guinea and Australia were settled more than 40,000 years ago by ancestral Australoid populations who spoke languages ancestral to the present Australian and Papuan phyla. The early New Guinea industry of flake tools,

1.9 *A tomb lined and roofed with pillars of prismatic basalt in the walled burial enclosure of Nan Douwas, Nan Madol, Ponape Island. (Photo courtesy of the 1963 Smithsonian expedition to Ponape, directed by Saul H. Riesenberg, ethnologist, with Clifford Evans and Betty J. Meggers, archaeologists.)*

ax/adzes, and waisted tools is at present without exact parallel in surrounding regions. This early phase of settlement may have extended into the Solomons and Santa Cruz islands, but definite information is lacking.

(b) In the period around 3000 B.C. the first Austronesian speakers entered Melanesia. New Guinea at this time already had its own tradition of horticulture and pig husbandry, but the Austronesians may have introduced these elements to the islands beyond. Cultural contact and intermarriage with Papuan-speaking populations were followed by a consolidation of Austronesian settlement in the islands to as far east as New Caledonia and the New Hebrides. Archaeological assemblages from this early Austronesian phase are lacking, and it is not known whether pottery was in use.

(c) Around 1500 B.C. another group of Austronesians, the makers of Lapita pottery, occupied a number of coastal niches in Melanesia. These people were (on circumstantial grounds) more Mongoloid than their predecessors, and they were clearly adept at canoe construction and navigation.

(d) By about 1300 B.C. one or more groups of Lapita potters, who may have been relatively little influenced by Melanesian populations, moved east to settle Fiji and West Polynesia. Fijian traditions and physical anthropology suggest that this island group received later Melanesian settlers, while the Polynesians—and possibly the central and eastern Micronesians—are direct descendants of the original Lapita settlers.

(e) Complex population interaction and movement in Melanesia within the past 2,500 years have given rise to the present ethnic pattern of the area (Chowning 1977). The Melanesian phenotype, and such cultural factors as dominance of unilineal kinship reckoning and rarity of genealogical ranking, probably reflect Papuan influence. The Micronesians and Polynesians, who have not interacted with preceding populations to the same extent, have preserved what may be an ancient pattern of hereditary ranking, together with many aspects of a Mongoloid physical type.

PETER S. BELLWOOD

References

Allen, J. 1972. Nebira 4: an early Austronesian site in central Papua. *Archaeology and Physical Anthropology in Oceania* 7:92–124.

Bellwood, P. S. 1975. The prehistory of Oceania. *Current Anthropology* 16:9–28.

———. 1976a. Prehistoric plant and animal domestication in Austronesia. In *Problems in economic and social archaeology*, ed. G. de G. Sieveking, I. H. Longworth, and D. E. Wilson, pp. 153–168. London: Duckworth.

———. 1976b. Indonesia, the Philippines and Oceanic prehistory. In *IXe Congrès union internationale des sciences préhistoriques et protohistoriques, colloque XXII*, pp. 7–26. Paris: Centre National de la Recherche Scientifique.

———. 1977. *Man's conquest of the Pacific.* London and Auckland: Collins.

———. 1978. *The Polynesians.* London: Thames and Hudson.

Blust, R. 1974. Eastern Austronesian: a note. *Working Papers in Linguistics* 6, no. 4:101–107. Department of Linguistics, University of Hawaii.

Bulmer, R. 1964. Edible seeds and prehistoric stone mortars in the highlands of East New Guinea. *Man* 64:147–150.

Bulmer, Susan. 1975. Settlement and economy in prehistoric Papua New Guinea. *Journal de la Société des Océanistes* 31:7–75.

Burrows, E. G. 1938. *Western Polynesia: a study of cultural differentiation.* Ethnologiska Studier no. 7, Gothenburg.

Chowning, Ann. 1977. *Peoples and cultures of Melanesia*, 2nd ed. Menlo Park, California: Cummings.

Curtain, C. C. 1976. On genetic markers in Oceania. *Current Anthropology* 17:530–531.

Davidson, J. M. 1971. *Archaeology on Nukuoro atoll. Auckland Institute and Museum Bulletin* 9.

Dixon, R. B. 1932. The problem of the sweet potato in Oceania. *American Anthropologist* 34:40–66.

Douglas, G. 1969. Checklist of Pacific oceanic islands. *Micronesica* 5:327–464.

Dyen, Isidore. 1965. *A lexicostatistical classification of the Austronesian languages.* International Journal of American Linguistics Memoir no. 19.

Egami, T., and F. Saito. 1973. Archaeological excavations on Pagan in the Marianas Islands. *Journal of the Anthropological Society of Nippon (Jinruigaku zasshi)* 81·203–226.

Garanger, José. 1971. Incised and applied-relief pottery, its chronology and development in southeastern Melanesia, and extra areal comparisons. In *Studies in Oceanic culture history*, ed. R. C. Green and Marion Kelly, vol. 2. *Pacific Anthropological Records* 12:53–66.

———. 1972. *Archéologie des Nouvelles-Hébrides.* Publication de la Société des Océanistes no. 30, Paris.

Gifford, E. W., and D. S. Gifford. 1959. Archaeological investigations in Yap. *University of California Anthropological Records* 18, no. 2.

Goldman, Irving. 1970. *Ancient Polynesian society.* Chicago: University of Chicago Press.

Golson, Jack. 1977. No room at the top: agricultural intensification in the New Guinea highlands. In *Sunda and Sahul: prehistoric studies in Southeast Asia, Melanesia and Australia*, ed. Jim Allen, Jack Golson, and Rhys Jones, pp. 601–638. London: Academic Press.

Green, R. C. 1966. Linguistic subgrouping within Polynesia: the implications for prehistoric settlement. *Journal of the Polynesian Society* 75:6–38.

Hambruch, P. 1936. Ponape: die Ruinen. In *Ergebnisse der Südsee-Expedition 1908–1910, vol. 2. B7-3, Ponape*, ed. G. Thilenius, pp. 3–103. Hamburg: Friedrichsen de Gruyter.

Howells, W. W. 1973. *The Pacific islanders.* New York: Scribners.

Kirk, R. L. 1965. Population genetic studies of the indigenous peoples of Australia and New Guinea. *Progress in Medical Genetics* 4:202–214.

———. 1971. Genetic evidence and its implications for aboriginal prehistory. In *Aboriginal man and environment in Australia*, ed. D. J. Mulvaney and Jack Golson, pp. 326–343. Canberra: Australian National University Press.

Lessa, W. 1950. Ulithi and the outer native world. *American Anthropologist* 52:27–52.

Levison, Michael, R. G. Ward, and J. W. Webb. 1973. *The settlement of Polynesia: a computer simulation.* Minneapolis: University of Minnesota Press.

Marck, J. C. 1975. On the origin and dispersal of the proto-nuclear Micronesians. Master's thesis, University of Iowa.

Mason, L. 1968. The ethnology of Micronesia. In *Peoples and cultures of the Pacific*, ed. A. P. Vayda, pp. 275–298. New York: Natural History Press.

Osborne, D. 1966. *The archaeology of the Palau islands.* Bishop Museum Bulletin no. 230, Honolulu.

Palmer, B. 1972. Pottery in the South Pacific. In *Early Chinese art and its possible influence in the Pacific basin,* ed. N. Barnard, vol. 3, pp. 693–722. New York: Intercultural Arts Press.

Pawley, A. K. 1966. Polynesian languages: a subgrouping based on shared innovations in morphology. *Journal of the Polynesian Society* 75:39–64.

———. 1972. On the internal relationships of Eastern Oceanic languages. In *Studies in Oceanic culture history,* ed. R. C. Green and Marion Kelly, vol. 3. *Pacific Anthropological Records* 13:1–142.

———. 1974. Austronesian languages. *Encyclopaedia Britannica, 15th ed.* Macropaedia vol. 2, pp. 484–494.

——— and R. C. Green. 1973. Dating the dispersal of the Oceanic languages. *Oceanic Linguistics* 12:1–67.

Pretty, G. L. 1965. Two stone pestles from western Papua and their relationship to prehistoric pestles and mortars from New Guinea. *Records of the South Australian Museum* 15:119–130.

Sahlins, M. D. 1958. *Social stratification in Polynesia.* Seattle: University of Washington Press.

Shutler, Richard, and J. C. Marck. 1975. On the dispersal of the Austronesian horticulturalists. *Archaeology and Physical Anthropology in Oceania* 10:81–113.

Simmons, R. T. 1962. Blood group genes in Polynesians and comparisons with other Pacific peoples. *Oceania* 32:198–210.

Specht, J. 1972. Evidence for early trade in northern Melanesia. *Mankind* 8:310–312.

Spoehr, A. 1957. *Marianas prehistory.* Fieldiana: Anthropology 48. Chicago: Natural History Museum.

Takayama, J., and M. Intoh. 1976. *Archaeological excavation of Latte site (M-13), Rota, in the Marianas.* Reports of the Pacific Archaeological Survey 4. Hiratsuka City: Tokai University Press.

Takayama, J., and T. Seki. 1973. *Preliminary archaeological investigations on the island of Tol in Truk.* Reports of the Pacific Archaeological Survey 2. Hiratsuka City: Tokai University Press.

Thomas, W. L. 1967. The Pacific basin: an introduction. In *The Pacific basin: a history of its geographical exploration,* ed. H. R. Friis, pp. 1–17. New York: American Geographical Society.

Watson, J. B. 1965. The significance of a recent ecological change in the central highlands of New Guinea. *Journal of the Polynesian Society* 74:438–450.

White, J. P. 1972. Carbon dates from New Ireland. *Mankind* 8:309–310.

Wurm, S. 1967. Linguistics and the prehistory of the southwestern Pacific. *Journal of Pacific History* 2:25–38.

———. 1972. Linguistic research in Australia, New Guinea and Oceania. *Linguistics* 87:87–107.

Yen, D. E. 1974. *The sweet potato and Oceania: an essay in ethnobotany.* Bishop Museum Bulletin no. 236, Honolulu.

Lapita

CHAPTER 2

ROGER C. GREEN

This chapter describes the distinctive Oceanic cultural complex that eventually would prove to be ancestral to Polynesian culture in the western area of the Polynesian triangle. Its recognition took place slowly. Yet sites associated with an easily identifiable style of pottery we now call Lapita have been known for years (see Fig. 2.1). The initial discovery of this pottery was made by Father Otto Meyer in 1908–1909 at the village of Rakival on the small island of Watom, some 6.5 km off the northeastern end of New Britain in the Bismarck Archipelago (Fig. 2.2, locality no. 3). He reported these finds in 1909 and 1910 in the major anthropological journal *Anthropos*.

The next discovery was made on a beach of the peninsula of Foué, on the central west coast of New Caledonia (Fig. 2.2, no. 9), by the geologist Maurice Piroutet; it was reported in 1917 in a study describing the stratigraphy of New Caledonia. His report appears to relate to the locality of "site 13" where Gifford and Shutler (1956) excavated in 1952. It is the name for this locality—Lapita—that has subsequently served to designate both the pottery and the cultural complex.

In this period yet a third discovery was that of McKern in the Tonga group in 1921. He found a few potsherds each from Pangaimotu and Motutapu, 23 from two sites on Eua, and 1,577 from three sites on Tongatapu. McKern's account of his discovery, along with a photograph of typical decorated sherds, was published in a Bishop

2.1 Anthropomorphic face from a large shoulder jar found in site SE-RF-2, Nenumbo Village, Main Reef Islands, and dating to circa 1100 B.C.

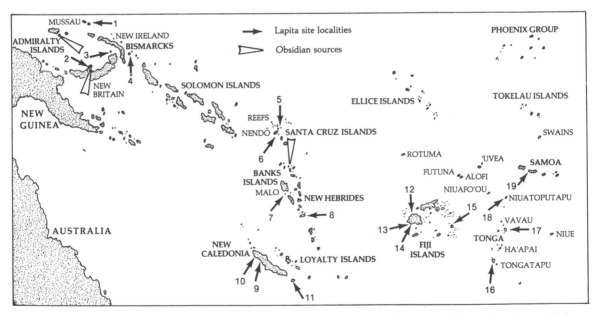

2.2 Map of island Melanesia and West Polynesia. The numbers indicate locations of the Lapita sites and obsidian sources discussed in the text. (Each location may have more than one site.)

ROGER C. GREEN

Museum Bulletin in 1929. In it McKern concluded that the use of pottery in Tonga was general, rather than peculiarly local, and while it was "probable that Tongan pottery had its original conception in Fiji" (1929:116), it seemed to him rather improbable, given its extensive use in Tonga, that Tongans went to Fiji for their pots. Still, the prevailing view that Polynesians did not make pottery persisted, and the lack of recognition of any connection of the Tongan pottery with that already reported from Watom and New Caledonia meant that the comparisons McKern attempted were with much later types of pottery from Fiji, an island group Tongans were known to have visited.

In 1948 Lenormand reported on new finds of Lapita-style pottery at the beach of Saint-François on the Île des Pins off the southeast coast of New Caledonia. Knowledge of this find allowed Avias (1950) to establish at last its close similarity to some of the pottery found by Meyer at Watom and lodged at the Musée de l'Homme by Father O'Reilly, who at about the same time provided independent confirmation of the relationship. It was only after Gifford and Shutler's excavations at "site 13," however, that recognition of the stylistic relationships was extended to the Lapita locality itself and given greater precision. Gifford and Shutler (1956) also used the occasion to draw attention to similar surface sherds from a site in the Sigatoka area on the south coast of Viti Levu in Fiji and to McKern's sherds from Tonga.

Oceanic archaeology during the 1950s and 1960s was moving into a modern phase, and it was not long before previously reported Lapita sites were systematically reexamined and new ones discovered, excavated, and dated. For example, in 1957 Golson (1959) confirmed McKern's findings for Tonga and reported the discovery of a similar though undecorated pottery from Samoa. Shortly thereafter he investigated the site on the Île des Pins, and in 1965 one of his students, Specht (1968), reinvestigated the sites reported by Meyer

on Watom. The Birkses (1967) followed up Golson's discovery of pottery in the Mangaia mound on Tongatapu and another of Golson's students, Poulsen (1967, 1972), continued the efforts there by defining a pottery sequence based on excavations at six additional sites.

The dating by Gifford and Shutler of the Lapita materials from "site 13" to some time in the first millennium B.C., and the Samoa materials by Golson to the first century A.D., allowed Golson (1959, 1961) to postulate that there once had been continuity of culture straddling the boundary between Polynesia and Melanesia, which in West Polynesia had given rise to the historic Polynesian cultures of that region. In this period the finding of a related pottery of similar antiquity in the Marquesas allowed Suggs (1960, 1961a) to lend his support to these views and amplify them from the perspective of East Polynesia.

The 1960s and 1970s have been marked by a steady succession of reports on additional Lapita sites. However, a real appreciation of some of the more important aspects of this cultural complex has developed only in the last few years. For a time problems of chronology, site integrity (because of stratigraphic disturbance), plus a tendency to direct much of the analytic attention to the decorated pottery, precluded a more rounded view of either the ceramic assemblage or the culture as a whole. Recent work has resolved some of these problems and partially corrected the imbalance. Pottery, however, continues to dominate much of the discussion.

Review of Nonceramic Lapita Evidence

I shall endeavor to compensate for the heavily pottery-based approach by reviewing initially the nonceramic Lapita evidence. The appendix to this chapter provides a much-needed survey of the principal sites, data on which are uneven and appear in widely scattered, sometimes unpublished sources. The survey begins in the west in the Bismarck Archipelago and moves east to Polynesia. It is from the western sites that the main evidence for this chapter is derived. Since a description of these sites—important though they are —would prove tedious for the nonprofessional reader, I merely list them by group. Figure 2.2 should be consulted as the list is reviewed.

What should be realized is that the Lapita villages, while variable in size, often show evidence of permanent habitation and inferential evidence of horticulture. They are most often located on low islets, although some are in appropriate coastal environments on large islands. Eastward from New Guinea the first locations are in the Bismarck group, where at least 13 separate sites are known. One is the site of the first Lapita discovery at Rakival on Watom Island. The obsidian from the source known as Talasea, on the north coast of New Britain, which was widely traded eastward over Oceania, occurs in most of these sites. One site is on a small island east of New Ireland, but none have been reported from the Solomons. I list 9 from Santa Cruz; about a dozen are known in the New Hebrides, 4 in New Caledonia, and at least 7 in Fiji. The sites to the east, in Polynesia proper, are better known and integrated into the published literature as well as being covered in other chapters of this book. It is, however, necessary to bring out several points. One is that on Tongatapu (Fig. 2.2, 16) the distribution of sites with Lapita pottery is highly correlated with a fairly narrow band of land along the north coast and the lagoon edge, a zone also associated with either a former marine beachline or with marine terraces raised to 10 m above the present sea level (Groube 1971). Less is known of the Lapita sites that occur in the Ha'apai and Vavau groups (Fig. 2.2, 17), but on Niuatoputapu at the northern end of the Tongan group (Fig. 2.2, 18), they are again confined to a narrow band associated with a raised marine beach terrace around the steeper central core of the island

(Rogers 1974). There the more recently emerged area of former lagoon surrounding this zone lacks sites with pottery. These situations recall the distribution of Lapita sites on Malo in the New Hebrides.

Eight and perhaps nine Lapita sites, out of a larger but unknown number, have been excavated on Tongatapu (Fig. 2.2, 16) by McKern, Golson, the Birkses, Poulsen and Groube. On Niuatoputapu Kirch, using transects and systematic sampling procedures similar to those used in the Main Reef/Santa Cruz group, has recently completed an excavation program totaling 127 m². Descriptions of Lapita sites on Tongatapu (Suggs 1961b; Poulsen 1967; Groube 1971) indicate they usually take the form of large, low, usually flat, and barely discernible mounds that rest directly on deposits of marine beach sand, even though they are no longer located on the lagoon or beach front. Only at the Mangaia and TO-1 sites were clay deposits present in the underlying zone; at TO-1, now 400 to 500 m from the lagoon, the deposits indicate there had been a 2 m transgression by the sea to the vicinity of the site at the time of occupation (Poulsen 1967). Evidence supporting a change in sea level relative to land and in the lagoon environment is also available from the base of TO-5 (Poulsen 1967).

All Lapita sites in Tongatapu have also been badly disturbed by more recent cultural and natural activities (Poulsen 1967). For example, Groube (1971) estimates that in the case of Vuki's mound "multitudinous disturbances" had destroyed over 60 percent of the 40 m² of excavation area exposed. Failure by Poulsen to adequately control for this problem during excavation led to major difficulties in determining the age of his sites.

Groube (1971) records that the largest Lapita site he saw on Tongatapu was uncovered when bulldozers cleared the land for new police barracks at the rear of the town of Nukualofa. The Mangaia mound covers about 3,000 m² (Suggs 1961b). Based on 200 test holes Poulsen estimated his TO-1 site to cover between 4,300 and 4,500 m², part of which had been bulldozed for a school-ground. He excavated 67.5 m² there in five sections, sampling 1.5 percent of the site. Site TO-3 is described as covering 2,150 m², TO-5 something over 1,000 m², and TO-6 between 1,400 and 1,500 m². Only small trenches were excavated at sites TO-2 to 5, but 69 m² (4.6 percent) was excavated at TO-6. All sites, even though stratified, seem to be shallow, varying from 0.5 to 1.5 m deep.

If Lapita sites in Tonga are frequently somewhat elevated above present sea level, those in Samoa from before 600 B.C. are apparently submerged. The one known early site (SU-MU-1), at the western end of Upolu (Fig. 2.2, 19), is under 1.5 m of water and 0.75 m of well-cemented coral beachrock. Recordings from a series of dredge sweeps across a turning basin for boats being constructed in the shallow lagoon revealed that the pottery occurred in a lineal zone some 35 m wide and more than 110 m long (Jennings 1974). From the conformation of the lagoon floor and stratigraphy, it appears that the site when occupied would have been on a beach at the inland end of an elongated embayment that led to a small bay with a good passage through the reef to the sea.

General Characteristics of Lapita Archaeology

Surprising though it may seem, no one has previously attempted a detailed survey of Lapita sites. Instead, the pattern has been to list the better-known sites, briefly describe the composition of the one most recently found, and spend the remainder of the report on description and analysis of the pottery, with comparison where relevant to pottery in other Lapita sites. A survey (above and appendix) has been necessary, therefore, to provide the basis for a number of important generalizations independent of the pottery.

(a) The integrity of deposits in Lapita sites represents a major and continuing problem.

Completely undisturbed occupation layers are seldom encountered. Rather, most Lapita sites have proved difficult to excavate and interpret because of natural and cultural events subsequent to the occupancy, in addition to the usual crab and root holes and gardening activities.

(b) Lapita sites are intimately associated with a number of natural events of some interest, particularly as they are used to reconstruct former environments associated with the period when they were occupied. Among these events are changes in land elevation relative to sea level, the pumice enrichment of former marine-sand beach deposits on which settlement occurred, occasional volcanic ash falls or dune formations following Lapita occupation, and changes in coastlines and local marine habitats accompanied by the flooding of sites via stream and sea action.

(c) Where Lapita deposits remain intact, subsequent cultural activities—both today and in the past—often have modified them extensively. Consequently, despite excavations (totaling not less than 1950 m²) in at least 32 Lapita sites, only a few have revealed any wealth of structural features.

(d) Lapita sites have proved to be reasonably large. Based on pottery distribution they apparently range in size from those between 800 and 2,000 m² to many in the 2,000 to 10,000 m² group, plus a number in the category greater than 10,000 m². They correspond reasonably well in size to self-sufficient sedentary village sites, both ethnographic and prehistoric, identified by similar means in the Shortland Islands of the Solomons (Irwin 1973).

(e) Because of their large size and the degree of subsequent disturbance, Lapita sites in general have been poorly sampled by archaeologists. Except for the most numerous type of artifact, the potsherd, one can not place too great reliance on the representativeness of the other items recovered. Even with potsherds there are problems, for in many cases only a portion derive from the primary context.

(f) Excavations of sites that have produced reasonably significant samples from secure contexts appear to number three. The largest sample is from Sigatoka, where the control over the pottery assemblage from 938 m², especially for reconstruction of vessel shape and size, is excellent. However, an equivalent amount of associated technological, economic, and structural data for a variety of reasons is lacking. Despite combined excavation of some 157 m² at Vatcha on the Île des Pins, the secure data in large part derive from about 20 m² of a lower occupation floor. This and an area of 153 m² excavated at the Main Reef Island site of Nenumbo provide the best integrated data on all aspects of a Lapita settlement. It is no wonder then that most of the discussion about Lapita has centered on its pottery.

(g) Lapita sites in general are found in remarkably similar environments whether they occur on large continental islands, small high islands, or raised coral reefs. Moreover, small islands represent a disproportionate part of the total. Although Lapita sites today exhibit a rather diverse range of ecological settings, these often do not accurately reflect the situation at the time the sites were occupied. What comes to the fore in any consideration of the original locations is their situation on raised coral platforms, marine terraces, and marine sand beaches from which the sea had fairly recently retreated. Lapita settlements when occupied were situated so as to maintain ready access to the sea and permit launching and beaching of large canoes. At Sigatoka (Birks 1973), Malo (Hedrick, personal communication), and in the Reef and Santa Cruz islands, the occurrence of Lapita sites in localities suitable for taking turtles has also been noted.

(h) Groube (1971) correctly claimed that the largest concentration of Lapita sites in the Western Pacific was in the Tongan archipelago. However, his statement that "elsewhere sites with Lapita pottery are isolated discoveries" is incorrect. Lapita sites elsewhere occur in centers or localities in which a number of sites are typically recorded, but only a few have been investigated.

Age of Lapita Sites

The list of radiocarbon dates given in Table 2.1 does not include all known chronometric estimations for the age of Lapita sites. Additional radiocarbon results have been published, and in the case of the Ambitle and the Main Reef and Santa Cruz island Lapita sites, the hydration rims on obsidian flakes have also been measured and experimental ages calculated on the basis of intrinsic rates (Green 1974a; Ambrose 1976a). The rejected ¹⁴C dates include one from Western Samoa, a whole series from

Tongatapu and Malo, one from the Île des Pins, and several from Ambitle Island. In the Samoan case, although the age of the shell sample has been accepted, the probability of recrystallization of the surrounding coral cementing agent, which was also dated, has led to rejection of the result as too young (Green and Richards 1975). In the case of 4010 ± 130 B.P. date for a *Placostylus senilis* (Gassiès) shell from Horizon IV at Vatcha (Frimigacci 1971), the result has been rejected because it is known that living land snails of the species *P. fibratus* (Martyn) have an age of 640 years before the present through taking up about 8 percent of a theoretically possible 12 percent of dead carbon as part of the carbonate that forms the shells (Rafter et al., 1972). It is also known that extinct and living species of *Placostylus* yield slightly younger age estimates than associated carbonate samples from New Caledonian sites, as well as ages of much greater antiquity. It is certain on stratigraphic grounds that the age of Horizon IV is older than the 1110 ± 165 B.C. date for Horizon II—but, on the same evidence, not 1,000 years earlier. Rather the motif analysis of the pottery (see below) suggests its comparability with the earliest sites in the age range 1300 to 1500 B.C.

The problem with the remaining reasonably reliable ¹⁴C dates for Lapita sites (Table 2.1) is that they do not provide any secure age estimates for sites to the west of the Main Reef and Santa Cruz islands. Yet this area constitutes the probable immediate home area from which the Lapita complex originated. Work on the obsidian hydration rims at the Ambitle site, plus close parallels between the pottery motifs in sites on Ambitle and Watom and dated sites in the Reef Islands, suggest ages in the 1000 to 1100 B.C. range. Statistical comparisons between the earliest estimates for sites in Santa Cruz, Malo, Fiji, and Tongatapu reveal no significant difference in their ages. Given this result and the probability of a comparable age for Horizon IV at Vatcha in New Caledonia, it is difficult to argue for any trend to Lapita settlement on the basis

ROGER C. GREEN

Table 2.1   The most reliable radiocarbon age estimates for Lapita sites.

Site	Sample identification	Years B.P.[a]	Age[b]	Comment
Watom Island				
Rakival	ANU 37b	2420 ± 110	540 ± 100 b.c. + ?	Bone, human burials; site FAC is as old or older than this date.
Main Reef Islands				
Nenumbo	I 5747	2955 ± 95	1130 ± 69 B.C.	Pooled mean, site BS-RL-2.
	I 5748	2775 ± 100		
Ngamanie	I 5749	2530 ± 95	680 ± 67 B.C.	Pooled mean, site BS-RL-6.
	I 5750	2460 ± 95		
Santa Cruz				
Nanggu	SUA 111	3250 ± 70	1400 ± 70 b.c. + ?	Shell; site BS-SZ-8.
Nanggu	SUA 112	3140 ± 70	1290 ± 70 b.c. + ?	Shell; site BS-SZ-8.
New Hebrides				
Malo	ANU 1135	3150 ± 70	1300 ± 70 b.c. + ?	Shell; site MH Ma-8.
Malo	ANU 1134	2980 ± 70	1120 ± 70 b.c. + ?	Shell; site MH Ma-8.
Erueti	GX 1145	2300 ± 95	510 ± 95 B.C.	—
New Caledonia				
Site 13	M 341	2800 ± 350	900 ± 263 B.C.	Pooled mean, rectangle Cl-2, Dl-2, first location.
	M 336	2435 ± 400		
Site 13	GIF 1983	2250 ± 100	370 ± 100 b.c. + ?	Shell; location A.
Île des Pins				
Vatcha	ANU 262	2855 ± 165	1110 ± 165 B.C.	Horizon II.
Fiji				
Natunuku	GAK 1218	3240 ± 100	1590 ± 100 B.C.	Lowest level, site VL 1/1.
Yanuca	GAK 1226	2980 ± 90	1310 ± 90 B.C.	Lowest level, site VL 16/81.
Sigatoka	GAK 946	2460 ± 90	620 ± 90 B.C.	Lowest level, site VL 16/1.
Tongatapu				
TO-2	ANU 541	3090 ± 95	1230 ± 95 b.c. + ?	Shell, bottom spits.
Mangaia mound	NZ 727A	2630 ± 50	760 ± 50 b.c. + ?	Shell, layer 3.
Vuki's mound	ANU 441	2440 ± 110	630 ± 91 B.C.	Pooled mean for charcoal from fireplace, layer 14.
	ANU 424	2540 ± 160		
TO-6	NZ 636A	2380 ± 51	590 ± 49 B.C.	Pooled mean for charcoal from fireplaces, base of site.
	ANU 24	2350 ± 200		
Western Samoa				
Ferry Berth	NZ 1958A	2890 ± 80	1030 ± 80 b.c. + ?	Shell; site SU-MU-1.
Faleasi'u	NZ 2726A	2440 ± 60	560 ± 60 b.c. + ?	Shell; site SU-FL-1, stratum I.
	RL 464	2220 ± 110	340 ± 110 b.c. + ?	Shell; site SU-FL-1, stratum I.

[a] = 5568 half-life.

[b] = probable calendrical age (1972 MASCA correction); b.c. = shell or bone, secular correction unknown.

of radiocarbon results. Together they tell us simply that Lapita sites as a cultural horizon date from between 1600 and 500 B.C. In New Caledonia there is some evidence that sites with decorated Lapita pottery may continue until the time of Christ (Frimigacci 1976). In Samoa and Tonga also, the plain pottery component of Lapita pottery continues up to the third century A.D. with some technological change (Groube 1971; Jennings et al. 1976). However, the elaborate vessel shapes on which most of the Lapita-style decoration occurs cease around 500 B.C., leaving only what I call Polynesian plain ware. Elsewhere, evidence for continuation of the Lapita style of pottery after 500 B.C. is currently lacking.

Relative Sea Level Change

The general evidence of the last 18,000 years in the southwest Pacific region is for a lowered sea level that rose continuously to its present level about 4,000 years ago (Chappell 1976). There is also New Zealand and Pacific evidence of first-order transgressions of 1 to 2 m by the sea in the periods 3500 and 2800 B.P. (Schofield 1977) just before and during the time when many of the earlier Lapita sites were occupied. Similar evidence of higher sea stands at roughly comparable times are known from New Caledonia (Launay and Recy 1970; Coudray and Delibrias 1972). As the review of Lapita sites shows, a number of the earlier sites provide the kind of evidence that could easily be accommodated within this eustatic framework. Others, however, provide evidence that is just as likely to be the result of tectonic uplift or tilting as well as submergence. The issues, which are complex and important to both the geologist and the archaeologist, clearly warrant the combined attention of both (Green and Richards 1975).

The Lapita Cultural Complex

Lapita has been referred to as both a cultural horizon and a cultural tradition, and as Golson (1971) observed, it contains elements of both concepts. Certainly no other set of archaeological assemblages in the Pacific forms so distinctive a time horizon or has such a wide distribution. It is also usual, in each region where the data are adequate, for Lapita sites to outline a sequence of 700 to 1,000 years of local cultural development. Interregional cultural traditions called eastern and western Lapita can also be distinguished. These exhibit quite separate developmental histories, although their origins were similar. The use, therefore, of the term "Lapita cultural complex" seems the most satisfactory way to encompass the dimensions of both a horizon and tradition. While the Lapita ceramics with their characteristic designs have provided the most obvious traits used to identify the cultural complex, a better understanding can be achieved if other aspects of the complex are summarized without reference to the pottery.

Lapita Settlements

Despite the limited evidence available, it seems certain that Lapita settlements were internally differentiated, self-sufficient villages occupied by sedentary populations and thus analogous to many of the more recent villages in Melanesia. The Lapita pattern of clustered coastal centers contrasts with the later Polynesian high-island pattern of dispersed households. There the preferred locations were in the intermediate zone, from which it was possible for related family groups to exploit with minimum effort both the agriculturally productive soils of inland valleys and the resources of the coast and adjacent sea. Since the substantial evidence for the size and beach location of Lapita settlements that bears on this point is reviewed in the Appendix, the more meager evidence of internal structural features is summarized here.

The basal layers of Tongan sites have revealed a common set of structural features that can be securely associated with Lapita

ROGER C. GREEN

horizon sites nearly everywhere. These include fires on the flat ground, scoop fire pits, basin-shaped cooking ovens usually containing ash and cooking stone, and a few postholes (cf. Poulsen 1967). In addition, small pits up to 1.5 m long and 0.5 m deep, some of them with undercut sides, are recorded in the basal horizons of the Mangaia mound (Suggs 1961b), Vuki's mound, and at a number of Poulsen's sites. Features restricted to Vuki's mound (Groube 1971:299) consist of "a series of house floors built one upon the other with an encircling collar of rich shell-fish midden"; the floors, where not refurbished by clean coral sand, are covered with scattered ash, charcoal, and the remains of scoop fireplaces and suggest structures used for complex cooking activities. Unfortunately no pattern emerged from the associated postholes. The Fijian evidence, repeating the Tongan, includes a few scoop fire pits, ovens, stake, and postholes. The one addition is the crouch burial in a pit at Natunuku, which recalls two burials in pits in Tonga, but those cannot with certainty be attributed to the Lapita horizon (Poulsen 1967).

In New Caledonia the general run of fire pits, ovens, and postholes may be attributed to the later Lapita sites. The more detailed evidence is confined to some 20 m² of a cooking area in Horizon IV at Vatcha, where two stone-lined hearths and indications of two others were found in association with patches of ash and charcoal, one of which formed a low mound of cooking waste and sherds of pottery. Shells of a large extinct landsnail—*Placostylus senilis* (Gassiès)—marine shells, the bones of turtle and of fish were distributed in patches over the surface. Because postholes are absent, the whole suggests an internally differentiated open-air cooking area (Frimigacci 1974).

As in many Lapita sites, postholes and shallow pits are attested to in the Malo sites of the New Hebrides, ovens in the Ngamanie site in the Main Reef Islands, and postholes and burials in site FAC on Watom (Fig. 2.2, 3). A full range of features, however, has been exposed in the Nenumbo site in the Main Reef Islands, dating to about 1100 B.C. Here two activity areas have been isolated—one in the middle of the site, rich in pottery, obsidian, and chert flakes, and another to the south of it. A number of cooking ovens, large deep postholes, and some shallow pits are located in the central area of the site. Then there is an area with few features. To the south of this is another, which has several large and deeper undercut pits (Fig. 2.3), more ovens, scoop fire pits, and one quite large, deep pit that was probably a well. To one side is an area in which the main features are alignments of postholes along the main axis of the site; some are at right angles, suggesting rectangular structures. Just as the differential distribution of the pottery on the surface had suggested (Green 1976a), there proved to be internally differentiated activity areas in the site. Although this is the only well-documented example, occasional comments in other accounts of Lapita sites suggest that the pattern applies elsewhere as well.

The Lapita Economy

The gathering of a wide range of shellfish from the lagoon and reef, and the taking of many fish from the same locations, is evident in most Lapita sites in which such materials survive. Fishbone and shellfish were also present in the Sigatoka site, although only traces remained (Birks 1973). Poulsen (1967) studied more atypical and possible changing conditions in the Tongatapu sites, where the diversity of shellfish species was restricted. There muddy-sand lagoon shells of *Gafrarium* species and shells of *Anadara antiquata* from the lagoon mouth and intertidal sandy coral reefs predominate in the middens. Elsewhere—in Samoa (Janetski 1976), in New Caledonia (Gifford and Shutler 1956), in the three excavated Main Reef and Santa Cruz island Lapita sites (Swadling 1975; Green 1976a), and probably in Lapita sites on Malo,

2.3 Site SE-RF-2, Nenumbo Village, Main Reef Islands, dating to circa 1100 B.C. Visible are the volcanic ash layer at the surface, the intact cultural occupation layer below, and posthole and pit features in section.

Watom, Eloaue, and the Fiji Islands (Specht 1968; Hedrick 1971; Groube 1971; Egloff 1975)—there is evidence of a typical diversity of shellfish species characteristic of the tropical island reef and foreshore. For the Main Reef and Santa Cruz island sites and the first locality at "site 13," relative abundances of different shellfish can be plotted as a species-diversity curve. Only a moderate tendency for selectivity of some of the more edible species is in evidence; the curves in general exhibit continuity with no sharp peaks or distinct clusters that would indicate preferred species.

Few fishbones other than those in the Lapita sites on Tongatapu and the Nenumbo

site in the Main Reef Islands have been identified more precisely. Nevertheless there is a high correlation between the two extant lists. Both include shark, eels, porcupine fish, several kinds of serranids (sea basses), and scarids (parrotfish), plus Monotaxis, a night high-tide feeder. Tonga also has wrasses and lethrinids. The complete lists consist predominantly of reef and shallow-water lagoon fish (Poulsen 1967; Green 1976a), in which only a few pelagic species are represented. Thus the majority of the fish are those most easily taken with nets, traps, and spears, data that are consistent with only minimal representation of one-piece fishhooks and no specialized gear

ROGER C. GREEN

such as lures for taking surface-feeding fish offshore.

Dugong is recorded for the Nenumbo and Eloaue Lapita sites. The single most numerous bone by weight and number at Nenumbo, is sea turtle, a situation repeated in the Malo sites (J. D. Hedrick, personal communication). There is record of turtle in both the early and the later Samoan sites; in all Tongan sites, with the greatest bulk being in the earliest site (TO-2) near the sea (Poulsen 1967); in both "site 13" and Vatcha in New Caledonia; and in the Eloaue Lapita sites of Mussau. Except for the turtle, marine resources seem to have been exploited by the Lapita people in an extensive rather than a selective manner, quite in keeping with other historic and prehistoric horticulturally based communities in Melanesia.

The hunting of a few birds is indicated by bird bones of uncertain type from Lapita sites on Eloaue, Watom, the Main Reef Islands, and Tonga. The bush turkey or megapod has been identified among the bird bones from Nenumbo, as has the flying fox, a bird-like bat. Wallabies and cuscus were included in the diet at Eloaue, with Polynesian rats recorded for several Lapita sites, although not in New Caledonia. There is also a Melanesian rat from Nenumbo. Hunting, it seems, was never an important part of the Lapita economy.

Two of the three expected Oceanic domesticates are well represented from a number of Lapita sites. One is the pig, recorded from the sites on Eloaue (Egloff 1975); from Watom both as bones and as an artifact (Specht 1968); from all three excavated sites in the Main Reef and Santa Cruz islands (Green 1976a), again as bones and as an artifact (see Fig. 2.5f); and as bones in Malo (Hedrick, personal communication) and as an artifact from Erueti (Garanger 1972) in the New Hebrides. Groube (1971), in challenging the security of Poulsen's ¹⁴C dates for Tongan Lapita sites, also challenged his assignment of pig bones to secure Lapita levels in those sites. I have pursued the matter and believe the pig to be in reason-

ably secure contexts at Horizon I in TO-1 and in the latest horizon at TO-6 (cf. Cram 1975; Poulsen and Scarlett, personal communication). The other certain domesticate is the chicken, in Lapita sites at Watom, Nenumbo, Malo, Tonga, and Samoa. The dog remains questionable but is possible at sites on Eloaue, Malo, and Tonga. The uncertainty relates to either its identification or the security of its context.

The evidence for horticulture of the expected root and tree crop variety in the Lapita economy is indirect but persuasive. Even the presence of the chicken, and more strongly of the pig, implies it. The need for horticulture is supported by the location of many Lapita sites. They are in situations that otherwise would require a far stronger commitment by the occupants than is evident to exploitation of marine resources or to hunting of birds and sea animals. Settlement size also demands that the residents must have maintained an economy in which horticulture was a mainstay. One very likely interpretation of the pits is in fact their use for storage of fermented banana, taro, or breadfruit. Finally, horticulture fits with the evidence of cooking ovens, pottery, cooking vessels, adzes, vegetable scrapers, and peelers in shell, and other tools typical of Oceanic societies that utilized tropical root and tree crops. I therefore question Groube's characterization (1971:312) of the Lapita potters as "Oceanic 'strandloopers' who, like the whalers and sealers in the European period, expanded ahead of colonization by agriculturists."

Exchange

No part of the Lapita evidence other than the pottery captures the imagination as much as the importation of items into Lapita sites from distances sufficiently far away to require open-sea voyaging for their transport. Although I avoid the word "trade" with respect to these items, not all writers do. My position is that what we have is evidence of imports—which in the case of the pottery, and probably the obsidian, came from other Lapita communities. At best, the evidence can be viewed as indicating no more than a network of reciprocal exchanges between related communities that maintained frequent contact.

The import list is dominated by obsidian, reasonable quantities of which were brought to Lapita sites on Eloaue, Watom, Ambitle, and the Main Reef–Santa Cruz islands for a period of up to 700 years. Some pieces were also taken to Malo, and a few to New Caledonia. The main source seems to have been Talasea, but the Lou source in the Admiralties and sources in the Banks Islands were also involved. In the one well-studied case (three sites in the Main Reef and Santa Cruz islands), all three obsidian sources were involved—the first instance in which a region to both the east and the west of a center have proved to be the source of a single material.

Importing of pots from other Lapita communities is widely indicated, although in every case most of the pottery proved to be made locally (Green 1976b). Thus few Lapita sherds of exotic origin have been found on Watom, and in the Reef–Santa Cruz, Malo, and Île des Pins sites. Most of the analytic work has been done by the geologist W. R. Dickinson (Dickinson and Shutler 1971), who finds that in the case of Watom and perhaps Talasea (Specht 1974) sources to the east are indicated; in the Reef–Santa Cruz case, the sources are to the west. An occasional two-way transfer of pots between the New Hebrides and New Caledonia is suggested by exotic sherds in both areas. Probably more important is that, on a general level, analyses of the decorative motifs have furnished evidence of a continuing interchange of ceramic information among communities.

Finished stone adzes and chert for flake tools were imported into the Reef–Santa Cruz sites from the southeast Solomons, while a chert-like material (phtanite) was imported into the Île des Pins from New Caledonia. Obsidian, adzes, and chert at times were transferred between sites in Fiji, Tonga, Samoa, and Futuna, but suffi-

2.4 A plano-lateral adz (lenticular section with flat sides) in a pale green meta-basalt rock from SE-RF-2, Nenumbo Village, Main Reef Islands, circa 1100 B.C.

cient evidence to indicate formal exchange is not available (Davidson 1977). However, no exchange items are known to have crossed the water gap between Fiji and the New Hebrides or New Caledonia at this time. Unusual imports include wallabies to the Eloaue sites in Mussau and a muscovite-garnet schist, perhaps from the New Guinea area, to the Reef and Santa Cruz island sites.

Apart from obsidian from Talasea (Specht and Sutherland 1975) and pots (with their contents?) from a number of sites, exports from specific Lapita sites are not in evidence. I suggest a yet to be discovered Lapita center in the southeast Solomons that made finished adzes of Lapita type in a distinctive pale green chloritic meta-basalt (Fig. 2.4); these were imported by Lapita

ROGER C. GREEN

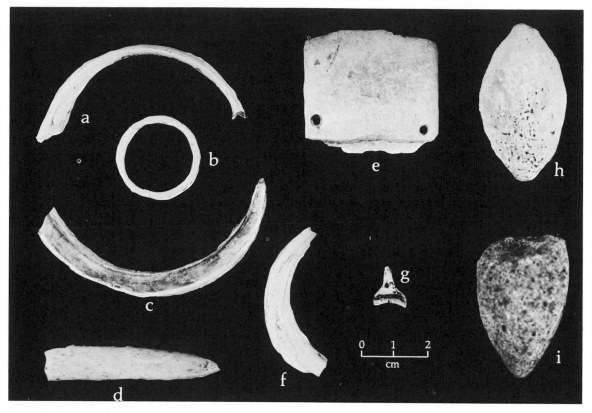

2.5 *A selection of portable artifacts, all but one of which are from SE-RF-2, Nenumbo Village, Main Reef Islands, circa 1100* B.C. *Items* a *and* c, *trochus shell arm rings;* d, *bone spear point;* e, *conus shell bracelet unit;* f, *worked pig-tusk piercing tool;* g, *drilled shark-tooth ornament;* h *and* i, *pointed-end slingstone of tridacna and basalt. Item* b *is a small shell ring from SE-RF-6, Ngamanie Village, Main Reef Islands, and dates to 700* B.C.

communities in the Reef and Santa Cruz islands and may also have been exchanged to the west.

Nonpottery Portable Artifacts

Because Lapita pottery is so distinctive, it is often thought that the rest of the cultural complex should be the same. However, given the great distribution of sites in space and time, it is more reasonable to anticipate variation and to focus on those processes that influence the cultural inventory from one area to the next, rather than concentrate on a few distinctive items found almost everywhere. From this point of view the Lapita cultural complex exhibits a full range of portable artifacts typical of many Oceanic assemblages. What is distinctive is

that many items in the Lapita sites of a particular area are not present in other cultural complexes either contemporary with it or later, often because they had to be imported.

A general inventory of the artifacts includes stone adzes with plano-lateral (Fig. 2.4), plano-convex, oval, and rectangular cross sections; shell adzes made from the giant clam; flake tools of chert and obsidian; shell scrapers and peelers; stone and coral files; and stone grinders, anvils, polishers, plus the so-called round-stone gaming disks. Other items include shell and stone slingstones with pointed ends (Fig. 2.5h,i).

Ornaments range from large (Fig. 2.5a,c) and small shell rings (Fig. 2.5b) through several types of shell bracelet units (Fig.

2.5*e*). There are also long shell beads perforated at the ends, pearl shell disks, and perforated shark teeth (Fig. 2.5*g*). Bone items consist of needles, awls, tattooing chisels, and spear points (Fig. 2.5*d*).

Simple shell fishhooks, though rare, are known from the Lapita sites in the Île des Pins, in Tonga, and in Samoa. Net sinkers and pumice floats are also in evidence.

The Lapita Ceramic Series and Design System

An extensive and detailed literature describes, analyzes, and interprets Lapita pottery. By and large it is of interest to the specialist only, particularly as it tends to deal with the minutiae of potsherds and their features. What attracts attention is that the pottery comes in an unexpected variety of vessel shapes with elaborate designs. The use of a set of comb-like toothed stamps to produce the dentate design impressions, probably filled with lime or some other white substance, is especially distinctive. However, other types of impressing, as well as incising, modeling, appliqué, and cut-away relief, were also used as decorative techniques.

The pottery is a sandy-textured low-fired earthenware whose surface is sometimes burnished or is slipped with a reddish clay. Pots were probably fired in the open, as is still the common Oceanic practice, and made by a combination of methods. The use of slab-building techniques on bases and at shoulder junctures is very evident, as is the careful wiping of the surface with a soft-textured material that obliterates any trace of the manufacturing techniques employed. Bonding of joints and compaction of vessel walls was certainly achieved at times by use of paddle and anvil. Ring building and hand molding and modeling (Fig. 2.6) have also been suggested as methods of performing at least some of the specialized tasks.

The Lapita ceramic series consists of vessel forms such as various shouldered pots (Fig. 2.7), open-mouthed jars, and flat-bottomed dishes (Fig. 2.8) with widely varying amounts of dentate-stamped, notched, and incised decoration. In addition, there is a range of infrequently decorated bowls of simple shapes and varying sizes, plus several forms of rather more frequently decorated subglobular pots (Fig. 2.9). Decoration on these vessels comprises elements and motifs whose occurrence can be listed and compared. To date 29 basic elements, including 8 zone markers, 18 two-dimensional, and 4 three-dimensional design elements have been identified; rules formulated for their combination lead to over 140 individual motifs. The restricted number of rules needed to generate the Lapita style from its elements, and the demonstration of a substantial corpus of early motifs spread from Watom to Samoa, are the most convincing evidence available that the style reflects a unified system known to the makers of the pots everywhere. The likelihood that we are dealing culturally with a series of closely related communities is therefore great. Yet each center or region also has its own unique motifs and developmental sequence and, as might be expected, early western and early and late eastern Lapita styles can be recognized by differences in vessel shapes, in motifs, in the style and frequency of decoration, and by the divergent trends in ceramic change in the two areas.

Decoration on Lapita pottery has been the subject of a careful and intensive analysis by investigators whose primary concern is developing formal methods for the study of Maori and Polynesian art (Mead et al. 1975). This work, which allows controlled comparisons of the design system from one pottery assemblage to another, has been extended by students and colleagues (Donovan 1973; Green 1976b; Hedrick, personal communication) to some 18 separate Lapita sites from 7 regions: Watom, Reef/Santa Cruz, New Hebrides, New Caledonia, Fiji, Tonga, and Samoa. When I did the analysis reported below, the data for the New

2.6　*Bird's head of modeled pottery from SE-SZ-8, Nanggu Village, Nendo (Santa Cruz) Island, dating to circa 1400* B.C.

2.7　*Reconstruction of type B vessel shape found at Paoancarai lagoon, Malo Island, New Hebrides. The decoration has been dusted with talc for photographic purposes. (Photo courtesy of J. D. Hedrick.)*

2.8　*Flat-bottomed dish from SE-RF-2, Nenumbo Village, Main Reef Islands, about 1100* B.C.

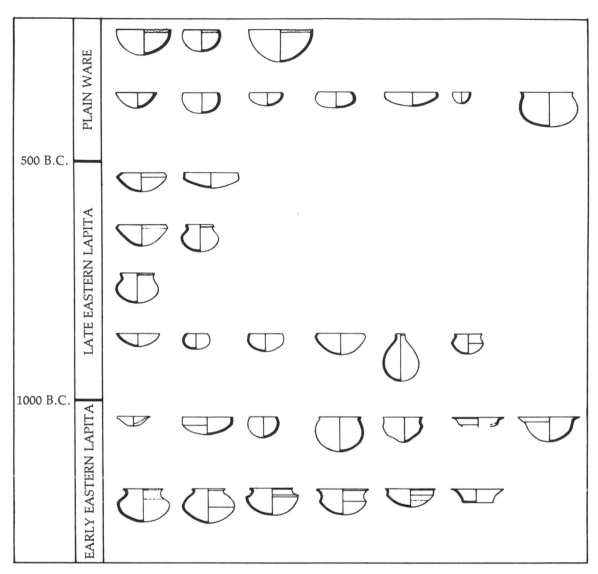

2.9 Simplified version of an analysis (Green 1974b) of change in vessel shape in the eastern Lapita cultural complex. The highly decorated vessels are complicated early shapes; later decoration, if any, is confined largely to the rims of the simpler vessel forms.

Hebrides were not available. However, the material since supplied by Hedrick for the Malo sites indicates further support for my conclusions.

Various techniques of analysis, often with the aid of a computer, have allowed sorting of the data and testing of a number of hypotheses (Green 1976b). One was the suggestion that the movement was from west to east, in an orderly geographic progression, with one branchoff to New Caledonia, and the other to the Fiji-Tonga-Samoa region. The results revealed an overall west-to-east trend indicative of distance decay in the Lapita design system, from the rather ornate curvilinear and fairly elaborate rectilinear design patterns of the western Lapita to the more simplified and generally rectilinear forms of the eastern Lapita. They also indicate that exchange of

ROGER C. GREEN

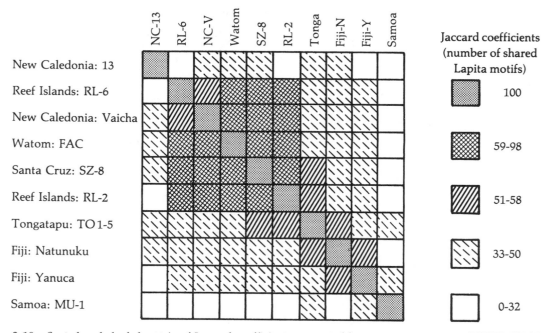

New Caledonia: 13

Reef Islands: RL-6

New Caledonia: Vaicha

Watom: FAC

Santa Cruz: SZ-8

Reef Islands: RL-2

Tongatapu: TO 1-5

Fiji: Natunuku

Fiji: Yanuca

Samoa: MU-1

Jaccard coefficients
(number of shared
Lapita motifs)

100

59-98

51-58

33-50

0-32

2.10 *Sorted and shaded matrix of Jaccard coefficients generated by computer programs COEFRAN (Q mode)
and MATRIX SORT for 54 motifs shared between at least two sites. In Tonga data for TO 1-5 are treated as a
tenth single site.*

motifs among the more westerly sites continued to occur, while in the eastern area Fiji, Tonga, and Samoa tended to remain in contact with one another but not with the regions to the west. Another analysis was a computer-sorted matrix of the shared motifs of nine individual Lapita sites, plus the Tongan sites TO 1-5 taken together as a tenth entity (Fig. 2.10). Although the matrix of individual sites did not seriate along a single dimension because it encompassed factors of spatial as well as temporal variability, it did identify the New Caledonian and later western Lapita sites at one end of the matrix, the eastern Lapita sites at the other end, and the early sites that were most closely related in the center.

Other analyses of 54 of the motifs shared between two or more sites allowed identification of motifs that were common, early, and widespread (Fig. 2.11). They also permitted identification of motifs characteristic of the western and eastern Lapita decoration styles. We are now well on the way toward distinguishing separate style areas as

well as demonstrating the core around which continuity in the Lapita decorative system was maintained over 4,000 km of space and up to 1,000 years in time.

Analyses of the decorative systems through time reveals other differences between the western and eastern Lapita sequences. In western sequences such as those from the Reef-Santa Cruz island group, there is an indication of some impoverishment of the local design system through time. This, however, is not related to the loss, as in the eastern Lapita ceramic assemblages, of the more elaborate vessel forms on which such decoration occurs. Rather the western Lapita ceramics retain their array of shoulder jars, bowls, and flat-bottomed dishes, with their highly complex decorative designs throughout the sequence. In the New Hebrides there are fewer vessel forms, and incising becomes the main decorative technique. By contrast, in the eastern Lapita sequences of Fiji, Tonga, and Samoa, the more elaborate and highly decorated vessel forms disappear

Early, widespread Lapita motifs:

Western motifs:

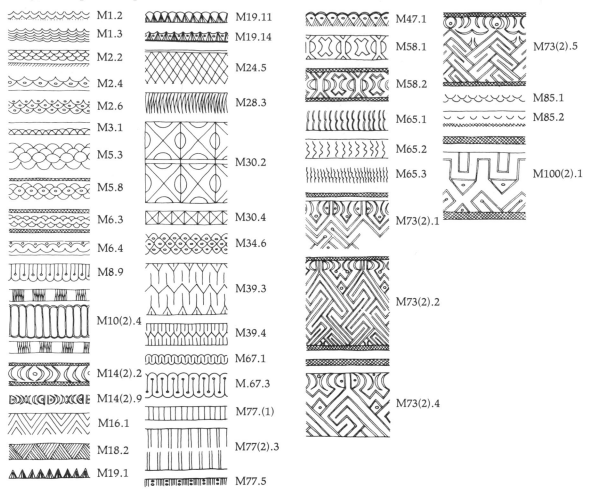

2.11 *Main Reef and Santa Cruz island examples of early, widespread Lapita motifs, and of more restricted motifs typical of the western Lapita sites, as determined from a cluster analysis of the 54 Lapita motifs shared by Lapita sites of two or more regions.*

during the second half of the sequence, and by the end only simple bowls and a globular jar shape with little or no decoration remain (Fig. 2.9). It seems that in the one case continued exchange of pots, as well as other items, provided a high degree of continuity and integration within the western Lapita exchange system. In the other cases isolation from this network resulted not only in a drift away from the original system, but also, in eastern Lapita, in a quite separate line of ceramic simplification that

led to the plain-ware pottery assemblages of Polynesia from Futuna, Samoa, Tonga, and the Marquesas.

Finally, it is worth noting that a formal comparison between the Lapita design system and Polynesian art, especially the design motifs retained in tattooing and bark cloth (Green 1978) indicates that the Lapita art style, which probably extended to tattooing and bark cloth as well as to pottery, is a likely basis for much of the Polynesian art style.

ROGER C. GREEN

Interpretations

Origins

There seems no way of avoiding the inevitable question about the ultimate origins of the Lapita cultural complex. The short answer, archaeologically, is that we do not know. No satisfactory ancestral cultural complex either in Melanesia or Island Southeast Asia has yet been excavated. An eastern area of Island Southeast Asia is certainly a very likely site on the grounds of language, food plants, domestic animals, technology, watercraft, and voyaging capability, as well as other aspects of the cultural content.

The question of Lapita's immediate origins within the currently known distribution of sites can be answered more positively. Howells (1973), for example, tentatively postulated that Lapita ancestors were reef fishers with no domestic animals and little in the way of agriculture, who came from eastern Micronesia to eastern Melanesia to establish in the New Hebrides a center from which they spread both east and west. Later they borrowed from their Melanesian neighbors the horticultural plants and domestic animals they lacked. This theory, which may assist in interpreting the evidence of physical anthropology, draws heavily on the view of the Lapita economy taken by Groube, which is not strongly supported by more recent archaeological evidence. The alternative route through Melanesia is, as Howells observes, logical and direct and has the lands necessary for keeping domestic animals and plants without the need of later borrowing to explain their more recent presence in Fiji and Polynesia.

My arguments are similar. The hypothesis I advance is that the original Lapita adaptation was to an area with a complex continental island environment, which possessed a wide range of resources that related communities could assemble through exchange. This I place in the New Britain–New Ireland area, from which for 700 years communities far to the east obtained obsidian. It seems to me unlikely that the Lapita cultural complex—with its emphasis on pottery, stone adzes, obsidian, chert, other continental rock types, and domesticated animals such as pigs and chickens—derives from eastern Micronesia; nor am I able to see its origin in the Reef and Santa Cruz island region. In fact, I have argued that the original Lapita adaptation could be maintained in the more restricted environments of the Reef and Santa Cruz islands only by the maintenance of long-distance as well as local exchange networks (Green 1976a).

The strongest support for the immediate Lapita homeland being in the New Britain–New Ireland area is that based on the study of the pottery, in particular on the results of the analyses of the decorative system. The fact that sites in the New Britain–New Ireland area, as early as any to the east of them, have not yet been excavated and dated can easily be explained by the difficulties archaeologists have faced in finding and excavating intact sites. That sites there as early as those elsewhere are to be expected is indicated by obsidian in the area from two sources—one of them a main source—turning up in the early sites far to the west, even though sources in the Banks Islands much closer to the Santa Cruz and Malo sites were known and used. The occurrence of other imports in the sites of the Reef and Santa Cruz islands (pottery, chert, meta-basalt stone adzes, abraded pieces of muscovite-garnet-schist) also point to the west rather than to equally close sites in Howell's postulated Lapita center in the New Hebrides.

Voyaging

A capability for effective two-way voyaging—A to B to A and then back to B—must underlie any exchange network in the Pacific that serves communities as widely distributed as the Lapita. Several studies have shown that effective two-way voyaging is most easily maintained over distances of up

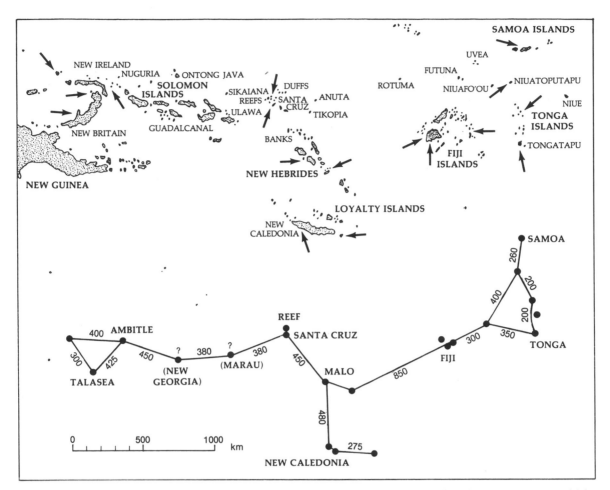

2.12 *An analysis showing the distances involved if a voyaging network connected all known centers in which Lapita sites occur, or hypothetical centers if suitable islands but no sites existed within a two-way voyaging range of 600 km. The map is oriented slightly west of north, so the impression of an east-west alignment of all except the New Caledonian sites is heightened.*

to 310 nautical miles (357 statute miles or 574 km). Most islands in the Pacific are in fact no more distant from one another than that and authorities, otherwise at odds, such as Sharp (1963) and Lewis (1972) are in general agreement that regular and historically well-attested two-way voyaging did in fact occur over such distances.

Further insight into the distribution of Lapita sites results if they are analyzed into a network of local centers, each with its own set and sequence of sites, and the centers are then used to formulate the points between which two-way open-ocean voyaging occurred. Starting with known

Lapita centers in the west and moving eastward to wherever there are suitable islands for settlement within an otherwise vast expanse of ocean led to an open-ended network of linked centers in which no known centers are unconnected if there is suitable land within 600 km (Fig. 2.12). One result was the postulation of three (then unverified) centers in the chain: one in the Lau group of Fiji, since found; one toward the eastern end of the Solomon Islands proper, indicated with a high probability by products from that area in the Reef–Santa Cruz Lapita sites; and one or probably more, still to be discovered, in the area between there

ROGER C. GREEN

and the Ambitle site at the eastern end of the Bismarck Archipelago.

Only east of the New Hebrides or New Caledonia is no center possible within the usual range of two-way voyaging. Moreover, computer simulation studies of the potential for one-way drift voyages across this water gap to settle Fiji, indicate little likelihood that the gap was often crossed by chance (Levison et al. 1972). To cross it in an easterly direction would have involved deliberate one-way voyages of more than 515 nautical miles (954 km)—a not impossible task, as a few deliberate voyages of such length without intervening land are known from the period of first contact of Pacific islanders with Europeans. The point is that this water gap presented a significant barrier to two-way voyaging and constitutes a significant break in the Lapita exchange network across which few, if any, goods flowed. As a result, events in the eastern Lapita area of Fiji, Tonga, and Samoa, once these areas were settled, proceeded in their own fashion more or less in isolation from events in Lapita communities farther west.

Contemporary and Earlier Cultural Complexes

Writers such as Shutler and Marck have attributed the arrival of Austronesian horticulturists in most areas of island Melanesia to the Lapita cultural complex. In particular, they claim (1975:95) that enough work has been done in the New Hebrides, New Caledonia, Fiji, and Polynesia "to reasonably suggest the temporal priority of Lapita over other horticultural traditions." Although the claim appears likely for Polynesia and probably for Fiji, elsewhere in Melanesia it is open to question. In fact, all would probably agree it does not apply in the Bismarck Archipelago (see Chapter 15), the location I propose as the immediate homeland of the Lapita cultural complex. Settlement of the Bismarcks by other Austronesian horticulturists with and without pottery at dates contemporary with, as well

as much earlier than, Lapita are either known or are to be expected, as is much earlier settlement by non-Austronesians.

Eastward to the Solomons, there is on Guadalcanal a nonpottery but otherwise neolithic Oceanic cultural complex beginning as early as the Lapita. Represented in several occupation layers at the base of Fotoruma cave on the Poha River, occupation continues at intervals between rockfalls almost to the present (Black and Green 1977). Other cultural assemblages of the same age as Lapita are known from Anuta (Kirch and Rosendahl 1976) and from Santa Ana (Swadling 1976; Black and Green 1977); they exhibit different styles of pottery and other items that identify them as separate complexes.

In the New Hebrides Garanger (1972) demonstrated the temporal overlap between a quite different and widely dispersed early Mangaasi pottery complex and the later end of the Lapita sequence. There is every indication he did not find the earliest Mangaasi sites. My impression is that in the central New Hebrides the earliest Mangaasi is more likely to be the founding cultural complex, and Lapita the intrusive one, as the occurrence of a few Mangaasi sherds in the Erueti sites suggests. Also, Shutler (1971) has demonstrated the existence of nonpottery Oceanic horticulturists in the southern New Hebrides from circa 500 B.C. and suggests the evidence gives reason to expect settlement there from at least 3,000 years ago. The first direct evidence of such horticultural activities from 200 B.C. in this region, supplied by Groube (1975), is certainly not the earliest.

The New Caledonian case is more complicated and cannot be discussed fully here. Suffice it to say that Smart (1969) obtained radiocarbon dates for ceramic sites on the west coast of New Caledonia with either plain or paddle-impressed pottery. These indicated a complete chronological overlap with Lapita, which suggested to him the possibility of contemporary pottery complexes. More recent evidence of paddle-impressed sherds in the Lapita horizons of sites in New Caledonia, including paddle-impressed techniques evidenced by some Lapita-style sherds, has been presented by Frimigacci (1976). Finally there are the tumuli, without pottery, but in both coastal and inland locations—a fact that demands their makers be horticulturists in order to subsist. On the evidence available from the admittedly difficult to interpret ^{14}C dates (Rafter et al. 1972), from the lack of pottery belonging to any later horizon, and from the association with the same extinct species of *Placostylus* land snail as in the Lapita sites, the tumuli should be as early or earlier than the Lapita (Pawley and Green 1973; Shutler and Marck 1975).

Language

Pawley and Green (1973) have outlined in detail the basic arguments for equating the eastern Lapita cultural complex with the protolanguage of the central Pacific subgroup of eastern Oceanic languages, the latter being the easternmost group of the Austronesian language family. Central Pacific includes the languages of Fiji and Polynesia; eastern Oceanic, as most recently defined by Pawley (1978), includes all the central Pacific languages, and those of the Northern Banks and central New Hebrides. To this subgroup the languages of eastern Micronesia can also be assigned with an increasing degree of confidence (Shutler and Marck 1975; Pawley, personal communication). Shutler and Marck, in a more recent consideration of the linguistic affiliations of the Lapita, have accepted the correlation of eastern Lapita and the central Pacific protolanguage. They extend the correlation, however, to include the New Hebridean Lapita and the northern New Hebridean protolanguage, and even to suggest possible correlation of all Lapita with a higher level subgrouping of the Oceanic Austronesian languages. There is little to support their case, which they concede is speculative. Rather, having examined this question for Lapita sites in the Solomons and then for all Lapita sites (Green 1976c), I would

warn against any attempt to assign a linguistic identity to the people responsible for the western Lapita sites. There are several possible ways the eastern Lapita populations could have acquired their central Pacific language, none of which can be excluded at present.

Physical Type

The state of the argument for the genetic identity of the bearers of the Lapita cultural complex is very like the linguistic one. A difference is that when more Lapita skeletal remains are recovered, the discrepancies may be resolved in part by direct evidence. The most satisfactory current hypothesis is the one argued by Howells (1973), which concludes that the eastern Lapita people are to be correlated with the unified and reasonably homogeneous ancestral Polynesian and pre-Polynesian populations as reconstructed from more recent skeletal materials and living populations. A weaker although still plausible hypothesis is that people belonging to the pre-Polynesian population of Howells are the bearers of the Lapita culture in the New Hebrides and New Caledonia. It is more difficult, without substantial direct evidence, to attempt to guess the genetic affinities of the people responsible for the western Lapita sites. The problem is providing all the necessary controls; the available data are largely from recent populations who are the result of three to four thousand years of genetic change in an area with a complex and little-known prehistory.

Polynesian Origins

For a decade now Emory's (1959) proposal that, instead of looking for a migration of Polynesians, we seek their development as Polynesians within Polynesia itself has steadily gained acceptance (Green 1967; Groube 1971). Today in a volume on Polynesia it is still necessary to deal with a migration, but one by Lapita ancestors, most of whom remained in Melanesia. We do

ROGER C. GREEN

not currently know what became of the Lapita populations who remained there; while the issue is an important one, it is not crucial in the present context, except in that it stresses that becoming Polynesian in Polynesia is one of the few aspects of the Lapita migration that can be traced with any confidence. Elsewhere these populations may have suffered cultural collapse and absorption as the result of a failure in their exchange system, or they may have been replaced or their population overwhelmed and their culture modified by new immigrants, or they may have developed their exchange network to take in unrelated neighbors and thus become ancestors of the more specialized traders characteristic of a number of later Melanesian societies. The possibilities are multiple.

In Fiji and Polynesia at least, some possibilities are excluded by the growing body of data that strongly support the proposals advanced here. They make it reasonable to suppose that one group of eastern Lapita became Polynesian in Polynesia as Emory suggested, and another played a leading role among the founding populations of Fiji. Moreover, it was the Lapita ancestors who developed many of the preadaptations in voyaging and navigation, who established viable populations with their plants and animals on the less well endowed islands of Melanesia, and who pursued what Buck (1938) called a Viking-like quest to continue exploration ever into the sunrise that allowed their Polynesian descendants to fill the remaining empty zone of the Pacific in something like a thousand years.

The Lapita cultural complex in my view is an important step in an adaptive series that has permitted man's expansion throughout the Pacific (Green 1976b). The people involved represent a migration of an innovative kind that has allowed the filling of little-used niches in Melanesia, as well as the pioneering of unsettled islands beyond. This view should bring joy to the heart of all those romantics who have so long sought the origins of the Polynesians in intrepid voyagers from one or more quarters of the Pacific. Their only disappointment will be that the Polynesians were not yet Polynesian, and that the logical and direct route through Melanesia long favored by the "establishment" has proved to contain the vital evidence.

Appendix to Chapter 2

Size and Number of Lapita Sites by Locality

I believe it probable that the westernmost Lapita sites in Oceania are still to be discovered. The most western sites known thus far are on Eloaue Island, a low, flat coral island on the southeast side of the high island of Mussau in the St. Matthias group (Fig. 2.2, 1). One locality, ECB, was an irregular shallow midden only 20 m in diameter, from which badly eroded sherds, some obsidian, and a few pieces of bone were recovered in test pits covering 4 m². In the other locality, ECA, excavations totaling 12 m² tested several shallow midden areas, one of which was reasonably productive (Egloff 1975). Two of the middens, with their long axis parallel to and several hundred meters inland from the respective coastlines (here about 900 m apart) have been cut by the construction of an airstrip across the island. They are separated by some 200 m, with a smaller patch of midden in between. Dimensions of the two larger middens are about 150 × 50 m.

The central part of the Willaumez Peninsula on the north coast of New Britain is the source of the Talasea obsidian found in many Lapita sites throughout Melanesia (Fig. 2.2, 2). Only one Lapita sherd has been found within the limits of the obsidian flows; Lapita sites, however, are close by (Specht 1974; Specht and Sutherland 1975). On the east side of the Talasea Peninsula, areas of old coral reef form low raised platforms indicating either uplift or periods of higher sea level. It is on these that the Lapita sites occur. Four sites have been reported, but none have been excavated—either because the sites have been very disturbed or because the conditions preclude excavation. The two sites on the peninsula itself, FCN and FCS, have been virtually destroyed by bulldozing and road building. Still, eroded material along the beach front of one indicates it extended for a distance of approximately 800 m. Plain and decorated sherds, obsidian flakes, and stone tools in a pale green imported rock have been recovered from both sites. The other two sites are on small offshore islands in Garua harbor. As on the mainland, the Buduna Island site rests on a raised coral platform, with the Lapita materials cemented in a calcareous beach rock that is covered at high tide. The Lapita site on Garua Island today is concealed by mangrove swamp.

Father Meyer's Watom site of Rakival now has the number FAC (Fig. 2.2, 3). Two locations within the missionary area of the village, where Meyer carried out most of his investigation, were carefully re-examined by Specht (1968). A stream that flows along the base of a limestone cliff, first exposing the pottery, defines the southern end of the site. Next to the stream Specht excavated a series of squares covering 100 m²; in all but 10 m² he reached pottery deposits at depths up to 3 m, having penetrated up to 2 m of overburden that consisted mainly of redeposited volcanic ash and small lenses of silt. Fifty meters to the north Specht put in two test squares of 16 m². His results there suggest that the southern end of the site lay in what was formerly a low-lying rocky area. This was subject to waterlogging from the stream

and its associated embayment, which at that time were somewhat north of their present position. The stream separated this area from a slightly raised and well-drained coralline sand dune to the north. The low rocky area Specht interpreted as a refuse dump, which by the fourth century A.D. had become a swamp. The dune was believed to be the habitation area. In it some postholes and three roughly contemporary burials were encountered; the bones from two of these were used for a radiocarbon date.

North from the mission compound, underlain by a former sand dune, the beach flat again narrows. Latrine and rubbish pits here occasionally show signs of the pottery occupation. Meyer also recovered pottery from the main village flat in a second little valley several hundred meters to the north. This locality which, following Specht, I would regard as a separate site, was tested but proved to be badly disturbed. A third Lapita site, situated at a tip of the raised limestone cliff under 1.5 m of ash, was discovered about 600 m west of the main village site, and another, some 4 km to the south behind the coastal village of Vunakabai, was reported by Meyer but not located again by Specht. On the evidence presented by Specht, a habitation area exceeding 50 × 35 m in an area 150 to 200 m long would seem to be indicated for the main FAC site.

The Malekolon Lapita site (Fig. 2.2, 4) designated as EAQ is found on a small flattish peninsula at the north end of Ambitle, a small volcanic island off the southeast coast of New Ireland (White and Specht 1971). The main pottery-bearing deposits, some 500 m from the present beach and 3 m above the high-water mark, show clear signs of disturbance, probably from major flooding. Obsidian and pottery are present in a fine sandy volcanic ash from near the surface to a depth of about 1.5 m, where the ash merges into an underlying clay and clay-and-gravel mixture. The majority of the sherds are said to occur below 50 cm in depth. Ambrose (personal communication)

ROGER C. GREEN

excavated a total of 19 m² in four separate areas over a distance of 45 m. Augering to a depth of 2 m at a grid interval of 20 m indicated that there was at least 4,000 m² of deposit containing an estimated 12 tons of pottery. The site could in fact be larger, as pottery has also been found in an eroding stream bank 150 m away. Other sites may also be present, for pottery and obsidian occur in sparse scatterings elsewhere along the 6-km track around the peninsula.

While Lapita sites may be predicted to occur at several places in the Solomon Islands chain west of the next known region of sites in the Santa Cruz Island group, they have not yet been found. Most of the Solomon Islands are still a blank on the archaeological map, and there have been few site surveys in likely areas. Lapita sites have not been found in the better-surveyed islands of the Shortlands, in the western Solomons, nor in Ulawa, Uki, San Cristobal, Santa Ana, or Santa Catalina in the southeast Solomons. Plain pottery of appropriate age has been found in Santa Ana, but I do not regard it as Lapita (Swadling 1976). The same applies to a few sherds of pottery recovered from a site on Bellona of slightly younger age (Poulsen 1972) and some surface sherds of pottery from Ontong Java.

In the Santa Cruz group, six Lapita sites have been found on two of the Main Reef Islands of Ngalo and Fenualoa (Fig. 2.2, 5), which are slightly uplifted, low, flat, recrystallized coral limestone platforms (Green 1976a). One of the sites (SE-RF-7) consists of a small separate scatter of sherds between two larger sites on Te Motu Taibä, but the other five sites on surface evidence are more extensive (Fig. 2.13). The Nenumbo site (SE-RF-2) on Te Motu Taibä in the Ngaua district has a well-defined surface size of between 800 and 1,100 m², of which 14 percent or 153 m², largely in the southern half of the site, has been excavated. Its long axis, which parallels the coast, is 160 m from the lagoon beach. The settlement was made on white coral beach sand containing waterborne pumice, at present

about 2.4 m above the average high-tide mark. Later the site was covered by 30 to 40 cm of a now decomposed volcanic ash tuff, in which the Lapita materials have been incorporated through years of gardening. The ash is from the nearby and still active volcano of Tinakula. In the underlying charcoal-stained grey sand occupation layer, however, major structural features are well preserved (Fig. 2.3).

The other two much larger Lapita sites on Te Motu Taibä are also parallel to the coast but set back from it, with SE-RF-4 being on a raised beach surface now several meters above the high-tide mark. So far only the Ngamanie Lapita site (SE-RF-6) has been found in the Ngaua district on the larger island of Neuwa, also called Lomlom (Fig. 2.13). The site runs parallel and next to the now mangrove-choked channel between Te Motu Taibä and Neuwa. With a sampling interval of one square meter in every nine and stratified, systematic, unaligned selection procedures, a 180-m² transect across the site was investigated by means of excavations that totaled 20 m². The width of the site is about 40 m, and its length on surface evidence is 270 m; the surface area is therefore 10,800 m². Excavations revealed a thin grey sand occupation layer that increased to more than a meter's depth toward the beach. The ash-rich surface deposit has been disturbed by yam gardening. The occupation layer is underlain by the raised coral limestone.

One Lapita site, of size comparable to RF-6, has been recorded on Ngasinue (Fenualoa) (Fig. 2.13).

Three Lapita sites are known from Nendö or Santa Cruz Island (Green 1976a). Two are on the southeast raised coralline coast of the main island, and the other on the adjacent raised coral island of Tömotu Noi (Fig. 2.2, 6). Only one, the Nanggu site (SE-SZ-8), has been investigated in detail. Again, the site is some 468 m inland from the present coastline, with one and perhaps two raised beaches in between. On the surface evidence of pottery distribution, the site is 70 to 100 m wide and 250 m long

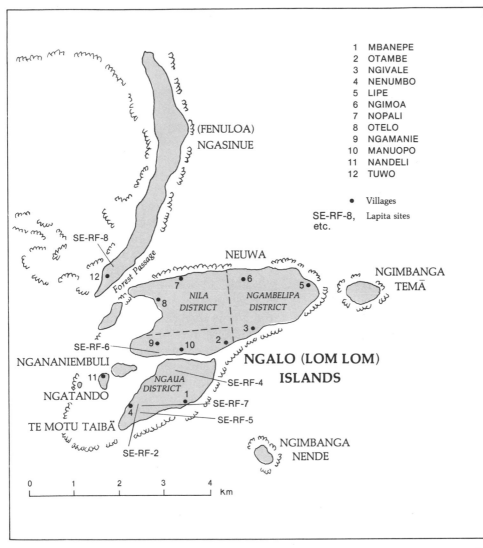

1 MBANEPE
2 OTAMBE
3 NGIVALE
4 NENUMBO
5 LIPE
6 NGIMOA
7 NOPALI
8 OTELO
9 NGAMANIE
10 MANUOPO
11 NANDELI
12 TUWO

● Villages

SE-RF-8,   Lapita sites
etc.

2.13   Map of Lapita sites in the Main Reef Islands. Adoption of the official Solomon Island Site Survey Registry numbers has altered the site codes as used by Green (1976a). Further information relating to multiple names in two languages for each of the individual islands within the reef, some confusion between district and individual island names, and the recent appearance of the name Ngalo (once Lomlom) on official maps for all land included within the surrounding reef system have led to the present version of this map.

and covers an area of some 14,000 m². Of this a T-shaped sampling transect of 459 m² toward the southern end of the site was laid out; with a sampling interval of one square meter in nine and stratified, systematic, unaligned selection procedures, a total of 51 m² was excavated. Charcoal-stained occupation deposits in the coral sand soil reached depths of 60 cm before coral lime-stone was struck; the surface deposits have been intensively gardened, and those at lower levels sufficiently disturbed so that few features were recorded.

Lapita sites in the New Hebrides are known from two localities. One is the small offshore islands of Malo and adjacent Aore at the southern end of Espiritu Santo; the other is on the southern coast of the island

ROGER C. GREEN

of Efate. Malo Island lies on a tilt block fault, and the older sites on it have been subjected to changes in land level (Fig. 2.2, 7). The first Lapita site there was initially described as a low mound at Avunatori (NH-MA-7) composed of a series of deposits dating to the first millennium A.D. (Hedrick 1971). It has now been demonstrated that while the mound's formation is of that age, the sherds in its deposits are not. Rather, they were incorporated in the mound when it was formed by later people scooping up much earlier primary deposits with Lapita pottery from the surrounding area.

More recent investigations on Malo by Hedrick (personal communication) have shown that a continuous line of occupation sites or area utilizations extends for more than 10 km along a 9- to 10-m-high raised beach terrace some distance back from the present shore. No Lapita material occurs in place on the higher ground above this terrace or below it in the former lagoon bed, and little or no Lapita pottery is found more than 100 m from the terrace. This closely parallels the environmental setting and distribution of Lapita sites on Niuatoputapu in the northern Tongan group (Rogers 1974).

Hedrick is currently completing his analysis of three excavated site locations: NH-MA-7, NH-MA-8, and NH-MA-101. All have a configuration similar to that of the dated site NH-MA-8, where three shallow layers in a deposit with a total depth of 35 cm indicate the repeated disturbance of the former occupation layer. The upper layer is a recent garden soil, with numerous irregular pits and holes that penetrate all other layers. Below this is a 15- to 20-cm-thick midden, then a thinner occupation layer associated with some pit features. The base is a culturally sterile fine sand, once part of the lagoon front.

The Erueti site on Efate is 400 m from the beach at the back of a bay protected by two islands too low for habitation (Fig. 2.2, 8). Again the 80-cm-deep deposits proved highly disturbed and without visible stratigraphy. They overlie a low Pleistocene coral limestone platform on which a soil had developed before occupation of the site began. The distribution of surface sherds indicated a former settlement some 250 m in diameter, of which Garanger (1972) excavated 38 m² in a series of levels. Most of the sherds and portable artifacts were recovered from depths between 40 and 70 cm, the dated charcoal sample coming from the 65-cm level. It seems likely this zone represents an occupation layer, because most of the sherds that could be fitted together came from this zone. Also, given that 5.2 percent of the pottery decoration is confined to the lip area and only 1.26 percent is found on body sherds, it is significant that the 20- to 40-cm level (which has the least amount of pottery) has 7.5 percent of the decorated pieces versus 2.6 and 1.9 percent for the two levels below. This suggests that the rims of formerly more complete pots from the 40- to 70-cm occupation level below have ended up in this level (Garanger 1972).

Three Lapita localities are known from New Caledonia, all of which present problems of interpretation, especially in determining which deposits are primary and which reworked. The first to be excavated was that of Lapita (site 13) located along a south-facing beach on the Foué Peninsula of the west coast of central New Caledonia (Fig. 2.2, 9). Here Gifford and Shutler (1956) excavated at two localities 400 m apart, the first yielding less than half the density of sherds of the second. In the first location potsherds, shell, bone, and charcoal were concentrated between 69 and 99 cm in depth below the surface in what is described as "beach debris," overlain by 60 cm of "black to brown adobe" (clay). Two test pits, each 1.7 m² and about 2.5 m apart, were excavated. A second series of excavations was carried out in location A, 400 m east of the first, where along 400 m of an exposed beach front, midden sherds were visible in section. At the previous location all 40 percent of the sherds carried Lapita decoration; here only 33 percent did, while the other 3 percent were of a paddle-impressed type, for the most part with what Gifford and Shutler (1956) called ribbed-relief decoration. Although one excavation of 1.7 m² in this location was abandoned as unproductive, those in an aligned series of rectangles beginning some 18 m back from the sea and extending inland opened up 11.7 m² of deposit. The results demonstrated that the 400-m exposure of midden in the beach front was at least 30 m wide. Shutler (1971) reports the deposits as having been disturbed by yam gardening.

A more recent section by Frimigacci (1975) shows the beach front at location A of site 13 to comprise 70 cm of archaeological deposits mixed with grey pumice; it contains the same kind of pottery as found there by Gifford and Shutler. The occupation layer rests on a 3-m-high Holocene marine terrace of unconsolidated fine sand, which has yellow pumice at its top. Shells from the bottom of the cultural deposits recently have been dated, giving an age compatible with the far more general first millennium B.C. radiocarbon estimates based on the early stages of CO_2 gas proportional counting reported by Gifford and Shutler (see Table 2.1).

The Lapita site of Boirra, near Koumac, is located on an embayment on the west coast of the northern part of New Caledonia (Fig. 2.2, 10). The site begins approximately 30 m back from the beach and continues inland more than 80 m. Here isolated dunes with stratified archaeological deposits are found for several hundred meters behind a beach sheltered by Paudop Point to the north. The dunes are developed on an old and level Holocene marine terrace composed of shelly beach sand with yellow pumice on its surface. The terrace is 1.8 m above present mean sea level. Sections cut through two dunes over 100 m apart revealed a very similar stratigraphy (Frimigacci 1975). At the base archaeological deposits lie horizontally on the raised beach surface; in one case a second fairly thin horizontal occupation lens is incorporated

in the beginnings of the subsequent dune formation. This lens has been radiocarbon dated to the second century A.D. (Frimigacci, personal communication). The upper pottery-bearing deposits have a similar archaeological content, but undulate over the sterile lenses of dune sand that separate them from the earlier occupation layer. I am not certain whether these deposits constitute an intact later occupation, as Frimigacci believes, or are simply reworked deposits from the underlying occupation.

The Lapita site of Vatcha, near Vao, on the Île des Pins (Fig. 2.2, 11) has been referred to both as the St. Maurice site and as a site on the beach of St. Francis (Frimigacci 1974). Unlike the other two Lapita sites, this one has more certain evidence of a stratigraphically intact earlier occupation as well as a later one. Moreover, the underlying occupation at this site is, on geologic grounds, earlier than the Lapita occupations at the previous two sites, for it is associated with the earlier sandy deposits prior to the yellow pumice rather than with the later raised-beach-terrace deposits. Accordingly, it is the overlying Lapita deposits at this site that are directly associated first with the yellow and then with the grey pumice.

The initial Lapita occupation at Vatcha is situated on old and indurated shelly marine beach sand, exposed by a former retreat of the sea to a level near the present one. Occupation on the unconsolidated upper surface of the beach turned the deposit grey (Horizon IV). In an area of 35 m² Frimigacci exposed an undisturbed living floor with a midden dump, hearths, and other features covering some 20 m². Two test squares, one 20 m inland and another 90 m west along the beach from the main area, revealed the same horizon, but with only vestiges of human occupation.

A dune (Horizon III), which subsequently covered the site, had its formation interrupted by a change of sea level that planed its surface and deposited a lens of yellow pumice. On this surface further Lapita occupation (Horizon II), associated with a posthole, an oven, and some other features, occurred. However, as some 23 percent of the sherds in Horizon II are rolled or eroded, the deposit apparently has been disturbed, at least in places. On the evidence of nine widely distributed test pits of 10 m², this occupation covered an area of more than 30 × 90 m. It corresponds to the occupation horizon excavated by Golson (1962). He excavated a series of four test pits totaling 26 m² along the beach frontage over a distance of 126 m and found them to be uniformly rich in material. Another 6-m² test pit 29 m from the beach had less material, while one 69 m inland produced almost nothing.

In one place, at the base of the uppermost deposit (Horizon I), Frimigacci discovered what appears to be part of an intact Lapita occupation (Horizon Ib) in association with yellow pumice and with only a few rolled or eroded sherds. By contrast, some 43 percent of the sherds in the rest of this sand, grey pumice, and humus deposit (Horizon Ia) are rolled and eroded. Golson remarks that the upper levels of the site had been turned over and their contents mixed by past agricultural activities. He also states that the pottery therefore was more fragmentary, and only at lower levels were distinct and distinctive layers undeniably present.

Palmer (1966) reported five known or potential Lapita sites on Viti Levu in the Fiji group, to which several others have now been added. However, only four of these and one more recently found on Lakeba in the Lau group have been excavated. The oldest is the Natunuku site (VL 1/1) located on a small tidal embayment between Ba and Tavua on the northwest side of Viti Levu (Fig. 2.2, 12). It comprises one or perhaps two adjacent Lapita settlements reflected by deposits that now extend inland from the rapidly eroding beach front only a few meters away. A number of lines of evidence suggest that within the last 40 years some 50 to 80 m of this beach front has been removed. Shaw (1975 and personal

communication) excavated test rectangles at three localities along it, the first two being 100 m apart and the third 175 m beyond. Cultural deposits of Lapita age around the first locality extended along the beach for 50 to 75 m and around the third locality for up to 200 m. Materials also were picked up as much as 100 m out onto the tidal mudflats in front of the site. Six layers approximately a meter thick were distinguished in the excavated deposits. The upper four contained cultural materials of several origins (European, paddle impressed, incised, and Lapita pottery), which from the extensive disturbance by grave digging, gardening, and natural agencies are now somewhat mixed. It is only in the fairly restricted white coralline beach sand of layer 5, and the more yellow beach sands of layer 6, that materials restricted to the Lapita cultural complex are encountered. These deposits, attesting to a former sandy-beach foreshore on which Lapita settlement once occurred, rest on blocks of consolidated beach rock formed when mean sea level was at about that height. The sea, which had retreated from this locality some time before Lapita settlement, has again returned, and at present the deposits are being removed by a prograding sea and retreating shorelines. No structural features were identified, but one young adult burial in crouch position was found in locality C, layer 5a.

The Lapita site (VL 16/81) on Yanuca, an island about 200 m off the south coast of Viti Levu, runs along the base of a sea-eroded cliff of coral limestone 6 m high and faces onto a shallow channel between Yanuca and Viti Levu (Fig. 2.2, 13). The site, which is 143 m long, is partially protected to the rear by the overhang of the limestone cliff (Fig. 2.14). Excavation was limited to 15 m at its western end, in which area 55 m² of deposits were removed to a depth of 1.8 m (Birks and Birks 1967). Because of the construction of a road between the sea-edge and the cliff, only 4.5 m width of deposits were still intact; before then, they may have been 6 to 8 m wide and the

2.14 *Excavations in progress in a limestone rock shelter, VL 16/81, on Yanuca Island, Fiji, dating to circa 1300 B.C. Lapita materials occur in lowest 46 cm of 1.8 m of deposit.*

site initially may have covered about 840 m². The 46 cm of cultural deposits at the base, which contained almost all the Lapita sherds, were laid down on a 61-cm-deep deposit of sand and marine shell that rested on the base of the wave-cut notch in the limestone cliff. This former beach surface is 1.6 m above the present high-tide level.

The Lapita occupation (VL 16/1) at Sigatoka occurs on the lowest of three humus-rich paleosols formed during periods when the immense dune system in the area was for a while stable and covered with vegetation (Fig. 2.2, 14). The paleosol horizon of Level 1, traced along the base of the dunes for over 177 m, begins only 14 m back from the present beach front (Fig. 2.15). In occu-

pied areas the grey-brown sand of Level 1 averages about 28 cm in depth and lies directly on top of a yellow beach sand. This has a fairly level surface, now 1.7 m above the mean high-water mark. Cultural deposits in Level 1 were limited to two zones, one 67 × 23 m and the other 40 × 18 m, separated from each other by a 37-m interval. Whether one site or two separate though nearly contemporary sites are involved is not certain. Two seem likely, as sufficient testing (55.7 m²) was carried out in the area between to demonstrate its lack of pottery or evidence of other occupation. In the two areas of occupation an amazing total of 938 m² was excavated, which yielded data on 114 partially restorable vessels (Birks 1973). Structural features, on the

ROGER C. GREEN

2.15 *Area excavations in progress at the windswept dune site of Sigatoka, VL 16/1, Viti Levu, Fiji, dating to circa 600* B.C. *Debris inland of the posts, which mark a 6.1-m grid, traces the approximate edge of the lowest of three horizons in which the Lapita deposits occur.*

other hand, were few—a handful of stake holes and three possible firepits.

A test excavation of 4.2 m² was also carried out in a steep eroding bank (VL 16/22) behind the beach in the area of reef-protected coast 4.8 km west of Sigatoka. Again the basal deposits rested on hard yellow beach sand, in which seven postholes and a firepit were found. Lapita and other pottery types were found in the four cultural layers above (Birks and Birks 1967).

The most recently excavated site in Fiji with Lapita pottery at its base is on Lakeba Island in the Lau group (Fig. 2.2, 15). Here a rock shelter formed from the wave-cut notch in the limestone cliff has long served as a shelter in which cultural deposits of several periods have accumulated to a depth of 4.5 m. In and on the basal beach-sand deposits, which occur at levels above the current highwater mark, Lapita sherds have been found (Best, personal communication).

References

Ambrose, W. R. 1976a. Intrinsic hydration rate dating of obsidian. In *Advances in obsidian glass studies: archaeological and geochemical perspectives,* ed. R. E. Taylor, pp. 81–105. Park Ridge: Noyes.

———. 1976b. Obsidian and its prehistoric distribution in Melanesia. In *Ancient Chinese bronzes and Southeast Asian metal and other archaeological artifacts,* ed. N. Barnard, pp. 351–378. Melbourne: National Art Gallery of Victoria.

Avias, J. 1950. Poteries canaques et poteries préhistoriques en Nouvelle-Calédonia. *Journal de la Société des Océanistes* 6:111–140.

Birks, Lawrence. 1973. *Archaeological excavations at Sigatoka dune site, Fiji.* Bulletin of the Fiji Museum no. 1, Suva.

——— and Helen Birks. 1967. A brief report on excavations at Sigatoka, Fiji. *New Zealand Archaeological Association Newsletter* 10:16–25.

Black, S. J., and R. C. Green. 1977. *Radiocarbon dates from the Solomon Islands to 1975.* Oceanic Prehistory Records no. 4, Auckland.

Buck, P. H. (Te Rangi Hiroa). 1938. *Vikings of the sunrise*. New York: Lippincott.

Chappell, J. M. A. 1976. Aspects of late Quaternary palaeogeography of the Australian-East Indonesian region. In *The origin of the Australians*, ed. R. L. Kirk and A. G. Thorne, pp. 11–22. Canberra: Australian Institute of Aboriginal Studies.

Coudray, Jean, and Georgette Delibrias. 1972. Variations du niveau marin au-dessus de l'actuel en Nouvelle-Calédonie depuis 6000 ans. *Comptes Rendus de l'Académie des Sciences de Paris*, 271:2623–2626.

Cram, C. L. 1975. Osteoarchaeology in Oceania. In *Archaeozoological studies*, ed. A. T. Clason, pp. 309–321. Amsterdam: North-Holland Publishing Co.

Davidson, J. M. 1977. Western Polynesia and Fiji: the archaeological evidence. Paper presented at 150th Anniversary Symposium of the Australian Museum on Exchange Systems in Australia and the Pacific Islands, Sydney.

Dickinson, W. R. and Richard Shutler, Jr. 1971. Temper sands in the prehistoric pottery of the Pacific Islands. *Archaeology and Physical Anthropology in Oceania* 6:191–203.

Donovan, L. J. 1973. A study of the decorative system of the Lapita potters in the Reef and Santa Cruz Islands. Master's thesis, University of Auckland.

Egloff, B. J. 1975. Archaeological investigations in the coastal Madang area and on Eloaue Island of the St Matthias Group. *Records of the Papua New Guinea Public Museum and Art Gallery* 5:15–31.

Emory, K. P. 1959. Origin of the Hawaiians. *Journal of the Polynesian Society* 68:29–35.

Frimigacci, Daniel. 1971. Une datation par méthode du C.14 du site Lapita de Vatcha (pres de Vao) Île des Pins. Études Mélanésiennes 21–25:43–44.

———. 1974. Les deux niveaux à poterie du site du Vatcha. *Journal de la Société des Océanistes* 30:25–70.

———. 1975. La préhistoire Néo-Calédonienne. Doctoral dissertation, University of Paris.

———. 1976. La poterie imprimée au battoir en Nouvelle-Calédonie: ses rapports avec le Lapita. Paper presented at IXᵉ Congrès Union Internationale des Sciences Préhistoriques et Protohistoriques, Nice.

Garanger, José. 1972. *Archéologie des Nouvelles-Hébrides*. Publication de la Société des Océanistes no. 30, Paris.

Gifford, E. W., and Richard Shutler, Jr. 1956. Archaeological excavations in New Caledonia. *University of California Anthropological Records* 18:1–148.

Golson, Jack. 1959. L'archéologie du Pacifique Sud: résultats et perspectives. *Journal de la Société des Océanistes* 15:5–54.

———. 1961. Report on New Zealand, western Polynesia, New Caledonia, and Fiji. *Asian Perspectives* 5:166–180.

———. 1962. Rapport sur les fouilles effectuées à l'Île des Pins (Nouvelle-Calédonie) de décembre 1959 à février 1960. *Études Mélanésiennes* 14–17:11–23.

———. 1971. Lapita ware and its transformations. In *Studies in Oceanic culture history*, ed. R. C. Green and Marion Kelly, vol. 2. *Pacific Anthropological Records* 12:67–76.

Green, R. C. 1967. The immediate origins of the Polynesians. In *Polynesian culture history: essays in honor of Kenneth P. Emory*, ed. G. A. Highland et al., pp. 215–240. Bishop Museum Special Publication no. 56, Honolulu.

———. 1974a. Sites with Lapita pottery: importing and voyaging. *Mankind* 9:253–259.

———. 1974b. A review of portable artifacts from Western Samoa. In *Archaeology in Western Samoa*, ed. R. C. Green and J. M. Davidson. vol. 2. *Auckland Institute and Museum Bulletin* 7:245–275.

———. 1976a. Lapita sites in the Santa Cruz group. In *Southeast Solomon Islands cultural history*, ed. R. C. Green and M. M. Cresswell. *Royal Society of New Zéaland Bulletin* 11:245–265.

———. 1976b. New sites with Lapita pottery and their implications for an understanding of the settlement of the Western Pacific. Paper presented at IXᵉ Congrès Union Internationale des Sciences Préhistoriques et Protohistoriques, Nice. Revised version: Working Paper 51 in Anthropology, Archaeology, Linguistics, and Maori Studies, Department of Anthropology, University of Auckland.

———. 1976c. Languages of the southeast Solomons and their historical relationships. In *Southeast Solomon Islands cultural history*, ed. R. C. Green and M. M. Cresswell. *Royal Society of New Zealand Bulletin* 11:47–60.

———. 1978. Early Lapita art from Polynesia and Island Melanesia. In *Exploring the Art of Oceania*, ed. S. M. Mead. Honolulu: University Press of Hawaii. Forthcoming.

——— and H. G. Richards. 1975. Lapita pottery

and lower sea level in Western Samoa. *Pacific Science* 29:309–315.

Groube, L. M. 1971. Tonga, Lapita pottery, and Polynesian origins. *Journal of the Polynesian Society* 80:278–316.

———. 1975. Archaeological research in Aneityum. *South Pacific Bulletin*, 3rd qtr. 1975: 27–30.

Hedrick, J. D. 1971. Lapita-style pottery from Malo Island. *Journal of the Polynesian Society* 80:15–19.

Howells, W. W. 1973. *The Pacific islanders*. London: Weidenfeld and Nicolson.

Irwin, G. J. 1973. Man-land relationships in Melanesia: an investigation of prehistoric settlement in the islands of the Bougainville Strait. *Archaeology and Physical Anthropology in Oceania* 8:226–252.

Janetski, J. C. 1976. Dietary remains from Jane's camp—a midden site. In *Excavations on Upolu, Western Samoa. Pacific Anthropological Records* 25:33–40.

Jennings, J. D. 1974. The Ferry Berth site, Mulifanua district, Upolu. In *Archaeology in Western Samoa,* ed. R. C. Green and J. M. Davidson, vol. 2. *Auckland Institute and Museum Bulletin* 7:176–178.

———, R. N. Holmer, J. C. Janetski, and H. L. Smith. 1976. Excavations on Upolu, Western Samoa. *Pacific Anthropological Records* 25:1–113.

Kirch, P. V., and P. H. Rosendahl. 1976. Early Anutan settlement and the position of Anuta in the prehistory of the Southwest Pacific. In *Southeast Solomon Islands cultural history,* ed. R. C. Green and M. M. Cresswell. *Royal Society of New Zealand Bulletin* 11:225–244.

Launay, Jean, and Jacques Recy. 1970. Nouvelles données sur une variation relative récente du niveau de la mer dans toute la région Nouvelle-Calédonie-îles Loyauté. *Comptes Rendus de l'Académie des Sciences de Paris*, 270:2159–2161.

Lenormand, M. H. 1948. Découverte d'un gisement de poteries indigènes à l'Île des Pins. *Études Mélanésiennes* 3:54–58.

Levison, Michael, R. G. Ward, and J. W. Webb. 1972. The settlement of Polynesia: a report on a computer simulation. *Archaeology and Physical Anthropology in Oceania* 7:234–245.

Lewis, David. 1972. *We, the navigators*. Canberra: Australian National University Press.

McKern, W. C. 1929. *Archaeology of Tonga*. Bishop Museum Bulletin no. 60, Honolulu.

Mead, S. M., Lawrence Birks, Helen Birks, and Elizabeth Shaw. 1975. *The Lapita pottery style of Fiji and its associations*. Polynesian Society Memoir no. 38, Wellington.

Meyer, Otto. 1909. Funde prähistorischer Töpferei und Steinmesser auf Vuatom, Bismarck Archipel. *Anthropos* 4:215–252, 1093–1095.

———. 1910. Funde von Menschen- und Tierkochen, von prähistorischer Töpferei und Steinwerkzeugen auf Vuatom, Bismarck-Archipel. *Anthropos* 5:1160–1161.

Palmer, Bruce. 1966. Lapita style potsherds from Fiji. *Journal of the Polynesian Society* 75:373–377.

Pawley, A. K. 1978. On redefining "Eastern Oceanic." Manuscript.

——— and R. C. Green. 1973. Dating the dispersal of the Oceanic languages. *Oceanic Linguistics* 12:1–67.

Poulsen, Jens. 1967. A contribution to the prehistory of the Tongan Islands. Ph.D. dissertation, Australian National University.

———. 1972. Outlier archaeology: Bellona, a preliminary report on fieldwork and radiocarbon dates. Part I—archaeology. *Archaeology and Physical Anthropology in Oceania* 7:184–205.

Rafter, T. A., H. S. Jansen, L. Lockerbie, and M. M. Trotter. 1972. New Zealand radiocarbon reference standards. In *Proceedings of the 8th International Conference on Radiocarbon Dating,* compiled by T. A. Rafter and T. Grant-Taylor, pp. 625–675. Royal Society of New Zealand, Wellington.

Rogers, Garth. 1974. Archaeological discoveries on Niuatoputapu Island, Tonga. *Journal of the Polynesian Society* 83:308–348.

Schofield, J. C. 1977. Late Holocene sea-level, Gilbert and Ellice islands, west central Pacific Ocean. *New Zealand Journal of Geology and Geophysics* 20.

Sharp, Andrew. 1963. *Ancient voyagers in Polynesia*. Auckland: Paul's Book Arcade.

Shaw, Elizabeth. 1975. The decorative system of Natunuku, Fiji. In *The Lapita pottery style of Fiji and its associations*, S. M. Mead, Lawrence Birks, Helen Birks, and Elizabeth Shaw. Polynesian Society Memoir no. 38, Wellington.

Shutler, Richard, Jr. 1971. Pacific Island radiocarbon dates, an overview. In *Studies in Oceanic culture history,* ed. R. C. Green and Marion Kelly. vol. 2. *Pacific Anthropological Records* 12:13–27.

——— and J. C. Marck. 1975. On the dispersal

of the Austronesian horticulturalists. *Archaeology and Physical Anthropology in Oceania* 10: 81–113.

Smart, C. D. 1969. Notes on the pottery sequence obtained from southern New Caledonia. Rapport confidentiel à l'Gouvernement de Nouvelle Calédonie, Musée Néo-Calédonien.

Specht, J. R. 1968. Preliminary report on excavations on Watom Island. *Journal of the Polynesian Society* 77:117–134.

———. 1974. Lapita pottery at Talasea, West New Britain, Papua New Guinea. *Antiquity* 48:302–306.

——— and F. L. Sutherland. 1975. Talasea: an obsidian source in New Britain. Paper presented at 46th ANZASS Congress, Canberra.

Suggs, R. C. 1960. *The island civilizations of Polynesia.* New York: Mentor Books.

———. 1961a. The archaeology of Nuku Hiva, Marquesas Islands, French Polynesia. *Anthropological Papers of the American Museum of Natural History* 49:1–205.

———. 1961b. Polynesia—regional report. *Asian Perspectives* 5:88–94.

Swadling, Pamela. 1975. Analysis of molluscs from excavated Lapita sites. Manuscript, University of Auckland.

———. 1976. The occupation sequence and settlement pattern on Santa Ana. In *Southeast Solomon Islands cultural history*, ed. R. C. Green and M. M. Cresswell. *Royal Society of New Zealand Bulletin* 11:123–132.

White, J. P., and J. R. Specht. 1971. Prehistoric pottery from Ambitle Island, Bismarck Archipelago. *Asian Perspectives* 14:88–94.

Fiji

CHAPTER 3

EVERETT L. FROST

 The Fiji Islands are a cluster of over 300 islands located at the border between the two Pacific cultures of Melanesia and Polynesia. They lie in the center of the southwest Pacific between latitudes 15° and 22° south, 450 km below the equator. Their western edge is about 900 km east of the Melanesian New Hebrides islands. Eastern Fiji, the Lau group, is about 275 km west of the Polynesian island cluster of Tonga.

Fiji's borderline position has resulted in a prehistoric and historic mixture of cultural, linguistic, and physical traits of the two zones—a blend that has complicated the analysis of Fijian culture since the time of the earliest European explorers. For example, Horatio Hale (1846), philologist of the 1838–1842 United States Exploring Expedition to the Pacific, considered the Fijians as an example of Melanesian culture but repeatedly noted their similarities to Polynesians in language, social structure, and physique. The extent of Hale's uncertainty about the proper cultural classification of the Fijians is revealed in his chart of oceanic migration. All Pacific islands, with the single exception of Fiji, are encircled within one of the clusters of Polynesia, Melanesia, Micronesia, Malaisia [sic], or Australia; Fiji stands alone as an apparently unclassifiable product of many influences.

In the last thirty years, systematic archaeological research coupled with linguistic and physical anthropological studies have confirmed Hale's chart. The reconstruction that emerges from evidence in the ground,

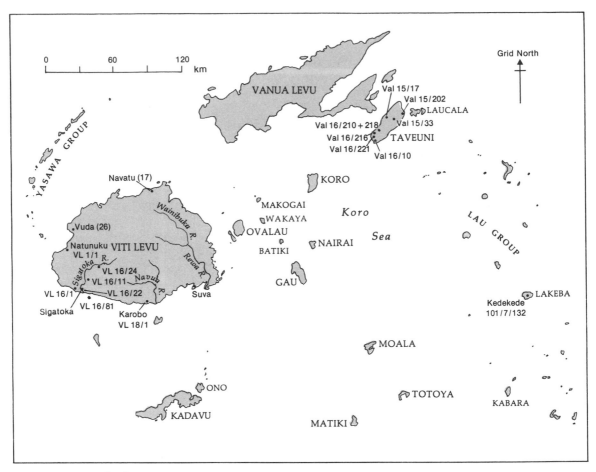

3.1   The Fijian Islands.

from studies of Fijian society and speech, and from archaeology in neighboring island clusters reveals an interweaving of influences that has produced a complexity not typical of the more homogeneous cultural sequences in Polynesia. Some of this complexity resulted from the ebb and flow of Oceanic migrants who sailed to and sometimes through Fiji during the eastward populating of the Pacific islands. The natural and cultural adaptive experiences unique to the populations adjusting to the ecology of the Fijian islands was another factor. This chapter will sketch these patterns and influences as they are known and interpreted today.

A geographic review reveals that the size and geologic heterogeneity of the Fiji cluster is significantly greater than that of island clusters in the Polynesian area (with the exception of New Zealand). The Fiji group lies west of the "andesite line," a geologic boundary that divides the continental islands associated with the formation of Asia and Australia. Islands east of the andesite line (most of Polynesia) are younger and lack the diverse natural resources of the continental islands. The Fiji group, then, provides a different kind of natural resource potential than the Polynesian islands, although it is quite similar to the Melanesian cluster.

The total land area of the Fiji Archipelago (Fig. 3.1) is over 18,000 km². Two islands, Viti Levu and Vanua Levu, make up about 90 percent of the total area and contain about the same percentage of the popula-

EVERETT L. FROST

tion. The largest island is Viti Levu, with over 10,000 km² of land; Vanua Levu is about half as large. Viti Levu, which dates from the Upper Paleozoic, is the oldest of the Fiji group and has several mature drainages and well-developed alluvial plains. Vanua Levu has small rivers that are still down-cutting into Tertiary deposits. Its topography is rugged, its coastline is jagged, and some of its landforms are the result of relatively recent volcanic activity. Taveuni, the third largest island, is perhaps the youngest in the group, with archaeologically dated evidence of volcanic activity at or after 100 B.C.

To the northwest of these large islands is a line of smaller ones called the Yasawa group. There are six principal islands, all but one primarily volcanic with hilly configuration and a relatively dry climate. On the east side of the Fiji group is another line, the Lau group, a 450-km chain of volcanic, limestone, or composite islands. Between the two big islands and the Lau group is the Koro Sea and the seven principal islands (Gau, Ovalau, Koro, Wakaya, Nairai, Batiki, and Makogai) that make up the Lomaiviti group. South of Lomaiviti is the Moala cluster (Moala, Totoya, and Matiki) and west of this group and south of Viti Levu are the islands of Kadavu and Ono.

The larger islands have some large high mountains (over 6,400 m) that block the path of prevailing winds; as a result, heavy rainfall (250 to 500 cm per year) prevails on the windward sides. These support dense tropical vegetation, while the leeward sides are seasonally wet and dry with grass and tree-covered bottom lands and forested hills and mountains. The two larger islands have navigable rivers, extensive flood plains, and regionally variable bountiful supplies of fresh water. The smaller islands, especially the younger ones, have less reliable water resources and limited agricultural soils.

The current population of all the islands is nearly 600,000, including about 260,000 Fijians. Almost 300,000 of the nonnative peoples are Indians who are immigrants or descendants of nineteenth-century laborers brought to Fiji as an agricultural work force. The precontact Fijian population is estimated to have been between 150,000 and 200,000, but over half these individuals died in the mid-nineteenth century because of disease and other post-European contact factors.

Initial Research

Anthropological research in Fiji has been extensive since the earliest ethnographic efforts of Fison in the 1870s and Hocart in the early 1900s. Over fifteen major monographs on the cultural history or ethnology of Fiji have been published by an international range of anthropologists. Despite the early and intensive interest, systematic archaeological research was the last to be started in the group. Gifford's pioneer excavations on Viti Levu in 1947 stood alone until the late 1950s, when investigations into the prehistory of the Pacific accelerated. This impact was first felt through evaluation of Gifford's results (1951, 1955) by Golson (1959) and Green (1963). They were able to review the 1947 material in the light of newer techniques and field remains from other island groups and to formulate a more definitive interpretation of the Fiji sequence, at the same time relating it to a broader range of then known Pacific prehistoric events.

Since then, the two most important influences on modern Fijian archaeology have been the appointment in 1962 of the late J. Bruce Palmer as director of the Fiji Museum and the allocation of funds for further excavations in Fiji by the Bernice P. Bishop Museum in Honolulu. Palmer coordinated the efforts of several researchers, including excavations by the two Birkses in the Sigatoka region, Shaw's survey of Taveuni and excavations at Natunuku, Smart's survey of Kabara in the Lau group, the research of the Fiji Museum staff and others in the Sigatoka project, the Wakaya survey, and several other efforts. Further contributions have been made by Parke's analysis of specialized sites on Vanua Levu and Frost's 1968–1969 excavations of fortified sites on Taveuni. Palmer's sudden death in 1974 brought to an unfortunate end his ongoing efforts in Fiji and slowed progress there. Work in the mid-1970s has been limited to a cultural history research project in Lau directed by Young, with associated excavations on Lakeba reported by Best and a survey and test excavation program on Laucala island conducted by Frost.

While these several projects of survey and excavation have been reported for Fiji, the amount of research is not great when compared to that on other groups of islands such as Samoa, Tonga, New Zealand, and Hawaii. The resultant prehistoric picture is quite incomplete.

The Ceramic Outline of Fijian Prehistory

In Fijian archaeological sites the most frequent surviving prehistoric artifact, and one that is often a diagnostic of temporal and cultural variation, is pottery. The analysis of Fijian ceramics and comparison to those found elsewhere in the Pacific have resulted in the definition of three general ceramic traditions that vary in their characteristic vessel forms and techniques of decoration. The distribution of these traditions through time and within sites, and their association with similar ceramics that have cultural and linguistic affiliations in other island groups, have led to the definition of four temporal phases of Fijian cultural history. These three traditions and four phases are indicated in Table 3.1 and form the general framework within which events in Fijian prehistory are sorted.

Two of the ceramic traditions were first defined and described by Gifford (1951) in the report of his 1949 pioneer excavations at the Navatu site and at the Vuda site in Ra province, both on Viti Levu island. Other surveys and excavations since that time have confirmed and amended the definition of these two traditions (the Impressed and Incised), and their occurrence

in the three most recent temporal phases, Navatu, Vuda, and Ra—named after Gifford's site locations.

In 1959 Golson noted the presence of a third and earliest ceramic complex (Lapita —see Chapter 2), and Green (1963) defined the fourth and earliest phases of Fijian prehistory, the Sigatoka. A reanalysis of Gifford's pottery by Shaw (1967), coupled with new survey and excavation collections, now makes evident the following ceramic outline of Fijian prehistory, elaborated with the description of nonceramic field evidence that gives broader cultural definition of the island group's past.

Lapita Ceramics and the Sigatoka Phase

Lapita is a ceramic tradition characterized by distinctive vessel forms and *pointillé* (dentate-stamped) decorations (Figs. 2.1, 2.8, 2.9). Its distribution is early throughout Melanesia and West Polynesia, and it is defined as the diagnostic of the proto-Polynesian population whose west-to-east voyage trail leads to Fiji as the staging area for Polynesian occupation. Lapita pottery is the earliest evidence for occupation in the Fiji Islands, with sherd collections dating at 1290 B.C. taken from Natunuku, near the Nadi River on the northeast coast of Viti Levu. The other dated collections of Lapita pottery in Fiji are all drawn from the Sigatoka region on the south coast of Viti Levu. There at least three stratified sites have been excavated, within which Lapita sherds form the lowest and earliest deposits. The Fijian Lapita collection has some unique vessel forms that include elaborate pot stands and disk-shaped ceramic pot lids, but the range of decorations is consistent with the general Lapita range and the eastern regional Lapita cluster. The oldest date for the next later ceramic tradition (Impressed) is 110 B.C. at the Yanuca shelter site. These dates therefore establish the Sigatoka phase and the Lapita tradition as persisting from 1290 B.C. through 110 B.C.

As the earliest evidence for Fijian occupation, the Sigatoka phase and its asso-

Table 3.1   Fijian ceramic traditions and their site chronology.

Ceramic tradition	Phase	Site name and number	Site location/type	Date	Source
Lapita	Sigatoka	Natunuku (VL 16/1)	Beach habitation	1290 B.C.	Shaw 1975
		Yanuca shelter (VL 16/81)	Rock shelter midden	1030 B.C.	Palmer 1968
		Yanuca shelter (VL 16/81)	Rock shelter midden	710 B.C.	Palmer 1968
		Sigatoka dune (VL 16/1)	Beach habitation	510 B.C.	Birks 1973
Impressed	Navatu	Yanuca shelter (VL 16/81)	Rock shelter midden	110 B.C.	Palmer 1968
		Navolivoli (VaL 16/10)	Inland hill habitation	100 B.C.	Frost 1974
		Navatu (17a)	Coastal habitation	50 B.C.	Gifford 1955
		Sigatoka dune (VL 16/1)	Beach habitation	A.D. 230	Birks 1973
		Navatu (17b)	Coastal habitation	A.D. 650	Gifford 1955
		Navatu (17b)	Coastal habitation	A.D. 750	Gifford 1955
		Navatu (17a)	Coastal habitation	A.D. 1000	Gifford 1955
Incised	Vuda	- - - (VaL 16/210)	Ring-ditch fort	A.D. 1210	Frost 1974
		Navolivoli (VaL 16/10)	Inland hill fort	A.D. 1240	Frost 1974
		Nawa (VaL 16/216)	Ring-ditch fort	A.D. 1240	Frost 1974
		Vuda (26)	Coastal habitation	A.D. 1250	Gifford 1955
		Vuda (26)	Coastal habitation	A.D. 1300	Gifford 1955
		- - - (VaL 16/202)	Ring-ditch fort	A.D. 1330	Frost 1974
	Ra	Nayalayala (VaL 15/17)	Inland hill fort	A.D. 1610	Frost 1974
		Qalau (VaL 16/221)	Inland ring-ditch fort	A.D. 1670	Frost 1974
		Navuga (VaL 15/33)	Inland ridge fort	A.D. 1870 (historic source)	Frost 1974

ciated sites and artifacts are the logical point to begin explanations of the nature of ancestral Fijian culture. Golson (1959, 1961) and Green (1963) were the first to note the ceramic continuity between Melanesia and Polynesia through Fiji. This led to Green's speculations on Fijian ancestral ties to Polynesia. Further, linguists have long noted that of the several hundred Pacific languages, Fijian is probably the one most similar to the ancestral Polynesian language. Though physical anthropologists recognize the resemblance between Fijian and Melanesian skin color and hair form, intensive study suggests to some that these characteristics are the result of relatively recent Melanesian intrusions and that there are strong resemblances between Fijians, Samoans, and Tongans. As early as 1933, Howells proposed that "it is possible that before the eleventh century Fiji was en-

tirely Polynesian" (1933:335). The Sigatoka-phase Lapita pottery shows a continuous distribution from eastern Melanesia to western Polynesia, while later Fijian ceramic traditions have no Polynesian ties and have apparent affiliations in Melanesia. This combination of evidence convinced Green that Lapita pottery was the broad Pacific ceramic tradition that tied the Sigatoka phase to an Austronesian-speaking, ancestral Polynesian population and that these peoples had moved through the Melanesian region to its eastern jumping-off point (Fiji) for the occupation of western Polynesia and from there, eventually, the entire Polynesian triangle.

The artifact inventory of the Sigatoka phase is small and the potential for cultural reconstruction limited. A worked shell paring knife and bracelet, and quadrangular, subrectangular-plano-convex and subtriangular adzes make up the nonperishable collection, while animal (unidentified) and fishbone fragments represent some of the subsistence base. The settlement pattern is coastal with no known structural forms. Birks (1973) has hypothesized that the Sigatoka dune site (VL 16/1) was a seasonal turtle-hunting station. Beyond these minimal dimensions, there are unpublished and informal reports of Lapita sherds from coastal Vanua Levu and the Lau group islands that imply a wide distribution of the early Sigatoka-phase peoples.

Impressed Ceramics and the Navatu Phase

Following the Lapita tradition, and separated by a possible cultural discontinuity and actual stratigraphic discontinuity at some sites (VL 16/1, VL 16/22), is the Impressed tradition, which marks the Navatu phase. Radiocarbon dates from many sites establish the range of this phase from 100 B.C. to A.D. 1100. Impressed ceramics (Fig. 3.2) are predominantly decorated by working a carved paddle against the body of the vessel before it is dry, to leave a raised pattern. The paddles are carved to produce patterns of diamond, square, or rectangular cross-relief, parallel ribs, zigzag lines, wavy relief, and spot relief. Another characteristic motif, called "pinched nubbins," is produced by using a finger inside the wet pot to push out a protrusion at the shoulder level. This protrusion is then apparently pinched between the thumb and finger to leave a ridged bump often with fingernail marks on either side of its base. Also associated with this tradition are sherds decorated by "chicken-bone" tool impressing, fine-line incising, and rims with hatching. Vessel forms include rounded, wide-mouthed cooking pots (*koro*), pots with angled joints around the side (shouldered pots), and—unique to the Sigatoka region—flat, crudely made ceramic trays or platters. The trays are usually circular in plan, with low side rims and with impressions from large leaves or grass mats on their undersurfaces, perhaps as a result of the surface on which they were made. L. Birks notes (1973) that there are several possible functions for this vessel form, including use as a fire container, serving dish, coconut-oil manufacturing vessel, or salt-water evaporation dish (to recover salt).

The nonceramic evidence for the Navatu phase is more extensive than for the Sigatoka. One site associated with this phase is particularly important because of the unique preservation of material caused by its salt-water-immersed location. The Karobo site (VL 18/1) located on the south central coast of Viti Levu yielded a wooden fishhook and stone sinker, thus providing the first clear testimony to line fishing as a Navatu-phase subsistence activity. Several kinds of plant remains were recovered. Six edible fruits and nuts were found in the layer, along with *makita* and candlenuts—both critical ingredients in processing coconut oil. In the lowest level of the site a piece of palm wood, possibly coconut, was recovered. In association with one fire hearth at the site, Palmer exposed a large, flat stone typical of those used to beat nuts open for extracting oil. Palmer (1965) correlates all this evidence to support the proposition that the site was a coconut-oil processing location in which the ceramic trays were used for heating and cracking the nuts and for holding the oil while it was separated and eventually skimmed off. Other botanical dimensions for the site and phase interpretation come from the leaf imprints on the bases of the flat-bottomed vessels. These include a possible banana leaf as well as *kuta*, a reed used in mat weaving. Pandanus nuts found in the lowest level testify to the presence of a second important mat-weaving resource. The Karobo site thus provides an impressive addition to our knowledge of the economic condition of the Navatu-phase peoples.

Other Navatu-phase sites show evidence of shell fishing and turtle hunting. Pig bone supports the argument for either feral pig hunting or pig husbandry or both. More important is the probability of root

EVERETT L. FROST

3.2 *Fijian pottery of the Impressed tradition.*

A to O, *carved-paddle impressed motifs: A—ribbed; B to H—cross-relief; I—cross-relief with applied, notched ridge; J—zigzag; K—scalloped ribbed relief; L—toothed ribbed relief; M—spot relief; N—elongated spot relief; O—triangular spot relief.*

P to T, *tool-impressed motifs: P and Q—wedge impressed; R—wedge impressed with spot relief; S— chicken-bone impressed; T—shell impressed.*

crop horticulture, which is typically associated with the distribution of pigs. Chicken and dog bones also occur. Lenticular and rounded rectangular adzes make up the stone tool inventory, and ornaments include a pottery disk and a child's shell ring. The cultural affiliation of this phase, somewhat tenuous, rests on ties to a generally similar technology of paddle-impressed pottery occurring in New Caledonia between 1200 B.C. and A.D. 300 and known from as far west as Southeast Asia (Golson 1971).

Incised Ceramics and the Vuda and Ra Phases

The third Fijian ceramic tradition, the Incised (Fig. 3.3), has some variation in decoration, vessel form, and temporal occurrence. This has led to the definition of two phases, the Vuda and Ra. The earliest occurrence of the Incised tradition is measured from the appearance of the following pattern of sherd distribution: very high frequencies of plain wares (80 to 90 percent), reduced frequencies of Impressed-tradition motifs (5 to 10 percent), and small frequencies of new, Incised motifs (up to 5 percent). These distributions occur in deposits dated from A.D. 1100 to the time of European contact (about A.D. 1600) and define the limits of the Vuda phase. Then the Ra phase occurs, with a significant increase in Incised-ware motifs and their association with European diffused artifacts. Since some Ra-phase ceramic traditions still continue in modern Fijian communities, their temporal dimensions are listed as A.D. 1600 to present.

The diagnostic motifs and techniques for the Incised tradition are most easily defined from the later Ra-phase deposits, where decoration is more frequent. Especially characteristic of this later phase are flat-rimmed bowls (dari), comb incising, buttressed shoulders, gash incising on vessel-lip edges, shell impressions on restricted orifice water jars, appliqué elements, tool impressions, and complex

combinations of all of these. The earlier Incised-tradition motifs were primarily simple tool incisions on the rim, neck, and shoulder of the pots, sometimes combined with appliqué relief designs.

The transition from the Impressed tradition to the Incised is hard to define. Both traditions include some kinds of tool impressing, incising, and modeling decorations. Also, there is evidence of a continuity of carved paddle-impressed motifs from the beginning of the Navatu phase through to the Ra phase. It is not possible from present collections to define in either ceramic analysis or site-context description a discontinuity between the two traditions. What seems most significant in the current data is the sudden decrease in carved paddle-impressed motifs and other Impressed-ware variants that tends to occur in site deposits from the vicinity of A.D. 1100. It is also important to note that these changes coincide in some sites with the appearance of fortifications, as documented later in this chapter. Finally, these changes that first occur in A.D. 1100 seem to be the starting point for a continuous development that is most elaborate in the Ra-phase Incised complex. The changes first seen in the Vuda period apparently did reflect the beginning of some kind of cultural change that led to the decline of the Impressed tradition and the development of an Incised tradition. Particularly, the Ra-phase Incised wares have close parallels to pottery west of Fiji, especially in the New Hebrides, which ties at least the later Incised tradition to Melanesian sources.

Nonceramic artifacts of the Vuda phase include pig, chicken, turtle, dog, and flying-fox bones as well as evidence of shell and line fishing. Human bone appears in unarticulated patterns as well as articulated burials. Adzes vary from rounded rectangular to elliptical, and some are made of shell. A coral fragment shows evidence of use as a bark-cloth (tapa) decorating tool. House platforms are stone faced and rounded in shape. The later Ra-phase material adds

3.3 *Fijian pottery of the Incised tradition.*

A to F, *Vuda phase:* A—*shell impressed with modeled knob;* B and C—*shell impressed;* D—*tool incised in triangular motif;* E—*tool incised in net motif;* F—*tool incised and pointed-tool impressed.*

G to Q, *Ra phase:* G—*tool-notched ridge;* H—*appliqué spots;* I—*comb incised;* J—*tool incised and pointed-tool impressed;* K—*tool incised with modeled knobs;* L—*appliqué spot and tool impress;* M—*shell impressed with appliqué ridges;* N—*tool impressed with appliqué ridges;* O—*tool impressed;* P—*appliqué spots with modeled ridges and shell impressing;* Q—*modeled ridge with shell impressing.*

evidence of European cattle and goats, as well as metal axes, buttons, glass, and ceramics. House platforms during this later period are frequently rectangular in shape.

Problem-Oriented Archaeology in Fiji

Fortified Sites

The most frequent kind of Fijian archaeological settlement, and often the most spectacular, is the fortification. There are thousands of them throughout the Fiji group. The task of explaining their occurrence and distribution is critical to Fiji prehistory, because fortifications and the warfare associated with them have many implications concerning internal and external sociocultural processes and developments. Construction of a fort may imply that there exists a certain level of cooperation, leadership, surplus production, planning, anticipation of offense, and necessity to maintain territorial control. If, as may be the case in Fiji, many groups are fortifying locations at the same time the implications are even more complex. What are the conditions that led to the Fijian pattern? Why did they occur in Fiji with such frequency? These questions cannot be definitely answered, but some assertions have been made.

Fortified sites in Fiji have been classified into both morphological and locational categories. The main classes are ring-ditched sites and ridge forts. Ring-ditch sites were constructed in relatively flat land areas. Most of them basically consisted of a ditch dug to encircle a habitation or occupation area, the ditches being crossed at certain points (usually four equidistant locations) by earthen causeways. The ditches might be dry or might contain water. There might be a bank of earth on the outside edge of the ditch and, much more rarely, on the inside edge. A palisade, often made of bamboo, might be constructed around the inside edge of the ditch, and the more elaborate forts might have fighting platforms (stages) built above the gateways op-

posite the causeways. Sometimes thorny bushes were planted around the ditches and banks, and sharpened bamboo splinters were hidden point up in the grasses filling the ditch bottom. Occasionally stone walls were constructed. The basic single-ditch, four-causeway system might be elaborated by multiple ditches with offset causeways or complex ditch systems enclosing or interconnecting two or more occupation areas. Some ring-ditch sites have house foundations and midden deposits within, supporting an interpretation that they were fortified areas of permanent habitation. Others show little occupation evidence; however, possible association with unprotected nearby habitations implies that these forts were used as temporary redoubts during times of siege. The flatland context of ring-ditch sites indicates that their distribution tended to be in coastal areas or the alluvial plains of river valleys.

Topography is the factor that brings about the greatest contrasts between ring-ditch sites and the second category, ridge forts. The ridge forts were defensive sites located on ridges, hills, headlands, or any kind of natural promontory that offered natural defense because of its isolation or difficulty of access; furthermore, they allowed good visibility of the lands surrounding the site. Sometimes habitation evidence is found on a ridge top with no associated architectural evidence to confirm a defensive function. Often ridges are found to display the same defensive modifications that occurred with ring-ditch sites —that is, ditching, banking, and palisades. Fijian ridge forts also have been found with terracing, artificial escarping to steepen ridge sides, transverse ditching and banking to restrict travel along ridge tops, and so forth. Like ring-ditch sites, ridge forts might enclose relatively permanent or elaborate habitation sites with house mounds and other settlement features, or they might simply provide defended, undeveloped space for refuge and function as a temporary redoubt.

Palmer (1967a, 1969) noted that the basic

morphology of the ring-ditch pattern seems to have been imposed on ridge and headland fort designs, sometimes when inappropriate. Even where steep topography makes the total encirclement of a ridge by a ditch apparently unnecessary, there are several Fijian sites that follow such a configuration. This patterning led Palmer to speculate that ring-ditch sites were the first developed in Fiji and have served subsequently as the mental template for fortifications in the uplands, even where such a duplication of form was not required. Confirmation of this hypothesis would require evidence that ring-ditch fortifications as a class date earlier than fortified ridges, headlands, hills, and volcanic cones. The evidence is not yet available to confirm the proposed chronology.

Fortified sites are not unique to Fiji, but occur in a number of other areas in Melanesia and Polynesia. Several papers have been written (Best 1927; Green 1967) aimed at interpreting the interrelations of these special site types from one area to the next. Some have suggested that clusters of island groups in the entire Polynesian/East Melanesian region have a shared heritage of fortification techniques that explains similarities and differences in fortification patterns. Just as reasonably it can be suggested that there are a limited number of ways, short of fleeing a habitation, that a people with a neolithic technology can respond to defensive needs and that these limitations lead to similarities rather than the diffusion of a pattern. Considering the terrain and available tools and weapons, the practices of ditching, banking, palisading, using stone walls, terracing, and transverse ditching are logical responses to a defensive need. It seems reasonable that they might have developed independently in several locations in the Pacific. This assertion is supported in part by the occurrence of fortifications similar to the Pacific ones in both the Old and New Worlds among neolithic cultural complexes. As with the other hypotheses, there is not yet enough information to test the assertions.

Windward Viti Levu Ring-Ditch Forts

The analysis of Fijian fortifications has also focused on more limited problems, and a few regional studies illustrate the importance of the prehistoric issues raised by research oriented to smaller-scale interpretations than those outlined above. One of the most interesting distributions of fortified sites is that described by Palmer (1969) for the windward region of Viti Levu.

An inspection of aerial photographs of a large portion of the southeastern portion of the island revealed several hundred ring-ditch sites scattered along the coastal flatlands, especially in the alluvial plains and delta areas of the Navua, Rewa, and Wainibuku rivers and around Viti Levu Bay. To provide some sort of limit to a mapping study, Palmer and his aides arbitrarily selected the 250-ft contour and plotted all sites relative to this contour. Recognizing that some sites would be obscured by vegetation or covered by post-European contact activities, Palmer still reports an association of the highest frequencies of forts with undifferentiated alluvial soils. Far fewer forts are found north or west of this general windward region.

Palmer notes two other associations with this distribution of sites. First, the densest distributions fall where two important food resources, *dalo* (taro) and *via kana* (a taro-like plant), are intensely cultivated today. Via kana is a critical food resource, in that it is flood resistant and once matured (three years after planting) it is available year round. The second association is with the distribution of the powerful nineteenth-century Fijian chiefdoms (Verata, Rewa, Bau). These were composed of political units whose leaders exacted tribute from villages and towns, using the surplus production to support the military activities of their polities. The settlement pattern of these areas with their nucleated villages and dense populations is contrasted to that of the uplands, where Palmer says agricultural technology was of a slash-and-burn variety with more scattered, less intensely productive crops and a dispersed-hamlet settlement pattern. Thus the upland country would probably support fewer people and result in smaller surpluses; defensive needs might be lower, inasmuch as the restricted surpluses would make these regions less attractive territory than the lowlands.

Palmer's argument, then, is that forts are not only denser in the flatlands because wet flatland agriculture can support more people, but also the land itself is a more important resource for an enterprising chief to control, so there is a greater need for defensive tactics. Palmer's research on the windward Viti Levu forts did not extend to an excavation program, and his hypotheses, including his assertion of the temporal priority of lowland fortification forms over upland forms, have neither been confirmed nor disproved. But his case for the association of the windward forts with the distribution of dalo and via kana intensive agriculture and the surplus productive needs of the nineteenth-century chiefdoms seems reasonable. The extent of this pattern of warfare and fortification before the nineteenth century is not defined, but the dalo and via kana technology is complex enough that one may be confident that the system existed some years previously.

Sigatoka Forts

In addition to the windward ring-ditch forts on Viti Levu, a research program in Sigatoka Valley led to the cataloging of many other elaborate ring-ditch and upland ridge fortifications and a frequent pattern of stone-wall defensive construction. The survey (Palmer 1967b) revealed that ring-ditched sites in the Sigatoka area tend to occur with more double ditches and causeways and other elaborated ditch defensive systems than those in the windward region. Several are built on limestone ridges. One example, Nabociwa (VL 16/24), is built on a ridge backed by a cliff and encircled in front by stone walls built on steep slopes. This defensive system encloses sev-

eral house foundations. Outside the stone walls are carefully constructed stone-faced terraces. The unique forms of Sigatoka fortifications are too numerous to describe in detail, but there are many more as complex as Nabociwa. Where surface pottery was collected from these sites, it seems to be of the Impressed tradition. Some of the Sigatoka forts are associated with an apparent influx of Tongans into the region in the eighteenth century. Perhaps the most impressive of these is Tavuni (VL 16/11), a ridge site that stands above a wide bend on the Sigatoka River. The site extends along several hundred meters of the ridge and has at least 37 stone-faced house foundations and 20 stone-faced terraces. An upright stone monument, over 1 m high, marks the downstream end of the site, where there is an impressive view of the lower Sigatoka River.

Wakaya Forts

Wakaya is a small, high volcanic island of nearly 8 km² located in the Koro Sea to the east of Viti Levu. There eight fortified sites, two ring-ditch types and six ridge forts, were discovered. Two ridge sites with several house mounds but lacking earthworks were visited. Their location would suggest that they served as good naturally defended sites; however, there is no evidence that they were fortifications.

An important contribution of the Wakaya survey to the analysis of Fijian fortifications is the surface collections of ceramics from the sites. Inasmuch as this pottery did not result from excavation, its association is not a strong one. Yet it does provide some basis for establishing a fortification chronology. Three of the Wakaya forts yielded Impressed-phase, carved-paddle decorated ceramics. Mixed with these sherds were Incised-phase ceramics, including comb-incised and appliqué patterns considered indicative of the Ra phase. The Wakaya collections include an elaborate range of decorated variants of a vessel form that was, until the Wakaya research, infrequently recovered in Fiji. This form is the *dari,* a shallow, thick-walled bowl with a wide flat rim that is usually elaborately decorated by appliqué, incision, and tool impression. The dari vessel form is thought by some to be reminiscent of the form of wooden kava bowls. Its association with comb-incised sherds and elaborately decorated waterpots characteristic of the Ra phase suggests that it too is a diagnostic artifact of the immediately precontact or contact period of Fiji.

Taveuni Forts

In 1966–1967 Shaw discovered a variety of forts, including several ditched and terraced ridge forts, on Taveuni Island. Later, the Frosts carried out a year-long program of testing of several of the sites. Neither Shaw's survey nor the Frosts' work revealed any Lapita pottery on the island. The earliest material found was exposed in deposits underlying a fortified component of a site built on a small inactive volcanic hill. This site, Navolivoli (VaL 16/10), had surface remains of 13 round and oval stone-faced, earthen-cored house foundations arranged around the rim of the hill with a fortifying ditch that encircled two-thirds of the hill below the house mounds. The other third of the hill was steep enough to make access difficult without any modification. Excavation revealed that underlying the fortified component, and sometimes covered by up to 2 m of sterile volcanic ash, was a second, earlier component that lacked any architectural features and consisted of ceramics distributed along a living surface that covered the entire hilltop. Charcoal concentrated in one area of the living surface and associated with a crushed pot yielded a radiocarbon date of 100 B.C. for the Navatu-phase Impressed-ware ceramics that were recovered. These included cross-relief, ribbed relief, wicker relief, spot relief and elongated spot relief, carved-paddle impressed pot fragments, as well as a waterpot ring handle with pouring spouts on either side (very similar to one found at

Gifford's site 17 in the lowest Navatu levels). The 100 B.C. date also measured the time at or after which a volcanic eruption occurred that covered at least the south half of Taveuni with lava flows and heavy ash deposits. At Navolivoli the upper layers of this ash were eventually transformed into soil. Upon that surface the later-fortified, house-mound component was constructed. Charcoal from a hearth within one of the house mounds yielded a radiocarbon date of A.D. 1240. The ceramics of this later component included Navatu-phase Impressed wares, and also several motifs characteristic of the Incised tradition including tool-impressed, shell-impressed, modeled, appliqué, and incised decorated sherds with some of these sherds having complex combinations of the above techniques. On the surface and in some subsurface contexts within this later component were Ra-phase Incised wares such as comb-incised sherds, buttressed rims, and decorated dari rims. This mixture of Impressed and Incised sherds of three phases from controlled, excavated contexts duplicates the pattern found on the surface of forts on Wakaya Island. The layers of sterile volcanic ash made it easy to detect disturbance between the upper and lower component, and it was clear that the Navatu-phase ceramics in the upper component were not the result of mixture from below. The upper-component sherd distribution showed no evidence of stratification except for the Ra-phase dari rims and comb-incised sherds, which were mostly in surface contexts. The house mounds and ditch were built on top of and cut into the volcanic ash layer and clearly were associated with Impressed and Incised ceramics of the upper component as well as with the A.D. 1240 date.

The Navolivoli site was not the only one on Taveuni to yield this pattern of Impressed and Incised ceramics co-occurring in a fortification at about the same time period. Site VaL 16/216 (Nawa) consisted of seven ditch-encircled areas constructed in a relatively unweathered lava flow several hundred meters from the beach at the southwest end of Taveuni. The angular rocky terrain was difficult to walk in, and the ditch system that interconnected the seven areas must have been extremely hard to excavate. No evidence of habitation was found in the seven components except for a few pottery sherds in each and a 10-cm-deep fire hearth in one. The charcoal from this hearth also dated at A.D. 1240. The ceramics included both Impressed- and Incised-tradition sherds. This terrain is so inhospitable and the habitation debris so thin that one must infer that the fortification served as a refuge and not a permanent dwelling.

There is then on Taveuni a consistent pattern of fortifications built between A.D. 1200 and 1400, with both Impressed- and Incised-tradition ceramics. Excavation of these sites does not reveal evidence that this combination of the ceramics of two traditions was brought about by anything but common use of vessels of the two ceramic traditions. Such a pattern is not unique to Taveuni, inasmuch as sherd distributions from Gifford's sites show a continued occurrence of Impressed-ware sherds throughout the upper Vuda- and Ra-phase, Incised-tradition layers. Also, as mentioned above, surface collections from Wakaya fortifications show the same pattern. The Taveuni sites do serve to establish the details of this pattern more clearly from excavated contexts.

Two other forts excavated on Taveuni had a few Impressed-ware sherds with high percentages of Vuda- and Ra-phase Incised wares dated to A.D. 1610 (VaL 15/17) and 1670 (VaL 16/221). Another ridge fort known to be of postcontact age had only a few Impressed-ware sherds but very large frequencies of dari rim sherds, appliqué, and incised waterpot sherds and comb-incised sherds.

Lau Forts

Two areas in the Lau group have been archaeologically investigated. In southern Lau, Kabara Island was studied in the mid-1960s by Smart, who discovered 12 fortified sites. Smart (1965) found primarily Incised-tradition pottery at the forts and therefore argues they are a late settlement development in Kabara.

A more precise dating of fortifications in Lau has resulted from 1976 work on Lakeba, in the central Lau group. While no detailed analysis of this research has yet been published, the preliminary report by Best (1977) indicates that a wide variety of fortification types were studied. One such site, a ridge fortification on the center of the island named Kedekede (101/7/132), had a very complex pattern of terracing and ditching along three ridges leading to a central flattened peak. On the peak were a few mounds and some stone-wall defenses. Two radiocarbon dates were established: one, near the surface, was A.D. 1830, and another, 2.5 m below the surface of a house mound and in an oval pit (2 m in diameter, 1.1 m deep), was A.D. 1270. The ceramic assemblage has not yet been reported.

Summary of Fortifications

While fortifications are perhaps the most frequent type of settlement found in Fiji, they have been excavated in only two areas, Taveuni and Lakeba. They occur in very diverse forms, which are in part a response to the topographic circumstance. In Taveuni and Lakeba, both ring-ditch and ridge forms have been dated to A.D. 1200 or later. The Taveuni forts show a combination of Impressed and Incised ceramics with a clear pattern of reduced frequencies of Impressed wares and increased Ra-phase Incised-tradition sherds in postcontact forts. Where oral traditions have been recorded concerning these sites, they explain the warfare as a result of internal political realignments, population shifts, and Tongan invasions. Palmer has suggested that the unique agricultural potential of the windward Viti Levu alluvial flatlands explains the high frequency of ring-ditch forts there. Frost has suggested that the occurrence of fortifications on Taveuni coincides with the addition of Incised-tradition ceramics to an ongoing tradition of Impressed wares. Green has suggested that these Incised ceramics have a New Hebridean derivation. It is tempting to suggest that the simultaneous addition of a new ceramic tradition and the development of fortification is a pattern reflecting a Melanesian population movement into Fiji. Perhaps the two events led to the warfare, population movements, mixture, and political realignments reflected in many Fijian oral traditions and in the physical and linguistic patterns of Fiji as well. It is risky to base such an interpretation on the Taveuni evidence alone, inasmuch as the known recent volcanic activity on that island may have made it uninhabitable for a long period of time and hence made the chronology of fortifications there atypical of the rest of Fiji. But Taveuni may *not* be atypical, because the Wakaya forts have a ceramic pattern similar to the Taveuni ones and the dated Lakeba fort is about the same age as the Taveuni ones. The development of the windward Viti Levu forts could have occurred at the same time or even later, as the population increased and the nineteenth-century political realms began to take form.

At this time only enough is known about Fijian fortifications to allow the raising, not the resolution, of hypotheses explaining them. They remain a class of settlements whose study has great potential for interpretation of the sociopolitical nature of Fijian prehistory. Such study must involve the extensive nineteenth-century warfare between the paramount chiefdoms of Fiji, well documented in the historic literature.

Naga and Ceremonial Sites

There are two clusters of unique walled sites with limited distribution on Viti Levu and Vanua Levu. These sites, especially the Viti Levu ones, are referred to as *naga* sites and are assumed to have been used for ceremonial functions associated with a secret society, male initiation rites, and the be-

ginning of the Fijian new year. While some of the sites have been surveyed, none have been excavated; the evidence to date, including their limited distribution, suggests they are a relatively recent phenomenon.

The sites most frequently referred to as naga sites are those found on Viti Levu in an ethnohistorically defined zone that starts at the coast on either side of the Nadi River and runs east into the highlands through the headwater region of the Sigatoka River to the headwaters of the Wainimala River. A narrow band of distribution extends from the Wainimal district to Korolevu beach on Viti Levu's south shore. Ethnohistoric sources on the naga sites and their probable associated *baki* rites suggest that the cult that constructed and used the sites originated on the west coast of Viti Levu at Nadi at a time when two strangers arrived from the sea to the west. Each of these men organized one portion of a dual organization with themselves as leaders, and in alternate years each would lead the ceremonies at the naga. The information indicates that every third year a new site (or an addition to an old one) was constructed.

Several sites near the headwaters of the Sigatoka River (Palmer 1971b) were mapped and proved to be rather different from those described in the ethnographic literature. Before field research began, the naga had been described as two parallel walls traversed by four walls with center gaps, thus forming a three-sectioned rectangle; round house structures were thought to be situated on a raised earth foundation outside one end of the rectangle. The sites proved to be less symmetrical than this, and more complex. One site, Togalevu (Palmer 1971b), is a series of rectangular enclosures made of stone walls 1 to 2 m high, or sometimes just single-row stone alignments. The total complex is over 160 m long and has three independent walled units. The simplest is a 53-m-long rectangle, 10 m wide at one end and 18 m wide at the other. Two interior walls divide the rectangle into segments of about equal length. One of the interior walls has a gap (walkway?) in its center, the other is solid. The interior walls and the wall at the widest end are thick and high (1 to 1.6 m), while the long side walls are single- or double-row surface-level alignments. The second unit at Togalevu is a slightly arcuate, four-section, north/south oriented, rectilinear stone-walled complex. There is an earthen mound outside the north end. The unit, 71 m long, averages 11 m in width and has a gap in the north end wall and the northernmost interior. Most of the east side and south end of the structure consists of only a surface-level stone alignment, whereas most of the interior dividers and the east side and north end are stone walls 0.4 to 1.2 m high. The third and most complex walled unit has an irregular triple parallel north/south wall system with end and interior walls subdividing the area into 12 sections. Some upright stones and stone slabs are found inside this 136-m-long unit. The sections average 10 m wide, with one double-width (19.5 m) unit at the north end. A fragmentary pot and pot stand were found at the site as was a pit, which could have been used either for breadfruit fermentation or as an earth oven.

The other six sites recorded in the region were simpler, usually with only two or three completely enclosed segments and sometimes with just free-standing walls or stone alignments.

The ethnohistorical accounts indicate that the complexes were used by adult males and adolescent initiates who walked and/or crawled through, sat in, and laid within and about the structures during the Fiji new year ceremony (October–November). This practice apparently was never observed by Westerners and was only remembered and recounted by a few older men. The use of the sites must have ended soon after contact, perhaps abruptly following mid- and late-nineteenth-century attempts to pacify isolated populations in the central Viti Levu highlands. Some analysts attribute the practice to older populations on the island that were driven east by the later influxes of immigrant Melanesians. Others argue the practices were brought by the immigrant Melanesians and locally adapted. A third position is that the practices and sites resemble those of the Polynesian *marae*.

This discussion of the Viti Levu naga sites can also logically include a geographic cluster of specialized sites on Vanua Levu. These sites were recently mapped, described, and analyzed by Parke. Eleven of the sites, mostly from the interior and northern end of Vanua Levu, are now recorded. Each consists of two parallel earthen walls with stone facing and paving, or stone walls with lesser earthen cores. Sometimes the walls are of about equal length, sometimes one is shorter than the other. There is a great deal of variation in the length of the parallel walls (from 8.5 m to 161.5 m). The average distance between walls, leaving a clear flat space, is 8.4 m (the range of width is 6.7 m to 10.7 m). Parke (1971) identifies two categories: those oriented north/south (six) and those oriented east/west (five). Three sites of the first category have a mound, platform, or terrace on one or the other or both ends of the site. All of the sites in the second category have such features. Nine have gaps in either (four) or both (five) walls (up to five gaps per wall). Eight sites have upright stones set on either (four) or both (four) walls.

Informants provided varying information about the use of the sites for purposes that included the killing and preparing of people to be eaten and the calling of ancestors; playing a game associated with yam harvest fertility ceremonies; and ceremonial exchange of gifts (*solevu*). Parke notes the similarity of these sites to the Viti Levu sites, but also comments on the more symmetrical construction techniques and the emphasis on upright stones in the Vanua Levu sites. Furthermore, the Viti Levu sites usually have transverse end and interior walls not found in the Vanua Levu complexes. Lester (1953) has noted that there may be a descent tie between the peoples using the Viti Levu naga sites and the Vanua Levu parallel-wall complexes.

Recent Research in Eastern Fiji

Two recently reported archaeological projects were completed in eastern Fiji in 1976. The Lakeba project has been mentioned in the discussion of fortifications. It is important to note also the excavation of a rock-shelter site on Lakeba that contained a 3.95-m continuous cultural deposit. The ceramic sequence reported there by Best (1977) is the following, from top to bottom: plain ware, elongated spot relief, paddle-impressed cross relief, plain and vertical-line relief coarse-textured ware, red slipped ware, and coarse-textured plain ware. The radiocarbon dates for this sequence run from 310 B.C. to A.D. 1860. Best also reports flake tools of chert-like material from Lakeba, with the possibility of composite tools. He found 17 types of sites on Lakeba, reporting a total of 188 sites spread throughout the 55 km² of the island.

The second recent project was a survey with brief test excavations by the Frosts on Laucala Island. Located northeast of Taveuni, this small island is traditionally associated with polities of both Taveuni and the Lau group. The survey revealed beach midden sites, undefended house mound villages, and fortified sites. Test excavation of the beach sites exposed up to 2 m of deposits that yielded low frequencies of Incised and Impressed wares underlain by red slipped and coarse-textured plain sherds.

Both the Lakeba and Laucala research contribute refined ceramic evidence to the general Fiji sequence, with their discovery of red slipped wares that occur elsewhere in Fiji but are usually associated with dentate-stamped Lapita pottery. The final reports of Best's Lakeba work will be an important addition to detailing the sequence of developments within the more general ceramic traditions. It is also important to note that the eastern Fijian research shows the same general sequence as the rest of Fiji and that the area's proximity to West Polynesia did not result in primary developmental affiliations with Polynesia even though postcontact records make it clear that there was much intercommunication.

Summary

Many students of Pacific cultural history have been uncomfortable with classification of the Fijian people, language, or culture as primarily either Melanesian or Polynesian. While the preceding pages have made occasional reference to the issue of cultural origins and affiliations, it seems useful to close this chapter by returning to the linguistic, physical, and archaeological data to see if the developmental position of Fiji can now be better defined.

As a starting point this summary will focus on internal variation within Fiji. No recent study has measured regional differences in the physical anthropology of the Fijian populations. One is left with the impression from previous studies that Polynesian traits are more predominant in the east and Melanesian in the west, but that in general Fijians are, as Howells has said, "Melanesianized Polynesians."

In the area of linguistics our evidence is better. In 1971 Pawley and Sayaba offered evidence that there are two Fijian dialects, eastern and western; each of these is made up of a series of communalects, none of which is as significantly different as those opposed in the east/west contrast. The dividing line for these dialect groups coincides with the major mountain range that divides inland Viti Levu. The two linguists claim that the dialect division is an old one, and that as early as 2,000 years ago proto-Fijian divided into proto-eastern-Fijian and proto-western-Fijian. The origins of proto-Fijian are found in the breakup of proto–Central Pacific, an Austronesian protolanguage. Looking to archaeological evidence and glottochronological estimates, Pawley and Sayaba tie proto–Central Pacific to the Lapita archaeological complex and suggest that it divided into proto-Fijian and proto-Polynesian some 3,000 to 4,000 years ago. They argue that the archaeological evidence of the period during which the Fijian dialect division started to take place (Sigatoka phase) affirms that the Lapita complex (and by inference the proto-Fijian language) spread through most of the coastal region of Viti Levu, if not much of the Fiji group. No evidence is found in this Lapita complex of more than one material culture complex, as would be necessary to suggest a cultural division similar to the linguistic one.

In fact, throughout the Fijian archaeological sequence there is no strong evidence in artifact distribution that would support a hypothesis of strong east/west cultural division. The admittedly limited amount of archaeological research completed so far shows a few minor variations in the distribution of ceramic forms. Navatu-phase flat-bottomed trays and the pinched nubbin motif occur in Viti Levu sites, while the Ra-phase dari bowls occur most frequently east of Viti Levu. Ethnohistoric evidence and present potting traditions suggest that some Ra-phase ceramic decoration motifs were geographically centered within certain villages. Palmer (1971a) suggests that there is some evidence that in the past, potters were wives of fishermen who lived on small islands near the mouths of major river drainages on the two largest islands, and that their locally unique ceramics were traded by their husbands along with the fish they caught. The evidence indicates that Fiji was divided into several paramount chiefdoms whose boundaries changed with each succeeding war, but whose distribution never seemed to match the east/west Viti Levu linguistic division.

What, then, was the process that led to the linguistic differentiation, and why has it not been detected in the archaeological assemblages? Pawley and Sayaba make reference to Groube's 1971 assertion that the assumed primarily maritime adaptation of Lapita peoples would have kept early inhabitants from spreading inland. At some later date, as populations did achieve the land-based subsistence skills necessary for inland adaptation, the central mountain range of Viti Levu would have served as the appropriately placed geographic barrier to account for inland linguistic diversification. Linguists discount this argument because it fails to account for occurrence of the dialect division in coastal Viti Levu contexts where no geographic barriers stand to cause isolation and diversification. Recent work by Kirch (1976) in Futuna and the pattern of early inland settlement in Samoa (Green and Davidson 1969, 1974) suggest that the Lapita technology may have included horticultural skills that could have supported inland populations. It may not be appropriate, therefore, to infer the several centuries' difference between coastal and inland settlement that would bring about dialect differences.

Another direction in which to look for the cause of the Fijian dialect division is external. Hocart (1952), having collected extensive traditional reports of migrant populations moving from unknown points in the west into Fiji, explained the east/west variation as the result of an overlay of new customs brought in by intrusive, but eventually integrated, populations. He notes widespread acceptance by Fijian informants of the claim that there were once "old states" of Fiji, such as Verata and Vuna, and that, before and during European contact, these were made subservient to new states, such as Bau and Cakaudrove, led chiefly by recent migrants from the west. Hocart was also intrigued by the pattern of dual organization in eastern Fiji, which he thought to be an archaic pattern with interesting parallels in western Melanesia, Australia, and India.

The archaeological evidence of Fiji suggests that following the initial Lapita settlement, two later ceramic traditions were introduced into the group and became widespread and long-lived. The earliest of these is the Impressed tradition, primarily characterized by carved-paddle impressed decorated pottery. Beginning no later than 100 B.C. this tradition replaced the Lapita ceramic complex in both decorative techniques and vessel form (Birks 1973; Pawley and Green 1975). The occurrence of paddle-impressed pottery has been documented to Southeast Asia and Melanesia with a New Caledonia distribution from 1200 B.C. to A.D. 300 (Golson 1971; Birks 1973; Pawley and Green 1975). While Groube (1971) has suggested that the Fijian paddle-impressed tradition could have developed from the Lapita complex, this possibility is discounted by Birks (1973). The current consensus is that Fiji's Impressed tradition and Navatu phase can be ascribed to Melanesian influences. Little is known of the cultural dynamics of this post-Lapita ceramic change and whether indigenous populations were replaced or whether intruding populations simply produced a circumstance where the Lapita ceramic complex, already moving toward plain ware, was abandoned and replaced with the Impressed-ware complex.

The linguistic and archaeological evidence has convinced Pawley and Sayaba (1971) and Pawley and Green (1975) that the Impressed-ware populations were not the originators of the ancestral Fijian language. They argue that the time required for linguistic diversification in Fiji is too great to be explained by the 100 B.C. initiation of the Impressed phase. They also argue that the Fijian language shows primary affiliation to proto–Central Pacific and proto–Polynesian and not to the languages of eastern Melanesia, to which the earliest Pacific Impressed-ware traditions would logically be tied. Pawley and Sayaba argue that Tongan is the only language to which significant borrowing by Fijian can be attributed, and this borrowing does not affect the basic vocabulary. Since proto-Polynesian and proto–Central Pacific are the language groups most logically associated with the western Polynesian Lapita assemblage and proto-Fijian is most clearly tied to these, Pawley and Green claim that it is most reasonable to infer that the Lapita culture is the source of the Fijian language and that the circumstance of the Impressed-

ware intrusion from Melanesia into Fiji had little impact on the linguistic continuity. This Sigatoka-Navatu phase transition remains one of the most complex problems of Fijian prehistory; there is a clear need to focus on research programs that will extract information on the late Lapita, early Impressed period.

A second post-Lapita Melanesian ceramic intrusion occurred with the introduction in about A.D. 1100 of Incised-tradition appliqué, modeled, and incised motifs that can reasonably be attributed to earlier central New Hebridean sources (Garanger 1971; Golson 1971, 1972). The cultural circumstances of this ceramic change are better understood than those of the Impressed-ware introduction. First, this change occurred much too late to have affected the general character or distribution of the Fijian languages. Second, rather than being a ceramic replacement in the way Impressed wares apparently were, the intrusive Incised motifs appear in association with Impressed wares; the two traditions co-occur in continuity, with a gradual drop in frequency of Impressed wares. When this co-occurrence was observed in Gifford's excavation results, the hypothesis of post-occupational mixture was suggested. More recent excavations have found it to be a consistent pattern, and it is possible that some carved-paddle impressing lasted up to the time of contact (Palmer 1971a; Frost 1974). A third factor important to the circumstance of the Incised-ware intrusion is the simultaneous appearance of fortifications and, by implication, of warfare. While the dating of forts from Taveuni and Lakeba may prove to be atypical of the Fiji group, it seems more than coincidental that forts and intrusive Incised ceramics co-occur.

The evidence makes clear that there is no simple answer to the question of Fijian antecedents and affiliations. Yet it seems fair to argue that the physical, linguistic, and cultural base to Fijian culture was one shared with the ancestral Polynesians and different from that of the Melanesians. While there is clear evidence of ceramic intrusion from Melanesia, of sociocultural diffusion of the sort noted by Hocart, and of Melanesian gene flow as pointed out by Howells and others, these apparently did not overwhelm the Polynesian vector of Fijian culture. If one must classify Fiji at all, it seems most logical to group it with West Polynesia. Furthermore, the issues of antecedents and affiliations focus largely on Fiji's external relations. Present evidence suggests that the development of Fijian culture is independent of the groups to the east and west and is internally quite complex. One may hope that future research will be able to delve into the processes of ecological adaptation and sociocultural development that led to the unique aspects of Fijian prehistory.

References

Belshaw, Cyril. 1964. *Under the ivi tree*. Berkeley: University of California Press.

Best, Elsdon. 1927. *The Pa Maori*. New Zealand Dominion Museum Bulletin no. 6, Wellington.

Best, Simon. 1977. Archaeological investigations on Lakeba, Lau group, Fiji. *New Zealand Archaeological Association Newsletter* 20:28.

Birks, Lawrence. 1973. *Archaeological excavations at Sigatoka dune site, Fiji*. Bulletin of the Fiji Museum no. 1, Suva.

———— and Helen Birks. 1967. A brief report on excavations at Sigatoka, Fiji. *New Zealand Archaeological Association Newsletter* 10:16–25.

Frost, E. L. 1974. *Archaeological excavations of fortified sites on Taveuni, Fiji*. Asian and Pacific Archaeology Series no. 6, Honolulu.

———— and J. O. Frost. 1979. *Preliminary definition of cultural history of Laucala Island, Fiji*. Mimeographed, Eastern New Mexico University.

Garanger, José. 1971. Incised and applied-relief pottery, its chronology and development in southeastern Melanesia, and extra areal comparisons. In *Studies in Oceanic culture history*, ed. R. C. Green and Marion Kelly, vol. 2. *Pacific Anthropological Records* 12:53–66.

Gifford, E. W. 1951. Archaeological excavations in Fiji. *University of California Anthropological Records* 13:189–288.

————. 1955. Six Fijian radiocarbon dates. *Journal of the Polynesian Society* 64:240.

Golson, Jack. 1959. L'archéologie du Pacific Sud: resultats et perspectives. *Journal de la Société des Océanistes* 15:5–54.

————. 1961. Report on New Zealand, western Polynesia, New Caledonia, and Fiji. *Asian Perspectives* 5:166–180.

————. 1964. *Excavation of quadrant no. 2 (southwest) of square A2 at Karobo*. Mimeographed, Australian National University.

————. 1971. Lapita ware and its transformations. In *Studies in Oceanic culture history*, ed. R. C. Green and Marion Kelly, vol. 2. *Pacific Anthropological Records* 12:67–76.

————. 1972. Both sides of the Wallace Line: New Guinea, Australia, Island Melanesia and Asian prehistory. In *Early Chinese Art and its possible influence in the Pacific basin*, ed. N. Barnard, pp. 533–596. New York: Intercultural Arts Press.

Green, R. C. 1963. A suggested revision of the Fijian sequence. *Journal of the Polynesian Society* 72:235–253.

————. 1967. Fortifications in other parts of tropical Polynesia. *New Zealand Archaeological Association Newsletter* 10:96–113.

———— and J. M. Davidson, eds. 1969. *Archaeology in Western Samoa*, vol. 1. *Auckland Institute and Museum Bulletin* 6.

————. 1974. *Archaeology in Western Samoa*, vol. 2. *Auckland Institute and Museum Bulletin* 7.

Groube, Leslie. 1971. Tonga, Lapita pottery and Polynesian origins. *Journal of the Polynesian Society* 80:278–316.

Hale, Horatio. 1846. *United States Exploring Expedition. During the years 1838, 1839, 1840, 1841, 1842, under the command of Charles Wilkes, U.S.N.* vol. 6, Ethnography and Philology. Philadelphia: C. Sherman.

Hocart, A. M. 1915. Ethnographic sketch of Fiji. *Man* 15:73–77.

————. 1952. *The northern states of Fiji*. Occasional Publication no. 11, Royal Anthropological Institute of Great Britain and Ireland, London.

Howells, W. W. 1933. Anthropometry and blood types in Fiji and the Solomon Islands. (Based on data of Dr. William L. Moss.) *Anthropological Papers of the American Museum of Natural History* 33:279–339.

Kirch, P. V. 1976. Ethno-archaeological investigations in Futuna and Uvea (western Polynesia): a preliminary report. *Journal of the Polynesian Society* 85:27–69.

Lester, R. H. 1953. Secret societies of Viti Levu. *Transactions of the Fiji Society* 2:117–134.

EVERETT L. FROST

Palmer, J. B. 1965. Excavations at Karobo, Viti Levu. *New Zealand Archaeological Association Newsletter* 8:26–33.

———. 1967a. *Archaeological sites of Wakaya Island*. Records of the Fiji Museum, vol. 1, no. 2, Suva.

———. 1967b. Sigatoka research project—preliminary report. *New Zealand Archaeological Association Newsletter* 10:2–15.

———. 1968. Recent results from the Sigatoka archaeological program. In *Prehistoric culture in Oceania*, ed. Ichito Yawata and Y. H. Sinoto, pp. 19–28. Honolulu: Bishop Museum Press.

———. 1969. Ring-ditch fortifications on windward Viti Levu, Fiji. *Archaeology and Physical Anthropology in Oceania* 4:181–197.

———. 1971a. Fijian pottery technologies: their relevance to certain problems of south-west Pacific prehistory. In *Studies in Oceanic culture history*, ed. R. C. Green and Marion Kelly, vol. 2. *Pacific Anthropological Records* 12:77–85.

———. 1971b. Naga ceremonial sites in Navosa upper Sigatoka Valley, final report no. 1. *Sigatoka Research Project Miscellaneous Papers*. Records of the Fiji Museum, vol. 1, no. 5, Suva.

Parke, A. L. 1971. Some prehistoric Fijian ceremonial sites on the island of Vanua Levu, Fiji, part 1. *Archaeology and Physical Anthropology in Oceania* 6:243–267.

———. 1972. Some prehistoric Fijian ceremonial sites on the island of Vanua Levu, Fiji, part 2. *Archaeology and Physical Anthropology in Oceania* 7:56–78.

Pawley, A. K. and R. C. Green. 1973. Dating the dispersal of the Oceanic languages. *Oceanic Linguistics* 12:1–67.

——— and Timoci Sayaba. 1971. Fijian dialect divisions: eastern and western Fijian. *Journal of the Polynesian Society* 80:405–436.

Roth, G. K. 1953. *Fijian way of life*. Melbourne: Oxford University Press.

Sahlins, M. D. 1962. Moala: culture and nature on a Fijian island. Ann Arbor: University of Michigan Press.

Shaw, Elizabeth. 1967. *A reanalysis of pottery from Navatu and Vuda, Fiji*. Master's thesis, University of Auckland.

———. 1975. The decorative system of Natunuku, Fiji. In *The Lapita pottery style of Fiji and its associations*, S. M. Mead, Lawrence Birks, Helen Birks, and Elizabeth Shaw, pp. 44–55. Polynesian Society Memoir no. 38, Wellington.

Smart, C. D. 1965. An outline of Kabara prehistory. *New Zealand Archaeological Association Newsletter* 8:43–52.

Spencer, Dorothy. 1941. *Disease, religion, and society in the Fiji Islands*. American Ethnological Society Monograph no. 11, Philadelphia.

Thompson, Laura. 1940. *Southern Lau, Fiji: an ethnography*. Bishop Museum Bulletin no. 162, Honolulu.

Ward, R. G. 1965. *Land use and population in Fiji: a geographical study*. London: Her Majesty's Stationery Office.

Samoa and Tonga

CHAPTER 4

JANET M. DAVIDSON

The evidence on the prehistory of Samoa and Tonga, the two principal island groups of West Polynesia, is divided into three periods. In the early or ceramic period, the emphasis is on material culture and economy, since almost nothing is known of settlement patterns, structures, or social organization. Only limited remarks can be made about change in this period; however, it was during the 1,000 to 1,500 years from the initial settlement of Samoa and Tonga to the cessation of pottery manufacture early in the Christian era that most or all of the developments probably took place that laid the foundations for Polynesian language, culture, and society as we know them. There is little information about the succeeding period, which corresponds roughly to the first millennium A.D. Continuity of occupation is assumed in view of the lack of evidence of intrusion. For the recent period, historical and traditional as well as archaeological evidence can be invoked. Here the emphasis is on structures, settlements, burial customs, and social organization, rather than on material culture or economy.

Samoa and Tonga, with the larger archipelago of Fiji, lie at the western gateway to Polynesia. Although these islands have long been regarded as important in the development of Polynesian culture, it took modern archaeological methods and the technique of radiocarbon dating to demonstrate the length of their prehistory—some 3,000 years—and their true significance as the hearth where distinctively Polynesian culture probably first developed.

Ethnologists have long distinguished subdivisions within Polynesian culture based on geographic groupings. In particular, a West Polynesian culture area has been identified, which has often been shown to share a significant range of traits with Fiji (Burrows 1938; see also Green 1968). Samoa and Tonga are the principal groups in this culture area, others being the smaller and more isolated islands of Futuna/Alofi and 'Uvea. Niue and the atolls of the Ellice and Tokelau groups to the northwest and north are sometimes included (see Fig. 2.2). Recent research suggests that although the cultures of Samoa and Tonga share a common origin, modern similarities also result from continued contact and communication between the archipelagoes throughout their history.

Present-day Samoa is politically divided. Upolu and Savai'i and their satellites constitute the independent nation of Western Samoa; Tutuila and Manu'a are a United States territory administered by the Department of the Interior. Archaeological research in Samoa has been somewhat affected by this division. The entire Tongan Archipelago, on the other hand, including the northern outliers, forms the independent Kingdom of Tonga.

Most residents of Tonga and Samoa today are Polynesians, descendants of the inhabitants described by the first European explorers to visit the two archipelagoes. A separate Polynesian language is spoken throughout each group; these languages are not mutually intelligible. Although Tongan is now spoken in Niuatoputapu, a word list collected by the first European to visit that island, LeMaire in 1616, suggests that at that time a different language, more closely related to Samoan, was spoken there (Biggs 1972).

Following the discovery of the northern outliers by LeMaire and Schouten in 1616, the next visitor to Tonga was Tasman in 1643, who discovered 'Ata, 'Eua, Tonga-

tapu, and Nomuka. Cook visited these islands plus Ha'apai on his second and third voyages, but Vava'u was first visited by Maurelle in 1781. The first missionary endeavor began in Tonga in 1797 but was unsuccessful. Activities leading to conversion resumed in the 1820s. Cook named the Tongan group the Friendly Isles because of the apparently peaceful and friendly way of life of the inhabitants. Following his visits, however, Tonga was plagued by wars that subsided only with the establishment of the present royal dynasty in 1845.

Several European visitors left accounts of Tongan life in the eighteenth and early nineteenth centuries; these provide a rich source of ethnohistoric information. They reveal fascinating glimpses of the political, social, and economic upheavals in the group during the period after European contact but before conversion to Christianity and adoption of a European-imposed peace.

By contrast, little is known of Samoa before 1830 and historical records remain poor until after 1840. The group was first sighted by Roggeveen, who sailed past Manu'a in 1722. Neither he nor Bougainville in 1768 landed, although some contact was made with the inhabitants, whose skill with canoes led Bougainville to name Samoa "The Navigators." The first detailed observations were made in 1787 by La Pérouse. A tragic incident on Tutuila, in which several of La Pérouse's men were killed, gave Samoa a bad name; other than a brief call by H.M.S. *Pandora* in 1791, no literate Europeans visited the group again until missionary activity began in 1830 with a visit by Williams. By that time there was already a substantial population of beachcombers, and Samoans were aware of and anxious for the benefits of European contact. This relative lack of information about Samoa during the initial contact period is important to archaeologists, for it means that later accounts by resident Europeans describe a society already much changed by knowledge obtained from beachcombers, Tongans, and other islanders. Descriptions of Samoan society and settlement patterns in 1840 cannot be regarded as a record of a society unaffected by European contact.

Samoa and Tonga are among the larger Polynesian archipelagoes (Fig. 4.1), with the greatest land areas after New Zealand and Hawaii, although they are dominated by their larger neighbor to the west, Fiji. Samoa is a relatively compact group of volcanic origin. Its two largest islands, Savai'i and Upolu, are in the western portion of the archipelago, separated by a relatively narrow strait in which lie the two smaller inhabited islands of Apolima and Manono. Savai'i has a land area of 1,814 km² and rises to a height of nearly 1,850 m. Upolu has a land area of 1,115 km² and a maximum elevation of 1,100 m. Tutuila, some 70 km southeast of Upolu, has an area of 145 km²; farther east again are the smaller islands of the Manu'a group.

The islands are composed of basalts of varying ages. In general, the older rocks are in the east and the younger in the west. Thus Tutuila and some eastern parts of Upolu have very rugged, dissected landscapes; these areas are well watered with permanent streams. By contrast, there have been three phases of volcanic activity on Savai'i in recent times—approximately 1760, 1902, and 1905 to 1911. The varying ages of the underlying rocks throughout the group are reflected in soil development, relief, water supply, and to some extent coral reef formation and lagoon development. These variations in turn have some effect on the nature and distribution of prehistoric settlement.

The climate of Samoa is humid and tropical, with only weakly developed seasonal variations in temperature and precipitation. Nor is there marked variation in rainfall between one side of an island and the other. Rainfall is greatest in the center of the larger islands; the annual mean in the highlands of Savai'i is considerably more than 6,000 mm. The western extremities of Upolu and Savai'i are driest, with approximately 2,500 mm of rainfall.

The Tongan group provides several marked contrasts to Samoa. It is much more extensive: about 200 islands with a total area of approximately 700 km². Most of the islands, including all the principal inhabited ones, are raised coral blanketed with fertile volcanic ash. There is, however, a chain of volcanic islands (some still active) in the western portion of the group.

Apart from the now uninhabited southern outlier of 'Ata, the southernmost cluster of the Tongan archipelago consists of the largest island, Tongatapu (275 km²), and its offshore islets and the higher island of 'Eua. Tongatapu is a tilted limestone island, with an extensive shallow lagoon on the north bordering a low-lying and indented coastline, and limestone cliffs reaching an elevation of 82 m on the eastern (*liku*) coast.

In the center of the archipelago are the numerous densely inhabited islands of the Nomuka and Ha'apai clusters, with the volcanic islands of Kao and Tofua to the west. Farther north is the Vava'u group, which consists of one large and numerous smaller raised coral islands. Vava'u, like Tongatapu, is tilted; in this case the highest point is in the north, where the limestone cliffs reach a height of more than 200 m. The southern coast of the main island has many indentations, and the smaller islands lie to the south and southwest, providing extensive areas of sheltered and often shallow waterways and lagoon.

Several northern outliers are now politically part of the Kingdom of Tonga. Niuatoputapu and its uninhabited neighbor Tafahi lie almost equidistant between Vava'u and Samoa—297 km from the former and 310 km from Upolu. Their nearest neighbor is the other northern Tongan outlier, Niuafo'ou, 190 km away. These islands are volcanic in origin; Niuafo'ou has been active very recently.

The bulk of the Tongan population is now concentrated on the raised coral islands. This was probably also the case in prehistoric times, although the volcanic islands contained important resources, notably basalt and other stone for tools. The

JANET M. DAVIDSON

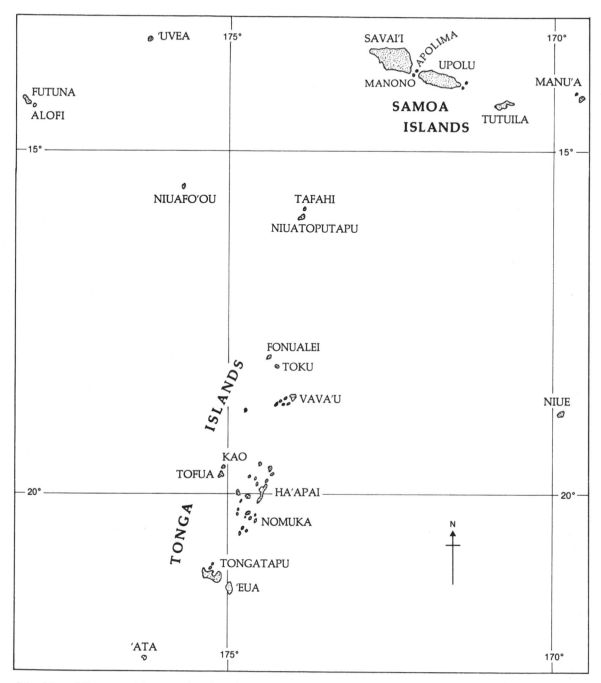

4.1 *Map of Tonga and Samoa, showing also some of the smaller West Polynesian islands.*

coral islands are fertile and most are associated with extensive lagoons. Fresh water is restricted in Tonga, unlike most parts of Samoa. It is most readily available in the low-lying areas, also attractive for settlement because of their proximity to the lagoon.

The climate in Tonga is less consistently

warm and humid than in Samoa. There is much more marked seasonal variation and a tendency toward periodic droughts in some islands. Mean annual rainfall in Tongatapu is about 1,600 mm, but the amount increases progressively northward to about 2,700 mm in Niuafo'ou.

Archaeological study in Samoa and Tonga has not been directed primarily toward environmental questions, despite a growing interest in subsistence economy. In this region, unlike New Zealand for example, possible effects of climatic change have not been evaluated, although minor changes in precipitation and wind regimes would have seriously affected the lives of the inhabitants. Nor have other environmental changes been studied. Yet there is little doubt that the initial impact of man's arrival on a hitherto uninhabited archipelago must have been considerable on both land and marine resources. More obvious forms of environmental change are those brought about by tectonic and volcanic activity, and by the changes in land/sea relationships that have occurred during human occupation of the region.

In both Tongatapu and Vava'u, the earliest known archaeological sites are associated with former shorelines (Fig. 4.2). The distance from the present beach is not great, however, and the increase in land area probably has not been very significant. The effects of such changes on the lagoon and particularly on shellfish populations are unknown, although a change from shellfish found in more open water conditions to those typical of the enclosed inner lagoon has been recorded in several early sites on Tongatapu. In Niuatoputapu, on the other hand, the effects of uplift and progradation have been considerable, for the land area there has more than doubled during human occupation. Conversely, an early Samoan site has been submerged rather than left high and dry. It remains unclear whether the coast of Upolu has been uniformly inundated or whether the

island has tilted. The continuing lack of early Lapita pottery from coastal sites suggests the former.

Another factor causing loss of habitable land in Samoa has been volcanic eruption. Large areas on Savai'i were affected by historic lava flows, and lesser flows are known to have occurred on both Upolu and Savai'i during the past 3,000 years. These would have caused at least short-term displacement of populations with repercussions elsewhere. The effect of volcanic eruptions in Tonga was probably less serious, or at least more localized. Temporary restriction of access to stone resources on Tofua, for example, is quite possible. The more catastrophic effects of volcanic activity on Niuafo'ou resulted in evacuation of the island between 1946 and 1958. Gardens on Vava'u were damaged by ash from the uninhabited island of Fonualei in 1846.

The pioneering archaeological study in West Polynesia was McKern's survey in Tonga in 1920–1921 (McKern 1929). This was largely an analysis of the more striking field monuments of Tonga, but limited excavations were carried out and pottery was found, including sherds with the distinctive decoration now known as Lapita. No comparable work exists for Samoa. Apart from incidental field observations by Buck (1930) and brief descriptions of individual field monuments by Thomson (1927) and Freeman (1943, 1944a,b,c), Samoa has been largely neglected. Modern research in this general area began with a visit by Golson in 1957 (Golson, n.d.; Green and Davidson 1969). In Tonga, Golson tested six sites, including two previously investigated by McKern; then, in Samoa, he laid the basis for future surveys and settlement pattern studies with an account of the principal field remains. He also conducted several test excavations, one of which (at Vailele) yielded pottery and stone adzes and gave three radiocarbon dates of the first century A.D. The Golson studies thus indicated for the first time the antiquity of settlement in

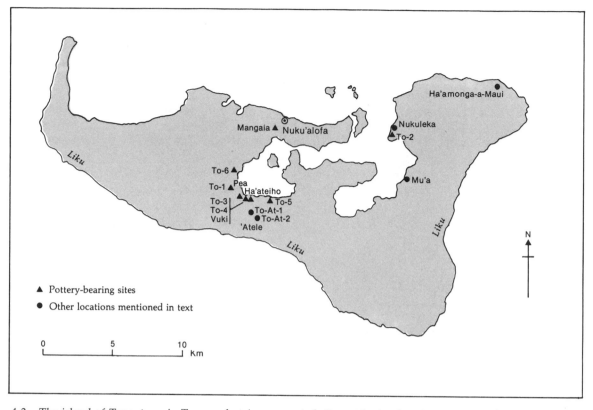

4.2 *The island of Tongatapu in Tonga, showing excavated sites and other locations mentioned in the text.*

West Polynesia and outlined the scope of future archaeological research.

The significance of the Lapita decoration on Tongan sherds then began to be recognized. Golson promoted further work on pottery-bearing sites in Tonga. All the excavations were on the southern and largest island of Tongatapu, and all have been concerned with pottery-bearing sites, except for my own excavation (Davidson 1969a) of two burial mounds that date to the post-ceramic period. A preliminary site survey was carried out on Vava'u in 1969 (Davidson 1971), but no excavations have taken place. Detailed research has, however, been undertaken on the northern outlier of Niuatoputapu, first with a site survey and test excavations by Rogers (1974) and recently with a more intensive project by Kirch (1977, 1978) that involved ethnoarchaeological study of modern subsistence, detailed

site survey, and excavations in both ceramic and aceramic sites. Much of what is known about Tongan prehistory, therefore, derives from excavations in pottery-bearing sites on Tongatapu, supplemented by surface evidence throughout the group, and reinforced by the recent data from Niuatoputapu.

In Samoa more ambitious and broadly based projects have been carried out, and the results have been more fully published. As part of the Polynesian prehistory programs of the Bishop Museum, Honolulu, in the 1960s, fieldwork in American Samoa was conducted by museum personnel (Kikuchi 1963; Emory and Sinoto 1965), and in Western Samoa by Green and his associates (Green and Davidson 1969, 1974). The Western Samoan program concentrated on the island of Upolu, with site surveys and excavations in several areas (Fig. 4.3), and

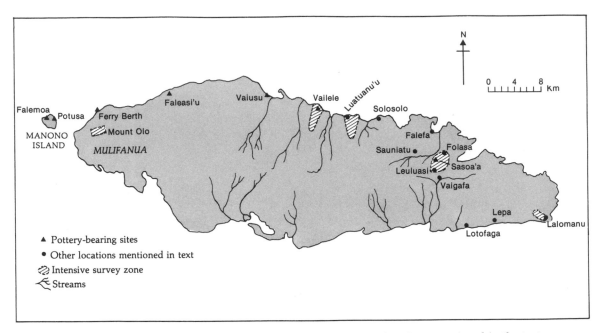

4.3 *The island of Upolu in Samoa, showing excavated sites and other locations mentioned in the text.*

with limited reconnaissance surveys on the island of Savai'i. Excavated sites ranged from deposits 2,000 years old to structures that dated from the early to middle nineteenth century. Since the conclusion of this project, a new program has been instituted in Western Samoa by Jennings and his associates (1976). This has involved intensive settlement pattern studies and excavation of early sites in western Upolu and Manono, areas relatively neglected by Green, who concentrated on eastern and central Upolu. In American Samoa work has recently been carried out on Tutuila by J. Frost (1976).

The results from Samoa provide a greater range of data than those from Tonga and include information lacking for Tonga about settlement patterns, structures, and field monuments. The evidence of the earliest settlement of Samoa is still very sparse, however, and the range of Samoan artifacts is much more restricted than that from early Tongan sites. These factors inhibit comparisons and hinder our understanding of the extent of communication,

contact, and exchange of ideas between the two groups.

The Early Period

The early settlement of Samoa and Tonga cannot be considered in isolation from the settlement of neighboring Fiji, since it is evident that the three archipelagoes were discovered and colonized fairly rapidly —slightly more than 3,000 years ago—by closely related people. The vital clue has been the discovery of distinctive Lapita pottery throughout the region. In Fiji (see Chapter 3), Lapita sites have been excavated at several locations on Viti Levu, and more recently on Lakeba in the Lau Islands. On Tongatapu, Poulsen (1966, 1967, 1968, 1972, 1974, 1976) excavated six pottery-bearing sites and Groube (1971) one; evidence from the Mangaia mound, variously tested by McKern (1929), Golson, and the Birkses (Suggs 1961; Golson 1962), can also be considered. Although there have been no excavations in Ha'apai or Vava'u, surface

JANET M. DAVIDSON

finds of pottery, including a few sherds with Lapita decoration, have been made. In Niuatoputapu, Rogers' (1974) identification of a narrow zone of pottery-bearing deposits following an old beach line around the entire circumference of the island has been confirmed by Kirch (1977, 1978), who excavated in ten localities around this zone. No pottery has yet been found in American Samoa, but several pottery-bearing sites are now known in Western Samoa. The only site in Samoa to yield distinctively decorated Lapita sherds thus far, however, is the Ferry Berth site at Mulifanua, western Upolu. This site, completely submerged, now lies about 110 m offshore in the lagoon and was revealed by dredging during wharf construction.

Detailed studies since 1957 of Samoan and Tongan pottery have gradually defined a ceramic sequence that probably spans considerably more than a millennium. It begins with the settlement of the region by people who made elaborate and finely decorated vessels in a variety of forms, using techniques and motifs that are also recognizable in Lapita assemblages over a wide area of the western Pacific. During the sequence vessel forms became more restricted, with decoration becoming scarcer and eventually disappearing. In Samoa, at least, plain pottery became increasingly thick and coarse. Pottery manufacture finally was abandoned in both Samoa and Tonga by about the beginning of the Christian era. In Fiji, however, new wares appeared, with pottery manufacture continuing in some areas until the present day.

On present evidence it is impossible to say which islands in the Tonga/Samoa archipelagoes were settled first. At the moment Tongatapu has slightly earlier radiocarbon dates and more early Lapita evidence available. However, this could result from the greater amount of archaeological effort that has been specifically directed toward Lapita sites in Tonga and the probable submergence of similar sites in Samoa. Rather than argue about which islands

were settled first, it seems more worthwhile to review in general terms our knowledge of Lapita and early Polynesian material culture, economy, and settlement pattern, using such evidence as is available and ignoring differences among islands from causes that are not understood.

Pottery-Bearing Sites

The early sites in Tongatapu (Fig. 4.2) are found along an old shoreline and originally would have been very close to the shore. The earliest deposits identified by Poulsen (1967), on the basis of pottery seriation, are at Nukuleka in the east of the island and the lowest deposits in the vicinity of Ha'ateiho and Pea. A radiocarbon date of 1140 B.C. ± 95 for the base of Nukuleka is matched by a date of 1180 B.C. ± 70 indicating activity at the Mangaia mound near Nuku'alofa. Both these dates were on shell samples and cannot be corrected for secular effect; nonetheless, it is probable that the true ages are somewhat older. These two dates together with the undated but comparable earliest ceramics at another site indicate established settlement at three different locations on the attractive foreshore of Tongatapu before the end of the second millennium B.C. There is also a shell date of 820 B.C. ± 100 from Pea.

Poulsen originally divided his material into two periods, the early period probably corresponding roughly to Green's early eastern Lapita and the late period to late eastern Lapita and Polynesian plain ware. In particular, the pottery from the upper levels belongs to the Polynesian plain ware. To this may be added the bulk of the material from Vuki's mound, excavated by Groube, while the Mangaia mound probably included late eastern Lapita and Polynesian plain ware deposits. Poulsen's other excavations were more limited and serve mainly to provide further evidence of the extent of pottery-bearing deposits.

Groube (1971), in support of his hypothesis that Tongatapu was settled first and that colonization proceeded gradually north from there, has argued that pottery-bearing deposits are more numerous in Tongatapu than in other parts of the Tongan group. However, sufficient pottery has now been found in Ha'apai and especially Vava'u to suggest the existence of extensive pottery-bearing deposits there.

The pottery-bearing sites tested by Kirch (1978) on Niuatoputapu appear to span most or all of the known sequence given above. His three principal sites are located on what at the time would have been the northern shore of the island. Even allowing for drastic changes in the island's area, this shore would have been the most attractive zone for settlement (as the equivalent northern shore is now). The three principal sites are Lolokoka, ceramics from which are tentatively assigned to early eastern Lapita on the basis of vessel form and design; Lotoa, tentatively assigned to late eastern Lapita, since decoration is confined to rims; and Pome'e, with entirely plain ware. Seven other sites supplement the information from these three.

The earliest known site in Samoa is the submerged Ferry Berth site (Fig. 4.3). There is a radiocarbon date on shell of 940 B.C. ± 80, which although slightly younger than the earliest Tongan dates is of comparable order. The site was probably on the fore-shore at that time. The sherds came from a relatively narrow elongated zone roughly parallel with the present shore. Studies of the probable shoreline at the lower sea level suggest that the site was probably on the inner edge of an embayment. The cemented coral crust that now seals the deposit (and contained a few sherds) gave a date of 220 B.C. ± 70.

Despite the difficulties experienced in finding pottery in Samoa after the initial chance discovery at Vailele, it is now evident that sites containing pottery are widespread in both coastal and inland locations. Intense work at Vailele revealed primary pottery-bearing deposits sealed beneath two of the four later mounds investigated,

and scattered sherds in and beneath the other two. Intensive work in another area, the inner part of the large Falefa Valley in eastern Upolu, led to the accidental discovery of a major pottery-bearing site at Sasoa'a, with sporadic finds of isolated sherds in several other valley sites. In exactly the same way, isolated sherds have been encountered near relatively late structural sites in inland Mulifanua—investigated, like the Falefa Valley sites, as part of a major settlement pattern study. Isolated sherds suggest a long occupation history and the almost certain presence of primary pottery-bearing deposits in the vicinity.

Other coastal pottery finds include a scatter of secondarily deposited sherds at the Paradise site at Vaiusu, on Apolima, and the more extensive and richer sites at Faleasi'u on Upolu, and at Falemoa and Potusa on Manono. Although the finds at Vailele and Sasoa'a were in clay soils, in which organic material and artifacts of bone and shell did not survive, Faleasi'u, Falemoa, and Potusa were in sandier soils with good preservation of bone and shell (both midden and artifacts). Whereas at Vailele and Sasoa'a the pottery-bearing deposits were sealed so that the associations of pottery and other finds were certain, at the other three sites pottery-bearing deposits graded into later layers with some possible mixing of material. The problem was acute only at Potusa. At Faleasi'u all the layers except the uppermost seem to have been deposited during the latter half of the first millennium B.C. and the same is true of Falemoa.

Material Culture

There is little doubt that the ceramic sequence in Tonga and Samoa represents the continuous development (or decline) of a single tradition. A principal-components analysis of Samoan sherds from the Ferry Berth site and two plain pottery sites showed continuity in technology (Jennings et al. 1976). Terms such as "Lapitan" or "Lapitoid" can be applied not only to the tradition in West Polynesia and Fiji, but

JANET M. DAVIDSON

also over a wide area of the western Pacific in which the end points of traditions of comparable length may be quite different from that of Polynesian plain ware. For this reason the ceramic tradition in West Polynesia should probably be distinguished as eastern Lapitoid.

Some breakdown in such a long sequence is certainly necessary. Green's divisions of early eastern Lapita, late eastern Lapita, and Polynesian plain ware—based on criteria of decoration and vessel form (Green and Davidson 1974)—are undoubtedly useful and can be applied to new discoveries. Kirch has been able to use these categories for sites of different ages on Niuatoputapu. He has also been able to apply them in Futuna and 'Uvea, where late eastern Lapita and Polynesian plain ware are found. Within Samoa, Green's distinction between an earlier thin fine (plain) ware and a later thick coarse (plain) ware continues to be useful, despite chronological overlap between the two.

Study of decoration from early sites has shown that some differentiation between Tongan and Fijian motif inventories had already taken place (Mead et al. 1975). The Tongan assemblages contain a series of motifs at present unique to Tonga, suggesting some initial development of decoration in Tonga during the early eastern Lapita phase there. Subsequently, however, the trend was one of decline in variety, extent, and execution of design. Vessel forms in Vuki's mound were limited to globular plain cooking pots and plain open bowls; in the even later Samoan plain-ware sites, only bowls were found. Despite the gaps in the record and the different representations from the various islands, it does appear that a very similar pottery sequence was followed throughout the Tongan and Samoan groups—so similar, in fact, that the resemblances must be the result of contact and interchange of ideas, not of coincidence. Futuna and 'Uvea can probably be included in this intercommunicating zone; pottery there is much like pottery of comparable age elsewhere in the region, al-

though early eastern Lapita so far has not been found there (Kirch 1976).

The pots appear to have been locally produced on each island. Analysis of temper sands in sherds from a number of sites has suggested that the materials are locally derived, because they seem to conform in each case to what is known of local geology. In other words, there is no present evidence for trade or transfer of pots between islands. This is particularly important in the case of the Ferry Berth sherds from Samoa, since the circumstances of discovery prompted the hypothesis that the sherds were derived from the wreckage of a Tongan or Fijian trading canoe. The sherds themselves rule this out. There is, of course, evidence for Fijian pottery in Tonga long after the Tongans themselves ceased to make pottery. For the early period, however, no such evidence has been found.

A major problem is posed by the abandonment of pottery manufacture throughout the region. An explanation from the time when pottery was unknown in Polynesia—that there were no suitable materials—clearly does not hold. Moreover, Tongans continued to use Fijian pots occasionally until the eighteenth century. Green and Davidson (1974) have shown that ultimately the vessel forms of the final phase of pottery manufacture in Samoa were subsequently manufactured in wood. Many reasons can be advanced about why the Polynesians moved away from the use of pottery, such as the importance of cooking in earth-ovens and particularly the development of wooden kava bowls. Even so, reasons for the loss of the art not merely in one island, but throughout two archipelagoes and several isolated islands, will continue to excite speculation and interest.

By far the fullest inventory of artifacts associated with pottery comes from Poulsen's (1967, 1968) excavations on Tongatapu, although the development of stone adzes is best documented by the Samoan collections (Green and Davidson 1974). The earliest known Tongan adz kit included stone and shell adzes, mostly of types that were also found in later deposits—where they were joined by several new forms. The stone adz component of this assemblage is also found in pottery-bearing deposits in Samoa, where Green has documented the expansion of the Samoa adz kit during the final phase of the ceramic period by the addition of adzes with triangular sections that became important in the inventory of East Polynesian adzes (Green and Davidson 1974). Shell adzes are not typical of Samoan collections. However, one fragment of a shell adz was found at Falemoa, and it is probable that the shell adz will prove to be a component of the earliest Samoan assemblages. Both stone and shell adzes have been found on Niuatoputapu.

On present evidence, Samoan adzes appear to show the development and variety necessary to provide the basis for the more varied and elegant East Polynesian adz assemblages. Without knowledge of adz development in Futuna, 'Uvea, or the northern parts of the Tonga group, however, it is premature to insist that the East Polynesian adz kit was actually derived from Samoa.

The Tongatapu sites yielded a variety of industrial tools. Most of these appear to have been used for working shell, since waste material of *Tridacna* and *Conus* was present at all sites. Worked bone was comparatively rare. Only stone industrial tools were found at Vailele and Sasoa'a. The three coastal sites of Faleasi'u, Falemoa, and Potusa have somewhat expanded the Samoan inventory (Jennings 1976).

Obsidian and chert were used by pottery-making people throughout the region. Siliceous flakes and two pieces of obsidian (both imports) were found in Tongatapu. Obsidian from Tafahi was used on Niuatoputapu, as was chert, which was probably imported from farther afield. In Samoa obsidian, possibly local, is largely confined to ceramic sites. Occasional chert flakes are also found. Determination of the sources of these rocks will help to document inter-island contacts.

Personal ornaments from Tongan sites include large rings (probably arm rings) of *Tridacna* and *Conus*; small shell rings; various biperforated units (perhaps beads); small beads of shell, bone, and stone; pearl shell pendants; a *pule* (cowrie) shell pendant; and various fragments. Shell rings and beads are reported from Niuatoputapu. Among recent discoveries from Samoa are shell rings and two biperforate units, probably of ivory. These discoveries suggest that early Samoans may have had a range of ornaments similar to that of their contemporaries in Tonga, although comparably rich sites are not yet known in Samoa. The presence of bone tattooing chisels in early deposits in Tonga shows that this very widespread Polynesian practice was probably introduced to Tonga by the first settlers.

A major concern has been the identification of artifacts directly related to subsistence activities, notably fishing and horticulture. In view of the undoubted importance of fishing in Polynesian economies, it is somewhat of a paradox that fishing gear has been rare to nonexistent in both Samoan and Tongan sites. The item most often identified (not always very securely) is the cowrie-shell cap of the octopus lure. One shell fishhook, a hook blank, and a gorge were found in early Tongan sites. Net fishing apparently was more important there. A few shell hooks have recently been found in Niuatoputapu.

Four shell hook fragments from Manono, and one from the later site of Lotofaga on Upolu, constitute the only evidence of one-piece hooks from Samoa. Not all the Manono hooks are conclusively associated with pottery, one having been found in a historic period deposit. On present evidence it can only be said that one-piece shell hooks were of minor importance throughout Samoan prehistory. Nevertheless, the presence of early one-piece hooks on the Polynesian outlier of Anuta (in the Solomon Islands) and recent discoveries of shell hooks associated with pottery on Lakeba (Fiji) together with the few Tongan and Samoan finds suggest that one-piece shell hooks were a part—if only a minor part —of the inventory of the earliest settlers of Polynesia, as indeed the reconstruction of a proto-Polynesian word *matau* for fishhook indicates. On the other hand, evidence for the early existence of trolling lures is still lacking. None were found in Tonga, and although one complete example and two blanks were found at Potusa, the complete example (which is identical to ethnographic specimens) and the more convincing blank were in the top layer associated with European artifacts, and even the context of the more questionable blank is uncertain.

The principal artifactual indication of agriculture is the indirect evidence of various shell scrapers and peelers. Such items, made from various shells, have been found in the later Tongatapu sites and at Faleasi'u, Potusa, and Falemoa. On Niuatoputapu cowrie scrapers were present in one site. Apart from a *Strombus* scraper on Tongatapu, however, there is little evidence for their presence in the earliest sites anywhere in the region.

It is customary to scrutinize the early material of West Polynesia both for links to earlier settlement in the west, and for links to colonization of East Polynesia. By and large, only the most general resemblances can be detected. Lapita pottery provides indisputable and close links with certain sites in the western Pacific, but most of the associated early material reflects widespread and general Oceanic traditions of material culture rather than specific links. In the other direction, the development of new adz types, which were further elaborated in East Polynesia, provides the most convincing link between that area and Samoa. Other links to the east again are general rather than specific. One-piece fishhooks have recently been emphasized, but the fishhooks of Samoa, Tonga, and Anuta are part of a widespread early Oceanic tradition found also throughout Micronesia. Fishhooks may very well turn out to be as widely represented archaeologically in parts

of Melanesia, where one-piece hooks are as lacking from the ethnographic record, as they are in Fiji, Tonga, and Samoa.

Subsistence and Social Patterns

Two conflicting hypotheses have been advanced about the subsistence base of the first settlers of Tonga and Samoa. One view suggests that they arrived with a virtually complete inventory of domestic plants and animals, and that their economy from the beginning included exploitation of both land and sea resources according to the widespread later Polynesian pattern. The conflicting view (Groube 1971) is that Lapita colonists were "Oceanic strand-loopers," lacking some or most of the cultigens of the later Polynesian economies and depending heavily on marine resources. Groube based his view on the very large quantity of shell midden associated with Tongan pottery sites; the apparent absence of later, aceramic middens in Tonga; and the lack of comparable middens in Samoa. However, direct comparisons of middens in Tonga and Somoa can be misleading in view of the different lagoon conditions and shellfish availability. The best evidence to date is probably from Niuatoputapu, where ceramic and postceramic sites are spatially differentiated and postceramic middens have been found.

An even more difficult problem is the identification of early horticulture in West Polynesia. In the absence of plant remains or evidence of earthworks or irrigation, cultivation must be inferred from such indirect evidence as food storage and fermentation pits, and vegetable peelers. The very location of some of the ceramic sites in Samoa—notably Sasoa'a, several kilometers inland in the Falefa Valley on Upolu—suggests dependence on horticulture; pits sealed beneath the earliest deposits at Vailele and Sasoa'a provide further evidence, as do the peelers from the Samoan coastal sites. The problem is not whether horticulture was fully developed by the time of

Polynesian plain ware, but whether it was introduced by the earliest Lapita settlers or at some later date in the ceramic period. Despite Groube's arguments, Poulsen (1967) presents reasonably convincing evidence for food pits in his early period on Tongatapu and very substantial evidence for such pits in his late period. He also has fairly secure support for the early presence of chicken, and slight but significant support for the early presence of pig. On Niuatoputapu, Kirch (1978) reports the pig at his earliest site. He strongly supports the view that the earliest colonizers were horticulturists with domestic animals and that they practiced a broad-spectrum economy involving both cultivation and marine exploitation. The evidence thus seems to favor the argument that at least the earliest settlers of Tonga brought with them most or all the elements of later Polynesian subsistence (trolling with shell lures being a probable exception).

Although horticulture in Samoa is suggested by pits and peelers, the early presence of domestic animals remains uncertain. Chicken has been definitely identified at Faleasi'u, but no pigbone is securely associated with pottery-bearing deposits in any of the three excavated coastal middens. This may be a result of the small amount of bone in the sites, the nature of the deposits themselves, or prohibitions on the disposal of pig remains; or the pig simply may have been introduced later. All in all, the view of the early West Polynesian economy proposed by Kirch on the basis of the evidence from Niuatoputapu appears to be the most acceptable at the present time.

Very little can be said about the early societies of Samoa and Tonga. The known distribution of settlement in Tonga was coastal. In Samoa before the end of the ceramic period, inland areas had begun to be cleared and colonized, a fact that suggests considerable buildup of population and probably the beginning of the kind of settlement pattern and social organization known in later times. Part of an oval house, a stone pavement, and other features at Sasoa'a foreshadow the structures of later Samoan sites. There is some slight evidence that burials were in shallow pits perhaps in or near settlements, but nothing has yet been learned from anthropological study of the bones themselves.

In Tongatapu small quantities of human bones were found scattered throughout the midden deposits. At least some of these may imply cannibalism. An old man buried at one of the sites appeared to have suffered a blow on the front of the face. These slight indications suggest, if not organized warfare, then a fairly typical Polynesian pattern of personal violence against stray individuals.

The Dark Ages

Although the end of pottery manufacture in Samoa and Tonga is not precisely dated, it must fall early in the Christian era. The succeeding centuries until about 1,000 years ago are poorly known. This is unfortunate, for it was presumably during this period that colonists left for East Polynesia. During these centuries also, many of the new developments that are characteristic of West Polynesia, but unknown in the east, probably began.

By 2,000 years ago in Upolu, not only the coast but several inland locations were settled. The flat, fertile bottom of the Falefa Valley was inhabited up to 8 km inland by pottery-using people; agricultural clearance, and probably habitation, had taken place on the ridges inland of Luatuanu'u; and some activity, including habitation, is suggested by stray sherds well inland at Mulifanua. The evidence from Falefa suggests that already the basis of Samoan settlement and economy was firmly established, with indications of stone pavements, fences, earth-ovens and hearths, food pits, and probably round-ended or oval houses. Succeeding centuries saw continued bush clearance and the extension of settlement to steeper, less fertile areas on the sides of the Falefa Valley, as well as continued use of the central valley floor. Similar activities took place on the ridges extending far inland behind Luatuanu'u, on the ridges behind Vailele, at inland Mulifanua, and no doubt in many other places. The evidence comes largely from dated deposits in stratified sites. However, more is known of the cultural content of earlier or later occupations at these sites than about the deposits of this period. Without pottery, continuity in material culture is indicated only by adzes and other stone tools. Absence of midden in the clay soils makes it difficult to draw economic inferences. It can only be assumed that the horticultural pattern continued.

In Tongatapu during the same period, the evidence is minimal. Continued if transient use of some of the earlier sites (Vuki's mound, the Mangaia mound, and others) either for habitation or for gardening is indicated by radiocarbon dates.

There is little evidence until late in the first millennium A.D. of the monumental sites, particularly the earthen and stone mounds, that are now such a feature of the archaeological landscapes of both Samoa and Tonga. On the other hand, it is likely that the practice of constructing houses on slightly raised platforms or on terraces on sloping ground was already established in Samoa, and that stone was used for paving and for walls and paths.

Nothing is known of social and political organization. The reasons that caused settlers to depart from one West Polynesian island or another to seek new land in the east remain unknown. It is possible that cannibalism had long been present in Tonga, and perhaps therefore in Samoa also. Organized warfare that would require the use of earthwork fortifications, as opposed to individual violence and the sporadic capture of isolated and unwary members of other groups, however, is largely undocumented. Of significance is a radiocarbon date of A.D. 450 ± 80 for charcoal near the base of the bank of a large fortification at Luatuanu'u. This date cannot be accepted without reservation, because the charcoal could antedate the building of the bank. Nonetheless, warfare and fort construction in Samoa could easily date back that far.

Toward the end of the first millennium of our era, new developments of uncertain origin began to occur. In particular, the construction of monumental mounds of various kinds appears to mark the beginning of the most recent phase of West Polynesian prehistory. In Samoa, mounds were constructed as foundations for houses of various kinds—dwellings, chiefs' houses, community houses, god-houses—and sometimes, apparently, as specialized edifices of a religious kind. In Tonga, mounds were constructed as burial places for both chiefs and commoners, as specialized structures, and possibly also as house foundations. The appearance of these structures marks the beginnings of the archaeological landscape of today. At the same time we approach an era touched upon by the oral traditions of the Samoans and Tongans themselves. For the latter part of this era, historical and ethnographic evidence can be of direct benefit to archaeological interpretation. It should not be forgotten, however, that the foundations of this recent era were laid during the preceding archaeological dark age.

The Recent Period

Initial field surveys in Samoa were only intended to discover something of the range and distribution of sites. As knowledge accumulated, the emphasis shifted to more intensive work in defined areas as a basis for settlement pattern studies. Present knowledge derives from both forms of investigation. In Tonga, on the other hand, only reconnaissance surveys have been undertaken, with a view to checking and refining McKern's work and extending coverage to areas such as Vava'u, which he dealt with only briefly. The most thorough study has been that on Niuatoputapu (Kirch 1977, 1978); for the rest of Tonga, detailed site surveys and settlement pattern studies are lacking, as are a range of excavations in recent sites to provide detailed evidence on house construction, material culture, and economy.

In Samoa field evidence varies from area to area according to the terrain and the underlying geology. House foundations in the older eastern parts of Upolu are of earth, or earth with stone facing and paving; the houses are outlined with waterworn curbstones and paved with small pebbles or river gravel. In the geologically younger areas, however, foundations are constructed of the rougher stones and boulders that are so abundant locally; curbstones and pebble paving are usually absent. Greater use is made of walls and stone paths in stony areas. House foundations are often located so as to take advantage of a natural eminence or small outcrop as the core of the structure.

Archaeologists have used arbitrary criteria to distinguish between platforms and large and small mounds. In fact, there is a continuous range from small, low structures to large, high structures, including also high structures of limited area and low but very extensive structures. The larger structures may have base dimensions of 30 m or more and be several meters high; the smallest platforms are barely large enough to provide the floor for a small pole and thatch house. Platform sides may be vertical or sloping, while a few mounds are stepped or tiered.

Most mounds and platforms are rectangular, but some are round. In eastern Upolu and Tutuila, if not elsewhere, there is a recognizable category of oval house platform, slightly raised, with a sloping stone pavement concentric with the house outline. An important category of mound is star shaped, with five to eleven protruding arms, and there is an apparently related category of irregularly shaped structures. The elaborate structures appear to derive from the last few centuries, and their disposition over the present landscape reflects the settlement pattern of the most recent prehistoric period. This is certainly true of those in-

vestigated closely by detailed mapping or excavation.

The bulk of the modern population lives in coastal settlements, and this has been the case since the 1830s. There is abundant archaeological evidence, however, that coastal concentration was a response to the beginning of European contact, and that until the early nineteenth century the population was much more evenly distributed over both coastal and inland areas in a form of dispersed settlement, probably with clusters around the residences of people of high status. Abandonment of the inland areas in the early nineteenth century was rapid, and in favorable localities complete plans of former settlements are preserved in plantations or in bush.

In the Falefa Valley former settlement remains in several areas in the rear of the valley were surveyed (Green and Davidson 1974). At Leuluasi on the fertile flats at the very back of the valley, settlement remains cover about 35 ha. Seventy separate sites were recorded, of which two-thirds were residential sites and the remainder walls, paths, and large earth-ovens. Houses were grouped together in twos or threes, partially or entirely surrounded by stone walls and sometimes connected by stone paths. Preservation of sites varied, but the dimensions of 14 houses were obtained from surface features. Two of these houses were excavated. More extensive excavations revealed that the site itself had been occupied sporadically for 2,000 years, with intensive use of the house foundation in its final form between the sixteenth and eighteenth centuries (Fig. 4.4); no evidence of post-European occupation was found.

On the slopes of the valley greater use was made of terracing for dwellings. At Folasa and other localities on the eastern slopes extensive terraces are found; house outlines are situated on terraces, often surrounded by walls and/or linked by paths. Excavation of a well-preserved house site at Folasa revealed successive construction of at least nine separate houses on the terrace during the last few centuries (Fig. 4.5); ini-

JANET M. DAVIDSON

4.4 *Excavation of a late prehistoric Samoan house site at Leuluasi, Upolu. (Photo courtesy of Anthropology Department, University of Auckland.)*

tial use of the locality, according to a radiocarbon date beneath the terrace, probably began 1,000 years earlier.

In contrast to some other areas, the inner Falefa Valley is not characterized by large or unusual mounds. A few small star-shaped and irregular structures are found high on the mountain walls of the valley, but not in the main residential areas. Some earthen mounds are found in the center of the valley. Excavation of one showed intensive use of its surface for houses, again during the last three centuries.

The majority of the remains in the Falefa Valley appear to relate to the everyday life of ordinary people. Traditions do not refer to residences of high-status people farther inland in the valley than the general vicinity of Folasa and the earthen mounds. This may explain the absence of star mounds and other large or unusual features, since these are likely to be associated with high-status people.

Extensive inland remains are not unique to the Falefa Valley. In this part of Upolu remains of similar extent have been noted, although studied in less detail, at neighboring Sauniatu, and running inland from Solosolo and Luatuanu'u. The extensive settlement of Vaigafa lies just on the other side of the central mountain ridge; remains extend between Vaigafa and the coast at Lotofaga and run inland from Lepa and Lalomanu. In the Lalomanu survey area, a particularly large number of star mounds was found, 13 in all. Many of these are in the remote bush and do not appear to be associated with other settlement remains, although extensive abandoned settlement areas are found closer to the coast. A similar concentration of star mounds is described at Pava'ia'i on Tutuila.

In marked contrast to the generally modest domestic character of much of the evidence of the Falefa Valley are the large earthen mounds of Vailele. Here, both on

4.5 *Superimposed Samoan houses on a single platform at Folasa in the Falefa Valley, Upolu. (Photo courtesy of Anthropology Department, University of Auckland.)*

the coast and some distance inland, are found large mounds including the four excavated coastal mounds previously described. The principal archaeological significance of these mounds has been the preservation of pottery-bearing deposits beneath two of them; their final use, however, and the purpose for which they virtually all were constructed, was as house mounds and it was in this capacity that they were used during the last few centuries. The mounds extend for some distance inland. Of particular interest is a cluster of very large ones, including the largest known earthen mound, Laupule, with base dimensions of 105 × 95 m and upper surface dimensions of 58 × 44 m. Traditional evidence associates Laupule and nearby large mounds with a despotic chief named Tupuivao, who probably lived in

the first half of the seventeenth century. There is a clear connection between high status and power, and the construction of large field monuments.

In addition to its concentration of large mounds, the Vailele area is unusual in its shortage of stone. There is an almost complete absence here of stone walls and stone paths; instead, paths are indicated by sunken ways, a feature also found at Luatuanu'u and Solosolo, in the same part of Upolu.

The most extensive and thorough survey of field remains to date has been the mapping of the Mount Olo tract at Mulifanua (Jennings 1976; Jennings et al. 1976). In this geologically more recent and very stony part of western Upolu, structural features are more difficult to identify than in the Falefa Valley. The fact that the area from coast

JANET M. DAVIDSON

to remote inland has been used for commercial plantations since the 1860s has led to unusual preservation and mapping conditions. At Mulifanua the continuous distribution of structures from the coast for 4 or 5 km inland testifies to the impossibility of distinguishing between "coastal" and "inland" settlements except in the most arbitrary fashion. A preliminary survey in 1966 of a narrow strip of land running inland for about 4 km from the coast recorded 227 mounds or platforms, as well as numerous stone paths and walls. Several star mounds were present among mounds of more orthodox shape. Holmer's survey of a tract inland of the original strip (Jennings et al. 1976) has, over two seasons, covered in detail several square kilometers and mapped more than 500 features. The Mount Olo settlements are thought to have been abandoned in the eighteenth century; as at Leuluasi, the great bulk of the remains probably reflect the final phase of occupation in the area.

Statistical analysis of mound size at Mount Olo has shown that when mounds from a single locality are considered, they can be segregated into three size categories according to volume. The smallest group can be correlated with ordinary house sites, and the two larger with chiefs' houses and community houses, and possibly communal god-houses. The relation of height to area is significant. Size categories can be defined within a given locality, but what ranks as a large mound in one locality may be equivalent to a medium-sized mound in another. These considerations appear to be related to status; this is confirmed at Mount Olo by the association of more and larger walls and walkways with larger mounds. Chronological factors may also be involved. Three clusters were initially identified at Mount Olo. Further work there has resulted in the definition of what are called Household Units (HHUs)—usually one large or two small platforms more than 75 percent enclosed by walls and paths, with a possible garden area within the enclosure. These units appear to correspond to similar units

recognized but not explicitly defined at Leuluasi. If so, a basic settlement unit can be identified in areas that use different construction and superficially appear rather unlike as a result of the underlying geological variations.

At Mount Olo star mounds are included in settlement areas. In view of the size range of the mounds, it is reasonable to assume that these were probably higher-status settlements than those of the inner Falefa Valley. Mapping and analysis similar to that at Mount Olo is now being extended to abandoned settlements inland of Sapapali'i and Palauli on Savai'i, where large and imposing remains, including the exceptionally large stone mound, Pulemelei (Fig. 4.6), were reported during earlier surveys (Green and Davidson 1969).

Drawing together the evidence of this kind in Samoa reveals that the most common archaeological feature is the mound or platform constructed as a foundation for a house. The majority are residences of ordinary people; large, high examples are possibly chiefs' houses or important god-houses, while large, low examples are more likely to be community houses. These interpretations are derived from the ethnographic literature (Davidson 1969b). Dividing walls and raised and sunken interconnecting paths advance interpretation and identification of HHUs. Scattered among the settlements are large earth-ovens and star mounds, to both of which are ascribed special functions related to high status at Mount Olo. However, these two features are not always found in association with settlements. Ethnographic evidence interprets the large ovens as having been used for cooking the root of the ti plant (*Cordyline fruticosa*), for which an initial high temperature and a long cooking period was required.

The interpretation of star mounds has caused considerable difficulty. Modern informants tend to view them as pigeon-snaring mounds (pigeon snaring used to be a chiefly sport in Samoa). The sole ethnographic reference discovered suggests a pri-

4.6   *The large stone mound of Pulemelei on the island of Savai'i in Samoa. (Photo courtesy of Anthropology Department, University of Auckland.)*

marily religious function that involved divination by pigeon snaring but lacked the sporting and competitive elements. Two star mounds have now been excavated, an earthen example at Luatuanu'u and a stone example at Mount Olo. In both cases the sites are relatively late; otherwise the results were negative, in that no evidence of use for habitation or burial was found. The interpretation as pigeon-snaring mounds, with or without the religious element, therefore gains some support. The remote location of some examples, notably those at Lalomanu and on Tutuila, suggests competitive pigeon snaring, since the mounds are situated in places frequently described by informants as suitable for this purpose. The Mount Olo examples, however, appear to be integral parts of substantial settlements, which probably fits the religious interpretation better.

Substantial data on house construction were obtained from excavations at Leuluasi and other Falefa Valley settlements. One of the most important of the excavations was Sasoa'a, site of a historic nineteenth-century settlement as well as of the ceramic deposits previously discussed. Sasoa'a differs significantly from Leuluasi in that it is very tightly clustered—fourteen houses occupy an area that at Leuluasi might include three. At Sasoa'a, moreover, features to define household units are lacking. The details of house size and construction, however, vary not at all—evidence of a remarkable continuity from late prehistoric to early historic times. At both Leuluasi and Sasoa'a two or more central posts supported a ridge pole from which the roof was suspended to rest on side posts set around the oval perimeter of the house. There is as yet no archaeological evidence

JANET M. DAVIDSON

of the *fale afolau*, a more complicated construction in which the ridge pole was supported by a king pin, tie beam, and parallel rows of internal side posts. In the nineteenth century this type of house was considered a recent Tongan introduction to Samoa. Its absence from the archaeological record appears to support this.

Fourteen houses at Leuluasi had floor areas ranging between 14 m² and 59 m², with a mean of 30 m². At Sasoa'a the range was from 14 m² to 53 m², with one exceptionally large house of 95 m² and a mean of 37 m² (19 houses in all). At Folasa, 10 houses ranged from 14 m² to 66 m², mean 32.9 m². These figures are probably a good indication of the size range of Samoan dwellings. A floor area of 90 m² or more is thought to distinguish a community house.

Burial customs, like house construction, show marked continuity from late prehistoric to early historic times. Burials were generally in the extended position, in shallow pits beneath or near the house floor. In the acid soils bones deteriorate rapidly, and burials are often represented only by a stain in the soil and a few teeth. No grave goods have been found, although traces of red ocher are often present. Interments of this kind have been found at Folasa, Leuluasi, Sasoa'a, and Mount Olo. The oldest example is of eleventh- to thirteenth-century date at Leuluasi. A burial in a house platform at Leone, Tutuila, is dated to A.D. 1410 ± 80. Historical evidence shows that missionaries put a stop to burials of this sort in the mid-nineteenth century. Yet similar burials took place in stone platforms, for one was discovered at Tausagi, Mount Olo. The burials at Faleasi'u, much older than any of those discussed here, suggest the considerable antiquity of the practice.

The most prominent other field monuments are fortifications. In Samoa these most often take the form of transverse trenches, some of considerable size, across narrow ridges in the interior (although other forms, such as terraced peaks, are also known). Apart from the large example

inland from Luatuanu'u, which may first have been constructed 1,500 years ago, none have been excavated. Some were certainly last used in the wars of the nineteenth century. Others are clearly prehistoric, and by their very number and diversity testify to a long period of warfare and conflict in prehistoric times.

The above emphasis on inland habitation and the remains of abandoned settlements may give the reader the impression that coastal settlement and marine resources were unimportant in recent times. This would be quite incorrect. In many parts of Samoa recent evidence of coastal settlement is obscured by modern villages, but many of those villages rest on midden deposits 1 to 2 m deep. Only one such site has been excavated, at Lotofaga. Here a low-lying sandy flat that is now part of the modern village first became habitable as a result of shoreline changes between 800 and 1,400 years ago. An oven containing human bone at the base of the midden gave a date of A.D. 1215 ± 85, this being the first clear evidence of cannibalism in Samoa. Thereafter stratified midden deposits containing only sparse artifactual and food remains gradually accumulated. At various points in the deposits were found postholes, ovens, hearths, a stone alignment, the corner of a house platform, and a burial—all evidence of early coastal habitation. The sparse midden remains reflect relatively slight dependence on the lagoon, restricted here in comparison with other parts of Upolu. Artifacts include a broken unfinished one-piece *Turbo* shell hook and a broken lure shank, both of which date to late prehistoric times.

Before archaeological work began in Samoa, the present pattern of almost entirely coastal settlement in planned nucleated villages was assumed to be of considerable antiquity. However, archaeological research combined with careful use of historical records has shown that there was a rapid and far-reaching change in the distribution of settlement in the late eighteenth and early nineteenth centuries, and that the late prehistoric pattern involved dispersed settlement fairly equally distributed over coastal and inland locations—a pattern similar to that described historically for Tonga. The numerous large mounds of both orthodox and star shape suggest the development of considerable social stratification and the ability of certain individuals such as Tupuivao to construct monumental house platforms for themselves. They also suggest that the modern Samoan propensity for building large churches has a firm precedent in the prehistoric past, since some large mounds were almost certainly the foundations of god-houses. Prehistoric Samoan religion appears to have involved the worship of supralocal deities who required large edifices built by communal labor, as well as the recognition of less important personal and family deities whose residences may be archaeologically insignificant.

Despite the change in settlement pattern in the early historic period, there does not appear to have been a comparable change in social organization. The flexible Samoan system could function at a local level regardless of whether settlement was nucleated, dispersed, or a combination of both. The essentials of a community were the widespread Polynesian features of meeting ground (*malae*), chief's house, community house, and god-house; the spatial arrangements of these and of ordinary dwellings could and did vary considerably.

Population size and growth in Samoa pose important problems. It is generally conceded that Samoa theoretically could support a much higher population than it had in the nineteenth century, and that unrestrained increase at even the most modest rate from first settlement would have produced a much higher population than existed at European contact. Some depopulation at the onset of European contact is widely accepted, but the factors affecting or controlling population growth in prehistoric times are not fully understood.

A small-scale archaeological approach to the problem has been to estimate the population of individual settlements. Estimates

based on floor space requirements recorded ethnographically in Samoan villages suggest between 45 and 55 people for Sasoa'a, 35 to 40 for Leuluasi, and 450 for the three Mount Olo clusters.

Little comparable information exists for Tonga, where archaeological evidence about houses and settlement patterns is lacking.

Mounds in Tonga are round or rectangular with considerable size range. Some are unfaced earthen mounds, others are faced with cut slabs of coral limestone (Fig. 4.7) and others are faced with coral boulders. Most rectangular faced mounds are believed to be the burial places of important people—members of the supreme and sacred Tui Tonga line, whose graves are called *langi*, or of other high-ranking people, whose graves are called *faitoka*. Such structures, found throughout Tonga, are probably most numerous in Tongatapu, where most of the Tui Tonga family resided. Some faced mounds are believed to be *esi*, or chiefly resting places—a uniquely Tongan invention. Some faced burial mounds are still in use; esi have been constructed, particularly for members of the royal family, in the present century.

McKern described a number of round mounds that he was told were pigeon mounds. Many have one or more external ramps (Fig. 4.8) and a central pit. Some round mounds are now regarded as house sites or esi. This may, however, be a rationalization. Evidence on pigeon snaring in Tonga is slight, and it is not clear whether the competitive or religious element dominated.

By far the most numerous mounds, at least in Tongatapu, are unfaced earthen mounds, usually circular. On many, but by no means all, traces of white coral sand can be seen. These are almost certainly the burial mounds of commoners. Excavation of two such mounds at 'Atele (Figs. 4.9 and 4.10) revealed their construction (Davidson 1969a). At both sites the locality had previously been used for habitation or gardening, and the first burials were made at the

JANET M. DAVIDSON

4.7 *Partially cut slabs for facing large monuments at Vava'u, Tonga. (Photo by author.)*

4.8 *Sia Longo, a large earthen mound with access ramps at Vava'u, Tonga. (Photo by author.)*

SAMOA AND TONGA

4.9 *A small burial mound, estimated to contain 100 individuals, under excavation at 'Atele, Tongatapu. (Photo by author.)*

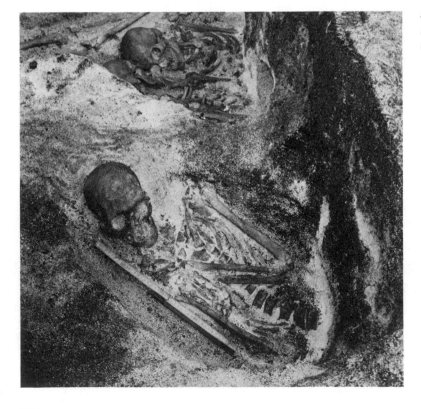

4.10 *Partially excavated burials at 'Atele, Tongatapu. (Photo by author.)*

JANET M. DAVIDSON

ground-surface level. A low mound was then constructed of earth from a surrounding ditch, and numerous burials were made at the new surface. In one case (at To-At-2) the mound was enlarged and heightened by the addition of another layer taken from a second surrounding ditch. More burials were made on the new surface. Graves were relatively shallow pits partially or wholly filled with white coral sand, which effectively preserved the bone. Orientations and positions of the bodies varied, although most burials were in extended position. No grave goods other than fragments of dark-colored tapa were recovered. Radiocarbon dates from these two sites are imprecise but suggest a late prehistoric age.

Excavations in a coral-pebble paved mound and in a large rectangular faced mound on Niuatoputapu revealed burials in both, apparently with white-sand grave fill. Test excavation of a mound of pigeon-snaring type revealed no midden, habitation evidence, or burials; a specialized function is therefore likely, as with the star mounds of Samoa.

Activity on the surfaces of the Mangaia mound, To-1, and To-5 between the fifteenth and seventeenth centuries is suggested by radiocarbon dates. A burial-mound phase that has sealed over the ceramic deposits at To-2, burial mounds tested by McKern, and possibly other sites tested by McKern and Golson may belong to the recent period. Almost no artifacts were associated with these deposits.

Isolated sherds reminiscent of later Fijian wares have occasionally been found throughout Tonga. Temper analysis of one such sherd from Tungua on Ha'apai has shown that it is almost certainly an import from the Rewa Delta area of Fiji (Dickinson and Shutler 1974). This is important support for historical accounts suggesting that Tongans occasionally obtained pots from Fiji.

Little can be said about the economy. The middens at the 'Atele burial mounds appeared similar to those of much earlier sites, although potsherds were not present. In Niuatoputapu, exploitation and dumping of shells certainly continued after the cessation of pottery manufacture. Tongan sites contain more and larger food storage pits than Samoan sites; agricultural practice may have varied, perhaps in response to the greater likelihood of drought and seasonal shortage in Tonga.

Initial historical descriptions of Tonga depict an idyllic, well-cultivated, and well-ordered landscape with dispersed hamlets linked by roads, and a few major clusters of structures. Most important of these was the ceremonial center at Mu'a on Tongatapu (Fig. 4.11), traditionally the residence and burial place of the Tui Tonga line since about the twelfth century. The amazing concentration of large structures here, enclosed by a substantial and apparently ancient fortification, has drawn the attention of every archaeologist to visit Tonga. Equally fascinating is the monumental trilithon, Ha'amonga-a-Maui (Fig. 4.12), at Hahake, an area sometimes regarded as the predecessor of Mu'a. Other islands also had their ceremonial center. The one at Feletoa in Vava'u was described in some detail in the nineteenth century when a large fortification was built there.

A change in settlement pattern took place in Tonga after Cook's visits. The wars of the late eighteenth and early nineteenth centuries resulted in the concentration of population in large fortifications for considerable lengths of time, and from these fortifications the modern villages of Tonga are believed to have developed. It is not clear whether this clustering into forts was an entirely new development, or whether there had been periods in prehistory also when Tongans gathered together for defense.

Tongan forts are of two main types —large circular or rectangular enclosures comparable in scale to British Iron Age forts and including multivallate examples (with several concentric ditches), and linear defenses that cut off whole segments of

4.11 *Paepae o Telea, one of the royal tombs at Mu'a, Tongatapu, showing facing of massive cut limestone slabs. (Photo courtesy of Anthropology Department, University of Auckland.)*

4.12 *The Ha'amonga-a-Maui, a massive trilithon at Hahake in Tonga—unique in Polynesia. (Photo by author.)*

islands. The most notable example of the latter is Kele-a-Pelehake in western Tongatapu; two examples are also known in Vava'u. Although most of the enclosed forts are known to have been used in historic times, the linear earthworks of Vava'u are said to be older.

Throughout much of Tongan prehistory, occupation sites have tended to cluster around the edge of the lagoon. In Tongatapu and Vava'u at least, burial mounds are often located away from residential areas in gardens or on the *liku* coast. A similar separation of habitation sites and burial mounds is evident on Niuatoputapu. Such separation, however, is by no means mutually exclusive.

It has been suggested that mounds of various kinds spread relatively recently from Tongatapu to the north of the Tonga group. Burial mounds, which are most distinctively Tongan, do appear to be oldest and most numerous in Tongatapu. Their appearance farther north, therefore, may relate to classic Tongan expansion. Other mounds—including the problematical pigeon mounds, which appear to be allied to Samoan forms—could on present evidence have spread through the Tonga group in either direction at any time in the last millennium.

Conclusion

Archaeological research in the last 20 years has given Tonga and Samoa the outlines of a prehistory very different from that assigned to them before stratigraphic excavation began. Only the bare outlines are known, however, and it is reasonable to expect many changes in detail and possibly more fundamental changes in outline to result from future research.

The orthodox view now depicts Lapita colonists moving into the region and spreading rapidly through it in the latter part of the second millennium B.C. There is no evidence of a long period of isolation and separate development on one island.

Instead, related populations on a number of islands appear to have maintained contact with one another and shared similar changes in material culture throughout the ceramic period. The point at which a recognizably Polynesian material culture had evolved cannot be precisely determined on present evidence. By 2,000 years ago, in Samoa at least, the foundations of the later settlement pattern and of the economy had been well laid. However, continuity between this and later periods is largely assumed, simply because there is no good evidence for intrusion. Still, it is unwise to be too complacent. Present evidence in West Polynesia does not yet permit the identification of a time or a place, even in the most general terms, for the departure of colonists for East Polynesia. Indeed there is still a real gap between the earliest evidence from East Polynesia and that of West Polynesia. Dendrogram models of linguistic relationships, faith in west-to-east migrations, and a handful of artifacts rather than firm archaeological evidence cement the relationship between East and West Polynesia in the first millennium A.D. On existing *archaeological* evidence it could even be suggested that Hawaii was settled directly from West Polynesia.

For the past millennium, archaeologists can devote themselves to the development of West Polynesian culture as it was recorded ethnographically, and to the fascinating problems of similarity and difference between Samoa and Tonga. The spread of mounds and forts, the development of fundamental differences in burial practices, and the probable similarities in settlement patterns despite differing emphases in social organization are all important issues. The supplementary data of oral tradition and historical records, combined with the splendid field monuments of the period, make the recent era of West Polynesian prehistory in its own way as rewarding as the more remote—and to many people more romantic—era of Lapita colonization and Polynesian beginnings.

References

Biggs, B. G. 1972. Implications of linguistic subgrouping with special reference to Polynesia. In *Studies in Oceanic cultural history*, ed. R. C. Green and Marion Kelly, vol. 3. *Pacific Anthropological Records* 13:143–152.

Buck, P. H. (Te Rangi Hiroa). 1930. *Samoan material culture*. Bishop Museum Bulletin no. 75, Honolulu.

Burrows, E. G. 1938. *Western Polynesia: a study of cultural differentiation*. Etnologisker Studier no. 7, Gothenburg.

Davidson, J. M. 1969a. Archaeological excavations in two burial mounds at 'Atele, Tongatapu. *Records of the Auckland Institute and Museum* 6:251–286.

———. 1969b. Settlement patterns in Samoa before 1840. *Journal of the Polynesian Society* 78:44–82.

———. 1971. Preliminary report on an archaeological survey of the Vava'u group, Tonga. *Royal Society of New Zealand Bulletin* 8:29–40.

Dickinson, W. R., and Richard Shutler, Jr. 1974. Probable Fijian origin of quartzose temper sands in prehistoric pottery from Tonga and the Marquesas. *Science* 185:454–457.

Emory, K. P., and Y. H. Sinoto. 1965. Preliminary report on the archaeological investigations in Polynesia: fieldwork in the Society and Tuamotu islands, French Polynesia, and American Samoa in 1962, 1963, 1964. Manuscript.

Freeman, J. D. 1943. The Seuao Cave. *Journal of the Polynesian Society* 52:101–109.

———. 1944a. Falemauga caves. *Journal of the Polynesian Society* 53:86–106.

———. 1944b. 'O le fale o le fe'e. *Journal of the Polynesian Society* 53:121–144.

———. 1944c. The Vailele earthmounds. *Journal of the Polynesian Society* 53:145–162.

Frost, J. O. 1976. Summary report of archaeological investigations on Tutuila Island, American Samoa. *New Zealand Archaeological Association Newsletter* 19:30–37.

Golson, Jack. n.d. Report to TRIPP on archaeological fieldwork in Samoa and Tonga. Mimeographed, Auckland.

———. 1962. Report on New Zealand, Western Polynesia, New Caledonia, and Fiji. *Asian Perspectives* 5:166–180.

Green, R. C. 1968. West Polynesian prehistory. In *Prehistoric culture in Oceania*, ed. Ichito Yawata and Y. H. Sinoto, pp. 99–109. Honolulu: Bishop Museum Press.

——— and J. M. Davidson, eds. 1969. *Archaeology in Western Samoa*, vol. 1. *Auckland Institute and Museum Bulletin* 6.

——— and J. M. Davidson, eds. 1974. *Archaeology in Western Samoa*, vol. 2. *Auckland Institute and Museum Bulletin* 7.

Groube, L. M. 1971. Tonga, Lapita pottery, and Polynesian origins. *Journal of the Polynesian Society* 80:278–316.

Jennings, J. D. 1976. University of Utah Samoan archeological program, 1976. Preliminary report.

———, R. N. Holmer, J. C. Janetski, and H. L. Smith. 1976. Excavations on Upolu, Western Samoa. *Pacific Anthropological Records* 25:1–113.

Kikuchi, W. K. 1963. Archaeological surface ruins in American Samoa. Master's thesis, University of Hawaii.

Kirch, P. V. 1976. Ethnoarchaeological investigations in Futuna and Uvea (Western Polynesia): a preliminary report. *Journal of the Polynesian Society* 85:27–69.

———. 1977. Ethnoarchaeological investigations in Nuiatoputapu, Tonga (Western Polynesia): a preliminary report. Manuscript, Bishop Museum, Honolulu.

———. 1978. The Lapitoid period in West Polynesia: excavations and survey in Niuatoputapu, Tonga. *Journal of Field Archaeology* 5:1–13.

McKern, W. C. 1929. *Archaeology of Tonga*. Bishop Museum Bulletin no. 60, Honolulu.

Mead, S. M., Lawrence Birks, Helen Birks, and Elizabeth Shaw. 1975. *The Lapita pottery style of Fiji and its associations*. Polynesian Society Memoir no. 38, Wellington.

Poulsen, Jens. 1966. Preliminary report on pottery finds in Tonga. *Asian Perspectives* 8:184–195.

———. 1967. A contribution to the prehistory of the Tongan Islands. Ph.D. dissertation, Australian National University.

———. 1968. Archaeological excavations on Tongatapu. In *Prehistoric culture in Oceania*, ed. Ichito Yawata and Y. H. Sinoto, pp. 85–92. Honolulu: Bishop Museum Press.

———. 1972. On the processing of pottery data. *Jysk Arkaeologisk Selskab Håndbøger* no. 2, Copenhagen.

———. 1974. Archaeology and ethnic problems. *Mankind* 9:260–267.

———. 1976. The chronology of early Tongan prehistory and the Lapita ware. In *La Préhistoire océanienne*, pp. 223–250. Paris: Centre Nationale de la Pecherche Scientifique.

Rogers, Garth. 1974. Archaeological discoveries on Niuatoputapu Island, Tonga. *Journal of the Polynesian Society* 83:308–348.

Suggs, R. C. 1961. Polynesia. *Asian Perspectives* 4:101–109.

Thomson, Andrew. 1927. Earthmounds in Samoa. *Journal of the Polynesian Society* 36: 118–121.

The Marquesas

CHAPTER 5

YOSIHIKO H. SINOTO

In the original version of this chapter (Sinoto 1970), I presented a hypothesis that proposed the Marquesas Islands as a dispersal center for the rest of East Polynesia. This proposal was based on the material culture sequence of the Hane site on Uahuka Island. Subsequently five monographs and articles relating to Marquesan prehistory have been published by other researchers (Kellum-Ottino 1971; Bellwood 1972; Skjölsvold 1972; Kirch 1973; and Pietrusewsky 1976), and I have reported on my own research on Mangareva, Henderson, and Pitcairn islands (Sinoto 1973, 1976). The recent important discovery of the Vaitootia site, Huahine, Society Islands (Sinoto 1974, 1977; Sinoto and McCoy 1975) further supported the hypothesis. The present chapter incorporates revisions and corrections derived from this more recent research, and includes explanatory descriptions of artifacts for readers who may not be familiar with Polynesian cultural material.

The Marquesas Archipelago in French Polynesia comprises ten islands and is located approximately 800 km northeast of Tahiti, between 8 and 10 degrees south latitude and 138 and 140 degrees west longitude (Fig. 5.1). The islands range in size from 0.8 to 200 km² and are divided into a northern and a southern group. The northern group includes the inhabited islands of Nukuhiva, Uahuka, and Uapou, and the southern group includes Hivaoa, Tahuata, and Fatuhiva. The islands are the peaks

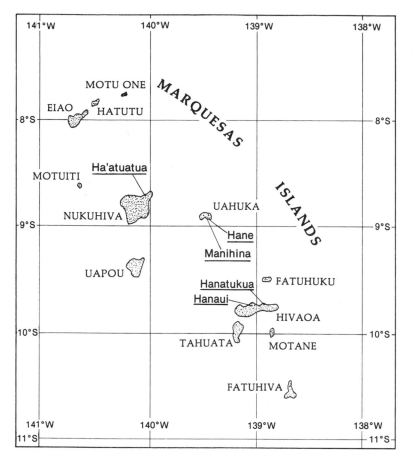

of a submarine volcano elevated about 1,200 m above sea level. There are no surrounding reefs. Heavy erosion has caused extremely rugged mountains and high cliffs and created some valleys that can be reached only from the sea. The lack of low coastal flatlands confined habitation and agriculture to valley floors, although the larger islands had some usable plateaus, especially in historic times. The archipelago is close to the equator and has persistent trade winds. The mean temperature at sea level is 22°C, with an annual range of only about 4 degrees. The humidity rarely goes below 80 percent. Rainfall ranges from 75 to 250 cm annually; intensive drought, however, sometimes continues for several months, severely affecting the important crop trees of coconuts and breadfruit (Freeman 1951).

The Spanish navigator Alvaro Mendana is credited with being the European discoverer of the southern group of the archipelago, in July 1595. He named the group Las Marquesas de Mendoca after the lady of the Viceroy of Peru. Today the shortened name, Marquesas, applies to the entire archipelago. Though not pleasant, the two-week encounter of the Spanish with the inhabitants of Tahuata and Fatuhiva islands resulted in the first ethnographic description of the Polynesian people (Buck 1953). It was nearly 200 years before the Marquesans saw Europeans again. Cook rediscovered the southern group in 1774, and an American named Joseph Ingraham found the northern group in 1791. Thus the impact of Western culture in the Marquesas dates from the nineteenth century. France annexed the islands in 1842. The pre-European population was estimated as 80,000, with only slight differences in physical and cultural aspects between the island groups. The introduced diseases, constant tribal warfare, and collapse of the old culture reduced the Marquesan population drastically —to a little over 2,000 by 1926. The 1970 census showed a slightly enlarged population of 5,400.

Cultural Sequence

The first framework of a Marquesan cultural history was established by Suggs in 1961. After the excavation of the Hane Dune site on Uahuka Island and the Ha'atuatua site on Nukuhiva, I had problems with some of Suggs's interpretations. The Nukuhiva and Uahuka materials are the principal sources I used in establishing a preliminary cultural sequence (Sinoto 1966), somewhat different from that of Suggs, for the northern Marquesas. In addition, my archaeological investigations on the northern coast of Hivaoa in the southern Marquesas in 1967–68 yielded materials that were comparable to those of the northern islands of Nukuhiva and Uahuka. These, together with Skjölsvold's (1972) results, Figueroa and Sanchez's (1965) materials and radiocarbon dates, and Smith's (1964) radiocarbon dates, have made it possible to establish a preliminary outline of the prehistoric cultural sequence for the southern Marquesas Islands. Despite the earlier postulations of occupational sequence for the Marquesas Islands (Handy 1925), it appears at the moment that the early—if not the first—settlers arrived in the northern group and then moved into the southern group. Both island groups have basically identical material cultures.

Phase I (Initial Settlement), A.D. 300–600

Sites representing phase I are located at Hane, Uahuka, and probably at Ha'atuatua, Nukuhiva, where pinpointing a precise position is difficult.

From the evidence we have at present, the northern Marquesas Islands were occupied initially by people who lived in the coastal areas. The earliest evidence of a habitation area in Hane showed rectangular house foundations with postholes. Some of the postholes had stone braces on the walls of the holes. No evidence has been found of oval thatched houses that had stone braces without holes (Suggs 1961). Later in this same location rectangular, single-stone-thick floor pavements were built. There is substantial evidence that these house floors were rebuilt several times.

A maritime-oriented economy was evidenced by the presence of a large quantity of fishing gear, especially for hook-and-line fishing. One-piece hooks predominated, but trolling hooks, or so-called bonito lures and points, were quite common in this early stage. One-piece hooks were made mainly of pearl shell, but some were made of porpoise bone, a distinguishing feature of this phase (Fig. 5.2). The usual form was the rotating type; either the shank or the point was incurved. Two other forms were significant to this phase. One was a jabbing type of hook with a straight shank and point. The cross sections of the shank and point of this hook were round, that of the shank being much thicker than the point. The line-lashing device was a single, horizontal groove just below the flat, blunt head (Fig. 5.2g).

Files used in hook manufacturing were made from pieces of *Porites* coral and from spines of the slate-pencil sea urchin, but the latter decreased in number in the later phases. No octopus-lure sinkers of the coffee-bean type (Fig. 5.3d) typical of the later phases were found, but a sinker form ancestral to both the conical West Polynesian type (Fig. 5.3e) and the coffee-bean type was used in this period. This ancestral sinker had a conical form with one longitudinally flat side (Fig. 5.3c).

Adzes were the most common stone artifacts in this phase. The flat quadrangular (Fig. 5.4a), the flat reversed-trapezoidal untanged (Fig. 5.4b), and the plano-convex types (Fig. 5.4c) were most frequently

YOSIHIKO H. SINOTO

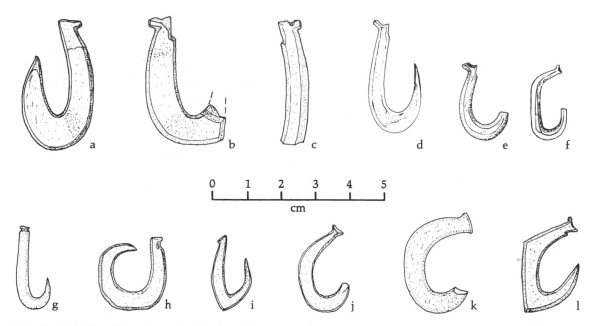

5.2   *Pearl-shell and bone one-piece hooks of phases I and II in the Marquesas Islands. Hooks a, b, d, e, and f are from Hivaoa Island; c is from Nukuhiva Island; the rest are from Uahuka Island. The hook in k is made of porpoise bone. (After Sinoto 1970.)*

found. Adz forms with the narrow or ridge-front face of the tall trapezoidal and triangular types (Suggs's Koma type) were present in an incipient form, as well as definitely tanged adzes, although these were very rare. Tangs were formed only by the pecking technique (Fig. 5.4*d*, *e*).

Chisels were made only of *Cassis* shell. The lip of the shell, the thickest part, was broken off. The broken edge was ground so that one end was formed into a cutting edge; the other end sometimes retained a curvature somewhat similar to that of an umbrella handle (Fig. 5.5*a*, *b*). Although some of the chisels did not retain this curvature, all had only one cutting edge (Fig. 5.5*c*).

Pounders for taro or breadfruit did not appear in this phase. Two types of graters (probably for coconuts), one hand held and the other made for attachment to a stand, were quite common in this phase (Fig. 5.3*f*), but there were no vegetable-peeling artifacts of any kind.

Pendants made from the teeth of small species of whales and porpoises (Fig.

5.3*g*, *h*) and a thin, round disk of *Conus* shell with a hole in the center (see Fig. 5.11*a*) were the characteristic ornaments of this phase, although a single pendant made from the perforated tooth of a dog was located. Pearl-shell pendants of a type particular to Hane (Fig. 5.3*i*) were also found. The shaped whale-tooth pendants (see Fig. 5.11*i*–*l*) similar to those from the Maupiti burial site, Society Islands (Emory and Sinoto 1964), and from the Wairau Bar sites, New Zealand (Duff 1956), were significant ornaments, but these were probably made near the end of phase I. No imitation whale-tooth pendants were found. Cloak pins (Fig. 5.3*k*) were made in this phase, however (Sinoto 1968b).

Tattooing needles made of bird bone, pearl shell, and shark tooth (Fig. 5.3*l*–*n*) were also uncovered from this phase. Although only a small quantity of pottery was found, there is evidence from the materials that it was used and possibly was of local manufacture (Dickinson 1967).

Dogs were present; however, the fact that only dog teeth and no bones were found in

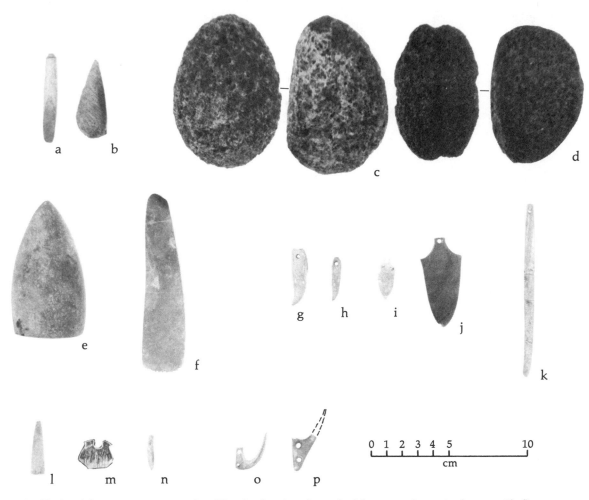

5.3 *Tools, sinkers, ornaments, and trolling-hook points from the Marquesas (except when specified): a, sea-urchin-spine file; b, Porites-coral file; c, conical-shaped octopus sinker; d, coffee-bean-type octopus sinker; e, Samoan octopus sinker; f, pearl-shell grater; g, whale-tooth pendant; h, porpoise-tooth pendant; i, pearl-shell ornament; j, pearl-shell ornament from Vaitootia site, Society Islands; k, bone cloak pin; l, bone tattooing comb; m, pearl-shell tattooing comb; n, shark-tooth tattooing comb; o, West Polynesian-type trolling-hook point; p, East Polynesian-type trolling hook point. (From the Bishop Museum collection.)*

the midden materials suggests that they were scarce. No clearly identifiable pig bones were found. This is interpreted to mean that if there were pigs, they were extremely few in number. No chicken skeletal materials have been identified, leaving their presence uncertain. Seabird bones, shearwater, petrel, and booby (Kirch 1973) were plentiful, especially at the beginning of phase I. There is some evidence that rats existed.

Based on the artifacts, it is difficult to determine whether or not breadfruit and taro were cultivated at this time. If the presence of cone-shaped stone pounders and vegetable peelers would imply the existence of these food plants, the evidence is negative. However, the presence of graters suggests that there was coconut. Midden-material analysis shows that fish, turtle, and seabird were the main sources of protein. Shellfish remains were unexpectedly negligible in

114

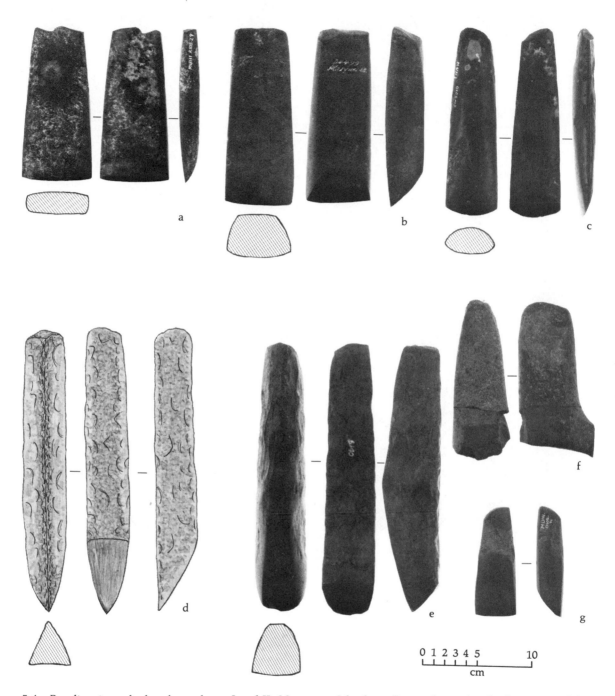

5.4 *Basalt untanged adzes from phases I and II, Marquesas Islands; a, flat quadrangular; b, flat trapezoidal; c, plano-convex; d, triangular beaked; e, high trapezoidal; f and g, pecked tanged. The inserts are cross sections taken at the midpoints and show characteristics of the particular adz type. (From the Bishop Museum collection.)*

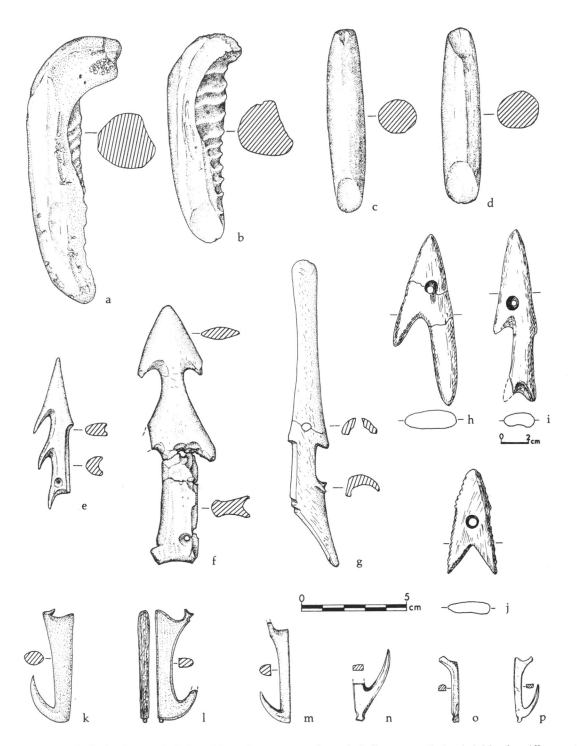

5.5 Cassis-*shell chisels, pearl-shell and bone harpoons, and pearl-shell compound-shank fishhooks. All except* h–j *are from the Marquesas Islands:* a–c, Cassis-*shell chisels, phase I, and* d, *phase II;* e, *pearl-shell, and* f, *bone harpoon heads, variety 2, both from phase I;* g, *bone harpoon heads, variety 1, phase IV;* h–j, *bone harpoon heads from New Zealand, varieties 3–5 (after Skinner 1937);* k–m, *pearl-shell compound-shank fishhooks, phases I and II, and* n–p, *phases III and IV. (After Sinoto 1970.)*

YOSIHIKO H. SINOTO

quantity. Of course, the bones of turtles and birds weigh more and are more bulky than most shellfish remains, so probably it takes several years of shellfish midden deposits to weigh as much as the remains of one turtle.

Phase II (Developmental Stage), A.D. 600–1300

Sites representing this phase were located at Hane and Manihina (Sinoto and Kellum 1965) on Uahuka Island and at Ha'atuatua on Nukuhiva Island in the northern group, and at Hanatukua and Hanaui on Hivaoa Island in the southern group. By this phase people already had started to spread out, not only along the coastal areas, but also into the valleys and plateaus.

While the material culture of this phase did not vary greatly from that of the earlier phase, there were some changes. Fishhooks became larger, and there was an increase in the relative number of the jabbing type (see Fig. 5.2a–d). In the northern group in phase II only pearl shell was used to make fishhooks. In the southern group bone was used also, but in small quantity. The bone hooks were very seldom made with shank barbs (Fig. 5.10d). Sea-urchin files were scarce.

In phase II the number of trolling hooks decreased, as did the size of the shanks. The proximal end of the base on trolling-hook points extended upward, and there were two holes for lashing the point to the shank (Fig. 5.3o). In the later portion of phase II, the proximal extension of the base became reduced in size and some points evidenced an extension of the distal end (Fig. 5.3p).

At this time appears, in incipient form, the typical Marquesan compound-shank hook, which later developed into a double-shank fishhook. There are two parent forms: on one the single shank has a rounded stem (Fig. 5.5k–m), which does not provide for the fastening of a second shank stem; on the other the back of the shank is flat (Fig. 5.5m–p). These unique

Marquesan compound-shank hooks of early type have been uncovered recently at the Vaitootia site, Huahine (Sinoto 1976). The coffee-bean type of octopus-lure sinker appears in this phase (Fig. 5.3d).

Adz types did not change much between phases I and II. The narrow and high trapezoidal, incipient Koma type and incipiently tanged adzes increased in numbers. Cassis-shell chisels were also present, but they were in a straight, cylindrical form; some had cutting edges at both ends (Fig. 5.5d).

Although conical stone pounders (Fig. 5.6d) still were not in evidence in phase II, a type of pounder was found that was gripped with both hands. It appears to be an incipient form of the Hawaiian stirrup pounder (Buck 1957) (Fig. 5.6a, b).

Peelers made of Purpura persica shells appeared in this phase in both the northern and southern island groups (Fig. 5.6e). Vegetable scrapers made from Tonna shells have been reported by Suggs (1961) and by me (1966); however, mine were incorrectly identified. The correct identification of the shell is Purpura persica (Linnaeus). If Suggs's illustrated scraper (see his fig. 29g) is representative of the eight vegetable scrapers from Ha'atuatua, it appears that his scrapers also were made from P. persica rather than Tonna.

Pottery apparently was still used in phase II, but so far the slim evidence shows up only in the northern group (Suggs 1961).

Shaped whale-tooth pendants still survive, but so far have not been found from the southern group. Shell imitations of whale-tooth pendants were also being made, as were pearl-shell disks with one center hole and serrations around the outer edge (Fig. 5.11b–d). In addition a carved stone image of simple design, unlike the typical late Marquesan design of Fig. 5.7b, was found.

Rectangular house foundations, paved with a single course of stones, were still being used.

Pigs were definitely in the Marquesas in this phase, although still scarce. A pig burial and a few pig bones were found in the

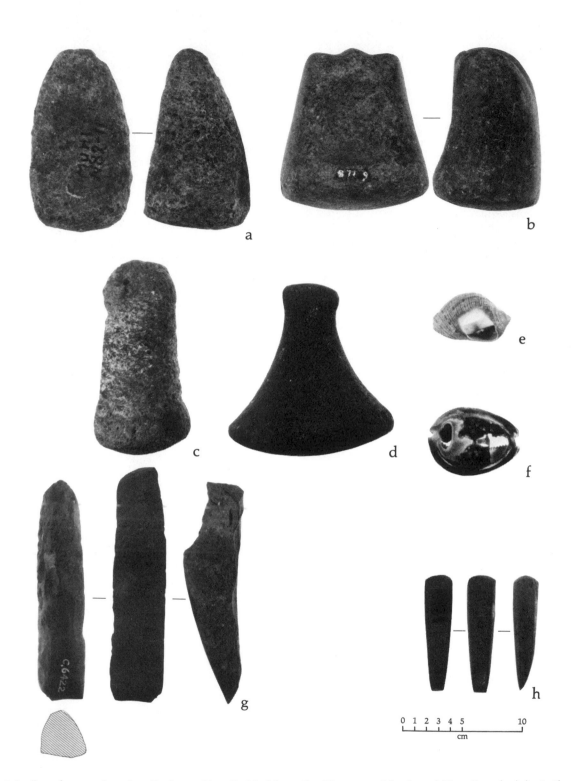

5.6   *Pounders, peelers, basalt adz, and basalt chisel from the Marquesas Islands and Hawaii:* a, *incipient stirrup pounder from Uahuka;* b, *stirrup pounder from Kauai, Hawaii;* c, *incipient pounder from Uahuka;* d, *conical knob-head pounder from Uahuka;* e, Purpura persica *shell peeler;* f, *cowrie-shell peeler;* g, Koma-type *adz;* h, *basalt chisel. (From the Bishop Museum collection.)*

YOSIHIKO H. SINOTO

5.7 *Stone images of Hane Valley, Uahuka:* a, *front view of image found on platform of inland religious site (see Fig. 5.13);* b, *front view of image found used as paving stone in phase II pavement, Hane Dune site. (After Sinoto 1970.)*

midden materials. Evidence of dog burials were found, which suggests that they were man's companion rather than his food.

Phase III (Expansion Stage), A.D. 1300–1600

It is likely that with the expansion of the population during this phase and into the beginning of phase IV, people settled throughout all inhabitable areas, mainly in valleys, on all the islands. Some significant artifacts, such as shaped whale-tooth pendants and *Conus*-shell disks, drop out of the cultural inventory and new artifacts appear. The population spread into inland areas coincides with structural changes in housing during this period. There is evidence that house foundations of the low-platform type with divided sleeping quarters and a front terrace were used (Suggs 1961).

A number of sites surveyed for this phase were found on Uahuka, Nukuhiva, and Hivaoa Islands, and were quite widely spread along the coastal and inland areas. Use of rock shelters was common.

Adzes, except for the smaller ones, showed a marked change and stabilization of forms. The earlier, incipient Koma-type adzes had developed into a unique form

with a high trapezoidal cross section and a definite tang (Fig. 5.6g). The pecking technique was no longer evident; only the chipping and grinding technique had survived. *Cassis*-shell chisels were not popular; instead, stone chisels appeared (Fig. 5.6h). Conical-type pounders were found in this phase, but still with plain heads.

Fishhooks were smaller in size and less varied in form. In general, they tended to be of the jabbing-hook type with heads like those in Fig. 5.8. These were the most popular features of fishhooks in this phase, and the ones by which they can be recognized. The compound-shank hooks have a flat shank to which a flat reinforcing stem is fastened. They appear to be less well formed and finished from this phase on into historic times (Linton 1923). Trolling hooks were extremely scarce everywhere. The dearth of both large one-piece hooks and trolling hooks seems to indicate that fishing was confined for the most part to inshore efforts. Octopus fishing was still practiced, and the stone sinkers of the coffee-bean type were narrower and higher than their predecessors. What was formerly a longitudinal groove on the bottom was expanded, and the whole bottom became convex.

Cowrie-shell vegetable peelers completely replaced *Purpura*-shell peelers in this phase

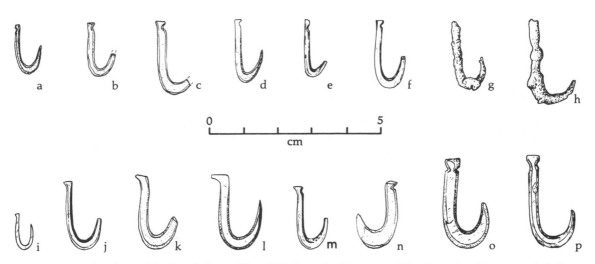

5.8 *Pearl-shell and metal hooks of phases III and IV from the Marquesas Islands: a–f and i–p, pearl shell; g and h, metal. (After Sinoto 1970.)*

(Fig. 5.6*f*). Pottery dropped out of the inventory.

Shellfish and human bone dominate the midden. Pieces of human bone with charring were found quite often in this phase and suggest cannibalism. The ratio of fish bones to other midden materials is not so high as it appeared to be in phase II, but judging from the quantity of fishhooks, a great many fish were caught. One small shelter in Hanaui yielded over 500 fishhooks. When we consider the numbers of small, inshore fish that were eaten whole, and the reluctance of the occupants to drop fish bones with sharp spines onto the house floor, recovery of skeletal remains of most of the eaten fish is impossible.

No dog bones were identified in this phase; they might have been near extinction. Pigs, on the other hand, were increasing steadily from this phase to the next (Kirch 1973).

Phase IV (Classic Stage), A.D. 1600–1800

No significant change in artifacts from the expansion to the classic period is seen in the material culture excavated from subsurface deposits. However, certain structural developments, especially of religious and ceremonial structures, occurred during this

time. Also, by the evidence of grave goods found in caves and crevices in late historic time, perishable materials flourished. However, their placement in the cultural sequence will have to wait for further investigations in the Marquesas.

Artifacts in Space and Time

Pottery

A total of only twelve small potsherds have been found thus far in the Marquesas Islands: nine from Ha'atuatua, one from Ho'oumi, and two from Hane, Uahuka. Because of the scarcity of sherds, my initial assumption was that they had been imported by the first settlers. However, petrographic analysis by Dickinson (1967) revealed otherwise. He examined one sherd and three pieces of baked clay from the Hane site. The temper sand of all the specimens is virtually identical, and Dickinson unequivocally stated that "there is no reason to doubt that the sherd is indigenous and was made locally." Similar results were arrived at by x-ray diffraction-pattern studies of pottery and clay samples from Hane (Sinoto 1968a). However, Dickinson recently altered his interpretation; because of finding quartz mineral among the temper of the same sherds

YOSIHIKO H. SINOTO

examined previously, he felt that the sherds could have been imported from Fiji, the nearest quartz resource area, or via Tonga (Dickinson and Shutler 1974).

Adzes

Studies of Polynesian adzes, especially those with archaeological contexts, have been made by Emory (1968) and Green and Davidson (1969). Green (1968) summarized the distribution of adzes in East Melanesia, West Polynesia, and East Polynesia in the initial stages. It is not necessary to repeat his conclusions here, but the adz complex of the Marquesan phases I and II most closely relates to that of Samoa.

One point which should be mentioned is that the grip or tang, which is an East Polynesia characteristic, now appears to be found in incipient form among the adzes of Samoa (Kikuchi 1963) and Tonga (Poulsen 1968); in East Polynesia it flourished.

Over a hundred classifiable adzes of phases I and II from Hane demonstrate two predominant manufacturing techniques—chipping and grinding. On the others, the surface was completely pecked. Tanged adzes are few, but were formed by the pecking technique.

Similarly, in the adz collection from the Maupiti burial sites (Emory and Sinoto 1964) in the Society Islands, either the whole surface or a portion of the tang is pecked on one-third of the adzes. A careful look at both Hane and Maupiti adzes made by the pecking technique reveals that they have thick oval or quadrangular cross sections with rounded corners. Controlling such curvatures by pecking would seem much easier than by chipping. The object was to achieve the rounded corners. On Easter Island the pecking technique continued in use and survived (Figueroa and Sanchez 1965). Not only adzes, but fishhooks and even *ahu* (religious structure) segments persist in their original forms or types there. One factor may be the geographic isolation of Easter Island. The pecking technique, a method that definitely existed

early in the Marquesas, and the adz types retained, which were particularly easily formed by the pecking technique, are interacting factors.

Hawaiian adzes were also studied and summarized by Emory. He states (1968:162) that "no place in Eastern Polynesia is there exhibited such a steadfast adherence to one form of adz as . . . in Hawaii." Until recently Hawaiian archaeology has concentrated on coastal sites, and finding adzes in fishing-oriented sites was an extremely rare occurrence. However, adzes from three major South Point sites (on the island of Hawaii) show the ratio of the quadrangular adzes to both reversed triangular and trapezoidal adzes to be 41 (87 percent) to 6 (13 percent) in the Sand Dune site, 16 (89 percent) to 2 (11 percent) in the Waiahukini site, and 9 (90 percent) to 1 (10 percent) in the Makalei site (Sinoto 1978). These ratios suggest that at least 10 percent of the Hawaiian adzes found in these archaeological sites do not have a quadrangular cross section, and the ratio is slightly higher in the earlier sites. Quadrangular adzes found in the Sand Dune site are tanged, but not markedly bent at the shoulder. Reversed trapezoidal and reversed triangular adzes are small in size and number and have an incipient tang. These types were also located in museum collections without provenience, but they are rare.

In the early Marquesan assemblages, were adzes ranging from similar to identical to the early Hawaiian types. However, from present evidence it seems that the differences between Hawaiian and Marquesan adzes are greater than between the adzes of Easter Island and the Marquesas, or those of the Societies and the Marquesas. In Hawaii the manufacturing method used was exclusively chipping and grinding. An obvious question is, why the pecking technique was not used in Hawaiian adz making. Although we do not know when stone pounders appeared in the Hawaiian cultural inventory, they were made by the pecking technique. Hawaiians knew and used this technique on pounders and other stone objects, but not on adzes. When pounders came into the archaeological sequence, chipped and ground adzes continued to exist. This is an evidence of preferred technique for certain types of artifacts. A quadrangular cross section and the chipping method seem to have a close relation. Hawaiians apparently selected the technique of chipping and grinding to make adzes, and its use may predetermine the adz form. The reverse may be equally true, that the preferred adz form may require chipping and grinding as a manufacturing technique. Elsewhere I have questioned whether the bottom layers of the South Point and Waiahukini sites really represent the initial stage of Hawaiian culture. The presence of well-developed two-piece hooks (shanks and points made separately and lashed together to form hooks) implies that there must be still older sites in the Hawaiian Islands (Sinoto 1967). If so, some pecked adzes may well show up among the nonquadrangular adz types.

Turning to the Society Islands, we are able to add the excellent collection of adzes from the Vaitootia site (Sinoto and McCoy 1975; Sinoto, 1977) to those from the Maupiti burial sites for the earliest adz assemblage in the islands. All the adzes from these sites had counterparts in the early Marquesan adzes and also in some lenticular, plano-convex, and trapezoidal adzes in Samoa (Green and Davidson 1969), Tonga (Poulson 1968), and Fiji (Gifford 1951). The adz assemblage from the Vaitootia site is more closely related to the Marquesan phase I and II assemblages than to that of the Maupiti burials in terms of form and frequency of incipiently tanged adzes. The dominant form of reverse triangular, or so-called Tahitian triangular, adzes (see Fig. 8.2) in the later period was not found in the above sites. How and when this form of adz appeared in the Society Islands is still a question, but it was probably during the 200-year period before A.D. 1350. Suggs (1961) thinks the simultaneous appearance of the Koma-type adz in the Marquesas in

the expansion period and in New Zealand after Wairau Bar may be the result of contact from Tahiti. The Koma-type adz could have developed in both places from a triangular adz, with or without a tang. It did not have a horizontal cutting edge, only a beaked triangular cutting point (Fig. 5.4d). If the straight ridge, which is the apex of its triangular cross section, were ground down to any degree, it would become the high trapezoidal, Koma-type adz (Fig. 5.4e or Fig. 5.6g). A good example of this was reported from Samoa (Green and Davidson 1969).

Stone Pounders

Polynesian pounders in general have a round grip with a flared base, the diameter of which is much larger than the grip (Fig. 5.6d). They are usually described as taro or breadfruit pounders. Although the grip and base have a uniform shape, the head portion of the grip differs through time from island group to island group and among islands within a group.

Marquesan pounders are of the conical or knobbed type (Buck 1957), originally with a head that was simply a rounded knob, and later with a more elaborate head carved with an image. In the archaeological context, such plain, conical, knob-headed pounders began to appear in the later part of phase III. One specimen from level 3 of the Hane site is an unfinished pounder. Its overall form is much like a pestle with a base that is slightly larger than the grip, but the reduction of the grip was quite evident. Two pounders found in Manihina Dune site, from the beginning of phase IV (Sinoto and Kellum, 1965), are plain, conical, knob-headed pounders.

Whether the pounders were an innovation of the Marquesans or an intrusion is still a question. Suggs (1961) raised similar problems, but he put the emphasis on Tahitian influence in the Marquesas. The difficulty again is a lack of information on Tahitian pounders. We have no evidence to

YOSIHIKO H. SINOTO

tell us when such pounders appeared in the Society Islands. The Maupiti and Vaitootia sites did not yield pounders.

If the pestle form of the unfinished pounder from Hane is evidence of an incipient pounder that was to develop into the typical later item, it would seem to be too late to have moved to islands beyond the Marquesas. However, if we adopt Suggs's view, the Hane pounder would be interpreted as evidence of a possible Tahitian contact during phase III, the expansion period, or of independent development in both places.

Pounders in Tahiti developed a very elaborate head form with an eared bar on top of the grip (Fig. 5.9a). The existence there also of knob-headed pounders suggests that they are the predecessors of the eared-bar type. However, because of the lack of evidence of pounders in New Zealand, Groube (1968) implies that they were not developed in Tahiti before A.D. 800—in other words, not before the settlers of New Zealand left Tahiti.

In Hawaii the appearance of the pounder is rather late. This may be because of the concentration on excavation of sites in the coastal areas. Here the Hawaiians again persistently continued one form—that of the plain, conical pounder—with no elaboration or modification. If the pounders were the result of Tahitian influence, the Tahitians who went to Hawaii would have left their homeland before any elaboration of pounders took place there.

There are two outstanding examples in the Hawaiian Islands of nonconical pounders: ring (Fig. 5.9b) and stirrup (Fig. 5.6b) pounders, restricted for the most part to the island of Kauai. Although they were used to pound taro, Emory (1975) has suggested that the original function of these artifacts may have been different. He based his theory of another use on his observations in the Tuamotus of a pandanus-key cracker, which was held in both hands in much the same way a Hawaiian stirrup pounder was gripped. In the case of the Tuamotuan pounder, a simple, roughly shaped coral slab was used instead of a more deliberately formed stone. The ring and particularly the stirrup pounder, because of their forms, are difficult to hold in one hand. When poi is made with a conical pounder, one hand adds water while the other operates the pounder. If the pounder had to be gripped with both hands, like the Tuamotuan pandanus-key pounder, the material being pounded might have been something other than taro. Even though we have only a surface collection of pounders from Kauai, there is a strong indication that they went through typological changes from the stirrup form to the ring form.

Two stone objects from phase II at the Hane site (Fig. 5.6a) strongly suggest an incipient stirrup-pounder form. Although similar objects were not found in subsequent levels, or in ethnologic collections, they evidence a strong morphological relation to the Kauai stirrup pounders.

Harpoon Heads

Outside of the Marquesas, bone, whale-tooth, and pearl-shell harpoon heads have been reported from Mangareva (Green 1960), the Vaitootia site, Society Islands (Sinoto and McCoy 1975), and New Zealand Archaic culture. Skinner (1937) classified New Zealand harpoon heads into five varieties. However, since there are two basic techniques for securing the harpoon shaft to the head, I have arbitrarily classified them into two types: type A combines Skinner's variety 1 and variety 2 (Fig. 5.5e, g). Harpoons of this type are flat or rounded (variety 1), or grooved (variety 2) along one side (opposite a distal foot) where the shaft is placed. There is a hole in the midsection for tying a long line. Type B includes Skinner's varieties 3 to 5 (Fig. 5.5h–j). These harpoons have a bifurcate base. The shaft for type A can be a plain, long pointed stick, but for type B the tip of the shaft must be split to hold the harpoon head. Type A harpoons are found

5.9 *Artifacts from the Society and Hawaiian islands: a, eared-bar pounder from Society; b, ring pounder from Kauai, Hawaii; c, octopus lure from Hawaii; d, pearl-shell trolling-hook shank, archaic type, from Marquesas; e, pearl-shell ventrodorsal perforated trolling-hook shank from Marquesas; f, whale-tooth pendant from Hawaii. (From the Bishop Museum collection.)*

in all three areas (the Vaitootia specimen is too fragmental to classify), but type B is found only in New Zealand. There are no adequate stratigraphic records of harpoons in New Zealand that enable us to place them in typological sequence and chronology, but there is no doubt of their antiquity there (Skinner 1937; Duff 1956). Three

variety 2 harpoons from Wairau Bar are recorded by Duff. Distribution in the three areas suggests that type A is older than type B. In the Marquesas, the harpoons of type A are found in two different phases—variety 2 in phase II, and variety 1 in phase IV—and continue to be evident into historic times. Although there is some evi-

YOSIHIKO H. SINOTO

dence of local variation, it does not seem feasible to view these three places—the Marquesas, Mangareva, and New Zealand—as having independently developed harpoons of basically the same type. What is more likely is that they are derived from one source, probably the Marquesas. Amazingly similar harpoons are distributed in the areas along the northern Pacific coast (Leroi-Gourhan 1946; Watanabe 1964). Although the outline of these harpoons is identical, the technique of securing a shaft is different: in the northern Pacific coastal sites the shaft is placed into a socket at the base of the harpoon (closed socket), instead of along the side of the harpoon shaft (open socket). Despite such differences, we cannot simply ignore their occurrence both in the middle of the Pacific and in the northern Pacific coastal areas.

Fishhooks

Fishhooks have been used as a diagnostic device for establishing chronology within an area (Emory et al. 1968) and for comparative studies among island groups. I have discussed this subject elsewhere, particularly with regard to the relations of the Hawaiian, Society, and Marquesas islands (Sinoto 1967). The head forms of one-piece hooks, the materials, the ratio between the length of the shank and the point, manufacturing methods, and tools are the main criteria for judging relations between early Marquesan fishhooks and early Hawaiian, Tahitian, and New Zealand fishhooks. Although only one hook was found in the Maupiti burials, the same type of hook has been found on the main island of Maupiti and recently was among a few hundred fishhooks collected at the surface in the rest of the Society Islands. Two phase II bone-hook fragments from the Hanatukua shelter (Bellwood 1972) represent the first discovery of a barbed-shank fishhook in central Polynesia. The additional discovery of a drill head (Fig. 5.10g) and chisels (Fig. 5.10i) made from spindle shells was made at the same site. The drill head was identi-

cal to those found at the South Point and Waiahukini sites (Fig. 5.10h) in Hawaii (Emory et al. 1968), and the chisels (Fig. 5.10j) were identical to those uncovered in Hawaii (Tuohy 1965), which were mistakenly classified as drill heads.

A very sensible interpretation of the Easter Island fishhooks was made by Golson (1965). Although we do not know much about the hook assemblage of the early period, the general characteristics of the head types of the middle and late periods show a similarity to those of the Marquesan hooks of phase I and phase II. As Easter Islanders retained the earlier adz types, they seem also to have retained the earlier fishhook forms.

Mangarevan archaeological fishhooks excavated and studied by Green (1960) are similar to the early Marquesan hook types, except for one type that was a later, local development. Even the wiggly-shank hook was found in the southern Marquesas in phase II (Fig. 5.10a–c).

Two-piece hooks are characteristic of the fringe areas of Polynesia, and no similar hooks are found in central Polynesia. They were apparently developed independently in three areas: Hawaii, Easter, and New Zealand. Their development was probably triggered by a limited supply, or a complete lack, of pearl shell. The elements of trolling-hook structure on which the two-piece fishhook is based were already possessed by the people in these areas.

Biflanged and inset fishhook points were reported from Ha'atuatua and Nahotoa cave (Suggs 1961). The latter site is classified as dating from the expansion through the classic periods. Both types of points are also found in Hanatukua shelter on Hivaoa (Fig. 5.10e, f) from phase II layers. The biflanged point from Hanatukua is disproportionally long and has notches near its midpoint that would render it too weak to use for a trolling hook point. It may have been used as a point on the octopus lure of the Hawaiian type (Fig. 5.9c), since a sinker of the coffee-bean type and some cowrie lures were found in the same layer. The inset-type

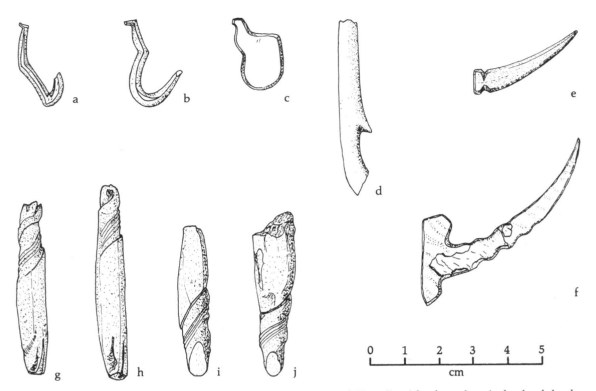

5.10 *Fishhooks, drill heads, and chisels from the Marquesas and Hawaiian islands: a, b, wiggly-shank hooks, and c, their blank; d, bone one-piece fishhook shank with barb; e, pearl-shell inset point; f, pearl-shell bi-flanged point; g, Marquesan, and h, Hawaiian, spindle-shell drill heads; i, Marquesan, and j, Hawaiian, spindle-shell chisels. (After Sinoto 1970.)*

point of pearl shell found at Hanatukua shelter is the same shape as the one illustrated by Suggs (1961), but is shorter and has a notch on both sides near the end of its blunt base. Both biflanged and inset points could be inserted into shanks in a fashion similar to the barracuda hooks of the classic Maori New Zealand assemblage (Buck 1949; Golson 1959).

Present evidence of the distribution of trolling-hook types in East Polynesia rather clearly indicates a Marquesan dispersal. The pearl-shell lure shank of wide, triangular form with a blunt, proximal end and a perforation for a line attachment (Fig. 5.9d) is found in phases I and II in the Marquesas, at Vaitootia, and at Maupiti. The point with a proximal base extension and with two lashing holes is also in these areas, at South Point sites in Hawaii, on Moorea (Green et al. 1967), and at Archaic

sites in New Zealand. The lure shank with the flat form or a triangular proximal end and a ventrodorsal perforation for line attachment is found in phase II in Hane and in Archaic New Zealand sites. In this case a pearl-shell specimen was uncovered in New Zealand (Green 1967). Examples are still rare, but barracuda-hook points might have followed the same path from the Marquesas.

Ornaments

Among the ornaments in phase I are two *Conus*-shell disks, each with a hole in the center. The apex end of the shell in each instance was carefully ground flat to a thickness of 1.5 to 2.0 mm and made into an almost perfect round disk about 25 mm in diameter (Fig. 5.7a). These are among the most beautifully made artifacts from the

YOSIHIKO H. SINOTO

Hane site. Suggs (1961) found pearl-shell disks from Ha'atuatua and related them to *kapkap* ornaments of Melanesia. While it seems to me that his pearl-shell disks may eventually relate to kapkap ornaments, it is difficult to see any direct morphological connection between them. The Ha'atuatua disks (Fig. 5.11*e*) have two holes in the center, and grooves are cut radially around the edge on one surface but are not visible on the other side. Kapkap mounts in Melanesia are round, plain *Conus*-shell disks with only one perforation in the center (Reichard 1933).

In phases II and IV at Hane site, pearl-shell disks appeared with serrated edges and a single hole in the center. Phase IV disks (Fig. 5.11*c, d*) are thicker and more crudely made than the phase II disks. Some of the latter are almost paper thin, and the two holes are as small as the eye of a metal needle (Fig. 5.11*b, g, h*). These serrated disks might have been used for the Marquesan headband, although I have not seen this in the ethnologic collections.

Pearl-shell breast ornaments and pearl-shell scrapers or spoons were discovered with the Maupiti burials (Emory and Sinoto 1964). The breast ornaments are whole pearl shells on which the rough exterior surface had been ground smooth and the iridescent inner shell revealed. The circumference edge was also ground smooth. A small perforation at the beak was made for suspension. The scrapers or spoons were taken from a center section of the pearl shell that extended from the beak to the ventral margin. They were also well polished, with the convex edge ground to a sharp edge. Specimens identical to these plates and scrapers were found in Hane phase I (Fig. 5.12*a, b*). At Hane they are not from burials, but from the cultural deposits, as were the shaped whale-tooth pendants. This marked resemblance seems to provide additional data to suggest a link between the Marquesas and the Society islands.

Shaped whale-tooth pendants were found at Hane (Fig. 5.11*i, j*), Maupiti (Fig. 5.11*l*)

and in Archaic New Zealand sites (Golson 1959). In 1965 Emory found a small, shaped whale-tooth pendant on a coral islet called Iriru off the coast of Avera, Raiatea (Fig. 5.11*k*). Preliminary test excavations did not yield further information, but I believe that a thorough investigation of the islet might uncover burials similar to those of Maupiti. In 1973 the Vaitootia site was uncovered, and three excavation sessions recovered five shaped whale-tooth pendants.

Except for shaped varieties, whale-tooth pendants are spread widely throughout Polynesia. These pendants have three major variations: variety 1—unmodified whale tooth, or simulated whale-tooth form made of other material with a suspension hole; variety 2—whale-tooth, or other material, with a long, rounded stem and a pointed, outward-protruding distal end (good examples of this variety are from Samoa and Tonga); variety 3—usually made of shell, but also of whale tooth, with the whale-tooth profile, but flattened and with side perforations near the top. Variety 1 is found in Hawaii, Mangareva, the Marquesas, Easter Island, Samoa, and Tonga. Variety 2 is from Hawaii (Fig. 5.11*o, p*), the Marquesas (Fig. 5.11*m, n*), New Zealand (Duff 1956), Samoa, and Tonga. In the Marquesas shaped whale-tooth pendants seem to have appeared first in phase I. Then, in phase II, variety 2 appeared, but the shaped whale-tooth pendant was still used. Varieties 1 and 3 probably soon replaced the shaped pendant and variety 2, and both continued into historic times.

Hanatukua Dune site on Hivaoa yielded artifacts of fishhooks and adzes contemporary with phase II. In a cache containing adz blanks was found a shell imitation of a whale-tooth pendant. Although it is unfinished and without perforations, its form belongs to variety 2 (Fig. 5.11*n*). So far, there is no evidence of shaped, variety 1 whale-tooth pendants in the southern Marquesas Islands.

Hawaii has not yielded shaped whale-tooth pendants of the Maupiti and Wairau Bar type. Only variety 2 pendants were

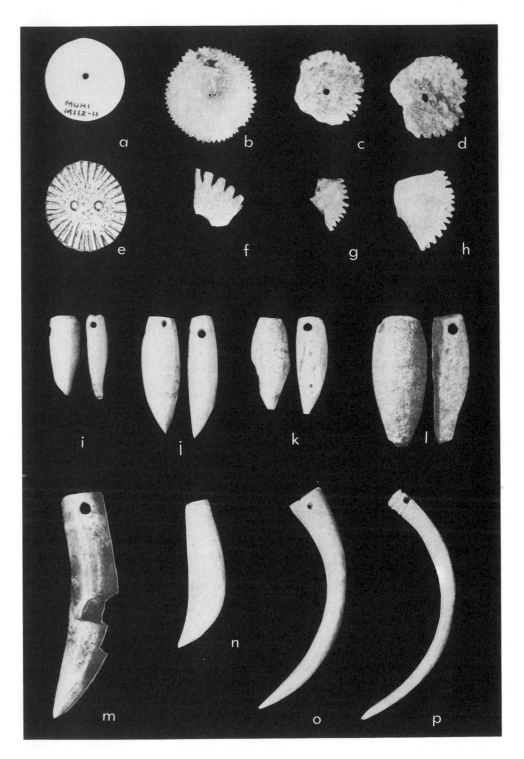

5.11 Shell, whale-tooth, and pig-tusk ornaments from the Marquesas (a–j, m and n), Society (k and l), and Hawaiian islands (o and p): a, Conus-shell disk; b–d, g, h, pearl-shell serrated disks; e, f, pearl-shell grooved disks (e, after Suggs 1961); i–l, shaped whale-tooth pendants; m–p, whale-tooth pendants, variety 2 (m, whale tooth; n, shell; o, p, pig tusks). (After Sinoto 1970.)

YOSIHIKO H. SINOTO

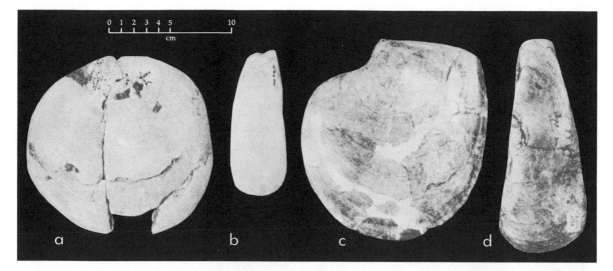

5.12 Pearl-shell breastplates and scrapers; a, b, *from the Hane Dune site;* c, d, *from burial site 1, Maupiti, Society Islands. (After Sinoto 1970.)*

found at the very bottom of the Waiahukini site, one of the oldest cultural deposits in Hawaii. Variety 3 pendants appeared later, but no contexual data are available. Meanwhile, the historically well-known typical Hawaiian whale-tooth pendant (*niho palaoa*) (Fig. 5.9*f*) developed locally (Sinoto 1963). The distribution of whale-tooth pendants in East Polynesia suggests dispersal from the Marquesas. Here again the time depth of variety 2 in West Polynesia is still in question.

Religious Structures

The religious structures in the Marquesas are very complicated in physical layout and in function (Linton 1925). Very few detailed studies have been made using modern archaeological methods. A religious site *me'ae* with elaborated architectural features could have existed in phase III. Smith (1964) surveyed and excavated the Pekia me'ae at Atuona, Hivaoa. Radiocarbon dates of the samples collected are A.D. 1300 ± 200, A.D. 1390 ± 100, A.D. 1720 ± 80, and A.D. 1730 ± 80. These dates fit well into phases III and IV. Smith, in a personal

communication, wrote: "I interpret the useful dates as follows: The oldest datable construction occurred in the 14th century. Construction was also carried out in the 15th century. Major expansion and rebuilding occurred about 1700."

A structure found deep in Hane Valley, Uahuka, was the one farthest inland, and its elevation was the highest in the valley. Although there were some terraces and retaining walls across the axis of the slope, at the back end of this structure, in the center of the court, was a low rectangular platform that was incorporated into the upward sloping ground. On top of this platform, in the middle, was an image of dark, reddish-tuff stone. This 39-cm-high oblong stone image has eyes, and open mouth, and both arms resting on the stomach. Although it was found lying down, most likely the image originally stood on the platform (Figs. 5.13 and 5.7*a*). Unlike most Marquesan images, it is similar to typical Tahitian in style. While the emphasis has been put on the discovery of this image on the platform, the platform itself, without the upright stones, has features reminiscent of the Necker Island, Hawaii, religious structures

5.13 *Stone image found in the Hane inland religious site. Although in the photograph it is standing, the image was found lying on the platform. (After Sinoto 1970.)*

(Emory 1928) and also of those of Easter Island. The earlier form of Society Island religious structure was discovered inland, where there was less destruction caused by later rebuilding or stylistic changes. If this is extrapolated to the Marquesan case, the Hane inland structure could represent the survival of an earlier form, a variation of which is found on Necker and Easter islands. Should this be so, religious structures—or more precisely the relative position of the principal platform and image—found in the Marquesas could be related to those found in other parts of East Polynesia. This Hane me'ae structure then could be placed in phase III and later, because of the unusually large pig skulls. More than ten of them were excavated from under the surface deposit at the foot of the platform, where they were probably placed as offerings. With these skulls was an unfinished, small image with a squarish body.

Concluding Remarks

On balance, there is fairly good evidence with which to evaluate the role of the Marquesas in early East Polynesian prehistory. The discovery of the Vaitootia site, Huahine Island, throws light on the cultural assemblage of the Society Islands at the time of the settlement period and is the beginning of our knowledge to fill the archaeological blank of this important island group (Sinoto 1976). The Vaitootia cultural assemblage is remarkably similar to those of phases I and II of the Marquesas Islands, except for the perishable artifacts from Vaitootia—a canoe paddle, a bow, adz handles, a ceremonial spear, hand clubs similar to the Maori *patu*, the structural remains of storage houses, and the kava plant (*Piper methysticum*) (Sinoto and McCoy 1975; Sinoto, 1977). The inference is that such wooden artifacts probably existed in the Marquesas. Compound-shank fish-

YOSIHIKO H. SINOTO

hooks and pearl-shell pendants, previously thought to be unique to the Marquesas, were also found at Vaitootia.

Pearl-shell one-piece fishhooks, found from the lowest layer of the Henderson Island cave shelter (about 160 km northwest of Pitcairn Island), are Marquesan phase II types (Sinoto 1976). *Porites*-coral files (Suggs 1961; Emory et al. 1968) are of the Hawaiian-Marquesan type and, like the basalt adzes associated with the pearl-shell hooks from Henderson, these materials are not indigenous. After these imported materials had been used up, the locally available resources—fossilized *Tridacna* shells and hammer-oyster shells—were utilized. The early Henderson material culture had a close affiliation with the early Marquesan culture, although personal ornaments were not found from Henderson. Charcoal at the bottom of the site yielded a radiocarbon date of A.D. 1160 ± 110.

The occupation of Pitcairn Island might be a similar case, based on its date and possible material linked with Henderson (Sinoto 1973). As far as we know today, the history of human occupation in East Polynesia goes back approximately 2,000 years. The Marquesas Islands yielded the earliest date, along with material cultural assemblages that establish a fairly solid cultural sequence from the settlement period to the historic period. It is also possible to see a cultural progression from the Marquesas to the Societies to New Zealand.

Problems still remain in interpreting the settlement of the Hawaiian Islands. The South Point sites and two others, one on Oahu (Pearson et al. 1971) and one on Molokai (Kirch and Kelly 1975), dated respectively at the sixth and seventh centuries A.D., have not yielded any diagnostic early Marquesan material culture such as shaped whale-tooth pendants, harpoons, or adzes, except for some one-piece hooks from the South Point sites. This situation weakens the argument for the Marquesas Islands as the primary homeland for the ancestors of the Hawaiians, since the Society Islands did have these diagnostic materials. More

survey in the southern Marquesas group is required.

However, there is one point that may be important to consider. The southern Marquesas also lacked the shaped whale-tooth pendants and harpoons and may have been occupied later than the north, beginning in phase II. The southern group accordingly may have been settled from the north. If the hypothesis is valid that this diagnostic material culture, which substantiates the link between the Marquesas, the Societies, and New Zealand, was not in the southern group, then the impact moved from the northern group to the Societies, and then to New Zealand.

Hawaii, on the other hand, had an impact from the southern group. Some of the southern Marquesas material culture indicates a closer link to that of Hawaii; Mangareva, Henderson, and Pitcairn may be in a similar situation. If the evidence presented here is reliable, despite the many unsolved problems, dispersal from the Marquesas to other island groups probably took place initially early in phase II, with no significant movements in subsequent phases, except for the possibility of a later movement to New Zealand (Emory and Sinoto 1965; Green 1967).

There is good evidence of occupation of almost every valley in the Marquesas, and the population density might have been higher than we estimate. The ruins in the valleys belong mostly to phase III and later. The population probably reached its climax in the early part of phase IV. If the islands could support such a large population, why was it that the people who settled there for a short while moved out again? There should be reasons other than those connected with the limited economic potential of the islands. Early dispersal to the Society Islands, Hawaii, and Easter Island probably took place between A.D. 650 and 800 (Emory and Sinoto 1965; Golson 1965; Emory and Sinoto 1969; Sinoto 1976) and to Mangareva about A.D. 1200 (Suggs 1962).

Finally, there are problems in determining the land of origin of the Marquesas Islands. There is still the question of line-fishing gear, which does not have clear connection with West Polynesia. However, archaeological shell hooks from Tonga (Poulsen 1968) and a surface hook found there by Golson (personal communication), plus one example of an unfinished *Turbo*-shell hook (Davidson 1969) and five specimens made of pearl shell (Jennings 1976) from Samoa are encouraging discoveries.

In any case, so far there is little evidence to connect the Marquesas and West Polynesia as far as line-fishing gear is concerned. The situation with respect to trolling hooks is somewhat odd. The Hane site clearly shows a typological change from so-called West Polynesian–type trolling points (Fig. 5.3*o*) to the East Polynesian type (Fig. 5.3*p*). The former was found chronologically early from Hawaii, the Societies, and New Zealand. Excavations in West Polynesia have not yielded a single example of trolling-hook points, although there are many trolling hooks in the ethnologic collections from Samoa and Tonga. The development of trolling hooks in Oceania poses an important and interesting research topic. There are two possibilities: either this fishing gear developed in the Marquesas or it was intrusive from unknown islands in West Polynesia or Micronesia. If the first, there must be an earlier site than Hane to allow the time needed for the form to develop within the islands.

The adz assemblage of the early Marquesas demonstrates a strong tie with Samoa. But some items in the Marquesan inventory—kapkap-type ornaments, whale-tooth pendants, bows, hand clubs, and even use of kava plants—are still unknown in archaeological contexts in West Polynesia, Melanesia, and Micronesia. Despite these unsolved problems, we have archaeological, anthropological, and linguistic evidence that indicates a strong link between West Polynesia and East Polynesia. More work must be done before we can proceed to speculate.

References

Bellwood, P. S. 1972. A settlement pattern survey, Hanatekua Valley, Hiva Oa, Marquesas Islands. *Pacific Anthropological Records* 17.

Buck, P. H. (Te Rangi Hiroa). 1949. *The coming of the Maori.* Wellington.

———. 1953. *Explorers of the Pacific.* Bishop Museum Special Publication no. 43, Honolulu.

———. 1957. *Arts and crafts of Hawaii.* Bishop Museum Special Publication no. 45, Honolulu.

Davidson, J. M. 1969. Excavation of a coastal midden deposit Su-Lo-l. In *Archaeology in Western Samoa,* ed. R. C. Green and J. M. Davidson, vol. 1. *Auckland Institute and Museum Bulletin* 6:224–252.

Dickinson, W. R. 1967. Temper in Marquesan sherds. Petroglyphic Report WRD-25 (12-20-67).

——— and Richard Shutler, Jr. 1974. Probable Fijian origin of quartzose temper sands in prehistoric pottery from Tonga and the Marquesas. *Science* 185:454–457.

Duff, R. S. 1956. *The moa-hunter period of Maori culture,* 2nd ed. Wellington: Government Printer.

Emory, K. P. 1928. *Archaeology of Nihoa and Necker islands.* Bishop Museum Bulletin no. 53, Honolulu.

———. 1968. East Polynesian relationships as revealed through adzes. In *Prehistoric culture in Oceania,* ed. Ichito Yawata and Y. H. Sinoto, pp. 151–169. Honolulu: Bishop Museum Press.

———. 1975. Material culture in the Tuamotu Archipelago. *Pacific Anthropoligical Records* 22.

——— and Y. H. Sinoto. 1964. Eastern Polynesian burials at Maupiti. *Journal of the Polynesian Society* 73:143–160.

——— and Y. H. Sinoto. 1965. Preliminary report on the archaeological investigations in Polynesia: fieldwork in the Society and Tuamotu islands, French Polynesia, and American Samoa in 1962, 1963, 1964. Manuscript.

——— and Y. H. Sinoto. 1969. Age of the sites in the South Point area, Ka'u, Hawaii. *Pacific Anthropological Records* 8.

———, W. J. Bonk, and Y. H. Sinoto. 1968. *Hawaiian archaeology: fishhooks,* 2nd ed. Bishop Museum Special Publication no. 47, Honolulu.

Figueroa, Gonzalo, and Eduardo Sanchez. 1965. Adzes from certain islands of Eastern Polynesia. In *Reports of the Norwegian archaeological expedition to Easter Island and the East Pacific,* ed. Thor Heyerdahl, and E. N. Ferdon, Jr. vol.

2, pp. 169–254. Santa Fe: School of American Research Museum.

Freeman, O. W. 1951. Eastern Polynesia. In *Geography of the Pacific,* ed. O. W. Freeman, pp. 364–393. New York: John Wiley & Sons.

Gifford, E. W. 1951. Archaeological excavations in Fiji. *University of California Anthropological Records* 13:189–288.

Golson, Jack. 1959. Culture change in prehistoric New Zealand. In *Anthropology in the South Seas,* ed. J. D. Freeman and W. R. Geddes, pp. 29–74. New Plymouth, New Zealand: Avery.

——. 1965. Thor Heyerdahl and the prehistory of Easter Island. *Oceania* 36:38–83.

Green, R. C. 1960. *The archaeology of the Mangarevan Archipelago, French Polynesia.* American Museum of Natural History expedition. Manuscript, Bishop Museum, Honolulu.

——. 1967. Sources of New Zealand's Eastern Polynesian culture: the evidence of a pearl-shell lure shank. *Archaeology and Physical Anthropology in Oceania* 2:81–90.

——. 1968. West Polynesian prehistory. In *Prehistoric culture in Oceania,* ed. Ichito Yawata and Y. H. Sinoto, pp. 99–110. Honolulu: Bishop Museum Press.

—— and J. M. Davidson, eds. 1969. *Archaeology in Western Samoa,* vol. 1. *Auckland Institute and Museum Bulletin* 6.

—— and J. M. Davidson, eds. 1974. *Archaeology in Western Samoa,* vol. 2. *Auckland Institute and Museum Bulletin* 7.

——, K. Green, R. A. Rappaport, Ann Rappaport, and J. M. Davidson. 1967. *Archaeology on the island of Mo'orea, French Polynesia.* Anthropological Paper no. 51, pt. 2, American Museum of Natural History, New York.

Groube, L. M. 1968. Research in New Zealand prehistory since 1956. In *Prehistoric culture in Oceania,* ed. Ichito Yawata and Y. H. Sinoto, pp. 141–149. Honolulu: Bishop Museum Press.

Handy, E. S. C. 1925. *The native culture in the Marquesas.* Bishop Museum Bulletin no. 9, Honolulu.

Jennings, J. D. 1976. University of Utah Samoan archeological program, 1976. Preliminary report.

Kellum-Ottino, Marimari. 1971. *Archaéologie d'une valée des îles marquises: évolution des structures de l'habitat à Hane, Ua Huka.* Publication de la Société des Océanistes no. 26, Paris.

Kikuchi, W. K. 1963. Archaeological surface ruins in American Samoa. Master's thesis, University of Hawaii.

Kirch, P. V. 1973. Prehistoric subsistence patterns in the northern Marquesas Islands, French Polynesia. *Archaeology and Physical Anthropology in Oceania* 8:24–40.

—— and Marion Kelly, eds. 1975. Prehistory and ecology in a windward Hawaiian valley: Halawa Valley, Molokai. *Pacific Anthropological Records* 24.

Leroi-Gourhan, André. 1946. *Archaéologie du Pacifique-Nord. Materiaux pour l'étude des relations entre les peuples riverians d'Asie et d'Amerique.* Paris: Institut d'Ethnologie.

Linton, Ralph. 1923. *The material culture of the Marquesas Islands.* Bishop Museum Memoir, vol. 8, no. 5, Honolulu.

——. 1925. *Archaeology of the Marquesas Islands.* Bishop Museum Bulletin no. 23, Honolulu.

Pearson, Richard, P. V. Kirch, and Michael Pietrusewsky. 1971. An early prehistoric site at Bellows Beach, Waimanalo, Oahu, Hawaiian Islands. *Archaeology and Anthropology in Oceania* 6:204–234.

Pietrusewsky, Michael. 1976. *Prehistoric human skeletal remains from Papua New Guinea and the Marquesas.* Asian and Pacific Archaeology Series no. 7, University of Hawaii.

Poulsen, Jens. 1968. Archaeological excavations on Tongatapu. In *Prehistoric culture in Oceania,* ed. Ichito Yawata and Y. H. Sinoto, pp. 85–92. Honolulu: Bishop Museum Press.

Reichard, G. A. 1933. *Melanesian design: a study of style in wood and tortoise shell carving.* New York: Columbia University Press.

Sinoto, Y. H. 1963. Analysis of Hawaiian ornaments and a tentative chronology. Typescript of paper read at meeting of Hawaiian Anthropological Society.

——. 1966. A tentative prehistoric cultural sequence in the northern Marquesas Islands, French Polynesia. *Journal of the Polynesian Society* 75:286–303.

——. 1967. Artifacts from excavated sites in the Hawaiian, Marquesas, and Society islands: a comparative study. In *Polynesian culture history: essays in honor of Kenneth P. Emory,* ed. G. A. Highland et al., pp. 341–361. Bishop Museum Special Publication no. 56, Honolulu.

——. 1968a. Position of the Marquesas Islands in East Polynesian prehistory. In *Prehistoric culture in Oceania,* ed. Ichito Yawata and Y. H.

Sinoto, pp. 111–118. Honolulu: Bishop Museum Press.

———. 1968b. Sources of New Zealand's Eastern Polynesian culture: evidence of the cloak-pin. *Archaeology and Physical Anthropology in Oceania* 3:30–32.

———. 1970. An archaeologically based assessment of the Marquesas Islands as a dispersal center in East Polynesia. In *Studies in Oceanic culture history*, ed. R. C. Green and Marion Kelly, vol. 1. *Pacific Anthropological Records* 11:105–130.

———. 1973. Polynesian occupations on Pitcairn and Henderson islands, Southwest Pacific. Paper read at the 38th annual meeting of the Society for American Archaeology, San Francisco.

———. 1974. A patu from Huahine, Society Islands. *Journal of the Polynesian Society* 83:366–367.

———. 1976. Polynesian migrations based on archaeological assessments. Paper read at the International Union of Prehistoric and Protohistoric Sciences, 9th congress, Nice.

———. 1977. Archaeological excavations of the Vaito'otia site on Huahine Island, French Polynesia (1975 excavation). Manuscript.

———. 1978. Artifacts from excavated sites, Ka'u, Hawaii. In preparation.

——— and Marimari Kellum. 1965. Preliminary report on excavations in the Marquesas Islands, French Polynesia. Mimeographed.

——— and P. C. McCoy. 1975. Report on the preliminary excavation of an early habitation site on Huahine, Society Islands. *Journal de la Société des Océanistes*, 31:143–186.

Skinner, H. D. 1937. Maori use of the harpoon. *Journal of the Polynesian Society* 46:63–73.

Skjölsvold, Arne. 1972. Excavation of a habitation cave, Hanapete'o Valley, Hiva Oa, Marquesas Islands. *Pacific Anthropological Records* 16.

Smith, C. S. 1964. Archaeological investigations at Pekia, Hiva Oa, Marquesas Islands. Typescript of paper read at the Ethnological Congress, Moscow.

Suggs, R. C. 1961. The archaeology of Nuku Hiva, Marquesas Islands, French Polynesia. *Anthropological Papers of the American Museum of Natural History* 49:1–205.

———. 1962. Polynesia—regional report. *Asian Perspectives* 5:88–94.

Tuohy, D. R. 1965. Salvage excavations at City of Refuge National Historical Park, Honaunau, Kona, Hawaii. Manuscript, Bishop Museum, Honolulu.

Watanabe, Makoto. 1964. On the bone harpoons from Iwaki province. *Arukaia* 3 and 4. Text in Japanese.

Yaata, Ichito, and Y. H. Sinoto, eds. 1968. *Prehistoric culture in Oceania: a symposium.* Honolulu: Bishop Museum Press.

Easter Island

CHAPTER 6

PATRICK C. McCOY

Easter Island (27°9′ south latitude, 109°26′ west longitude), 3,200 km west of the South American continent and 2,000 km southeast of the nearest inhabitable island (Pitcairn), is one of the most isolated landmasses in the world. The vast distances separating Easter Island from other islands, and its extreme windward position, effectively prohibited two-way voyaging, so that there was probably little or no contact with other Polynesian groups after first settlement (see Chapter 14). Further correlates of isolation are biotic impoverishment and hence resource scarcity; and increased susceptibility of endemic flora to extinction with the advent of new species and human alteration of the landscape (Fosberg 1963; Simberloff 1974). In addition to being extremely insular, Easter Island is relatively small (total land area 160 km²). Viewed in terms of the far-reaching limitations posed by isolation to the input of ideas from outside, and spatial and ecological constraints on population growth, the first millennium of Easter Island prehistory is an anthropological paradox.

The prehistoric culture of Easter Island attained a level of advancement that resulted in one of the most highly evolved technologies in the world at a Neolithic level. Its best known manifestations are (1) monolithic stone statues or images (*moai*); (2) megalithic religious structures (*ahu*); (3) a written "script" called *rongorongo;* and (4) a highly sophisticated system of solar observation, occasionally used in the orientation of ahu facades. The image-carving and stone-working traditions of Easter Island were superior to any in Polynesia, as was the apparent fund of knowledge about solar phenomena. The written language, although possibly owing its origin to European influence, is unique to Easter Island and the climaxing symbol of a remarkably ingenious population. These and other unique aspects of Easter Island culture have made this remote island one of the most fascinating and intellectually intriguing locales in world prehistory.

A direct expression of the intellectual curiosity about Easter Island prehistory is the extensive background of archaeological investigations and the vast popular literature on the island's so-called mysterious remains. It is significant that Easter Island has a longer history of archaeological research than any of the more centrally located, accessible islands in Polynesia, except possibly New Zealand. As a consequence the general outlines of Easter Island culture history are reasonably well known. At the same time, Easter Island has the dubious distinction of being one of the most widely misinterpreted and misunderstood areas of its size in the world. There are a number of widely held misconceptions about Easter Island culture history as the result of not altogether factual or accurate accounts in appealing books such as *Aku-Aku* (Heyerdahl 1958), *Mysteries of Easter Island* (Maziere 1968), and *Chariots of the Gods?* (Von Däniken 1969). These and other writings have been successful in exploiting the complexities of local prehistory, commonly expressed in the phrase "the mysteries of Easter Island." The by-product of this romanticism is a badly informed public holding to beliefs that are difficult to dispel.

The "mysteries" of Easter Island prehistory were created by a series of historical events that resulted in the loss of information about the past and thus the inability to comprehend it readily. The modern enigma began with internal cultural degradation that had progressed to the point where there was a great disparity between Easter Island culture as it existed at the time of first European contact in the eighteenth century and earlier, grandiose cultural achievements. This incongruity resulted from a deterioration in socioeconomic conditions, accompanied by population decline and gradual abandonment of certain established traditions and practices (such as the carving of monolithic statues).

In a period of little more than 150 years after European rediscovery of the island by the Dutch on Easter Sunday in 1722 (Roggeveen 1908), Easter Island culture was on the verge of extinction. In 1862–1863, between 1,000 and 1,500 inhabitants were taken prisoner to work the guano deposits on the Chincha Islands off the Peruvian coast—an act finally terminated through the protests of a Catholic bishop in Tahiti. The result was near-total decimation of the Easter Island population because of a high death rate caused by miserable working conditions and disease, subsequently introduced to the island by the few survivors of the Peruvian slave raids. An 1877 census revealed an indigenous population of only 110 individuals.

The arrival of missionaries in the early 1860s and rapid conversion to Christianity contributed to the already serious loss of information about the past stemming from earlier population decline. The slave raids, followed quickly by missionization, had a profoundly adverse effect on the quantity and breadth of ethnographic information available to later researchers, including archaeologists. The scantiness of the ethnographic data base is paralleled, unfortunately, by the brevity of ethnohistoric accounts of the early contact period in the eighteenth and nineteenth centuries. The important scientific expeditions that reached Easter Island in the eighteenth century (Cook in 1774, La Perouse in 1786) spent little time there because of the lack of safe anchorages, the scarcity of resources for replenishing depleted provisions, and the suspicious attitude of the local people after several had been killed in a skirmish with the Dutch in 1722. The first reports on

PATRICK C. McCOY

Easter Island culture therefore are rather superficial and incomplete. The paucity of ethnohistoric and ethnographic data for Easter Island is particularly lamentable because of its rich archaeological heritage and the largely unique prehistoric developments that characterize this easternmost island in Polynesia.

A critical assessment of the popular works of Heyerdahl and others is outside the scope of this chapter, which aims instead at presenting a broad overview of what is currently known or suggested in the large corpus of data on Easter Island cultural development. The emphasis is on articulating the geographic and ecological factors that influenced the course of local prehistory, and the degree to which it is notably divergent from the culture histories of other East Polynesian islands.

Easter Island Field Archaeology

Despite its remote geographic location, and the consequent logistic difficulties in organizing expeditions until regular air service was instituted in 1967, Easter Island has a long history of archaeological research that dates back to the latter part of the nineteenth century. From its inception in 1886, local archaeology understandably has focused on the investigation of statues and ceremonial centers, since these are both the most impressive and the most intriguing remains. In this respect the orientation of Easter Island archaeology parallels the historical development of archaeology in most of East Polynesia and other areas of the world where monumental structures exist.

The earliest archaeological work on Easter Island was fundamentally descriptive; as elsewhere in Polynesia, it involved the simultaneous collection of ethnologic materials and ethnographic data. Until recently, most of the archaeology on the island has been undertaken with the primary aim of developing a culture-historical outline of local prehistory. Two primary research biases are evident: a pioneering concern for knowledge of time depth, with a resultant emphasis on chronology and formulation of a cultural sequence; and a strong interest in determining cultural origins and non-Polynesian affinities, if any. In the period since 1960, a number of ceremonial centers and associated domestic structures have been restored, providing new data to evaluate a previously accepted three-period sequence. Beginning in 1968, a series of investigations has been directed at the collection of data to develop models of settlement and subsistence patterns. This research reflects a broader interest in the processes of cultural adaptation and culture change.

The first archaeological investigations in 1886, carried out by Thomson and Cooke of the U.S.S. *Mohican*, comprised a quick reconnaissance survey plus more detailed recording of a great number of ahu and the ceremonial center of Orongo in the southwestern corner of the island (Thomson 1891; Cooke 1899). A privately funded British expedition under the direction of Routledge spent 17 months on the island in 1914–1915, during which she and her associates made important studies of the statue quarry at Rano Raraku, of ahu and other architectural features, and of Orongo Village. Although the complete results of this work were never published before Routledge's death and the expedition's field notes were subsequently lost, she did publish several short journal articles and an informative book.

The next important contribution to Easter Island archaeology was made by a joint Franco-Belgian expedition in 1934–1935. Lavachery (1935, 1936) made a survey of selected sites and undertook an exhaustive study of petroglyphs and pictographs, which resulted in a two-volume work (Lavachery 1939) that is still the best statement on rock art. Metraux, the expedition ethnographer, also collected archaeological data; these are presented in several short papers and in his monumental volume, *Ethnology of Easter Island*.

A year after the departure of the Franco-Belgian expedition, a Capuchin priest, Father Englert, arrived on the island and until his death in 1969 devoted a considerable part of his nonclerical life to the study of Easter Island language and culture, including prehistory. He made the first complete survey of ahu which was published along with other valuable ethnographic and linguistic data (Englert 1948, 1970).

The advent of modern scientific archaeology on Easter Island and other areas of East Polynesia is marked by the 1955–1956 Norwegian expedition organized by Heyerdahl. He assembled an international group of archaeologists which, in a six-month period, carried out systematic reconnaissance surveys and excavations of ahu, the statue quarry, Orongo Village, houses, habitation caves, the site of an alleged battle between two warring groups (the "Long Ears" and the "Short Ears") and several other features. The excavations produced the first radiocarbon dates for the island and the first obsidian-hydration age determinations in the Pacific. On the basis of the ahu excavations a provisional three-period sequence was established, which provided for the first time an integrated culture-historical framework.

The interest in ahu has continued, beginning with the first of a series of excavations and restorations in 1960 directed by Mulloy (Mulloy 1968, 1970, 1973, 1975a and b; Ayres 1971, 1973; Mulloy and Figueroa 1978). The first stage of a proposed island-wide intensive site survey was initiated in 1968 (McCoy 1973, 1976a). Excavations of habitation sites were conducted in 1968 (McCoy 1973) and again in 1973 (Ayres 1975).

Biogeoclimatic Background Information

Geology, Soils, and Hydrology

Easter Island is a composite of three Pliocene- to Holocene-age volcanic centers, not the remnant of a sunken continent as earlier suggested (Brown 1924). Because of its volcanic origin it is classified as a "high"

island, but it attains a maximum elevation of only 510 m above sea level (Fig. 6.1). Poike, a strato-volcano forming the east headland of the island, is the oldest of the three centers, with a potassium-argon date of 3 million years on lavas near the base of sea cliffs on its north side (Baker et al. 1974). Rano Kau is an intermediate-age (1 million ± years) strato-volcano on the southwest side (Isaacson and Heinrichs 1976). Its center is a large collapsed caldera with an impounded freshwater lake at the bottom (Fig. 6.2). Most of the island's mass was formed by Maunga Terevaka, a complex fissure-volcano, and its approximately 70 eruptive centers. Lavas at the base of sea cliffs on the north flank of Maunga Terevaka have been dated at 300,000 years (Baker et al. 1974). On present evidence volcanic activity ceased prior to human settlement of the island. There is no mention of volcanism in local folklore, and radiometric age determinations of about 2,000 years for the most recent lava flows on the west coast predate settlement by at least 500 years (Baker 1967).

The Easter Island landscape has a distinctive rolling, hilly appearance that results from the large number of eruptive centers. Most of these are cinder, ash, and scoria cones such as Puna Pau, where topknots for ahu images were made of a welded red scoria. A notable exception is the tuff cone of Rano Raraku, the site of the statue quarry. Obsidian, another economically important rock type, is found on the southwestern corner of the island, occurring in the largest quantity on Maunga Orito.

The flanks of many hills (*maunga*) and intervening lava plains are characteristically stony, with loose rocks covering as much as 80 to 95 percent of the surface in some localities. In clearer areas such as Poike, where the stone cover is reduced to less than 10 or 15 percent, soils are deep and of finer texture. Easter Island soils are predominantly loams and clays developed from volcanic parent materials that are mostly basalts and differentiated andesitic

PATRICK C. McCOY

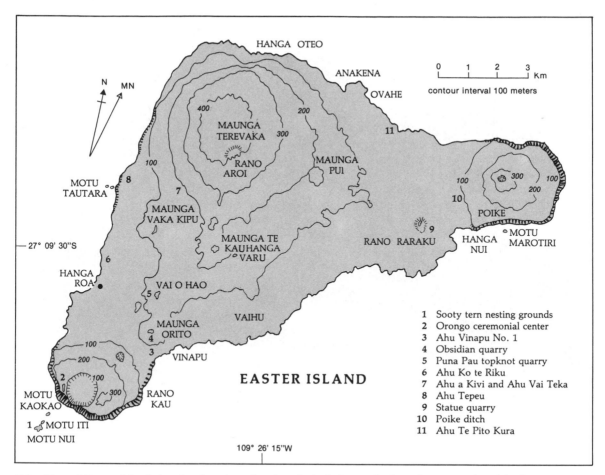

6.1 *Map of Easter Island showing location of archaeological sites and other places mentioned in the text.*

rocks. Leaching is common because of relatively rapid chemical weathering that results from high temperature and humidity. Elevated soil temperatures account in part for a high evaporation rate (Wright and Diaz 1962).

The net effect of rapid evaporation and porous soils is a poorly developed drainage system with no perennial streams. There is one intermittent stream originating on the south flank of Maunga Terevaka that flows toward the sea during heavy rains. The most reliable sources of fresh water are the lakes inside Rano Aroi, Rano Raraku, and Rano Kau. Groups in former times that inhabited lands away from these lakes were dependent on brackish-water springs and

pools located inside lava tubes. The problem of obtaining sufficient drinking water is reflected in the development of pecked-stone catchment basins called *taheta*.

Climate

Easter Island is at the southern, poleward limit of the tropics, and the climate consequently is subtropical to temperate. The average annual temperature is about 22° C. Summer and winter temperatures are more variable than in the islands of the central Pacific. Rainfall is moderate, with the average between 1,250 and 1,500 mm per annum; however, the amount can vary considerably from the norm. Southeast trade

6.2 *Partial view of the collapsed caldera of Rano Kau, taken from the southern end of Orongo Village. The impounded, largely reed-covered freshwater lake at the bottom is 300 m below the rim. (Bishop Museum photo.)*

winds blow fairly constantly from October to April, and there are but few days in the year when there is no wind at all.

Fauna and Flora

The extreme geographic isolation of Easter Island is reflected in a markedly impoverished biota. There are no indigenous land mammals, few insects, and the only reptiles present are two species of small lizards. A fair variety of migratory seabirds has been recorded (Metraux 1940), but their numbers have dwindled in recent times with the result that they are no longer of much economic importance. Marine mammals and turtles appear never to have been especially abundant in the waters around Easter Island, to judge from the small amount of

bone found in archaeological sites. The fish fauna are likewise impoverished by Oceanic standards, with only 109 species identified at present (Randall 1970). There is no coral reef, so that the marine invertebrate fauna are highly restricted in variety and population size.

Fauna introduced prior to European contact were limited to the Polynesian rat (*Rattus exulans*) and the chicken (*Gallus gallus*). If the dog and pig were successfully carried to the island in voyaging canoes, they did not survive long; their remains have not been recovered in archaeological deposits. The absence of dogs and pigs and the restricted marine fauna had an important bearing on the economy. One of the effects was an unusual dependence on chickens for food and for gift exchange.

PATRICK C. McCOY

While the pauperization of the modern Easter Island flora has invited many comments, there is no better general characterization than that of Skottsberg (1928:489): "There does not exist another island of the size of Easter Island and with such a fine climate where the native flora is so poor." Skottsberg, who carried out the most detailed botanical survey ever made on the island, was able to record no more than 30 species that could be regarded as indigenous. However, he was led to believe in the former existence of "a kind of savanna forest, a parklike formation with scattered, stunted *Sophora* trees and a grass cover" (Skottsberg 1928:492) because of the wide-ranging uses of the now extinct *Sophora* tree (*toromiro*).

Pollen samples, collected by the Norwegian expedition and partially analyzed by Selling, confirm Skottsberg's suspicion of a former forest. Heyerdahl (1965, 1976) has reported the occurrence of a now extinct palm, referred to by Selling as the genus *Pritchardia*, a conifer (*Ephedra* sp.), and has noted evidence for a greater abundance of woody plants in the past. In addition, he has described the presence of sooty particles (presumably charcoal flecks) together with introduced plant pollens, which he interprets as evidence of early forest clearance for agricultural purposes. Root molds in some archaeological excavations lend credence to a denser vegetative cover in the past (see Heyerdahl 1961).

Culture in the Ethnographic Present

A brief sketch of Easter Island culture in the ethnographic present is presented for the dual purposes of providing a general, but integrative overview of the traditional culture; and of characterizing conditions as they existed at the end of the prehistoric period. It was an era distinguished by social disintegration and general cultural decadence. The probable cause of decadence and the evidence of early-contact-period culture change are discussed later in the chapter. For historical reasons already noted, including the disruptive effects of cultural instability in the ethnographic present, some aspects of the traditional culture are poorly known. However, some valuable material does exist; it is reviewed below.

The markedly stratified Easter Island society consisted in a series of internally ranked, segmentary unilineal kin groups that traced descent to a common ancestor. The lowest in the hierarchy of ranked levels or ramages was the household—a patrilocal extended family (*ivi* or *paenga*), probably headed by the senior male. The household owned land in common and its members constituted a task unit that cultivated its garden plots. Closely related households formed lineages (*ure*), each of which apparently had its own ceremonial center (ahu) where deceased kin were buried. The major social unit was the *mata* (translated by Metraux as "tribe," but regarded by others as equivalent to a clan), which developed by the same process of segmentation or fissioning.

By the ethnographic present there were 10 mata whose members no longer occupied socially discrete territories as in earlier times, but instead were dispersed within one of two districts, referred to in the literature as western (Tuu) and eastern (Hotu Iti). The development of this dualism can be attributed to the formation of tribal alliances prompted by warfare, which on traditional evidence was internecine conflict between high- and low-ranking mata (Goldman 1970).

An apparent result of warfare, and sign of political instability, was the ascendancy of powerful warriors (*matatoa*) to positions of secular authority. Some of them assumed temporary sanctity of office as well (Metraux 1940; Goldman 1970). In the end there was a dual status system at the highest level of Easter Island society: one based on stable, inherited position; the other temporary and dependent on military supremacy—similar to that of Mangaia in the

Cook Islands. Chiefs of plebeian tribes had become the secular rulers of the island, but the source of the paramount priest-chief (*ariki-mau*) was still in one aristocratic tribe, the Miru.

Information on social classes is sketchy, but there were at least two basic status grades: chiefs (*ariki*) and commoners (*huru-manu*). Metraux (1940) also included in his list of classes: (1) priests (*ivi-atua*); (2) warriors (*matatoa*); (3) servants or farmers (*kio*); and (4) occupational specialists known by the terms *maori* or *tohunga*. Kio have been described as "defeated people who were obliged to serve their conquerors or to pay tribute to them with the produce of their lands" (Metraux 1940:139).

The Easter Island economy was diversified in the same general way as all Polynesian economies, with a dependence on agriculture, exploitation of marine resources, animal husbandry, and—to a lesser degree—naturally occurring food sources such as seabirds and wild plants. Agriculture was the most dependable source of food, but the variety of root and tree crops was more restricted than in other islands of East Polynesia. The staple was sweet potatoes (*kumara*). Taro, yams, bananas, and sugarcane were the other principal cultigens. Shellfish gathering contributed little food, and by the beginning of the eighteenth century there must have been a reduction in the amount of fish consumed, owing to the fact that there were few canoes. Decreased fish yields appear to have stimulated an increased level of production of domestic fowl. Food shortages are reflected in the emergence of cannibalism, to which there are numerous references in traditions on warfare.

An overlapping stewardship in the tenure of land and sea resources involved both tribal chiefs and the paramount religious leader, who had supreme powers over agricultural production and fishing. Harvests and fishing were regulated by tabus and involved first-fruits rites. Little is known of economic redistribution and reciprocity, except that the nobility were the focal points of accumulation. Redistribution of food frequently resulted in bitter feuds and a new cycle of wars because of assertions of inequitable gifts.

One of the clearest signs of decadence in the ethnographic present is the purposeful destruction of religious structures. Ahu images were toppled from their platforms, and many ahu were reduced to rubble piles that continued to function only as burial depositories. Others were abandoned altogether. The earlier cessation of statue carving and overthrow of images representing deceased chiefs must have had a serious effect on the traditional system of ancestor worship. As a result of these internal depredations and the later Peruvian slave raids, little is known about Easter Island religion, although we are aware of certain of its peculiarities, including the lesser importance of the great gods and mythological heroes of other Polynesian religions. The greatest god of Easter Island was Make-make, who was venerated in an annual feast of the birdman (*tangata manu*), a ceremony through which the secular chiefs could attain temporary sanctity of office. Supernatural spirits, both good and evil, were called *aku-aku*.

At the time of first European contact in the early eighteenth century, the population of Easter Island probably did not exceed 3,000—and may in fact have been considerably lower. The earliest ethnohistoric accounts describe small, dispersed coastal settlements of low, elliptical-shaped thatched houses inland of ceremonial centers. Chiefs and higher ranking individuals occupied the houses nearest the ahu, while commoners were dispersed farther inland in and around agricultural plantations.

Cultural Origins

No single aspect of Easter Island prehistory has generated more theories and controversy than cultural origins. Debate has centered on the probable source of such seemingly non-Polynesian traits as the rongorongo script and the stylistically unique stone statues. Diffusionists have favored the interpretation of dual origin from separate cultural traditions. Other scholars, such as Metraux (1940), have advocated a unitary origin in East Polynesia, whereby the aberrant features of Easter Island culture are explained as local adaptations or the result of independent invention.

Heyerdahl's theory of Easter Island settlement is the best known of various composite culture hypotheses and the only one that is in any sense still viable. Briefly, he has argued for first settlement by people from the Andean area of South America, followed by a late Polynesian migration. His theory has met with considerable criticism, but it is one that merits discussion, particularly in view of the fact that a New World contact cannot be categorically dismissed. Most Polynesian archaeologists are open to such a possibility, but strongly disagree with Heyerdahl in its temporal precedence over Polynesian colonization and relative influence on local cultural development.

Easter Island is one of two focal points in Heyerdahl's broader view on Polynesian origins (1941, 1952). He proposed that the first movements into Polynesia were from the east, from the Americas, rather than through Micronesia and Melanesia as was the widely accepted view at the time. Heyerdahl argued that: (1) Easter Island had been settled by a group of maritime Tiahuanaco people from the Peruvian coast in approximately A.D. 500; (2) a forced migration from North America of Kwakiutl Indians from the Northwest Coast had resulted in colonization of the Hawaiian Islands in about A.D. 1100; and (3) in the later settlement of other islands, the Amerindians were met by a dark-skinned people known as *Menehune*. Extensive research has failed to produce any supporting evidence for the latter two points, and they have been largely forgotten.

Heyerdahl considered a variety of evidence in formulating his Easter Island settlement theory: linguistic data, physical characteristics, plant species distributions, masonry styles and techniques, and stone image styles. Though substantially different from earlier applications of the comparative method that evaluated a single trait or several unrelated ones, Heyerdahl's approach is nevertheless bothersome in the highly selective choice of data in a theory far too involved to allow a comprehensive review of every detail. He has repeatedly emphasized (1968a and b) a certain few key elements of fundamental importance to his claim for a strong South American cultural affinity:

(1) The linguistic aspect of Heyerdahl's theory is based on studies of: (a) lexical terms for the numerals 1 to 10 collected by a Spanish expedition in 1770; (b) the Easter Island term for sweet potato (*kumara*); (c) the rongorongo script; and (d) selected place names. The derivation of the pan-Polynesian term for sweet potato (the protoform is *kuumala*) from Quechua *cumar* has been widely accepted by scholars, and it may come as a surprise that the word *cumar* "is not a Quechua word; and the word *cumar* never was used for sweet potato anywhere along the coast of South America" (Brand 1971:361). There are, in fact, no known precontact borrow words in the Easter Island language (commonly referred to as Rapanui).

(2) Heyerdahl has cited botanical evidence for New World contact in the human introduction of numerous American plant species: the sweet potato (*Ipomoea batatas*); the bulrush (*Scirpus riparius*), also referred to in the literature as *Scirpus totora; Polygonum acuminatum*; an economically important tree *Sophora toromiro*; the chili pepper (*Capsicum* sp.); cotton (*Gossypium*); the bottle gourd (*Lagenaria siceraria*); and several others (Heyerdahl 1961a). The pre-European occurrence of some, such as the chili pepper, is doubtful, while questions remain about the agent of dispersal for others. For lack of space, further remarks are limited to the two species of central importance to Heyerdahl's ethnobotanical argument—the sweet potato and the bulrush reed commonly called *totora*.

The sweet potato has long been accepted as a New World plant, but that it was first introduced to Easter Island as argued by Heyerdahl (1961a) is doubtful. On linguistic evidence alone it is more probable that the sweet potato was carried to central East Polynesia between the third and eighth centuries A.D., and from there was widely dispersed (see Yen 1971, 1974). There are even more compelling reasons for questioning the claim for a South American source of the Easter Island bulrush. First, there is the possibility that the seeds of *Scirpus* were carried to the island on the feet of migratory seabirds (Heiser 1974), in which case it is unnecessary to think in terms of a human agent alone. Secondly, the Easter Island and Andean species of *Scirpus* are not identical, as Heyerdahl has assumed (Heiser 1974), nor is the distribution of this plant limited to Easter Island and South America (Heyerdahl 1966). Emory (1972) has presented linguistic evidence to the contrary, which also demonstrates that Easter Island must have been settled before the migration to Hawaii.

(3) An important part of Heyerdahl's composite culture theory, one that derives from a comparative study of Easter Island house types by Ferdon (1961b), is the idea that there were two building traditions on the island—one Polynesian, the other most probably of South American origin. The "Short Ears" (Polynesians), presumed to have inhabited the western part of the island, purportedly were the architects of pole and thatch houses, while the "Long Ears" (South American Indians), supposedly living on the eastern end, were credited with the introduction of a sophisticated stone technology, manifested in thick-walled masonry houses, corbeled-roof houses, ahu walls, and statues. Elsewhere I have suggested that corbeled-roof houses are a local invention stimulated by the availability of a particularly amenable form of raw material (flat, thin basalt slabs), and furthermore that the appearance of thick-walled masonry houses reflects an adaptation to increasing scarcity of materials for continued construction of traditional pole and thatch structures.

The general similarities between dressed stone masonry in some Easter Island ahu and structures in the Andean highlands at localities such as Cuzco add considerable strength to Heyerdahl's thesis of a South American contact. The problem is in Heyerdahl's insistence on an early date for this masonry on Easter Island. In reviewing the possibility of a South American source, Lanning (1970:175) has noted: "Mortarless polygonal-block masonry on Easter Island and in Cuzco would be meaningful only if the Polynesian case could be shown to date after A.D. 1440, when the technique had its inception in Peru." The earliest available date for an ahu with dressed stonework is about A.D. 1200. While it more closely approximates the Peruvian dating, it also allows time for the in situ development of this technique, which is unevenly distributed elsewhere in East Polynesia and nowhere common.

This abbreviated review of Heyerdahl's composite culture hypothesis has disclosed serious objections and widespread skepticism, which in large part derive from "the subjective nature of the comparisons due to lack of attention to problems of dating and distribution" (Lanning 1970:175; see also Meggers 1963; Green 1967). While there is no conclusive proof for any part of Heyerdahl's theory, this does not negate the chance of a South American contact. It would appear to be a remote possibility, however, for a further reason that has not been addressed: wind and current patterns. As Heyerdahl's own Kon-Tiki raft voyage demonstrated, the most likely landfall from the east in Polynesia would be the Tuamotu Archipelago or the Marquesas. Heyerdahl nonetheless has had a positive effect on the growth of Polynesian archaeology. His theory has prompted careful review of earlier assumptions and has generated new research.

It remains to summarize the more widely accepted view of Easter Island cultural origins. Local settlement traditions relate the arrival of the first chief, Hotu Matu'a, from a place called Marae Renga or Marae Toe Hau. There are numerous versions of this legend, which differ in details but are in agreement on one important point: that Hotu Matu'a was preceded by an advance party of six men who planted yams on Rano Kau. The names for the homeland and the reference to a Polynesian cultigen are undeniable evidence for an East Polynesian source of the Easter Island population. The agreement between glottochronological and radiocarbon dates places the settlement of the island at A.D. 400 to 500. Supporting evidence for early colonization by an as yet largely undifferentiated Archaic East Polynesian population includes: (1) the retention of an Archaic linguistic trait (see Chapter 10); (2) the presence of early East Polynesian adz forms; and (3) the absence of certain widespread material items known to be of somewhat later origin than A.D. 500 in the primary dispersal centers of East Polynesia.

Settlement and Subsistence Patterns

Substantive data on Easter Island settlement and subsistence patterns are limited to the period postdating A.D. 1500; few habitation sites of an earlier age have been located. Excavations in the Anakena area on the north coast have not been successful in confirming the existence of an early beach site described in settlement legends. On present evidence the earliest population centers were located in the southwestern corner of the island, but dates comparable to or earlier than those for the first phases of ahu construction at Tahai (A.D. 690 ± 130) and Vinapu (A.D. 857 ± 200) can be expected in the future for other coastal areas. Late prehistoric-protohistoric settlement and subsistence patterns appear to reflect adaptations to environmental change and should not be regarded as fully representative of earlier patterns, particularly at the household level of organization.

The late prehistoric-protohistoric house-hold settlement pattern is characterized by normally small groupings of two or three sleeping houses, probably occupied by closely related extended families. On the bases of ethnohistoric descriptions and archaeological evidence, the commonest house type in the period after A.D. 1500 was a low, elliptical-shaped thatched structure generally less than 2 m wide and 15 m long (Fig. 6.3). Class distinctions in this house form are recognized on the basis of differences in the foundation and exterior pavement bordering the front of the house (Metraux 1940; McCoy 1976b). The dwellings of high-ranking individuals, known as *hare paenga,* are distinguished by dressed curbstone foundations for the insertion of poles to form the suprastructure, and by well-made, crescent-shaped pavements of selected waterworn beach cobbles or boulders. Commoners' residences lack stone foundations, and the pavements are both smaller and different in the use of angular lava rock.

In addition to the elliptical shape, circular and rectangular forms have been recorded, all of which have parallels in East Polynesia. The round house, called *hare oka,* was a temporary dwelling. The oldest dated house (to our knowledge) on the island is a rectangular structure on the east rim of Rano Kau with a single radiocarbon date of A.D. 770 ± 230 years (McCoy 1973). There are several distinctive varieties of stone houses: (1) low-walled enclosures, generally oval to round in shape; (2) elliptical to subrectangular corbeled-roof structures at Orongo Village (Fig. 6.4); and (3) a small number of unevenly distributed thick-walled, tower-like structures called *tupa* (Fig. 6.5).

In close proximity to the sleeping house and almost universally located on the front, seaward side are one or more of the following features: a cooking oven (*umu*), garden enclosures (*manavai*), and/or stone chicken houses (*hare moa*). Spatial analysis indicates that all of these features, if present, are generally within 20 m of the house. One variety of Easter Island earth oven, called

6.3 The curbstone foundation of a house type called hare paenga, *occupied by nobility. (Bishop Museum photo.)*

an *umu pae*, was stone-lined with the rim projecting above the ground. A detailed analysis of such ovens, where the form was determinable, indicates the popularity of three geometric shapes—pentagonal, rectangular, and circular—which on current dating are contemporary forms in the late part of the cultural sequence. No consistent relationship between oven form and social class is indicated (McCoy 1978a). The infrequent remains of cookhouses reveal an apparently standardized circular thatched structure that averaged about 4 m in diameter at the base.

The garden enclosures are of two varieties: (1) free-standing masonry-walled structures of varied form and breadth, but averaging 1 to 1.5 m in height; and (2) excavated pits of oval to circular shape averaging about 4 m in diameter and 1 to 1.5 m deep. They functioned to retain

moisture, block out wind, and shade the leaves of plants (such as the paper mulberry) from the sun. The hare moa is a peculiarly Easter Island innovation designed to protect fowl from nighttime raids. It is a low, subrectangular or occasionally circular, thick-walled stone structure with a ground-level entry and central chamber (Ferdon 1961c; McCoy 1976b).

Easter Island settlements conform to Chang's description (1972:16) of a "self-contained village" in the presence of components within which are found "varying kinds of complementary activities that indicate a self-contained cycle of subsistence on a year round basis." The components include: (1) small dispersed clusters of commoners' residences adjacent to or within agricultural plantations; (2) further seaward, a community center usually composed of one large feast house and the

146

6.4 *The entrance to a corbeled-roof house at the ceremonial center of Orongo, before restoration. (Photo by author.)*

6.5 *A stone-walled dwelling called a* tupa; *the entrance is at ground level immediately to the left of the tower-like section. (Bishop Museum photo.)*

surrounding dwellings of nobility in a nucleated pattern; and (3) well removed from these, the lineage ahu (McCoy 1976b).

There is no recognizably consistent plan in the layout of the three components. The amorphous character of settlements and the differential degree of clustering between components is typical of the general Polynesian settlement pattern:

The most common internal patterning in Polynesia ranges from dispersed to loosely clustered, though largely unplanned settlements which are organized in relation to the localized kin-group ownership of land. Thus it was only at the communal or political level, where the residence of a principal chief or a community complex of religious structures provided a focus, that any tendency towards nucleation appeared and only occasionally was the clustering transformed into permanently occupied and formally planned villages (Green 1970:32).

Further research is required to establish the time depth of this community-level pattern, which is presently unknown.

Examination of the broad distribution of sites in the southwestern corner of the island (the only area for which there are detailed data) reveals important differences in land utilization patterns and settlement density. A large area, comprising almost all of Rano Kau except for the lower flank at Vinapu, appears to have been largely abandoned as a site for permanent occupation in later times. Dense agglomerations of sites around the rim of Rano Kau are primarily temporary habitations occupied seasonally during the bird cult ceremonies that took place at Orongo. These sites have been labeled camps on the basis of characteristics that indicate short-term occupation (McCoy 1976b). Other sites provisionally considered to be camps for similar reasons are located at the primary source of obsidian on Maunga Orito.

A site density analysis for a segment of the southeast coast revealed a sharp decrease in the number of sites between 1 and 1.5 km back of the shoreline. This band would appear to mark the boundary between preferred and marginal habitation zones. Population aggregation on the coast was hypothesized to have been determined by the availability of fresh water and access to marine resources (McCoy 1976b).

Apart from general data on the spatial distribution of household garden enclosures and chicken houses for the southwestern corner of the island (McCoy 1976b), there is relatively little information on prehistoric subsistence. Easter Island agricultural fields were not walled and were only occasionally demarcated by a single course of stones around the perimeter. Field systems thus are not readily recognizable on the ground and no effort has yet been made to identify them from aerial photographs. The one notable exception to poor archaeological visibility of plantations is a complex of terraced gardens on the steep interior slopes of Rano Kau volcano (Ferdon 1961d; McCoy 1976b). Ferdon's investigation of one of the several Rano Kau terrace systems constitutes the only research of prehistoric agriculture to date. The sadly inadequate data on dietary patterns and marine resource exploitation are being supplemented by current midden analyses of a number of recently excavated habitation sites.

Portable Artifacts

Easter Island portable artifacts on the whole are similar to most other East Polynesian high-island assemblages in the range of functional classes present. This is not surprising because of a historical continuity in exploitative technologies and crafts. Yet there is a predictable degree of variability in Easter Island assemblages because of long-term development in isolation, and adaptation to local conditions such as the scarcity of certain raw materials. For example, there are relatively few tools made of shell. The adaptive response in this case is an elaborated stone tool industry, the commonest and most diversified examples of which are obsidian flake tools.

Apart from rather detailed studies of adzes, fishhooks, and one specialized obsidian implement, data on Easter Island artifacts are extremely poor. There is little information, for example, on assemblage variability in time and space, or flake tool manufacture and use. In large part this is a result of the disproportionate amount of attention given to the investigation of ahu. The collections from ahu are primarily surface finds, which lack a precise temporal context. The same problem is encountered in relating subsurface artifacts in ahu to a time-stratigraphic unit, because they most often occur in the fill of walls or in cremation pits (*avanga*) used over an extended period, which means that they could be earlier than the context in which they are found.

The best known class of tools, and the one showing the most detailed similarities to Archaic East Polynesian assemblages, is that of stone adzes. Easter Island adzes are distinctive in the absence of the tang, although a few of one type exhibit a functionally analogous groove on the butt end. An analysis of 675 Easter Island adzes has shown considerable diversity in types (described in terms of the cross section at the midpoint of untanged adzes), but a high frequency of only two forms. In this sample 310, or 45.9 percent, were described as "quadrangular or irregular in cross-section with the front always wider than the back." The only other common type (24.9 percent) is described as "thick with cross-sections basically varying to trapezoidal and rectangular and obscured by markedly convex sides which result in apparent oblate ovoid, oblate circular, or oblate elliptical contours" (Figueroa and Sanchez 1965:171–172). Other distinctive characteristics of the Easter Island adz complex are the fairly common occurrence of specimens made of obsidian, and examples in basalt with a double bevel. According to established definitions, these double-bitted forms should be reclassified as axes.

Easter Island fishhooks include one-piece and two-piece forms, the former being made of both bone (human) and stone (Fig. 6.6). One-piece hooks are of the "jabbing"

and "rotating" types, occasionally with barbs on the shank (Emory et al. 1959). Head forms are variable. Stone hooks would appear to be a local innovation, although counterparts are known from Pitcairn and the Chatham Islands. On present evidence two-piece hooks are limited to the geographically marginal islands of East Polynesia: New Zealand, Hawaii, and Easter. Fishhook manufacturing tools consist of coral abraders and files and perhaps obsidian drills.

The only other commonly made bone artifact found on Easter Island is an eyed needle normally manufactured from a split long bone of chicken or seabird. Its inferred use was in sewing together strips of tapa cloth—a method apparently unique to Easter Island. Less common are simple bone pendants with one or two perforations.

The bulk of the stone artifacts found in surface and buried contexts are amorphous obsidian flake tools and cores of varied form, including recently reported percussion blades and blade cores (McCoy 1976a). Occasional cores show edge damage suggestive of use as scrapers, but the majority appear to be nonutilized by-products of flake removal. The variable edge properties of flake tools indicate use in both scraping and cutting. While most flake tools tend to be amorphous (McCoy 1973), there is a considerably higher frequency of patterned forms on Easter Island than is true of other Polynesian assemblages with the possible exception of New Zealand. There are items that resemble gravers, perforators or drills, some scrapers, and a tanged or stemmed, broad-faced "blade" called a *mata'a*.

The mata'a is an item of considerable importance in local archaeology because of its presumed social context as an implement of war and its late appearance in the cultural sequence. At present it is the only artifact type that can be used as a "horizon marker." The mata'a seems to have appeared after A.D. 1600 in a period coinciding with prolonged internal strife between kin groups. Native testimony on the use of the mata'a and ethnographic specimens are

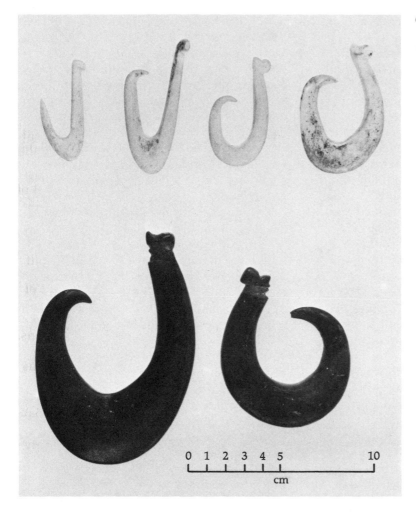

6.6 *Bone* (above) *and stone* (below) *one-piece fishhooks.* (*Bishop Museum photo.*)

clear in establishing its primary function as a spearpoint hafted to a wooden shaft of variable length—but variability in the shape of the distal edges opposite the tang raises the question of multiple use (Fig. 6.7). It is difficult to believe that the sharp, thin edges of the mata'a would not have been utilized as knives, if only infrequently. A recent, preliminary examination of the flake scars on some mata'a and obsidian drills suggests the possibility that pressure flaking was employed in the final stage of manufacture.

Other objects made of stone include hammer stones, pecking stones, digging tools, files, small round disks of obsidian inserted into the eye sockets of wooden images, stone pillows, grinding slabs, slingstones, and crescent-shaped, edge-ground knives. The latter, resembling the Eskimo *ulu*, are unevenly distributed in Polynesia. Stone pillows are elongated, waterworn beach boulders. The absence of wooden headrests suggests that the stones are a late adaptation to the scarcity of wood. Slingstones are curiously rare despite the prevalence of warfare. Notably lacking or rare on Easter Island are stone food pounders, common to East Polynesia (the other important exception being New Zealand). Several fragments have been found on Easter Island in surface contexts, but these may be historic introductions from Tahiti or elsewhere.

PATRICK C. McCOY

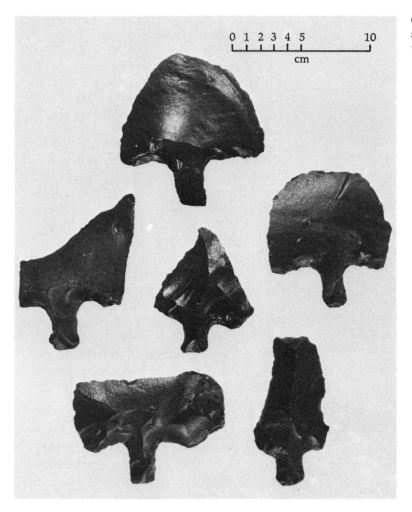

6.7 *Common forms of obsidian spearpoints (mata'a). Note the variability in the edge shapes. (Bishop Museum photo.)*

Religious Efflorescence: Art and Architectural Expression

The archaeological landscape of Easter Island is testimony to an unusual preoccupation with religion and ancestor worship, which was productive of some of the most stylized and technologically advanced forms of megalithic art and architecture in Polynesia. A building and carving compulsion for religious purposes is manifested in ahu, statues, and the houses and petroglyphs at Orongo Village.

Various explanations have been given for the efflorescence of religious activity on Easter Island, including "the desire for display" and "tribal pride and competitive instinct" (Metraux 1940:307). There is no reason to doubt these motives, but they do not explain the localized elaboration of statue carving, since all three qualities are cultural constants in Polynesia. Sahlins (1955:1051) formulated an alternative hypothesis for the development of Easter Island stone imagery, based on an assessment of local environmental constraints:

Environmental features . . . precluded the use of communal and specialist labor in subsistence production. As a result, these efforts were channeled into an esoteric domain of culture. Perhaps facilitated by a tradition of carving, a limited amount of wood and the availability of easily worked tuff, the canalization toward esoteric production took the particular direction that resulted in the renowned stone heads of Easter Island.

There are various interpretations of the significance of the Easter Island statues (Skjölsvold 1961), but the most popular view is that they represent chiefs and, perhaps, other deceased individuals of high rank. Members of Captain Cook's party in 1774 heard the term *ariki* applied to some images, from which they concluded that they were "monuments erected to the memory of some areekees, or kings" (Forster 1777:375). The images were given names, such as "Twisted Neck," "Tattooed One," and "Stinker"—which is grounds for rejecting the belief that they were representations of gods.

Most of the more than 600 statues on the island are a single stylistic form carved at the quarries on Rano Raraku of a consolidated lapilli tuff (Fig. 6.8). The highly conventionalized Easter Island image is best described by Mulloy (1970:5):

The classic form is that of a usually male human figure from the hips upward with arms held stiffly at the sides and hands turned unnaturally toward each other. The lower belly protrudes greatly and has a convex profile. Above the navel the belly recedes in a concave profile which continues over the chest. The head is an elongated rectangle with a slightly concave nose and compressed lips. Ear lobes are carved to appear perforated and extended to hang far down the sides of the face. The backs of some statues bear detailed designs which appear to represent tattooing.

Finished statues on ahu vary from 2 to 9.8 m in height, with the average estimated at about 6 m. The largest one (called *Paro*) at Ahu Te Pito Kura has an estimated weight of 82 metric tons (Smith 1961a). It appears that images became more stylized and progressively larger through time. There is also evidence that the statues farthest from the quarries are consistently smaller, suggesting an atemporal relationship between size and transport distance.

The earliest available date for the classic image of Rano Raraku tuff is A.D. 1110 to 1205 from Ahu Ko te Riku on the west coast, just north of Hanga Roa (Mulloy and Figueroa 1978). The height of this statue (5.2 m) suggests an early limiting date of perhaps A.D. 900 for the appearance of the model form, assuming that the first statues were indeed smaller. Even earlier dates have been postulated for aberrant forms, which are few in number and generally made of other materials, such as basalt and scoria. They tend to be smaller than the stylized image and less well made. An exception is a unique kneeling statue uncovered on the exterior slope at Rano Raraku (Skjölsvold 1961). This and other aberrant statues generally have more rounded heads and lack the extended earlobes of the classic form. They bear some similarity to stone statuary from the Marquesas, Pitcairn, and Raivavae in the Austral Islands, but according to Heyerdahl (1952, 1961a) there is a greater degree of resemblance to South American stone imagery, especially that of Tiahuanaco.

There are few archaeological locales in the world more impressive than Rano Raraku, an isolated tuff cone with a small summit lake 150 m above a grass-covered plain. The eastern and southern sides are steep rock faces cut by marine erosion and further reduced by image-carving specialists over a period of perhaps 800 years. Quarrying was not limited to the exterior slopes, but took place also on the southern interior rim of the cone. A total of 299 statues in various stages of completion has been recorded in the immediate environs of Rano Raraku; more can be expected.

The unfinished quarry statues are as varied in size as those on ahu, although several are considerably larger than any that were ever transported to a ceremonial center. One essentially finished statue that stands vertically on the exterior south flank has a height of 11.4 m, while the outline of another higher up in the quarry measures 20.9 m and has an estimated weight of 300 tons (Skjölsvold 1961). It is doubtful that it could ever have been successfully moved and erected on an ahu platform.

PATRICK C. McCOY

6.8 *Partially buried images on the southern exterior slope of the statue quarry at Rano Raraku. (Bishop Museum photo.)*

The presence of about 70 standing statues on the lower slopes of both the exterior and interior quarries has puzzled observers for some time. Metraux (1940) considered them to be different from ahu images, from which he concluded that the standing quarry images were never intended to be placed on ahu. Detailed observations on the processes and stages of manufacture evident in the quarries led Skjölsvold and others to conclude that the statues had been set up vertically to finish carving the backs. It was reasoned that the desired profile could not have been achieved until the image was erect, since the back was the last area to be freed from the bedrock. There is one important difference between quarry and ahu images—the former lack eyes, indicating that the final finishing stage took place outside the quarry.

Members of the Norwegian expedition employed local men in an experiment designed to calculate the length of time required to carve an average-sized statue. Abandoned stone picks (*toki*) littering the quarries were utilized, and the bedrock was dampened with water to facilitate cutting, according to what was said to be an established tradition in stone cutting. Although the project was not completed and the number of determining variables was obviously hard to control for, it was estimated that a 5-m statue would take almost a year to complete (Skjölsvold 1961).

Other experiments were organized by Heyerdahl in the 1955–1956 research project to provide some insight on the long-standing controversial problem of transporting and then erecting statues on ahu. A measure of success was attained in dragging

6.9   *The Ahu Ko te Riku* (left) *and the Ahu Tahai, both restored in 1968.* (*Photo by Herb Pownall.*)

statues on the ground with ropes and levering them into position with timbers while simultaneously building a stone platform beneath. Mulloy (1970) has subsequently demonstrated the greater mechanical advantage and efficiency of employing fork sledges and a bipod of large timbers to transport statues in an upright position. This use of the bipod conforms to the local tradition that the statues "walked" from the quarries, advancing a short distance each day. The principal routes are clearly marked by abandoned, broken images all lying face down. They are examples of rare failures in the engineering skills of the prehistoric population.

Another expression of engineering capabilities was the placement of cylindrical stone topknots weighing up to 11 tons on the heads of some statues (Fig. 6.9). Topknots were carved of a welded red scoria at another quarry on Puna Pau, located near Hanga Roa. The meaning of the topknots is ambiguous. Metraux (1940) was under the impression that they were a representation of a hair bun, on the basis of early European descriptions of people wearing their hair up with a knot on top. Topknots were not placed on all statues, which suggests that they were a later feature added for embellishment.

The focal point of religious activity and ritual was the lineage ahu, a stone platform with its direct structural-functional counterpart in the marae of Central and East Polynesia. In the southern Marquesas, Tuamotu, Society, and Austral islands the term *ahu* referred only to the raised platform at the end of a rectangular court, while on Easter Island and in Nukuhiva and Ua Pou (in the northern Marquesas) it was applied to the entire ceremonial center (Linton 1925). The Easter Island ahu images are deemed analogous to the upright slabs on the raised platforms of Central and East Polynesian marae.

There are approximately 300 ahu on Easter Island, most located on the coastline, with occasional occurrences some kilometers inland. There are several formally

PATRICK C. McCOY

6.10 *Yosihiko Sinoto on the central platform of the restored Ahu a Kivi. (Bishop Museum photo.)*

6.11 *Excavation and restoration of the Ahu Tahai in progress. (Photo by Herb Pownall.)*

distinctive types of structures known as *ahu* (Smith 1961a; Ayres 1973; McCoy 1976b). All but the numerically more common image ahu (referred to by Englert as Ahu Moai) would appear to have been constructed for the primary function of housing burials. Although few nonimage ahu have been investigated, most are thought to be of late prehistoric age.

The typical image ahu (Fig. 6.10) consists of: (1) a raised central platform of rubble contained by facades of fitted stones; (2) offset, lateral extensions on one or both sides of the platform, called wings; (3) a stone-paved sloping ramp on the landward side (Fig. 6.11), abutting the central platform; and (4) a leveled rectangular court area (usually described as a plaza), occasionally bounded on three sides by an earthen embankment. The number of statues erected on ahu range from one to a maximum of fifteen. The ramp and wing extensions are known only on Easter Island, and until an extraisland source can be demonstrated, they are interpreted as localized stylistic elaborations of the basic East Polynesian marae structure.

Easter Island image ahu exhibit features characteristic of considerable advance planning, such as bilateral symmetry in the construction of the wings and in the case of the restored Ahu a Kivi (Fig. 6.10), a bilateral symmetry in the heights of the seven statues on the central platform (Mulloy and Figueroa 1978). The most marked evidence of planning is the astronomical orientation of the facades of some ahu. Mulloy (1961, 1975a) has described orientations perpendicular to the azimuths of the rising or setting sun at the solstices and equinoxes.

There are major architectural differences in the construction of the seawalls of some ahu (Fig. 6.12), which have been assumed to have chronological significance. The Norwegian expedition tripartite cultural sequence is based in large part on the assumed universality of a change from cut and precisely fitted dry stone masonry in the early period (A.D. 400 to 1100) to the construction of larger, but less carefully made, walls to accommodate statues in the middle period (A.D. 1100 to 1680). The acceptability of this architectural change is examined more fully in a later discussion on developmental sequences. At this point it is sufficient to note that internal variability in the construction of ahu walls is clear-cut evidence for multiple phases of rebuilding, which seems to have been quite common.

The outstanding example of Easter Island dressed-stone masonry is the seawall of Ahu Vinapu No. 1 (Fig. 6.13), located at Vinapu on the southeast coast. The wall consists of two courses of cut and precisely fitted quadrangular blocks of stone whose exterior surfaces curve slightly outward from the joints. This wall has been repeatedly compared to Andean masonry, which it resembles in a general way, including the quality of precision fitting and slightly convex profile of the slabs. Unfortunately, no dates were obtained for the construction of the central platform wall to compare with the age of comparable quality masonry of the Andean region. The wall must predate the radiocarbon age determination of A.D. 1516 ± 100 years for the rebuilding of the landward ramp.

The religious efflorescence of Easter Island was manifest not only in image carving and the quality of ahu architecture, but also in the development of a unique bird cult:

Until the second half of the nineteenth century the annual feast of the bird man (*tangata manu*), held at Orongo, was extremely important to Easter Islanders. The rites performed were not only connected with the cult of the greatest god of the island, Makemake, but were endowed with special social significance, since ideas of prestige and economic privileges were closely associated with these ceremonies. The ostensible purpose of the ceremony was to obtain the first egg of the *manu tara* (*Sterna hirundo*, sooty tern), the quest of which was entrusted to servants (*hopu*). The chief whose servant discovered the first egg received the envied title of birdman (*tangata*

6.12   A section of the seaward facade of the Ahu Tepeu. Note the variability in construction and the use of curbstones robbed from a hara paenga house foundation. (Bishop Museum photo.)

6.13   The late William Mulloy in front of the seaward facade of Ahu Vinapu No. 1. This is the best example of dressed-stone masonry on the island, and in Polynesia. (Bishop Museum photo.)

manu). This title, surrounded with tapus, brought to its holder and to members of his lineage certain material advantages and vast moral and religious benefits (Metraux 1940:331).

The cult was apparently controlled by the chiefs of plebeian tribes who, through victory in the annual competition, assumed a temporary sanctity of office. The winner lived in seclusion in a special house built for him on the lower slopes of Rano Raraku. Those who did not acknowledge his special status had their houses and fields burnt. This and other depradations by the victor seemingly prompted a new series of wars that effectively decided the contenders for the next year's competition (Goldman 1970).

The ceremonial center of Orongo, located on the southwestern rim of Rano Kau overlooking the crater lake and three offshore islets (*motu*), is one of the most interesting sites on the island. There are approximately 47 stone houses with corbeled roofs arranged in two groups, reflecting the dual political division of the island. To the north of the house complex is a plaza and early ahu, where a solar equinox determination device of stone was found (Ferdon 1961e). On the southern edge of the site is an impressive grouping of high-relief petroglyphs, most of them depicting a birdman or the god Makemake. Available radiocarbon dates indicate that the first phase of construction at Orongo dates to the fifteenth century (Ferdon 1961e), but many houses may postdate A.D. 1500 to 1550 (Golson 1965).

The search for the sooty tern egg took place on Motu Nui, a small islet about 2 km off the southwestern coast below Orongo. The servants occupied caves, several of which have pictographs similar in design to those found in the interiors of some Orongo houses. Survey has revealed the presence of 20 caves which, like the houses at Orongo, were secondarily utilized by young boys and girls in adolescent initiation rites (Metraux 1940; McCoy 1978b).

Part of the bird cult ceremonies at

Orongo involved the recitation of chants and prayers by priests or bards called *tangata rongorongo*, who read from wooden tablets of inscribed hieroglyphic characters collectively known as *kohau rongorongo* (Fig. 6.14). This pictorial script, the only known example in Polynesia, is the climax of Easter Island culture. Like so many other aspects of local cultural development, there is little first-hand information about the meaning and manner in which the script was used. Moreover, there are few surviving tablets (24 total) and most of these are fragmentary. The possibilities of decipherment thus are greatly reduced, with the further complication that specific translations will always be somewhat suspect.

The tablets consist of directionally alternating lines of incised anthropomorphic zoomorphic, and geometric characters. This type of script, known as reversed boustrophedon, requires turning the tablet 180 degrees at the end of each line. Some figures may represent words, but there is no conclusive proof of complete sentences or a grammar. In all probability the tablets were simply mnemonic devices to aid in the presentation of oral traditions and royal genealogies. The kohau rongorongo were said to be tabu and were handled only by the priests and their servants. Selected initiates, instructed in the reading of scripts at special "schools," were tested at public readings held annually at Anakena (Metraux 1940).

The origin and antiquity of the Easter Island script have been widely discussed. Heyerdahl has attempted to show a genetic relationship with several South American scripts, but all of the ones to which he refers are post-European. Barthel, the leading scholar in the decipherment of rongorongo texts, has postulated an East Polynesian origin on Huahine and Raiatea in the leeward Society Islands. He attributes the introduction of the script to a second wave of Polynesian immigrants led by Hotu Matu'a at about A.D. 1400 ± 100 years (Barthel 1971). Emory has reviewed the rongorongo problem and concluded that "the

PATRICK C. McCOY

6.14 *A rongorongo board in the collection of the Bishop Museum, Honolulu. Below is a close-up view of the incised figures in the same script. (Bishop Museum photo.)*

script definitely indicates non-Polynesian influence" (Emory 1972:63). He suggests that it was inspired by the ceremony that made the island the property of Spain in 1770, during which the chiefs of the island affixed their "signatures" to the document of annexation. There is no mention of the tablets in early European accounts, and no archaeological evidence of it, facts that Emory uses in his interpretation that the script is a post-European innovation dating after 1770.

Cultural Degradation: An Ecological Perspective

In sharp contrast to the first millennium of progressive development that produced Easter Island's world-renowned statuary and megalithic architecture, the final 200 years of prehistory were a period of general decadence. Cultural instability is attested to in a wealth of traditions on tribal warfare, which is known to have resulted in famines, the emergence of cannibalism, and widespread destruction of image ahu. The overthrow of ahu images and the cessation of statue carving are the chief distinguishing characteristics of the Norwegian expedition's late period, genealogically and archaeologically dated A.D. 1680 to 1868 (Ferdon 1961a). Ethnohistoric accounts and archaeological data suggest an escalation in the rate of cultural deterioration after 1722, accompanied by a steady decline in economic prosperity, and in population as well. A renewed period of general stability has some support (see La Perouse 1799), but it appears to have been of short duration.

Earlier speculations on the probable causes of cultural devolution include theories of volcanic catastrophism (Forster 1777) and a late Polynesian invasion leading to interracial conflict for control of the island (Heyerdahl 1958). The volcanism theory is rejected on geological evidence, while Heyerdahl's hypothesis is untenable on two accounts: (1) the absence of supporting data for the existence of two "racial" types (Shapiro in Metraux 1940; Murrill 1965), and (2) abundant evidence for first settlement by Polynesians.

Ecological and archaeological data suggest man-induced environmental change as an alternative explanation for cultural decadence. The long-term cumulative effects of population growth on land and flora are identified with an irreversible process of environmental degradation. Archaeological evidence of late prehistoric culture change has been viewed in terms of new adaptive strategies to cope with a heightened level of resource scarcity (McCoy 1976b). This model does not exclude the possibility that environmental change resulted in part from natural causes such as climatic fluctuations, but at present there is no conclusive proof of anything more than periodic droughts in historic times.

On the basis of an agricultural carrying-capacity estimate (Routledge 1919) and present archaeological indications, it has been conjectured that a peak population upward of 7,000 was attained by approximately A.D. 1550, or roughly 1,200 years after colonization of the island (McCoy 1976b). Even if the maximum population was only 4,000 to 5,000, it is easy to envision the eventuality of near-total deforestation in a relatively short time, assuming that the early forest was indeed a savanna-parkland type formation of scattered trees and shrubs. One thing is certain—only a small remnant of a forest remained at the beginning of the eighteenth century. There are repeated references in early ethnohistoric accounts to a barren landscape and the paucity of canoes, all small (3 m long), patchwork constructions of short planks

sewed together (Herve 1770; Forster 1777; Roggeveen 1908). Since these conditions held true as early as 1722, it can be inferred that extensive deforestation had occurred by A.D. 1600 or shortly thereafter.

Forest clearance and eradication of shrubby vegetation and grasslands are understandable in terms of cultural needs and practices. First, there is a demonstrable historical continuity in a culture dependent on the broad exploitation of wood and plant resources (for example, pole and thatch house building, canoe making, manufacture of utilitarian and ritual objects). Agricultural expansion and the practice of burning property (houses and plantations) in warfare are regarded as other major factors in the decimation of the local flora. It is important to note here that the vegetation of Easter Island is particularly susceptible to modification by burning, owing to a highly erratic moisture regime (Wright and Diaz 1962). Finally, the necessity for large timbers or logs in the transport and placement of statues on ahu (Mulloy 1970) implies a continuous, long-term exploitation of large trees. The magnitude of this specialized use pattern undoubtedly hastened the process of forest decline.

Deforestation and ground-cover removal had multivariate effects that are manifested archaeologically. If we accept the hypothesis that large trees were a prerequisite for the continued production of images for ahu, there is notable agreement of the projected sixteenth- to seventeenth-century dates for statue quarry abandonment and deforestation. The scarcity of wood and thatching materials is correlated with changes in domestic architecture and patterns of habitation. Rectangular houses, which require larger timbers for corner posts, do not appear to have been constructed in the late part of the local cultural sequence. Low elliptical houses, the model form in the late prehistoric and protohistoric periods, utilized poles of 5 to 10 cm diameter for the suprastructure. The decrease in building materials has been provisionally related also to the loss of the fully enclosed cookhouse (McCoy 1978a). La Perouse (1799) did not report the occurrence of any cook-houses in 1786, noting that ovens instead were simply protected on one side by a low windbreak. Deforestation is seen also as having prompted the construction of stone houses and greater utilization of caves for permanent habitation. The Spanish expedition of 1770 reported that many people were living in caves, and archaeological dates for cave habitations indicate increasing use after A.D. 1500.

The increasingly barren landscape is considered to have had a profound effect on the economy. The late prehistoric appearance of agricultural enclosures is viewed as an adaptive response to the need to protect plants from wind and sun, and to retain soil moisture because of the deleterious effects of tree and ground-cover removal. A decrease in crop yields is predictable. The information on eighteenth-century canoes suggests reduced catches of deep-sea fish, which would have placed a greater importance on domestic fowl especially as a source of protein, since there were no dogs or pigs. Weights of fish and chicken bones for recently excavated sites are in general agreement with this conjecture. The innovation of a stone-walled chicken house to alleviate thievery is seen as another adaptive response to the general nonavailability of traditional building materials. On present evidence this is a protohistoric change, because fowl are reported to have been kept in "little runs scraped out in the ground and thatched over" as late as 1770 (Herve 1770:122). The "boundedness" of garden enclosures and chicken houses is considered to be an expression of intensified production in a period of economic stress. A common form of high-island food-production intensification in Polynesia, irrigation agriculture, was an impossible option in view of the hydrologic characteristics of Easter Island.

An ultimately important social consequence of deforestation was the impossibility of emigration for people defeated in war. Eighteenth-century canoes were inca-pable of long-distance voyaging. Temporary escape was possible by hiding in refuge caves (*ana kionga*) (Fig. 6.15) or fleeing to near-shore islets; but neither ensured a good chance of survival or freedom from eventual captivity to become slaves (*kio*) (McCoy, 1978b).

Developmental Sequences

The 1955–1956 Norwegian expedition to Easter Island was more or less successful in achieving the project's research goals in the elucidation of five problems of primary importance to the interpretation of local prehistory (Heyerdahl 1961a and b). In their analysis of the varied research results obtained, the members of the expedition concluded that the prehistory of the island could be ordered into a provisional tripartite cultural sequence. The divisions of the sequence were given temporal designations: early period (A.D. 400 to 1100), middle period (A.D. 1100 to 1680), and late period (A.D. 1680 to 1868). The distinguishing characteristics of each period are outlined by Smith (1962) and discussed in some detail by Ferdon (1961a). The primary foundation of the sequence, ahu architecture and function, is briefly summarized and assessed here in terms of its continued utility as a valid outline of local prehistory.

The early and middle periods were defined primarily on the basis of architectural changes in ahu wall construction observed by Mulloy at two Vinapu structures and by Smith at seven others. Walls of the early period were identified as those with cut and precisely fitted slabs oriented either horizontally or vertically. The middle architectural period was distinguished by

sea walls built of stones fitted primarily by selection, although a minor amount of pecking and grinding is sometimes present. In general, the walls are somewhat irregular, because of the forms of the stone and the lack of dressing on the outer surfaces. Boulders, somewhat cube-like in form, seemed to have been preferred in contrast with the large flat slabs of the Early Period (Smith 1961a:214).

6.15 *The crawlway inside a specially designed refuge cave (ana kionga); the walls and roof of hara paenga curbstones enclose a natural overhang. (Photo by author.)*

There are indications that the differences in masonry styles between the two periods were not caused by the inability of later workers to fit stones in the neat manner evidenced earlier. Rather, it appears that more attention was given to preparing the central platform for the support of statues which, if they existed in the early period, were probably placed on the plaza. Mulloy (1961:160) described this temporal change as a shift in emphasis "from architecture to sculpture."

The late period was characterized by the cessation of statue carving and widespread destruction of ahu, including the ultimately complete overthrow of statues (the last report of erect statues appeared in 1838). The ramps and open areas beneath fallen statues were subsequently used for burial. The beginning date for this period, and thus for decadence, was based on the correlation of genealogical and archaeological dates for the legendary battle between the "Long Ears" (*Hanau eepe*) and the "Short Ears" (*Hanau momoko*) at the Poike ditch. Excavations of the "ditch" (Smith, 1961b) produced an early ^{14}C date of A.D. 386 ± 100 years and a later one of A.D. 1676 ± 100 years, which approximate Englert's genealogical date of about A.D. 1680 for this event. The earlier date is in question, although it is a reasonable estimation for the settlement of the island.

In the interpretation of this architectural sequence and other data from excavations, Heyerdahl (1961a:497) was led to conclude:

Certainly, archaeological evidence does not indicate continuity or stability of one homogeneous culture, nor does it indicate a long sequence of unbroken architectural development culminating in structures with precisely dressed masonry such as that of Vinapu. On the contrary, the last two centuries are marked by cultural decadence, and the previous era of florescence is divisible

162

into two periods, each with its own clearly defined and characteristic religious-ceremonial concepts in architecture.

This sweeping generalization of Easter Island prehistory is based on the assumption that the architectural changes in the nine investigated ahu are representative of an island-wide sequence. Two reviews of this sequence present evidence to the contrary.

The most perceptive critique of the three-period sequence is that of Golson; on analysis of the data contained in the Norwegian expedition reports, he arrived at quite different conclusions. He demonstrated continuity in image ahu "siting, planning, construction, and general if not detailed use" (Golson 1965:51) to show the absence of the hypothesized cultural break between the early and middle periods. He also showed that the chronological order of masonry techniques can be reversed—that is, that ahu with cruder walls of uncut, vertically oriented stones and showing the greatest similarities to East Polynesian marae are older than structures made of dressed and precisely fitted slabs.

In the final report on their work at Ahu a Kivi and Ahu Vai Teka in the interior, on the western side of the island, Mulloy and Figueroa (1978) reviewed the chronological and architectural data for 11 image ahu. The results are in agreement with Golson's earlier demonstration of historical continuity in ahu in terms of conception, apparent function, and detailed architectural characteristics. The same view is adhered to in a revised developmental sequence, which differs in that it uses *phases* rather than *periods* (Ayres 1973). In conclusion, there is evidence for an uninterrupted cultural sequence and strong supporting evidence for the existence of a single, coherent, but changing, cultural tradition.

Acknowledgments

The late William Mulloy made my Easter Island research possible. He invited me to conduct the first phase of a proposed long-term intensive site survey of the entire island. Beginning with his participation in the Norwegian archaeological expedition to Easter Island and other areas of East Polynesia in 1955–1956, Mulloy contributed more to an understanding of Easter Island prehistory than any other individual. Although the last decade of his work on the island was restricted to restoration and the study of architectural variability in ahu, he actively encouraged others to pursue different interests. The success he achieved in preserving Easter Island's world-renowned monuments was shared with the island's inhabitants, who through his concerted efforts have a greatly enlarged sense of cultural pride in their fascinating past.

References

Ayres, W. S. 1971. Radiocarbon dates from Easter Island, East Polynesia. *Journal of the Polynesian Society* 80:497–504.

———. 1973. The cultural context of Easter Island religious structures. Ph.D. dissertation, Tulane University.

———. 1975. Easter Island: investigations in prehistoric cultural dynamics. Manuscript.

Baker, P. E. 1967. Preliminary account of recent geological investigations on Easter Island. *Geological Magazine* 104:116–122.

———, F. Buckley, and J. G. Holland. 1974. Petrology and geochemistry of Easter Island. *Contributions to Mineralogy and Petrology* 44:85–100.

Barthel, T. S. 1971. Pre-contact writing in Oceania. In *Current trends in linguistics,* ed. Thomas Sebeok, pp. 1165–1186. The Hague: Mouton.

Brand, D. D. 1971. The sweet potato: an exercise in methodology. In *Man across the sea,* ed. C. L. Riley et al., pp. 343–365. Austin: University of Texas Press.

Brown, J. M. 1924. *The riddle of the Pacific.* London: T. Fisher Unwin.

Chang, K. C. 1972. *Settlement patterns in archaeology.* Addison-Wesley Modular Publications 24, pp. 1–26. Indianapolis: Addison-Wesley Publishing Co.

Cooke, G. H. 1899. Te Pito Te Henua, known as Rapa Nui, commonly called Easter Island, South Pacific Ocean. *Report of U.S. National Museum for 1897,* pp. 689–723. Washington, D. C.: Government Printing Office.

Emory, K. P. 1972. Easter Island's position in the

prehistory of Polynesia. *Journal of the Polynesian Society*, 81:57–69.

————, W. J. Bonk, and Y. H. Sinoto. 1959. *Hawaiian archaeology: fishhooks*. Bishop Museum Special Publication no. 47, Honolulu.

Englert, P. S. (Father Sebastian). 1948. *La tierra de Hotu Matu'a: historia, etnologia, y lengua de la Isla de Pascua*. Santiago, Chile: Padre las Casas.

————. 1970. *Island at the center of the world: new light on Easter Island*. New York: Charles Scribner's Sons.

Ferdon, E. N., Jr. 1961a. A summary of the excavated record of Easter Island prehistory. In *Reports of the Norwegian archaeological expedition to Easter Island and the East Pacific*, ed. Thor Heyerdahl and E. N. Ferdon, Jr., vol. 1, pp. 527–535. Santa Fe: School of American Research Museum.

————. 1961b. Easter Island house types. In *Reports of the Norwegian archaeological expedition to Easter Island and the East Pacific*, ed. Thor Heyerdahl and E. N. Ferdon, Jr., vol. 1, pp. 329–338. Santa Fe: School of American Research Museum.

————. 1961c. Site E-6, an Easter Island hare moa. In *Reports of the Norwegian archaeological expedition to Easter Island and the East Pacific*, ed. Thor Heyerdahl and E. N. Ferdon, Jr., vol. 1, pp. 381–383. Santa Fe: School of American Research Museum.

————. 1961d. Stone houses in the terraces of Site E-21. In *Reports of the Norwegian archaeological expedition to Easter Island and the East Pacific*, ed. Thor Heyerdahl and E. N. Ferdon, Jr., vol. 1, pp. 313–321. Santa Fe: School of American Research Museum.

————. 1961e. The ceremonial center of Orongo. In *Reports of the Norwegian archaeological expedition to Easter Island and the East Pacific*, ed. Thor Heyerdahl and E. N. Ferdon, Jr., vol. 1, pp. 221–255. Santa Fe: School of American Research Museum.

Figueroa, Gonzalo, and Eduardo Sanchez. 1965. Adzes from certain islands of Eastern Polynesia. In *Reports of the Norwegian archaeological expedition to Easter Island and the East Pacific*, ed. Thor Heyerdahl and E. N. Ferdon, Jr., vol. 2, pp. 169–254. Santa Fe: School of American Research Museum.

Forster, George. 1777. *A voyage round the world in H. B. M.'s sloop "Resolution" (1772–75)*. London: White.

Fosberg, F. R. 1963. The island ecosystem. In *Man's place in the island ecosystem*, ed. F. R. Fosberg, pp. 1–6. Honolulu: Bishop Museum Press.

Goldman, Irving. 1970. *Ancient Polynesian society*. Chicago: University of Chicago Press.

Golson, Jack. 1965. Thor Heyerdahl and the prehistory of Easter Island. *Oceania* 36:38–83.

Green, R. C. 1967. The immediate origins of the Polynesians. In *Polynesian culture history: essays in honor of Kenneth P. Emory*, ed. G. A. Highland et al., pp. 215–240. Bishop Museum Special Publication no. 56, Honolulu.

————. 1970. Settlement pattern archaeology in Polynesia. In *Studies in Oceanic culture history*, ed. R. C. Green and Marion Kelly, vol. 1. *Pacific Anthropological Records* 11:13–32.

Heiser, C. B., Jr. 1974. Totoras, taxonomy, and Thor. *Plant Science Bulletin* 20:22–26.

Herve, J. 1770. Narrative of the expedition undertaken by order of His Excellency Don Manuel de Amat, Viceroy of Peru . . . to the Island of David in 1770. *Hakluyt Society*, ser. 2, vol. 13, 1908. Cambridge.

Heyerdahl, Thor. 1941. Did Polynesian culture originate in America? *International Science* 1.

————. 1952. *American Indians in the Pacific*. London: Allen and Unwin.

————. 1958. *Aku-aku*. New York: Rand McNally.

————. 1961a. General discussion. In *Reports of the Norwegian archaeological expedition to Easter Island and the East Pacific*, ed. Thor Heyerdahl and E. N. Ferdon, Jr., vol. 1, pp. 493–526. Santa Fe: School of American Research Museum.

————. 1961b. The objectives of the expedition. In *Reports of the Norwegian archaeological expedition to Easter Island and the East Pacific*, ed. Thor Heyerdahl and E. N. Ferdon, Jr., vol. 1, pp. 7–13. Santa Fe: School of American Research Museum.

————. 1965. The statues of the Oipona *Me'ae*, with a comparative analysis of possibly related stone monuments. In *Reports of the Norwegian archaeological expedition to Easter Island and the East Pacific*, ed. Thor Heyerdahl and E. N. Ferdon, Jr., vol. 2, pp. 123–151. Santa Fe: School of American Research Museum.

————. 1966. Discussions of transoceanic contacts: isolationism, diffusion or middle course? *Anthropos* 61:689–707.

————. 1968a. *Sea routes to Polynesia*. New York: Rand McNally.

PATRICK C. McCOY

————. 1968b. The prehistoric culture of Easter Island. In *Prehistoric culture in Oceania*, ed. Ichito Yawata and Y. H. Sinoto, pp. 133–140. Honolulu: Bishop Museum Press.

————. 1976. *The art of Easter Island*. New York: Doubleday.

———— and E. N. Ferdon, Jr., eds. 1961, 1965. *Reports of the Norwegian archaeological expedition to Easter Island and the East Pacific*, vols. 1 and 2. Santa Fe: School of American Research Museum.

Isaacson, L. B., and D. F. Heinrichs. 1976. Paleomagnetism and secular variation of Easter Island basalts. *Journal of Geophysical Research*, 81:1476–1482.

Lanning, E. P. 1970. South America as a source for aspects of Polynesian cultures. In *Studies in Oceanic culture history*, ed. R. C. Green and Marion Kelly, vol. 1. *Pacific Anthropological Records* 11.

La Perouse, J. F. G. de. 1797, 1799. A voyage round the world . . . 1785–88 by the "Boussole" and "Astrolabe." 3 vols. French ed. 1797. London: Robinson.

Lavachery, Henri. 1935. La Mission Franco-Belge dans I'Île de Pacques. *Société Royale de Géographie d'Anvers Bulletin* 55:313–361.

————. 1936. Easter Island, Polynesia. *Annual Report of the Board of Regents of the Smithsonian Institution*, pp. 391–396.

————. 1939. *Les Petroglyphes de l'Île de Paques*. Antwerp: De Sikkel.

Linton, Ralph. 1925. *Archaeology of the Marquesas Islands*. Bishop Museum Bulletin no. 23, Honolulu.

McCoy, P. C. 1973. Excavation of a rectangular house on the east rim of Rano Kau volcano, Easter Island. *Archaeology and Physical Anthropology in Oceania*, 8:51–67.

————. 1976a. A note on Easter Island obsidian cores and blades. *Journal of the Polynesian Society*, 85:327–338.

————. 1976b. *Easter Island settlement patterns in the late prehistoric and protohistoric periods*. Bulletin 5, Easter Island Committee. New York: International Fund for Monuments.

————. 1978a. Stone-lined earth ovens in Easter Island. *Antiquity* 52:204–216.

————. 1978b. The place of near-shore islets in Easter Island prehistory. *Journal of the Polynesian Society:* in press.

Maziere, Francis. 1968. *Mysteries of Easter Island*. New York: W. W. Norton.

Meggers, B. J. 1963. Review of Thor Heyerdahl, *Archaeology of Easter Island*. *American Journal of Archaeology* 67:330–331.

Metraux, Alfred. 1940. *Ethnology of Easter Island*. Bishop Museum Bulletin no. 160, Honolulu.

Mulloy, William. 1961. The ceremonial center of Vinapu. In *Reports of the Norwegian archaeological expedition to Easter Island and the East Pacific*, ed. Thor Heyerdahl and E. N. Ferdon, Jr., vol. 1, pp. 93–180. Santa Fe: School of American Research Museum.

————. 1968. *Preliminary report of archaeological field work February–July 1968, Easter Island*. Bulletin 1, Easter Island Committee. New York: International Fund for Monuments (reprinted 1975).

————. 1970. *Preliminary report of the restoration of Ahu Vai Uri, Easter Island*. Bulletin 2, Easter Island Committee. New York: International Fund for Monuments.

————. 1973. *Preliminary report of the restoration of Ahu Huri a Urenga and two unnamed ahu of Hanga Kio'e, Easter Island*. Bulletin 3, Easter Island Committee. New York: International Fund for Monuments.

————. 1975a. A solstice oriented *ahu* on Easter Island. *Archaeology and Physical Anthropology in Oceania* 10:1–39.

————. 1975b. *Investigation and restoration of the ceremonial center of Orongo, Easter Island*. Bulletin 4, Easter Island Committee. New York: International Fund for Monuments.

———— and Gonzalo Figueroa, G.-H. 1978. *The A Kivi-Vai Teka complex and its relationship to Easter Island architectural prehistory*. Asian and Pacific Archaeological Series No. 8, Social Sciences and Linguistic Institute, Honolulu.

Murrill, R. I. 1965. A study of cranial and postcranial material from Easter Island. In *Reports of the Norwegian archaeological expedition to Easter Island and the East Pacific*, ed. Thor Heyerdahl and E. N. Ferdon, Jr., vol. 2, pp. 255–324. Santa Fe: School of American Research Museum.

Randall, J. E. 1970. Easter Island: an ichthyological expedition. *Oceans* 3:48–59.

Roggeveen, Jacob. 1908. Extracts from the official log of Mynheer J. Roggeveen (1721–22). *Hakluyt Society*, ser. 2, vol. 13. Cambridge.

Routledge, Mrs. Scoresby. 1919. *The mystery of Easter Island*. London: Hazell, Watson, and Viney.

Sahlins, M. D. 1955. Esoteric efflorescence in Easter Island. *American Anthropologist* 57:1045–1052.

———. 1958. *Social stratification in Polynesia.* Seattle: University of Washington Press.

Schuhmacher, W. W. 1976. On the linguistic aspect of Thor Heyerdahl's theory: the so-called non-Polynesian number names from Easter Island. *Anthropos* 71:806–847.

Simberloff, D. S. 1974. Equilibrium theory of island biogeography and ecology. *Annual Review of Ecology and Systematics* 5:161–182.

Skjölsvold, Arne. 1961. The stone statues and quarries of Rano Raraku. In *Reports of the Norwegian archaeological expedition to Easter Island and the East Pacific,* ed. Thor Heyerdahl and E. N. Ferdon, Jr., vol. 1, pp. 339–379. Santa Fe: School of American Research Museum.

Skottsberg, Carl. 1928. The vegetation of Easter Island. In *The natural history of Juan Fernandez and Easter Island,* vol. 2, pt. 4, no. 17. Uppsala: Almquist and Wiksells.

Smith, C. S. 1961a. A temporal sequence derived from certain *ahu.* In *Reports of the Norwegian archaeological expedition to Easter Island and the East Pacific,* ed. Thor Heyerdahl and E. N. Ferdon, Jr., vol. 1, pp. 181–219. Santa Fe: School of American Research Museum.

———. 1961b. The Poike ditch. In *Reports of the Norwegian archaeological expedition to Easter Island and the East Pacific,* ed. Thor Heyerdahl and E. N. Ferdon, Jr., vol. 1, pp. 385–391. Santa Fe: School of American Research Museum.

———. 1962. An outline of Easter Island archaeology. *Asian Perspectives* 6:239–243.

Thomson, W. J. 1891. *Te Pito te Henua, or Easter Island.* U. S. National Museum Annual Report for 1889, pp. 447–552.

Von Däniken, Erich. 1969. *Chariots of the gods?* London: Souvenir Press.

Wright, C. S., and Carlos Diaz, V. 1962. Soils and agricultural development of Easter Island. *UNESCO Quarterly Report, suppl.* 1.

Yen, D. E. 1971. Construction of the hypothesis for distribution of the sweet potato. In *Man across the sea,* ed. C. L. Riley et al., pp. 328–342. Austin: University of Texas Press.

———. 1974. *The sweet potato and Oceania: an essay in ethnobotany.* Bishop Museum Bulletin no. 236, Honolulu.

Hawaii

CHAPTER 7

H. DAVID TUGGLE

 Some of the broad goals of archaeology include the description of events and the understanding of change in prehistory. Hawaiian archaeology is, in part, concerned with the problems of how the people who settled a group of islands in the North Pacific came to be "Hawaiian" —that is, certainly Polynesian, but nonetheless unique. The answer involves determining the origin and culture of the first settlers. It involves exploring the way in which these settlers and their descendants met the possibilities and limitations of an island environment over a period of some 1,500 years. And it involves understanding the consequences of isolation from the rest of the Polynesian world. The theme of Hawaiian prehistory thus becomes the human use of an isolated and bounded environment, which resulted in the culture encountered by Europeans in 1778.

The Hawaiian World at Contact

The Hawaiian archipelago lies over 4,000 km north of the Society Islands and nearly 5,000 km due west of the Jalisco coast of Mexico. The islands stretch across the Tropic of Cancer, with the main groups toward the southeast and a string of island remnants toward the northwest. These subtropical islands, volcanic in origin, have great diversity in landform, rainfall, and vegetation (Figs. 7.1 and 7.2). If an island is visualized as once a cone (or several cones), its topography may be understood as a consequence of the amount of erosion of

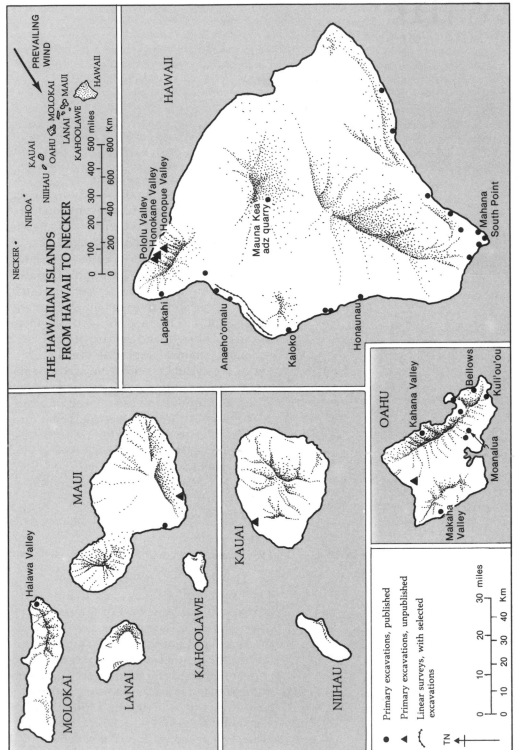
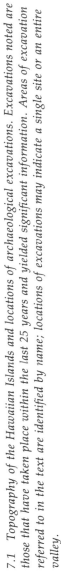

7.1 Topography of the Hawaiian Islands and locations of archaeological excavations. Excavations noted are those that have taken place within the last 25 years and yielded significant information. Areas of excavation referred to in the text are identified by name; locations of excavations may indicate a single site or an entire valley.

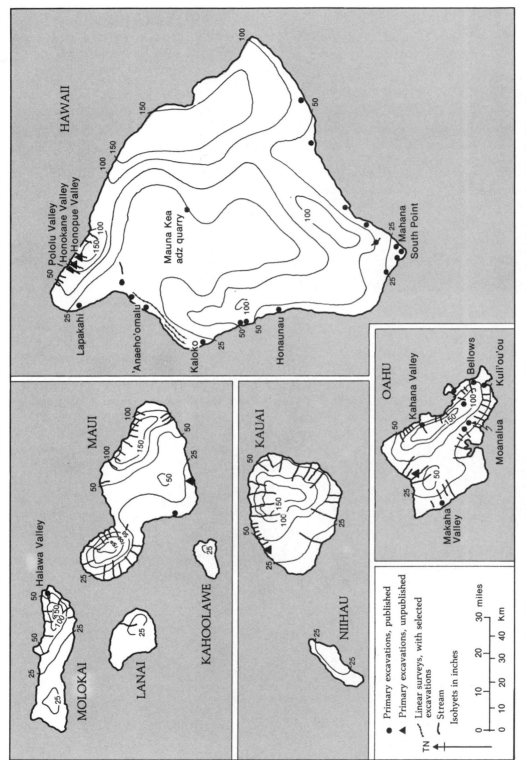

7.2 Rainfall, streams used for prehistoric irrigation, and location of archaeological excavations in the Hawaiian Islands. The streams provide a general indication of areas that were under irrigation at the time of contact.

7.3 *Waipio Valley, island of Hawaii. Modern irrigated taro fields can be seen on the valley floor; they are probably modified and rebuilt remnants of those that existed at the time of European contact. This valley is unusually large, but it has features common to many windward valleys: steep sides, flat bottom, alluvial floor, and a permanent stream—generally ideal conditions for irrigation. Waipio is about 1.2 km wide at the mouth and extends inland for some 5 km.*

7.4 *The upland field system of Lapakahi, Hawaii. The low field borders of stone and earth run parallel to the contour of the undissected slopes on the leeward side of the Kohala Mountains. Traditional cultivation in this area was rainfall dependent. The fields shown are located about 4 km from the coast at an elevation of 350 m above sea level (see Fig. 7.17). The field borders are about 50 cm high, and the alignments run 5 to 10 m apart.*

H. DAVID TUGGLE

7.5 *The leeward side of the Koolau Mountains, Oahu. Houses extend up Wa'ahila Ridge* (center), *probably traditionally used for dry cultivation. The valleys to either side were under intensive irrigation prior to contact. At the coast, present-day Waikiki Beach was the location of taro fields, numerous fishponds, and residences of chiefs.*

the cone's surface. To windward (northeast), the direction of the prevailing wind and rain, erosion has formed deep valleys, usually with permanent streams, on the older cones (Fig. 7.3). To leeward, the cone sides are poorly dissected or are cut by valleys usually shallower than those to windward (Figs. 7.4 to 7.6). Coastal plains have formed in some areas, with trough-like valleys behind them (Fig. 7.5). The coastlines include wave-cut cliffs, rocky slopes, and beaches of cobbles or sand.

In 1778 this landscape of Hawaii was a human landscape. The Hawaiians were farmers. They cleared vegetation by cutting and burning; controlled streams through the construction of dams, canals, and terraces; cultivated the soil of slopes and valley bottoms; and constructed field lines of stone to restrict erosion. The Hawaiians were builders. Under a complex social system, massive temples of piled stone were constructed and are still visible in imposing locations around the islands. As far north along the chain as Necker Island and as high as the upper slopes of the volcano called Mauna Kea, the Hawaiians left their imprint on the land.

The effective world of the Hawaiians in 1778 was eight major islands, with a total land area of 16,558 km², spread along an arc some 500 km long (Fig. 7.1). According to Hawaiian tradition, there had been no contact with other areas of Polynesia for some twenty generations prior to European contact. Two small islands, Nihoa and Necker, to the northwest of the main group, have archaeological remains but were not occupied at contact. Hawaiians traveled between islands by paddling or sailing canoes; however, several wide and often dangerous channels, up to 115 km across, limited communication. The wider channels created four interaction areas, areas with stronger ties internally than externally: Kauai and Niihau; Oahu; Maui, Molokai, Lanai, and Kahoolawe; and Hawaii. Under the best of conditions communication between Kauai and Hawaii may have taken five or six days with the use of special runners and canoe crews.

The largest island, Hawaii, is composed of five volcanoes, the highest of which is 4,205 m above sea level. The island has 10,415 km² of land and 425 km of coastline. Kahoolawe, the smallest of the major islands, was formed by a single volcano and is 450 m high, with 116 km² of land and

7.6 *Fishponds along the leeward coast of Molokai. The walls, constructed of stacked stone, are partially submerged. The pond to the left measures approximately 80 m across; vegetation, primarily mangrove, is spreading along the walls.*

46 km of coastline. Transportation across islands before contact was on foot because there are only a few kilometers of navigable streams and there were no pack animals at the time. An extensive system of trails had been developed which, combined with coastal travel by canoe, allowed relatively rapid communication on each island.

The remains of such trails provide the clearest record of Hawaiian movement and are found extending inland and along the coast. Trails were marked in a variety of ways. Waterworn stones were placed across rough lava fields, and small cairns were placed as markers particularly atop knolls. Many sections of trail are corridors through field structures. Often a trail may be identified by a shallow trough-like depression and a scattering of discarded sea shells. Caves or small sheltering walls of piled stone were used as resting places where trails ran for long distances through uninhabited territory.

Petroglyphs (rock carvings) are frequently found in association with trails, particularly in areas of smooth lava. Although petroglyphs served many purposes, those associated with trails probably were mementos left by travelers—perhaps to record events

of importance, perhaps for luck. The petroglyphic depictions include canoes, travelers, and carrying poles, and so provide evidence for several forms of transportation used by the islanders.

Resource Use

For the Hawaiians as farmers, the major resources of the land were fertile soil and water. Flowing water was used to irrigate the alluvial bottoms of valleys and sections of coastal plains. Canals, led from streams or springs and brought to irrigated fields, were constructed of earth and stone embankments (Figs. 7.7 and 7.8). In many areas the beds of small streams were terraced and converted to pond fields. There is a general relation between landform and the development of irrigation: the steeper the land, the less likely it was to have been irrigated; and with land that was irrigated, the steeper the slope, the smaller the plot size. Thus while the extent of irrigation was considerable, construction labor was kept to a minimum.

The staple grown in the irrigated fields was taro (*Colocasia esculenta*), a plant with many varieties that were cultivated also

172

7.7   *Abandoned irrigation terraces in the valley of 'Ahuimanu, Oahu. The terraces were constructed on a steep slope, and the fields consequently are narrow (about 3 m); the stone facings are about 1.2 m in height. (Photo by Bert Davis.)*

under nonirrigated conditions. The other major food plant, the sweet potato (*Ipomoea batatas*), was exclusively a dryland crop. It was grown in fields that had 60 to 200 cm of rain per year with adequate sunlight. The dry taro could be grown primarily where rainfall exceeded 120 cm per year.

Other cultigens included coconut (*Cocos nucifera*), banana (*Musa paradisica*), and breadfruit (*Artocarpus incisus*). Where possible these and other plants were grown in concert with sweet potatoes and taro, even though the largest percentage of land was devoted to the latter two. The agriculture was multicrop, and agricultural techniques were mixed. Irrigated and nonirrigated fields were often adjacent, and the dry cultivation techniques ranged from swidden to permanent field. Taro grown in irrigated wet valleys and sweet potatoes grown on dry slopes represent the extremes of the system.

Irrigation fields on Kauai were described in this way in the late 1700s:

The whole plantation is laid out with great neatness and is intersected by small elevated banks conveying little streams from the above aqueduct to flood distant fields on each side at pleasure. (Menzies 1920:29)

This same observer provided an account of the dryland field system above Kealakekua Bay, Hawaii:

The space between these [breadfruit] trees did not lay idle. It was chiefly planted with sweet potatoes and rows of cloth plant. . . For several miles around us there was not a spot that would admit of it but what was with great labor and industry cleared of the loose stones and planted. (Menzies 1920:77)

Only some 10 to 15 percent of the island of Hawaii was under cultivation at contact because agriculture was constrained in great inland stretches by low rainfall, recent lava

7.8　*Exposure of irrigation terrace deposits, Honokane Nui Valley, island of Hawaii. In recent times the stream has eroded laterally, destroying the terrace facings on the stream side and exposing the soils of the pondfields, which appear as a shallow (20 to 40 cm) band of light-colored clay accumulated on top of the massive alluvium. The terraces can be seen stepped in a downstream direction* (right to left), *with one facing of stone in the upper right and one on the left.*

flows, or high altitude. A much greater percentage of each of the other large islands was under cultivation. The total agricultural complex included pig (*Sus scrofa*), dog (*Canis familiaris*), fowl (*Gallus gallus*), and several species of fish. All of these were dependent to some extent upon agricultural production or the agricultural environment. Fishponds were often incorporated into the lower areas of the large irrigation complexes. The primary tools used in agriculture were adzes for vegetation clearance (used in conjunction with fire), a simple wooden digging stick for tilling, and cutting implements (perhaps bamboo and basaltic-glass—a variety of obsidian) for plant trimming.

Other resources of the land came from the upland forests. Items collected included some food plants, fibers, wood for house and canoe construction, and a few animals —particularly birds, which were hunted for food and as a source of feathers for cloaks and headdresses. Some cultigens, especially taro and banana, were planted in the forests and allowed to go wild to serve as potential food supply in case of crop failure. Streams were also a source of food where fish (particularly of the family *Gobiidae*) and prawns could be collected.

Another major resource of the land was stone. Stones of every variety—waterworn cobbles, talus fragments, volcanic cinder blocks—were used in construction. Locales with stone of particular qualities were quarried for the manufacture of tools: fine-grained basalt for adzes, basaltic-glass for cutting implements, and scoracious basalt for abraders.

The ocean was the primary source of pro-

H. DAVID TUGGLE

tein for the Hawaiians. They obtained fish, shellfish, squid, crustaceans, and, on occasion, marine mammals. The most diversified tool assemblage of the Hawaiians was for ocean resource exploitation and included fishhooks, nets with sinkers, traps, and octopus lures, as well as manufacturing tools (such as abraders made of sea-urchin spines or coral) and canoes for transport.

Saltwater fishponds were constructed on all of the main islands (Fig. 7.6) by extending a wall from the shoreline over a shallow reef to form an enclosing pond, or by walling off the mouth of an estuary. Fish were not simply trapped within the ponds but planted, cared for, and fed.

Furthermore, the ocean provided salt. It was collected in dry coastal areas by evaporation, frequently in prepared "saltpans"— large stones with basin-like depressions, either natural or manufactured by pecking.

An environment not only provides resources, it poses hazards. In Hawaii, tsunamis (tidal waves), mud and rock slides, and volcanic eruptions (on Maui and Hawaii) were all hazards to life and property, but the greatest threat came from drought and flood, the hazards to agriculture. Dryland farming was subject to periodic failure, particularly in areas of marginal rainfall. Flash floods even now are quite common in the islands and can easily destroy fields and settlements. Floods and drought-produced famines are recorded in the traditional literature and in early historic records.

The archaeological remains of Hawaiian resource use are extensive, although many have been destroyed by the same hazards the early Hawaiians faced, especially tsunamis and floods. Yet many Hawaiian structures were well engineered. A number of fishponds continue to survive the pounding of the ocean and are still in use today. Remnants of irrigation fields can be found in the upper portions of the valleys on Oahu, while whole irrigation complexes, some also still in use, exist in the valleys of other islands (Fig. 7.3). The terrace

facings of stacked stone are still in evidence, some as high as 2 and 3 m (Fig. 7.7); stone-lined canals can be traced; and, on occasion, a terrace soil is still naturally irrigated, long after abandonment, and wild taro continues to grow. In dry valleys and on slopes, dry agricultural features of stone alignments, terraces, low walls, and mounds have been identified. These features are seldom imposing, but in some areas they are dramatic because of their extent (Fig. 7.4). Excavations into agricultural fields have shown that pondfields commonly developed fine clay above a hardpan as well as a zone of heavy iron staining (Fig. 7.8), while dry fields show the disturbance of cultivation and frequently a heavy scatter of charcoal fragments.

Portable artifacts are found primarily in areas of manufacture, storage, or discard, rather than in places of use. Adzes are found in the largest numbers at the quarry sites where they were roughed out, or they are located in association with structures where they were being finished or sharpened. The adzes produced at about the time of contact varied widely in size, but tended to be quadrangular in cross section and tanged or flat. They were often finely ground and polished on at least two sides (Fig. 7.9).

The greatest percentage of fishhooks are located in sites that were the temporary shelters of fishermen. Fishhooks made of wood, bone, and shell were manufactured in a variety of sizes and shapes, but at contact three forms predominated: a single-piece hook with either a jabbing or rotating point; a two-piece hook; and a trolling hook. The line attachment for single-piece hooks was generally knob shaped (Fig. 7.10).

A wide variety of other nonperishable portable artifacts, such as pestles, pounders, and stone flakes, was employed in obtaining or processing food. Flakes of volcanic glass, rarely more than 2 cm in length, were produced for cutting and scraping. Perishable artifacts, such as matting and gourd containers, are found occasionally in dry caves.

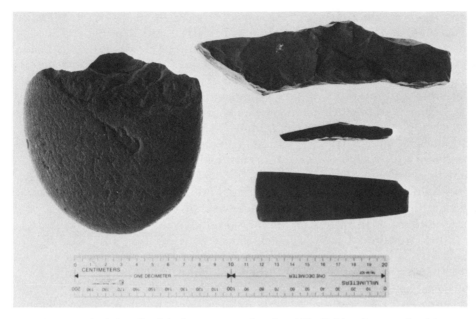

7.9 *Stone tools: bifacially flaked, waterworn basalt cobble (left); adzes, made of fine-grain basalt, are all rectangular in cross section (right). The top specimen (side view) has not been polished; the middle specimen (side view) and the lower one (front or top view) have been polished.*

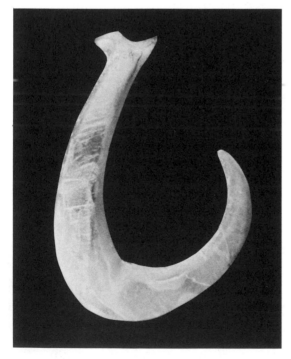

7.10 *One-piece rotating fishhook with knobbed line attachment, made of shell; the shank length is 15 cm.*

The resources used by the Hawaiians fall into concentric zones on each island: the ocean, occasional reef, and shoreline; agricultural lands of the valleys and slopes; and upland forest. In general, resources were exploited by means of the basic Hawaiian land unit, the *ahupua'a,* which extended from the coast inland, thereby cutting across the resource zones. Each island was divided radially by numerous ahupua'a, the boundaries of which tended to follow natural topography (Fig. 7.11). Ahupua'a varied in size, but few were more than 2 km wide at the coast. They extended from 5 to 20 km inland.

The nature of ahupua'a social and economic organization has long been a problem in Hawaiian anthropology. Recent work suggests that the people who lived within an ahupua'a tended to form an economically self-sufficient unit (Earle 1977a). Not every scholar agrees with this notion, however, and much more research on material distribution is needed. Although some form of distribution of items from localized resources, high-quality adzes

H. DAVID TUGGLE

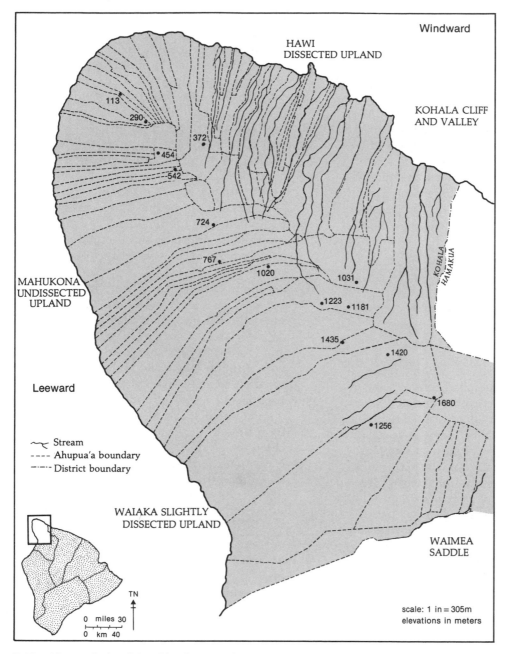

Windward

HAWI
DISSECTED UPLAND

KOHALA CLIFF
AND VALLEY

113
290
372
454
542
724
767
1020
1031
1223 1181
1435
1420
1680
1256

KOHALA
HAMAKUA

MAHUKONA
UNDISSECTED
UPLAND

Leeward

⌇ Stream
- - - Ahupua'a boundary
-·-·- District boundary

WAIAKA SLIGHTLY
DISSECTED UPLAND

WAIMEA
SADDLE

TN

0 miles 30
0 km 40

scale: 1 in = 305m
elevations in meters

7.11 Ahupua'a (traditional land units) of a portion of the Kohala district, Hawaii. The ahupua'a are shown in relation to permanent streams and physiographic zones. Those of the windward area generally included a stream, used for irrigation, and dry agricultural land. The leeward ahupua'a incorporated upland dry agricultural land and had boundaries that were somewhat more arbitrarily defined than those of the windward ahupua'a. Note the subdivision of the Waimea Saddle zone, a particularly rich agricultural area. The ahupua'a boundaries were obtained from nineteenth-century records and are probably close approximations of boundaries at contact.

for example, probably took place, the mechanisms for such distributions are unknown.

Ahupua'a boundaries were of major importance because they defined the territories of use. They were marked with cairns or identified by natural landmarks such as rock outcrops or valley rims. The word *ahupua'a* itself is composed of two words meaning pig altar or pig cairn, thought by some to refer to a structure, sometimes called an altar, located at the border of an ahupua'a for the placement of tribute (symbolized by the pig). No such tribute cairn has been identified archaeologically, but markers that follow historically recorded ahupua'a boundaries have been noticed in a number of areas. Inland trails may also have served as boundaries.

Organization of People

Hawaiian society was divided into two major classes, so-called commoners and chiefs, the latter subdivided into at least two ranks, with an additional segment forming a special category of priests. Local populations were organized into family units, although among all social ranks males ate separately from females in a special men's house, which also housed a local shrine and was used for a number of activities, such as adz manufacture. The common people of an ahupua'a maintained a certain amount of social distance from members of other ahupua'a by local endogamy. In contrast, the chiefs developed geographically extensive marriage networks.

The ahupua'a were organized into large political units, each of which was under the control of a ruling chief, usually a male, who "owned" the land and its produce. He or his representative allocated the use of the land to the commoners, who supported themselves and the chiefs from its production. An overseer, usually a low-ranking chief, represented the interests of the ruling chief within each ahupua'a. The commoners generally remained on the land through succeeding generations, as the

land was reassigned to them as the chiefs' administrations changed.

The ideological support for the hereditary ranking system lay in the belief that chiefs were chiefs because they were genealogically closer to the gods than were commoners. This relationship was ratified through the actions of the priests, who carried out ceremonies of propitiation and dedication on behalf of the chiefs. The gods were also considered to be the power behind natural forces that brought rain and good fortune on the one hand and drought and misfortune on the other. Thus the actions of the priests as representatives of the chiefs provided ideological security for the commoners.

Among the chiefs intense competition for power for themselves and their lines expressed itself through diplomacy, marriage, and warfare. At the time of contact, there were four independent chiefdoms, each with a ruling chief. The four territories centered on Kauai, Oahu, Maui, and Hawaii. Each island was subdivided into political districts, which according to the traditions from time to time had been independent chiefdoms (Fig. 7.12). The ruling chief of Hawaii at the time of contact had acquired his domain by first taking control of two districts of the island, then conquering the ruling chief of the remaining four districts.

Hawaii had one of the most complex Polynesian societies, as defined by the sharply bounded endogamous classes, the number of chiefly ranks, and the power held by the ruling chiefs. The development of this complexity is a problem of much concern in Hawaiian anthropology and an important issue in the archaeology of the islands.

The material reflections of social relations are often inadequate, but there is some evidence for Hawaiian class separation and social units. As suggested by recent detailed analysis of residence patterns (Cordy 1978), a commoner's family ordinarily occupied one or two structures, a sleeping house and perhaps a cooking or utility house. These took the archaeological form of pavings, low platforms, or enclosures, averaging

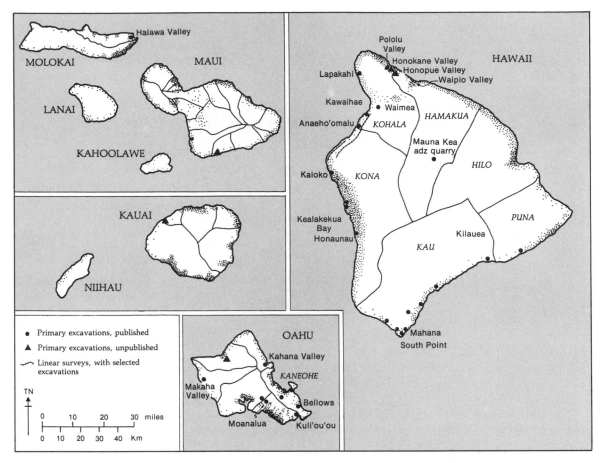

7.12 *Hawaiian population distribution, aboriginal districts, and locations of archaeological excavations. Population distribution and concentration at about the time of contact are indicated by stippling; the population distribution provides a general indication of the location of settlements prior to historic destruction. The traditional political districts are shown for each island, but only those on the island of Hawaii are identified (large caps); place names mentioned in the text are also identified.*

about 35 m² in area (Fig. 7.13), which served as the foundation for pole-and-thatch houses. Small hearths are found in sleeping houses in some instances, while cooking houses may have an earth-oven and perhaps an additional hearth. A number of structures have been archaeologically identified as men's houses (Kirch 1971; Cordy 1976). They are platforms or enclosures, averaging over 100 sq m in size, and may include several stepped terraces. Unworked pieces of coral and a platform, perhaps shrine features, are also indicative of a men's house.

The household of a chief resided in a cluster of several structures, including one or more of the following: a sleeping house, a men's house, a female eating house, a storehouse, and perhaps a canoe shed and house temple. The rank of the chief, Cordy (1977) argues, can be related to the number of structures or to the overall labor expenditure in housing construction relative to that of other clusters.

Habitation complexes of chiefs and commoners have been located on bare lava fields, in areas with some soil buildup around the structures, or buried in alluvial deposits or sand dunes. Excavations have evidenced multiple construction or rebuilding of structures and usually have produced scatterings of shell, flakes of basalt or basal-

7.13 A house platform located in the Honopue Valley, island of Hawaii. Part of a large complex of structures, this platform is constructed of stone cobbles and measures about 3 × 5 m. A pole-and-thatch structure was probably built atop this platform.

tic-glass, and fragments of adzes, fish-hooks, and abrading tools. The most common features are earthen ovens or hearths of various forms.

Two other kinds of structures, slides and temples, were primarily associated with the activities of the chiefs. The slides are long ramps of stone used for a toboggan-like sport. The temples (*heiau*) have been described in great detail ethnographically but have not been studied recently as a structural class. A good many of the major temples in use at contact have survived (Fig. 7.14). They are stone structures, as much as 4,000 m² in area. Some are stone-filled platforms, many with sides several meters high. Others are constructed as a series of large, stepped platforms or have great walled enclosures. These originally served as the foundation or enclosure for a number of structures of pole and thatch, where ceremonies were carried out. The major temples are usually conspicuously located on hilltops above bays, on high sand dunes, or at the upper edge of ridges on valley sides.

Burial pattern has been argued to be a reflection of differences between chiefs and commoners, but the contact practices are not well-known. In some areas burial platforms were constructed, and it has been suggested that platform size was related to the rank of the buried chief (Tainter 1973, 1976); however, there is some uncertainty about the dating of these structures. The data may also be skewed by the reported practice of hiding bones to prevent their use in magical practices. By the time of contact, in some areas, the bones of ruling chiefs were placed in mausoleums—places of great sanctity—one of which is still preserved at Honaunau, Hawaii, as a National Historic Park. The house of the chiefs' bones is there associated with two temples and a huge wall that isolates the sacred area on a spit of lava at the ocean edge.

The archaeological remains of warfare between competing chiefs are primarily sanctuaries, either ridge forts or refuge caves, defensible areas in which small groups of people could hide during conflict. Ridge-top refuges are found on most of the islands; these are located on knife-edge ridges with trenches 3 to 4 m deep cut across the ridges to leave a central area of isolation. Stones could then be dropped on attackers as they crossed the trenches. Many caves were used for hiding, and a

7.14 *The temple of Pu'ukohola, near Kawaihae, island of Hawaii. The temple combines platforms and a high standing wall for an imposing effect. It is constructed of stacked stone cobbles and covers an area of more than 2,000 m². Probably constructed in several phases, the structure was last modified in 1791 under the command of King Kamehameha I.*

number of fortified caves have been found on the island of Hawaii. Located in lava fields, they are entered through the collapsed roof of a lava tube or bubble. Their openings are walled to allow passage for only one person in a stooped position and give those inside the best defensive advantage.

Although fields and structures are reported to have been destroyed in warfare, no direct evidence of this has been noted archaeologically.

Population and Settlement Pattern

The Hawaiian population at contact is estimated to have been between 200,000 and 250,000, with the following geographic breakdown (Schmitt 1971): Hawaii, 80,000 to 100,000; Maui, 45,000 to 60,000; Oahu, 35,000 to 50,000; Kauai, 20,000 to 30,000; Molokai, 8,000 to 10,000; Lanai, 3,000 to 4,000; and Niihau, 500 to 1,000 (no estimate for Kahoolawe).

The first census records from the early 1800s indicate a great range of population size per ahupua'a. In a detailed study in one area of Kauai it was found that the size of ahupua'a populations, which ranged

from 85 to 522 in an 1832 census, correlated strongly with the amount of agricultural land within the unit (Earle 1977a and b). Ahupua'a that contained irrigation complexes such as those on Kauai were generally defined by the limits of the drainage area. Thus the larger the irrigation resource base (drainage basin), the larger the population of the ahupua'a. However, in areas with nonirrigated agriculture populations were of approximately equal size per ahupua'a, with each ahupua'a having an approximately equal production base. In other words, the richer the resources, the smaller the ahupua'a; and the poorer the resources, the larger the ahupua'a, a situation that resulted in more or less equal population distribution per unit. In each case, people were concentrated where food was concentrated.

If a wide range of resources is considered, four types of resource areas can be defined.

(1) Maximum resource areas. Concentration of the greatest variety and most productive resources; agricultural land (good alluvial valley or optimum rainfall) with associated animal population, fishponds, coastal collection area, and offshore fishing.

Such areas include Kaneohe, Oahu; Waipio, Hawaii; and central Kona, Hawaii.

(2) Secondary resource areas. Productive zones, but limited in size or lacking one or two highly productive areas; smaller alluvial valleys or regions adjacent to the maximum zones where rainfall may be less than optimum.

(3) Minimum resource areas. Areas with only one or two resource zones providing limited productivity; coastal areas with poor fishing; and marginal inland agriculture. An example is the coast of north Kona, Hawaii.

(4) Specialized resource areas. Areas with high productivity of only one resource—for example, areas with excellent coastal fishing, but little or no adjacent agriculture; inland areas suitable for productive agriculture but well removed from the coast (such as Waimea, Hawaii); and the inland areas of some of the deepest valleys.

At contact, population distribution was positively correlated with the first three categories (Fig. 7.12). Land subdivision was also correlated with these resource areas, as the smaller ahupua'a and the greatest populations were in the maximum to secondary resource areas. A third correlation was with district boundaries. Districts centered on maximum resource areas, and boundaries between districts fell in secondary to minimum resource areas or along natural boundaries dividing such areas.

The majority of people maintained their permanent residence along the coast with temporary-use shelters inland for specialized work, particularly in the agricultural fields. There were two exceptions to this. Scattered permanent residences appear to have existed inland in association with extensive irrigation fields, and small-scale permanent settlements may have been located in at least some of the inland specialized agricultural areas, such as Waimea, Hawaii. Permanent inland settlement in dry agricultural fields has been suggested but not clearly demonstrated.

The chiefs of a district resided predominantly in the largest centers of population, that is, in the maximum resource areas. The many chiefs and their retainers required a large amount of food, including a preponderance of fishpond production and a great share of the pigs and dogs. Goods from outlying areas were collected for the chiefs, who also moved about the district, particularly to good surfing or fishing areas, helping to distribute the burden of their support.

In areas not destroyed by modern culture, the archaeological sites reflect the contact settlement. Maximum resource areas are dense with permanent sites composed of stone platforms and low walls, many structures being of massive boulder construction. In contrast, only a few scattered structures can be found along a coastline of minimum resources.

Many temporary-use sites are also found archaeologically. These include caves and stacked, stone-wall windbreaks (Fig. 7.15). The cave sites at the coast served as fishermen's shelters and those inland as rest areas or temporary shelters for exploitation of specialized resources, such as adz stone quarries. The low-walled shelters are frequently found in nonirrigated inland agricultural areas. Excavations in these sites have produced evidence of sporadic occupation, such as superimposed hearths and lenses of debris. Coastal caves commonly have relatively deep midden deposits (over 30 or 40 cm) and numbers of fishhook fragments.

Research Background

The first known European sighting of Hawaii was made on January 18, 1778, by an English expedition under Captain James Cook, heading north from the South Pacific in search of a northwest passage across America.

We continued to see birds every day, of the sorts last mentioned sometimes in greater numbers than at others: and between the latitude of ten and 11 we saw several turtle. All these are looked upon as signs of the vecinity of land; we however saw none til day break in the Morning

H. DAVID TUGGLE

7.15 *A stone shelter, located in Lapakahi, island of Hawaii. This structure is a part of the upland field complex of Lapakahi (see Fig. 7.17); it was probably a sporadically occupied, short-term field shelter.*

of the 18th when an island was descovered bearing NEBE and soon after we saw more land bearing North and intirely ditatched from the first. (Cook, in Beaglehole 1967:263)

This was the first recording of what would become a major source of information about early historic Hawaii: the observations of explorers, travelers, and traders. As Hawaii became westernized in the nineteenth century, voluminous descriptions of Hawaiian life and events became part of the archival material: records of missionaries and planters; tax, marriage, and census records; land claims; court cases; and newspapers. The "memory" culture of Hawaii was also recorded during this period by island residents, Hawaiian and European. Some Hawaiian writers called on their own experiences in recording material about the Hawaiian past. The Europeans and many of the Hawaiians also collected great quantities of information from Hawaiian informants about traditional customs, myths, legends, and histories.

As in the history of all contact, however, the people making the observations were also involved in events that changed what they were observing. Venereal disease was immediately introduced. Iron nails were converted to fishhooks before the eyes of the first Europeans to reach Kealakekua Bay, Hawaii. From the first encounter, the observations and records were of an increasingly "acculturated" Hawaii. Those collections of traditional cultural data are subject to the problems of misunderstanding, omission, and leveling of regional and social differences. Archaeology, despite its many limitations, provides an independent reference to the past. It is a source of information about the period before contact, the culture at contact, and the events following contact. To understand how sites can be used, it is first necessary to explore their history per se, that is, how they became sites and whether those that remain after years of destruction are representative of the range of past occupation.

When Cook arrived, there was little that could be called archaeological: there were few abandoned areas; no major ruins of earlier or different peoples (although legends referred to such people); no lost cities; mysterious mounds, or decaying monuments. The "sites" were alive and well, lived in and lived upon. European contact changed this. Areas of Hawaiian occupation would become Hawaiian ruins.

Beginning in the early 1800s some areas began to lose population, the use of the land began to change, and old ways of life were transformed. The infant death rate increased and the birth rate declined as the population was reduced by some 50 percent in the first 60 years of contact. Political and economic changes brought redistribution of the population. The islands were consolidated into a single Hawaiian monarchy, and European trade became a major factor in the economy. Areas favorable for the anchorage of European vessels saw the growth of new centers of population and trade. Introduction of new plants and animals altered agricultural practices.

While many of these changes occurred gradually or without sharp boundaries, a major socioreligous change occurred in 1819 with the deliberate abandonment of the old "state" religion and the practices associated with it, particularly the separation of male and female activities. This led to the abandonment or destruction of temples and men's houses, and changed relationships within the family unit.

As some structures were being abandoned, many more were modified where Hawaiians remained on the land but altered the ways in which they lived. European artifacts of metal and glass were added to or replaced the traditional assemblage. Homesteads and settlements were reorganized or rebuilt. The nineteenth century became the century of the stone wall. Houses, yards, fields, and roads were enclosed or lined with stacked stone walls, in response to the great numbers of animals to be controlled, to new concepts of property, and to the make-work needs for prisoners. Toward the end of the nineteenth century many Hawaiian settlements were abandoned as economic independence was lost, as commercial demands lured people into towns or plantations, as transportation of produce became too costly, or as property was lost through indebtedness.

There are areas in Hawaii today where these nineteenth-century abandoned settlements, and the occupations that existed before them, may be found as archaeological sites. But large-scale eradication of sites began with nineteenth-century plantation agriculture and has continued to the present with urban and resort expansion. No one has assessed how much this distorts knowledge of Hawaiian archaeology, but for some islands—certainly Oahu—the remains of much of the past have perished.

The origin of archaeology in Hawaii is firmly linked with the founding in 1889 of the Bernice Pauahi Bishop Museum for Polynesian Ethnology and Natural History. Although there was an interest in antiquities prior to this time, the museum brought organization to the study of Hawaiian material culture and sites, particularly temples, fishponds, and petroglyphs (Newman 1968). Archaeological field surveys were begun around the turn of the century, and the first controlled excavation in Hawaii was the digging of a shelter deposit on Kahoolawe in 1913. Only very limited excavations were carried out over the next 37 years, a period characterized by broad-scale surveys aimed at the location and categorization of major surface features on each island and the collection of local information about their history.

This archaeological work produced no "prehistory." There are several ways to explain this, one of which is by examination of the relation between data and problems. A conference held in Honolulu in 1920 emphasized the difficulties with Polynesian origins and suggested a program of ethnographic and archaeological survey in Polynesia for the collection of comparative data. Stratigraphic excavation was suggested, and culture area and age area were the theoretical frameworks for explanation. In Hawaii Emory began a problem-oriented survey, but no substantial excavations were carried out. The archaeological material in Hawaii proved hard to control typologically and chronologically. Artifacts such as adzes and temples did not lend themselves to easy comparison, because they lacked the stylistic variability of pottery or projectile points, which was leading to success in

H. DAVID TUGGLE

mainland American archaeology in the creation of archaeological "cultures" and diffusion patterns. The sites in Hawaii were generally thought to be shallow and unsuitable for excavation (despite the results on Kahoolawe), surface structures were hard to categorize, and portable artifacts were generally few in number and limited in variety. The research carried out stimulated no controversy; there was nothing like the Moa-hunter material of New Zealand. McAllister (1933), who conducted surveys on Kahoolawe and Oahu, noted that the material from Stokes's 1913 excavation yielded some artifacts adequate in number for comparison, but with no variation throughout the site. In other words, there was no evidence for significant change in the archaeological record, and without change, what was to be explained? There was nothing to cast doubt on the Polynesian origins of the Hawaiians, but neither was there much evidence to aid in determining the specific Hawaiian homeland.

Oral traditions and linguistics (in other words, nonarchaeological data) proved more valuable in dealing with problems of prehistory than did archaeology. The Hawaiian traditions furnished detailed accounts of voyaging, wars, famines, and other major events, with an accompanying time-scale of genealogies that could be converted to years. Furthermore, comparative ethnology and linguistics were used to postulate migration and contact histories.

In the 1950s archaeological data and archaeological questions began to match. The beginnings of radiocarbon dating meant specific sites could be dated, so that some sort of "absolute" time scale for early Hawaii could be determined. Stimulus came also from a field school excavation of a rock shelter that produced a variety of artifacts. The possibility of prehistoric change was revived (Emory 1968). A program to develop a framework for Hawaiian archaeology was devised, which focused on a search for early components in relatively deep stratified sites. Cave and sand dune

deposits provided the models for this kind of site and led to excavations at South Point, Hawaii. This research produced evidence of relatively early Hawaiian occupation and a clear demonstration of artifact change through time, primarily morphology (Emory et al. 1968). This change was used to develop a seriation, with a stratigraphic base, that could be used for temporal references—the first use of archaeological data to solve an archaeological problem in Hawaii. Specific ideas about Hawaiian culture history also came from this work.

In the 1960s work on settlement pattern, subsistence, and social organization was begun and emphasized the study of local regions. This orientation, primarily inspired by Green's concept of settlement archaeology (1967), aligned Hawaiian archaeological problems with the kind of data of greatest abundance and variety in Hawaii: agricultural and residential structures. Current problems thus include not only Hawaiian origins, but patterns of resource use, agricultural change, trade patterns, stone technology, and the development of complex ranking.

The locations of most of the important excavations of the last 25 years are indicated in Figs. 7.1, 7.2, and 7.12. In Fig. 7.12 excavations are shown in relation to population density, an approximation of habitation site density. In Fig. 7.2 the excavations are shown in relation to irrigated streams. It is evident that many areas have not been studied, so conclusions about the Hawaiian past are still very tentative.

A number of dating methods have been used in Hawaiian archaeology. Many sites are referred to in Hawaiian traditions and thus may be "dated" genealogically. But no such date has been tested by archaeological means. Relative chronological control through artifact seriation has been used with success in the South Point area of the island of Hawaii, but broad areal application has yet to be demonstrated. Radiocarbon dates have been obtained from most of the islands, but use of the radiocarbon method has been hampered by the wide error range and by some erratic results particularly in samples from early sites. In recent years Hawaiian chronology has become increasingly dependent on the results of the hydration dating method applied to volcanic glass flakes (Morgenstein and Riley 1975). In the following discussion the "dates" given are based on the excavators' analyses of radiocarbon and hydration age determinations; they should be taken as generalized. Detailed age determination data can be found in the references.

Regional Studies

Hawaiian research in recent years has centered on regional studies rather than on individual sites. Two of these studies are summarized here as examples of local cultural change.

Halawa Valley (Fig. 7.16), an ahupua'a on the northeast coast of Molokai, extends some 3 km inland from a deep bay and a sandy shore about 500 m in width. Comparable to most windward Hawaiian valleys in form, it has steep sides and ends in an amphitheater head, where two waterfalls drain from the mountain watershed. The alluvial valley floor has one main stream and is bordered by talus slopes. Rainfall is less than 50 cm at the coast and increases to over 150 cm per year at the head. Survey and excavations were conducted over several seasons from 1964 through 1970 (Kirch and Kelly 1975).

The lower, wider portion of the valley floor is covered with remnants of extensive irrigation, two large complexes divided by the main stream. Each complex (one with 231 fields, the other with 366) covers nearly 10 ha and is fed by ditches that run the length of the complex, carrying water from the main stream. The major ditches, each several hundred meters in length, discharge water laterally to the fields. Five smaller irrigation complexes are found farther upstream in poor alluvial or side slope locations. These terraces depended upon perennial streams, but other water-control

features, particularly spreader terraces or check dams, are in gulches with intermittent flow. There is also evidence that the talus slopes were used for swidden cultivation.

Scattered along the talus slopes above the irrigation complexes are residential structures, small rectangular platforms of earth or gravel with stone facings. Excavations indicated that these were sleeping and cooking houses with hearths, earth-ovens, and subfloor burials; the artifacts are generally limited to adzes, grindstones, and stone flakes. A number of stepped terrace structures have been identified as either men's houses or small temples. There are also two major temples in the valley, but they were not excavated. These are associated with residential clusters and indicate a local social group organization. Although no structures were visible on the dune at the front of the valley, excavations revealed a stratified habitation deposit containing food remains, tools, and house outlines formed by postmolds and stone lines. Dating revealed that this deposit contained the earliest occupation uncovered in the valley.

Detailed archaeological study of Halawa has resulted in the most complete picture of the development of settlement and subsistence available for a windward valley. The evidence indicates that the coast was the locale of an early settlement, perhaps founded as early as A.D. 650, with occupation continuing until around A.D. 1350. Subsistence included marine collection and some agriculture, with a gradual shift toward greater dependence on agriculture. Around A.D. 1200 to 1400, permanent settlement began to move inland and created residential clusters, with associated men's houses (or temples) as a full development by at least A.D. 1500. It is postulated that this inland movement was related to increased dependence on irrigation agriculture. The population of the valley was recorded as 506 in 1863, with the maximum population before contact estimated at around 600.

A second regional study was of Lapakahi

H. DAVID TUGGLE

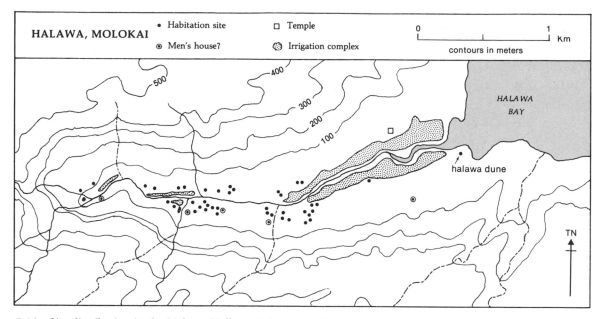

• Habitation site   □ Temple

◎ Men's house?   ⊛ Irrigation complex

0   1
Km

contours in meters

HALAWA BAY

halawa dune

TN

7.16 *Site distribution in the Halawa Valley, Molokai. Additional sites, including a large temple, were found in a gulch slightly to the north of the main valley. The area constituted one ahupua'a.*

(Figs. 7.4, 7.15, and 7.17), an ahupua'a in the district of Kohala, Hawaii. It lies on the dry leeward side of Kohala volcano and has an expansive, sloping terrain dissected by small gullies. The Lapakahi study area, perhaps containing ahupua'a adjacent to Lapakahi proper, is over 1 km wide and extends inland for 7 km, up to an elevation of about 600 m above sea level. The archaeological study of this area from 1968 through 1970 was comparable to the Halawa work in its focus on settlement and subsistence.

The rocky coastline of Lapakahi is composed of low sea cliffs up to 15 m high and a few gravel-bottom inlets; rainfall averages about 25 cm per year. Soil accumulation along the coast is very shallow. The coastal occupation sites are combinations of stone platforms, stone walls, and stone enclosures, with few structures located more than 100 m inland.

On the slope extending inland from the coastal occupation is a zone largely barren of archaeological sites for a distance of 2.5 km, where at an elevation of approximately 250 m the lower limits of an agricultural field system are reached. Running

throughout the barren zone are a number of trails, which connect the coastal settlement with the upland agricultural area. The agricultural fields continue to the upper limits of the Lapakahi area. The fields are one part of a vast field system (Fig. 7.4) that extends laterally an estimated 25 km along the leeward Kohala slope. The lower boundary of the Lapakahi fields has around 60 cm of rain annually, and the upper area has an annual rainfall of about 150 cm.

The agricultural fields are defined by low stone alignments that create a pattern of long rectangles (as narrow as 7 m and as long as 284 m) paralleling the coast. The dominant crop grown in these fields was sweet potato, but ethnohistoric accounts and the variety of agricultural features indicate that a number of other plants including sugarcane (*Saccurum officiarum*) and paper mulberry (*Broussonetia papyrifera*) were also planted. Nonagricultural structures are scattered throughout the fields. Many of these are low shelter walls of stacked stone (Fig. 7.15). Excavation of the occupation areas has yielded multiple fireplaces, portable artifacts, and food remains.

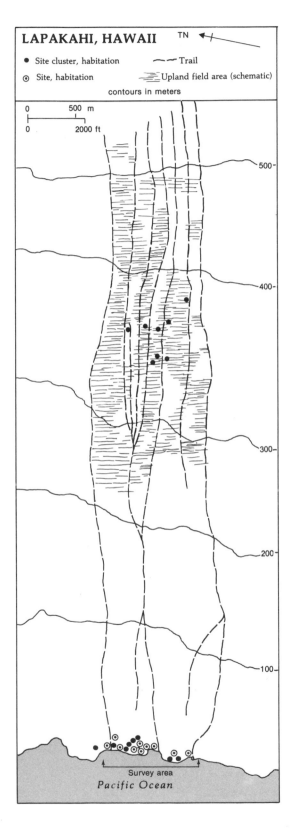

LAPAKAHI, HAWAII

● Site cluster, habitation   - - - Trail

⊙ Site, habitation   ≡≡≡ Upland field area (schematic)

contours in meters

0   500 m

0   2000 ft

Survey area

Pacific Ocean

7.17   Site distribution in the Lapakahi area of the island of Hawaii. Habitation sites continue in both directions along the coast, and the field area also extends laterally far beyond the study area shown. Site clusters include one or more habitation structures and a men's house. The number of ahupua'a in the area is uncertain.

The structures are thought to be field shelters for temporary use during periods of cultivation. Dates obtained from material within the shelters indicate that upland occupation and cultivation began at least as early as A.D. 1400. Structures postulated as small agricultural temples are also located within the field area.

The Lapakahi coastal occupation began around A.D. 1300 and expanded along the coast for two or three centuries, perhaps in association with an increase of upland area in cultivation. The coastal habitation revealed by excavation involved heavy use of marine resources in addition to the agricultural exploitation. The original interpretation of the coastal settlement suggested that clusters of structures represented the residences of single families. A reanalysis (Cordy 1978) indicates that each cluster included sleeping houses for several families, and the use of a common men's house. Although most of the clusters are thought to be the residences of commoners, one large complex may have been the occupation area of a chiefly family. This complex contains a massive wall (over 30 m long and up to 3 m high) that forms a boundary on one side of a number of platforms, some faced with boulders. The construction of the wall occurred sometime after A.D. 1500. Maximum expansion probably was reached around A.D. 1700, with a population estimated at about 150 to 200.

Culture History and Culture Change

There have been few attempts to construct archaeological phases or periods for the cultural development of Hawaii. The following discussion instead presents trends and changes that led to Hawaiian culture in

H. DAVID TUGGLE

1778. It should be clear that this is a tentative generalization, which represents only one of several possible arrangements of the data. As examination of Fig. 7.1 will indicate, the preponderance of archaeological excavation has been on Hawaii, so discussion of regional change concentrates on this island. Even there the work is too limited to allow formulation of a proper prehistory.

Comparative ethnology, linguistics, and archaeology leave little doubt that Hawaiians were East Polynesian in origin. The dominant culture historical problems are the specific origin area, the time of initial settlement, and the number of periods of migration.

At various times either the Society Islands or the Marquesas have been favored as the Hawaiian homeland, but recent research indicates that the early assemblages of these islands were very similar. They are referred to as the remains of an "archaic" East Polynesian culture (Kirch 1975a). The cultures of Hawaii, New Zealand, and Easter Island are thought to be derived from this early culture, and thus it remains uncertain whether a specific island origin can be established.

The evidence for the early occupation of Hawaii has been analyzed in detail (Kirch 1973, 1974, 1975a). Sites that have been dated prior to A.D. 800 to 1000 or that produced artifacts thought to have early styles include Bellows Dune and Kuli'ou'ou Shelter, Oahu; Halawa Dune, Molokai; Waiahukini Shelter, South Point, and one complex at 'Anaeho'omalu, Hawaii; several sites on Maui; and, possibly, sites on Nihoa and Necker. The Sand Dune site at South Point, Hawaii, and sites at Mahana Bay, north of South Point, may be added to this list (Hunt 1976).

Kirch argues that the earliest components yet excavated in Hawaii are the two bottom strata of the Bellows Dune. The material from these two strata and an upper stratum has a number of traits that show close resemblance to the archaic East Polynesian assemblage: one-piece pearl-shell fishhooks with distinctive head types, adzes with re-verse-triangular or plano-convex cross sections, chisels, an imitation sea-mammal tooth pendant, and a coconut grater (Kirch 1975a). The first occupation at Bellows may date as early as A.D. 375, although many of the artifacts listed above come from higher strata that may date to about A.D. 900. The other early sites have artifacts whose forms indicate some degree of local change, but with enough similarity to the Bellows material to suggest a common origin.

These early sites thus indicate that the first significant settlement of the islands was by people with a cultural assemblage similar to that of archaic East Polynesia and that this settlement occurred sometime prior to A.D. 400. These people became "Hawaiian" as their population increased, as their culture adjusted to the environment of the islands, as they interacted with one another, and as they remained largely isolated from changes in other areas of Polynesia. The number of people, vessels, or voyages involved in the earliest settlement will never be known with certainty, but there is no reason at present to suspect that these numbers were large. It is conceivable that a single voyage could have accounted for Hawaiian settlement.

Hawaiian traditions are ambiguous about Hawaiian origins. They are, however, explicit about a period of two-way voyaging between Hawaii and places to the south. Using genealogies for time reckoning, scholars have estimated that this voyaging would have occurred sometime between A.D. 950 and 1350 if it did in fact take place. Contact with other areas of Polynesia is said to have resulted in significant changes in Hawaii, particularly with regard to religion (the introduction of a new form of temple, human sacrifice as a religious rite, and symbols of sacred prohibition). This sounds suspiciously like external justification for internal consolidation of elite power, but the final arguments about two-way voyaging will ultimately depend upon archaeology. The primary archaeological argument used to support a second migration period is that changes in styles of fishhooks found in the South Point sites occurred between A.D. 1150 and 1450 as a result of Tahitian influence (Sinoto 1967). Corroborating information is required in the light of alternative explanations, such as indigenous development. The determination of contact and influence is always elusive in archaeology—and certainly so in Polynesia, where cultural similarities are great and where variability in artifact styles is limited.

Population Growth, Expansion, and Settlement Pattern

Although the number of voyages to Hawaii cannot be documented, it is assumed that they were relatively few and that the distribution of people (sites) occurred primarily as a result of local population growth and settlement expansion. Island population growth may have been very erratic (McArthur et al. 1976), so a great deal of information will have to be collected before a Hawaiian pattern can be demonstrated. Some of the sets of possibilities for the history of expansion, which may be considered in future research, include:

Expansion Pattern

A. (1) Concentrated. Population growth was contained within the early settlement areas, with agricultural intensification inland, until a large population was reached and budding off occurred.
(2) Dispersed. Population growth in early settlement centers led to budding at an early stage.

B. (1) Linear. Once settlements budded, the colonies were located near the original settlement until they again budded and expansion moved another step away.
(2) Spaced. Once early settlements budded, the new pioneer communities moved to the richest resource area between the parent community and the nearest settlement like the parent community.

Political Control of Expansion

(1) Centralized control. Regardless of the pattern of budding, the new settlement maintained ties with the parent community and remained under centralized political control.
(2) Decentralized control. Regardless of the pattern of budding, the new community was established as politically independent.

In each set it is assumed that the earliest settlements were in maximum resource areas. It is possible, of course, that there were no permanent settlements during the early period of occupation. Wide-ranging groups with scheduled returns to cultivation areas could be postulated. These and other possibilities need to be examined.

Of the early Hawaiian sites the two most likely candidates for permanent occupation (although argument against permanence is possible in each case) are Bellows Dune, Oahu, and Halawa Dune, Molokai. Halawa is located in a maximum resource area and Bellows is on the periphery of one. Other early sites were for temporary use and located in areas of specialized resources. The identified early sites are widely distributed. If this pattern holds, it will argue that the first period of expansion was spaced—a small number of permanent settlements spread to the maximum resource zones with a wide-ranging search for specialized resource areas (fishing grounds, basalt and basaltic-glass sources). This type of colonization might have involved exploration voyages along the island chain, and could have resulted in sites such as those on Nihoa and Necker.

The sites that date from A.D. 800 to 1400 include temporary occupation in various locales and permanent settlements on the leeward Hawaii coast at 'Anaeho'omalu (A.D. 1400), Kaloko (A.D. 1100), and Lapakahi (A.D. 1300). The first lies beside a bay, but is removed from agricultural land, whereas the latter two settlements are not far from cultivated inland areas. None of these lie in the maximum resource areas of leeward Hawaii, the most important of which is central Kona, one of the richest rainfall agricultural zones in the islands. The earliest date (A.D. 1100) comes from an

H. DAVID TUGGLE

inland shelter associated with agriculture, but few excavations have been conducted in this area. Coastal sites should prove to be earlier. No work has been conducted in maximum resource areas along the windward coast, such as Waipio Valley and Hilo. The earliest date from this coast comes from a small valley, Honopue, and dates permanent settlement at least as early as A.D. 1200.

The problem of coastal expansion has been considered in detail by Cordy (1978) in a study of 15 ahupua'a in north Kona. The resources of this barren coast vary from secondary, where some fields are located inland, to near minimum. The section of the coast studied is located between 'Anaeho'omalu and Kaloko, areas with permanent settlements dated from A.D. 1100 to 1400. In the study area no evidence was found for permanent occupation prior to A.D. 1400, but settlements were established during the period A.D. 1450 to 1500.

Hommon (1976) has analyzed the excavation information for the islands and argues that inland expansion was generally after A.D. 1400. As he notes, this is expansion into inland dry agricultural areas, not permanent settlement. He suggests that population growth is not necessarily the only cause for this, and proposes agricultural innovation—perhaps introduction of the sweet potato—and climatic change as reasons for the increased amount of land under agricultural production. Nonetheless, population increase along the shore in areas of prime settlement was probably an important element.

In Halawa, Molokai, expansion of the irrigation complexes was associated with a shift of permanent settlement inland, although it is probable that permanent settlement remained on the coast as well. In the inland dry areas of Lapakahi and Makaha there was more attention to agriculture during this period, but the problem of related permanent settlement has not been solved.

I postulate that for the island of Hawaii a settlement expansion of a dispersed, spaced, and possibly decentralized nature

lasted until about A.D. 1300 to 1400. Slow at first, population growth was increasing rapidly by A.D. 1200, with a continual budding of colonies to the best unoccupied and isolated environment available. The population remained coastal, exploiting marine resources and agricultural land adjacent to the coast. After A.D. 1400 population growth continued but new colonization was largely confined to marginal coastal areas and perhaps to specialized inland agricultural areas. Settlement budding declined, and older settlements in maximum resource areas increased in population. This settlement concentration was accompanied by expansion and intensification of agriculture.

Use and Organization of Resources

Although the land provided Hawaiians with the soil and water for agriculture, it provided few plants for domestication. All of the major cultigens and domesticated animals used by the Hawaiians were introduced by the Polynesians. It is assumed that agriculture was part of early Hawaiian subsistence, but no swidden or irrigation fields have yet been dated prior to the A.D. 1200s (dated fields are from Halawa, Molokai; Makaha, Oahu; and Honopue, Hawaii). The location of early agricultural features remains a research priority. Archaeological material from early sites does include pig and dog remains, although none as yet of domesticated fowl. The best record of long-term subsistence comes from Halawa, where an early heavy dependence on marine products gave way to an increasing reliance on agricultural production.

Two aspects of agricultural change may be postulated on the basis of present evidence from a number of areas. The first is that dry cultivation was occurring inland after about A.D. 1200 to 1400. The second change was the conversion of dry fields to irrigation, as indicated by the superposition of irrigation terraces over soils thought to have been under swidden cultivation. There is evidence for this from several areas, including Moanalua and Makaha, Oahu; Halawa, Molokai; and Honopue, Hawaii. This evident intensification was occurring at least as early as A.D. 1300 in some areas. The large irrigation complexes may have been constructed or completed late in the precontact period.

There is additional evidence that an effort was made on the island of Hawaii to develop most of the areas with agricultural potential. Irrigation complexes were constructed nearly to the head of the 7 km extent of Honokane Nui Valley. In Pololu Valley an irrigation system was built in spite of a poor water source and intermittent water shortage. The intensive use of these two valleys occurred after A.D. 1500. Surveys along the Kohala-Hamakua coast indicate that most irrigable areas, even those in isolated locations or with limited land, were developed to some extent for irrigation. At Lapakahi the lower portions of the dryland fields had been pushed into an agriculturally marginal rainfall zone. In barren inland areas of southern Kohala, small settlements with agricultural features developed around A.D. 1600 on small alluvial fans of intermittent streams.

The development of the agricultural systems on the island of Hawaii probably did not reach a "maximum," particularly with respect to mountain terracing. It is evident, however, that one level of expansion was reached, which contrasts with that of other islands, particularly Oahu and Kauai where many areas suitable for irrigation were under dry cultivation or were not cultivated in any manner (Ayres 1970; Earle 1977b). Production demands perhaps had not reached the level of those on Hawaii, where the irrigation potential was much greater than that of Kauai and Oahu. Thus agricultural histories may have to be considered separately for each island.

The elaboration of fishponds (Fig. 7.6) is a unique Hawaiian feature within Polynesia. The ponds may have developed from an earlier practice of maintaining fish within irrigated taro plots, but no sequences have been worked out. Fishponds

are referred to in Hawaiian traditions in association with individuals whose genealogies indicate a time period as early as the fourteenth century (Kikuchi 1976).

The development of fishponds and the expansion of irrigation-field areas are forms of subsistence intensification. Although population increase accounts in part for this, other factors were probably involved. It will be of particular interest in future research to determine whether class stratification increased also, a process that presumably would remove the chiefs from the working force and increase the demands for ritual production.

The location of raw materials, particularly stone, was perhaps one of the major goals of the postulated early settlement pattern (shifting or permanent camps, with wide-ranging exploration and collection). An early date from a site within Haleakala crater on Maui may indicate such activity. Further, the early occupation at Halawa contained basaltic-glass thought to have come from a small offshore island and adzes made of material originating at the other end of the island. At Bellows the basaltic-glass in the lowest component indicates active search for resources. Although local sources were used for adzes in most occupations, regardless of time period, it is postulated that there was a distribution of adzes over most of the islands from the major quarry on Mauna Kea, Hawaii. Recent surveys and excavation (McCoy 1977) indicate that this quarry is vast in extent, with quarrying locations spread over 17 km². The date of initial use of this area, located at 4,000 m above sea level, is unknown, but probably it was rather early.

The artifact assemblage associated with resource use at the time of contact was developed within the Hawaiian Islands, generally from the original archaic Polynesian base. However, the variation of Hawaiian artifacts in space and time remains poorly known and is a persistent problem of research. The two-piece fishhook was developed in Hawaii, and barbing was elaborated. Kirch (1975) considers the base of the

H. DAVID TUGGLE

two-piece points from Bellows and Halawa to have "incipient" knobbing which, after A.D. 1000, developed into full knobbing for attachment to the two-piece shank. Local variation in base attachment form is indicated by notching of the points of two-piece hooks found at South Point in deposits contemporaneous with or somewhat later than those from Bellows and Halawa. It is thought that this attachment style also developed into knobbing, a style that predominated at the time of contact. For one-piece hooks, the variety in one-piece head attachment decreased through time, so that knobbed-head attachment predominated at contact. It has also been noted that functional classes may cut across the one-piece versus two-piece categories.

Adzes found in early components have a variety of cross sections (including plano-convex, reverse-triangular, reverse-trapezoidal, and quadrangular) and tend to be untanged or minimally tanged. The dominant adz form at contact was quadrangular in cross section and tanged, but the majority of preforms found at the Mauna Kea adz quarry are quadrangular and untanged. The temporal change of Hawaiian adzes is by no means clear, but there is some possibility of a reduction in variety.

The development of the ahupua'a as an organized means of access to resources cannot be ascertained, but there is enough evidence to consider some possibilities. The last significant establishment of new settlements on Hawaii may have occurred no later than about A.D. 1650, although the population probably continued to move about to a limited extent. It may be argued that contact ahupua'a boundaries became set at about this time, with associated economic self-sufficiency. However, there seems to be even greater reason to argue for the economic independence of earlier settlements than for later ones. There was greater concentration on marine resources and agriculture near the coast. Pressure on resources would have been less with a smaller population. The fewer the settlements the greater the possibilities for wide-ranging exploitation. If the spaced settlement pattern interpretation is supported, it is possible that the basic ahupua'a economic and social pattern was established very early in Hawaiian history. At the same time, the mechanism of intercommunity trade and its effect on community relationships remains unknown for virtually all Hawaiian history prior to contact.

Organization of People

All studies of Hawaiian social system assume a beginning with some version of the Polynesian distinction between chiefs and commoners, but without class stratification. The problems presently addressed in Hawaiian social change are the development of ranks among chiefs, the origin of class distinction, the loss of kinship ties between chiefs and commoners, and the economic separation into producing commoners and nonproducing elite. Oral traditions recorded after contact have long been used as a basis for defining changes that took place in Hawaiian society, but data are becoming available for archaeological evaluations of ideas about social change. There is little evidence yet to define the early relation between chiefs and commoners—or even to test the assumption that such a distinction existed.

The positive evidence for chief-commoner separation is probably best derived from the development of structures that marked class division at contact. These structures are primarily residences, major temples, or burials, but the burials as a rule cannot be dated. The earliest evidence, dating about A.D. 1100, for a contact pattern of commoners' residence is found at Kaloko, Hawaii. The first evidence for any pattern of settlement of chiefs in relation to commoners occurs also at Kaloko (A.D. 1450 to 1600) and at Lapakahi (after A.D. 1500). In each case the chief's house is within a local center of population. However, the maximum resource zones, the areas that might contain the earliest structures of chiefs, have not been thoroughly investigated. Only two of the many large temples in Hawaii have been excavated. Each of these, one at Honaunau, Hawaii, and one at Makaha, Oahu, was constructed in a series of building stages. Kaneaki temple in Makaha has a date of around A.D. 1460 for the first construction stage, while 'Alealea at Honaunau yielded an uncertain set of dates. The increasing size of these structures through successive building phases could be taken as a measure of greater sociopolitical power if a higher expenditure of labor was involved. At least the result was ever more imposing structures. The walling of many temples (although yet undated) is a further indication of the symbolic separation of those involved in the activities of the temple—the chiefs—and those not involved—the commoners.

It has long been suggested that the traditional districts of Hawaii were centers of earlier independent chiefdoms. The fact that each of the districts is centered on a major resource area (Fig. 7.12) indicates this possibility, and it is supported by the pattern of settlement presented above. Recent additional evidence comes from an indication of unoccupied zones between these centers before A.D. 1450. One area is Pololu and Honokane Nui valleys, near the Kohala-Hamakua windward border; another is northern Kona, adjacent to the Kohala border. The fragmentation of the buffer zones by A.D. 1500 may mark the end of independent chiefdoms on Hawaii and the beginning of a unified island political structure. Increasing homogeneity of the style of portable artifacts also suggests enlarged interaction spheres, perhaps through the breakdown of chiefdom independence (although trade and political borders do not necessarily coincide).

Major changes were certainly occurring on Hawaii between A.D. 1400 and 1500. Irrigation agriculture had probably been well developed and inland dry cultivation was expanding during the beginning of the period. Population grew rapidly and then perhaps leveled off. Significant distinctions appeared in residence structures, and large temples were being constructed. The contact pattern of sociopolitical organization may have been reached during the last hundred years of this period.

The Processes of Change

A documentation of "natural" environmental change and of environmental changes precipitated by human activity is ultimately necessary before human adaptation can be understood; yet there is currently little information available for Hawaii. Virtually no studies of Holocene climatic change have been carried out, but there is some evidence for recent variation in the Mauna Kea climate, which would have limited human exploitation of the quarry. Hommon (1976) has noted evidence for world climatic changes around A.D. 1000 to 1200, and he suggests these may have had an effect on the Hawaiian rainfall pattern. Sea-level fluctuations occurred during human habitation, but probably had little effect on settlements. Volcanic activity on Maui and Hawaii certainly affected settlement, in that it destroyed old land areas and created new ones. In historic times a fishpond on the Kona coast, an adz quarry on Kilauea, and a number of settlements have been destroyed by lava flows.

The Hawaiians changed portions of their environment through agriculture, by such methods as forest clearing, field burning, and damming of streams. Fire may have been used for plant selection. It has been argued that some of these activities contributed to erosion, with resulting damage to the Hawaiian land. Seabird and some crustacean populations were decimated by exploitation, and animals introduced by the Polynesians probably damaged the biota (Kirch 1973). Human adaptation in Hawaii thus required response to human-induced change.

Random "cultural drift" probably accounts for some change in minor elements

H. DAVID TUGGLE

of Hawaiian culture, possibly in such things as adz cross section. Other variations (as Sinoto has suggested in a personal communication) are functional innovations designed to meet demands of the environment, such as the development of the two-piece fishhook in the absence of good pearl shell for manufacturing larger hooks. The extensive construction of irrigation complexes may be related to the quality of alluvial land available (Earle 1977b). Some alterations, such as sweet potato cultivation or fishhook style change, could represent local modification of outside introductions.

The major changes can probably best be viewed as adaptation in isolation, an elaboration of a cultural pattern through local social group interaction within a particular environment. The cultural pattern was set by the original migrant group. In a situation of relative isolation there was no competition between different cultures, no extensive interregional trade, no network for the dissemination of innovation. It is this feature of internal development that gives the variations on the Polynesian cultural pattern such a fascinating cast in places like Hawaii, Easter Island, and New Zealand.

It is assumed that the basic Polynesian cultural pattern was a fishing-farming economy and a conical-clan social structure, and that this pattern characterized early settlements. The assumption must still be tested by archaeology, but in the meantime it is the baseline of virtually all discussion of Polynesian adaptation.

The cultural pattern of a pioneering group has its origins elsewhere. In the case of Polynesians, it is reasonable to argue that the pattern developed in the early adaptation of the culture, an adaptation that certainly involved island pioneer settlement. Still, adaptation was not only to islands but to long-distance voyaging between islands. The conical-clan structure is well suited to both voyaging and island colonization. Authority is built into such a system by seniority, supported in Polynesia by the ideology of *mana*. Unquestioned authority is perhaps the key to success in long-distance voyaging. The conical clan, adapted to voyaging, is in turn suitable for settlement: contained in the authority structure through seniority is a potential for easy segmentation, so that expansion is one potential of the structure.

Widely spaced early settlements, organized as conical clans and established in maximum-resource zones, may have been economically, politically, and socially independent. These settlements could form nuclei for chiefdoms, which would become increasingly competitive and within which the numbers of ranks would increase over time; the eventual result would be the social system described at contact.

The origin of the complex Hawaiian ranking system has long been discussed, but only recently has archaeology begun to produce solid evidence regarding the nature and temporal sequence of social change. While much remains to be learned, it is evident that social distance marked by differences in house size and temple construction was occurring in some areas prior to A.D. 1400. It has been suggested (Hommon 1976) that ahupua'a economic independence occurred at this time, tending to localize isolate groups of commoners while chiefs maintained contact in the political suprastructure. Over time, chiefs increased their separation with multiplying demands for subsistence and luxury goods. Production demands brought increased needs to exercise physical force for internal social control and for external conquest warfare. This explanation and others that involve the role of trade, population increase, warfare, and centralized management are currently much debated.

The Polynesian social system—the conical clan—certainly contained the elements for elaboration into a class system. The problem is to isolate the elements that led to centralization of authority in a society with potential economically independent subunits and a fissionable structure. It will be important in future research to refine archaeological measures of rank and to compare the development of rank on different islands, where a number of variables, including population size and resource productivity, may be controlled.

Hawaii is often cited as a prime example of a complex-ranked society, an isolated population whose numbers may have been ideal for the development of competing polities. It may also prove to have the ideal archaeological data, the structures, and the datable material to allow a well-defined history of the development of complexity. At stake is information on one of the most compelling issues in anthropology, the origin and elaboration of hereditary ranking (see Flannery 1977). A fascinating aspect of the history of archaeological research is the time it takes to understand how best to use archaeological data to solve problems of history and change.

Acknowledgments

I am extremely grateful to those who read the first draft of this chapter and made substantial contributions: Ross Cordy, Timothy Earle, Roger Green, Patrick McCoy, Thomas Riley, and Myra Tomonari-Tuggle.

Bibliographic Notes

References in the body of the paper have been kept to a minimum, with additional selected sources indicated below.

Some general sources on the Hawaiian environment include Gosline and Brock (1960), Carlquist (1970), Macdonald and Abbott (1970), and Armstrong (1973). Several of the major sources on traditional Hawaiian culture are Vancouver (1801), Ellis (1827), Lyons (1875), Menzies (1920), Malo (1951), Ii (1959), Kamakau (1961, 1976), Beaglehole (1967), and Fornander (1967). Note that these are not all original publication dates. Analytic studies of Hawaiian culture at contact include Sahlins (1958), Davenport (1969), and Goldman (1970), while a general history of Hawaii after contact is given in Kuykendall (1968).

Early archaeological field reports are represented by Emory (1922, 1928), Bennett (1931), and McAllister (1933). Most current Hawaiian ar-

chaeological fieldwork published at monograph length is found in two series of the Bishop Museum in Honolulu: *Pacific Anthropological Records* and the *Department of Anthropology Report Series;* and in contract research reports of Archaeological Research Center of Hawaii. Recent summaries of Hawaiian archaeology are those of Hommon (1976) and Cordy (1978), and a history of archaeological research in Hawaii is given in Newman (1968). Recent selected archaeological field studies, most of which refer to dated sites, include Emory and Sinoto (1961), Pearson (1962, 1968), Emory et al. (1969), Green (1969, 1970), Ayres (1970), Barrera (1971), Crozier (1971), Ladd and Yen (1972), Rosendahl (1972), Riley (1973), Tuggle and Griffin (1973), Kirch and Kelly (1975), and Kirch (1975b).

Specific studies involve trails (Apple 1965; Kaschko 1973), petroglyphs (Cox and Stasack 1970), resource use and Hawaiian portable artifacts (Titcomb 1952; Buck 1957; Green 1961; Emory et al. 1968; Newman 1970; Handy and Handy 1972; Yen 1974), ahupua'a (Kelly 1956; Earle 1977a), early Hawaiian sites and migration (Emory et al. 1969; Green 1971; Pearson et al. 1971; Kirch 1973, 1974, 1975a; Cordy 1974b; Cordy and Tuggle 1976), and Hawaiian sociopolitical change (Cordy 1974a; Hommon 1976; Earle 1977b). Material on the valleys of Pololu, Honokane, and Honopue is from my own research with manuscripts in preparation. Spellings and definitions of Hawaiian words are based on Pukui and Elbert (1971).

References

Apple, R. A. 1965. *Trails: from steppingstones to kerbstones.* Bishop Museum Special Publication no. 53, Honolulu.

Armstrong, R. W., ed. 1973. *Atlas of Hawaii.* Honolulu: University of Hawaii Press.

Ayres, W. S. 1970. *Archaeological survey and excavations, Kamana-Nui Valley, Moanalua Ahupua'a, South Halawa Valley, Halawa Ahupua'a.* Bishop Museum Department of Anthropology Report 70–8, Honolulu.

Barrera, William. 1971. Anaehoomalu: a Hawaiian oasis. *Pacific Anthropological Records* 15.

Beaglehole, J. C., ed. 1967. *The journals of Captain James Cook on his voyages of discovery,* vol. 3. Cambridge: Cambridge University Press, for the Hakluyt Society.

Bennett, W. C. 1931. *Archaeology of Kauai.* Bishop Museum Bulletin no. 80, Honolulu.

Buck, P. H. (Te Rangi Hiroa). 1957. *Arts and crafts of Hawaii.* Bishop Museum Special Publication no. 45, Honolulu.

Carlquist, S. J. 1970. *Hawaii: a natural history.* New York: Natural History Press.

Cordy, R. H. 1974a. Complex-rank cultural systems in the Hawaiian Islands: suggested explanation for their origins. *Archaeology and Physical Anthropology in Oceania* 9:89–109.

————. 1974b. The Tahitian migration to Hawaii ca. 1100–1300 A.D.: an argument against its occurrence. *New Zealand Archaeological Association Newsletter* 17:65–76.

————. 1976. Problems in the use of ethnoarchaeological models: a Hawaiian case. *Archaeology and Physical Anthropology in Oceania* 11:18–31.

————. 1978. *New approaches to an old problem: the development of complex societies in the Hawaiian Islands.* Draft Ph.D. dissertation, University of Hawaii.

———— and H. D. Tuggle. 1976. Bellows, Oahu, Hawaiian Islands: new work and new interpretation. *Archaeology and Physical Anthropology in Oceania* 9:207–235.

Cox, J. H., and Edward Stasack. 1970. *Hawaiian petroglyphs.* Bishop Museum Special Publication no. 60, Honolulu.

Crozier, S. N. 1971. *Archaeological excavation at Kamehameha III road, North Kona, island of Hawaii, phase II.* Bishop Museum Department of Anthropology Report 71–11, Honolulu.

Davenport, William. 1969. The "Hawaiian cultural revolution": some political and economic considerations. *American Anthropologist* 71:1–20.

Earle, T. K. 1977a. A reappraisal of redistribution: complex Hawaiian chiefdoms. In *Exchange systems in prehistory*, ed. T. K. Earle and J. E. Ericson. New York: Academic Press.

————. 1977b. *Economic and social organization of a complex chiefdom: the Halelea district, Kaua'i, Hawaii.* Anthropological Paper no. 64. Museum of Anthropology, University of Michigan.

Ellis, William. 1827. *Journal of William Ellis.* Honolulu: Advertiser Publishing.

Emory, K. P. 1922. *The island of Lanai: a survey of native culture.* Bishop Museum Bulletin no. 12, Honolulu.

————. 1928. *Archaeology of Nihoa and Necker islands.* Bishop Museum Bulletin no. 53, Honolulu.

————. 1968. Preface. In *Hawaiian archaeology: fishhooks* by K. P. Emory, W. J. Bonk, and Y. H. Sinoto, pp. vii–ix. Bishop Museum Special Publication no. 47, 2nd ed., Honolulu.

———— and Y. H. Sinoto. 1961. *Hawaiian archaeology: Oahu excavations.* Bishop Museum Special Publication no. 49, Honolulu.

————, W. J. Bonk, and Y. H. Sinoto. 1968. *Hawaiian archaeology: fishhooks*, 2nd ed. Bishop Museum Special Publication no. 47, Honolulu.

————, W. J. Bonk, and Y. H. Sinoto. 1969. Waiahukini shelter, site H8, Ka'u, Hawaii. *Pacific Anthropological Records* 7.

Flannery, K. V. 1977. Review of *The Valley of Mexico*, edited by Eric R. Wolf. *Science* 196:759–761.

Fornander, Abraham. 1969. *An account of the Polynesian race, its origin and migrations.* Tokyo: Charles E. Tuttle Co. (originally published 1878, 1880, 1885).

Goldman, Irving. 1970. *Ancient Polynesian society.* Chicago: University of Chicago Press.

Gosline, W. A., and V. E. Brock. 1960. *Handbook of Hawaiian fishes.* Honolulu: University of Hawaii Press.

Green, R. C. 1961. Review of *Hawaiian archaeology: fishhooks*, by Kenneth P. Emory, William Bonk, and Yosihiko H. Sinoto. *Journal of the Polynesian Society* 70:139–144.

————. 1967. Settlement patterns: four case studies from Polynesia. In *Archaeology at the Eleventh Pacific Science Congress*, ed. W. G. Solheim. Asian and Pacific Archaeology Series no. 1, Honolulu.

————. 1969. Makaha Valley historical project: interim report no. 1. Pacific *Anthropological Records* 4.

————. 1970. Makaha Valley historical project: interim report no. 2. Pacific *Anthropological Records* 10.

————. 1971. The chronology and age of sites at South Point, Hawaii. *Archaeology and Physical Anthropology in Oceania* 6:170–176.

Handy, E. S. C., and E. G. Handy. 1972. *Native planters in old Hawaii: their life, lore, and environment.* Bishop Museum Bulletin no. 223, Honolulu.

Hommon, R. J. 1976. The formation of primitive states in pre-contact Hawaii. Ph.D. dissertation, University of Arizona.

Hunt, T. L. 1976. Hydration-rind dates from archaeological sites in the South Point area: a contribution to Hawaiian prehistory. Paper presented at the 1976 First Conference in Natural Sciences in Hawaii.

Ii, J. P. 1959. *Fragments of Hawaiian history.* Honolulu: Bishop Museum Press.

Kamakau, S. M. 1961. *Ruling chiefs of Hawaii.* Honolulu: Kamehameha Schools Press.

———. 1976. *The works of the people of old.* Bishop Museum Special Publication no. 61, Honolulu.

Kaschko, M. W. 1973. Functional analysis of the trail system of the Lapakahi area, North Kohala. In *Lapakahi, Hawaii: archaeological studies*, ed. H. D. Tuggle and P. B. Griffin, pp. 127–144. Asian and Pacific Archaeology Series no. 5, Honolulu.

Kelly, Marion. 1956. Changes in land tenure in Hawaii, 1778–1850. Master's thesis, University of Hawaii.

Kikuchi, W. K. 1976. Prehistoric Hawaiian fishponds. *Science* 193:295–299.

Kirch, P. V. 1971. Archaeological excavation at Palauea, South-east Maui, Hawaiian Islands. *Archaeology and Physical Anthropology in Oceania* 6:62–86.

———. 1973. Early settlement and initial adaptational models in the Hawaiian Islands. Paper presented at the 38th meeting of the Society for American Archaeology, San Francisco.

———. 1974. The chronology of early Hawaiian settlement. *Archaeology and Physical Anthropology in Oceania* 9:110–119.

———. 1975a. Excavations at site A1-3 and A1-4: early settlement and ecology in Halawa Valley. In *Prehistory and ecology in a windward Hawaiian valley: Halawa Valley, Molokai*, ed. P. V. Kirch and Marion Kelly. *Pacific Anthropological Records* 24:17–70.

———. 1975b. Radiocarbon and hydration-rind dating of prehistoric sites in Halawa Valley. In *Prehistory and ecology in a windward Hawaiian valley: Halawa Valley, Molokai*, ed. P. V. Kirch and Marion Kelly. *Pacific Anthropological Records* 24:161–166.

——— and Marion Kelly, eds. 1975. *Prehistory and ecology in a windward Hawaiian valley: Halawa Valley, Molokai. Pacific Anthropological Records* 24.

Kuykendall, R. S. 1968. *The Hawaiian kingdom*, vol. 1. Honolulu: University of Hawaii Press.

Ladd, E. J. 1973. Kaneaki temple site: an excavation report. In Makaha Valley historical project interim report no. 4, ed. E. J. Ladd. *Pacific Anthropological Records* 19:1–30.

——— and D. E. Yen. 1972. Makaha Valley historical project: interim report no. 3. *Pacific Anthropological Records* 18.

Lyons, C. J. 1875. Land matters in Hawaii. *Islands* 1:103–104.

McAllister, J. G. 1933. *Archaeology of Kahoolawe.* Bishop Museum Bulletin no. 115, Honolulu.

McArthur, Norma, I. W. Saunders, and R. L. Tweedie. 1976. Small population isolates: a micro-simulation study. *Journal of the Polynesian Society* 85:307–326.

McCoy, P. C. 1977. The Mauna Kea adz quarry project: a summary of the 1975 field investigations. *Journal of the Polynesian Society* 86:223–244.

Macdonald, G. A., and A. T. Abbott. 1970. *Volcanoes in the sea.* Honolulu: University of Hawaii Press.

Malo, David. 1951. *Hawaiian antiquities.* Bishop Museum Special Publication no. 2, 2nd ed. (originally published 1898).

Menzies, Archibald. 1920. *Hawaii Nei 128 years ago: journal of Archibald Menzies.* Honolulu: [The New Freedom].

Morgenstein, Maury, and T. J. Riley. 1975. Hydration-rind dating of basaltic-glass: a new method for archaeological chronologies. *Asian Perspectives* 17:145–159.

Newman, T. S. 1968. Hawaiian archaeology: an historical review. *New Zealand Archaeological Association Newsletter* 11:131–150.

———. 1970. *Hawaiian fishing and farming on the island of Hawaii, A.D. 1778.* Department of Land and Natural Resources, Honolulu.

Pearson, Richard. 1962. Some bases for ecological inferences about the aboriginal population of the Hanapepe Valley, Kauai. *Journal of the Polynesian Society* 71:379–385.

———, ed. 1968. Excavations at Lapakahi, North Kohala, Hawaii Island, 1968. *State Archaeological Journal* 69-2:1–130.

———, P. V. Kirch, and Michael Pietrusewsky. 1971. An early prehistoric site at Bellows Beach, Waimanalo, Oahu, Hawaiian Islands. *Archaeology and Physical Anthropology in Oceania* 6:204–234.

Pukui, M. K., and S. H. Elbert. 1971. *Hawaiian dictionary.* Honolulu: University of Hawaii Press.

Riley, T. J. 1973. Wet and dry in a Hawaiian valley. Ph.D. dissertation, University of Hawaii.

Rosendahl, Paul. 1972. Aboriginal agriculture and residence patterns in upland Lapakahi, island of Hawaii. Ph.D. dissertation, University of Hawaii.

Sahlins, M. D. 1958. *Social stratification in Polynesia.* Seattle: University of Washington Press.

Schmitt, R. C. 1971. New estimates of the precensal population of Hawaii. *Journal of the Polynesian Society* 80:237–243.

Sinoto, Y. H. 1967. Artifacts from excavated sites in the Hawaiian, Marquesas, and Society islands: a comparative study. In *Polynesian culture history: essays in honor of Kenneth P. Emory*, ed. G. A. Highland et al., pp. 341–361. Bishop Museum Special Publication no. 56, Honolulu.

Tainter, J. A. 1973. The social correlates of mortuary patterning at Kaloko, North Kona, Hawaii. *Archaeology and Physical Anthropology in Oceania* 8:1–11.

———. 1976. Spatial organization and social patterning in the Kaloko cemetery, North Kona, Hawaii. *Archaeology and Physical Anthropology in Oceania* 11:91–105.

Titcomb, Margaret. 1952. *Native use of fish in Hawaii.* Polynesian Society Memoir no. 29, New Plymouth, New Zealand.

Tuggle, H. D., and P. B. Griffin, eds. 1973. *Lapakahi, Hawaii: archaeological studies.* Asian and Pacific Archaeology Series no. 5, Honolulu.

Vancouver, C. 1801. *A voyage of discovery to the North Pacific Ocean and round the world.* New York: Da Capo Press.

Yen, D. E. 1974. *The sweet potato and Oceania: an essay in ethnobotany.* Bishop Museum Bulletin no. 236, Honolulu.

The Societies

CHAPTER 8

KENNETH P. EMORY

Lying in the heart of Polynesia—more specifically in the center of East Polynesia —are the Society Islands, of which Tahiti is the largest. In the popular literature Tahiti has given its name to the Society Islands as a whole, so that "in Tahiti" usually means "in the Societies." If one wishes to refer to the island of Tahiti, "on Tahiti" is the correct phrase. Furthermore, the Societies are divided into the Windward Society Islands (including Tahiti) and the Leeward Society Islands. The inhabitants of these islands, the Tahitians, are often thought of as the typical Polynesians. Their islands were not the first within Polynesia to be discovered by Polynesians, however, nor the first to be discovered by European explorers.

The island of Tahiti, lying 18 degrees south of the equator, was discovered by Captain Samuel Wallis in 1767. The following year Louis de Bougainville arrived and thought he had made the discovery. Captain James Cook reached Tahiti in 1769, then made a second visit to the Societies in 1773–1774, and a third in 1777. The Spaniards under Don Boenechea visited Tahiti in 1772, between Cook's first and second voyages, and again in 1774–1775, between his second and third voyages. From these first explorers we have descriptions and illustrations depicting the people, their canoes, their dress, their utensils, their way of life. The Reverend William Ellis, who followed the first missionaries from England, left descriptions of the culture as it was in his time, 1817 to 1825, again from a European point of view. The Reverend J. M. Ormond, in the islands from 1817 to 1856, recorded a wealth of traditional lore, including genealogies of the ruling chiefs, which has been published by his granddaughter, Teuira Henry (1928). Douglas Oliver, in a project extending over 20 years, gathered and studied original source materials and presented the results in a monumental three-volume work titled *Ancient Tahitian Society*, published in 1974. In time, archaeological findings will be studied along with these and other descriptions and analyses, in the effort to follow the culture from its beginnings.

Field research into the prehistory of the Society Islands has been carried out through the Bernice P. Bishop Museum of Honolulu intermittently since 1923. The American Museum of Natural History financed an intensive investigation of the archaeology of the Opunohu Valley and shore on the island of Moorea during 1960–1962, by Green and Davidson. The first French participation was by Verin, of the Office de la Recherche Scientifique et Technique Outre Mer (ORSTOM), who joined the Bishop Museum party in 1960–1961 (Verin 1964). Then in 1963–1964 the Centre National de la Recherche Scientifique (CNRS) sponsored an archaeological survey of the Tautira Valley on Tahiti (Garanger 1964, 1967). More recently the CNRS has conducted an investigation of archaeological remains in the part of the Papenoo Valley on Tahiti that is due to be submerged under the waters of a dam (Chazine 1977). ORSTOM also put an archaeological team on an archaic site discovered at Vaihi on Raiatea (Semah et al. 1978).

Tahitian culture and history cannot be understood only in terms of what is found in the Societies themselves, but through study and comparison of the cultures (including genealogies) of the islands from which ancestors of the Tahitians came and those on which they later settled (Emory 1978). Through linguistic and archaeological research we can reach back objectively to the very beginnings. Therefore I shall consider mainly the results in these two areas of study, in an attempt to trace the origin and development of the indigenous Tahitian culture.

Tahitian Prehistory Reconstructed through Linguistics

While it has become clear that the languages of East Polynesia belong in a group that shared a protolanguage that was its last major Polynesian branch, it has not been clear on linguistic evidence alone whether the Society Islands or the Marquesas Islands were the place where this branch began (Biggs 1967, 1972; Green and Pawley 1973). Whichever group was inhabited first would, of course, be the locale, because the two archipelagoes are too far apart (1500 km) to have been a joint center.

Biggs (1972:148) found it incredible that the Marquesas, "separated by more than 2,000 miles and many intervening island chains" from West Polynesia, could have been the area of East Polynesia first settled, and so ruled out its candidacy as the first dispersal center for the East Polynesian language. But if archaeological evidence establishes that it was the first settled, then it automatically becomes the first dispersal center.

Green (1966), taking advantage of the uniquely shared vocabularies which I years ago began to assemble (Emory 1946), found it necessary to place Hawaiian, Marquesan, and Mangarevan in one subgroup, with the Marquesas the logical center of dispersal. Tahitian, languages of the Cook group, and Maori were placed in another subgroup, with the Society Islands its logical center of dispersal. Green has the Marquesic group break away from the family stem before the Tahitic.

In my comparison of the names of the lunar months and nights of the moon, I was able to show that the changes made by the Tahitians had definitely exerted influence on the Hawaiian language. But Hawaiians have retained the original Marquesan names, revealing a dual heritage in their vocabulary (Emory 1946).

Tahitian Prehistory Reconstructed through Archaeology

For the reconstruction of Tahitian prehistory we needed sites that would yield artifacts demonstrably belonging to the beginning phase of Tahitian culture. The groundwork for discovery was laid when reconnaissance surveys for the remains of significant stone structures throughout the islands were carried out by the Bishop Museum from 1923 to 1931 (Emory 1933). These surveys called the attention of the local people to the importance of local remains. An island-by-island search for artifacts on the surface, to determine their distribution and also to locate potentially valuable sites for excavation, was begun by the Bishop Museum in 1960 (Emory 1962). The inhabitants were encouraged to watch constantly for artifacts while clearing and cultivating their land.

In June 1962 a clue led to the discovery of a very early-period burial ground on Maupiti, in the Leeward Islands at the western end of the Tahitian chain. A workman digging a posthole exposed a skull with a stone adz and two shaped whale-tooth ornaments lying beside it. These artifacts were given to the local medical practitioner, who brought them to Papeete for us to examine. We were startled to see for the first time ornaments from Tahiti that were identical in form to necklaces found with Moahunter burials in New Zealand, and to several excavated by Sinoto from his earliest-known site, Uahuka, in the Marquesas (Sinoto 1968). We went immediately to the Maupiti site. From this burial ground, on an islet, we uncovered 13 skeletons in 1962–1963. Seven of them were laid out full length, three were in a flexed position, three were in other positions (Emory and Sinoto 1964). The burial goods, differing from historic types, totaled 16 shaped whale-tooth pendants, 18 adzes of six different archaic types, 7 pearl-shell bonito lures, and a pearl-shell hook (Emory and Sinoto 1964, 1965). A collagen date from human bone at this site was A.D. 860 ± 85, which is consistent with expectations if the ancestors of the Moa-hunters came from the Societies were they used similar burial goods.

In 1972 a somewhat earlier site was located, a habitation site on the island of Huahine, the easternmost of the Leeward Islands. Artifacts picked out of the dredgings for a pond behind the Hotel Bali Hai Huahine, at Fare, and shown to Sinoto by Richard Soupine led to discovery of the Huahine site. The adzes and bonito lures were typologically similar to those of the Maupiti burial site, but most significantly there was a whalebone hand club similar to a Maori *patu* (Fig. 8.1).

Certain that abutting on the pond there would be deposits containing similar early artifacts, Sinoto took a Bishop Museum excavation team there in August 1973 (Sinoto and McCoy 1975a). They came upon a cultural layer that yielded such artifacts 250 m from the beach. Some 20 cm of coral sand and pebbles had been deposited over the cultural layer by storm waves or a tidal wave. The cultural stratum averaged 20 cm thick and lay just below sea level, so that ground water came into it and created a water-logging condition that preserved the wood and vegetable materials. A rising of sea level or a sinking of land had taken place since the habitation which left the cultural layer. The discovery of an intact wooden patu on the last day of the eight-day digging period brought the full realization that here we could find preserved and in situ a fuller range of the remains of activities of an early Polynesian settlement than had ever been available before. Also we could expect to find a cross section of the activities at the moment the waves had destroyed the habitations.

Sinoto was able to return to this Huahine site three more times—September 20 to November 30, 1974 (Sinoto and McCoy 1975b); August 31 to October 5, 1975 (Si-

8.1 *Whalebone hand club picked out of dredging for a pond at Fare, Huahine, in 1972. In the Musée de Tahiti et des Îles. (Bishop Museum photo.)*

noto 1976); and July 23 to September 2, 1977 (Sinoto 1978). The last excavation came about as a result of Soupine's report that a backhoe, digging for sand in an adjacent area north of the earlier excavation, had brought up wooden hand clubs, a tapa beater, and archaic adzes. As the expanding hotel would require more of this area, an urgent salvage operation was called for and was made possible by an emergency grant from the National Geographic Society. The effort was magnificently rewarded by producing the 7-m-long end boards of the deck of a large double canoe; its steering paddle, having a blade 3.8 m long; and its 49-cm-long bailer. Sinoto found that if the planks were used in the position shown on a Bishop Museum model of a Tuamotu canoe made in the middle of the last century, the extrapolated length of the canoe would have been 20 m. Three more whalebone patu were found during the 1977 excavation, as well as an extensive array of other items.

The artifacts retrieved from this early Huahine site constitute a treasure. In addition to the canoe parts enumerated above, we now have several regular canoe paddles; two of what are apparently dancing paddles; a wooden grip instrument for pulling canoe lashings taut; one end of a sophisti-

cated bow; 6 unfinished adz handles; a sword club (?); a wooden foreshaft for mounting a harpoon head; a whalebone harpoon head; 8 whalebone and 2 wooden patu; 3 tapa beaters; 5 flat beaters; a whalebone spear; more than 100 stone adzes, many of them unfinished; Terebra-shell chisels; a Cameo-shell chisel; a stone chisel; unifacial and bifacial stone knives; stone abraders, scrapers, and choppers; turtle-bone and pearl-shell scrapers; pearl-shell coconut graters; pearl-shell fishhooks and fishhook blanks; bonito-lure shanks (but no points); a pearl-shell compound shank hook, Marquesan type (see Fig. 8.13*d*, *e*); pearl-shell pendants, Maupiti, New Zealand style; 4 pendants, each cut from pearl shell, in a shape resembling an arrow point with a short stem and identical to several from the Hane site in the Marquesas excavated by Sinoto (1966); a porpoise-tooth pendant; and pearl-shell tattooing needles. A grindstone and a stone that seems to have served as an anvil in the beating of tapa were found in situ. No human burials appeared, but the bones of turtle, dog, chicken, and rat were present. The absence of pig bones should be noted, as well as the absence of the well-known Tahitian pounder. Remains of pandanus, coconut, gourd, and the *awa* plant were present.

In the southern part of the area, posts and floorboards of four small buildings whose floors were propped up on half-meter-high stone pillars indicated storehouses. It was possible for Sinoto (1977) to reconstruct the appearance of one. The houses were rectangular, and the rafters came to the ground. Much more study and further excavation are required before other buildings can be reconstructed.

The following radiocarbon dates of items found in the early cultural layer buried at Huahine have been obtained (Sinoto and McCoy 1975b; Sinoto 1977):

From a whale rib	A.D. 850 ± 70
From charcoal	A.D. 1180 ± 90
From coconut shell	A.D. 1180 ± 85
From wood	A.D. 935
From wood	A.D. 1200

These dates give a range from A.D. 780 to 1270, which seems to us too late. Other dates are pending.

The third early site was discovered in 1977 on Raiatea when a French team from ORSTOM in Papeete and the Musée de Tahiti undertook excavation in an area at Vaihi, where a road was to be built (Semah et al. 1978). Test excavations had indicated that it might hold a site as early as that on Huahine. Based on diggings in December 1977 and January–February 1978, there can be no doubt that the situation was parallel to that at Huahine. Again, at some distance from the lagoon and at a similar depth, lay an intact, water-logged cultural layer containing worked wooden pieces and adzes, fishhooks, a Terebra chisel, and scrapers. Lacking in the Raiatea assemblage, which is much smaller than that from Huahine, are the patu, the ornaments, and the Marquesan type of pearl-shell compound-shank hook.

None of the other excavated sites in the Societies have produced artifacts giving assurance, because of their form and stratigraphic position, that they extend back to the period reflected in the culture of the early Maupiti, Raiatea, and Huahine sites.

Thus there is a gap in the transition from early to late forms of prehistoric artifacts such as adzes and fishhooks. We have not been able to fill this gap because we have not yet found a site showing continuous occupation from early to late prehistoric times. The search is made difficult because the roots of trees and plants and, on the coastal plain, land-crab burrows have greatly disrupted the stratigraphy. The only extensive excavations of what proved to be later habitation sites have been on Moorea, where a Bishop Museum team uncovered a small habitation area near Afareaitu Village (Emory and Sinoto 1965), and at Opunohu, where an American Museum party under Green explored the whole valley. They mapped the ruins of the settlement clusters in the interior of the valley and sites around its bay and at the adjacent village of Papetoai (Green 1961, 1967). At the Afareaitu site 4 marae, one feasting platform, and one house foundation were excavated, yielding 20 fishhooks, 6 adzes, a human bone, a *Conus*-shell chisel, 2 sea-urchin files, and many branch-coral files. "The whole complex of the Afareaitu site is characteristic of the late period of Tahitian prehistoric culture, some of which was retained into historic times" (Sinoto 1962; Emory and Sinoto 1965:57).

Green (1967) counted the number of different structures in the Opunohu Valley to be 81 marae, 56 shrines, 5 council (assembly) platforms, 3 archery platforms, a large assembly-house platform, and 160 house sites. Evidently family groups needed to have their own separate marae and shrines. Council platforms were for community groups, and archery platforms for the elite. Green said, "Archaeologically, a radiocarbon date sets occupation as far back as the thirteenth century, although the sustained occupation appears, again on the basis of a number of radiocarbon dates, between the seventeenth and early nineteenth centuries" (Green 1967:220). Several excavations within the Opunohu Valley yielded very few artifacts, but those at the shore were more numerous and varied.

KENNETH P. EMORY

Within the east portion of the valley, from the site of a large, round-ended house were taken one complete nonflaring pounder, 6 adzes, 3 adz chips, 2 fragments of pounders, and 2 slingstones. From another large, round-ended house site came 3 tanged adzes, an adz blade, 2 adz fragments, and several slingstones. In the west portion of Opunohu Valley, from still another large, round-ended house site came 2 broken adzes of the typical Tahitian triangular form and a flake tool.

Settlement Patterns

The importance of establishing the development of settlement patterns has been demonstrated by Green with his intensive survey accompanied by test excavation of the Opunohu coast and valley on the island of Moorea in 1960. Size of population could be estimated, demographic distribution explained on ecological grounds, social organization revealed, and economic activities envisioned. Green thus could conclude:

The bulk of the population on Mo'orea need not have been concentrated on the seashore along the coralline part of the coastal flat as it is at present, nor aggregated into villages. Rather, for a people who relied essentially on cultivable foods, the more scattered, homestead-like pattern of settlement described by the early European explorers, with focal concentrations in ecologically favorable zones inland, seems to be more understandable in terms of both the archaeological record and the economic requirements of Tahitian food production. It is our belief, then, that the territorial base of political and social units in Mo'orea involved both "inland" and "coastal" zones. They comprised one or more valleys and their shorelines, according to the variations in the local ecology and the degree of social and political integration that had been achieved as a result of historical circumstances. Settlements, at least in Mo'orea, may not be divided into two qualitatively distinct types, coastal and inland. Instead, the settlement of each strip of coast and its associated interior valleys must be viewed as a unit, with situations differing according to the local ecology. (Green et al. 1967:216–217)

Structural Remains

Dwellings

Houses at habitation sites are usually outlined by curbstones revealing a rectangular or oval house plan, on the ground or on a stone platform, and so constitute a record also of size. At the time of European contact, houses of chiefs and meeting or assembly houses were round-ended. Was this a feature in the beginning of habitation, or did it develop later independently or through diffusion from West Polynesia, where round-ended houses are the dominant form? The only certain record we have of a house plan of the settlement period on Huahine is a small rectangular house on piles, probably a storehouse, at Vaitootia, excavated by Sinoto in 1973 (Sinoto and McCoy 1975b).

The French team digging at Vaihi, Raiatea, found embedded worked curbstones defining a very open "V" and so indicating a round-ended house contemporary with their early-period site (Semah et al. 1978).

Religious Structures

The religious structures called *marae* are the most conspicuous and the most specialized of Tahitian stone remains. Except along the coast of Tahiti, a large number of marae have survived. Many of these have been located and described in archaeological surveys (Emory 1933; Emory and Sinoto 1965; Green 1967). Basically, an elongated platform known as an *ahu* is set across one end of a rectangular court defined by a paving or a low stone enclosing wall. Upright stones or slabs on the ahu mark the positions of the deities invoked or of the principal worshippers. Three additional upright slabs are on or in front of the ahu (Fig. 8.2).

The smaller marae exhibit variations of the basic type (Green 1961). The court may or may not be enclosed by a stone wall; in very small marae, the ahu may be omitted and only upright stones identify the area as a marae (Fig. 8.2a). The larger marae,

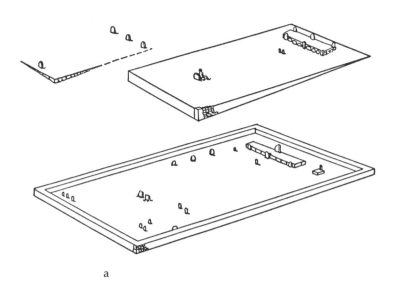

8.2 *Marae types on Tahiti and Moorea:* a, *the simplest version, found in numbers inland;* b, *the stepped-platform marae, typical of those found along the coasts;* c, *the ten-step Mahaiatea marae. (From Emory 1933.)*

a

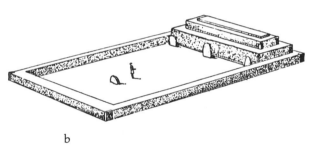

b

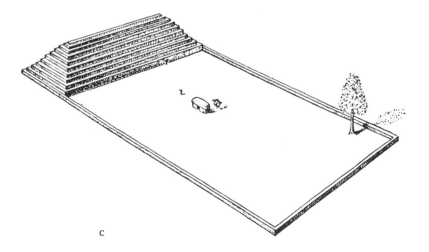

c

KENNETH P. EMORY

which are those of the important families, have a high ahu with uprights along the court face rather than on the ahu (Fig. 8.2b).

In the Windward Islands, Tahiti, and Moorea, the high platforms are stepped, with no more than five steps—except for the famous Mahaiatea marae on Tahiti, built in 1769, which has ten steps (Fig. 8.2c). Dressed stones face the ahu and enclosing walls of the marae of high-ranking families (Green 1968).

In the Leeward Islands the marae are not enclosed, and the ahu is a simple platform faced with a single course of limestone slabs set on edge or on end, except that there are three marae with two-stepped platforms, described below. During the restoration of the ahu of the chief marae of the Societies (that of Taputapuatea at Opoa on Raiatea) Sinoto (1969) discovered that it completely encased a smaller, two-stepped ahu of an earlier stage. Only two other examples of two-stepped ahu are known for the Leeward Islands—those of the leading marae of Huahine Nui, named Manunu, and of the leading marae of Huahine Iti, named Anini. These are shown in Fig. 8.3. The enlarging of Taputapuatea's ahu may be regarded as the result of a desire to make its size comparable to that of the two later marae (Emory 1932, 1933).

In the Tuamotus we learned that the ahu uprights served as backrests for the gods. Thus we can see in the platforms also called ahu on Easter Island a reflection of this type of religious structure, which is a feature of East Polynesian culture that distinguishes it from West Polynesia. On Easter Island the ancestral gods are represented by seated stone figures instead of a row of backrest slabs.

A simple form of Tahitian marae having a low, single ahu platform with an uneven number of upright slabs on it has been found throughout the Tuamotus and on Hawaii, Maui, Nihoa, and Necker in the Hawaiian Islands. Because of its small size and low profile, and the ease with which

upright stones can be removed, the marae can be easily disrupted or covered by tropical growth and its identity thereby lost.

The simple marae of a single platform and three upright slabs along the front still was being built at the time of Cook's visit, as evidenced by the one found in Paea (Emory 1933).

Council Platforms

A structure that was unrecognized prior to archaeological surveys is a stone platform which is not a marae in the usual sense, or an archery platform, or a house site. One at Maeva, Huahine, had slab backrests along its sides (Fig. 8.4a); fortunately, its function was identified by the missionary Tyerman, who wrote that it was for "councils, when the kings, priests, chiefs, and land-owners assembled to determine questions respecting peace, war, or other great public concerns" (Emory 1933:17). An old resident called it a *tahua umu pua'a* (pig oven *tahua*, or assembly place). But it also bears the name *Marae Fare Toa* (House of Warriors' Marae).

A large platform excavated in the vicinity of the Taputapuatea marae on Raiatea was strewn with pig bones from feastings (Emory and Sinoto 1965). A small one excavated at Afareaitu on Moorea, from the quantity of animal bones, obviously was also a feasting place. Charcoal from the Raiatea structure gave a radiocarbon date that would put its construction in the sixteenth century (Emory 1933). Green (1967) has located six such platforms in the interior of Moorea that could be classified as council platforms or tahua, and which he termed "assembly platforms." Others have now been recorded on Huahine and Raiatea. Equivalent sites are bound to exist elsewhere in East Polynesia. For example, within the ruins of the village of Kaunolu on Lanai in the Hawaiian Islands is a large platform at the mouth of Kaunolu gulch that could qualify for such an identification.

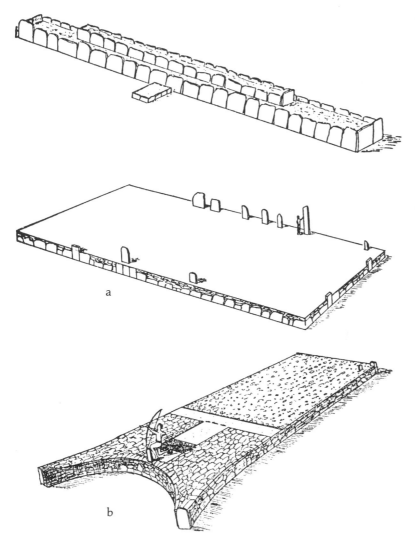

8.3 *Type of Leeward Island marae having two steps, such as the Manunu and Anini marae on Huahine. (From Emory 1933.)*

8.4 *Ceremonial structures: a, council platform at Maeva, Huahine; b, archery platform at Vaihi, Papenoo Valley, Tahiti. (From Emory 1933.)*

Archery Platforms

Unique structures in Polynesia are the Society Island platforms built to accommodate archers participating in what had become a sacred sport of the upper class, one that required the donning of sacred apparel. Although well described by the Reverend William Ellis, the platforms first came to the notice of archaeologists when pig-hunter guides in 1925 led me to several, deep in the valley of Papenoo, on Tahiti (Emory 1933). The platforms are easily recognized by their concave front, which also is wider than the back, and by divisions of the pavement to accommodate the archer (Fig. 8.4b).

Tahitian arrowheads were plain points of ironwood fitted to a reed shaft. Two barbed arrowheads of pearl shell were picked up in front of the platform of the Taputapuatea marae on Raiatea (Fig. 8.5a). Nearly a hundred meters distant and facing the marae is an archery platform. The distance between this platform and the marae platform is about the maximum range a Tahitian bow could send an arrow. The competition, we know, was not for accuracy but for distance, with the arrows apparently shot in the direction of the marae. The sport at this

KENNETH P. EMORY

location may have continued to the time when arriving foreign ships may have brought someone familiar with American Indian arrows, who introduced the making of barbed arrows. In 1965, in a reef islet (Iriru) opposite the Taputapuatea marae, we found a delicate barbed pearl-shell object (Fig. 8.5b), which adds to the puzzle of the barbed arrow, a non-Polynesian feature. From the presence of the head of a well-formed bow at the ancient Huahine site, it would seem that even at that time a bow was held in high esteem.

Petroglyphs

Tahitian petroglyphs are few and widely scattered. Most frequently represented are groups of turtles on boulders or on facing slabs of marae. The body may be divided by concentric circles or by lines making a cross. As turtles are favorite offerings at marae, the petroglyphs may stand for these offerings. On an isolated boulder at Faaa, Tahiti, a face appears having a circle within a circle to represent eyes (Emory 1933), so we know that concentric circles alone may have different meanings. Human and fish figures occur (Fig. 8.6).

An unusual figure—which appears to be twins attached back to back, with an appendage that looks like an umbilical cord—is remarkably well carved and occupies the whole surface of a flat slab roughly 150 × 200 cm lying beside a brook in Tipaerui, Tahiti (Fig. 8.7). A local tradition claims it was carved in memory of the wife and twin children of one Tetaurii, but it may well be a place where attached twins were delivered at birth. Also noteworthy is the fact that the human figure is represented by double lines outlining the body, a technique used in the Marquesas.

Four canoe petroglyphs appear on three adjacent slabs of the seaward facing of the Rauhuru marae at Maeva Village, Huahine. Because of the upturned ends and what seems to represent a raised platform, these may have been meant to depict a Tahitian war canoe (Fig. 8.8). No other canoe petro-

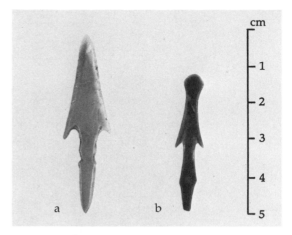

8.5 *Arrowhead-type artifacts collected at Raiatea: a, pearl-shell arrowhead of American Indian shape; b, pearl-shell ornament (?), reflecting barbed arrowhead. (Bishop Museum photo.)*

glyphs have been reported (Emory 1933).

Most interesting of all the petroglyphs are those representing the mask and headdress of the head mourner at the death of a chief (Fig. 8.9). A group of these was found at Vaiote on Tahiti, and a single one on a stone of a council platform at Tevaitoa on Raiatea (Figs. 8.10 and 8.11) (Emory 1927, 1933).

Artifacts

The numbers and varieties of portable artifacts from stratified sites in the Societies is distressingly limited except for the earliest site on Huahine, which alone yielded a wide range of wooden artifacts. It is on excavated artifacts that we depend in order to place in time and locale artifacts that have been picked up on the surface or that have found their way into collections without indication of origin. And it is on the assemblages of artifacts in archaeological sites that we often have to depend for identifying tool kits and the functions and methods of making of specific artifacts. I shall take up just a few categories of artifacts that have been most helpful in reconstructing history.

8.6 *Figures on a boulder in Haapapara Valley, Raiatea. (From Bishop Museum unpublished preliminary report on the archaeological investigations in the Society Islands, 1962–1964.)*

8.7 *A petroglyph boulder at Tipaerui, Tahiti. (Bishop Museum photo by the author.)*

KENNETH P. EMORY

8.8   *Petroglyphs of canoes, on slabs of the Rauhuru marae in Huahine. (Bishop Museum photo by the author.)*

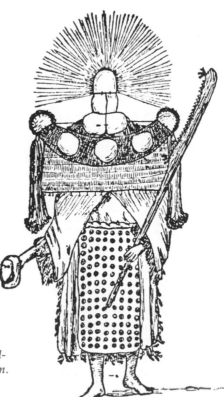

8.9   *Sketch of the chief mourner's costume, sword-club, and pearl-shell clapper in the British Museum. Compare with the petroglyphs in Figs. 8.10 and 8.11. (From Emory 1927.)*

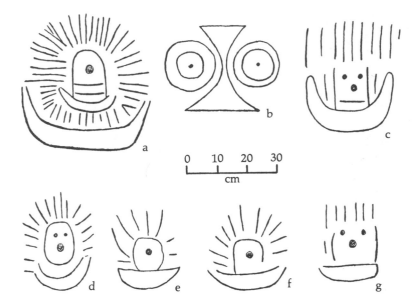

8.10 *Petroglyphs representing the headdress of the chief mourner, on boulders at Vaiote, Tahiti, except for* b, *which is the face on a boulder in Faaa, Tahiti. (From Emory 1933.)*

8.11 *Petroglyph representing a mourner's headdress, on a facing stone of a council platform at Te-vaitoa, Raiatea. (From Emory 1933.)*

KENNETH P. EMORY

Adzes

Because stone adzes are relatively inde-
structible, Polynesian adzes, by virtue of
their unique forms, are the most useful
tools for identifying areas of origin and
periods, once we have determined through
excavations the place and period to which
they belong.

The basic features used to classify adzes
are, first, the cross section at the middle of
the adz, and second, the presence or absence of a modification of the top of the
butt over which pass the lashings that bind
the adz to its wooden haft. The major cross
sections are: rectangular, quadrangular,
trapezoidal, triangular, reverse triangular,
and plano-convex (Emory 1968). If the modification of the butt is present, we say that
the adz is tanged (Fig. 8.12).

More than 100 adzes have been available
for classifying from the three excavations of
settlement-period sites in the Leeward Islands, giving us the range of forms then
current—from Maupiti, 15; from Huahine,
86 (36 from the Vaitootia excavations and
50 from the Faahia excavations); from Raiatea, 3. We have no more than 10 adzes
from excavations later than the early Leeward sites, however.

From the surface of Maupiti, 52 adzes
were classified, plus 47 more that were recovered by divers in the pass into the Maupiti lagoon. From the surface of Raiatea,
224 adzes have been classified. From the
private collection of Henry Picard, now in
the Tahiti museum, 469 adzes, mainly from
Tahiti and Moorea, have been classified
(Emory 1968).

For classifying the adzes in use by the
Tahitians at the time of discovery by the
British, we can depend on the large number of hafted adzes collected by Cook's
party; we know of 25, and as many as 50
more are preserved in museums and recorded in the Bishop Museum's ethnophoto
file. These adzes, so far as can be determined, are all tanged and reverse triangular
in cross section, except for one which is
triangular.

From the 15 adzes possessed by those
who buried their dead on Paeao islet, Maupiti, we know that these implements of that
early period are untanged (6 examples) or
have only a slightly developed tang (8),
with one tanged adz that has a sharply
triangular cross section. None of the others
have this cross section, although one untanged adz approaches it in being trapezoidal. Four adzes are plano-convex untanged
and have a curved cutting edge; of the remaining 9, 2 are rectangular, 5 are quadrangular, and 2 are reverse subtriangular
(Emory and Sinoto 1964).

If we now study the 78 classified adzes
from the early Huahine site, we find that
Sinoto has categorized them all as untanged
or incipiently tanged, and divided them
into the five forms noted below (Sinoto and
McCoy 1975a and b; Sinoto 1978):

(a) Square, with or without round corners—4 (5.1 percent)

(b) Quadrangular to trapezoidal, base
wider than face—9 (11.6 percent)

(c) Quadrangular, face wider than base,
31 (39.8 percent)

(d) Reverse triangular—26 (33.3 percent)

(e) Semicircular (quadrangular-oval and
plano-convex) with curved cutting edge—8
(10.2 percent).

The largest percentage of these adzes
(37.3) are quadrangular with the face narrower than the base, but if we add to them
the other quadrangular adzes of the first
two forms, then that type predominates
(52.9 percent) as it does at Maupiti.

Although these early forms of Maupiti-
Huahine adzes appear in surface collections, they are rare, as exemplified in the
surface collection of 52 adzes from Maupiti,
where the trapezoidal and plano-convex
adzes number only 3, or 5.7 percent, as
compared with 33 percent in its earliest site
(Emory 1968).

In the general collection of 489 Tahitian
adzes that we studied, 49.9 percent were
reverse triangular in cross section, 28 percent triangular, and only 11.5 percent quadrangular, as compared with 52.9 percent
quadrangular in the early Huahine site. In

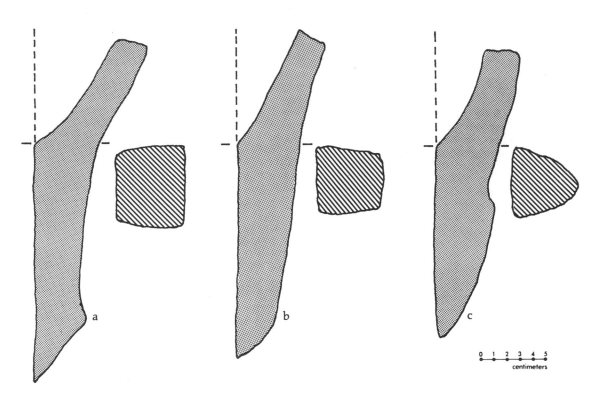

8.12 *Tanged angle adzes of East Polynesia:* a, *Tahitian quadrangular cross section;* b, *Hawaiian quadrangular cross section;* c, *Tahitian reverse triangular cross section.*

the time since the early Huahine settlement, adzes of triangular cross section were proliferating and those of quadrangular cross section were not.

The abandoning of untanged adzes is most evident in the results we obtained from the classification of 224 Raiatea adzes collected from the surface. Only 25, or 11 percent, were untanged.

Divers in the boat pass into Maupiti's lagoon came up with 47 adzes, of which 9 (19 percent) were untanged, mute evidence of canoes capsizing in the pass in early settlement times (Emory 1968).

From the surface collections we know that, between the early adzes of Maupiti and Huahine and those of the time of British discovery, there developed in the quadrangular adzes a modification through which the top of the butt is at an angle with the blade, and the bases of many of these adzes have a concave curve in profile (Fig.

8.12). Such adzes appear in the Tuamotus and are most distinctive of the Hawaiian adzes, unmistakably linking the Societies and Hawaii. It is certain that Hawaiian prehistory began with the rectangular, tanged adz but the angle feature may have appeared then or later. In any case, it brings out a historic connection between the two groups after the time of the Huahine settlement. It is certain, from its rarity, that this angled adz became obsolete in Tahiti and had a short span of preference, so that if it were to be found in a datable, stratified archaeological site in the Societies, the time of the Tahiti-Hawaii connection would be established.

The standard Tahitian adz in Cook's time was the reverse triangular tanged adz that we see in all the hafted adzes his group collected, and that predominate in the surface collections since then. With its haft, this adz became the favorite form of the

KENNETH P. EMORY

Austral and Cook islands (with slight modifications), but did not spread beyond Tahiti's neighboring islands.

Noteworthy is the change that took place in the wooden hafts. Those excavated from the Huahine site have a heel and a toe at the end of the handle, as do the hafts of the Hawaiian adzes collected by members of the Cook expedition; the historic Tahitian adzes lack the toe entirely.

Through the adzes that have become available for study, we not only have knowledge of the forms from the beginning of settlement of the Society Islands to the time of European discovery, but also of the forms used in the other island groups of Polynesia. Early forms of the untanged adzes of West Polynesia in the beginning were carried to the Marquesas and from there to the Societies and to Easter Island. From the Societies, after development of the tang, they were carried to New Zealand; and from the Marquesas or Tahiti or both, again after development of the tang, several of the early forms were carried to Hawaii. In each of these East Polynesian colonies local development resulted in distinctive indigenous adz forms.

Food Pounders

We have descriptions of 15 Tahitian food pounders collected by the Cook expedition (Kaeppler 1978). There are two types of tops: those that are forked, often called "eared," or those that have a cross bar, often called "barred." The bottoms are flared (see Fig. 5.6). A barred pounder of black basalt has come to be known in Tahiti as the Maupiti pounder. Because of this it has been assumed by some that barred pounders were typical of the Leeward Islands and eared pounders of the Windward Islands.

Pounders rarely break and are always reusable; therefore it is not surprising that only two have been archaeologically excavated, both on Moorea and both by Green (Green et al. 1967). One was in the village of Papetoai at the bottom of a deposit with a radiocarbon date of A.D. 1200. It has a nonflaring base, a neck that is oval in cross section, a head with lateral projections, and a center ridge. It could well be the prototype of the typical flaring eared pounders of Tahiti. Another with a similar body but simple lateral projections of the head was found in the fill of a pit at a house site inland. No such food pounders have been found in the early site on Huahine, giving us some reason to assume they had not yet appeared.

Food pounders are not found in West Polynesia, on Easter Island, or in New Zealand. Except for a block form, they are not found in the early levels of Marquesan sites. Therefore we have assumed that the obviously related food pounders of Tahiti-Hawaii-Marquesas developed in central East Polynesia after the primary dispersal of Polynesians to the distal corners of the Polynesian triangle. As the typical Tahitian pounders do not appear in Hawaii, but the Hawaiian pounder is very closely akin to the Marquesan, it seems that we need to place the Tahitian pounders in a period after the early Huahine site and assume that if Tahitians arrived in Hawaii with a Tahitian form of pounder, the Marquesan form was already established. The origin and spread of the forms of the East Polynesian food pounder remain very much of a puzzle and call for a statistical study and comparison of Polynesian pounders, with more archaeologically excavated examples.

Fishhooks

Tahitian fishhooks, because of their typological and structural features, are also proving essential in reconstructing prehistory. We are familiar with the forms at the time of Cook, through more than 40 hooks collected during his expeditions (Kaeppler 1978). These have the following striking differences from the archaic Maupiti-Huahine forms:

(a) The shank of the later simple hook ends in a sharp point instead of being flat (Fig. 8.13a to c).

(b) The point of the later trolling hook

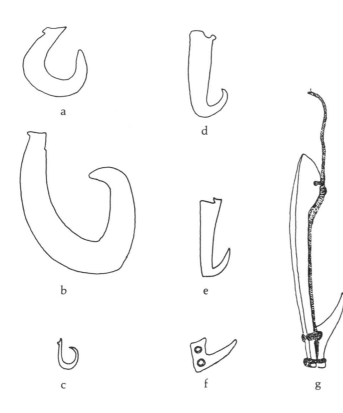

8.13   Tahitian pearl-shell fish-hooks: a and b, ancient rotating hooks with flat heads—in a the shank is curved, in b the point is curved; c, historic rotating hook with pointed head; d, compound-shank hook from Vaitootia, Hua-hine, compared with e, Marque-san equivalent; f, ancient-type point of bonito-lure hook, from Moorea; g, historic bonito-lure hook, in the Peabody Museum, Salem, Massachusetts.

has a downward-projecting rather than an upward-projecting base and has one instead of two holes for lashing the point to the pearl-shell lure (Fig. 8.13*f*,*g*).

(c) The lure of the later trolling hook no longer has sharp shoulders at the top (Fig. 8.13*g*).

The above changes also appear in the Hawaiian hooks, but the first two did not take place in the Marquesas and so can be attributed to Tahitian influence. However, we have not come across simple, rotating hooks in the early Tahitian assemblage in which the shank only is curved, the point being straight. These are characteristic of both archaic Hawaiian and Marquesan hooks and so support the belief that Marquesans settled in Hawaii before the first two changes above took place.

Octopus Lures

The use of cowrie shells attached to a stone sinker to attract and capture octopus is well-known in Polynesia. Several examples of the Tahitian contraption may be observed in the Cook collection (Kaeppler 1978). Tops of cowrie shell are attached together around a grooved oval stone and tied to a stick thought to represent the tail of a rat (Fig. 8.14). We have not yet identified these lures and their sinkers in the excavated sites, but we have recorded four "coffee-bean" octopus-lure sinkers characteristic of the Hawaiian lure, one picked up on Raiatea and three from one district of Tahiti. They could have been made and used by Hawaiian visitors in post-European times. What is important to note is that in the Societies, the Hawaiian-Marquesan type of sinker was not in use at the time of European contact. It would seem to have been dropped in favor of a nondescript stone or coral sinker, or else reliance was put simply on the weight of the shells tied to the stick. When the device is compared with the West Polynesian lure (Fig. 8.14), we see that in a Tongan specimen the sinker is shaped like a cone, flat on the bottom and at one end. This type has

KENNETH P. EMORY

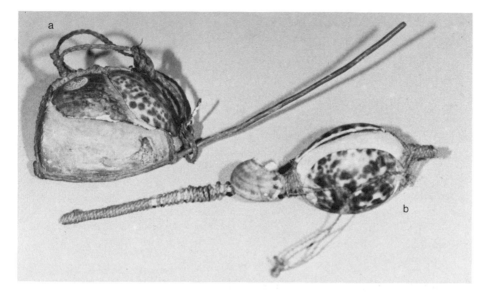

8.14 *Octopus lures and sinkers: a, West Polynesian type from Tonga; b, Tahitian type, in National Museum of Ireland, Dublin. (Bishop Museum photo.)*

turned up in the earliest strata of the Marquesan sand-dune site at Hane and precedes the coffee-bean type (oval, flat on the bottom, grooved) that appears throughout the site at Hatuatua. It is the occurrence of the Marquesan coffee-bean form in Hawaii that is good grounds for belief in a settlement from the Marquesas.

Hand Clubs

Totally unknown as a weapon ever wielded by Tahitians were hand clubs such as the Maori *patu*, until in 1972 one of whalebone (Fig. 8.1) was picked out of the dredgings of a pond. By 1978 four more of whalebone and three of wood had been recovered from this prehistoric site at Fare, Huahine. The excavation of a wooden patu in situ at the bottom of the site proved its existence before the time of settlement of New Zealand and therefore indicates it as an ancestral form.

Notched Quoits

Five notched stone disks—convex on one side, flat on the other—have been picked up on Raiatea. They can be identified as quoits used in the Polynesian game of twirling a disk toward a goal. Fifteen identical quoits have been found, widely distributed, in the Hawaiian Islands, their rarity indicating them to be archaic. A quoit from Fetuna, Raiatea, is exactly similar to a Hawaiian one, as shown in Fig. 8.15. Because Havai'i is the ancient and present poetical name of Raiatea, we can speculate that this is the Hawai'i to which Hawaiian legends refer as the land from which their ruling chiefs came.

Conclusion

The search into the prehistory of Tahiti has revealed that this land was not the first occupied in East Polynesia by those Polynesians sailing ever eastward to discover and occupy the most remote islands of the Pacific Ocean. Language relationships have shown that Tahiti shares in a common heritage that separates East Polynesia from West Polynesia. Even though this protolanguage seems to have come into existence in the Marquesas, Tahiti—as in all other aspects of culture—has had a powerful role in the prehistory of its neighbor islands and of New Zealand and Hawaii.

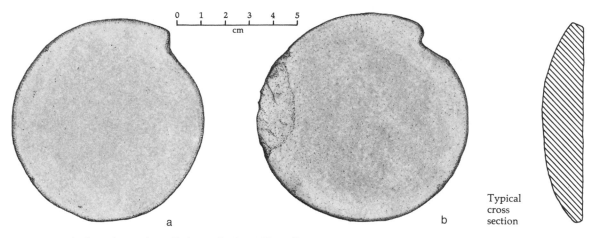

8.15 *Notched quoits:* a, *from Raiatea;* b, *from Hawaii.*

Adzes, fishhooks, ornaments, even a notched-disk gamestone, tell what the Society Islands received and what was passed on, what was modified and what diffused. It is the time over which these events took place that is still uncertain, still to be resolved because of the inconsistencies in our dating results. A chronology arrived at through sequences determined in stratified sites, however, is helping us to arrive at approximate times on which we can place some reliance.

The marae became all-important in the life of the Tahitians. It has become clear from their stone remains and a knowledge of their functions that essentially the marae marked a sacred rectangular area, one end of which was reserved for the deities invoked, who occupied a raised platform, the ahu, and whose seated positions as well as those of principal worshippers were marked by upright stone slabs. In Tahiti only sorcery gods were objectified in stone images; these were small and placed on an adjacent shrine without a platform.

The appearance of marae similar to the Tahitian marae (a simple platform with a number of upright stones along the top) throughout the Tuamotus and in the prehistoric structures on several of the Hawaiian Islands—shrines of the adz makers of Mauna Kea on Hawaii, shrines of visitors to Haleakala Crater on Maui, and especially

those on Necker and Nihoa—establishes this form as the one used in the early expansion of the East Polynesians. The seated-image ahu of Easter Island clearly reflects this East Polynesian marae form also (Emory 1970, 1972).

As this form of marae has not been found in the Marquesas, it would appear that its occurrence in Hawaii and on Easter Island could be attributed only to migrants from Tahiti. These early marae of East Polynesia, however, being small, can so readily be destroyed or their identity lost that their apparent absence cannot be taken as proof that they never existed.

The people who erected the shrines on Necker thus cannot necessarily be considered descendants of Tahitian migrants, but could be descendants of Marquesan migrants. And if the settlers of New Zealand came from Tahiti, even though the Tahitian early marae do not appear there, we need not assume that at the time of their leaving Tahiti such marae did not exist in Tahiti. It may be that conditions were not favorable for their continuance in the form we have seen in the Tuamotus and on Necker.

In 1967 Green came to this conclusion: "All the data on the Society Islands . . . do not as yet warrant broad conclusions that attempt to outline the cultural sequence or to place it in context of Polynesian prehistory" (Green 1967:216).

KENNETH P. EMORY

In 1969 Bellwood, in a paper prepared for a symposium on prehistoric culture in Polynesia, prefaced it with the statement that he would show that "on present evidence we do not yet have the earliest sites in East Polynesia . . . No island group has . . . an unchallenged claim to recognition as the earliest dispersal center in East Polynesia" (Bellwood 1970:93).

At the same symposium Sinoto, who excavated the earliest site so far known in the Marquesas and had excavated the early Maupiti site, also presented a paper (Sinoto 1970). He brought out that his excavations at this site have enabled the establishment of an uninterrupted cultural sequence from settlement times, which can be illustrated by assemblages of a wide range of artifacts. Most importantly, the sequence of the development period embraces the artifacts from the Maupiti excavation as well as artifacts found with burials of the Moa-hunters in New Zealand. After two further years of excavation at the early Huahine site, Sinoto's tentative conclusion reads:

A comparative analysis of Vaitootia [at Fare, Huahine] artifacts and those from the Maupiti site and from Phases I and II [the settlement and expansion periods] of the Hane site, Uahuka Island [in the Marquesas] (Emory and Sinoto 1964; Sinoto 1970) has demonstrated that artifact types from Vaitootia are definitely related to Marquesan Phases I and II—indeed, they are nearly identical. It is significant that the material culture at that time was homogeneous, though from areas that are geographically far apart. In other words, so-called Marquesan and Tahitian culture were not distinguishable at that time. It seems necessary now to treat such a homogeneous culture without restriction of geographic boundaries in East Polynesia, and to classify the Marquesan and Vaitootia assemblages as "archaic East Polynesian cultural assemblages," even though one significant exception in the Vaitootia assemblage is lack of pottery, which was found in the Marquesan sites.

Chronologically the Marquesas are the oldest, followed by Vaitootia, as far as we know today. Polynesians who had East Polynesian culture left the Marquesas and at least one group of people settled at Huahine. Artifacts from the Maupiti burial site, especially the adz forms, indicate that the Maupiti site is chronologically slightly later than the Huahine. We still have, however, a gap of knowledge between the settlement and later prehistoric periods of the Society Islands' history. Between the two periods the so-called Tahitian reversed-triangle adz, the pounder, and the *marae* religious complex were developed. (Sinoto and McCoy 1975b:10–11)

Sinoto's two later excavation periods (1975, 1977) at the Huahine site have served to reinforce the above conclusions to the point where they are no longer tentative. The succession of artifacts and their distribution in East Polynesia have left no doubt in Sinoto's mind or mine that the northern Marquesas Islands were settled before the other groups in East Polynesia.

Sinoto states that the time period of the Huahine site is not earlier than the Marquesan Hane settlement period, to which he has assigned the time (arrived at through radiocarbon dates) of A.D. 300 to 600 (Sinoto 1976). Therefore the Huahine period should fall within A.D. 600 to 1300, the development period. The Huahine radiocarbon dates do cluster around A.D. 900 and A.D. 1200, with only one earlier date of A.D. 850 ± 70.

From typological comparisons of the cultural assemblages Sinoto believes that the beginning of the occupation of the Huahine site must be set earlier than A.D. 850 (Sinoto 1977). I believe we can at least be sure that New Zealand and Hawaii were settled after the Society Islands, and that the Society Islands were settled originally from the Marquesas Islands. Thereafter canoes would occasionally arrive from the Marquesas, or even elsewhere, bringing changes for Tahitian culture which we hope to detect in the artifacts of future excavations.

References

Bellwood, P. S. 1970. Dispersal centers in East Polynesia, with special reference to the Society and Marquesan islands. In *Studies in Oceanic* culture history, ed. R. C. Green and Marion Kelly, vol. 1. *Pacific Anthropological Records* 11:93–104.

Biggs, B. G. 1967. The past twenty years in Polynesian linguistics. In *Polynesian culture history: essays in honor of Kenneth P. Emory*, ed. G. A. Highland et al., pp. 377–396. Bishop Museum Special Publication no. 56, Honolulu.

———. 1972. Implications of linguistic subgrouping with special reference to Polynesia. In *Studies in Oceanic culture history*, ed. R. C. Green and Marion Kelly, vol. 3. *Pacific Anthropological Records* 13:143–152.

Chazine, J. M. 1977. Recherches archéologiques entreprises dans la vallée de la Papenoo à Tahiti. *Bulletin de la Société des Études Océaniennes* 16:707–711.

Emory, K. P. 1927. L'Art tahitien. *Bulletin de la Société des Études Océaniennes* 19:236–239.

———. 1932. Traditional history of Society Islands *marae*. Manuscript.

———. 1933. *Stone remains in the Society Islands*. Bishop Museum Bulletin no. 116, Honolulu.

———. 1946. Eastern Polynesia: its cultural relationships. Ph.D. dissertation, Yale University.

———. 1962. Report on Bishop Museum archaeological expeditions to the Society Islands in 1960 and 1961. *Journal of the Polynesian Society* 71:117–120.

———. 1968. East Polynesian relationships as revealed through adzes. In *Prehistoric culture in Oceania*, ed. Ichito Yawata and Y. H. Sinoto, pp. 151–169. Honolulu: Bishop Museum Press.

———. 1970. A reexamination of East Polynesian marae: many marae later. In *Studies in Oceanic culture history*, ed. R. C. Green and Marion Kelly, vol. 1. *Pacific Anthropological Records* 11:73–92.

———. 1972. Easter Island's position in the prehistory of Polynesia. *Journal of the Polynesian Society* 81:57–69.

———. 1978. Comparison of Polynesian genealogies in the Bishop Museum. *Pacific Studies 1.* Brigham Young University, Hawaii.

——— and Y. H. Sinoto. 1964. Eastern Polynesian burials at Maupiti. *Journal of the Polynesian Society* 73:143–160.

——— and Y. H. Sinoto. 1965. Preliminary report on the archaeological investigations in Polynesia: fieldwork in the Society and Tuamotu islands, French Polynesia, and American Samoa in 1962, 1963, 1964. Manuscript.

Garanger, José. 1964. Recherches archéologique dans le district de Tautira, Tahiti. Rapport preliminaire. *Journal de la Société des Océanistes* 20:5–21.

———. 1967. Archaeology and the Society Islands. In *Polynesian culture history: essays in honor of Kenneth P. Emory*, ed. G. A. Highland et al., pp. 377–396. Bishop Museum Special Publication no. 56, Honolulu.

Green, R. C. 1961. Moorean archaeology: a preliminary report. *Man* 61:169–172.

———. 1966. Linguistic subgrouping within Polynesia: the implications for prehistoric settlement. *Journal of the Polynesian Society* 75:6–38.

———. 1967. The immediate origins of the Polynesians. In *Polynesian culture history: essays in honor of Kenneth P. Emory*, ed. G. A. Highland et al., pp. 215–240. Bishop Museum Special Publication no. 56, Honolulu.

———. 1968. Religious structures of the windward Society Islands. *New Zealand Journal of History* 2:66–89.

——— and A. K. Pawley. 1973. Dating the dispersal of the Oceanic languages. *Oceanic Linguistics* 12:1–6.

———, K. Green, R. A. Rappaport, Ann Rappaport, and J. M. Davidson. 1967. *Archaeology on the island of Mo'orea, French Polynesia*. Anthropological Paper no. 51, pt. 2, American Museum of Natural History, New York.

Henry, Teuira. 1928. *Ancient Tahiti*. Bishop Museum Bulletin no. 48, Honolulu.

Kaeppler, A. L. 1978. *Artificial curiosities. An exposition of native manufactures collected on the three Pacific voyages of Captain James Cook*. Bishop Museum Special Publication no. 65, Honolulu.

Oliver, D. L. 1974. *Ancient Tahitian society*. Honolulu: University Press of Hawaii.

Semah, F., M. Charleux, and H. Ouwen. 1978. *Fouilles archéologiques sur Raiatea: Vaihi*. Papeete: Centre ORSTOM, Musée de Tahiti.

Sinoto, Y. H. 1962. A preliminary report on the excavations at Vairao, Tahiti and Afareaitu, Moorea. Manuscript.

———. 1966. A tentative prehistoric cultural sequence in the northern Marquesas Islands, French Polynesia. *Journal of the Polynesian Society* 75:286–303.

———. 1969. Restoration de marae aux îsles de la Société. *Bulletin des Études Océaniennes* 14:236–244.

———. 1970. An archaeologically based assessment of the Marquesas Islands as a dispersal center in East Polynesia. In *Studies in Oceanic culture history*, ed. R. C. Green and Marion Kelly, vol. 1. *Pacific Anthropological Records* 11:105–130.

————. 1976. Final phase of the excavation of an archaic habitation site on Huahine, Society Islands; preliminary report (1975 excavation). Manuscript.

————. 1977. Archaeological excavations of the Vaito'otia site on Huahine Island, French Polynesia (1975 excavation). Manuscript.

————. 1978. Preliminary report on the salvage archaeology at Faahi'a, Fare, Huahine, Society Islands, French Polynesia (1977 excavation). Manuscript.

———— and P. C. McCoy. 1975a. Report on the preliminary excavation of an early habitation site on Huahine, Society Islands. *Journal de la Société des Océanistes* 31:143–186.

———— and P. C. McCoy. 1975b. Excavations of an archaic habitation site on Huahine, Society Islands; preliminary report (1974 excavation). Manuscript.

Verin, Pierre. 1964. Notes sur les sites du plateau de Mahina, domain de Nono-Ahu, Tahiti. *Journal de la Société des Océanistes* 20:22–27.

New Zealand

CHAPTER 9

JANET M. DAVIDSON

 New Zealand differs in several important respects from the other Polynesian island groups discussed in this book. It is a much larger land mass, and the only one situated in a temperate latitude. In size it is comparable to New Guinea; in climate it resembles some temperate coastal parts of Australia. The study of archaeology in New Zealand has gone on for more than a century. This means, first, that there is a much more substantial body of data to consider than for any other part of Oceania. Secondly, current views on New Zealand prehistory are inevitably influenced to some extent by earlier hypotheses, many of which, although no longer accepted by professional archaeologists, are deeply embedded in the folklore of modern New Zealanders.

Prehistory in New Zealand is short—barely 1,000 years. And because of the size of the country, particularly its great length, Polynesian settlers encountered considerable regional diversity there. These two factors make it difficult to organize archaeological data into a series of tight chronological or developmental divisions. In the following review, therefore, after an initial introduction to the country, its people, and the course of archaeological research, changes in several aspects of the culture are discussed as a series of themes. No attempt is made to organize the data into phases and periods, although two standard reference points in New Zealand prehistory are used: archaeological evidence from known early sites, and ethnographic accounts of the eighteenth-century Maori.

New Zealand comprises two principal islands and numerous smaller islands that extend between 34° and 48° south latitude (Fig. 9.1). Both of the major islands are relatively long and narrow, with a combined length of more than 1,500 km and a maximum width of only 320 km. Rugged mountains form the backbone of each island, with the highest mountain in the South Island, Mount Cook, attaining a height of 3,764 m; Ruapehu, in the North Island, reaches 2,797 m. At least three-quarters of New Zealand's total land mass is more than 200 m above sea level (Wards 1976).

Geologically, New Zealand is relatively ancient compared with the tropical Polynesian islands, with a much greater variety of rocks and soils than Polynesian man encountered anywhere else in his island world. Its geographic isolation is reflected in the fact that before the arrival of man the only land mammals were two species of bat. The bird fauna had radiated to fill vacant niches, and a number of species of flightless birds occupied the land.

Although the whole of New Zealand has a temperate climate, the considerable distance from north to south results in marked environmental differences from one part of the country to another, some of which were significant to settlers from tropical Polynesia. For example, the far northern section of the North Island has a mean annual temperature of 15° C or more, while coastal areas in the far south range between 7.5° and 10° C. Some southern areas, however, have much greater extremes of both heat and cold than the milder north. The incidence of frost also varies considerably. Average rainfall varies from as little as 350 mm in Central Otago to more than 7,000 mm in the Southern Alps, although for much of the country it varies between 600 and 1,600 mm.

Some 880 km east of Christchurch lie the Chatham Islands, politically part of modern New Zealand but in prehistoric times in-habited by an isolated group of Polynesians, the Moriori. The prehistory of these islands is currently the subject of intensive research by archaeologists from the University of Otago. It is not yet fully reported so cannot be discussed meaningfully here.

The first European to visit New Zealand, Abel Tasman in A.D. 1642, had only a very brief encounter with the inhabitants, whom he found murderous and warlike. The next arrival, James Cook, both in 1769–1770 (Beaglehole 1955) and on subsequent visits during the 1770s (Beaglehole 1961, 1967) established contact with New Zealanders at a number of places and provided valuable accounts of their society at that time. To Cook the similarities, particularly of language, between the inhabitants of New Zealand and those of other Polynesian islands were striking. He had no doubt that the New Zealand Maori, as they were later to be called, and the Tahitians and Tongans shared a common origin, which he believed lay to the west.

Cook found inhabitants on much of the New Zealand coast, even in remote Fiordland in the southwest portion of the South Island. In some areas life appeared peaceful, whereas other groups were hostile or at war. Numerous fortifications were seen in the North Island and the northern South Island; in some places, however, people appeared to be living peacefully in small undefended hamlets. Extensive cultivations were observed in the Bay of Islands and elsewhere on the east coast of the North Island. Plants familiar to the explorers from Tahiti were recognized, notably taro (*Colocasia esculenta*), sweet potato (*Ipomoea batatas*), and gourd (*Lagenaria siceraria*). Yams (*Dioscorea* sp.) and paper mulberry (*Brousonettia papyrifera*) were also noted in the north. The importance of fish and the dried rhizome of the bracken fern was apparent everywhere. In the northern South Island, where cultivation was not seen and warfare was particularly intense, Banks, who accompanied Cook on his first voyage, flippantly remarked that the inhabitants

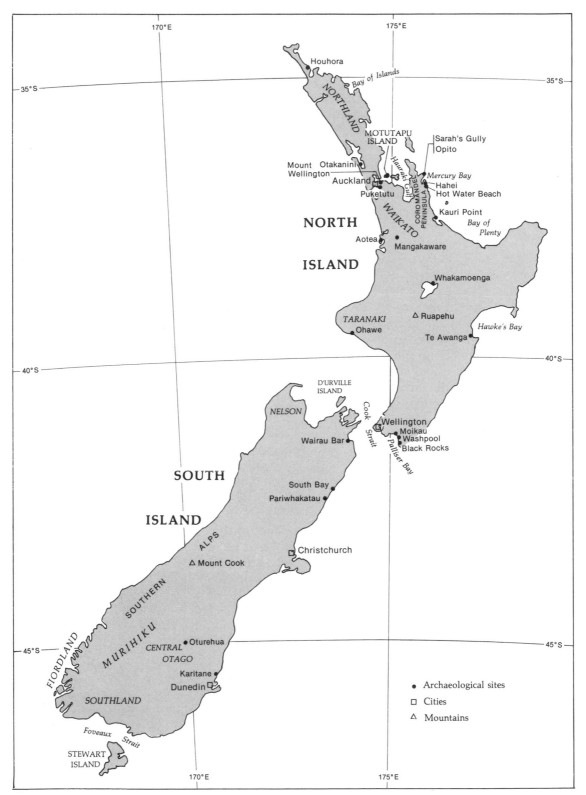

9.1 *Map of New Zealand, showing important locations.*

JANET M. DAVIDSON

appeared to live entirely on fish, dogs, and enemies (Beaglehole 1962). The practice of cannibalism aroused horror among the European observers.

Houses, settlements, costumes, weapons, tools, and ornaments were described, illustrated, and in the case of portable items collected by Cook's company. With similar information from subsequent European visitors, these accounts provide the basis for definition of what has been called Classic Maori culture—the New Zealand culture as it existed in the late eighteenth century, before it was significantly altered by contact with Europeans.

The similarities of language and appearance noted by early observers between the Maoris and other Polynesians have been borne out by studies in linguistics and physical anthropology. The Maori language belongs to the East Polynesian subgroup of Polynesian languages and is closely related to the languages of Tahiti and Rarotonga (Green 1966). The pioneering work of Scott (1893) in physical anthropology and subsequent studies by Buck (1922–1923), Shapiro (1940), Marshall and Snow (1956), Taylor (1962), Shima and Suzuki (1967), and others have demonstrated the Polynesian affiliation of the Maori people; some regional variation has also been documented.

Archaeology in New Zealand

In the early days of European settlement in New Zealand, archaeology was stimulated by the discovery of the bones of the giant extinct birds known as *moa* (order Dinornithiformes) and other extinct species such as the swan, goose, and eagle, and the even more exciting realization that these bones were often found in human campsites. Although these first discoveries were made before 1850, the great era of nineteenth-century archaeology was in the 1870s, when a number of papers describing the investigation of moa-hunter campsites were read before various branches of the New Zealand Institute. Intense controversy was provoked by Sir Julius von Haast

(1871, 1874), who proposed that the moa-hunters, as he called them, were a vanished, autochthonous, palaeolithic race of great antiquity who exterminated the moas; the neolithic Maoris, coming much later, subsisted on fish and shellfish rather than extinct birds. The contrary view, that the moa-hunters were simply the ancestors of the present Maoris who changed their diet as their initial food supply dwindled, gradually became accepted and by the 1890s this was the generally held opinion. During this period numerous sites (mostly in the South Island) were investigated, and in some cases detailed lists were published of the artifacts and faunal remains found. The principal investigators were natural scientists, well read in recent developments in European archaeology, who were involved not only in the excavation of sites and the identification of bones but in the determination of species of extinct birds—which in many cases were found in archaeological as well as natural deposits.

As this first efflorescence of archaeology died down, another important strand in the development of New Zealand prehistory began to dominate study. This was the study of Maori oral traditions, which had already begun with the collection and publication of traditions by various authorities (for instance, Grey 1854; Shortland 1854). It was stimulated by the search for Maori stories about the moa and gained impetus with the founding of the Polynesian Society in 1892. Not content with merely collecting traditions, the founders of this movement, particularly S. Percy Smith, extended the search for ever more esoteric lore relating to remote origins and migrations. Indeed, they looked for stories that appeared to interpret the archaeological finds of the earlier era. Although much that was of great value was recorded, it was at this time that many spurious traditions about origins gained wide acceptance—ideas that still bedevil the study of New Zealand prehistory. These include the beliefs that oral tradition reaches back far enough to describe Polynesian wanderings through countries as remote as Egypt and India; that New Zealand was first settled by an inferior race known as Moriori (confused with the Chatham Islanders) or Maruiwi, who were conquered by later Maoris; and that Maori traditions can be organized into a simple, coherent story known and accepted by all Maoris—a narrative of the successive discovery of New Zealand by heroes named Kupe and Toi, and of its subsequent settlement by a single great migration of canoes from the homeland known as Hawaiki.

The "Maruiwi myth," particularly, has been challenged on both traditional (Williams 1937) and archaeological grounds. In the 1920s a program of archaeological work was instituted by Skinner in the South Island to demonstrate the truly Polynesian nature of moa-hunter assemblages, thereby debunking the idea of an earlier and different race (see, for example, Skinner 1923; Teviotdale 1932). The demonstration was successful archaeologically, but the romantic Maruiwi myth lives on in New Zealand folklore, despite modern scholarly reassessment of the sources of the traditions (Simmons 1969a, 1976).

The archaeological work of the 1920s and 1930s was curiously lacking in any concept of sequence or change apart from the economic effects of the extermination of moas and other bird species. Regional but not chronological differences throughout New Zealand were recognized (Skinner 1921). Stratigraphy was largely ignored; consequently the rich assemblages recovered are now of limited use in modern archaeological studies.

Two of Skinner's pupils were responsible for significant new developments. The excavation by Duff at Wairau Bar in the northern South Island (Duff 1956) provided a very full definition of moa-hunter material culture, largely based on grave goods, although a great deal of other material was also recovered from the middens at Wairau. The East Polynesian nature of early New Zealand material culture was fully demonstrated at this site. Wairau was one of the first archaeological sites in New Zealand

to be dated by the radiocarbon method. Lockerbie, working in Otago and recognizing the importance of stratigraphy in a number of deep coastal sites (see, for example, Lockerbie 1940, 1959), demonstrated the changing economy and material culture of southern New Zealanders.

Until the mid-1950s virtually all major archaeological work had taken place in the South Island: by von Haast and his opponents, Skinner and his protégés, and finally Duff and Lockerbie. Yet the South Island is climatically less suitable for Polynesian settlement than the North Island, and in the eighteenth and nineteenth centuries only a very small proportion of the total Maori population was to be found there. Moreover, nearly all the spectacular field monuments are in the North Island (Fig. 9.2); yet they had been almost totally neglected, apart from isolated and exceptional studies such as that of Best (1927) on pā (fortifications). It thus came to be thought that the South Island was a focus of early moa-hunter occupation and that the North Island was only later intensively occupied, as new waves of Maori immigrants succeeded in introducing horticulture. With this stronger subsistence base, and with new and fiercer techniques of warfare, North Islanders became numerous and powerful, introducing both horticulture and warfare to the South Island and exterminating some of the allegedly peaceful moa-hunters in the process. This view of New Zealand prehistory is a mixture of archaeological evidence and oral traditions of doubtful authenticity. There has always been a tendency in New Zealand to fall back on oral traditions to interpret or fill gaps in archaeological evidence. The combination of South Island prehistory derived from archaeological evidence and tradition, and North Island prehistory derived almost entirely from selected traditions, has been particularly dangerous.

Since 1954 a great deal of investigation has been done in the North Island with modern excavation techniques and such additional aids as radiocarbon dating. Atten-

9.2 *Maori earthworks and a modern road on the eastern slopes of Mount Wellington, one of Auckland's volcanic cones. (Photo courtesy of Anthropology Department, University of Auckland.)*

tion has been directed not only toward coastal middens rich in artifacts and faunal remains, but toward the wealth of structural sites, so much more numerous in the North Island than the South, which contain the remains of houses, food storage structures, and fortifications (Fig. 9.3), but often relatively few artifacts. Thus the earlier one-sided view of New Zealand prehistory is gradually being revised.

Theoretical Perspectives

The need to organize the abundant and often disparate data of New Zealand prehistory has resulted in a number of theoretical contributions during the past 20 years. Golson (1959), drawing on both British and American archaeological theory, outlined a framework for New Zealand prehistory according to chronological phases and regional aspects. He left open the alternatives that Classic Maori culture was derived directly from the earlier founding culture, for which he proposed the term Archaic, or resulted from an admixture of Archaic with

another intruding culture; or whether two distinct cultures, or two phases of one culture, were involved. Green (1963) attempted to classify the somewhat diverse archaeological data already accumulating from the Auckland province according to a six-phase model, which included settlement pattern and economic criteria as well as material culture. He substituted the term "New Zealand Eastern Polynesian Culture" for Golson's Archaic. Meanwhile, Duff (1962) continued to elaborate his earlier model of South Island prehistory, in which a moa-hunter period was superseded by a Classic Maori period as a result of intrusion from the North Island. Other workers, notably Simmons (1969b), have proposed overall economic sequences for New Zealand prehistory, based on the decline and extinction of moas, changes in forest regeneration, and the increasing importance of horticulture. A major paper by Groube (1967) discussed alternative models of culture change in New Zealand and considered in particular the rate of culture change and the relevance of models tested in New

9.3 *Kauri Point Pā, Bay of Plenty, a small cliff-edge pā with double ditch and bank. (Photo courtesy of Anthropology Department, University of Auckland.)*

Zealand to areas with longer and more complex sequences.

Several problems have complicated most or all of these approaches. One is a tendency toward polarization; in separating the known earliest and latest materials it becomes difficult to recognize anything intermediate or transitional. Another has been the assumption that Classic Maori culture was a package involving not only certain types of artifacts but horticulture and various social aspects, notably the development of warfare, as well. A third has been the tendency to overlook the considerable regional diversity in New Zealand and propose similar sequences of economic and social change for widely separated regions.

At present, there appears to be a concentration on regional prehistory, particularly on the interaction of man and his environment through time. The emergent outlines of New Zealand prehistory are very different from those current only a few years ago.

Early Settlement

The date of the first settlement of New Zealand has not yet been reliably established,

nor is it certain that there was only one effective colonization. Some early regional differences in material culture, particularly in stone technology, suggest separate origins outside New Zealand, but these have yet to be identified. At present it can merely be said that by A.D. 1200 much of the coast of New Zealand and some inland regions had been settled by people of East Polynesian cultural affiliations. On this basis, first settlement is usually estimated at about A.D. 800, with some authorities preferring a slightly earlier date. By 1100 or 1200 there appears to have been differentiation between regions, with centers of population in the far north, the Coromandel Peninsula, South Taranaki, Cook Strait, Murihiku (southern South Island), and probably in other regions not yet adequately investigated, such as the central South Island. Whether some or all of these centers arose from the separate arrival of colonists from the same general region of East Polynesia, or whether they resulted from the splitting up and spread of a single original colonizing group, is not known. In later times considerable tribal migration took place; it is possible that the earliest settlers were equally mobile.

JANET M. DAVIDSON

9.4   *Excavations at the early site of Houhora, Northland. (Photo courtesy of Anthropology Department, University of Auckland.)*

The first arrivals, whether in one group or several, found New Zealand largely forested, apart from some areas of the eastern South Island, inhabited by a land-based avifauna never previously exposed to mammalian predators. They also found, importantly, a regional and climatic diversity sufficient to prevent a uniform economic adaptation.

Until recently it was widely believed that the first New Zealanders failed to bring with them, or failed to establish, the tropical plants that were cultivated by later Maoris in favorable parts of the country. Because moa-hunters in the southern South Island almost certainly practiced a hunting and gathering economy, as did the later inhabitants of Murihiku, it was assumed that moa-hunters elsewhere did likewise. One of the most important developments in New Zealand archaeology has been the demonstration that horticulture was certainly practiced in widely separated parts of the North Island in the twelfth century. It

can now be cautiously assumed that horticulture was a feature of Polynesian life there from the time of first settlement.

Of the animals that accompanied Polynesians across the Pacific, only the dog (*Canis familiaris*) and the Polynesian rat (*Rattus exulans*) reached New Zealand. No traces of pig or chicken have been found, but both dog and rat bones are common in early sites. The colonization of New Zealand by the rat, even if it was brought in deliberately by man as a food delicacy, appears to have been at least as rapid as its colonization by man.

The settlements of early New Zealanders that have been investigated are mostly coastal, at the mouths of streams, rivers, or harbors. Some, such as the northernmost properly excavated site (at Houhora in Northland, see Fig. 9.4), have been interpreted as summer camps of people who spent other seasons elsewhere (Shawcross 1972); others, such as the Washpool Village at Palliser Bay on the southern tip of the

North Island, have been seen as small year-round villages (B. F. Leach 1976); others again, such as Wairau Bar (Duff 1956), are viewed as large permanent villages. The prevailing pattern was probably one of villages close to gardens, as at Palliser Bay, with seasonal camps for fishing and fowling and perhaps other activities close to the appropriate resource.

Change

Change in all its aspects is of interest to New Zealand prehistorians. It can be broken down into several major if overlapping categories. Change in material culture, long the special province of archaeologists, is one important facet. Change in subsistence economy is another that has dominated thinking about New Zealand prehistory. Change in social life, particularly the development of warfare, has also been significant. Besides warfare this involves consideration of such social phenomena as settlements, community size and relationship, exchange and communication, ritual and belief, and burial customs—some of the most difficult and elusive aspects of culture for archaeologists to study. Finally there is environmental change, both that independent of man, such as climatic change or volcanic cataclysm, and that brought about by man himself in his impact on the environment.

The possibility of climatic fluctuations during the last millennium is a crucial point in New Zealand prehistory because of the marginal nature of tropical Polynesian horticulture. Climatic change was first suggested to explain apparent anomalies in forests and soils in parts of the South Island (Holloway 1954; Wardle 1963). It has also been recognized, however, that Polynesian use of fire had a significant effect on South Island forests (Molloy 1969). Recently, independent evidence about temperature curves has been obtained from isotope ratios in speleothems (Hendy and Wilson 1968), and from variations in gla-

ciers in the Southern Alps (Wardle 1973; Salinger 1976). Changes in precipitation and wind regimes appear to have been related to the temperature fluctuations (Wilson and Hendy 1971). All those factors would have been significant for Polynesian man in New Zealand. Increased storminess, particularly, would have affected both off-shore fishing and seaborne communication.

Both Yen (1961) and Green (1963) attempted to relate the introduction of horticulture in New Zealand, and especially the adaptation of the *kumara* or sweet potato, to deteriorating climatic conditions. It now appears, however, that not only horticulture but the unique New Zealand kumara storage techniques were already developed before significant declines in temperature took place. On the other hand, it is possible that Polynesian settlers arrived at the onset of an amelioration of climate during the ninth century that lasted for several hundred years, during which horticulture and storage became firmly established. Succeeding fluctuations would certainly have affected horticulture in marginal southern and inland zones, but not the nature or existence of horticulture itself.

Volcanic eruptions and seismic movements have had severe local effects in some parts of the North Island. The most devastating of the holocene eruptions took place before the arrival of man, and it now appears that vegetation and moas had recolonized much of the affected area before human settlement. However, later eruptions had considerable if localized impact, and tephra deposits provide important stratigraphic marker beds over wide areas (Wellman 1962).

The impact of Polynesian man on the environment, like climatic change, has been the subject of considerable controversy. Some writers have seen forest changes as almost entirely natural and moas as already on the verge of extinction when man arrived. Others have blamed man for the destruction of the forest, the extermination of moas and other birds, and the severe reduction in number and distribution of the

JANET M. DAVIDSON

tuatara (*Sphenodon punctatus*) and other creatures such as certain land snails (Fleming 1962)—a view that has gained popularity in recent years. This need not imply that man was deliberately and needlessly destructive, but rather that the arrival of man, with his fires and his accompanying rats and dogs, introduced important new factors into the ecology. The role of the rat in particular has probably been underestimated (Fleming 1969). The role of fire, however, has long been recognized. In the drier eastern South Island, large fires could have been accidental. In the North Island, on the other hand, progressive clearance of land for horticulture—a constant nibbling away of the forest fringe with an occasional accidental fire—probably brought about great change in both animal and plant communities over a long period of time. Whatever the cause, significant changes in forest and fauna took place during the pre-European period of human occupation of New Zealand.

The time has now been reached when broad general pictures must be replaced by more detailed regional studies of the impact of man on his environment. This has already been demonstrated in several areas, where changes not merely in the forest but in many aspects of the environment can be inferred from archaeological evidence. At Palliser Bay, for instance, clearance of forest resulted in erosion that affected not only the garden soils but also the coastal marine environment (H. M. Leach 1974).

The material culture of the earliest New Zealanders shows strong affinities with contemporary assemblages in the Society Islands and Marquesas (Green 1975), notably the sites of Maupiti, Vaitootia, and Hane, all of which could be described as Archaic East Polynesian. Similarities are evident in fishing gear, harpoons, ornaments (including reels, necklace units, real and imitation whale-tooth pendants as well as various other pendant units), needles and cloak pins, and stone adzes. There are a few problems, however. Phase II in the Marquesas (in which material most comparable to New Zealand assemblages is found) is only broadly dated between A.D. 600 and 1300, while the early Society Island sites are dated between A.D. 600 and 1200. New Zealand contains a greater variety of adz forms and probably fishing gear than is known from any other Polynesian island group at the same period. It is possible, therefore, that New Zealand was a sort of catch-all for migrants from every other part of East Polynesia, or that there was some return movement from New Zealand to tropical Polynesia, which took New Zealand inventions back there. Be this as it may, a recognizably East Polynesian material culture can be identified in early New Zealand sites, many features of which had been replaced or considerably modified by the eighteenth century.

Fishing gear. New Zealand trolling gear was a direct adaptation of Polynesian forms, with stone or bone shanks instead of pearl shell. It lasted in some areas on the east coast of the North Island until European times (Duff 1956). In the South Island, the so-called barracouta lure (a wooden shank with a bone point), which may or may not have an East Polynesian prototype, was present for much or all of the sequence, the points becoming progressively more ornate or "baroque" through time (Hjarno 1967). The other principal Classic Maori lure, the North Island kahawai lure (a wooden shank with *paua* shell plate and bone point), is hardly represented archaeologically and may be a very late development. One-piece hooks of bone and occasionally shell show increased use of barbs and more ornamentation through time, and there was a steady increase in the use of composite bait hooks, usually with wooden shanks and bone or shell points. Both barbs and two-piece points have been considered distinctively New Zealand developments. Their recent discovery in small numbers in early New Zealand sites (B. F. Leach 1976), and their occasional presence elsewhere in Polynesia, makes this attribution uncertain. In general, however, it can be said that New Zealand fishing gear shows an initial adaptation of Polynesian forms, followed by elaboration of some forms at the expense of others, and the development of regional variation. People on the Coromandel Peninsula were very conservative, for example, at least until about A.D. 1500, while in Murihiku they were much more innovative. Nonetheless, certain forms of late Maori fishhooks are apparently found from one end of the country to the other, and it is not yet possible to determine in which direction they spread.

Ornaments. Typical Archaic ornaments may have persisted until A.D. 1400 or 1500 in some areas. Some ornament forms, such as bird bone beads, *Dentalium nanum* shell beads, and simple pendants of bone and shell are found throughout the sequence. The first appearance of what are considered, on ethnographic evidence, as distinctively Classic Maori ornaments (Orchiston 1972) is difficult to document, since some of the most characteristic forms are seldom or never found in excavations. The use of nephrite for ornaments seems to be later than its use for tools; plain nephrite pendants appear in the archaeological record from about A.D. 1500 on, although they could well have been present earlier. The more elaborate nephrite pendants, including *hei tiki*, are very rare in archaeological sites. The same is true of other striking forms such as the whale-tooth *rei puta* pendants. Another typical Classic Maori adornment, the ornamental head comb, rarely found in excavations, is not so far recorded from Archaic assemblages except for a possible fragment from Hot Water Beach, Coromandel (Leahy 1974). In ethnographic times, however, combs were made of wood as well as of bone. Wooden combs have been dated to the fifteenth or sixteenth centuries at Kauri Point (Shawcross 1976; Green 1978).

Tattooing, fairly prevalent in eighteenth-century New Zealand, is shown to have been present throughout the sequence by the remains of bone tattooing chisels from sites of all ages. Development of typical Maori designs can only be guessed (Mead 1975), although it has been suggested that a change from broad to narrow chisels may relate to a change from rectilinear to curvilinear patterns.

Adzes. Whereas early adzes exhibit a variety of shapes, typical late adzes are ungripped specimens of rounded quadrangular section, which have often been considered inferior to earlier examples. Certainly the manufacturing technique can be considered inferior, since the late adzes are shaped by pecking and grinding; as a result, they are far less elegant than many early specimens made by craftsmen with a considerable mastery of flaking technique, particularly in the northern South Island. Recent functional study (Best 1975) suggests that for some purposes the later adzes may be more successful, however, so the question of improvement versus degeneration deserves a long, hard look. In general, the early adzes were made of stones selected for their flaking characteristics—stones similar to the basalts of tropical Polynesia. Large exchange networks were based on early quarries on the Coromandel Peninsula and in northeast Nelson, and lesser ones on quarries in Auckland and Southland. Later adzes are often made from a variety of stones of more local origin but still apparently carefully selected. In the South Island the development of nephrite adzes and their export replaced to a considerable extent an earlier trade from Nelson/D'Urville Island. Nephrite adzes were probably the most highly prized throughout the country. At the same time, a few stylistically early adzes apparently continued in use until very recently as heirlooms for special occasions (McKay 1973).

Stone technology. One of the most difficult and least studied aspects of New Zealand material culture is stone technology. Flaking techniques for adz manufacture apparently varied from region to region. There is a world of difference between the casually struck and unstandardized obsidian flake tools of most regions and the highly developed prismatic blade industry

JANET M. DAVIDSON

9.5 *Distribution of material from a blade manufacturing site at Oturehua, Central Otago, as reconstructed in the laboratory. (Photo courtesy of B. F. and H. M. Leach.)*

of Murihiku (Fig. 9.5). The latter was apparently fully developed by the twelfth century, then declined and largely disappeared after the fourteenth century, although some continuity in flaking technology in Murihiku throughout the sequence has been demonstrated (B. F. Leach 1969). The extent to which early variations are the result of separate settlement or the rapid loss of certain skills in some small populations remains to be determined.

Other items. Adzes, ornaments, fishing gear, and stone flakes are the items most commonly found by archaeologists. Relatively little can be said about other apparently important items because there have been so few finds from adequate archaeological contexts. Short fighting weapons, known as *patu* (see Fig. 8.1), long thought of as distinctively Maori, have recently been found at Vaitootia in the Society Islands in wood and whalebone (Sinoto and McCoy 1975). Thus it seems likely

that weapons of this kind, particularly in wood, were part of Archaic East Polynesian material culture, later dying out in the tropical islands while being elaborated in New Zealand. Some of the various whalebone examples from the South Island and one from the early site of Ohawe (or Waingongoro) in South Taranaki could well have come from Archaic contexts, although none have been found in controlled excavations. The development of the distinctive stone *patu ōnewa*, however, is probably a late North Island development; the only archaeological examples have been found in recent North Island sites.

One of the most significant aspects of change in material culture, the development of Classic Maori art styles, is probably the most difficult of all to document archaeologically (Mead 1975). Several notable swamp excavations, however, productive of water-logged wooden material, offer hope that further discoveries may be made. From

a small swamp at Kauri Point in the Bay of Plenty, thought to be a repository of *tapu* objects, items including a large assemblage of wooden combs that show stylistic change through time were found (Shawcross 1976). A variety of wooden material recovered from the bed of a small Waikato lake (Mangakaware) was probably associated with one or more relatively late fortified sites on its fringes (Bellwood 1971). Items that appear to be stylistically earlier have been uncovered recently in a site in Taranaki. Further finds of this sort, especially from sites for which radiocarbon dates can be obtained, will advance this field of study.

Horticulture and plant foods. Many archaeologists now agree that horticulture was probably established by the earliest settlers. However, direct evidence is still rare, for root crop horticulture by its nature is difficult to identify archaeologically. Evidence includes the numerous stone-walled gardens of Palliser Bay (Fig. 9.6) (H. M. Leach 1974, 1976), similar but more extensive field systems on the volcanic soils of the Auckland Isthmus (Sullivan 1972), and dated examples of "made soils"—soils to which charcoal, gravel or shell fragments have been added—in Northland. In all these examples the actual fields have been studied and dated. It can only be inferred that they were for kumara rather than some other crop. As H. M. Leach has demonstrated, the alternatives are limited, particularly in regions such as Palliser Bay. Of all the tropical crops available to migrating Polynesians, the kumara has adapted best to New Zealand conditions; it is reasonable to assume that the earliest settlers, like their later descendants, concentrated their attention on the most successful of their cultigens. Palliser Bay is now near the limits of kumara cultivation. Therefore it can be assumed that when the kumara was introduced to New Zealand, it could be grown at least to its present limits.

JANET M. DAVIDSON

The important change in this aspect of subsistence was not from nonhorticultural to horticultural, but the development of storage techniques. No storage pits other than small round or oval pits in the sand of living sites have been found associated with the early fields in Palliser Bay, and it has been suggested that these early crops were kept in baskets in houses. In much of New Zealand, however, crops were later stored in sunken structures, both *rua* (true pits not unlike the food fermentation pits of tropical Polynesia) and "cellars"—rectangular sunken buildings with floors well below ground level, covered with pitched roofs supported on one or more rows of posts in the floor of the pit (Fox 1974). These latter structures (Fig. 9.7) are a notable feature of the archaeology of horticultural parts of the country and on present evidence appear to be a distinctively New Zealand development.

The earliest dated pits include both rectangular and rua pits from Sarah's Gully and Opito on the Coromandel Peninsula, dated to the twelfth and thirteenth centuries (Davidson 1974). Comparable and even earlier dates have been obtained from the site of Te Awanga in Hawke's Bay (Fox 1975). These dates are for larger pits, including an example of the distinctive raised-rim type (Fig. 9.8), which is confined to the east coast of the southern North Island and northern South Island. Some doubt attaches to the antiquity of this type, as the sample dated at Te Awanga might have been old timber. No pits have been investigated in Northland—a likely region for the development of this type of storage. Neither the origin of pits nor the direction of their spread is yet known. It is probable that although storage pits first appeared at a fairly early date, the many variations and the very large examples (the biggest excavated pits are approximately 9×6 m in plan) are later developments.

The sheer size and number of pits discovered in excavations and field survey from the mid-1950s on led to the suggestion that they could not all be for storage

and that some must be dwellings. This view is still held by a number of archaeologists, particularly in the South Island, but the preferred interpretation at present is that the pits were for storage.

Fern root (more properly, the rhizome of bracken *Pteridium aquilinum* var. *esculentum*) was an important food in many areas in the eighteenth century. A great many wild plants were gathered and in some instances cultivated. Examples of the latter are flax (*Phormium tenax*; grown for fiber rather than food), karaka (*Corynocarpus laevigata*; a berry-producing tree), and native species of *Cordyline* (Colenso 1880). However, the prospects of identifying the full range of plants eaten at a particular time and place and of establishing the relative importance of each seem remote. Similarly, changes through time are difficult to document. Even the period in which fern root first became important has not been established. We can only imagine Polynesians attempting to cultivate whichever of their crops would grow and supplementing them to a greater or lesser extent with other plant foods available in the region.

Hunting and fishing. Undoubtedly one of the most dramatic changes in New Zealand prehistory was the decline and extinction of moas and other species of birds. However, it is unlikely that any Polynesians in New Zealand depended wholly or even largely on moas for food.

Evidence of hunting comes from numerous coastal sites and some inland sites in both islands. Only a few detailed quantitative analyses are available, and for some of the most famous "moa-hunter" sites in the South Island the evidence is no longer available to establish the actual importance of moas in the diet. Although the South Island has always been regarded as the center of moa-hunting, it now appears that a wider range of species was available until a later date in some parts of the North Island (notably the Coromandel Peninsula) than in the South Island. On the other hand, the medium-sized *Euryapteryx*, the principal moas hunted in the eastern South Island,

9.7 *Kumara storage pit at Kauri Point Pā, Bay of Plenty. (Photo courtesy of Anthropology Department, University of Auckland.)*

9.8 *Kumara storage pits of the raised-rim variety near Palliser Bay. (Photo courtesy of B. F. and H. M. Leach.)*

JANET M. DAVIDSON

may have been more numerous than their North Island counterparts (Scarlett 1974).

Where quantitative analysis has been carried out, moas do not dominate the diet to the extent that was once thought. At Houhora in the far north, the meat weight of 50 moas was estimated as considerably less than that of 43 seals and 2,332 snapper (Shawcross 1972). Indeed the importance of seals in the diet of early North Islanders and of South Islanders at most periods has only recently been recognized. The fur seal, in particular, must have been common around the New Zealand coast before man arrived and clearly formed a major part of the diet of the first arrivals.

In addition to moas, a wide range of other birds is found in early midden sites. These include bush birds, seabirds, open-country birds, and waterfowl. In Northland, Auckland, Coromandel, South Taranaki, and Wellington, as well as much of the South Island east coast, early middens typically contain moa, seal, dog, rat, sometimes other sea mammals, fish, and some 20 species of other birds. In some parts of the North Island, particularly Auckland, there is a rapid and dramatic change. Later middens consist almost entirely of fish and shellfish, with an occasional rat and dog (for example, the Sunde Site described by Scott 1970). Not only do moas and other extinct species disappear from the sites, but also birds that are still present in the area today. The change appears to be from broad-spectrum hunting to a concentration on those protein foods that were present in almost inexhaustible supply in harbors and estuaries and were amenable to gathering during most or all of the year, often by women and children.

The contrast between early bone-rich middens and later shellfish beds has always been one of the most striking aspects of New Zealand archaeology. While it was first commented on in relation to South Island sites, it is much more noticeable in some regions than in others. In the southern South Island, and indeed in more northern parts of the South Island also,

bird bones (although not moa) are often present in later sites and appear to reflect hunting activities similar to those of much earlier sites.

Ethnographic accounts of Maori fowling suggest that enormous quantities of certain species were taken. For example, godwits (*Limosa lapponica*) were harvested as they gathered in huge numbers in northern harbors in the autumn; so also were mutton birds (*Puffinus griseus*) breeding on the islands of Foveaux Strait in southern New Zealand and certain bush birds at particular seasons in the central North Island (Buck 1958). Middens reflecting these activities have not been found. Steady taking of burrow-nesting birds around the coasts of both islands is reflected in middens of various ages, but immature birds are seldom identified (Law 1972; Leahy 1974), so there is no evidence yet of the concentrated and specialized exploitation described in ethnographic reports. The reason, of course, could be that the appropriate sites simply have not been found, or it may be that these practices only developed to their fullest extent in post-European times.

Although many aspects of bone identification and midden analysis have been highly developed in New Zealand, the study of fish bone until recently has been neglected. Fish bones are ubiquitous in sites but have been ignored because they were widely considered unidentifiable. This picture is changing rapidly, and important results can be expected in the next few years. Regional differences in fishing are considerable and at present appear more significant than chronological differences.

What then can be concluded about hunting and fishing? The first settlers appear to have hunted selectively but without specialization. In many areas the fur seal was probably the principal game, and its distribution was reduced as a result; moas where available and a wide range of other birds were taken from a variety of habitats; fishing was a universal activity; other sea mammals (porpoises, sea lions, leopard

seals, and whales) added occasional variety. Only fishing and shellfish gathering continued throughout New Zealand prehistory as virtually universal activities. The decline of other forms of hunting varied greatly from region to region, depending probably on the availability of various kinds of game, the presence of alternatives (such as huge supplies of estuarine shellfish), and population density.

In an area such as Auckland, it is easy for the archaeologist to be overimpressed by the contrast between the few known early bone-rich middens and the enormous quantities of fish and shellfish midden that dominate the archaeological landscape. To balance the picture it is worth considering an early archaeological example and a later ethnographic example from two locations in the North Island. An early midden at Black Rocks, Palliser Bay (Fig. 9.9), contained 21,323 shellfish and crustaceans (including about 500 crayfish), 146 fish of 12 species, 59 birds of 18 species, and 1 moa. This site

is dated to the twelfth century and is thought to have been occupied twice for a period of about three months during the summer on each occasion (Anderson 1973). And in November 1769 Joseph Banks described a party of Maoris camped in Mercury Bay (Coromandel Peninsula) who had gathered a quantity of fern root to take away with them. Their supper consisted of shellfish, lobsters, fish, and birds. Evidently the summer seaside camp was a feature of the seasonal round over a long period of time.

The pattern of Maori society in early European times is not one that can be succinctly and accurately described, despite the wealth of ethnographic study devoted to it. It was characterized by flexibility and variety, and although it followed the general Polynesian preference for descent through the senior male line, it allowed more options than many Polynesian societies. The effective kin-based units of *whānau* (house-

9.10   *Living terraces and kumara storage pits on the volcanic cone of Puketutu, South Auckland. (Photo courtesy of Anthropology Department, University of Auckland.)*

hold group) and *hapū* (clan or subtribe) could vary greatly in size. The *iwi* (tribe) and *waka* (group of tribes claiming descent from the crew of one migratory canoe) were too large to be effective for most purposes. Even for late prehistoric or protohistoric times it is difficult to relate archaeological sites to units of social organization, although there have been a few brave attempts to correlate pā (fortification) size with hapū size (see, for example, Law 1969a; Bellwood 1971). For earlier periods we can only infer, in the most general terms, kin-based communities of generalized Polynesian pattern.

The New Zealand archaeologist has difficulty making useful inferences about society at this level. He can, however, study houses and settlements, and document patterns of exchange and communication, the development of warfare, and changes in burial practices. The Palliser Bay program summarized by B. F. Leach (1976) is a valuable example of this approach.

Settlements. The seasonal round of activities, involving at least some movement, and the variable size of social groups make it difficult to identify contemporary settlements or document precisely all the settlement components in a region. In the vicinity of Auckland, for example, archaeological sites range in size from an isolated group of two storage pits to the enormous and spectacular terraced settlements on the volcanic cones, each of which covers many hectares (Figs. 9.2 and 9.10). Smaller terraced hills, larger pit clusters, middens without visible associated features, field systems, burial caves, and fortified headlands contribute to the archaeological landscape, while the relentless advance of a modern conurbation has destroyed an unknown number of sites. Auckland is perhaps an extreme case, but in most parts of New Zealand problems of site conjunction are acute.

At the simplest level most sites where people actually stayed, even briefly, contained some provision for shelter, facilities for storing or processing whatever food was the immediate concern, a cooking area, and a refuse dump (Groube 1965). These elements are found in seasonal camps, in horticultural hamlets, and in those fortifications that were inhabited for any length of time. There were also, at various times, specialized components—particularly storage units, working areas, and burial places —that were segregated from residences.

In horticultural areas a reasonably permanent settlement was needed from which gardens could be supervised and tended, and in or near which crops could be stored during the winter. In the ethnographic period, permanent winter base villages were also a feature of the settlement pattern of some nonhorticultural South Island tribes (H. M. Leach 1969).

Early villages, such as Washpool and Wairau, encompass residence, tool making, cooking and dumping of food refuse, processing or storage of food, and even burial places. An eighteenth-century hamlet on Motutapu Island near Auckland also contains all these elements. Other examples have been recognized on the Coromandel Peninsula in the twelfth century (Davidson 1975), at Kauri Point in the fifteenth century (Green 1964, 1978), at Aotea on the west coast of the North Island in the sixteenth century, and on Motutapu in the eighteenth century (Davidson 1970, 1972; Leahy 1970, 1972). Most of these were probably occupied for only a few years by fairly mobile people, a fact that would explain the large number of such sites in the archaeological landscape.

Although horticultural hamlets close to gardens can be considered a constant component of the settlement pattern, they are only one part of the story. Fortified pā, separate burial places, and seasonal camps could all be used by the same group of people; depending on fluctuations of social groups and their political allegiances, the size varied greatly. Whereas the horticultural hamlet was a feature from earliest times (reflecting a universal Polynesian pattern), fortifications seem on present evidence to be a later development. In some areas also, there was a tendency toward increased segregation of various settlement components through time, notably the isolation of burial places to prevent violation and of certain food storage facilities to prevent plundering (B. F. Leach 1976). This tendency seems more obvious in an impoverished area such as Palliser Bay than in a naturally more fruitful area such as Motutapu. An opposing trend, the concentration of components (except perhaps burial places) in a single fortified settlement, can also be discerned in some areas.

Buildings. In recent years quite a few houses have been excavated. The earliest and one of the largest is at Moikau, Palliser Bay, and dates to the twelfth century (Prickett 1974). It displays the rectangular (but slightly asymmetrical) plan, with porch at one end, of the ethnographic *whare puni* (Firth 1926) from which the communal meeting house of modern Maori communities is derived (Fig. 9.11). At Moikau, however, there are no center posts and the door is differently positioned, whereas in a later prehistoric house at Palliser Bay, the door is in the same position as in modern houses. Examples of the whare puni house plan have been reported from various areas and periods. An interesting variation is provided by slightly sunken examples of protohistoric age from the central North Island. Other houses, lacking the open porch and sometimes much flimsier in construction, are nevertheless all rectangular in plan. It is thus clear that basic Maori house plans have persisted for some 750 years. The lack of archaeological data on houses from central East Polynesia is regrettable, since the Maori whare puni is very different from the oval houses of West Polynesia or the round-ended houses of East Polynesia. Its relationship, if any, to other Polynesian houses remains unknown.

In addition to sunken buildings for kumara storage, Maori settlements featured a variety of raised platforms and sometimes raised buildings for storage of other goods.

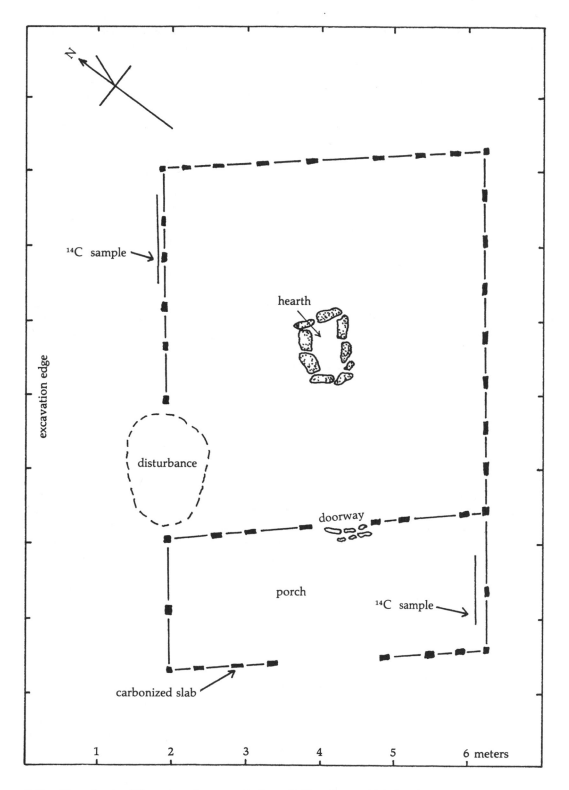

N

¹⁴C sample →

hearth

excavation edge

disturbance

doorway

porch

¹⁴C sample →

carbonized slab

1   2   3   4   5   6 meters

9.11   *Plan of a twelfth-century house at Moikau, Palliser Bay, which foreshadows the Maori whare puni of historic times. (After Prickett 1974 and B. F. Leach 1976.)*

NEW ZEALAND   241

These are the most perplexing of all structures to identify archaeologically, since they leave only postholes; and individual plans are very difficult to disentangle from the confusing mass of features often revealed by excavation.

In New Zealand, as elsewhere in Polynesia, cooking was done in earth-ovens outside residences. Ovens, oven debris, and the postholes of cooking shelters (of which rectangular and rare round examples have been identified) are among the commonest forms of archaeological evidence.

Both stone-edged and basin-shaped scoop hearths have been found inside the houses of New Zealand (H. M. Leach 1972), and also outside the houses as focal points of activity in places as far separated in space and time as twelfth-century Palliser Bay and the eighteenth-century far north. The stone-edged hearth is very similar to examples from Samoa, for instance, and is probably an ancient Polynesian trait. In New Zealand, such hearths were used for warmth as well as light.

Ritual. Many ethnographers have stressed the fact that ritual considerations, particularly those concerned with tapu, permeated all aspects of Maori life. Yet New Zealand lacks the spectacular religious edifices of some other parts of Polynesia. Consequently, only from ethnographic and historical records can anything be learned about this aspect of Maori life. From archaeology a few rare glimpses are obtained of ritual observance: the deliberate flaking of an adz into the fill of a grave; the careful burying of a dog jaw beside one of the main posts of a house (B. F. Leach 1976); the placing of stone adzes at the base of a palisade post (Bellwood 1971). A major concern of many Maori communities must have been the disposal of tapu objects. The precise placing of a variety of objects, particularly wooden head combs and obsidian flakes, in one part of a small swamp adjacent to a pā at Kauri Point is an indication of how one community evidently dealt with this problem (Shawcross 1976).

Like many other aspects of culture, burial practices exhibit regional diversity. Indeed this is an aspect particularly prone to regional variation in Polynesia, if the example of Samoa and Tonga is an indication. The general practice among early communities in New Zealand appears to have been burial on the fringe of the living site, in a cluster of shallow graves. There is a variety of position and orientation, although the preference was for the extended position. At some sites such as Wairau Bar, which may have been the residence of important tool-making specialists, people were buried with rich grave goods (Duff 1956). Elsewhere, as at Washpool, grave goods were less rich, and at Sarah's Gully on the Coromandel Peninsula none at all were found. At nearby Hahei, however, some burials apparently included ornaments similar to those of Wairau. Although most early burials are primary interments, secondary burial of disarticulated bones and removal of skulls from primary interments are recorded. There is a general trend toward increasing segregation of the dead from the living through time. In later periods bones were more often placed in caves and crevices, and highly diversified practices are documented ethnographically (Oppenheim 1973). Yet in some areas primary burials in or near settlements continued into the eighteenth century (Davidson 1970, 1972).

Warfare. Maori warfare in the late eighteenth century represented an extreme within Polynesia in its extensive development of earthwork fortification (Fig. 9.3). How this came about has been a major preoccupation of some New Zealand archaeologists.

It has been generally held that the earlier inhabitants of New Zealand were peaceful and that both warfare and fortifications arose simultaneously in the North Island and spread from there to the South Island. Yet evidence of personal violence among the early inhabitants of Palliser Bay (Sutton 1974), indications of probable cannibalism in an early site on the Coromandel Peninsula where the inhabitants appear to have consumed a man and a moa (Allo 1972),

JANET M. DAVIDSON

and the presence of patu at Vaitootia in the Society Islands suggest that the earliest settlers may well have brought with them warfare and violence of a fairly typical Polynesian pattern, even if fortifications initially were lacking.

Authorities have been cautious but divided on the question of whether earthwork fortifications arose independently in New Zealand or were introduced from elsewhere in Polynesia (see, for example, Groube 1964; Green 1967; Fox 1976). There has been similar division of opinion over the causes of pā warfare. Suggestions have included population pressure, pressure related to kumara horticulture—in particular, competition for good horticultural land (Duff 1967)—and competition for cleared land already available for both horticulture and fern root (Vayda 1960). Others have argued that there was more than enough cleared land for a greater population than most estimates would allow (Law 1969b). Whatever the reasons, Maoris invested enormous effort in the construction of their pā, among the most spectacular of Polynesian monuments. The total number has been conservatively estimated at between 4,000 and 6,000, of which 98 percent are in horticultural parts of the country (Groube 1970) (although these are also the areas where the population was probably greatest because of a combination of all food resources, not merely horticulture).

Pā, like other settlements, varied greatly in size, situation, and purpose (Fox 1976). Some relied heavily on naturally steep terrain, others on artificial defenses. Some were man-made mounds in swamps and lakes, defended by palisades. Some appear to have been built primarily as defended food stores, others have convincing evidence of intensive occupation. Several excavated pā have very complex histories during which their function fluctuated, others appear to have resulted from a decision to fortify an existing settlement.

Fewer than 50 pā have been excavated in even the most minimal way by archaeologists—less than 1 percent of the total (Fig.

9.12). Such evidence as there is, however, suggests an efflorescence of pā building between the fourteenth and sixteenth centuries. At this time forts were built in Auckland, Coromandel, the Bay of Plenty, and Hawke's Bay. Indeed, on a corrected sixteenth-century radiocarbon date, the South Island pā of Pariwhakatau (Duff 1961) would fall within this period. These results give no indication of where the concept originated. But by the end of the eighteenth century, fortification warfare had spread beyond the limits of horticulture. Warfare was as intense and cannibalism more evident in the South Island than in the North.

Trade and communication. Ethnographic accounts stress the importance of gift exchange in Maori society. Items exchanged included many kinds of foods such as preserved fish, birds, rats, seaweed, prepared kumara, fern root, and berries; commodities such as kōkōwai (red ocher), shark oil, and oven stones; manufactured goods such as garments and canoes; and stone resources such as obsidian and above all greenstone (Firth 1959). Not all of these can be equally well documented in the archaeological record. Some, however, particularly stone resources, provide the clearest possible indication that people throughout the country were in at least indirect communication with one another during the prehistoric era. By the twelfth century most of the stone resources important to the Maori had been discovered and were being widely distributed. People in Palliser Bay at this time received obsidian from the Bay of Plenty, Coromandel, and central North Island, metasomatized argillite from D'Urville Island, nephrite from the South Island west coast, silcrete from central Otago, and various other rocks from the southern North Island and northern South Island (B. F. Leach 1976). People at Houhora in the far north were obtaining basalt, obsidian, and probably siliceous sinter from the Coromandel Peninsula and the Bay of Plenty (Best 1975).

Obsidian is probably the most widely distributed and frequently found stone in

9.12   *Excavation of a pā at Waioneke, South Kaipara. (Photo courtesy of Anthropology Department, University of Auckland.)*

New Zealand archaeological sites. Eighteen petrographically distinct sources in eight major areas have now been identified (Ward 1974), and considerable work has been done on developing routine techniques for identifying the geologic sources of archaeological samples (B. F. Leach 1977). Other important stone resources are also being studied.

It has often been suggested that the development of warfare led to the breakdown of communication and to increasing regional isolation. Nonetheless, both obsidian and nephrite were still being widely distributed between the fourteenth and eighteenth centuries—the very period when this breakdown is supposed to have taken place. Moreover, ethnographic evidence provides little indication of any such deterioration. On the contrary, it seems likely that the exchange patterns provided

channels by which new ideas as well as physical items could travel and thereby impeded the development of regional differentiation.

Conclusion

Most discussions of New Zealand prehistory have sought not merely to document change but to explain it. In particular, archaeologists have longed for a single coherent explanation of Classic Maori culture, one that would cover not only changes in material culture but also the development of horticulture and warfare. Tribal migration and warfare rather than peaceful communication have been seen as the most likely vehicle for spreading change. An older generation of scholars, drawing more heavily and more overtly on available versions of Maori traditions, saw Classic

244

Maori culture as something imposed by victorious migrants who defeated earlier inhabitants. More recently, scholars have sought to relate the development of Classic Maori culture and warfare to the successful development of kumara horticulture somewhere in the North Island. Two authorities have selected Northland as the most likely location and tried to correlate the spread of certain kinds of stone adzes and fortifications with oral traditions, even suggesting that the famous migratory canoes of Maori tradition may have traveled from Northland to other parts of the North Island, rather than reaching New Zealand from tropical Polynesia (Groube 1970; Simmons 1971).

Eventually a unified explanation may be developed. At present, however, the separate strands of the story must still be disentangled and examined individually. Changes in material culture almost certainly took place at different places and different times but where and when cannot be stipulated. Recent developments in the study of horticulture show that it was well established and widespread long before the rise of fortifications or the appearance of most "Classic Maori" artifact forms.

The development of pā warfare poses perhaps the most vexing problems in New Zealand prehistory. If it could be correlated with developments in art styles and certain elements of ritual and belief, then perhaps the essence of the development of Classic Maori culture could be captured archaeologically; such correlation is not yet within the reach of the archaeological method. Alternatively, if both pā warfare and Maori art were separated from the Classic Maori package and considered in the contexts of Polynesian warfare and Polynesian art, they could probably be better understood.

To many Polynesianists, New Zealand prehistory is a thing apart. To the New Zealand prehistorian, on the other hand, it has proved to be absorbing, with the rest of Polynesia irrelevant. This is unfortunate, for New Zealand prehistory is firmly rooted in its Polynesian beginnings and is itself an important chapter in the total story of Polynesian prehistory. In many respects, New Zealand archaeology is far more sophisticated than archaeology anywhere else in Polynesia, but the many years of practice and modern expertise have merely shown how much there is left to learn.

References

Allo, Jan. 1972. The Whangamata Wharf site (N49/2): excavations on a Coromandel coastal midden. *Records of the Auckland Institute and Museum* 9:61–79.

Anderson, A. J. 1973. Archaeology and behaviour: prehistoric subsistence behaviour at Black Rocks Peninsula, Palliser Bay. Master's thesis, University of Otago.

Beaglehole, J. C., ed. 1955. *The Voyage of the Endeavour 1768–1771.* Cambridge: Cambridge University Press, for the Hakluyt Society.

———. 1961. *The Voyage of the Resolution and Adventure 1772–1775.* Cambridge: Cambridge University Press, for the Hakluyt Society.

———. 1962. *The Endeavour Journal of Joseph Banks 1768–1771.* Sydney: Trustees of the Public Library of New South Wales, in association with Angus and Robertson.

———. 1967. *The Voyage of the Resolution and Discovery 1776–1780.* Cambridge: Cambridge University Press, for the Hakluyt Society.

Bellwood, P. S. 1971. Fortifications and economy in prehistoric New Zealand. *Proceedings of the Prehistoric Society* 37:56–95.

Best, Elsdon. 1927. *The Pā Maori.* New Zealand Dominion Museum Bulletin no. 6, Wellington.

Best, S. E. 1975. Adzes, rocks and men. Master's thesis, University of Auckland.

Buck, P. H. (Te Rangi Hiroa). 1922–23. Maori somatology. *Journal of the Polynesian Society* 31:37–44, 145–153, 159–170; 32:21–28, 189–199.

———. 1958. *The coming of the Maori,* 2nd ed. Wellington: Maori Purposes Fund Board and Whitcombe and Tombs.

Colenso, William. 1880. On the vegetable food of the ancient New Zealanders before Cook's visit. *Transactions of the New Zealand Institute* 13:3–38 (issued 1881).

Davidson, J. M. 1970. Excavation of an "undefended" site, N38/37, on Motutapu Island, New Zealand. *Records of the Auckland Institute and Museum* 7:31–60.

———. 1972. Archaeological excavations on Motutapu Island, New Zealand. Introduction to recent fieldwork, and further results. *Records of the Auckland Institute and Museum* 9:1–14.

——. 1974. A radiocarbon date from Skipper's Ridge (N40/7). *New Zealand Archaeological Association Newsletter* 17:50–52.

——. 1975. The excavation of Skipper's Ridge (N40/7), Opito, Coromandel Peninsula, in 1959 and 1960. *Records of the Auckland Institute and Museum* 12:1–42.

Duff, R. S. 1956. *The Moa-hunter period of Maori culture,* 2nd ed. Wellington: Government Printer.

——. 1961. Excavation of house-pits at Pari Whakatau pa, Claverly, Marlborough. *Records of the Canterbury Museum* 7:269–302.

——. 1962. Aspects of the cultural succession in Canterbury-Marlborough with wider reference to the New Zealand area. *New Zealand Archaeological Association Newsletter* 5:205–209.

——. 1967. The evolution of Maori warfare. *New Zealand Archaeological Association Newsletter* 10:114–129.

Firth, Raymond. 1926. Wharepuni: a few remaining Maori dwellings of the old style. *Man* 26:54–59.

——. 1959. *Economics of the New Zealand Maori,* 2nd ed. Wellington: Government Printer.

Fleming, C. A. 1962. The extinction of moas and other animals during the Holocene period. *Notornis* 10:113–117.

——. 1969. Rats and moa extinction. *Notornis* 16:210–211.

Fox, Aileen. 1974. Prehistoric Maori storage pits: problems in interpretation. *Journal of the Polynesian Society* 83:141–154.

——. 1975. Some evidence for early agriculture in Hawke's Bay. *New Zealand Archaeological Association Newsletter* 18:200–205.

——. 1976. *Prehistoric Maori fortifications.* Auckland: Longman Paul.

Golson, Jack. 1959. Culture change in prehistoric New Zealand. In *Anthropology in the South Seas,* ed. J. D. Freeman and W. R. Geddes, pp. 29–74. New Plymouth, New Zealand: Avery.

Green, R. C. 1963. *A review of the prehistoric sequence of the Auckland Province.* New Zealand Archaeological Association Monograph no. 2.

——. 1964. An undefended settlement at Kauri Point, Tauranga district. *New Zealand Archaeological Association Newsletter* 7:11–17.

——. 1966. Linguistic subgrouping within Polynesia: the implications for prehistoric settlement. *Journal of the Polynesian Society* 75:6–38.

——. 1967. Fortifications in other parts of tropical Polynesia. *New Zealand Archaeological Association Newsletter* 10:96–113.

——. 1975. Adaptation and change in Maori culture. In *Biogeography and ecology in New Zealand,* ed. G. Kuschel, pp. 591–641. The Hague: Dr. W. Junk.

——. 1978. Dating the Kauri Point sequence. *Historical Review (Journal of the Whakatane and District Historical Society, New Zealand)* 26:32–45.

Grey, G. E. 1854. *Ko nga mahinga a nga tupuna Maori.* London: George Willis.

Groube, L. M. 1964. Settlement patterns in prehistoric New Zealand. Master's thesis, University of Auckland.

——. 1965. Settlement patterns in New Zealand prehistory. *Occasional Papers in Archaeology* 1, University of Otago.

——. 1967. Models in prehistory: a consideration of the New Zealand evidence. *Archaeology and Physical Anthropology in Oceania* 2:1–27.

——. 1970. The origin and development of earthwork fortifications in the Pacific. *Pacific Anthropological Records* 11:133–164.

Hendy, C. H., and A. T. Wilson. 1968. Palaeoclimatic data from speleothems. *Nature* 219:48–51.

Hjarno, Jan. 1967. Maori fish-hooks in southern New Zealand. *Records of the Otago Museum, Anthropology* 3.

Holloway, J. T. 1954. Forests and climates in the South Island of New Zealand, *Transactions of the Royal Society of New Zealand* 82:329–410.

Law, R. G. 1969a. Kohekohe ridge pā—a social reconstruction. *New Zealand Archaeological Association Newsletter* 12:20–37.

——. 1969b. Bracken fern and kumara in Maori settlement. Paper presented at New Zealand Archaeological Association conference, May 1969. Abstract in *New Zealand Archaeological Association Newsletter* 12:57.

——. 1972. Archaeology at Harataonga Bay, Great Barrier Island. *Records of the Auckland Institute and Museum* 9:81–123.

Leach, B. F. 1969. *The concept of similarity in prehistoric studies.* Studies in Prehistoric Anthropology 1, University of Otago.

——. 1976. Prehistoric communities in Palliser Bay, New Zealand. Ph.D. dissertation, University of Otago.

JANET M. DAVIDSON

———. 1977. Progress towards the routine sourcing of New Zealand obsidians. *New Zealand Archaeological Association Newsletter* 20:6–17.

Leach, H. M. 1969. Subsistence patterns in prehistoric New Zealand. *Studies in prehistoric anthropology* 2, University of Otago.

———. 1972. The hearth as an archaeological feature in New Zealand. *New Zealand Archaeological Association Newsletter* 15:59–75.

———. 1974. Man's use of nature. Pre-European (1). The first 500 years. *New Zealand's Nature Heritage* 1:117–122.

———. 1976. Horticulture in prehistoric New Zealand. An investigation into the function of the stone walls of Palliser Bay. Ph.D. dissertation, University of Otago.

Leahy, Anne. 1970. Excavations at site N38/30, Motutapu Island, New Zealand. *Records of the Auckland Institute and Museum* 7:61–82.

———. 1972. Further excavations at site N38/30, Motutapu Island, New Zealand. *Records of the Auckland Institute and Museum* 9:15–26.

———. 1974. Excavations at Hot Water Beach (N44/69), Coromandel Peninsula. *Records of the Auckland Institute and Museum* 11:23–76.

Lockerbie, Leslie. 1940. Excavations at King's Rock, Otago, with a discussion of the fish-hook barb as an ancient feature of Polynesian culture. *Journal of the Polynesian Society* 49:393–446.

———. 1959. From Moa-hunter to Classic Maori in southern New Zealand. In *Anthropology in the South Seas*, ed. J. D. Freeman and W. R. Geddes, pp. 75–110. New Plymouth: Avery.

McKay, A. 1973. Te Toki a te Maataariki. *Journal of the Polynesian Society* 82:412–413.

Marshall, D. S., and C. E. Snow. 1956. An evaluation of Polynesian craniology. *American Journal of Physical Anthropology* 14:405–427.

Mead, S. M. 1975. The origins of Maori art: Polynesian or Chinese? *Oceania* 45:173–211.

Molloy, B. P. J. 1969. Evidence for post-glacial climate change in New Zealand. *Journal of Hydrology (New Zealand)* 8:56–67.

Oppenheim, R. S. 1973. *Maori death customs.* Wellington: Reed.

Orchiston, D. W. 1972. Maori neck and ear ornaments of the 1770s: a study in protohistoric ethno-archaeology. *Journal of the Royal Society of New Zealand* 2:91–107.

Prickett, N. J. 1974. Houses and house life in prehistoric New Zealand. Master's thesis, University of Otago.

Salinger, M. J. 1976. New Zealand temperatures since 1300 A.D. *Nature* 260:310–311.

Scarlett, R. J. 1974. Moa and man in New Zealand. *Notornis* 21:1–12.

Scott, J. H. 1893. Contribution to the osteology of the aborigines of New Zealand and of the Chatham Islands. *Transactions of the New Zealand Institute* 26:1–64.

Scott, S. D. 1970. Excavations at the "Sunde Site," N38/24, Motutapu Island, New Zealand. *Records of the Auckland Institute and Museum* 7:13–30.

Shapiro, H. L. 1940. The physical anthropology of the Maori-Moriori. *Journal of the Polynesian Society* 49:1–15.

Shawcross, Wilfred. 1972. Energy and ecology: thermodynamic models in archaeology. In *Models in archaeology*, ed. D. L. Clarke, pp. 577–622. London: Methuen.

———. 1976. Kauri Point swamp: the ethnographic interpretation of a prehistoric site. In *Problems in economic and social archaeology*, ed. G. de G. Sieveking et al., pp. 277–305. London: Duckworth.

Shima, Goro, and Makoto Suzuki. 1967. Problems of race formation of the Maori and Moriori in terms of skulls. *Osaka City Medical Journal* 13:9–54.

Shortland, Edward. 1854. *Traditions and superstitions of the New Zealanders; with illustrations of their manners and customs.* London: Longman, Brown, Green and Longmans.

Simmons, D. R. 1969a. A New Zealand myth; Kupe, Toi and the 'fleet'. *New Zealand Journal of History* 3:14–31.

———. 1969b. Economic change in New Zealand prehistory. *Journal of the Polynesian Society* 78:3–34.

———. 1971. Regional traditions and culture history. *New Zealand Archaeological Association Newsletter* 14:92–97.

———. 1976. *The great New Zealand myth: a study of the discovery and origin traditions of the Maori.* Wellington: Reed.

Sinoto, Y. H. and P. C. McCoy. 1975. Report on the preliminary excavation of an early habitation site on Huahine, Society Islands. *Journal de la Société des Océanistes* 31:143–186.

Skinner, H. D. 1921. Culture areas in New Zealand. *Journal of the Polynesian Society* 30:71–78.

———. 1923. Archaeology of Canterbury, 1: Moa-bone Point Cave. *Records of the Canterbury Museum* 2:93–104.

Sullivan, Agnes. 1972. Stone walled complexes of

central Auckland. *New Zealand Archaeological Association Newsletter* 15:148–160.

Sutton, D. G. 1974. Resurrection of the prehistoric dead; the personal histories of sixteen ancient inhabitants of Eastern Palliser Bay. Master's thesis, University of Otago.

Taylor, R. M. S. 1962. Non-metrical studies of the human palate and dentition in Moriori and Maori skulls. *Journal of the Polynesian Society* 71:83–100, 167–187.

Teviotdale, David. 1932. The material culture of the moa-hunters in Murihiku. *Journal of the Polynesian Society* 41:81–120.

Vayda, A. P. 1960. *Maori warfare*. Wellington: Polynesian Society.

von Haast, Julius. 1871. Moas and moa hunters. *Transactions of the New Zealand Institute* 4:66–107 (issued 1872).

———. 1874. Researches and excavations carried on in and near the Moa-bone Point Cave, Sumner Road, in the year 1872. *Transactions of the New Zealand Institute* 7:54–85 (issued 1875).

Ward, G. K. 1974. A paradigm for sourcing New Zealand archaeological obsidians. *Journal of the Royal Society of New Zealand* 4:47–62.

Wardle, Peter. 1963. The regeneration gap of New Zealand gymnosperms. *New Zealand Journal of Botany* 1:301–315.

———. 1973. Variations of the glaciers of Westland National Park and the Hooker Range, New Zealand. *New Zealand Journal of Botany* 11:349–388.

Wards, Ian, ed. 1976. *New Zealand atlas*. Wellington: Government Printer.

Wellman, H. W. 1962. Holocene of the North Island of New Zealand: a coastal reconnaissance. *Transactions of the Royal Society of New Zealand (Geology)* 1:29–99.

Williams, H. W. 1937. The Maruiwi myth. *Journal of the Polynesian Society* 46:105–122.

Wilson, A. T., and C. H. Hendy. 1971. Past wind strength from isotope studies. *Nature* 234:344–345.

Yen, D. E. 1961. The adaptation of kumara by the New Zealand Maori. *Journal of the Polynesian Society* 70:338–348.

JANET M. DAVIDSON

Language

CHAPTER 10

ROSS CLARK

 On the afternoon of January 19, 1778, as Captain Cook's ships, the *Resolution* and the *Discovery*, sailed along the coast of Kauai, the first canoeloads of Hawaiians paddled out from the shore to visit the strange vessels. To the Europeans the appearance, the clothing, and the canoes of these natives indicated clearly that they were close kin to the people of the Society Islands, more than 3,200 km to the south. But, in the words of one officer, "what more than all surprised us, was our catching the sound of Otaheite words in their speech; and on asking them for hogs, breadfruit, and yams in that Dialect, we found we were understood" (Beaglehole 1967:263n). For the first time, the extraordinary geographic spread of the Polynesian peoples was fully apparent to Europeans, and it was the similarity of language that most strikingly marked their kinship. The same officer (James King, second lieutenant of the *Resolution*) later reflected on this fact:

There doubtless cannot be a subject more liable to error than in deducing the origin of a people from certain resemblances in their religious ceremonies, their arts and their manners . . . The same language, however, hardly requires any other proof of those who speak it being the same people, and originating from the same country. And that the language which is spoken at these isles, at New Zealand, at Easter Island and the Society and Friendly Isles is the same, is clear . . . not differing more than provincial dialects of the same nation. (Beaglehole 1967:1392)

Linguistic evidence has continued to play a leading part in the investigation of Polynesian prehistory ever since the time of Cook and King. This chapter will examine the nature of the evidence and the conclusions that have been drawn from it. First, however, we need to consider some general principles of historical and comparative linguistics.

Linguistic Change and Reconstruction

All languages are in a constant state of change. The English of our grandparents' time was not the same as the English we speak today. Shakespeare and the King James Bible, though recognizably our own language, present many unfamiliar features and problems of understanding. Chaucer is still more difficult, and the Old English of 1,000 years ago, while connected to today's English by an unbroken tradition, is almost as unintelligible to us as Dutch or Swedish. The historical linguist seeks to understand the processes by which languages change (while seeming to their speakers to remain "the same") and to discern the course of linguistic change in the past—sometimes through the evidence of written records (which are always imperfect, and sometimes actually misleading), but more often through reconstruction from the study and comparison of modern languages.

A language is the common property of a speech community, and the members of such a community continue to understand one another despite the accumulating changes in the language, because they all make the same changes. Their continuing linguistic interaction enables an emergent change, initiated by one speaker or group, to be imitated and adopted by others. The exact way in which innovations in language arise, the means by which they are diffused throughout the community, and the factors determining the "success" of some and not of others, still are by no means well understood. Until recently, linguists have been interested mainly in changes that are already complete.

Now it may happen that a speech community becomes divided into two or more groups that no longer communicate with one another regularly. The result is that the free spread of innovations is blocked; changes may arise and spread through one subcommunity but will not be passed to the others, and the speech of each subgroup will begin to diverge from the others. The situation can be represented by the type of diagram shown in Fig. 10.1.

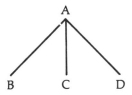

10.1 A protolanguage and its daughters.

Here A represents the language of the original unified community, and B, C, and D the languages of the now isolated subcommunities. At first the differences will be of a minor order, and B, C, and D can be considered variants, or dialects, of a single language. If isolation continues for a long enough time, however, the divergence of B, C, and D will reach the (ill-defined) point at which it becomes necessary to consider them as distinct languages. By virtue of their common historical relationship, however, B, C, and D are said to constitute a linguistic family. A is referred to as the *protolanguage* of this family (or as "Proto-BCD"), and B, C, and D as its daughter languages. Thus "Proto-Polynesian" is the name given to the postulated prehistoric language of which Tongan, Samoan, Hawaiian, and Maori are all daughters.

Of course, at any time one of the daughter languages may split in the same way as the original protolanguage, thus creating a family of more complex structure, such as that represented in Fig. 10.2. Here B has split into three daughter languages, whereas C and D have continued to develop without dividing. Within the language family EFGHI, then, E, F, and G are said to form a *subgroup* by virtue of their

ROSS CLARK

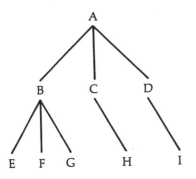

10.2 *A linguistic family with a subgroup.*

Table 10.1 *Cognate forms illustrating sound correspondences in three Polynesian languages.*

Maori	Tahitian	Hawaiian	Meaning
ingoa	i'oa	inoa	name
mata	mata	maka	eye
matangi	mata'i	makani	wind
mate	mate	make	dead
ngutu	'utu	nuku	mouth
tangata	ta'ata	kanaka	person
tangi	ta'i	kani	weep

common descent from the protolanguage B, which itself is a daughter of A, the protolanguage of the entire group. On the other hand, H and I have no special relation to each other beyond their common descent from A. Within the language family known as Indo-European, for example, such familiar language families as Celtic, Germanic, Romance, and Slavic are subgroups.

For the Polynesian family, as for the great majority of the world's languages, written records are available for only the most recent period. The direct evidence available to the linguist thus corresponds to the bottom layer of the family-tree diagram, and his task is to reconstruct the rest. The techniques of such reconstruction are a large part of the subject matter of classical comparative-historical linguistics and cannot be described here in detail. However, it is essential to discuss a few of the most basic principles of evidence and inference on which the conclusions of the later sections are based.

Principle 1: The primary criterion for inferring historical relationship between languages is the existence of systematic similarities too great to be explained by chance. The classic type of similarity is a set of regular sound correspondences in the vocabulary, as shown in Table 10.1. Here the vowels of each item are identical in all three languages. The consonants, while not identical, show regular and predictable relations. Thus Maori and Tahitian *t* regularly correspond to Hawaiian *k*, and Maori *ng* regularly corresponds to the glottal stop (') in Tahitian and to *n* in Hawaiian.

The existence of a body of words showing reg-

ular sound correspondences (hundreds of which could be added to the list for these particular languages) rules out the possibility that the languages in question happened by chance to develop words of corresponding form for the same meaning. Some historical connection must be supposed. One possibility is borrowing—the adoption of features by one language from another, possibly unrelated, language with which it comes into contact. (Borrowing will be discussed in more detail later on.) If borrowing can be ruled out for some reason, the only other possible conclusion is that the languages in question are members of one linguistic family, descended from a common protolanguage. The regular sound correspondences are the result of common inheritance of words from the protolanguage, subject to regular sound changes.

Once the sound correspondences are established, careful comparisons of the corresponding forms usually make it possible to reconstruct the protoforms from which they are derived. Thus from the data in Table 10.1 we can reconstruct the protoforms *ingoa* ("name"), *mata* ("eye"), and so on for the language (Proto–Central Eastern) from which Maori, Tahitian, and Hawaiian are descended. These reconstructed forms (starred because they are inferred, not actually attested) represent a hypothesis about the nature of the protolanguage and the history of its development. Together with a statement of the changes of the consonants (*t* and *ng*, as explained previously) they constitute a historical explanation of the observed data. Corresponding words in related languages are said to be *cognates*, and each of these is a *reflex* of the protoform from which it is descended.

Principle 2: Within a family, subgroups will show shared innovations from the protolanguage. Thus in Fig. 10.2, changes undergone by language B during the period between the breakup of A and the later breakup of B itself will—unless they are later lost—be reflected in E, F, and G, but not in H or I. For example, one of the defining characteristics of the Germanic subgroup of the Indo-European family is the set of consonant changes known as Grimm's Law, which took place in the history of Proto-Germanic. The present-day evidence of this change is in such sets as English *father*, German *Vater*, Dutch *vader*, Swedish *fader* (all with an initial *f* or *v*) compared with French *père*, Spanish *padre*, Modern Greek *pateras*, Persian *pedar*, Punjabi *pyta*, all of which retain the original *p* of the even earlier Proto-Indo-European. The most reliable way to establish the existence of a subgroup is to demonstrate the existence of shared innovations of this kind.

Linguistic and Historical Relationships

The relationships established by comparative reconstruction, such as those represented in Figs. 10.1 and 10.2, are purely linguistic conclusions. In themselves, they tell us very little about the human relationships that underlie the linguistic facts. This caution must be emphasized because it is frequently ignored, and unjustified conclusions are often drawn from linguistic data. For example, many people would describe the relationships shown in Fig. 10.3 by saying that F was the first to "branch off" or "split off" from the rest of the family, and might draw the conclusion that the historical event in question involved the departure of the ancestors of the speakers of F from wherever the protolanguage (A) was spoken, while the ancestors of the B, C, D, and E speakers remained at home. Such an inference is completely unjustified, however; Fig. 10.3 could equally well be the result of the departure of pre-BCDE speakers, leaving the pre-F speakers behind.

The translation of linguistic facts into historical hypotheses always involves certain extralinguistic assumptions, but many times these are not made explicit. The following is a list of a few such principles that appear to be reliable for our present purposes. (For some other attempts to set out explicit principles of inference, to which

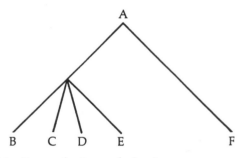

10.3 *Beware hasty conclusions!*

the present discussion owes a great deal, see Dyen 1956; Pawley and K. Green 1971; and Pawley 1975.)

Principle 3: Since daughter languages constantly diverge from one another, greater diversity of daughter languages implies a longer period of separation, hence a protolanguage further back in time and a more remote relationship.

Principle 4: The larger the number of shared innovations in a subgroup, the longer the period of separate development before breakup of the protolanguage. If the vertical axis in Fig. 10.4 represents time, we have a schematic representation of the conclusions that would be drawn if B and C showed a few common innovations and D and E a great many. In this case D and E would be said to form a strongly defined subgroup, B and C a less defined subgroup.

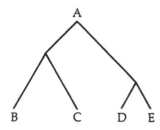

10.4 *A strong and a weak subgroup.*

Principle 5: The homeland of a language family (the place where its protolanguage was spoken) was some part of the territory over which its daughter languages are now spoken. While not a logical necessity, this assumption is confirmed by the great majority of cases for which independent evidence is available. In a sense it also follows from Principle 6.

ROSS CLARK

Principle 6: Other things being equal, that theory is to be preferred which postulates the fewest and shortest moves in order to account for the present observed language distributions and relationships.

Principle 7: On the assumption that the earliest migrations from the homeland were to nearby areas, and that later migrations populated successively more distant areas (and that no subsequent events have obscured this pattern), it follows that the highest-order divisions in the family—those that reflect the earliest split in the protolanguage community—will be represented in the area near the homeland. As a principle of inference, this leads us to expect the homeland to be in an area of maximal diversity—where neighboring languages are members of different highest-order subgroups.

The next three principles apply specifically to the Polynesian situation.

Principle 8: The Proto-Polynesian homeland was a single island or archipelago. Because of the ever-present tendency for isolated subcommunities to diversify linguistically, no language can maintain its unity for long if it extends beyond the limits of frequent communication imposed by its technology. As soon as Proto-Polynesian speakers had settled two or more islands or archipelagoes between which voyaging was infrequent or impossible, the linguistic breakup would have begun. The observed distribution of languages in early historic times suggests that this limit of coherence was not much greater than the average island group as geographically distinguished.

Principle 9: In Polynesia the normal occasion of linguistic split has been the migration of one part of a speech community from one island or archipelago to another.

Principle 10: It is rare for a small number of speakers to succeed in imposing their language on a large population. Hence we normally assume that linguistic continuity implies substantial genetic and cultural continuity as well. This does not, of course, exclude the possibility of borrowing or the effects of subsequent influence (as with some outlier communities that are physically and culturally Melanesian). It merely emphasizes the fact that languages are not exchanged like pots or pigs. For actual language replacement to happen, special social circumstances are required—for example, conquest and prolonged occupation by a foreign group; or a drastically reduced population on an atoll, which could be outnumbered by a single party of migrants.

The Polynesian Family

It cannot but strike the imagination, the immense space through which this nation has spread; the extent of its limits exceed all Europe, and is nearly equal to Africa, stretching in breadth from A'toui [Kauai] to New Zealand . . . and in length from Easter Island to the Friendly Isles [Tonga] . . . All the isles in the intermediate space are by their affinity or sameness in speech to be reckoned as forming one people. (Beaglehole 1955–67:III,1392–1393)

Thus Lieutenant King described what has become known as Polynesia in the geographic sense—a roughly triangular area with vertices at Hawaii, New Zealand, and Easter Island (see Fig. I.1). He correctly surmised that the few islands within the area that remained to be discovered would also turn out to be linguistically Polynesian. These "triangle languages" include the best-known and most thoroughly studied members of the family: Maori, Hawaiian, Tahitian, Samoan, and Tongan. It was already known in King's time, however, that Polynesian languages were not confined to the triangle. On his second voyage, Cook had heard the language of Futuna in the southern New Hebrides; he found it "nearly if not exactly the same as that spoke at the Friendly Islands" (Beaglehole 1955–67:II,504). By the end of the nineteenth century a whole series of small Polynesian-speaking communities (the largest having about 2,000 speakers) had been discovered in Melanesia and Micronesia, from the Loyalty Islands to the central Carolines. They are now referred to as the Polynesian outliers.

The Polynesian linguistic family is very clearly defined; there is no language whose membership in the family is at all doubtful or controversial. It is less easy to assign a precise number to the languages in the family, because there is no specific, nonarbitrary criterion for deciding whether two different forms of speech are distinct languages or simply dialects of a single language. Table 10.2 enumerates 33 Polynesian languages commonly distinguished by

Name	Location and comments	Name	Location and comments
	West Polynesia	Moriori	Chatham Islands. Extinct since late nineteenth century. Might be classed as a dialect of Maori.
Tongan	All islands in Tonga except Niuafo'ou.		
Niuean			
Samoan		Easter Island	
Tokelauan			
Tūvalu	Clear division between northern (Nanumea, Nanumanga, Niutao) and southern (Nukufetau, Vaitupu, Funafuti, Nukulaelae) dialects.		*Outliers*
		Nukuoro	Caroline Islands.
		Kapingamarangi	Caroline Islands.
		Nuguria	
		Takuu	North Solomons Province, Papua New Guinea.
		Nukumanu	
East Uvea	Wallis Island.	Luangiua	Ontong Java, Solomon Islands.
East Futuna	Hoorn Island.		
Niuafo'ou	Tonga.	Sikaiana	Solomon Islands.
Pukapuka	Cook Islands.	Rennellese	Rennell and Bellona, Solomon Islands.
	East Polynesia	Pileni	Reef Islands and Duff Islands (Taumako).
Hawaiian		Tikopia	
Marquesan	Strong division between northern (Nuku Hiva, Ua Pou, Ua Huka) and southern (Hivaoa, Fatu Hiva, Tahuata) dialects.	Anuta	Despite close cultural ties and some linguistic similarities to Tikopia, recent research (Green 1971; Feinberg 1977) suggests that Anuta should be considered a distinct tradition.
Tahitian	Society Islands and parts of Tuamotus.		
Tuamotuan			
Mangareva	Gambier Islands.	Mae	Makata Village, Emae Island, New Hebrides.
Austral	Scanty available information suggests recent or ongoing replacement of distinctive Austral language or languages by Tahitian.	Mele-Fila	Mele Village and Fila Island, Efate, New Hebrides.
Penrhyn	Tongareva, Cook Islands.	West Futuna	Futuna and Aniwa islands, New Hebrides.
Rarotongan	All Cook Islands except Penrhyn and Pukapuka.	West Uvea	Ouvea, Loyalty Islands.
Maori	New Zealand.		

linguists, with their conventional names. (For a more detailed survey see Biggs 1971.)

From the existence of this strong linguistic family we conclude that the populations of the triangle islands and the outlier communities are descended, at least in large part, from a single original community who spoke the language we refer to as Proto-Polynesian. Since only a modest degree of linguistic diversification has taken place—the relatedness of the languages is apparent at first glance even to nonlinguists—it is probable that the breakup of Proto-Polynesian took place in relatively recent times.

ROSS CLARK

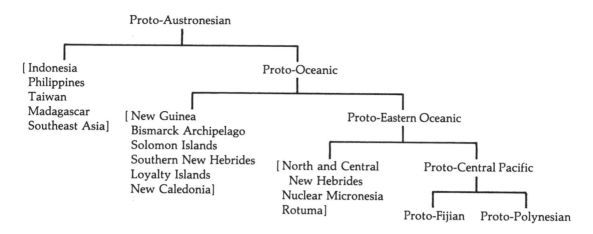

10.5 Subgrouping of the Austronesian family. (Names in square brackets refer to areas, not individual languages. More than one subgroup may be represented.)

External Relations

Polynesian is a small subgroup of the language family originally called Malayo-Polynesian, but now more commonly Austronesian (AN). With well over 500 daughter languages, this is numerically the largest well-established language family in the world. The geographic extent of its territory is also one of the largest, although much of the area included is water. The Austronesian-speaking area includes the islands of Polynesia, Micronesia, Melanesia, Indonesia, Madagascar, the Philippines, and Taiwan, as well as continental enclaves in Indochina and the Malay Peninsula. (For a recent general survey of Austronesian languages see Pawley 1974.) Within this territory virtually the only non-AN languages are found on the mainland of New Guinea and parts of some of the adjacent islands (eastern Indonesia, the Bismarck Archipelago, the Solomon Islands, and the Santa Cruz group). These non-Austronesian languages are often called "Papuan," but they are not members of a single family.

While the fundamental work on comparative Austronesian linguistics was done by Dempwolff in the 1920s and 1930s (see Dempwolff 1934–38), subgrouping of the Austronesian family is a matter of continuing debate. Many languages likely to be important eventually are only beginning to

be well described, and it will be some years before a well-supported theory and a comprehensive Austronesian family tree gain general acceptance. Figure 10.5 depicts the position of Polynesian within the Austronesian family in a way that would be accepted by many linguists. (Only the subgrouping that directly involves Polynesian has been shown.)

The Oceanic subgroup was recognized early by Kern (1886), the substantial evidence for its existence being provided by Dempwolff. (Dempwolff's term for it was "Urmelanesisch"; the use of "Oceanic" in this sense is fairly recent.) The subgroup includes almost all the AN languages of the Polynesian-Melanesian-Micronesian island world, the exceptions being at the western edges—some languages at the far western end of New Guinea, and Palauan, Chamorro, and possibly Yapese in Micronesia. The best-known innovation shared by the Oceanic languages is a series of simplifications of the Proto-Austronesian sound system, some of which are shown below.

Proto-Austronesian		Proto-Oceanic
*p, *b	$\longrightarrow$	*p
*s, *z, *c, *j	$\longrightarrow$	*s
*k, *g	$\longrightarrow$	*k

The grammatical system was modified in significant ways, which are only beginning to be understood (see Pawley 1973; Pawley and Reid 1976; Foley 1976), and there were, of course, lexical changes as well. The Proto-Austronesian word for a citrus fruit, *limaw, for example, which would have been expected to appear as *limo in Proto-Oceanic, turns up instead with its syllables reversed, as *moli.

Oceanic divides into a number of subgroups, the one of interest for our purposes being Eastern Oceanic. The most detailed discussion of this subgroup is by Pawley (1972); a number of earlier writers, however, had observed that among the languages of Melanesia, those of the southeast Solomons and the central and northern New Hebrides seemed to show the closest similarities to Fijian and Polynesian. Pawley argued for an Eastern Oceanic subgroup including all of these, plus Rotuman and the Oceanic languages of Micronesia. More recently he has suggested (Pawley 1978) that the languages of the southeast Solomons do not really belong in this group and that their apparent special resemblance to Polynesian and Fijian results from common grammatical and phonological conservatism rather than shared developments. Among the innovations that Pawley sees as characteristic of the newly defined Eastern Oceanic are the development of a new pronoun form *kamami ("we, not including you"), alongside the original *kami; the evolution of the preposition *ki, and possibly the addition of a new category of possession, "drinkable," alongside the "edible," "intimate," and "neutral" categories found in many other Oceanic languages.

The close relation between Polynesian and Fijian has long been apparent, though some writers (see Milner 1971), have attributed it to borrowing rather than to a common subgroup. Pawley (1972) uses the term "Central Pacific" for a subgroup that comprises only Fijian and Polynesian. Probable innovations of Proto–Central Pacific include the development of the "focus particle" *ko and the prefix *fia- ("want to"), and a change from subject first to verb first as the preferred sentence order. The nu-meral "four" also has the unexpected form *faa, where other Eastern Oceanic languages would have led us to expect *fati. (On Proto–Central Pacific see also Hockett 1976.)

The position of Rotuman relative to Central Pacific is still somewhat unclear. Grace (1959) proposed a Fijian-Rotuman-Polynesian subgroup; but after Biggs (1965) showed that much of the Rotuman-Polynesian resemblance was the result of borrowing, it was generally assumed that Grace's hypothesis would have to be discarded. Recently, however, Pawley (1978) has proposed that Rotuman be reincluded in Central Pacific, partly on the basis of new data on Fijian languages.

Let us now attempt to draw some historical conclusions from the above linguistic facts, a subject treated in detail by Pawley and R. Green (1973). The first observation to be made is that the facts agree well with the picture of a gradual movement of Austronesian-speaking people from Indonesia through the Melanesian islands into the remote Pacific. The hypothesis held by many early writers, of a number of direct migrations from particular areas of Indonesia into particular parts of Oceania, is not supported by the linguistic evidence. Such a hypothesis would predict the existence of a number of subgroups connecting different points within these two regions. Instead, all the AN languages beyond a certain geographic point belong to a single large subgroup (Oceanic), with features distinguishing them from all Indonesian languages. Likewise, the fact that the closest linguistic relatives of Polynesian are also its closest geographic neighbors argues against the once widely held belief in a long-distance migration of Polynesians from Indonesia into the Polynesian triangle, bypassing the already established Melanesians.

If we now plot a sequence of hypothetical homelands of the successive protolanguages ancestral to Proto-Polynesian, we shall have a rough indication of the possible path followed by these successive migrants over the centuries. The Proto-Austronesian homeland cannot be confidently located, of course, while the question of the primary subgrouping of the family is still unresolved; but it almost certainly lies inside the triangular area defined by Taiwan, Sumatra, and New Guinea. The homeland of Proto-Oceanic was most probably on the coast of northeastern New Guinea or on the nearby islands. Although the membership as well as the higher subgrouping of Eastern Oceanic are still uncertain, the northern New Hebrides would be a likely location for its homeland. Finally, virtually whatever the position of Rotuman, all evidence points to Fiji as the homeland of Proto–Central Pacific. We shall consider the Proto-Polynesian homeland in the following section of this chapter.

Internal Relations

The Polynesian family itself, as we have already seen, is very strongly defined, which suggests that the Proto-Polynesian (PPN) speech community underwent a long period of isolated development after its separation from Proto-Fijian. Some of the innovations that define the Polynesian family are shown in Table 10.3.

The presently accepted theory of Polynesian subgrouping is largely the work of Pawley (1966, 1967), whose major groups

Table 10.3   Proto-Polynesian innovations.

Phonology

Prenasalized stops become plain voiceless stops.

Fijian	Proto-Polynesian (PPN)	Meaning
ᵐbeka	*peka	bat
ⁿdalo	*talo	taro
ᵑgele	*kele	earth

Grammar

Common noun article *na disappears and is replaced by contrasting definite (*te) and indefinite (*sa) articles.

System of four categories of possession (inalienable, edible, drinkable, and neutral) is reduced to two categories (dominant and subordinate).

Fijian	Maori	Meaning
na ulu-na (inalienable)	t-oo-na uru (subordinate)	his head
na ke-na kumala (edible)	t-aa-na kuumara (dominant)	his sweet potato
na me-na wai (drinkable)	t-oo-na wai (subordinate)	his water
na no-na kato (neutral)	t-aa-na kete (dominant)	his basket

Vocabulary

PPN
*kai ("eat"); from Proto-Oceanic *kani
*poo ("night"); PO *mpoŋi
*raku ("scratch"); PO *karu
*tama ("child"); cf. PO *tama ("father")

Other items restricted to Polynesian

*la'aa ("sun")	*ma'uŋa ("mountain")
*kata ("laugh")	*kulii ("dog")
*moana ("sea")	*moɑ ("fowl")

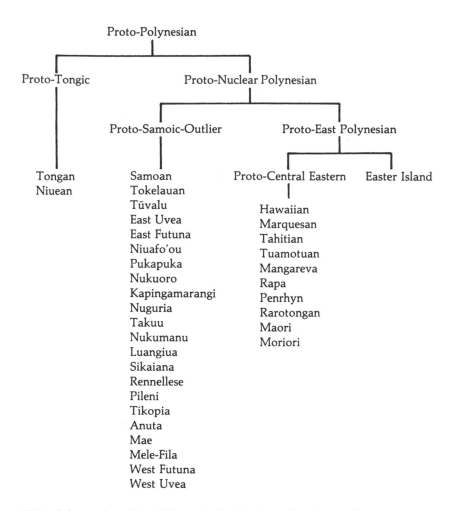

```
                           Proto-Polynesian
          ┌────────────────────────┴────────────────────────┐
   Proto-Tongic                        Proto-Nuclear Polynesian
       │                      ┌────────────────┴────────────────┐
       │            Proto-Samoic-Outlier            Proto-East Polynesian
       │                      │                 ┌────────────┴──────────┐
    Tongan               Samoan          Proto-Central Eastern    Easter Island
    Niuean               Tokelauan                │
                         Tūvalu              Hawaiian
                         East Uvea          Marquesan
                         East Futuna        Tahitian
                         Niuafo'ou          Tuamotuan
                         Pukapuka           Mangareva
                         Nukuoro            Rapa
                         Kapingamarangi     Penrhyn
                         Nuguria            Rarotongan
                         Takuu              Maori
                         Nukumanu           Moriori
                         Luangiua
                         Sikaiana
                         Rennellese
                         Pileni
                         Tikopia
                         Anuta
                         Mae
                         Mele-Fila
                         West Futuna
                         West Uvea
```

10.6 *Subgrouping of the Polynesian family (from Pawley 1966).*

are shown in Fig. 10.6. The most important and original feature of Pawley's categorization is the Nuclear Polynesian subgroup, which includes all members of the family except Tongan and Niuean. While not strongly defined, Nuclear Polynesian is supported by a few pieces of solid evidence, some of which are shown in Table 10.4.

Central Eastern is a very strongly defined subgroup, a fact that indicates a long period of common development after separation from the rest of Nuclear Polynesian. Some of its innovations are shown in Table 10.5. Easter Island shares some of these innovations, but not all.

The other primary subgroup of Nuclear Polynesian is Samoic-Outlier, the least clearly defined of the major groups. Pawley (1967) has suggested a number of innovations, but there are problems with most of them.

Tongic, the subgroup that includes only Tongan and Niuean, is fairly clearly defined. Its most conspicuous innovations are the loss of PPN *r and the replacement of the definite article *te by he or e.

The Nuclear Polynesian hypothesis implies that the first split of the PPN speech community separated the linguistic ancestors of the present Samoans and Tongans. According to the maximal diversity princi-

Table 10.4 Nuclear Polynesian innovations.

The Proto-Polynesian *h* is lost:

Proto-Polynesian (PPN)	Tongan	Niuean	Samoan	Maori	Meaning
*hiwa	hiva	hiva	iva	iwa	nine
*hala	hala	hala	ala	ara	road
*fohe	fohe	fohe	foe	hoe	paddle

The indefinite article, PPN *sa* (Tongan, Niue *ha*) is replaced by Proto–Nuclear Polynesian *se* (Samoan *se*, Maori *he*).

Second-person plural pronoun, PPN *kimoutolu* (Tongan *kimoutolu*, Niue *mutolu*) is reduced to Proto–Nuclear Polynesian *koutou* (Samoan *'outou*, Maori *koutou*).

ple, then, a likely location for the PPN homeland would be the area including Tonga, Samoa, and the nearby isolated islands. A Tongan homeland, for instance, with the primary split resulting from the first colonization of Samoa, would be consistent with this evidence.

A fundamental east-west division in Polynesia has long been assumed. While Pawley's East Polynesian corresponds to one side of this dichotomy, there is no similar "West Polynesian" subgroup. The Nuclear Polynesian hypothesis thus implies that the similarities between, for example, Samoan and Tongan are the result either of independent retention of original Proto-Polynesian characteristics or of later borrowing.

All the Polynesian islands east of 165° west longitude, as well as New Zealand, derive their languages from a single ancestor, Proto–East Polynesian. This single original colony in East Polynesia must have remained a coherent and isolated community for several centuries, during which only a single migration (to Easter Island) succeeded in establishing a separate language tradition.

The inclusion of all the outliers within the Samoic-Outlier subgroup of Nuclear Polynesian is evidence against the hypothesis (maintained, for example, by Capell 1962) that at least some of the outliers rep-

resent colonies left behind during the migration of the original Polynesian settlers toward the triangle. This hypothesis would require a primary split in subgrouping between the outliers and all the triangle languages. Instead, the Pawley subgrouping suggests that all outliers were colonized as a result of east-west voyages from the triangle area. The relatively weak evidence for the Samoic-Outlier subgroup itself may indicate that various groups began to disperse from the homeland relatively soon after the breakup of Proto–Nuclear Polynesian.

Some lower-order subgroupings have been proposed and may be briefly mentioned here. Pawley (1967) gave evidence for some small local subgroups among the outliers, such as (a) Kapingamarangi and Nukuoro; (b) a "North Solomons" group, which includes Sikaiana, Luangiua, Nukumanu, Takuu, and Nuguria; and (c) Mele-Fila and Futuna-Aniwa. (Further data now available strongly confirm the last grouping; see Clark 1979.)

Attempts to find linguistic evidence for connections between specific outliers and specific parts of West Polynesia have been less successful. Pawley proposed a subgrouping of the four southernmost outliers with East Futuna, and another of Tūvalu with the North Solomons and Micronesian outliers. While there is nothing implausible

Table 10.5   Central Eastern innovations.

Phonology

f . . . f sequences change to w . . . h.

Proto-Polynesian (PPN)	Hawaiian	Tahitian	Maori	Meaning
*fafie	wahie	vahie	wahie	firewood
*fafo	waho	vaho	waho	outside

Grammar

Negation with *kore*.
Tongan: 'Ikai te u 'ilo.
Samoan: 'Ou te lee iloa.
Hawaiian: *'A'ole* wau e 'ike.
Tahitian: *'Aore* au e 'ite.
Maori: *Kaahore* au e moohio.
Meaning: I do not know.

Preverbal subject pronouns are lost.

Progressive tense with *e* preceding and *ana* following the verb.

Vocabulary

*maitaki ("good")
*koorero ("speak")
*tomo ("enter")
*paŋo ("black")
*tiki ("carved image")

about these proposals, the evidence for them so far is not particularly strong. It can be expected that clearer hypotheses will emerge when more adequate data become available for the outliers, only a handful of which are well described.

Green (1966) proposed two major subgroups of Central Eastern: Tahitic, including Tahitian, Tuamotuan, Rarotongan, and Maori; and Marquesic, including Marquesan, Hawaiian, and probably Mangarevan. His evidence consisted of lexical data originally collected by Emory (1946), as well as some common sound changes and lexicostatistical figures. While the case for two such subgroups seems promising, a more extensive and careful study is required, preferably with better sources for such languages as Marquesan and Mangarevan.

Quantitative Methods: Lexicostatistics and Glottochronology

The arguments and conclusions discussed so far are all based on classical comparative methods. We must look now at a new method that has been widely applied in recent years.

The technique of lexicostatistics, first elaborated by Swadesh in the early 1950s, is an attempt to refine the rules of thumb stated above as Principles 3 and 4 into a quantitative measure. Swadesh drew up a list of 200 meanings intended to be, as nearly as possible, universally known and culture independent (items such as "and," "big," "drink," "head," "mother," "skin," "star," "throw"). Given two related languages, with a list of the basic words for these meanings in each, we can count the number of items for which the two languages have cognate forms. English and German, for example, have cognate forms for "and," "drink," "mother," and "star" (German *und, trinken, Mutter, Stern*), but not for "big," "head," "skin," and "throw" (German *gross, Kopf, Haut, werfen*). The number of cognates, expressed as a percentage of the total list, gives us a numerical measure of the closeness of the relation between the two languages.

Two dialects that have just recently been separated by a migration will share 100 percent cognates. If contact is not reestablished, this percentage will steadily decrease with time as one or the other language loses or replaces an item on the list. Given the assumptions that the rate of loss (replacement) is roughly constant within a given language family, that the particular items replaced are independent from language to language, and that factors such as borrowing do not complicate matters, the cognate percentages for various pairs of languages should be directly translatable into relative lengths of time since separation for each pair of languages, and thence into a subgrouping. Figure 10.7 shows an idealized example.

If we make the stronger assumption that the rate of replacement of items on the 200-word list is universally constant and can be determined, we have glottochronology, which offers the possibility of translating cognate percentages directly into dates. Swadesh "calibrated" this measure by investigating rates of replacement in several languages with long documented histories and found close agreement among them. He arrived at a figure of 19.5 percent replacement (or 80.5 percent retention) per 1,000 years. The time, t, since separation of a pair of languages can be computed from the formula:

$$t = \frac{\log C}{2 \log r},$$

where C is the percentage of cognates between the two languages and r is the reten-

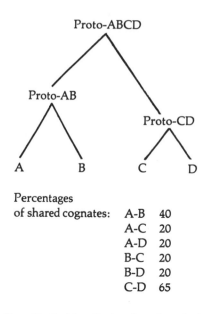

Percentages of shared cognates:

A-B	40
A-C	20
A-D	20
B-C	20
B-D	20
C-D	65

10.7 Hypothetical family tree based on lexicostatistical figures.

tion rate (here 0.805). Some representative figures are given in Table 10.6.

Lexicostatistics and glottochronology as concepts have provoked stormy scholarly interest since their first appearance. Almost all of their fundamental assumptions have been challenged, and the practical details of the technique are full of complications. The results are often hard to reconcile with those arrived at by more traditional methods. Yet the promise of glottochronology, in particular—ideally a linguistic equivalent of radiocarbon dating—is so attractive that even the skeptical majority of

Table 10.6 Glottochronological time depths for selected cognate percentages.

Percent cognates between related languages	Years since separation (with margin of uncertainty)
100	0
80	500 (± 100)
60	1,200 (± 200)
40	2,100 (± 350)
20	3,700 (± 500)
10	5,300 (± 800)

Table 10.7 Cognate percentages among selected Polynesian languages.

	Rar	Tah	Mqs	Haw	Eas	Sam	Ece	Tik	Pil	Ren	Kap	Nuk	Ton	Niu
Maori	56	41	50	51	54	44	49	50	47	43	44	39	45	47
Rarotongan		54	61	64	57	51	48	54	47	47	47	43	47	56
Tahitian			44	48	44	36	42	42	37	43	32	30	35	38
Marquesan				57	59	44	50	51	45	45	42	40	44	50
Hawaiian					59	48	54	54	50	49	43	42	44	51
Easter I.						51	56	56	49	50	46	44	50	55
Samoan							63	63	53	57	50	49	61	62
Ellice								67	57	60	53	51	65	63
Tikopia									61	63	54	53	63	60
Pileni										57	47	49	53	54
Rennellese											52	53	57	56
Kapinga												53	46	49
Nukuoro													46	49
Tongan														71

NOTE: Taken from Kirk and Epling 1972 (from Dyen). Rounded to nearest one percent.

linguists are reluctant to dismiss it altogether. Most would concede that it can provide at least a useful order-of-magnitude indication of the time depth of linguistic relationships. Laymen find the whole idea fascinating.

Lexicostatistical computations for various sets of Polynesian languages have been published by Elbert (1953), Grace (1959), Emory (1963), Walsh (1963), and Dyen (1965). Differences in method and in the languages treated make it difficult to compare results. The most comprehensive study is that of Dyen (1965). A selection of his figures is shown in Table 10.7. Dyen translated his cognate percentages into a subgrouping by isolating sets of languages in which each member was related to one of the others by a percentage higher than the greatest percentage of any member with a nonmember. The resulting subgrouping for Polynesian is shown in Fig. 10.8. Except for the Polynesian subfamily itself, the critical percentage (the difference between the internal and external percentages) is only a few points for each of the subgroups shown—not a large amount in comparison to the level of statistical uncertainty of lexicostatistical figures.

Dyen's subgrouping differs in important ways from that based on classical comparative methods (Fig. 10.6). Its West Polynesian cluster includes both Samoan and Tongan, which in Pawley's subgrouping are distinct at the highest level. Nor does Pawley find any justification for the isolated position in which Maori, Kapingamarangi, and Nukuoro appear in Dyen's scheme. Clearly Dyen's subgrouping is a faithful representation of a certain set of facts; but whether those facts can support direct historical interpretation is less clear. It seems likely that they could be explained in terms of a basic set of "ideal" percentages derived from the orthodox subgrouping, and subjected to complex distortions because of borrowing and accelerated replacement rates in some languages. A careful attempt to reconcile the two has not yet been made.

Of more immediate interest to prehistory are the absolute dates yielded by glottochronology. Bauan Fijian shows percentages in the low 20s with various Polynesian languages, suggesting that Proto-Polynesian and Proto-Fijian diverged in the neighborhood of 1500 B.C. The lowest percentages within the Polynesian family are

ROSS CLARK

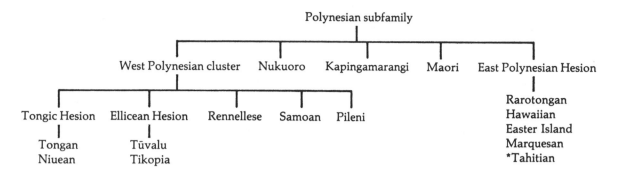

10.8 *Subgrouping of the Polynesian family (from Dyen 1965). (*Tahitian provisionally included on "corrected" figures.)*

around 40, suggesting a date of about A.D. 0 for the breakup of Proto-Polynesian. A date for Nuclear Polynesian is less easy to determine, but certain figures seem to show a difference of about 5 percent, which would indicate a date two or three centuries later than the PPN breakup. Easter Island's scores with the Central Eastern languages (in the mid-50s) indicate about 1,500 years of divergence, while an average of 60 within the Central Eastern group means a maximum of about 1,200 years since the first separation.

A careful inspection of Dyen's (or any other) lexicostatistical figures will reveal many deviations from the type of general pattern just described. In the next sections we shall examine two of the factors recognized as responsible for at least part of this distortion. (On this subject see also Dyen 1963.)

Borrowing

Borrowing is the direct adoption by one language of lexical items and other features from another language. It is perhaps the major factor that complicates the family-tree model of linguistic relationships outlined above and frustrates the linguist's attempts to reconstruct history. On the other hand, borrowing can provide valuable information on the time, extent, and nature of the cultural contacts that produced it.

In Polynesia we are concerned with the specific problem of borrowing among members of the same linguistic family. We need to be able to distinguish between a word that a language has "directly inherited"— by unbroken transmission since the proto-language—and one that it has borrowed at some point from a sister language that has inherited it directly (see Fig. 10.9). When

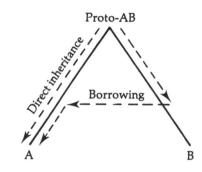

10.9 *Direct and indirect inheritance.*

the same word occurs twice in a given language, having arrived by two such dissimilar paths of transmission, we speak of a "doublet." With luck, the different histories will have exposed the word to unlike sequences of sound changes, resulting in variants of form from which the history can be inferred. In English, for example, words like *pedal* and *paternal* are revealed as borrowings from some non-Germanic language, since they have not undergone the *p* to *f* shift of Grimm's Law, unlike their directly inherited cognates *foot* and *father*.

Flower and *friar*, on the other hand, betray a Romance origin by having undergone the *bh* to *f* change characteristic of Latin, whereas the directly inherited *bloom* and *brother* preserve something closer to the Indo-European original consonant.

In the Polynesian family, with its rather simple phonological history, such diagnostic clues are often not available. This may be one of the reasons that relatively little attention has been paid to borrowing in this area. Another, perhaps, is the assumption that the natural isolation of the islands would make borrowing of negligible importance. Indications are that this is so only in certain exceptional cases such as Easter Island and Hawaii; but since so little detailed research has been done, we can only list some of the cases where borrowing appears to have taken place.

The best-documented instance involves the influence of a Polynesian on a non-Polynesian language. Biggs (1965) has shown that apparently inconsistent sound correspondences in Rotuman can be explained by borrowing from Tongan (and perhaps another Polynesian language as well).

Tongan linguistic influence, in fact, has been felt on almost all the surrounding islands. Many Tongan loanwords are found in the dialects of the Lau islands in eastern Fiji. The vocabularies collected in 1616 by Schouten and Lemaire at Niuatoputapu and Tafahi in northern Tonga show that a non-Tongic language was spoken there at that time. Yet when these islands were rediscovered by Europeans in the nineteenth century, the earlier language had been replaced by Tongan. East Uvea shows about 85 percent agreement with Tongan in basic vocabulary, so that Dyen classed the two, for purposes of his lexicostatistical survey, as dialects of a single language. Pawley (1967), however, has argued convincingly that East Uvea is fundamentally a Samoic language that has been subjected to heavy Tongan influence.

Niuean, as a number of features of its phonology and grammar clearly show, is an offshoot of the same major branch of the family as Tongan. However, there are various peculiarities suggesting that the linguistic history of Niue may be more complicated than simple Tongan colonization of a previously uninhabited island. The existence of doublets such as *akau* ("tree") and *laakau* ("shrub, plant")—both from PPN **ra'akau*, the former reflecting the Tongic development (Tongan *'akau*) and the latter the Nuclear Polynesian (Samoan *laa'au*)—suggest some inheritance of Nuclear Polynesian material, and there are even indications of a specifically East Polynesian influence, as in the word *mitaki* ("good"). Another word of apparently eastern origin is *Tafiti*, meaning "distant, remote" in Central Eastern languages, but on Niue used only as the name of one of the two districts of the island. The other is called *Motu* ("island"), and while these names are highly suggestive, the few dialect differences that have been noted between the two areas do not seem to follow any consistent historical pattern.

Samoa and Tonga, the two major archipelagoes of West Polynesia, probably have been in some degree of contact ever since the breakup of PPN; a degree of borrowing between them is to be expected and has generally been assumed. As yet, however, it has not been even perfunctorily investigated. Careful study will probably reveal a large number of such borrowings, though not enough to threaten the existence of either language or even to obscure its historical affiliations, as with East Uvea. To consider a single example: the semantic change by which PPN **'alu* ("follow") becomes the basic word for "go" (singular) is apparently reflected only in Samoan, Tongan, and East Uvea (known to have borrowed extensively from Tongan). Most other languages show a reflex of **fano*, the original Proto-Oceanic term, or (in the east) of **sa'ele*, originally meaning "walk, stroll." This distribution suggests Samoan-Tongan borrowing. A clue to the direction of borrowing is given by the plural form of the same verb, where both Samoan and Tongan have *oo*, whereas other languages show *olo* or *oro.* Given a PPN form **oro,* all reflexes could be explained as directly inherited (the loss of PPN **r* in Tongan is regular), except for Samoan. The irregular absence of *l* in Samoan could be explained if *oo* were a borrowing from Tongan. And this in turn would suggest that the singular of the same verb had been transmitted in the same direction.

Pukapuka shows some evidence of borrowing from other Cook Islands languages, including some grammatical features, though its basic structure is unquestionably Samoic. Elsewhere in East Polynesia the relatively wide separation of island groups would lead one to expect less borrowing, while the relatively close relatedness of the languages makes its detection all the more difficult. Green (1966) has suggested borrowing from Tahitian into Hawaiian to account for discrepancies in the distribution of evidence for his Tahitic subgroup. This would presumably be correlated with the often postulated "second migration" of Tahitians to Hawaii. There is no intrinsic evidence that the forms in question are borrowed, however; and their distribution can easily be explained in other ways.

Name Avoidance

At least since the time of Horatio Hale (1846), scholars have been intrigued by a body of words in the Tuamotuan dialects that have no obvious Polynesian etymologies, such as *neki* ("fire")—PPN **afi; rari* ("one")—PPN **tasa,* PNP **tasi;* and *hakoi* ("man")—PPN **taŋata* or **ta'ane.* This "non-Polynesian" component has been used as evidence for various unorthodox theories of Polynesian prehistory (most recently by Langdon 1975), but it must be emphasized that no connection with any other language family has ever been demonstrated, so that the term "non-Polynesian" or "foreign" suggests more than is really justified. In fact, there is no reason to think that any external influence is required to explain these words.

Every language contains words of obscure origin. English *bird* and *dog,* for example, cannot be clearly traced beyond Old English. Such cases are presumably the result of changes in form or meaning too drastic or too unpredictable to leave clear clues about their past. In the Tuamotuan case, however, we do have an unusually large number of these obscure words in the basic vocabulary, and the particular explanation is to be sought in the widespread Polynesian linguistic practice of name avoidance.

This custom has been most fully described in Tahiti (White 1967), where it was known as *pii.* White indicates that it probably prevailed in the Tuamotus as well, and it has also been reported in Samoa (Pratt 1911), New Zealand (Williams 1915), and Rapa (Stokes 1955). In essence, the idea was to avoid use of a chief's name in any context that might be considered disrespectful. The stricture extended to the use of any ordinary word that might be homophonous (identical in sound) with the chief's name or a part of it—and Polynesian languages are rich in homophones. In most cases the avoidance would not extend beyond the chief's sphere of influence or his lifetime; the old word would be remembered and reintroduced when there was no longer any danger. But in some cases the replacement could have become permanent. A well-documented historical instance in Tahitian is the replacement of *poo* ("night") by *ru'i* and of *mare* ("cough") by *hota* during the reign of Pomare I, the first "king" of Tahiti, in the early nineteenth century.

The name-avoidance custom (commonly referred to as word tabooing) is generally accepted as the explanation for a number of unexpected forms in the basic Tahitian vocabulary, and a similar explanation for the Tuamotuan words seems more plausible than an appeal to unidentified non-Polynesian sources. Unfortunately we have few details of how the custom worked, in particular of how the replacement words were chosen. In some cases they are clearly words of related meaning—as with *ru'i* ("dark") replacing *poo* ("night")—but many others have not been satisfactorily explained. Words may simply have been coined out of thin air whenever replacements were needed for names to be avoided.

The pii custom accounts for the abnormally high rate of vocabulary replacement in Tahitian, and its low cognate percentages with all other languages (see Table 10.7). A similar explanation seems likely for certain peculiar items in Samoan, such as *maile* ("dog") for PPN **kulii* and *tele* ("big") for PPN **lasi*; and certain lexicostatistical anomalies can be explained on the assumption that Samoan's percentages have been depressed by such a factor, though not to the same extent as Tahitian's.

The Proto-Polynesian World

Proto-Polynesian is a prehistoric language of only modest antiquity, and since we have a number of well-described daughter languages to work from, we can reconstruct it in some detail. (We now know more about the protolanguage, ironically, than about some of its more obscure daughters.) The possibility thus arises of examining the protolanguage itself, in particular its vocabulary, for information on what sort of world was inhabited by the Proto-Polynesian speakers. While phonological and grammatical structure are essentially independent of extralinguistic factors, the vocabulary of a language must unavoidably show some relation to the external world, because every language reflects those aspects of culture and environment of which its speakers are aware. The process of reasoning from the vocabulary of a reconstructed language to conclusions about the culture and environment of its speakers is often referred to as the *Wörter und Sachen* (words and things) technique.

Great care, of course, is required in reconstruction. Even if a number of languages in a family show apparently cognate forms with the same meaning, it is necessary to reckon with the possibility that the term was borrowed at some time after the breakup of the protolanguage, or that the original meaning was different and subsequently was changed in the same way by several languages. Negative inferences are very risky, since the probability of several languages losing a term is far higher than that of several independently changing the meaning in a particular direction. For example, Proto-Indo-European has a clearly reconstructible word for "snow," but none for "rain"; yet we can be sure that the Proto-Indo-Europeans were acquainted with rain and had a word for it.

Our confidence in the correctness of our inferences from reconstruction will be increased if we find a cluster of semantically related terms in the protolexicon. A familiar example is the "canoe complex" in Proto-Polynesian (Biggs 1972), where in addition to the general term for canoe (**waka*) we can reconstruct words for outrigger (**hama*), outrigger boom (**kiato*), the side of the canoe opposite the outrigger (**katea*), bilge (**liu*), paddle (**fohe*), mast (**tila*), and sail (**laa*), among others. This existence of this protocomplex would refute any claim, for example, that the Proto-Polynesians had only rafts, and that the word for raft (**waka*) was later transferred to outrigger canoes.

Quite a large Proto-Polynesian vocabulary has already been reconstructed. Walsh and Biggs (1966), in the major published source, list over 600 forms and subsequent research has more than doubled this number. But relatively little detailed attention has been paid to the meanings of the reconstructed forms, or to their implications for prehistory. The most comprehensive discussion so far has been that of Pawley and K. Green (1971), who classified about 400 items under various headings of environment and culture. Their main purpose was the location of the Proto-Polynesian homeland, and to this end they developed a picture of the PPN environment that is interesting to consider, even where it does no more than confirm what has been generally assumed or deduced from other evidence.

The marine environment of the PPN community is shown clearly in a number of words translating the English "sea": *tahi ("sea") as a basic direction, opposed to *'uta ("land"), hence seaward/landward or toward the shore/inland (*tahi also refers to salt water); *moana ("open sea"); and *wasa ("sea between two places"); there are also related terms *lili and *sou denoting rough seas; *peau ("wave, on the open sea"); *ŋalu ("wave, breaking"); and *hu'a ("high tide"). The presence of coral reefs is indicated by *hakau ("reef"); the words *puŋa, *feo, and *lase for kinds of coral; *awa ("channel"); and *loto ("lagoon").

A less predictable inference from the lexical data is that the PPN homeland included a high island or islands of some extent. Thus there are reconstructed words for mountain (*ma'uŋa), cliff or precipice (*mato), ridge (*tuŋasiwi), and landslide (*solo), as well as for various fresh-water features not found on atolls or the smaller volcanic islands: *waitafe ("river, stream"), though this could have been an independent formation from *wai ("fresh water") and *tafe ("flow"); *muriwai ("river or stream mouth"); *hafu ("waterfall"), *lolo ("flood"); and *rano ("lake, swamp").

Reconstructions for flora and fauna, as expected, indicate a homeland within the tropical Indo-Pacific region; for example, *niu ("coconut palm"), *fara ("pandanus"), *moli ("citrus"), and *tawake ("tropic bird"). The conclusion that the homeland was, or included, a high island of some size is further supported by the reconstruction of terms for a number of plant species, mainly trees, restricted to such environments: the mangrove (*toŋo); a nettle tree of the genus Laportia (*salato); the Polynesian chestnut, Inocarpus edulis (*'ifi); sandalwood (*asi); and the Malay apple, Eugenia malaccensis (*kafika).

Some of the biological lexicon, because of the limited distribution of species within Polynesia, further restricts the possible

range of Polynesian homelands. Pawley and Green argue that the reconstructibility of terms for the edible palolo worm (PPN *palolo), land snake (*ŋata), and the nut tree Pometia pinnata (*tawa), none of which occur in East Polynesia, eliminates the eastern islands as possible homelands. To these may be added the incubator bird, Megapodius freycinet (PPN *malau), found in the Polynesian triangle only on Niuafo'ou (Clark 1978).

If East Polynesia is eliminated, we are left with the West Polynesian high islands and those outliers that are on or near high islands in Melanesia. (It is difficult to eliminate these latter islands as homelands by the Wörter und Sachen technique, although the indications are clearly against them.)

The evidence considered by Pawley and Green implies that the Proto-Polynesians had gardens (*ma'ala) in which they grew such crops as taro (*talo), yams (*'ufi), bananas (*futi), and sugarcane (*toLo). The much-discussed case of the sweet potato (Ipomea batatas) requires special comment. Such Polynesian forms as Tongan kumala, Samoan 'umala, Tahitian 'umara, and Maori kuumara show regular sound correspondences that would support the reconstruction of PPN *kumala as a term for this plant, with the implication that the Proto-Polynesian community was acquainted with it. As with most other reconstructions, however, the attested forms could have resulted from the borrowing of an outside word into the individual languages sometime after the breakup of PPN. Only a very recent borrowing can be ruled out. (Tahitian, for example, substitutes t rather than ' for k in all post-European borrowings.)

Biggs (1972) has questioned the reliability of *kumala as a PPN reconstruction on the grounds of its allegedly unusual canonical shape and certain irregular reflexes (such as Mangaia tiimala and Hawaiian 'uala). I find these arguments unconvincing, however. On internal Polynesian linguistic evidence, *kumala is as secure (or insecure) as scores of other undisputed reconstructions. The only reasons for subjecting it to extraordinary scrutiny are the ethnobotanical controversy about the sweet potato's origin, and the existence of a possible South American cognate.

Many writers have pointed to the existence of a term for the sweet potato of the general form *kumar* in the Quechua language of Peru and Ecuador. (For discussion of the sources and lists of variants see Brand 1971 and Yen 1974.) The *kumar* form is documented as early as a 1586 dictionary, and attempts to argue that it was introduced into Quechua from Polynesian languages via Spanish (as does O'Brien 1972) seem both far-fetched and unnecessary. It has been pointed out, however, that *kumar* may denote only a certain variety of the tuber; that it may have been borrowed into Quechua from some language submerged by Inca expansion; and that it is attested only in certain dialect areas, all of them highland rather than coastal. Though these are relevant points, it must be added that our knowledge of the coastal languages of this region is extremely limited and that the issues of the *prehistoric* geographic distribution of languages, and distribution and precise meanings of the various terms for sweet potato have scarcely even been raised.

In view of these multiple uncertainties, it seems unwise to treat the linguistic evidence as a major component of the case for any hypothesis on sweet potato origins. The Polynesian credentials of **kumala* are sound, and there appears to be no good reason to question the status of *kumar* as a pre-Columbian word, whatever its precise meaning and distribution. In the last analysis, one must bear in mind that such resemblances do sometimes occur by chance, between languages with no historical connection.

In addition to their reconstruction of the natural environment, Pawley and K. Green (1971) list words in a number of areas of material culture, such as fishing, gardening, cooking, and house building, but do not discuss them at any length. Both ma-

terial culture and social organization in the Proto-Polynesian lexicon have received very little linguistic attention. We do not even have a full linguistic study of PPN kinship terminology. Rather, the pattern has been for social anthropologists and culture historians to use linguistic data as they see fit, to support their hypotheses—not always with happy results.

Language, as Captain Cook and Lieutenant King realized, can provide a uniquely powerful and subtle tool for the recovery of certain aspects of a people's past. In the Polynesian field, linguistic data have been the basis of some admirable interdisciplinary endeavors, and also of some of the wildest flights of pseudoscientific fancy. It is important that prehistorians should understand both the logical basis and the limitations of historical linguistics, in order that this tool may be used to its fullest advantage.

References

Beaglehole, J. C., ed. 1955–67. *The journals of Captain James Cook on his voyages of discovery.* Cambridge: Cambridge University Press, for the Hakluyt Society.

Biggs, B. G. 1965. Direct and indirect inheritance in Rotuman. *Lingua* 14:383–415.

———. 1971. The languages of Polynesia. In *Current trends in linguistics*, ed. T. A. Sebeok, vol. 8, pp. 466–505. The Hague: Mouton.

———. 1972. Implications of linguistic subgrouping with special reference to Polynesia. In *Studies in Oceanic culture history*, ed. R. C. Green and Marion Kelly, vol. 3. *Pacific Anthropological Records* 13:143–152.

Brand, D. D. 1971. The sweet potato: an exercise in methodology. In *Man across the sea: problems of pre-Columbian contacts*, ed. C. L. Riley et al., pp. 343–365. Austin: University of Texas Press.

Capell, Arthur. 1962. Oceanic linguistics today. *Current Anthropology* 3:371–428.

Clark, Ross. 1978. Proto-Polynesian birds. In preparation.

———. 1979. The New Hebridean outliers. In *Proceedings of the Second International Conference on Austronesian Linguistics.* Pacific

ROSS CLARK

Linguistics series. Canberra: Australian National University.

Dempwolff, Otto. 1934–38. *Vergleichende Lautlehre des austronesischen Wortschatzes.* Berlin: Dietrich Reimer.

Dyen, Isidore. 1956. Language distribution and migration theory. *Language* 32:611–626.

———. 1963. Lexicostatistically determined borrowing and taboo. *Language* 39:60–66.

———. 1965. *A lexicostatistical classification of the Austronesian languages.* International Journal of American Linguistics Memoir no. 19.

Elbert, S. H. 1953. Internal relationships of Polynesian languages and dialects. *Southwestern Journal of Anthropology* 9:147–173.

Emory, K. P. 1946. *Eastern Polynesia, its cultural relationships.* Ph.D. dissertation, Yale University.

———. 1963. East Polynesian relationships: settlement pattern and time involved as indicated by vocabulary agreements. *Journal of the Polynesian Society* 72:78–100.

Feinberg, Richard. 1977. *The Anuta language reconsidered: lexicon and grammar of a Polynesian outlier.* New Haven, Connecticut: Human Relations Area Files.

Foley, W. A. 1976. *Comparative syntax in Austronesian.* Ph.D. dissertation, University of California, Berkeley.

Grace, George. 1959. *The position of the Polynesian languages within the Austronesian (Malayo-Polynesian) family.* International Journal of American Linguistics Memoir no. 16, Baltimore.

Green, Roger. 1966. Linguistic subgrouping within Polynesia: the implications for prehistoric settlement. *Journal of the Polynesian Society* 75:6–38.

———. 1971. Anuta's position in the subgrouping of the Polynesian languages. *Journal of the Polynesian Society* 80:355–370.

Hale, Horatio. 1846. *United States Exploring Expedition, 1838–42: ethnography and philology.* Philadelphia: Lea and Blanchard.

Hockett, C. F. 1976. The reconstruction of Proto Central Pacific. *Anthropological Linguistics* 18:187–235.

Kern, J. C. H. 1886. De Fidjitaal vergeleken met hare verwanten in Indonesië en Polynesië. *Verhandelingen der Koninklijk Nederlandsche Akademie von Wetenschappen, Amsterdam, Afdeling Letterkunde* 16:1–242.

Kirk, Jerome, and P. J. Epling. 1972. The dispersal of the Polynesian peoples. Working Papers

in Methodology no. 6, Institute for Research in Social Science, University of North Carolina.

Langdon, Robert. 1975. *The lost caravel.* Sydney: Pacific Publications.

Milner, G. B. 1971. Fijian and Rotuman. In *Current trends in linguistics,* ed. T. A. Sebeok, vol. 8, pp. 397–425. The Hague: Mouton.

O'Brien, P. J. 1972. The sweet potato: its origin and dispersal. *American Anthropologist* 74:342–365.

Pawley, A. K. 1966. Polynesian languages: a subgrouping based on shared innovations in morphology. *Journal of the Polynesian Society* 75:39–64.

———. 1967. The relationships of Polynesian outlier languages. *Journal of the Polynesian Society* 76:259–296.

———. 1972. On the internal relationships of Eastern Oceanic languages. In *Studies in Oceanic culture history,* ed. R. C. Green and Marion Kelly, vol. 3. *Pacific Anthropological Records* 13:1–142.

———. 1973. Some problems in Proto-Oceanic grammar. *Oceanic Linguistics* 12:103–188.

———. 1974. Austronesian languages. In *Encyclopaedia Britannica,* 15th ed. Macropaedia, vol. 2, pp. 484–494.

———. 1975. The relationships of the Austronesian languages of Central Papua: a preliminary study. In *Studies in languages of Central and Southeast Papua,* ed. T. E. Dutton. Pacific Linguistics, ser. C, no. 29, Linguistic Circle of Canberra.

———. 1978. On redefining "Eastern Oceanic." Manuscript.

——— and K. Green. 1971. Lexical evidence for the Proto-Polynesian homeland. *Te Reo* 14:1–36.

——— and R. C. Green. 1973. Dating the dispersal of the Oceanic languages. *Oceanic Linguistics* 12:1–67.

——— and L. A. Reid. 1976. The evolution of transitive constructions in Austronesian. Working Papers in Linguistics, University of Hawaii 8(2):51–74.

Pratt, George. 1911. *Grammar and dictionary of the Samoan language,* 4th ed. Malua, Western Samoa: London Missionary Society.

Stokes, J. F. G. 1955. Language in Rapa. *Journal of the Polynesian Society* 64:315–340.

Walsh, D. S. 1963. Dictionaries versus informants: an aspect of glottochronology. *Te Reo* 6:30–38.

——— and Bruce Biggs. 1966. *Proto-Polynesian*

word list I. Te Reo Monographs. Linguistic Society of New Zealand, Auckland.

White, R. G. 1967. Onomastically induced word replacement in Tahitian. In *Polynesian culture history: essays in honor of Kenneth P. Emory,* ed. G. A. Highland et al. Honolulu: Bishop Museum Press.

Williams, William. 1915. *A dictionary of the New Zealand language,* 4th ed. Wellington: Whitcombe and Tombs.

Yen, D. E. 1974. *The sweet potato and Oceania: an essay in ethnobotany.* Bishop Museum Bulletin no. 236, Honolulu.

Physical Anthropology

CHAPTER 11

WILLIAM HOWELLS

The physique of the Polynesians is rich in clues to their origin and probable history, clues that in the past have been misread regularly, sometimes riotously. In part this has resulted from inadequate methods of reading the signals, in part from a predisposition among anthropologists and others to make the clues fit schemes erected on other kinds of data—linguistic, cultural, or legendary. As R. T. Simmons said in a paper presented at the Tenth Pacific Science Congress in 1961, "There does not appear to be a Polynesian problem other than that which we make for ourselves."

The approach of physical anthropology lies in interpreting the biological variety among the Polynesians themselves and taking this as a base for considering their likenesses to and differences from other peoples elsewhere. One handicap: in Polynesia the time depth is short and prehistoric skeletal evidence very meager. One caution: given the evidence, we are safer in trying to say what the Polynesians are not than what they are.

When the early voyagers had covered enough of the Pacific, they concluded that it held two kinds of people: the dark, fuzzy-haired Melanesians and the lighter, slightly Oriental-looking Polynesians. A century later anthropologists began to see local differences within each kind, differences that in Melanesia especially became more evident as the less hospitable islands were visited (even though simple description and recording are still incomplete). In

Polynesia, as anthropologists contemplated and measured skulls, and as the Bishop Museum in Honolulu sponsored systematic studies of the living, variation among individuals and among island groups was recognized. Yet these techniques—measurement and observation, later of blood groups also—introduced complexity without resolving it.

One attempt at resolution, and a popular one, was the recognition of "types" within a population, such types sometimes being distinguished by particular combinations of head and nose shape. These types were assumed, on no clear grounds, to correspond to the original ancestral "races" that had migrated from different homelands into the Pacific, perhaps all the way to Polynesia, before mixing; and their varying proportions in the island groups would account for the later physical differences among those groups. Once a population, or skulls thereof, had been categorized according to whether noses, for example, were wider or narrower, it became easier to suggest more specific relatives for each type in other regions. So the Polynesians became for a while some kind of amalgam of suspected Caucasoid, Mongoloid, and Negroid (specifically Melanesian) elements. And these became associated, depending on the author, with different hypothetical waves of migration, waves also reflected in culture and myth. Legendary black people, as the first settlers of New Zealand, became a supposed component of the Maori; less specifically, the kava drinkers of the West were suggested to stem from Vedic India (Caucasoids, perhaps) and the Tangaloa cult folk of the center from the South China coast. These are only examples, the latest and perhaps most original being Heyerdahl's derivation of Easter Islanders from Peru and Hawaiians from the Northwest Coast of North America, on the grounds of perceived cultural parallels.

Quite apart from being without the benefit of archaeological perspective, the entire approach misconceived the nature of genetic variation in a population. It assumed that ancestral races, or combinations of physical traits, could reappear indefinitely instead of being melded in a common gene pool; and it neglected the possibility of even the modest microevolution that could have differentiated Polynesians in Hawaii from those in Easter Island. Altogether, the atmosphere was one of tracing prehistoric migrations and diffusions from the vantage point of an armchair; the anthropologists had virtually made their own rules for the game. Later they learned to apply the rules of biology more carefully, and these, together with better methods of analysis, have done much to reduce the complexity of the formerly undigested data. In large measure we have come back to what the voyagers saw: two main complexes of Pacific peoples, each varied. Micronesians and Polynesians differ somewhat physically and biochemically, and Australians and Melanesians more so. Nonetheless, these pairs seem to constitute two main branches having essential differences from each other in form and in ultimate source.

It is difficult to be verbally specific about appearance. In general, Polynesians are (or were) large in size: relatively tall, large boned, and tending to corpulence. The small young women who greet tourists with leis in Hawaii or Tahiti are apt to be more Asiatic than Polynesian in parentage. Polynesian women may not all approach the truly majestic Queen Salote of Tonga or past royalty in other groups, but the females of Gauguin's paintings or living Maoris—both pictorially familiar—would be representative. Skin color is variable, usually a light brown. Hair also varies, seldom being either frizzly or perfectly straight, but instead slightly to markedly wavy, and always dark. Faces are large, high, and oblong, with noses that are neither prominent nor flat. Micronesians, on the other hand, although having a family resemblance to Polynesians, are shorter and seem somewhat more varied from one island group to another.

Melanesians (who in some locations clearly manifest past Micronesian or Poly-

WILLIAM HOWELLS

Table 11.1 *Mean measurements for some Polynesian and Micronesian population samples. Dimensions are in millimeters except for stature, which is given in centimeters.*

Location	Stature	Head		Face		Nose	
		Length	Breadth	Width	Height	Height	Width
Polynesia							
Tonga	173	191	155	144	128	58	44
Samoa	172	191	155	146	131	60	44
Society Islands	171	188	160	146	125	54	43
Marquesas Islands	170	193	153	143	124	53	43
Hawaii	170	188	158	144	125	56	44
New Zealand	171	196	153	146	124	53	40
Cook Islands							
Rarotonga	174	190	159	147	129	57	43
Aitutaki	172	188	159	148	130	58	43
Mangaia	170	194	156	147	123	55	42
Kapingamarangi	171	195	153	145	117[a]	53	45
Melanesia							
Fiji							
Coast	173	187	158	145	123	54	46
Interior	170	190	152	146	121	53	48
Micronesia							
Kusaie	160	188	147	136	117[b]	54[b]	42
Ponape	162	193	142	139	125[b]	57[b]	42
Truk	162	190	139	137	118[b]	53[b]	43
Yap	160	188	150	145	117	55	42
Palau	161	185	150	141	118[b]	52[b]	42

[a] As reported; a second sample seems to confirm.

[b] Adjusted for apparent errors in measuring (locating nasion point).

nesian admixture) are, of course, dark skinned and frizzly haired, with lower faces that project more, broader noses, and rather strong bony brows. The resemblance to Africans is superficial, not borne out in skull shape. Melanesians lack the small, quadrangular African ear, and throughout the region children tend to have blond hair that darkens with age, although it survives for a while in many young women. This trait is found in parts of Australia, but is absent from Africa and Polynesia alike.

In Table 11.1 are given averages (rounded to whole centimeters or millimeters) for certain measurements taken on samples of adult men in different island groups of Polynesia, Melanesia, and Micronesia. These are selections only, for rough com-

parison by inspection, although this procedure has never been more than a descriptive exercise. The figures show the uniformly tall stature, and the broad heads and faces of Polynesians (and Fijians), with some local variety in head breadth. From these figures and many others gathered in the past, Fig. 11.1 shows a tree of relationships among a total of 151 samples of Pacific peoples (from Howells 1970), based on the same seven measurements given in Table 11.1. ("Tree" is not a good word—the relationships show likeness, but not necessarily lines of descent.) Computer-assisted mathematics finds the simple, correct coordinates for positioning the populations relative to one another; it is a technique, not formerly available, for re-

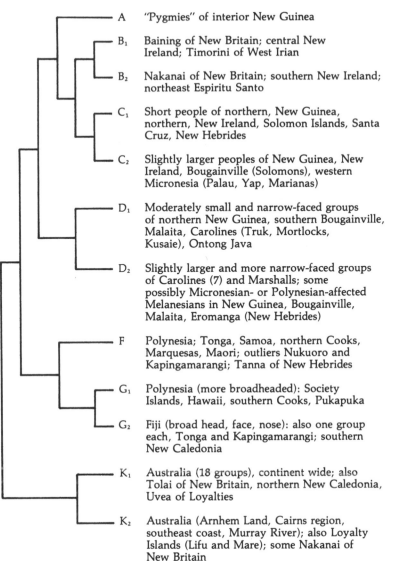

A   "Pygmies" of interior New Guinea

B₁   Baining of New Britain; central New Ireland; Timorini of West Irian

B₂   Nakanai of New Britain; southern New Ireland; northeast Espiritu Santo

C₁   Short people of northern, New Guinea, northern, New Ireland, Solomon Islands, Santa Cruz, New Hebrides

C₂   Slightly larger peoples of New Guinea, New Ireland, Bougainville (Solomons), western Micronesia (Palau, Yap, Marianas)

D₁   Moderately small and narrow-faced groups of northern New Guinea, southern Bougainville, Malaita, Carolines (Truk, Mortlocks, Kusaie), Ontong Java

D₂   Slightly larger and more narrow-faced groups of Carolines (7) and Marshalls; some possibly Micronesian- or Polynesian-affected Melanesians in New Guinea, Bougainville, Malaita, Eromanga (New Hebrides)

F   Polynesia; Tonga, Samoa, northern Cooks, Marquesas, Maori; outliers Nukuoro and Kapingamarangi; Tanna of New Hebrides

G₁   Polynesia (more broadheaded): Society Islands, Hawaii, southern Cooks, Pukapuka

G₂   Fiji (broad head, face, nose): also one group each, Tonga and Kapingamarangi; southern New Caledonia

K₁   Australia (18 groups), continent wide; also Tolai of New Britain, northern New Caledonia, Uvea of Loyalties

K₂   Australia (Arnhem Land, Cairns region, southeast coast, Murray River); also Loyalty Islands (Lifu and Mare); some Nakanai of New Britain

11.1   Dendrogram of relationships of 151 living Pacific populations (male), based on mean figures for seven measurements for each population (height, and length and breadth of head, face, and nose).

ducing the complexity of many measures of many groups to a set of "generalized distances" among them. The tree, or dendrogram (diagram of branchings), is computed from the distances.

The clustering analysis that produces the tree of Fig. 11.1 is also mechanical: the computer finds the smallest "distance" between two of all the 151 peoples, unites them as a first subgroup, then goes on to make up larger groups separated by ever larger total distances until major branches are formed. The figure actually shows only

one possible solution, depending on previous steps, but it is an informative one.

All the Australian samples (well over 20 from all regions) go in a single branch, together with certain Melanesians who actually look somewhat like Australians and have been recognized as such in the past. Polynesians also form a single main branch in which are included Fijians, who are Melanesian in external appearance but more Polynesian in shape and size. Melanesia and Micronesia, through organized fairly well within a large branch, overlap in

WILLIAM HOWELLS

a way that confirms a probable amount of intermigration and mixture, but that belies the different outward appearance of the two peoples. A degree of local mixture is highly probable: for example, the Melanesians of the Lau lagoon on Malaita in the Solomon Islands have strong traditions of connections with Ontong Java, a Polynesian outlier in the open ocean to the north, although the two peoples differ in physical appearance, language, and much of their culture.

A valuable source of information today is skulls, formerly used to generate misinformation as well in the days of segregating them by types. Skulls can be measured more precisely and fully than heads, they exhibit special traits not visible in heads, and they do not prejudice the observer by their deportment, cleanliness, or physical attractiveness. Museums hold collections of Polynesian crania from some areas where modern indigenous Polynesians are hardly available or are of dubious genealogy, like Hawaii or Easter Island. These two peoples, or rather their skulls, represent Polynesia among a set of the world's populations in Fig. 11.2a and b.

The plots in the two portions of this figure result from a kind of simplification similar to generalized distances, known as discriminant functions. The peoples included each furnish a series of about 50 male skulls (a good number for these purposes), in each case drawn from a restricted locality or community, not from a large and less specific area. The Norwegians come from a few parishes of medieval Oslo, Berg is a mountain village in Austria, the Australians are from two closely related tribes on the lower Murray River, the Hawaiians are from a precontact cemetery on Mokapu Peninsula, Oahu, and so forth. The Easter Islanders are localized only to that island, but are homogeneous statistically. Peruvian Indians are from local sites in a part of Yauyos province, and the Arikara are from a single protohistoric village. All the crania were subjected to 70 measurements and derived angles by a single individual, my-

self, and are therefore "controlled." All these data were submitted to discriminant analysis, which produced a series of transformed "measurements," based on those 26 measurements from the original 70 most likely to discriminate, in combination, among these particular populations. These new measurements, the discriminant functions, are so computed as to determine the maximum possible segregation among all the populations; they are uncorrelated, or totally independent of one another, unlike the original measurements in which skull breadth, biauricular breadth, and asterionic breadth, all taken near one another, necessarily repeat much of the same information. Discrimination among groups is most marked along the first function to be derived, and so a few functions will carry the bulk of the discriminating power of a large number of measurements. The individual crania are rescored on these functions and form more or less segregated clouds or clusters representing their groups, when plotted on these new measurements.

In Fig. 11.2a the average positions of the populations are plotted on the first and second functions (1 and 2), which together account for 52.5 percent of total discrimination. Figure 11.2b shows average positions for functions 3 and 4, which carry 24.8 percent. Altogether, it is necessary to imagine a space of four, not three, dimensions, in which 77.3 percent of the total possible dispersion orders the specimens and their averages (the latter are the points shown; points for all the individuals would form slightly overlapping clouds around the mean points). This is a powerful reduction in objective and explicit terms of the large numbers of original data. And the consistent distances on all four functions show that the populations are grouped together, or displaced from one another, in different parts of the complete 4-space (which cannot be drawn) with high coherence and consistency.

This astronomical-looking arrangement of populations sets them off in groups but

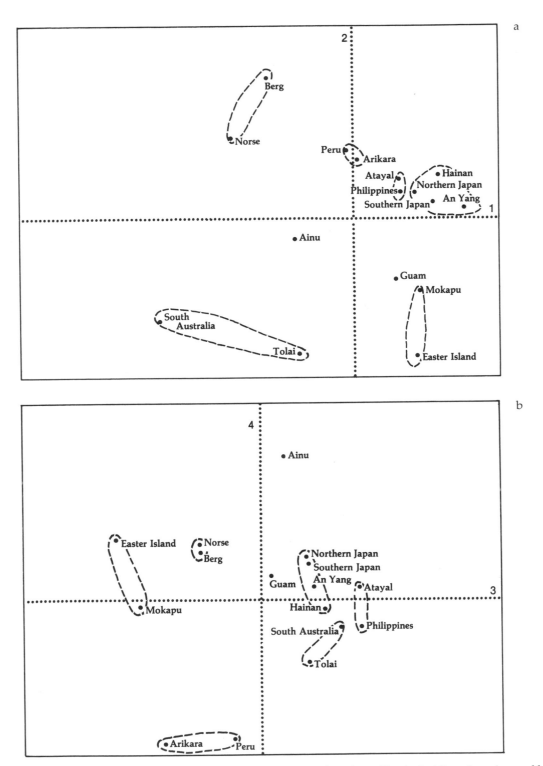

11.2 *Positioning of cranial series (males) by discriminant functions. The dashed lines have been added for ease in noting regional pairs or groups in the plots and have no numerical significance.* a, *plot of functions 1 and 2;* b, *plot of functions 3 and 4.*

WILLIAM HOWELLS

does not state the actual distinctions of skull shape that produce it. Other analyses of the data (such as Howells 1973a) find that Polynesians have a particular forward prominence of the upper face, especially just above the nose. In fact, in a total of 26 series of skulls from all parts of the world, which I measured in the way shown here, Easter Islanders and Hawaiians (the only Polynesians included) have the highest mean basion-nasion measurements of all—that is, the greatest distance from the foramen magnum at the skull base to the frontonasal junction. In addition, while certain Mongoloid groups—Eskimos and Siberian Buriats—approach Polynesians in this regard, the latter have a relatively retracted lower face that lacks the prognathism which is a marked feature of Australian and Melanesian skulls.

More generally, students experienced with Polynesian crania find them distinctive in various ways, regardless of island group. They show pronounced muscle markings, especially for the posterior neck muscles; they have fairly well-developed bony brows (though not like those of Australians and Melanesians) with an especially prominent glabella just above the frontonasal junction; the forehead tends to be sloping, although farther back the skull is high. A special Polynesian feature, prevalent everywhere, is the "rocker jaw"; the lower edge of the mandible is convex so that it will not sit firmly on a flat surface but rocks back and forth. Long unexplained, it has been diagnosed recently by Houghton (1977) as resulting from the Polynesian pattern of facial growth (hinted at in my own figures above). At about puberty the lower jaw rotates downward and backward. As it and the face grow, in skulls with high upper faces and a more open angle of the cranial base (this last being especially characteristic of Polynesians) there develops an acute angle at the back corner of the jaw and a convex lower border.

This trait alone argues strongly for a de-

gree of Polynesian unity and distinctiveness in the biological sense. So also do the teeth, in detailed statistical studies by Turner and associates. They have found the teeth of Hawaiians and Easter Islanders (the only Polynesian groups they have so far examined thoroughly) to be remarkably similar in all categories of traits used. Broadly, Katich and Turner (1974) report Australian and Melanesian teeth to be large but simple in pattern, those of Mongoloids and American Indians to be complex, and those of Polynesians to be Asian-like but simplified. (A significant point: Turner believes that such Micronesian dentitions as he has surveyed, particularly from Yap, approach those of Polynesians in their characteristics, distinguishing them from Melanesians; this is a counterweight to my failure, above, to find a simple segregation of Micronesian and Melanesian samples in the multivariate analysis of a relatively few measurements of the living.) In a specific and familiar trait, shovel-shaped incisors (which have raised edges along the inner surface, like a shovel) are highly characteristic of American Indian populations everywhere but are infrequent in Polynesia.

Multivariate work on a finer scale has not yet been particularly enlightening. A recent study by Pietrusewsky (1977) is broader but shallower than the preliminary results just cited. It includes crania from most Polynesian archipelagoes, several series from Melanesia, and a pair from the Marianas; the analyses are based on measurements and on nonmetric traits and thereby produce two different sets of distances. There are methodological problems, including small sample sizes, perhaps too-inclusive groupings, and mathematical questions in the computation of nonmetric distances (de Souza and Houghton 1977). At any rate, there are discrepancies in results between the sexes and among the several analyses, especially in the placing of Hawaiians, Fijians, and Micronesians. In the brute outcome, however, Melanesians of east and west (*including* Fijians) are separated from

Polynesians and Micronesians, although the morphological bases for this distinction are not stipulated by the analysis.

Blood genetic traits, best expressed as the frequencies or proportions of different genes in a population, have been an important kind of data, both in attempting to trace relationships and in studying micro-evolutionary processes. The latter, as we shall see, have to be borne in mind in attacking the former. Unfortunately, Polynesia has been sampled less than it deserves, especially for the many new enzyme and serum protein systems, including the important Gm gamma globulin system. The neglect may be partially a result of the recent rapid hybridizing with other peoples in many Polynesian islands, which would make the significance of findings more uncertain and which therefore reduces the interest of serologists in collecting such data. (Shapiro, in a private communication, has expressed to me his opinion that it would today be virtually impossible to find a "pure" Marquesan, for example.) In some cases also, as in Hawaii, the existing data are rather old.

Table 11.2 gives frequencies (as proportions of the gene pool) for those genes that have been reported for many Polynesian peoples. The figures are largely taken, and checked, from the two most interested and reliable compilers, Mourant (1976) and Simmons (1962). Such figures must always be looked on as approximations, since different samplings from the same population will vary somewhat and, furthermore, pooling logical groups (such as villages or islands of the same people) may hide some differences among them. The figures given, however, may be taken as presenting the situation reliably in broad outline.

We may note certain common genetic properties of the Polynesians, as compared with world-wide distributions, and also certain trends.

ABO system. The B gene is low or absent, and A is fairly high. This trend becomes more positive from the west, where B is present in amounts similar to Micronesia or parts of Melanesia, through the center to the margins, where A is indeed high and B is never high and is absent from a number of samplings.

MN system. These two genes are roughly balanced in many populations of the world. In Polynesians M tends to prevail, as it does in the American Indians. The opposite is true of Micronesia and much of Melanesia. Within the latter there is no obvious trend.

Rh system. The gene R_1 (CDe) is somewhat more frequent than R_2 (cDE), but not overridingly so as in Micronesia, Melanesia, and Indonesia. (However, the importance of the two genes together is an Oceanic trait generally.) Again, American Indians are not sharply distinguished from Polynesians.

Duffy system. The Fy^a gene varies but is relatively low compared with Melanesians; figures are more like those for American Indians.

Diego system. The Di^a gene, present very widely in the Americans—sometimes at a level of 0.20 or more—is also present in most Mongoloid peoples of Asia. It has not been found in Polynesia, although this particular antigen has been adequately tested for.

How can Polynesian connections be interpreted from such figures? (It must be repeated that the information for Polynesia is quite limited, compared to the present known panoply of testable systems.) Interpretation is ruled by the emphasis one gives to three factors. The first and simplest is the basic inertia of gene frequencies; they tend to remain the same from one generation to another and preserve the ancestral picture indefinitely, unless hybridization moves the frequencies somewhat in the direction of the second population, according to the proportions of the mixture. If this simple persistence were the actual situation for Polynesia, then the best fit for central and marginal Polynesians would be American Indians, at least in the systems shown here. It is true that South American Indians essentially lacked both A and B aboriginally (there is a little doubt about their total absence); however, certain North American tribes, including some on the Northwest Coast, lack B but have high A like the Polynesians. If this kind of derivation for the latter is entertained, then the

Table 11.2 *Typical blood group frequencies for Pacific and other peoples (from various sources). Frequencies are given as proportions of the gene pool.*

Location	Blood group					
	A	B	M	R_1	R_2	Fy^a
Western Polynesia						
Tonga	0.28	0.06	0.59	0.69	0.24	0.88
Samoa (U.S.)	.10	.12				
Samoa, Western	.24	.10				
Tavala (Ellice)	.19	.14	.62	.76	.13	.68
Tokalau	.23	.03	.44	.72	.22	.74
Outliers						
Kapingamarangi	.25	.00	.71	.75	.24	
Ontong Java	.29	.06	.45	.80	.13	
Rennell	.01	.35	.70	.54	.42	
Bellona	.01	.34	.69	.79	.18	
Central Polynesia						
Southern Cooks	.47	.04	.51	.49	.45	.32
Northern Cooks	.30	.04	.58	.53	.41	.40
Tahiti	.37	.03	.58	.54	.33	.62
Marquesas, Tuamotus, Tubuai	.33	.00	.49	.51	.48	.64
Marginal Polynesia						
Hawaii	.38	.01				
Easter	.42	.01	.37	.37	.57	.67
New Zealand, North Island	.33	.00	.53	.46	.54	.46
Micronesia						
Gilbert Islands	.47	.16	.37	.78	.17	.89
Marshall Islands	.13	.10	.22	.95	.04	.07
Truk	.32	.20	.34	.83	.12	
Guam	.18	.12	.49	.67	.13	.88
Yap	.13	.10	.24	.79	.08	
Palau	.14	.10	.34	.94	.03	
Melanesia and elsewhere						
Fiji	.34	.06	.35	.82	.14	.97
Island Melanesia	.18	.11	.18	.88	.09	.93
Ainu	.28	.21	.40	.56	.21	.92
Haida, North America	.13	.01	.82	.33	.53	.81
South America	.00	.00	.72	.41	.54	.73

West Polynesians would be viewed as having acquired their significant levels of B through Melanesian or Micronesian gene influx, possibilities for which a case might be made on certain cultural grounds. Mourant and Simmons, excellent authorities, are both inclined to think that the frequencies seen in the center and margins are more representative of the original Polynesian arrivals, without assuming that the arrival was from America. But the American connection is argued against by the total absence in Polynesia of the Diego antigen, which should have been imported to the Pacific and have survived there if Polynesian gene frequencies really reflect American ancestry as faithfully as the other systems might be taken to suggest.

There are countervailing forces to consider that would produce change, not imperturbability, in blood frequencies. One is natural selection of the most elementary Darwinian kind, presumed to be mainly through disease in the case of blood and serum factors. Unfortunately, too little is known in this field for useful application to Polynesia. The demonstrable effects on the Duffy system and the hemoglobin variants (especially the "sickling" gene), and on some other polymorphisms, of some of the malaria species do not serve to elucidate Polynesian frequencies in general or their possible connections with other peoples.

A third recognized agent is chance variation from generation to generation—genetic drift—which takes effect most rapidly when populations are small and isolated. In such groups chance is not merely impartial: a less frequent gene, of which B in the ABO set is a good example, tends to lose ground and in fact to disappear entirely, which is the point of irreversibility. There are various localities in the Pacific and elsewhere where this process seems to have operated against gene B, although in a few rare cases (as the exceptions that prove the rule) B has prevailed against A—sometimes completely, sometimes partially, as in the twin Polynesian outliers, Rennell and Bellona (see Table 11.2), where the frequencies of A and B are anomalous for any people in this part of ocean, and unusual anywhere.

The role of chance is enhanced if a group is somehow reduced in size and then expanded periodically, the bottleneck effect. An important and allied special case is the "founder principle," by which one segment of a population—in the human case apt to be composed of related families, possibly with a slightly unrepresentative set of genes—departs to colonize a new home. Vayda (1959) gives examples, actual and hypothetical, of the kind of tragedy that in reducing or dividing a Polynesian population (a tidal wave, a typhoon, a canoe being blown out to sea, even marriage rules) can distort gene frequencies accidentally by both the founder effect and population reduction. The founder principle has been seen at work among the Hutterites (Steinberg et al. 1977). They are an exclusive and strict anabaptist sect that originated several centuries ago in Central Europe; in a hundred years they have prospered greatly in numbers and economy in the American and Canadian plains. The Hutterites live in closed farming communities, which periodically have become too large to continue as single units; at this point they divide, and half the people (or families) take up new farmland elsewhere. These colonies are found to vary in blood gene frequencies to a significant degree; some, predictably, have lost gene B—highly uncharacteristic for a people of Central European ancestry.

Thus there is available a model genetic history for application to the populating of Polynesia, and one actually preferred by the majority of students. Its presentation here is hardly original. The same model can be applied to the bulk of Australian Aboriginal populations (south of the northern rim of the continent), and to the American Indians coming out of Asia. The diminution or loss of B has not been observed actually taking place in Polynesia as with the Hutterites; but since genetic drift *can* explain the situation in Polynesia, Australia, and America, this force, able to act over even a modest number of centuries, must be preferred (as an explanation of their similarities in some gene frequencies) over hypotheses of immediate kinship. We have noted that such authorities as Simmons and Mourant suspect that original Polynesians were more like the present eastern groups in their frequencies than are most Oceanic peoples, and that they did indeed have an ultimate Asiatic origin akin to that of the Americans. Once more, the figures should not be taken on face value as evidence of migrations from America direct to Polynesia. Contrariwise, if they do not point to

WILLIAM HOWELLS

any clear genetic connections with people in the other direction, such ancestral connections are not thereby ruled out.

We have not specifically considered variation within Polynesia; that is, those differences among archipelagoes that formerly gave rein to hypotheses of several migrations, including even some from America. For blood evidence, another look at Table 11.2 reveals Polynesian homogeneity rather than diversity. And such diversity as there is makes a logical pattern that does not refute a basic unity: the differences from east to west, especially the rise of B and the decline of A, are entirely explicable by (1) genetic drift over two or three millennia and/or (2) possible gene flow from Melanesian sources into western groups that formerly had A and B values closer to those of the east. While we wait for results on other systems not yet properly tested, we can say only that nothing in the blood data controverts the supposition of Polynesian unity.

When crania are considered, it can be seen that the typical interpretation of 50 and more years ago, based on discerned "types," was founded more on methodological misdirections than on intergroup differences. For example, a wave of "Melanesians" was present in virtually all parts, though in different proportions, in the eventual Polynesian populations. A more legitimate local difference lies in the cranial index: long heads in the margin (Hawaii excepted), rounder heads in the west and especially the center. This has been incorrectly interpreted as resulting from two waves of migrants, both Polynesian, of which the earlier, longer-headed type, has persisted in most of the marginal groups. (I cannot forbear remarking that anything as conservative as two related Polynesian waves has been far less appealing, whether to anthropologists, pseudoanthropologists, or laymen, than waves of Libyans, Aryans, Greeks, Melanesians, unspecified Mongoloids, or Incas. Such attitudes seem inescapable. Why is it that, in any illegitimate union of nutty astronomy and nutty an-

thropology such as *Chariots of the Gods,* it is anthropology that gets stuck with the baby?) Other measurable differences among the Polynesians are not so patterned as the cranial index. The question then becomes the significance of the index, which in fact is a feature known to have fluctuated over time within a single population. In my cranial analysis of many measurements, reported herein (Fig. 11.2) and in previous studies (Howells 1973a), cranial length and breadth can be shown not to be major discriminators of populations, whether within or outside Polynesia. In this analysis Easter Island and Hawaii (Mokapu), though contrasting in head form (70 vs 77 in the cranial index respectively), nevertheless remain closely associated on the four major discriminant axes (as do Norwegians and Austrians, similarly contrasted in head form), while being clearly set off from other population groups. In other words, none of the four most important axes of interpopulation cranial variation give evidence of recognizing this aspect of head shape as significant, obvious though the trait may be to the eye. And the other basic cranial features of Polynesians are common to all, in a pattern distinct both from Melanesians and from American Indians. It is not easy to state objectively, or numerically, the relative homogeneity of Polynesians vis-à-vis other major human groupings, but in multivariate measures, as in special features (dental patterns, rocker jaws), the fact is clear. The simpler grouping analysis of the living (described above) also sets the Polynesians off as a group. The grouping includes the Fijians and two southern Melanesian samples. This analysis, it should be noted, recognizes body and face size as one important axis of difference.

Pietrusewsky, in addition to his broader cranial analysis (1977), has done multivariate studies internal to Polynesia (1970, 1971, 1973). These include, as before, metric and nonmetric traits of crania, as well as observed physical (anthroposcopic) traits in the living, taken from previous publications by others. Figure 11.3 shows dendro-

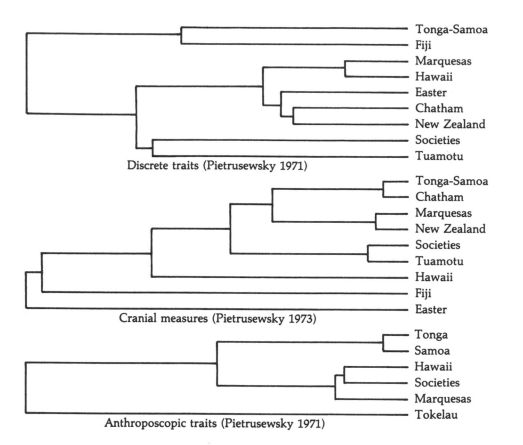

11.3 *Dendrograms of relationships by clustering of Polynesian series, adapted from Pietrusewsky (1971, 1973). Top,* nonmetric traits of skull; *center,* metric traits of skull; *bottom,* nonmetric observations of the living.

grams similar to Fig. 11.1 based on generalized distances using each kind of trait. Although the results are not consistent throughout, they suggest a geographic pattern akin to several proposed earlier: some isolation of Tonga and Samoa (and their alignment with Fiji), and some logical association of the marginal groups. In the measured traits, however, there is no explanation for the relative isolation of Hawaii, Fiji, and Easter, a repetition of Pietrusewsky's results in the larger study described above. More exact morphological relations might be revealed by more intensive cranial studies, that is, by the inclusion of many series (as Pietrusewsky has endeavored to do) but with a larger number of measurements of a more searching kind, and with closely defined samples as

in my own work—which has been limited in the number of Oceanic populations. But this is easier said than done; it may never be possible to locate the necessary material.

At the moment, then, a coherent picture of Polynesian cranial variation does not exist. Such a picture for the living, though possibly broader, is limited and to a considerable extent impressionistic; it does, however, support essential Polynesian unity, again if we allow for a modest degree of Melanesian (Fijian) gene flow in the west. The possible effect of genetic drift in causing other morphological local variation, such as that in the cranial index, would be very difficult to quantify; but its existence as a force has been made clear in close studies of limited regions in Melanesia (see for example Friedlaender 1975, on Bougain-

WILLIAM HOWELLS

ville). We might compare Polynesian and Micronesian internal variation systematically if more were known about Micronesia. I suspect that variation within Micronesia would emerge as the greater. There are some apparent mutual similarities among Micronesians, who are uniformly about 10 cm shorter than Polynesians, but (mainly from impressions) they seem to vary more in appearance; in blood gene frequencies the internal range is considerable.

In summary, all the physical evidence argues that the Polynesians are a genetically uniform people, who vary no more than the wide spread of their occupied archipelagoes would lead one to expect—if that much. Internal differences in blood group frequencies conform well to a probable history of repeated colonizations, each one deriving from a previous one, with subsequent isolation of different but considerable degrees. Variations in head form, unexplained but not necessarily mysterious, are apparently of little significance when seen against a specifically Polynesian pattern of cranial and dental form, a pattern that is evidently deep-seated and uniform, with no possibility of American or Melanesian origins. The tall stature and the marked skeletal robustness are also unexplained. A combination of a virtually disease-free environment and a generally protein-rich diet would foster large size. But more Melanesian communities might be expected to qualify, in spite of the presence there of malaria; and the variety of food of many Micronesian islands and atolls is comparable to that of Polynesia—without tall Micronesians as a product. We may presume that before colonization of the area the parental Polynesian group was already large bodied, compared to related peoples anywhere in or out of East Asia, if it produced such consistently tall progeny later on. African peoples in general probably have the genetic resources for a wide range of stature, but some African peoples have become genetically stabilized toward the taller (Tutsi) or shorter (Pygmy) ends

of the range. Such a deviation may apply to the parental Polynesians, for reasons unknown.

Concerning the specifics of their arrival, the biological picture is in close accord with the history now suggested by archaeology and linguistics: a first colonization of Fiji-Tonga-Samoa in the second half of the second millennium B.C., followed some time later by a series of secondary colonizations eastward and thence outward to the margins. Such a schedule allows from 1,500 to 3,000 years or more of occupation for different island groups, with whatever differentiation in blood and physique we may now perceive. If this is the case, the first occupants of Fiji biologically had to be Polynesian. The biological pattern, in external features but above all in the cranium, is too positive to leave any reasonable suspicion of an ancestral connection with Melanesians, and in fact it demands that the pre-Polynesians had no important gene exchange with Melanesians before or enroute to their colonization of Polynesia proper. The modern Fijians share so much of the Polynesian pattern that they can only be understood when thought of as Polynesians, secondarily admixed with later Melanesian colonists of Fiji. Certain other Polynesian-like peoples in East Melanesia, like the Tannese, might be of the same origin; on the other hand, they might be original Melanesian settlers who became admixed with Polynesians like those who settled the more distinctly Polynesian outliers, which are of smaller land mass. The main point is that the Polynesians of the east must certainly represent the ancestral group more faithfully than those of the west, who have been longer in contact with Melanesians; their fully un-Melanesian character proclaims the same for their ancestors of three millennia back. (We do not entertain revived talk to the effect that the easterners are really American Indians.)

Green, in this volume and in previous papers, has been arriving at a much more complete picture of the Lapita culture complex, its dates and its distribution. There can be no doubt that the pre-Polynesians of Fiji-Tonga-Samoa were Lapita-carrying people, and there can be no doubt that they were physically Polynesian. The historical problem is, were all the participants in the Lapita complex also physically Polynesian? It is difficult though not impossible to suppose that they could have been tribally varied: the Kula ring has embraced different groups, cargo cultism is not confined to Melanesia, and the ceremonial use of kava exists in Polynesia, Melanesia, and Micronesia. But somehow, the pre-Polynesians must be supposed to have reached the far end of the Lapita line (Samoa), however they entered it, without becoming physically Melanesianized to any significant extent along the way. This is something of a dilemma and formerly made me suggest (Howells 1973b) that consideration should be given to an arrival of Lapita users (that is, pre-Polynesians) from Micronesia. This was before evidence of early dates and occupations by the Lapita voyagers was established by Green and others for Central and West Melanesia.

As to the Micronesians, they do not grade into Polynesians anywhere today—there is no Micro-Polynesian "Fiji." The line, for example, between such neighbors as the Gilbert and Ellice groups seems, on little information to be sure, as definite physically as it is linguistically or culturally. Biologically, it is possible to hypothesize the original Polynesians as a restricted group drawn from the same matrix of peoples as the varied Micronesian populations, though a group probably exceptional in some ways such as the taller stature. We might not, on the other hand, suppose the Polynesians to have been drawn in this way from a Melanesian matrix. The latter matrix would have its roots (see Howells 1973b) in Southeast Asia and early Indonesia; the Micro-Polynesian complex must derive from a major population matrix somewhere north of the other one, with basically Mongoloid relationships, as also seen in the American Indians.

However, this is the simplest statement,

without the evidence of linguistics or archaeology. For the latter, Micronesia is still almost mute. In any case, we must relate the Polynesians to the Lapita phenomenon, as their actual channel of transmission to the Fiji-Tonga-Samoa hearth of Polynesia proper. Their degree of biological differentiation from the Micronesians may be a measure of the isolation of the latter peoples from the Lapita complex. Linguistics suggests a dispersal of most languages in Micronesia from east to west, through the Carolines, rather than by the seemingly natural settlement route from west to east. This might in turn suggest an early offshoot from a region in the Lapita network, and a related or later effect in the Gilbert Islands, linguistically closer to Polynesia and its linguistic parentage. All of this would have occurred before the development of the essential Polynesian culture in Fiji-Tonga-Samoa.

However, it is still possible to draw hypothetical arrows in too many directions. We need more Polynesian data; we need Lapita skeletons, Micronesian archaeology, and much more information on the prehistory of the East Asiatic shore and islands from Japan down through Indonesia. We have *begun* to see the Polynesians as a phenomenon in their own right, biologically and historically, but that is all that can be said.

References

de Souza, P., and Philip Houghton. 1977. The mean measure of divergence and the use of non-metric data on the estimation of biological distances. *Journal of Archaeological Science* 4:163–169.

Friedlaender, J. S. 1975. *Patterns of human variation: the demography, genetics, and phenetics of Bougainville Islanders.* Cambridge, Massachusetts: Harvard University Press.

Houghton, Philip. 1977. Rocker jaws. *American Journal of Physical Anthropology* 47:365–370.

Howells, W. W. 1970. Anthropometric grouping analysis of Pacific peoples. *Archaeology and Physical Anthropology in Oceania* 5:192–217.

———. 1973a. *Cranial variation in man. A study*

WILLIAM HOWELLS

by *multivariate analysis.* Peabody Museum Papers no. 67, Cambridge, Massachusetts.

———. 1973b. *The Pacific Islanders.* London: Weidenfeld and Nicolson. (Published also 1973 in Wellington: A. H. & A. W. Reed; 1974 in New York: Scribners.)

Katich, J. F., and C. G. Turner II. 1974. Peoples of the Pacific. II. The dentition of prehistoric Hawaiians and the question of New World origin of Polynesians. Paper presented at the XLI International Congress of Americanists, Mexico City, Sept. 2–7, 1974. Mimeographed.

Mourant, A. E., A. C. Kopec, and K. Domaniewska-Sobczak. 1976. *The distribution of the human blood groups and other polymorphisms,* 2nd ed. London: Oxford University Press.

Pietrusewsky, Michael. 1970. An osteological view of indigenous populations in Oceania. In *Studies in Oceanic culture history,* ed. R. C. Green and Marion Kelly, vol. 1. *Pacific Anthropological Records* 11:1–12.

———. 1971. Application of distance statistics to anthroposcopic data and a comparison of results with those obtained by using discrete traits of the skull. *Archaeology and Physical Anthropology in Oceania* 6:21–33.

———. 1973. A comparison of dendrograms based on craniological data from the Pacific and Southeast Asia. In *Genetic structure of populations,* ed. N. E. Morton. *Population Genetics Monographs* 3:211–216.

———. 1977. Études des relations entre les populations du Pacifique par les méthodes d'analyse multivariée appliquées aux variations crâniennes. *L'Anthropologie* 81:67–97.

Simmons, R. T. 1962. Blood group genes in Polynesia and comparisons with other Pacific peoples. *Oceania* 32:198–210.

Steinberg, A. G., T. J. Oliver, and John Buettner-Janusch. 1977. Gm and Inv studies on baboons, *Papio cynocephalus:* analysis of serum samples from Kenya, Ethiopia and South Africa. *American Journal of Physical Anthropology* 47:21–30.

Vayda, A. P. 1959. Polynesian cultural distribution in new perspective. *American Anthropologist* 61:817–828.

Subsistence and Ecology

CHAPTER 12

PATRICK V. KIRCH

Polynesia's diversity of cultural experiments on individual islands endows the region with unique qualities for the study of human ecology. Sahlins (1958:ix) puts the matter succinctly: "The Polynesian cultures derive from a common source; they are members of a single cultural genus that has filled in and adapted to a variety of local habitats." The biological analogy is well taken. The dispersal of Polynesian populations to a variety of insular situations—ranging from tiny atolls to near-continental New Zealand—provides tight controls for study in this extraordinary anthropological laboratory. Man's capacity for behavioral adaptation—a rapid alteration of behavioral response to environment—is probably not unique; nevertheless, it is of a greater order of magnitude than that of any other species. Not only does man alter his own behavior in response to his surroundings, but he displays an awesome capacity to modify the makeup and distribution of other species and, indeed, of entire landscapes.

Ethnologists in Polynesia have always included the culture-environment interface as a part of their investigative scope. Similarly, botanists and ethnobotanists, intrigued by the trans-Oceanic dispersal of Polynesian crop plants, have long been concerned with Oceanic subsistence; they have also noticed the important archaeological implications of their studies. Archaeologists, of course, have been quick to utilize the ecological data recovered in the middens and shell heaps of Oceanic islands.

Recent studies of settlement patterns, functional variability in fishing gear, agricultural soil horizons, and stone terracing, among others, have yielded new insights into Polynesian subsistence systems. These diverse anthropological approaches have much to gain from a consideration of ecological and biogeographic models (see Terrell 1976). My own recent work, in what I call ethnoarchaeology (Kirch 1978b) attempts to integrate ethnographic, ecological, and archaeological perspectives.

In short, the approach to Oceanic subsistence and economy has been eclectic. In this chapter I attempt to survey, on a sampling basis, some of the contributions in many fields. Because Polynesian cultural ecology as a field of study is developing rapidly, I have avoided a typological approach, making no effort to catalog Polynesian subsistence adaptations. Rather, the attempt is to illustrate the range of cultural variability displayed in the dispersal of Polynesians to every inhabitable island over more than 20 million km² of Pacific Ocean.

The Oceanic Environment

Like the cultures they support, Oceanic islands are endlessly varied; yet they share certain circumscribing features. Their isolation and limited size have had a dominant impact not only on man, but on the entire island biota. Isolation, as barrier and filter, accounts for much of the uniqueness of island life. Once a potential colonizing plant or animal passes through the hazards of natural overseas transport, however, it is likely to find an environment free of predators and competing species. Thus, one or a few successful colonizing stocks often gave rise to an amazing diversity of new species through adaptive radiation. The Hawaiian inventory of about 2,000 higher plants that arose from perhaps 275 ancestral immigrant stocks is a classic case in point.

Fosberg (1963) has listed other significant characteristics of island ecosystems, such as a limitation of resources, restriction of organic diversity, protection from outside species competition, a tendency toward climatic equability, and an extreme vulnerability when isolation is broken.

Except for New Zealand—a pre-Mesozoic continental remnant—all the Polynesian islands are volcanic in origin, composed of successive flows of basaltic or andesitic lavas. The subsequent erosion and alteration of these igneous masses produced islands of three classic forms: (1) high islands with volcanic soils, (2) low islands or atolls, and (3) raised coral islands. The latter are really coral caps on igneous cores. Niuatoputapu Island, in the Tongan group, combines all three forms: its central volcanic ridge is surrounded by an uplifted plain of coral reef and detritus, while its leeward coast and lagoon are protected by a barrier reef with offshore islets in typical atoll configuration.

The Polynesian flora and fauna that cover the islands are largely derived from Asia, particularly tropical Southeast Asia. For example, the typical Polynesian seaside vegetation of *Cocos, Pandanus, Tournefortia, Scaevola, Barringtonia, Hernandia*, and other species would be as familiar to a native of Tahiti as to an Indonesian or even an occupant of the Seychelles. Likewise, the mollusks and fish of the central Pacific form part of a great Indo-Pacific faunal province. The extension of the Indo-Malayan biotic realm into Polynesia is important, because the concepts of environment that were developed by early Austronesian-speaking populations in insular Southeast Asia were equally applicable in the more remote islands of Polynesia. The Polynesian biota is a pauperized version of the Asian one. In some cases such as Hawaii, it has evolved in the direction of extreme endemism. Among the most important consequences for Polynesians are the near-total absence of food plants and of most of the edible land mammals or reptiles. The wild relatives of all of the Oceanic crop plants do not occur eastward from the Solomon Islands. Farther east, in Polynesia, the domestic varieties were introduced.

New Zealand (see Chapter 9) contrasts

markedly with tropical Polynesia not only in its continental size and temperate climate, but in the adaptation of Polynesian ethnobiological concepts and cultural techniques that its particular characteristics required. With 501,776 km², New Zealand encompasses more land than the rest of the Polynesian islands combined (Cochrane 1973). Whereas the annual temperature in tropical Polynesia averages about 24° C, annual temperatures in New Zealand range from 16° C in the North Island to 10° C in the South Island. Thus the greater portion of New Zealand's acreage is unsuitable for tropical crop production. Nevertheless, a diverse and unique biota provided rich resources for the development of new hunting-and-gathering subsistence strategies (Shawcross 1967; Green 1974). Witness the exploitation—to the point of extinction—of some 24 species of flightless moa (in *Megalapteryx* and other genera) and the extensive use of uncultivated bracken fern (*Pteridium esculentum*) rhizome for food.

Archaeologists in Oceania have just begun to explore the concepts of environmental diversity and variability. Variability in spatial environment figured, of course, in earlier theories such as Sahlins' (1958) correlation of resources with social stratification. Recent fieldwork in West Polynesia tentatively suggests a correlation between environments in which agricultural systems could not be intensified by means of irrigation or drainage, and the development of centralized chiefdoms (Kirch 1976). Variation in environment as a function of time, however, has not been investigated to any extent, perhaps because this kind of temporal change is not readily apparent in short-term research projects. "Environmental hazards" (Vayda and McCay 1975) are significant in human ecology, and in Oceania these include infrequent—but temporally recurring and often disastrous—drought and cyclones.

A dynamic viewpoint is crucial to an understanding of man's adaptation to the Polynesian ecosystems. The island masses themselves are in movement, a point dem-

onstrated forcefully with the discovery of submerged Lapita pottery in Samoa (Chapter 4). The Pacific Basin is tectonically active, as is evident from the submergence or emergence of sizable land areas (Honaunau on Hawaii; Futuna and Niuatoputapu islands in West Polynesia). Furthermore, Oceanic islands are characterized by their vulnerability and susceptibility to rapid change once isolation is broken. The Polynesians extensively modified the biota of their surroundings and often the physical landscape as well. Easter Island and Mangareva were undoubtedly deforested as a direct result of Polynesian subsistence activities, and the lowland vegetation of every inhabited island was extensively altered. The extinction of the New Zealand moa and of several species of Hawaiian honeycreeper are further examples. In short, the total landscape of any Polynesian island must be viewed as the cumulative result of a complex and highly dynamic interaction between natural and cultural forces.

An Ethnographic Perspective

Although Polynesian cultures adapted themselves to a range of varying environments, their subsistence procurement systems remained in the general Southeast Asian mold. An ethnographic perspective allows us to observe the integration of these procurement patterns as a baseline for archaeology, where past subsistence behavior can only be inferred. The following ethnographic overview (an "ideal" view, not necessarily applicable to any single Polynesian society) is drawn from the literature and from recent fieldwork in western and outlier Polynesia.

Food is probably the most culturally valued product of Oceanic economic systems (Bell 1931), and its classification by Polynesians provides an analytically useful and culturally meaningful point of entry into the value systems. Firth (1936:53) remarked upon "the directness of the tie between man and his food" in Tikopia, saying,

"People in this island community do not arrive home to snatch a meal and return to work; the attainment of the meal itself is the fulfillment of their work." In Futuna, food (*kai*) is of two elemental types: *mangitsi* ("staple starch") and *kina* ("relishes"). Kina includes all animal foods, coconut, and a variety of vegetable foods such as sugarcane, nuts, and fruits, consumed more or less spontaneously in the bush or gardens. While kina is desirable and indeed vital for the entertainment of honored guests and at communal feasts, in and of itself kina does not constitute a meal. Only mangitsi, the product of agricultural labor, will satiate an empty Futunan stomach. This division of food describes Polynesian subsistence in general: a balance between cultivation of the dominant mangitsi and procurement of the less abundant but essential kina.

As has been mentioned in earlier chapters, the indigenous crop plants of Polynesia are, with the significant exception of the sweet potato, tropical East or Southeast Asian in origin (Table 12.1). As a complex, these cultigens exemplify what has been termed tropical vegeculture, with reproduction by vegetative propagation of tubers or cuttings. Some cultigens, for example the parthenocarpic bananas (Simmonds 1962), have entirely lost their potential for sexual reproduction, while many—including the yams and aroids or taros—are only infrequently seen in flower or seed.

Five groups of staple-starch-producing cultigens dominate Polynesian agricultural systems: aroids, yams, breadfruit, bananas, and the sweet potato. Of the aroids, most important are taro (*Colocasia esculenta*) and elephant ear (*Alocasia macrorrhiza*), although a third species, giant swamp taro or *pulaka* (*Cyrtosperma chamissonis*), is also cultivated in the westernmost islands. *Colocasia* is a hydrophile, and while it is frequently seen in nonirrigated swidden gardens, it will not tolerate dry conditions for any lengthy period. The yams, particularly *Dioscorea alata* and *D. esculenta*, are tropophytic, that is, they require dry condi-

tions during part of the year and humid conditions during the other part. As a result, the scheduling of yam planting and harvest is of major importance in Oceanic agricultural calendars. Three additional species of yam are found in Polynesia: *D. nummularia*, *D. pentaphylla*, and *D. bulbifera*—the last two only rarely reported in regular cultivation, although widely collected during food shortage and famine. Both seeded and seedless forms of breadfruit are present in Polynesia and usually bear two or three times per year (Wilder 1928). In some archipelagoes, especially the Marquesas, breadfruit became the dominant food source. The edible bananas include two sections: Eumusa and Australimusa. The Australimusa group, often termed *fehi* or *fe'i*, were of particular importance in the Society Islands (MacDaniels 1947).

Yen's (1974a) tripartite hypothesis of the distribution of the sweet potato has clarified the previously enigmatic status of this South American crop plant in Polynesia. In the presently accepted construction the sweet potato was transferred (by unspecified means) to Central Polynesia (Society and Marquesas islands) in prehistoric times, and from this center to the marginal islands of East Polynesia: New Zealand, Easter Island, and Hawaii. The microenvironmental adaptability of this species accounts for its importance in these "marginal" settings away from the tropical core of the Polynesian subsistence pattern. Contrary to one recently published formulation, the sweet potato does not appear to have been present in West Polynesia prehistorically, nor has it ever attained the status of a dominant in these western islands.

Many other cultigens are present in the Polynesian agricultural complex, and some of these are enumerated in Table 12.1; space precludes a detailed discussion of most, and the interested reader is referred to Barrau's excellent papers (1961, 1965b; Massal and Barrau 1956) for further discussion.

Polynesian systems of cultivation—the association of crop plants, tools, and partic-

Table 12.1   Some important Polynesian cultigens.

Botanical nomenclature	English vernacular	Polynesian vernacular[a]	Crop type[b]	Cultivation method[c]	Remarks
Dicotyledons					
Moraceae					
Artocarpus altilis (Park ex Z) Fosb.	Breadfruit	*kulu*	FF	A	Fruit preserved in pits
Piperaceae					
Piper methysticum Forst. f.	Kava	*kawa*	N	S	Narcotic infusion used ceremonially
Leguminosae					
Inocarpus fagiferus (Park ex Z) Fosb.	Tahitian chestnut	*ifi*	O	A	
Anacardiaceae					
Spondias dulcis Park.	Vi apple	*wii*	O	A	
Convolvulaceae					
Ipomoea batatas (L.) Lam.	Sweet potato		FT	S	American origin
Monocotyledons					
Liliaceae					
Cordyline terminalis (L.) Kunth	Ti	*tii*	S	S	Root baked in special oven
Taccaceae					
Tacca leontopetaloides (L.) Kuntze	Polynesian arrowroot	*pia?*	FT	S	
Dioscoraceae					
Dioscorea alata L.	Greater yam	*qufi*	FT	S	Tropophytic
Dioscorea esculenta (Lour.) Burkill	Lesser yam		FT	S	Tropophytic
Gramineae					
Saccharum officinarum L.	Sugarcane	*toLo*	S	S	
Palmae					
Cocos nucifera L.	Coconut	*niu*	O	A	
Araceae					
Alocasia macrorrhiza (L.) Schott	Elephant ear	*kape*	FT	S	
Colocasia esculenta (L.) Schott	Taro	*talo*	FT	S/W	Hydrophytic
Musaceae					
Musa, Section Eumusa	Banana	*futi*	FF	S	
Musa, Section Australimusa	Banana	*fehi?*	FF	S	

[a] Proto-Polynesian reconstructions, partially after Pawley and Green (1973).
[b] FF, farinaceous fruit; N, narcotic; O, other; FT, farinaceous tuber; S, sugar.
[c] A, arboriculture; S, shifting cultivation; W, water control (irrigation and/or drainage).

ular microenvironments with discrete patterns of agricultural behavior—are of two elemental types: extensive and intensive. By extensive, I refer to shifting cultivation in the characteristic Malayo-Oceanic pattern (Spencer 1966), where swidden garden plots (Fig. 12.1) are cleared, fired, cropped, and fallowed in a second-growth rotational sequence. Intensive cultivation involves the modification of hydrologic and edaphic

PATRICK V. KIRCH

12.1 *A typical mixed swidden garden on Niuatoputapu, Tonga. In the foreground is a first-year planting of* yams (Dioscorea alata) *and aroids* (Alocasia macrorrhiza). *Behind them is a third-year planting of manioc* (Manihot esculenta) *and bananas* (Musa). *Tree crops (breadfruit and coconut) are in the background. (Photo by author.)*

conditions so as to favor certain cultigens, and results in the creation and maintenance of relatively sophisticated water-control facilities (Wagner 1960). Barrau (1965a) pointed to the "wet and dry" as the single most significant key to Oceanic agriculture, based largely on the preferred microenvironments of the hydrophytic taro and the tropophytic yam. Intensive cultivation systems in Polynesia have focused largely on these two crops, either in the direction of water control (irrigation and drainage) or of dryland field systems. In marginal East Polynesia, the sweet potato has featured in intensive cultivation systems, of which La-

pakahi in Hawaii is an example (Rosendahl and Yen 1971).

The extensive-intensive dichotomy merely describes the extremes of a continuum, so the terms must not be applied indiscriminately. Intensive field systems (for example, Anuta—see Yen and Gordon 1973) demonstrate the modification of shifting cultivation to a more or less continuous crop rotation under pressures of population, environmental constraint, or frequently both.

Certain general characteristics define shifting cultures in Polynesia, with local variations in crop composition, scheduling, and agronomic treatment. The Uvean system (Kirch 1978c) illustrates some of these basic parameters. New swiddens are cut (during the dry season) in herbaceous second growth, and the slashed vegetation is allowed to dry out for several weeks prior to burning. Yams are planted at the same time as the firing, with aroids interplanted soon after. Bananas, sugarcane, and other cultigens may be put down, especially along field borders. This mixed crop assemblage in many respects comes to resemble the bush it has replaced; a "natural forest is transformed into a harvestable forest" (Geertz 1970:25). The yam crop matures in 7 to 9 months, and additional aroids are planted following the yam harvest. Planting of bananas after the aroid harvest (1 to 2 years after planting) extends the swidden's productive life into the third or even fourth year; its use actually overlaps with the beginning of second-growth regeneration. A fallow period of roughly 6 to 12 years follows before the plot is recropped.

Irrigation in Polynesia is directed toward taro and usually involves the diversion of water from a spring or stream into terraced pondfields, artificially leveled, bunded, and flooded (Figs. 12.2 and 12.3). Such pondfields may be cropped for extended periods, although they are generally let to fallow at repeated intervals (Kirch 1976). A reverse kind of water control is practiced in the swampy coastal plains of some islands (Uvea and Rarotonga, for instance), where reticulate drainage channels separate "garden-islands" on which taro is planted, usually with intensive mulching. The taro corms are thus allowed to tap the freely flowing fresh-water lens, and stagnation is averted.

Arboriculture, a third component of Polynesian agriculture, centers on breadfruit, although a number of other fruit- and nut-bearing trees are also cultivated. In Niuatoputapu the Tahitian chestnut (*Inocarpus fagiferus*) is extensively cultivated on the rich clay soils of the island's central terrace. The Marquesas (Handy 1923) represent the apo-gee of Polynesian tree culture, with dominant reliance on breadfruit.

Domestic animals—dog, chicken, but especially pig—are closely integrated with agricultural production in Polynesia. Pigs, widely fed on coconut, substandard tubers of taro or sweet potato, bananas, and food scraps in general, perform an important scavenging function in removal of human feces from village areas. Special structures have been developed in order to protect gardens from marauding pigs: extensive rock walls in Futuna and swidden fences in Niuatoputapu are examples.

It must not be forgotten that Oceanic culture is bound inextricably to the sea, so the procurement and exploitation of marine foods and resources have always been an important aspect of Polynesian economy. The structure and complexity of indigenous folk classifications of fish and other marine life (Titcomb 1952) reflect intense familiarity with the sea. In most Polynesian islands marine foods provided a daily source of protein, augmented irregularly with pigs, seabirds, and other land-derived meat. The extent to which any Polynesian culture emphasized cultivation or marine exploitation was, to some extent, always constrained by local environment. Atoll cultures in particular relied more heavily on marine resources.

The range of marine exploitation techniques practiced in Polynesia has been documented in the ethnographic literature (Reinman 1967), particularly with regard to the material culture associated with such exploitation: spears, hooks, traps, nets, weirs, and the like. Unfortunately, little is known of Polynesian fishing and shellfishing so far as the full range of procurement strategies is concerned (Fig. 12.4). Recent ethnoarchaeological research on Niuatoputapu Island (Kirch 1978a) documents the spatial distribution of eight major categories of marine exploitation across the island's littoral fringes, lagoon, windward and leeward reefs. The enormous variety of microhabitats exploited, as well as the

PATRICK V. KIRCH

12.2 *Irrigated pondfields planted in taro* (Colocasia esculenta) *on a steep valley slope on Futuna Island.* (*Photo by author.*)

12.3 *View of Nuku Village and environs, Futuna Island, with extensive irrigated pondfields on coastal plain. The village houses are scattered among the tree crops in the zone between the taro fields and the reef. Gradual tectonic uplift has resulted in an aggrading coastline, and old pottery-bearing occupation sites are now covered by the pondfields.* (*Photo by author.*)

SUBSISTENCE AND ECOLOGY

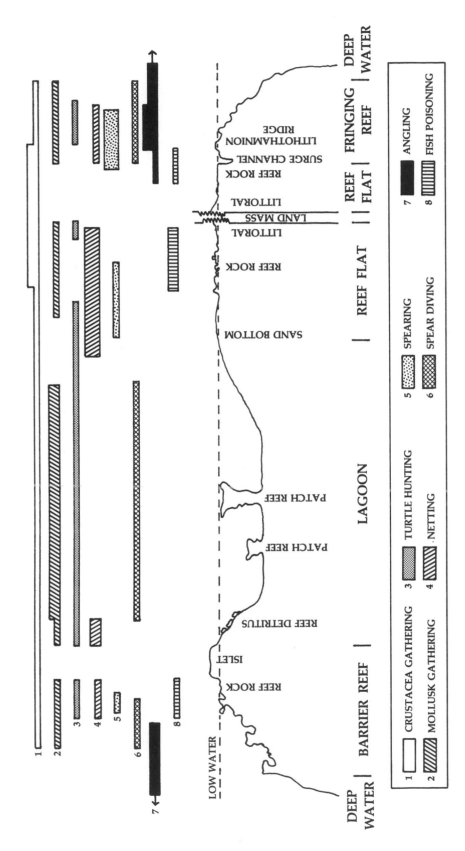

12.4 *Schematic section through windward and leeward marine environments of Niuatoputapu Island, Tonga, showing the zonal utilization of eight exploitation techniques. Bar thickness is an approximate indicator of the frequency of a given technique. The unbroken bar for crustacea gathering includes several species of land crabs that are classed with marine crabs in the local folk taxonomy.*

12.5 Communal weir fishing on Anuta Island, a Polynesian outlier in the Eastern Solomons. The advancing line of people drives the fish into the confines of the stone weir (visible at the right), where they are speared. (Photo courtesy of Bishop Museum, Honolulu.)

harvesting methods used, reflects the age-old intimacy of man-sea relations.

While many techniques can be applied successfully by a single individual, as in spear fishing or shellfish collecting, others require combined—sometimes communal—efforts. One of the group techniques is the use of weirs, either permanent structures of coral cobbles or temporary constructions of coconut fronds. On Anuta Island virtually the entire population participates in communal fish drives across the reef (Fig. 12.5), which may result in the capture of as much as 90 kg in two hours.

Social Aspects of Subsistence

The integration of subsistence activities into whole adaptive strategies brings us to the socioeconomic groupings that control or coordinate individual effort, because "co-operation, exchange, and multiform obligations weave the quest for food into a complex social pattern" (Firth 1936:53). Embedded in the social context of the household or extended family, Polynesian subsistence activity constitutes an example of what Sahlins has termed the "domestic mode of production." One's affiliation with such a group is determined by descent and residence choice. Variations in Polynesian social organization have been treated extensively in the ethnographic literature; we are concerned here merely with their general relevance to the structuring of economic activities. The household shows the same division of labor that is dominant in the entire society, so that the solidarity of the household is confirmed by the daily production and preparation of food, cooked in the group's earth oven, providing "a daily ritual of commensality that consecrates the group as a group" according to Sahlins (1972:94).

The extended family groups, such as the Futunan kainga, the Samoan 'ainga, or the Anutan patongia, serve other social purposes. They are units for ownership and transmission of major property, including arable land, houses, crops, food in general, pigs, and other items of material culture (canoes, food bowls, mats, and the like).

Individuals have rights of use through their affiliation with household and larger social groups, but it is the group, not the individual, through which property is transmitted. Transmission of land-use rights through local descent groups with strongly agnatic cores (Panoff 1970) is fraught with major implications for the population-resource relationship, which will be dealt with below.

Certain resources may be considered property of larger social groupings such as the village. In Futuna this is true of main irrigation ditches and of interior mountainous land where communal gardens are cut (Kirch 1976). Traditional Hawaiian society represents an interesting deviation from the general Polynesian pattern, as described in Chapter 7. There, development of a powerful chiefly stratum led to the alienation of land from the local kinship structure, although use rights apparently continued to be observed in most cases. (The Hawaiian term *makainana,* translated "commoners," is clearly cognate with West Polynesian *kainanga* or *kainga,* "local landholding descent groups.")

While the domestic mode of production tends toward a strategy of underproduction, this is countered by the demands of a public economy, in particular by production for social prestation and ritual (Brookfield 1972). In Futuna production for ritual occasions can be prodigious, as in a feast witnessed at Kolia Village in 1974, when some 250 medium-sized pigs (one year old), 40 mature hogs, and at least 10^3 kilos of yams were consumed or distributed. The role of chiefs in the production, and especially allocation, of scarce resources—particularly at times of ecological stress—has been noted (Yen 1976).

Origins and Development of Oceanic Adaptations

The derivation of agriculture from a Southeast Asian source must be viewed as more than the mere transferral of crop plants to the islands of remote Oceania. Anderson's concept of transported landscapes is useful:

"that unconsciously as well as deliberately man carries whole floras about the globe with him, that he now lives surrounded by transported landscapes, that our commonest everyday plants have been transformed by their long associations with us" (Anderson 1952:9). This concept was elaborated by Yen, who noted that the detachable parts of donor environments that become the founding environment include plant materials, tools, and the ideas or concepts behind their use. "Such basic concepts as that taro requires a wet edaphic medium and yams require a dry are as permanent as the species occupying roles in subsistence plant patterns. They remain a part of what has variously been described as the underlying lore or the ethno scientific basis of so-called primitive agricultures" (Yen 1973:70).

The development of the concept that Oceanic agriculture is Southeast Asian in origin has been largely in the work of the botanists and ethnobotanists. Archaeological research on Southeast Asian agriculture has been slight indeed. Gorman's (1969) finds from the Spirit Cave site in northwestern Thailand have more significant implications for the antiquity of certain man-plant associations than for plant domestication per se. (Note the presence of such culturally important genera as *Areca, Terminalia,* and *Aleurites,* for example.) To date, no archaeological finds of either of the two great Oceanic crop plants—taro and yam—have been reported from mainland or insular Southeast Asia. Archaeological evidence for animal domestication is likewise scanty, but some indications of domestic pig have been reported.

Perhaps the most important botanical and archaeological problem in the transfer of agriculture from Southeast Asia to Oceania is the absence of rice in the latter region. The alternative hypotheses, (1) that the Oceanic cultigen complex was transferred prior to the domestication of *Oryza* in Southeast Asia, or (2) that rice was lost in the transfer process, both have their supporters; nothing definitive on the problem is available, however.

PATRICK V. KIRCH

Table 12.2 *Some Austronesian lexical reconstructions associated with agriculture.*[a]

Gloss	PAN	POC	PPN	EFU
Taro	*tales*	*ntalo(s)*	*talo*	*talo*
Yam	*qubi(s)*	*qupi*	*qufi*	*'ufi*
Banana (*Eumusa*)	*pun(ti)i*	*punti*	*futi*	*futi*
Breadfruit	*kulur*	*kulu(r)*	*kulu*	*mei*[b]
Coconut	*niuR*	*niuR*	*niu*	*niu*
Inocarpus	*ipil*	*ipi(l)*	*ifi*	*ifi*
Fermented breadfruit	*kama(ng) (cs)i*	*masi*	*masi*	*masi*
To plant	*teba*	*topa*	—	*to*
Swidden	*quma*	*quma*	—	*'umanga*
Fallow land/to weed	*wawaw*	*wawo*	*wao*	*vao*
Sucker (of banana, taro)	*suli*	*suli*	*suli*	*'uli*

[a] Reconstructions after Pawley and Green (1973). PAN = Proto-Austronesian; POC = Proto-Oceanic; PPN = Proto-Polynesian; EFU = East Futunan, a West Polynesian language, used here as an example of a contemporary Polynesian language.
[b] *Ulu* in certain other Polynesian languages.

Linguistic evidence for an early Austronesia agricultural base is well-developed, with undisputed Proto-Austronesian reconstructions for all the major Oceanic crops (Table 12.2). Significantly, terms for or associated with rice are absent among the eastern Austronesian languages. Given a time depth of perhaps 6,000 to 8,000 years for Proto-Austronesian, it is evident that the origins of tropical vegeculture (Harris 1972) in Southeast Asia are ancient indeed.

Attention has recently focused on New Guinea and to a lesser extent on Melanesia as a secondary source for the domestication and/or further development of certain cultigens. Barrau (1965b) and Warner (1962) pointed to New Guinea as the probable center of origin for sugarcane, while Simmonds (1962) indicates that the Australimusa section of edible bananas probably originated there. Archaeological finds of pig bone in the highlands point to even earlier introduction of suids in coastal regions. These indirect suggestions for a New Guinea source have been bolstered by Golson's excavations at Kuk (Golson and Hughes 1976), where intricate drainage channels attest to sophisticated water-control technology as early as 4000 B.C. Farther to the east, Yen (1974b) has extensively documented the intensification of a whole arboricultural complex by selection for gigantism in several species of fruit- and nut-bearing trees. The potential importance of the Melanesia-Polynesia border area in past development of Oceanic subsistence is hinted at by certain other traits, including local elaboration of irrigation and terracing, as well as several food conversion-preservation methods in this region.

The association between Lapitoid assemblages—distributed from New Britain in the west to Tonga and Samoa in the east—and the dispersal of the Austronesian-speaking peoples is now widely accepted (Chapter 2). The archaeological evidence for Lapita horticulture is not direct, but depends upon such indications as: (1) the locations of Lapita settlements in areas with access to arable land; (2) the large size of Lapita settlements, comparable to those of present-day agricultural communities; (3) the presence of pig, intimately associated with agriculture in ethnographic contexts throughout Oceania; and (4) the presence of various portable artifacts and structural features—including shell scrapers and peelers, adzes, pottery vessels, cooking ovens, and storage pits—typical of agriculturally based economies. Groube's alternative hypothesis (1971) that the Lapita economy represents a kind of "Oceanic strandlooping" does not appear to be supported on present archaeological evidence, nor does it mesh well with the linguistic model noted earlier.

Green (1974, 1976a and b, and Chapter 2 of this volume) has summarized the evidence for Lapita exchange networks, involving the import and distribution of various items including chert, obsidian, various metamorphic and metavolcanic rocks, pottery, and presumably other perishable items as well. He says, "The original Lapita adaptation was one to an *area* with a complex continental island environment which possessed a wide range of resources able to be assembled in individual communities through exchange" (Green 1976a:72). Analogy with ethnographically documented exchange systems in Melanesia suggests that the Lapita system might have included valued or otherwise unequally available goods, such as women, pigs, or agricultural produce.

Tracing the Lapita adaptive series in both space and time to its eastern attenuation brings us to Polynesia proper and to the immediate origins of Polynesian culture in Fiji, Tonga, and Samoa. The Lapita populations that colonized the West Polynesian archipelagoes, while participating in a local exchange system, were effectively isolated from the ancestral Lapita communities to the west by a water gap of 800 to 1,000 km. Furthermore, in settling this region these Lapitoid populations first came into contact with true Oceanic islands and their implications for reduced environmental diversity. The Andesite Line, representing the tectonic contact between two crustal plates, passes through West Polynesia and marks the separation between complex sedimentary, metamorphic, and metavolcanic or andesitic rocks to the west and the relatively uniform basic basaltic volcanics to the east. Lithic technology, consequently, had to be adapted to the restricted range of available flaking materials. The flora and fauna of the true Oceanic islands are likewise impoverished versions of their western neighbors, with implications for hunting-and-

gathering strategies. It is in this West Polynesian region that classic Polynesian culture developed, as an adaptation to this set of particular environmental circumstances and constraints. Davidson in Chapter 4 reviews the archaeological sequences of West Polynesia, including the evidence pertaining to subsistence and economy.

The final stage in the adaptation of Austronesian cultural patterns to the problems of an Oceanic existence occurred with the colonization of central Polynesia (Marquesas and Society islands) and subsequent rapid dispersal to the marginal islands of the Polynesian triangle. There are suggestions that the earliest phase of settlement in the Marquesas may have been without domestic animals, although these were present by the developmental period (Kirch 1973). Certainly the Marquesan settlement period is marked by heavy reliance upon marine resources, although it seems likely that agriculture was also a component of the total subsistence system from initial settlement on.

The Vaitootia site on Huahine in the Society Islands (Chapter 8) has provided—largely because of its unique preservation of wooden and other normally perishable materials—a well-rounded picture of Archaic East Polynesian settlement. Direct macrofossil evidence of cultivated or exploited plants includes kava (*Piper methysticum*), gourd (*Lagenaria*), coconut, and *Pandanus*. The usual indirect evidence of artifacts, domestic animals, and settlement characteristics in conjunction with the plant remains leaves no doubt about the agrarian basis of this early East Polynesian community. Although the ecological setting of the Vaitootia site has yet to be exhaustively explored, the indications of formerly swampy conditions may be significant, as such microhabitats could have matched the wet edaphic needs of taro. A raised wooden structure exposed by Sinoto has been interpreted as a storage house, with yam as the suggested crop, and this correlates well with an ethnographic model. The structural similarities between the

Vaitootia storage house and certain Melanesian yam storehouses (see Malinowski 1935, for example), although widely separated in time and space, are indeed striking.

To recapitulate, Polynesian subsistence was molded in its general configuration by a tropical Southeast Asian ancestry. The adaptation of this broad-spectrum economic system, based both on agriculture and on extensive hunting-fishing-gathering, to the increasingly impoverished Oceanic islands, was a process requiring several millennia. The expansion of the Austronesian-speaking peoples through the southwestern Pacific into Polynesia is viewed by Green as an adaptive series. It was a continuing experiment in adjustment to insular conditions.

Elaborations of Oceanic Adaptations

The origins and development, as well as the general configuration, of Polynesian subsistence have been characterized above. It may be useful to consider briefly some examples of local elaborations.

Exploitation of Stone

Ground stone adzes have been utilized for years by prehistorians as *the* essential artifact of Polynesia, with variations in overall form and cross section providing the basis for culture-historical frameworks. Evidence from Lapita sites of the southwestern Pacific documents long-distance transport of scarce lithic resources, especially obsidian and chert. It is surprising that the specific problems of sources, exploitation procedures, and manufacture techniques associated with ground stone implements have been neglected for the most part by Pacific archaeologists. Only recently has any attention been directed to these problems, including the little-studied (and sometimes unreported or even discarded!) Polynesian flake industries in fine-grained rocks such as obsidian and basalt.

It is increasingly apparent that exploita-tion of stone in Polynesia involved the repeated utilization of specific quarries. The Tahanga quarry at Opito Bay, New Zealand, exemplifies such extraction sites. A 5 × 5 ft (1.5 × 1.5 m) excavation in one of the debitage piles yielded 39 adz preforms (Shaw 1963).

Quantitative and distance (numerical taxonomic) analyses have been performed on some New Zealand flake assemblages (Shawcross 1964; Leach 1969). In general, the New Zealand assemblages appear to be similar to many Oceanic flake industries, with emphasis on production of amorphous flakes with a sharp working edge, rather than the shaping of discrete tool "types" through extensive use of secondary retouch —although some limited retouch is present. "A feature which is common to the . . . archaeological assemblages is the low number or complete absence of repetitive forms of secondarily retouched flakes" (Shawcross 1964:22). Leach (1969), using models derived from numerical taxonomy, has explored the potential importance of flake assemblages in the analysis of inter-site variability.

One of the largest Neolithic stone quarries in the world—that on 4,205-m-high Mauna Kea in Hawaii—has been the focus of intensive and continuing investigations by the Bishop Museum (McCoy 1977). The Mauna Kea adz quarry complex includes "a series of extraction areas and chipping stations—large, clustered areas and smaller, isolated ones—with associated religious shrines, habitation rockshelters [Fig. 12.6], overhang shelters, and open-air shelters" spread out over about 2,000 ha (7.5 mi²) between 3,350 and 3,780 m above sea level. The problems confronting prehistoric Hawaiians in the exploitation of Mauna Kea's unique, fine-grained vitreous basalt must have been numerous, considering that periglacial conditions persisted at the quarry site throughout the term of human utilization. McCoy's research combines traditional techniques of survey and excavation with a rigorous sampling design and uses experiments to replicate the types of

12.6 *Shelter cave with debitage scree of flakes at the Mauna Kea adz quarry complex. Note the two adz preforms on the debitage pile. (Photo by P. C. McCoy, courtesy of Bishop Museum, Honolulu.)*

flakes removed in adz preform manufacture industry. His analysis provides a model for further analyses of Polynesian stone quarries and lithic technology.

The uneven distribution of lithic resources, and the consequent establishment of major quarries in key localities, leads to the question of how quarried material was distributed. Did particular social groups control access to quarries? Were specialists involved in the extraction of stone and production of tools? And did some version of formalized exchange serve to distribute these lithic artifacts to communities that lacked access to the raw material? These are questions that may never be satisfactorily answered on archaeological data, but that must be addressed in an ecologically oriented prehistory.

Marine Exploitation Technology

Fishhooks have been second only to adzes in their usefulness for developing local culture sequences, especially in East Polynesia (Emory et al. 1968; Sinoto 1968). Although some attention has been directed to a functional analysis of fishing gear (Reinman 1970; Kirch 1979), this has been overshadowed by the typological approach commonly used.

The earliest and most complex fishhook assemblage thus far reported from the Southwest Pacific is that excavated on tiny Anuta Island in the eastern Solomons, with a date of at least 800 B.C. (Kirch and Rosendahl 1976). The precise relation of the Anuta assemblage to other sites in the region is unclear; it appears to be somewhat

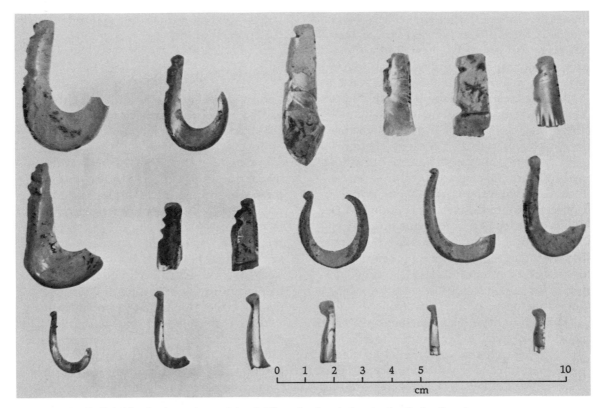

12.7 *Turbo-shell fishhooks from Anuta Island. These hooks, dating to the first milennium* B.C., *are among the earliest known finds of one-piece fishing gear from the western Pacific. (Photo courtesy of Bishop Museum, Honolulu.)*

related to the Lapita series and for various reasons may be considered as representing a fishhook complex ancestral to that of Polynesia proper. The 45 specimens (some of which are shown in Fig. 12.7) evidence a one-piece fishhook tradition in *Turbo* and other shell, including the rotating and probably also jabbing types. Three kinds of line-attachment devices are present. These hooks, furthermore, are associated with a manufacturing tool kit including branch-coral abraders, echinoid-spine abraders, coral rubbing stones, and flakes—all of which appear in the later, widely-documented fishhook complexes of East Polynesia.

Fishhooks very similar to those from Anuta have more recently been excavated in a Lapitoid pottery context in Tonga and Samoa. The Tonga materials (Kirch 1978a) are not only typologically identical to the Anutan hooks, but again are associated with the typical manufacturing tools. In sum, the elaborate fishing-gear assemblages of East Polynesia can now be traced to simpler, one-piece hook complexes in the Southwest Pacific that date as early as 800 B.C.

The East Polynesia fishhook assemblages themselves evidence particular adaptations to local environment. In Easter Island an apparent lack of suitable raw materials (especially pearl shell) led to the manufacture of hooks in stone as well as in bone; the bone was human, as there were no pigs or dogs. The development of two-piece hooks in Hawaii, Easter Island, and New Zealand perhaps can be traced to an ancestral form in Central Polynesia, or, alternatively, may represent independent adaptations to the problem of shear stress on the hook's weakest point, the bend. In Hawaii recent excavations and analyses (Kirch 1979) suggest that hook form and size may be closely correlated with certain features of environment, such as the extent of inshore reefs at particular fishing localities. These findings have important negative implications for the traditional application of formal typologies to assemblages from sites in a variety of local environmental conditions. For example, the anomalous concentration of fishhooks at South Point, Hawaii (Chapter 7), leads one to inquire about the ecological factors that must have contributed to this situation. The deep, sheltered water off South Point even today yields large fish such as skipjack and yellowfin, a fact that would not have escaped the notice of Hawaii's early Polynesian colonizers. Are the differences in archaeological fishhook assemblages then a reflection of variation in the marine resources at the sites? This question must be answered if intersite variation in fishhook assemblages is to be understood.

Ethnoarchaeology would appear to offer one of the most potentially rewarding avenues for investigation of Polynesian fishing. The analysis of marine exploitation strategies may provide models on which to base a more convincing interpretation of fishing gear and faunal remains. It is clear, for example, that many cultural and natural factors intervene between the capture of a fish and the final disposition of its remains in an archaeological context. Only the ethnographic discovery of those factors— whether they are regular patterns of cultural behavior or physical processes of site formation—can provide a reasonable basis for the interpretation of midden deposits. Ethnographic data, such as that partially displayed in Fig. 12.4, may further provide correlates among exploited species, particu-

lar capture techniques, and environmental variation.

The Sweet Potato

The sweet potato, now unquestionably regarded as being of American origin (Yen 1974a), has perhaps inspired more debate on its Polynesian sources than any other single item. Just how the tuber was introduced does not concern us here, but rather the fascinating range of agronomic adaptations applied by its Polynesian cultivators. In these areas, especially in New Zealand but also in Easter Island and Hawaii, the sweet potato became a dominant crop because of its adaptability to edaphic and climatic conditions only marginally suited to the usual Oceanic staples, taro and yam.

Yen has outlined a tripartite sequence for the introduction and consequent adaptation of *Ipomoea batatas* in New Zealand. Apparently still uncertain in this formulation is the role played by climatic change (the contention that there was a period of deteriorating climate during the period of human colonization being questioned by some students). Nevertheless, the tripartite model, with introductory, experimental, and systematic stages, appears to take account of the available evidence. It is apparent that even if such plants as coconut, breadfruit, and kava had been successfully transferred during the initial settlement from Central Polynesia, they must soon have succumbed to the temperate climate. Even taro was restricted to the low latitudes of the North Island. Yen has noted that the experimental stage probably involved a great concern with the field requirements of the growing plants. Most significant was the development of pit storage of the tubers and conversion to an annual cropping scheme. The association of developed sweet potato cultivation and a stable agricultural system during the systematic stage, with such cultural traits as the fortified *pā* settlement, continues as a focus of archaeological research (Chapter 9).

For Hawaii, Yen (1974a) has proposed a two-stage agricultural sequence—introductory and expansion—in which the sweet potato figured most prominently in the later era. The introductory phase involved the transfer of the tropical yam-taro crop complex, with settlement emphasis on valleys that provided the most desirable array of soil and water conditions. After population increases, settlement and agriculture expanded into ecologically more marginal zones such as leeward slopes and inspired the adaptation of slash-and-burn techniques to a field system with plots defined by stone borders. The Lapakahi field system on the Island of Hawaii (Chapter 7) perhaps best exemplifies the expansion stage in Hawaiian agricultural development. As in New Zealand, the hypothetical relations between such agricultural intensification and the social system—in Hawaii especially the rise of powerful chiefdoms—continue to be a research topic of major concern.

Environmental Instability and Food Preservation

Instability or temporal variation in rainfall (leading to drought) and damage from cyclones have always been important constraints in Oceania. One of the most striking technological responses of Polynesians to this temporal variability is the semianaerobic fermentation and pit ensilage of starchy food pastes, particularly breadfruit. Generally uncooked starch pastes are sealed in subterranean leaf-lined pits. Bacterial fermentation occurs, with the waste alcoholic by-products gradually decimating the microbial population and creating a steady-state system. The sealed supply of staple starch may be left in the ground for considerable periods, with reports of 10 years or more not uncommon. The fermented product is variously known in Polynesian languages as *ma* or *masi,* and the term may apparently be reconstructed to Proto-Oceanic (Table 12.2). Archaeological evidence for the antiquity of this technique in Polynesia has been claimed in West Polynesia; in Samoa and Tonga symmetrical pits (not containing charcoal or other evidence of fire) have been interpreted as food-fermentation silos. Such pits on Niuatoputapu, in sites with Polynesian plain-ware ceramics, are also associated with *Cypraea*-shell food scrapers.

A causal relation between cyclic, environmentally induced food shortage and the development of fermented starch-staple reserves seems clear and is a significant adaptation of normally perishable tropical crops to long-range food-surplus requirements. The technique appears to have reached its apogee in the Marquesas, where pits with volumes as great as 876 m³ have been reported (in Taipivai, Nukuhiva—Handy 1923). Suggs (1961) noted the presence of large ma pits on some of the Marquesan ridge-top fortifications (such as that at Taiohae), which date to the expansion period. The associations here between stress (famine), accumulated surplus, and warfare are obvious. The correlation between potential food shortage and masi production is not lost on the inhabitants of Futuna or Niuatoputapu, even though these islands ceased making masi more than 20 years ago because of the "insurance" provided by the availability of European food stocks (rice, flour, and the like). As one elderly Niuan agriculturist put it, in free translation: "It is the thing of the olden time, the protection of man. Should the famine descend, and there is no starch staple, sit then and eat this food."

Adaptation and Process

To appreciate the tremendous range of Polynesian adaptations to the environment, it is necessary to look beyond descriptive analyses of individual societies. Polynesian archaeology has matured to the point where the essential culture-historical sequences for the major archipelagoes and islands are known to some degree, as this volume testifies. Furthermore, the extensive literature of Oceanic anthropology has documented the structural bases of these societies. What is possible now is to search out and explain the consistencies and repeated patterns of cultural adaptation to environmental challenges. There are certain directions that might prove productive in the study of adaptation as process.

Emphasis in this chapter has repeatedly been placed on the importance of environmental variation. By this I mean the ecological diversity and variation within specific circumscribed territories to which populations adapt rather than the total environmental range of Polynesia. Such variations include not only spatial differences in terrain or biotic zoning, but temporal irregularities, cyclical or otherwise, in environmental parameters. A further consideration is "spacing" between either spatial or temporal components of environment; this has sometimes been referred to as the "grain" of the environment (either fine or coarse).

Perhaps the most important concept here is that of *constraint*. This is not a synonym for "determinism." It is rather the concept that environment imposes boundaries or limits on cultural strategies. While irrigation as a technique may be part of a population's cultural repertoire, the absence of permanent streams on a specific island is a constraint that necessarily channels the adaptive strategy of the population; it does not, however, direct that strategy along a no-alternative course. In addition, man more than any other species has developed the ability to modify his natural environment, and thus to alter or remove certain constraints (although his actions thereby frequently impose previously nonexistent constraints). Irrigation may not be feasible on coral atolls, but the excavation of artificial pits and consequent tapping of the fresh-water lens creates a microhabitat suitable for taro cultivation and thus effectively lessens the constraint imposed by natural conditions. Such cultural or behavioral strategies may or may not entirely eliminate constraint.

Population growth, size, and density obviously are factors of critical importance in the process of Polynesian adaptation, yet from the viewpoint of the anthropologist they are among the most complex elements theoretically and most elusive elements methodologically. There can be little doubt that the pressure of human numbers on finite, circumscribed resources (whether land, food, or something else) is a real force in man-environment relations; nonetheless, the calculation of carrying capacity is one of the most hotly debated issues in human ecology. And still, the prehistoric cultural sequences of Polynesia present the same scenario over and over: initial settlement by a numerically restricted group, rapid population growth, expansion into all habitable biotopes, and—frequently—intergroup conflict and degradation of the natural environment.

One reason why population is such a difficult concept is that it is so intimately bound up with aspects of social structure and organization. Kelly (1968) has shown that population pressure in highland New Guinea results from the complex interplay of many factors, including the structure of local social groups and the nature of land inheritance patterns. In Polynesia, where transmission of land-use rights frequently is via local descent groups with strongly agnatic cores, imbalance in male-female ratios over several generations could result in "pressure" on the allocation of arable land, even if the standard demographic variables of population size and density were to remain more or less constant.

Aspects of social and political structure have further implications for ecological adaptation. The organization of Polynesian social groups around a generational-seniority model results in a tendency for segmentation of junior lines. In a colonization situation such descent-group fissioning could and probably frequently did result in relatively rapid settlement of the most favorable environmental zones within a few generations after initial occupancy. The result was autonomous sociopolitical groups

PATRICK V. KIRCH

distributed throughout the island or archipelago.

The ecological significance of social stratification (Sahlins 1958) needs to be more thoroughly explored, particularly in light of the diachronic evidence accumulating through archaeological research. The important role played by chiefs in the allocation and distribution of scarce or limited resources at times of stress (when environmental constraint is especially critical) has been noted. In Polynesia chiefs were martial leaders as much as economic managers, and the ecological role of warfare has yet to be thoroughly analyzed. There are indications that the rise of powerful chiefdoms—for instance, in Tonga or in the Kona-Kohala region of Hawaii—may have been linked to similar environmental circumstances. Certainly the rise of such political units cannot be ascribed solely to status rivalry devoid of an ecological milieu. Polynesia has in the past contributed a full share to the development of anthropological theory; prospects for the future are no less exciting and equally challenging.

Acknowledgments

This chapter draws heavily on unpublished data from recent and continuing investigations in western and outlier Polynesia that have been generously supported by grants (GS-40294 and BNS-04782) from the National Science Foundation. I should like to thank Tom Dye, my assistant on the Tongan expedition, and my colleagues D. E. Yen and P. C. McCoy for sharing their data and their thoughts with me.

References

Anderson, Edgar. 1952. *Plants, man and life*, pp. 1–245. Boston: Little, Brown.

Barrau, Jacques. 1961. *Subsistence agriculture in Polynesia and Micronesia*. Bishop Museum Bulletin no. 223, Honolulu.

———. 1965a. L'Humide et le sec: an essay on ethnological adaptation to contrastive environments in the Indo-Pacific area. *Journal of the Polynesian Society* 74:329–346.

———. 1965b. Histoire et prehistoire horticoles de l'Océanie tropicale. *Journal de la Société des Océanistes* 21:55–78.

Bell, F. L. S. 1931. The place of food in the social life of Central Polynesia. *Oceania* 2:117–135.

Brookfield, H. C. 1972. Intensification and disintensification in Pacific agriculture: a theoretical approach. *Pacific Viewpoint* 13:30–48.

Cochrane, G. R. 1973. The general environment and New Zealand's biogeography. In *The natural history of New Zealand*, ed. G. R. Williams, pp. 1–27. Wellington: A. H. and A. W. Reed.

Emory, K. P., W. J. Bonk, and Y. H. Sinoto. 1968. *Hawaiian archaeology: fishhooks*, 2nd ed. Bishop Museum Special Publication no. 47, Honolulu.

Firth, Raymond. 1936. *We, the Tikopia*. London: George Allen and Unwin.

Fosberg, F. R. 1963. The island ecosystem. In *Man's place in the island ecosystem*, ed. F. R. Fosberg, pp. 1–6. Honolulu: Bishop Museum Press.

Geertz, Clifford. 1970. *Agricultural involution: the processes of ecological change in Indonesia*. Berkeley: University of California Press.

Golson, Jack, and P. J. Hughes. 1976. The appearance of plant and animal domestication in New Guinea. In *La Préhistoire océanienne*, ed. José Garanger. Paper presented at IXᵉ Congrès Union International des Sciences Préhistoriques et Protohistoriques, Nice, Colloque 22:88–100. Paris: Centre National de la Recherche Scientifique.

Gorman, C. F. 1969. Hoabinhian: a pebble-tool complex with early plant associations in Southeast Asia. *Science* 163:671–673.

Green, R. C. 1974. Sites with Lapita pottery: importing and voyaging. *Mankind* 9:253–259.

———. 1976a. New sites with Lapita pottery and their implications for an understanding of the settlement of the Western Pacific. Paper presented at IXᵉ Congrès Union Internationale des Sciences Préhistoriques et Protohistoriques, Nice. Revised version: Working Paper 51 in Anthropology, Archaeology, Linguistics, and Maori Studies, Department of Anthropology, University of Auckland.

———. 1976b. Lapita sites in the Santa Cruz group. In *Southeast Solomon Islands cultural history*, ed. R. C. Green and M. M. Cresswell. *Royal Society of New Zealand Bulletin* 11:245–265.

Groube, L. M. 1971. Tonga, Lapita pottery, and

Polynesian origins. *Journal of the Polynesian Society* 80:278–316.

Handy, E. S. C. 1923. *The native culture of the Marquesas.* Bishop Museum Bulletin no. 9, Honolulu.

Harris, D. R. 1972. The origins of agriculture in the tropics. *American Scientist* 60:180–193.

Kelly, R. C. 1968. Demographic pressure and descent group structure in the New Guinea highlands. *Oceania* 39:36–63.

Kirch, P. V. 1973. Prehistoric subsistence patterns in the northern Marquesas Islands, French Polynesia. *Archaeology and Physical Anthropology in Oceania* 8:24–40.

———. 1976. Ethno-archaeological investigations in Futuna and Uvea (Western Polynesia): a preliminary report. *Journal of the Polynesian Society* 85:27–69.

———. 1978a. The Lapitoid period in West Polynesia: excavations and survey in Niuatoputapu, Tonga. *Journal of Field Archaeology* 5:1–13.

———. 1978b. Ethnoarchaeological approaches to the study of agricultural systems in the humid tropics. In *Explorations in ethnoarchaeology,* ed. R. A. Gould, pp. 103–125. Albuquerque: University of New Mexico Press.

———. 1978c. Indigenous agriculture on Uvea, Western Polynesia. *Economic Botany* 32:157–181.

———. 1979. Marine exploitation in prehistoric Hawaii. *Pacific Anthropological Records* 29:in press.

——— and P. H. Rosendahl. 1976. Early Anutan settlement and the position of Anuta in the prehistory of the Southwest Pacific. In *Southeast Solomon Islands cultural history,* ed. R. C. Green and M. M. Cresswell. *Royal Society of New Zealand Bulletin* 11:225–244.

Leach, B. F. 1969. *The concept of similarity in prehistoric studies.* Studies in Prehistoric Anthropology 1, University of Otago.

McCoy, P. C. 1977. The Mauna Kea adz quarry project: a summary of the 1975 field investigations. *Journal of the Polynesian Society* 86:223–244.

MacDaniels, L. H. 1947. *A study of the Fe'i banana and its distribution with reference to Polynesian migrations.* Bishop Museum Bulletin no. 190, Honolulu.

Malinowski, Bronislaw. 1935. *Coral gardens and their magic,* vol. 1. London: George Allen and Unwin.

Massal, Emile, and Jacques Barrau. 1956. *Food*

plants of the South Sea Islands.* South Pacific Commission Technical Paper no. 94, Noumea.

Panoff, Michel. 1970. *La Terre et l'organization sociale en Polynesie.* Paris: Payot.

Pawley, A. K., and R. C. Green. 1973. Dating the dispersal of the Oceanic languages. *Oceanic Linguistics* 12:1–67.

Reinman, F. M. 1967. *Fishing: an aspect of Oceanic economy.* Fieldiana: Anthropology 56. Chicago: Natural History Museum.

———. 1970. Fishhook variability: implications for the history and distribution of fishing gear in Oceania. In *Studies in Oceanic culture history,* ed. R. C. Green and Marion Kelly. *Pacific Anthropological Records* 11:47–59.

Rosendahl, P. H., and D. E. Yen. 1971. Fossil sweet potato remains from Hawaii. *Journal of the Polynesian Society* 80:379–385.

Sahlins, M. D. 1958. *Social stratification in Polynesia.* Seattle: University of Washington Press.

———. 1972. *Stone age economics.* Chicago: Aldine.

Shaw, Elizabeth. 1963. Maori quarry, Tahanga Hill, Opito. *New Zealand Archaeological Association Newsletter* 6:34–36.

Shawcross, Kathleen. 1967. Fern-root, and the total scheme of the 18th century Maori food production in agricultural areas. *Journal of the Polynesian Society* 76:330–352.

Shawcross, Wilfred. 1964. Stone flake industries in New Zealand. *Journal of the Polynesian Society* 73:7–25.

Simmonds, N. W. 1962. *The evolution of the bananas.* London: Longmans.

Sinoto, Y. H. 1968. Fishhook typology and its significance for establishing prehistoric cultural sequences in Oceania. *Proceedings of the Eighth International Congress of Anthropological and Ethnological Sciences.* Science Council of Japan, Tokyo.

Spencer, J. E. 1966. *Shifting cultivation in southeastern Asia.* University of California Publications in Geography, no. 19, Berkeley.

Suggs, R. C. 1961. The archaeology of Nuku Hiva, Marquesas Islands, French Polynesia. *Anthropological Papers of the American Museum of Natural History* 49:1–205.

Terrell, John. 1976. Island biogeography and man in Melanesia. *Archaeology and Physical Anthropology in Oceania* 11:1–17.

Titcomb, Margaret. 1952. *Native use of fish in Hawaii.* Polynesian Society Memoir no. 29, New Plymouth, New Zealand.

Vayda, A. P., and Bonnie McCay. 1975. New directions in ecology and ecological anthropology. In *Annual Review of Anthropology*, ed. B. J. Siegel et al., vol. 4, pp. 293–306. Palo Alto, California.

Wagner, Philip. 1960. *The human use of the earth.* New York: Macmillan Co.

Warner, J. N. 1962. Sugar cane: an indigenous Papuan cultigen. *Ethnology* 1:405–411.

Wilder, G. P. 1928. *The breadfruit of Tahiti.* Bishop Museum Bulletin no. 50, Honolulu.

Yen, D. E. 1973. The origins of Oceanic agriculture. *Archaeology and Physical Anthropology in Oceania* 8:68–85.

———. 1974a. *The sweet potato and Oceania: an essay in ethnobotany.* Bishop Museum Bulletin no. 236, Honolulu.

———. 1974b. Arboriculture in the subsistence of Santa Cruz, Solomon Islands. *Economic Botany* 28:247–284.

———. 1976. Indigenous food processing in Oceania. In *Gastronomy: the anthropology of food and food habits,* ed. M. L. Arnott. Chicago: Aldine.

——— and Janet Gordon, eds. 1973. *Anuta: a Polynesian outlier in the Solomon Islands. Pacific Anthropological Records* 21.

Settlement Patterns

CHAPTER 13

PETER S. BELLWOOD

 A settlement pattern is a particularly important expression of past human activity in a landscape, and prehistoric settlement patterns in Polynesia are particularly important to the archaeologist owing to their easy visibility in many island groups. The Polynesians used a great deal of stone for pavements, platforms, walls, and other structures; much of this stonework has survived, together with other modifications of surface terrain such as terraces, ditches, and mounds. Because these structures are normally discrete, they adapt well to intensive survey methods.

The great majority of the structures that are visible above ground today probably were erected within the last thousand years, with the rate of survival becoming higher as one moves forward in time. Information on settlement patterns from earlier periods comes mainly from subsurface excavations and is therefore rather restricted. Even when structures can be surveyed without excavation, the archaeologist immediately runs into the basic problems of determining chronological relationships; these problems are of sufficient importance to require presentation here.

In the absence of pottery or architectural idiosyncrasies that can be referred to specific chronological brackets, it is very difficult to sort out from visible remains the sites and structures in use at a given time. Most structures are not deeply buried, so stratigraphic excavations and radiocarbon dating are of little assistance. Fossilized settlement patterns abandoned at an

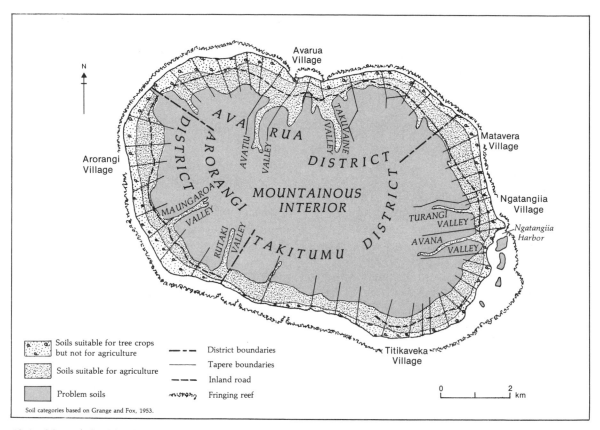

13.1 *Map of the island of Rarotonga, showing tapere boundaries, soil zonation, and the course of the prehistoric road.* (*Redrawn from Crocombe 1964.*)

earlier period, such as the one on Necker Island in the Hawaiian group (Emory 1928), have been considered unusual. However, large prehistoric village complexes that date from before A.D. 1500 are now being discovered and mapped in detail in Western Samoa, so they are becoming less rare as research proceeds.

Units and Patterns of Settlement

As noted earlier in this volume, Polynesian islands (excluding New Zealand) are of two distinct types: high volcanic islands with steep, rather inhospitable interiors; and atolls or raised coral islands. On the high volcanic islands (the Hawaiian, Marquesan, Society, Austral, southern Cook, and Samoan groups) populations were historically distributed around the coasts and in the

valleys that penetrate the interiors. Basic tribal land divisions in these groups were usually radial and incorporated a section of coast, the coastal lowland, and perhaps a valley (Fig. 13.1). Ideally shaped like pie segments, these divisions tapered off toward the island centers—for all land on Polynesian islands was claimed, even if it was too inaccessible to be utilized directly. Such radial divisions, called *tapere* in the Cooks, *ahupua'a* in the Hawaiian Islands, and *nu'u* in Samoa, form the basis for any ethnohistorical interpretation of overall settlement patterns.

The land within the major Polynesian divisions was under the titular control of the chief, who normally controlled any necessary rearrangement of land rights among the members of his group. Individual lineages theoretically would support themselves on a subsidiary radial slice of the tribal division, but a good deal of fragmentation occurred through reallocation as families died out or expanded. There was no private ownership of land in the English legal sense, although in practice a lineage or family had the right to use its land in perpetuity.

I propose now to examine the structures within which ancient Polynesian settlement patterns are preserved. In doing so, I draw heavily on ethnohistoric sources. I visualize four basic levels of analysis. First, there are what I term "primary settlement units"— individual structures such as houses (a large multifunctional category), tombs, temples, and so forth. In the field these primary units survive as a rather bewildering variety of platforms, walls, pavements, and amorphous heaps of stone or earth, and it should be realized that not all can be simply categorized from survey data alone into the classes I am using here. For example, is a ruinous and overgrown stone heap to be interpreted as a house foundation, as part of a religious structure, as a tomb, or as something unrecorded ethnographically?

The second level of analysis concerns the combined settlement unit, the third considers geographic spacing, while the fourth uses overall settlement patterns to support ecological and social generalizations.

Primary Settlement Units

In most island groups houses for all functions were built of timber and thatch; the main exceptions are the occasional corbeled stone houses on Easter Island (especially in Orongo Village), and the stone foundation walls used in the Hawaiian Islands. In some island groups, especially Samoa, Easter Island, and the Societies, the bases of the house walls were lined with a curbing of stones or coral. Unless stone was used in such ways, the actual shapes of the houses can only be recovered through the discovery of postholes where supports once stood.

However, in a number of islands the sites (but not necessarily the shapes) of

houses are visible owing to the construction of terraces, pavements, or raised platforms. Terraces, often stone faced, are common on the high islands of Polynesia, and surface pavements are widely reported in East Polynesia. In many of these the pavement was the floor for an open veranda and/or an unroofed approach area, while the back sleeping section of the house was often constructed on bare soil. The plans can only be recovered by excavation (Fig. 13.2). Raised stone platforms with paved and stepped tops (*paepae*) were particularly well constructed in the Marquesas Islands. The Samoans also frequently made rough stone or earthen house platforms.

According to both ethnographic reports and excavations, Polynesian houses were basically rectangular or oval in plan; circular and square variants are rare, and the circular form became truly popular only in Samoa. Oval houses were the main form there and were important also in Tonga (Fig. 13.3) and Easter Island; in addition, this form was used for large community houses in the Society Islands (Fig. 13.5). Elsewhere in East Polynesia the rectangular form was dominant (Fig. 13.4). However, house shapes in Polynesia vary so greatly that it is rather dangerous to generalize. In fact, both the oval and the rectangular forms go back to the early periods of settlement in Samoa and the Hawaiian Islands; they could indeed be part of the Lapita complex, although there is no direct evidence yet on Lapita house plans. Furthermore, there are no differences in house plans to differentiate West Polynesia as a whole from East Polynesia as a whole, and the characteristics used for this purpose by Burrows (1938; see also Chapter 1) were concerned mainly with roofing methods, which are not recovered archaeologically.

Tombs are not normally an important type of monument in Polynesia, since burial was often in caves or directly in earthen graves. It is only in Tonga and Uvea (Kirch 1976) that tombs are prominent features of the settlement pattern. Large numbers of Tongan mounds were constructed for

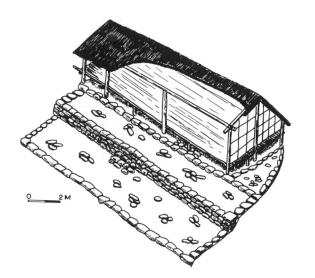

13.2 *A house with a slightly raised floor, constructed on an earthen terrace and fronted by two paved terraces, in the Upper Maungaroa Valley on Rarotonga. (Reconstruction drawing from excavations by the author.)*

13.3 *A round-ended chief's house in the Tongan Islands, drawn by Louis de Sainson on the voyage of the* Astrolabe, *under the command of Dumont D'Urville, in 1826 to 1829. (Courtesy of the National Library of Australia.)*

13.4 *A hamlet on Kauai, Hawaiian Islands; original drawn by John Webber in 1777. The complete version of this illustration is an inaccurate compilation of two separate original drawings by Webber. The left-hand half of the scene has been purposely omitted.*

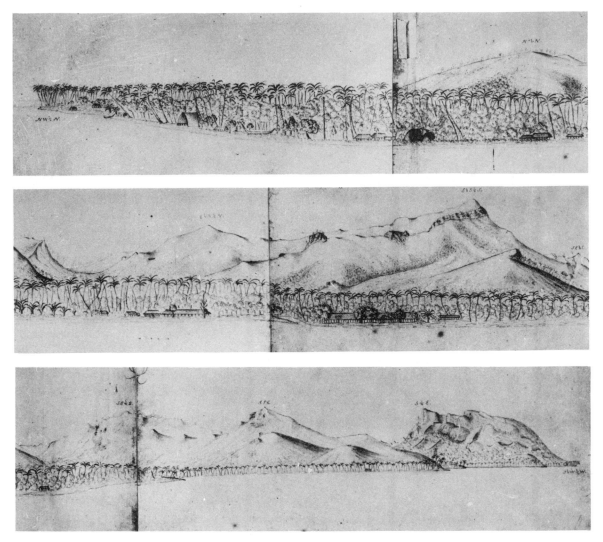

13.5 *A view of the island of Huahine in the Societies, drawn on Captain Cook's first voyage. The original drawing is continuous (starting at top left) and shows a fairly scattered settlement pattern: small rectangular sleeping houses, large round-ended community houses, and open-ended canoe houses fronting the beach. (Reproduced by permission of the British Library Board, Add. MS. 23921 f.3.)*

successive inhumation burials. There, the mounds for commoners' burials were entirely of earth (Davidson 1969a), while those for chiefs often had coral-slab burial cists and coral-slab faced terraces. According to early accounts the Tongans also constructed rather specialized earthen mounds for pigeon snaring and to serve as resting places for chiefs; the pigeon mounds are found in Samoa and Uvea as well, but not in East Polynesia. Samoa has no certain ex-

amples of burial mounds, but the placing of burials in stone platforms or cairns is quite widely reported in East Polynesia, especially from the Hawaiian, Marquesan, and Easter islands. The East Polynesian temples (*marae*) frequently served as locations for subsurface burials.

The most impressive remains of past Polynesian culture are perhaps the temples, especially in East Polynesia. Furthermore, these structures present an array of forms

PETER S. BELLWOOD

that make them useful for tracing inter-island relations. In West Polynesia temples were mainly of the god-house type, while in East Polynesia they usually comprised open-air courts and platforms. God-houses for the storage of images and other paraphernalia were certainly present on many East Polynesian temples, but they do not seem to have been the main focus for rituals, except possibly in the northern Marquesas. The West Polynesian god-houses are poorly recorded ethnographically and unknown archaeologically, unless the star mounds in Samoa supported such structures. The Tongans also constructed "consecrated houses" where gods, evidently those without their own priest, could be invoked (Mariner 1817), and houses for burial ceremonies were constructed on the tops of the burial mounds. The majority of the other islands in western and outlier Polynesia seem also to have had god-houses, although Green (1970a) has noted the use of upright stones to represent gods in an open space (*malae*) adjacent to the god-house in the Ellice and Tokelau islands, and on Tikopia and Nukuoro. In addition, Kirch (1976) has recently reported them from Alofi. Uprights of this type are found very widely in East Polynesia, but apparently not in Tonga and Samoa. Nevertheless, the use of stone uprights for this purpose is regarded as a trait of high antiquity in Polynesia. It may even predate the settlement of East Polynesia.

The open-air temples (the *marae* of central Polynesia, *ahu* of Easter Island and the northern Marquesas, *heiau* of the Hawaiian Islands) are perhaps the most interesting class of monuments of Polynesia (Emory 1970). The basic plan was a rectangular court, often paved or walled, with a stone platform running across one end (Fig. 13.6). Upright slabs to mark positions for the participants in various ceremonies were often placed about the court, with additional slabs representing positions for gods sometimes put on the platform. This basic plan is well recorded in the Society and Tuamotu islands, and on Easter Island (where

the upright slabs seemingly have been replaced by statues). The basic marae form seems to have developed in an early stage of East Polynesian settlement, and at least some version of it was taken to all parts of the region, although local variations in design had become quite marked by the time of European contact. In the Hawaiian and southern Marquesan islands the pattern was complicated by extensive use of terracing, but in the Austral and southern Cook islands more emphasis was placed on the use of uprights. Although stone temples are virtually absent in temperate New Zealand, there are occasional lines of upright stones (called *tuahu*), which indicate that the basic concept was known; frequent seasonal movement in the Archaic phase may have rendered the construction of large stone structures impracticable, however.

Other primary units that occur in the Polynesian settlement landscape include field walls, paved tracks and roads, fishponds and fish traps, fortification ditches, and cultivation terraces, to list perhaps the most important categories. These are considered below as components of combined settlement units.

Combined Settlement Units

The ethnographic record for Polynesia indicates that combined settlement units existed at two main social levels, those of the commoner and the chief. While commoner units tended to occupy one single plot of ground, chiefly units often comprised quite scattered facilities. Those social divisions should not be confused with factors of geographic spacing, which will be discussed separately.

Throughout Polynesia commoner units generally consisted of one or more sleeping houses, plus a separate cookhouse and perhaps a storehouse or canoe shed. Chiefly units were larger; in the Marquesas they comprised several sleeping houses for the chief and his retainers, often with separate houses used only by men (houses for unmarried men were especially widespread in

13.6 *A marae with walled court and stepped platform in Matavai Bay, Tahiti, drawn in 1768 on Captain Cook's first voyage. (Reproduced by permission of the British Library Board, Add. MS. 23921 f.27.)*

Polynesia). In addition, there were a number of communal structures such as temples and terraced dancing floors (*tohua*) under the titular control of the chief, although not necessarily in direct proximity (Bellwood 1972). Similar chiefly units occurred in most East Polynesian islands for which we have record, and in the Hawaiian Islands the chiefly unit in some regions also incorporated large coastal fishponds (Kikuchi 1976). In West Polynesia, in addition to dwellings, the chiefly unit often comprised an open space (malae) for ceremonies, a god-house, a house for young men, and a community house for council meetings (Green 1970a). Many of these structures were of course used communally, rather than by the chief and his family alone. They are considered here under the heading of chiefly unit because they were built at the behest of high-ranking individuals.

Although the existence of these units can be certified from the ethnographic record, in archaeological fieldwork they are often hard to identify. In areas where structures are distributed fairly evenly without visible clustering it may be impossible to recognize combined settlement units, and the difficulties of establishing contemporaneity of use have already been mentioned. While major ceremonial sites are often surrounded by a remarkably high density of other structures, in reality one can rarely attribute the individual structures to particular household types. Nevertheless, in a few cases archaeologists have claimed to recognize household units at a nonspecific level; for instance, Jennings (1976) has identified them in the Mount Olo tract on Upolu, Western Samoa, as areas enclosed by walls or paths that contain one or two platforms and a possible garden area. In my own Hanatekua Valley survey in the Marquesas (Bellwood 1972), I was able to recognize what I termed a discrete "economic and dwelling unit": several dwelling platforms, two small shrines, a breadfruit storage pit, and several gardening enclosures and ter-

PETER S. BELLWOOD

races. In New Zealand, such generalized household units probably occupied individual terraces in fortifications or in undefended terraced sites.

The Geographic Spacing of Polynesian Settlements

Because combined units at the social level discussed above are so hard to define archaeologically, most survey reports have been more concerned with factors of spacing, such as relative degrees of nucleation and dispersal. In general, Polynesian settlement patterns were dispersed (as in Fig. 13.5), but localized clusters of quite high density occurred often. True villages with clear outer boundaries, wherein houses were set close together around plazas and along streets, are rare.

The following are examples of discrete villages in Polynesia:

Easter Island. The Middle period ceremonial village of Orongo (Mulloy 1975), and possibly the now destroyed 1.6 km-long village of stone houses observed by Thomson (1889).

Rurutu. The linear village, about 1 km long, of round-ended houses and marae at Vitaria (Verin 1969).

New Zealand. The many fortifications that served as nucleated villages, although for economic reasons the total population was probably not in residence all year round (see Bellwood 1971a).

Tonga. The major ceremonial center and chiefly residence at Mu'a (McKern 1929).

Outliers. The formally planned village on Nukuoro atoll (Green 1970a) and its possible counterpart on Kapingamarangi. Kirch (1976) also reports a late prehistoric village of houses grouped around a malae at Loka on Alofi.

No doubt other investigators could provide other examples of such discrete villages; I have given the above list only to show that such settlements do exist in small numbers over a wide area. With European contact and the resulting missionary and trade stimuli the village settlement of course proliferated throughout Polynesia.

My present inclination is to regard the above examples as villages on the grounds of formal patterning and discrete boundaries. Examples of dense clustering are much more common; Captain Cook, for instance, reported clusters of up to 200 houses in the Hawaiian Islands—although formal villages of this size have not, to my knowledge, been identified archaeologically. The remarkable fortifications of Rapa in the Australs may also have served as nucleated villages (Ferdon 1965). (The Norwegian expedition's investigation of these structures did not produce any actual house plans, so one cannot automatically assume permanent occupation.) The same applies to the numerous ditched and terraced ridge forts reported particularly from the Samoan, Hawaiian, and Marquesan islands; many of these sites were probably only temporary refuges. In Samoa there is at least one inland planned village at Vaigafa on Upolu (Davidson 1974), although the archaeological evidence from this group indicates that the modern coastal Samoan villages appeared mainly after 1800 because of European stimuli (Davidson 1969b). Prehistoric Samoan sites show the same kind of dispersal with localized clustering characteristic of most other parts of Polynesia.

To illustrate the differing degrees of clustering and dispersal found in Polynesia, let me give two examples from my own surveys. The first is the Hanatekua Valley on Hivaoa in the Marquesas (Bellwood 1972). Hivaoa, like the other Marquesan islands, has a rugged interior and no coastal flats, so all settlement was concentrated ribbon-fashion along the radial valleys that penetrate the interior. In Hanatekua, where the settlement is 1.2 km long, the lower part of the valley was apparently used mainly for plantations, probably of coconut and breadfruit, with few dwelling structures. This may reflect vulnerability to tidal waves and coastal raiding parties from other valleys. Most of the dwellings, walled plantations perhaps (for breadfruit), breadfruit storage pits, temples, and a large walled fort are concentrated in the center of the valley, where the dwellings average between

10 and 40 m apart. The very narrow upper valley contained only terraced gardens and a few dwellings. Basically, this is a situation of fairly dense clustering imposed by ecological and social factors, and it seems to be quite typical of the group as a whole (for a similar Marquesan valley survey see Kellum-Ottino 1971).

My second example comes from Rarotonga in the Cook Islands (Bellwood 1971b). This island has a rugged interior like the Marquesas, but differs in having a broad coastal flat. Most of the settlements were located on this flat, on either side of a partially paved road (Fig. 13.1) that encircled the island, linking all the tribal districts. However, complete settlement patterns have survived only in remote valleys of Rarotonga and my own surveys were carried out in two on the southwestern side of the island—Maungaroa and Rutaki. The Rutaki Valley merely had a scattered number of dwelling pavements, between 10 and 100 or so m apart. The Maungaroa Valley had a much larger population, which was barred by enemies from access to the coast in the period before 1823. Because the Maungaroa Valley has little arable land, the settlements are clustered in four zones of poor land, reflecting the factors of safety in numbers and need to leave as much cultivatable land as possible free of structures. The dwellings and marae in these clusters are generally less than 50 m apart (Fig. 13.7). There is no sign of planning, except in one cluster that comprised about eight close-set terraced house floors on a ridge high above the valley. The latter may have served as an undefended fortress to which people could flee when necessary. The valley as a whole provides a good example of relative nucleation under stress. The coastal settlements were probably more scattered, although too few have survived to warrant study.

The Hanatekua and Rarotongan examples show both dispersal and clustering at work. There are many additional examples from other parts of Polynesia where extensive settlement pattern surveys have been car-

ried out, such as Samoa (numerous reports in Green and Davidson 1969, 1974), the Hawaiian Islands (see Chapter 7), the Society Islands (Green et al. 1967), and the Cook Islands (Bellwood 1978).

I should state here that settlement clustering, when present in Polynesia, did not normally result in ceremonial centers of the type so well known from the Mayan lowlands; it is quite rare to find temples clustered together at a single locus. This may be seen from the Lower Maungaroa plan (Fig. 13.7), where the marae are scattered fairly randomly among the houses. The implication is that low-ranking families built their own marae close to their houses, for in many cases the largest marae do not appear to have attracted any extraordinary density of surrounding structures. However, there are a number of notable exceptions, in particular the complex of tombs, dwellings, and god-houses at the chiefly center of Mu'a on Tongatapu, and the rather remarkable cluster of 25 marae at Maeva on Huahine in the Society Islands (Emory 1933). The massive stone platform known as the Pulemelei on Savai'i in Samoa seems also to have attracted a fair density of surrounding structures (Scott 1969), but many of these may have been dwellings. Otherwise, a fairly even spread of single temples, with the larger ones generally farther apart than the smaller ones, characterizes most surveyed regions of East Polynesia (witness the spread of ahu around the coast of Easter Island).

The pattern of settlement has drawn comment from Sahlins (1958), who suggested that dispersal of settlement in Polynesia was associated with dispersal of resources. He went on to relate dispersal of resources to the need for redistribution through a central chiefly node. This explanation of the genesis of the Polynesian chiefdoms (excluding Samoa in Sahlins' terminology, but see Bellwood 1971b) is now well known, but in my view it can be easily refuted. Polynesian islands tend to be small, and although resources may be relatively scattered in some cases, all populations seem to

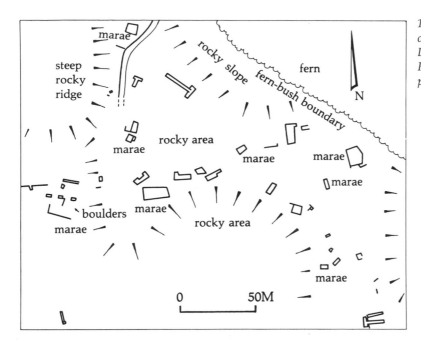

13.7 A scaled plan of the largest of the four site clusters in the Lower Maungaroa Valley on Rarotonga, with outlines of house pavements and marae.

have been able to fulfill their needs from their own territories without too much difficulty. The Polynesian chiefdoms probably developed prior to the settlement of Polynesia itself, and the prevalent dispersal of settlement relates more logically to a desire to live close to inherited plantation land. Such land, whether used for fruits or for tubers, for the most part was in fairly constant use and land rights would be strengthened by close residence. Given the small scale of the average Polynesian landscape, it is hard to see what advantages would have accrued from nucleated settlements, except in a few specialized cases involving defense or ceremonial activity.

Overall Settlement Patterns

All settlement patterns have specific and nonrecurring ecological correlations, since no two environments are absolutely identical. Nevertheless, it is apparent that populations tend to place their settlements in situations that give easiest access to all required resources. This means that settlements tend to be in environmental transi-

tion zones (or ecotones) and, in theory at least, such situations reduce to a minimum the amount of movement needed for combined subsistence activities. This may seem a gross oversimplification, but Polynesian settlements by and large do occur along ecotones.

Thus it appears that most early sites in each group, from Lapita times to the first settlements throughout East Polynesia, were located on coasts (which can be considered the basic ecotones between land and sea). Later sites were more complex, and increasing populations and increasing dependence on inland horticulture led to a much broader spread of settlement by the end of the first millennium B.C. in West Polynesia (especially Samoa and Uvea), and by A.D. 1200 in many parts of East Polynesia. It must be stressed again that Polynesian horticulture outside New Zealand was based on fairly permanent resources such as fruits (coconut and breadfruit, for instance) and irrigated taro, so that frequent shifting of settlements owing to slash-and-burn techniques was probably not necessary, except in Tonga and Samoa.

The general tendency toward ecotonal location may be illustrated from the southern Cook Islands (Bellwood 1971b). On Aitutaki, resources were zoned in an approximately concentric pattern with the best garden soils inland, surrounded by coastal sandy soils suitable only for coconut and pandanus, and then the lagoon. Settlements tended to be along the boundary between the inland garden soils and the coastal soils, rather than on the beachfront itself. On Rarotonga, the road around the island (mentioned earlier—see Fig. 13.1) occupied a similar ecotonal position with inland forests and valleys on one side, coastal taro plots and sand on the other. The island of Mangaia had a different distribution of settlement; resources there were not concentric, but bunched around localized swamps used to cultivate taro—the staple food of the inhabitants. Mangaian settlements were therefore concentrated around the swamps, although the ecotonal concept still applies. Even in the Maungaroa Valley on Rarotonga, settlements were clustered along the approximate boundary between cultivable soils and the forested rocky valley sides.

The individual Cook Islands are too small to be subject to major environmental or climatic differences from one side of an island to another. However, the much larger Hawaiian Islands have a more complex pattern of wet windward (eastern) sides and dry leeward sides, a pattern that results from island size and the prevailing direction of the trade winds. This circumstance means that large valleys on either side have different patterns of settlement and horticultural usage, particularly in the period after A.D. 1300 when increasing evidence appears for the construction of field boundaries and wet taro terraces.

The best example of a windward valley survey to date is that of the Halawa Valley on the eastern end of Molokai (Kirch and Kelly 1975; see Chapter 7). A small coastal habitation was established at the mouth of this valley by about A.D. 650. From here settlement spread inland after 1350 along the lower slopes at the valley side; the val-

ley floor itself may have been used for shifting cultivation, and stepped or staircase terraces for taro were constructed in tributary streambeds. Finally, after 1650, most of the valley floor was used for wet taro. The pattern of taro cultivation in the bed of the valley, with settlements along its sides and at its mouth, survived until European contact; it is in fact typical of many windward valleys in the group.

The leeward valleys developed a different pattern; the Makaha Valley on leeward Oahu (Green 1969, 1970b; Ladd and Yen 1972) was wet enough in its upper section for terraced cultivation of wet taro, but the lower part was much drier and only suitable for dry land cultivation on terraces and fields cleared of stones. Foundations of small shelters perhaps indicate seasonal settlement in this region, but most permanent settlements were located on the coast rather than in the valley itself. The differences between Halawa and Makaha are caused mainly by rainfall variation, although the Makaha Valley does not have the extensive flats in its bottom that Halawa does. This latter factor could also militate against the construction of extensive wet taro plots, regardless of water availability.

The Makaha leeward pattern is paralleled on the island of Hawaii, particularly on the northwestern coast where the land slopes gently up from the coast to an inner mountain range, without major valleys. (The lava flows here are so recent that they have not yet weathered into the ridge and valley formations present on the other islands of the group.) The Lapakahi pattern (Chapter 7) is characteristic of this dry region; settlements located along the coast, a dry barren belt of unutilized land running for 2 km or so inland, then dry fields with stone boundaries constructed in the higher zone where rainfall is sufficient for cultivation. The three Hawaiian examples just mentioned are, to my mind, the clearest examples in Polynesia of the close relationship between environment and overall settlement pattern.

The New Zealand case is naturally different in its specifics from all other parts of

Polynesia, although one can still make the same broad generalizations about ecotonal location and response to climatic factors—but more particularly to temperature rather than rainfall. During the Archaic phase, settlements appear for the most part to have been coastally oriented and seasonally occupied, based on an economy of hunting, gathering, and collecting, with restricted horticulture in the north. During the Classic phase, settlements in the South Island declined in numbers and emphasized even more a coastal orientation; the pattern may well reflect overexploitation of resources in this nonhorticultural region (Simmons 1973). The Classic phase in the North Island was characterized by increasing population and horticulture: thus developed the eighteenth-century pattern of large fortified villages (Fig. 13.8) in the warmer coastal and inland regions, together with a range of seasonally occupied middens and horticultural hamlets.

Some of the factors influencing location of individual sites in New Zealand have been examined intensively by Cassels (1972a and b) for a section of the Waikato, an inland region of the North Island. He points out that sites presumed to have been occupied year-round are widely spaced, about 3 to 6 km apart, but located within easy reach of many resources (lake edges were a favorite location). Sites presumed to have been occupied seasonally are more numerous, ecologically more specialized, and have fewer resources within easy reach. Using detailed soil and vegetation maps to support his reasoning, Cassels has been able to show, for instance, that some sites were located for sweet potato cultivation on a seasonal basis (from late spring to early autumn), and also that some sites are ecologically so specialized that they would not have been reasonably habitable unless European-introduced crops were present. The latter sites therefore may be presumed to postdate 1770. Cassels also suggests that the sites most advantageously placed are the earliest; if this view is correct, it could imply that Archaic sites were often occu-

pied on a more permanent (year-round) basis than hitherto realized.

The above examples drawn from all parts of Polynesia illustrate two rather important facts; settlements are not distributed at random in a landscape, and ecological factors operate in positive and identifiable ways to negate randomness. Social factors also operate within the ecological framework to determine individual settlement location in terms of clustering and dispersal, although it is complicated and perhaps pointless to try to separate the ecological from the social factors. A settlement pattern does of course represent elements in the social and political structures of any community, but in the case of Polynesia the difficulties connected with establishing contemporaneity of primary units render many hypotheses not only weak but circular. The sole period for which one can reasonably assume contemporaneity of use is that immediately prior to the abandonment, under European influence, of aboriginal settlements. Therefore, to close this chapter I shall give one excellent example wherein a late-eighteenth–early nineteenth-century settlement pattern has been related in a convincing way to ethnographic records about the structure of the society. The example comes from the Opunohu Valley on Moorea, in the Society Islands.

In this valley Green and his colleagues (1967) surveyed some 500 structures 2 to 3 km in from the coast; the coastal pattern itself was destroyed through modern developments. The structures included horticultural terraces, small rectangular dwelling houses and larger round-ended community houses, many marae, and some other specialized units such as archery platforms. The marae vary greatly in size and design and seem to reflect status levels within the society; that is, some were tribal structures, others merely household shrines. From ethnohistorical sources and the presence of two major clusters of sites, Green has suggested that at least two maximal ramages (high-order kinship groups) resided in the

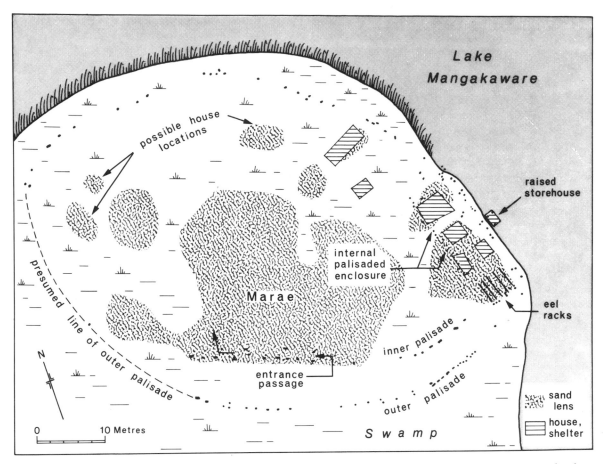

13.8 Plan of an excavated swamp fortification by Lake Mangakaware in the Waikato district, New Zealand. The plan shows the positions of defensive palisades, the line of houses along the lake edge, and the central open space (marae). (Drawn from excavations by the author.)

valley. The largest marae, which has a stepped ahu, is in the most densely settled area and was probably connected with the highest-ranking chiefly line. Eight marae of slightly smaller size, together with the round-ended houses, were perhaps connected with lesser ramage segments or individual powerful families, and finally there are 47 small marae that were perhaps used by individual extended families. It is not clear from the report whether the high-ranking structures are concentrated in one place or whether they are scattered evenly among the lesser units, but the general correlations between hierarchy of primary units based on size and complexity, and hierarchy within the society, are very con-

vincing. There have been other efforts to relate site hierarchy to social hierarchy, particularly by Cordy (1974) in his attempts to trace the genesis of the Hawaiian chiefdoms as recorded at contact.

Concluding Remarks

Polynesian settlement patterns have been examined at four levels: the primary settlement unit (or discrete structure), the combined settlement unit as recorded ethnographically, the variation in geographic spacing, and the overall pattern in relation to ecological and social factors. The most important archaeological surveys to date have taken place on high islands, mainly in

320

valley situations. Unfortunately the sample is rather biased, since the areas that had high-density prehistoric populations by and large are those that have undergone extensive development and site destruction today; this applies especially to the fertile coastal strips found on many islands. And some groups, such as the Tuamotuan atolls, Tonga, and most of the Societies, have received relatively little survey attention. Still, the broad generalizations that one can make about Polynesian settlement patterns are now fairly secure for the late prehistoric period, and the major difficulties will lie in recovery of the subsurface settlement patterns of the distant past.

References

Bellwood, P. S. 1971a. Fortifications and economy in prehistoric New Zealand. *Proceedings of the Prehistoric Society* 37:56–95.
———. 1971b. Varieties of ecological adaptation in the southern Cook Islands. *Archaeology and Physical Anthropology in Oceania* 6:145–169.
———. 1972. A settlement pattern survey, Hanatekua Valley, Hivaoa, Marquesas Islands. *Pacific Anthropological Records* 17.
———. 1978. Archaeological research in the Cook Islands. *Pacific Anthropological Records* 27.
Burrows, E. G. 1938. *Western Polynesia: a study of cultural differentiation.* Ethnologiska Studier no. 7, Gothenburg.
Cassels, R. J. S. 1972a. Locational analysis of prehistoric settlement in New Zealand. *Mankind* 8:212–122.
———. 1972b. Human ecology in the prehistoric Waikato. *Journal of the Polynesian Society* 81:196–247.
Cordy, R. H. 1974. Complex-rank cultural systems in the Hawaiian Islands: suggested explanations for their origins. *Archaeology and Physical Anthropology in Oceania* 9:89–109.
Crocombe, R. G. 1964. *Land tenure in the Cook Islands.* Melbourne: Oxford University Press.
Davidson, J. M. 1969a. Archaeological excavations in two burial mounds at 'Atele, Tongatapu. *Records of the Auckland Institute and Museum* 6:251–286.
———. 1969b. Settlement patterns in Samoa before 1840. *Journal of the Polynesian Society* 78:44–82.
———. 1974. Site surveys on Upolu. In *Archaeology in Western Samoa,* ed. R. C. Green and J. M. Davidson, vol. 2, pp. 181–204.
Emory, K. P. 1928. *Archaeology of Nihoa and Necker islands.* Bishop Museum Bulletin no. 53, Honolulu.
———. 1933. *Stone remains in the Society Islands.* Bishop Museum Bulletin no. 116, Honolulu.
———. 1970. A reexamination of East Polynesian marae: many marae later. In *Studies in Oceanic culture history,* ed. R. C. Green and Marion Kelly, vol. 1. *Pacific Anthropological Records* 11:73–92.
Ferdon, E. N., Jr. 1965. A summary of Rapa Iti fortified villages. In *Reports of the Norwegian archaeological expedition to Easter Island and the East Pacific,* ed. Thor Heyerdahl and E. N. Ferdon, Jr., vol. 2, pp. 69–76. Monographs of the School of American Research and the Kon-Tiki Museum no. 24, pt. 2.
Grange, L. I., and Fox, J. P. 1953. *Soils of the Lower Cook group.* Soil Bureau Bulletin no. 8. New Zealand Department of Scientific and Industrial Research, Wellington.
Green, R. C. 1969. Makaha Valley historical project: interim report no. 1. *Pacific Anthropological Records* 4.
———. 1970a. Settlement pattern archaeology in Polynesia. In *Studies in Oceanic culture history,* ed. R. C. Green and Marion Kelly, vol. 1. *Pacific Anthropological Records* 11:13–32.
———. 1970b. Makaha Valley historical project: interim report no. 2. *Pacific Anthropological Records* 10.
——— and J. M. Davidson, eds. 1969. *Archaeology in Western Samoa,* vol. 1. *Auckland Institute and Museum Bulletin* 6.
——— and J. M. Davidson, eds. 1974. *Archaeology in Western Samoa,* vol. 2. *Auckland Institute and Museum Bulletin* 7.
———, K. Green, R. A. Rappaport, Ann Rappaport, and J. M. Davidson. 1967. *Archaeology on the island of Mo'orea, French Polynesia.* Anthropological Paper no. 51, pt. 2, American Museum of Natural History, New York.
Jennings, J. D. 1976. University of Utah Samoan archeological program, 1976. Preliminary report.
Kellum-Ottino, Marimari. 1971. *Archéologie d'une vallée des îles marquises: évolution des structures de l'habitat à Hane, Ua Huka.* Publication de la Société des Océanistes no. 26. Paris.
Kikuchi, W. K. 1976. Prehistoric Hawaiian fishponds. *Science* 193:295–299.

Kirch, P. V. 1976. Ethno-archaeological investigations in Futuna and Uvea (western Polynesia): a preliminary report. *Journal of the Polynesian Society* 85:27–69.

Kirch, P. V., and Marion Kelly, eds. 1975. Prehistory and ecology in a windward Hawaiian valley: Halawa Valley, Molokai. *Pacific Anthropological Records* 24.

Ladd, E. J., and D. E. Yen. 1972. Makaha Valley historical project: interim report no. 3. *Pacific Anthropological Records* 18.

McKern, W. C. 1929. *Archaeology of Tonga*. Bishop Museum Bulletin no. 60, Honolulu.

Mariner, W. 1817. *An account of the natives of the Tonga Islands*. London: Constable.

Mulloy, William. 1975. *Investigation and restoration of the ceremonial center of Orongo, Easter Island*. Bulletin 4, Easter Island Committee.

New York: International Fund for Monuments.

Sahlins, M. D. 1958. *Social stratification in Polynesia*. Seattle: University of Washington Press.

Scott, S. D. 1969. Reconnaissance and some detailed site plans of major monuments of Savai'i. In *Archaeology in Western Samoa*, ed. R. C. Green and J. M. Davidson, vol. 1, pp. 69–90.

Simmons, D. R. 1973. Suggested periods in South Island prehistory. *Records of the Auckland Institute and Museum* 10:1–58.

Thomson, W. J. 1889. *Te Pito te Henua, or Easter Island*. U.S. National Museum Annual Report for 1889, pp. 447–552.

Verin, Pierre. 1969. *L'ancienne Civilisation de Rurutu*. Office des Recherches Scientifiques et Techniques Outre-Mer, Memoir no. 33, Paris.

Voyaging

CHAPTER 14

BEN R. FINNEY

 How were the many and far-flung islands of Polynesia discovered and settled? How could a Stone Age people, without ships or navigation instruments, have crossed much of the world's greatest ocean to colonize these islands? Such questions have intrigued us ever since explorers from another ocean first chanced on Polynesia. This chapter attempts to answer them by focusing on recent experimental research on Polynesian canoes and navigation, particularly on the 1976 voyage of the *Hōkūle'a* from Hawaii to Tahiti and back. Yet previous efforts to answer these questions cannot be ignored. The subject of Polynesian discovery and settlement is one that has filled the pages of many a book and journal. We need to begin our journey into the problem by examining how previous theories have shaped recent efforts to learn how Polynesian canoes sailed and how the ancient navigation system worked.

Some early theorists proposed an American origin of the Polynesians, and a few thought them to be autochthonous survivors, on mountaintops turned islands, of a sunken continent. But by the late 1800s most writers looked to the west, to Indonesia and the Asian continent beyond, for the Polynesian homeland. Among those who developed grandiose migration theories during this era two writers stand out: Abraham Fornander of Hawaii and S. Percy Smith of New Zealand.

Fornander and Smith were amateur scholars, fluent in Polynesian languages and conversant with Polynesian oral narratives. They focused particularly on the voyaging epics and based their schemes in large part on their often fanciful interpretations of these heroic stories. Both men also held a high opinion of Polynesian canoes and navigation techniques. Indeed, necessary to their schemes were the assumptions that Polynesians were near superhuman navigators and had a highly developed voyaging technology that enabled them to sail directly from Asia into the Pacific. But neither Fornander nor Smith were students of naval architecture or navigation, and they were vague about details of the voyaging craft and navigation techniques used in the postulated migrations. For example, Fornander devotes scarcely three pages to the subject in his massive three-volume work, *An Account of the Polynesian Race, Its Origins and Migration.*

The uncritical interpretation by these two authors of the voyaging epics, plus their undocumented assumptions concerning Polynesian canoes and navigation techniques, led to a romantic vision of Polynesian voyaging and migration that was to dominate thinking until the last few decades. For example, in 1923 Elsdon Best, a New Zealand colleague of Smith, wrote a monograph on Polynesian voyaging marked more by an adulation of voyagers who "traversed the vast expanse of the Pacific as western peoples explored a lake" than by an analysis of how they might have done it. Best accepted the Fornander-Smith reconstructions of legendary voyages and even went so far as to draft a map showing legendary voyaging routes, including one to the iceberg-filled seas of Antarctica.

In the 1930s two important books relating to Polynesian migration were published. In *Canoes of Oceania* A. C. Haddon and James Hornell surveyed canoe design and construction throughout the Pacific in order to trace the migration of Polynesian and other Pacific peoples. But again they did not address the sailing and navigational questions crucial to those migrations. In 1938 Sir

Peter Buck published *Vikings of the Sunrise,* a glowing description of Polynesian voyaging, settlement, and cultural development. Like previous scholars he looked to India as the ultimate Polynesian homeland. His description of events within Polynesia was phrased differently, however. Buck's mother was Polynesian, and Maori was his first language. He therefore could write with pride about the voyaging ability of his ancestors, who "conquered the Pacific with stone-age vessels that swept ever towards the sunrise." Like his predecessors, he neglected to explain how these vessels sailed or how their navigators guided them.

By midcentury, then, an orthodoxy had been firmly established. Polynesians came from the west—from Asia—and island-hopped their way into the Pacific, where they found and settled the islands now known as Polynesia. They were able to undertake this migration because they had large, seaworthy, and swift sailing canoes; because they were great navigators; and because they had a tremendous drive to explore. Although it was admitted that some discoveries might have been made accidentally when canoes were blown off course, it was thought that voyages of exploration and colonization were the primary means by which Polynesia was settled.

This orthodoxy was challenged by Thor Heyerdahl with his 1947 raft voyage from South America to Polynesia, followed by his massive book *American Indians in the Pacific* and other writings, and also by the New Zealand historian Andrew Sharp, who in 1956 published *Ancient Voyagers in the Pacific,* in which he attacked what he considered to be the modern mythology of Polynesian migrations. Both writers were critical of long cherished but largely unsupported assumptions concerning Polynesian voyaging. Heyerdahl maintained that canoes could not have sailed across the Pacific from west to east against easterly tradewinds and currents, and that settlement must therefore have come from the Americas by seafarers drifting and sailing from east to west before wind and current.

BEN R. FINNEY

Sharp, though agreeing with the accepted direction of Polynesian migration, claimed that settlement had been accomplished by accident, not design—by random drift and exile voyages. Settlement by drift came about when a canoe was blown off course during a coastal or short interisland trip and, after drifting before wind and current, fetched up on some uninhabited shore. Settlement by exile occurred when a group was driven from its island and, after randomly wandering over the sea, chanced upon another island. Sharp ridiculed the notion of planned expeditions setting out in search of new lands, and he categorically denied that settlement of distant islands could have come about through a deliberate process involving exploratory probes, return voyages to the homeland, and the mounting of fully equipped expeditions to the newfound lands.

Heyerdahl's theory of the American origin of the Polynesians attracted a large public following, but little support among scholars. In contrast, Sharp's debunking of the romantic image of Polynesian voyaging had little public appeal, yet was warmly received among some anthropologists and historians. His arguments were particularly welcomed by a new generation of scholars who had been taught to be wary of using legends to trace history. To them the reconstructions of Polynesian migrations worked out by Fornander, Smith, Best, and Buck were examples of the worst type of "conjectural history."

For example, those studying New Zealand prehistory were most appreciative of Sharp's denunciation of the historical value of legends. Smith in 1910 had developed a detailed settlement history from Maori legends that started with the discovery of New Zealand in A.D. 925 by a Tahitian chief and culminated with the arrival of the "Great Fleet" in A.D. 1350. Sharp's critique of this sequence appealed to young archaeologists fresh out of England, who were relieved to be able to work out archaeologically based sequences without having to make them congruent with fixed dates of discovery and settlement (Golson and Gathercole 1962).

While Sharp's critique of romantic interpretations of Polynesian voyaging epics was widely appreciated, a number of Pacific scholars who had an appreciation of the sea and of sailing objected to Sharp's dismissal of the possibility of deliberate long-distance voyaging. Sharp's case rested ultimately on a negative assessment of Polynesian voyaging technology. Deliberate colonization efforts, particularly those involving two-way voyaging, would have required seaworthy canoes, capable of sailing to windward as well as before the wind, and an accurate navigation system. To Sharp, Polynesian canoes were frail craft, unsuited for windward sailing and therefore unequal to the task. Similarly, since their navigation system was not as accurate as that used by modern navigators, Sharp judged that the early Polynesians could not have guided their canoes to distant landfalls. He was willing to acknowledge that Polynesians could intentionally sail between islands up to 550 km apart. Beyond that he believed that limitations of craft and navigation technique made intentional voyaging impossible.

The ensuing debate between Sharp and those who objected to this negative assessment foundered for want of data. The crucial information was simply not available. Legends are vague on technical details, and the growing archaeological record was largely mute on the nature of voyaging. Accounts of canoes and navigation found in the journals of early Western visitors contained much useful information, but usually the observations were neither precise enough nor systematic enough to prove a point definitively. (In fact, with judicious selection from early accounts it was possible to support either side of the debate.) And one could not go out and measure canoe performance or check on the accuracy of an indigenous navigator. The great voyaging canoes and the master navigators had disappeared from Polynesian waters—victims of modernization.

By the mid-1960s several researchers

began to experiment with new ways of approaching the problem. In 1965 David Lewis sailed his catamaran from Tahiti to New Zealand to test the utility of the Polynesian navigation system. While he was sailing in the South Pacific, in California I was building a replica of a traditional Hawaiian double canoe. The next year, in Hawaii, I used the canoe for a series of paddling and sailing experiments that provided the first good indication of double-canoe performance. At about this time R. Gerald Ward and his colleagues in England were starting a massive computer simulation study of Polynesian settlement that was to show the limitations of Sharp's drift-voyaging hypothesis. In 1968–1969 Lewis went to sea again to sail with canoe navigators from islands in Micronesia and Melanesia, where traditional navigation systems survive. Soon thereafter he combined information gained from these experiences with an analysis of the literature to develop a comprehensive picture of indigenous navigation systems.

As all this work was published, a clearer perspective on Polynesia began to emerge (Finney 1967; Lewis 1972; Levison et al. 1973). A group of us in Hawaii felt, however, that the topic could be further clarified by reconstructing an ancient voyaging canoe and then sailing it from Hawaii to Tahiti and back by means of traditional sailing and navigation methods. In 1973 C. Thomas Holmes, Herbert Kawainui Kane, and I formed the Polynesian Voyaging Society to sponsor the effort. We built the canoe *Hōkūle'a* in 1974–1975 and sailed it to Tahiti and back to Hawaii in 1976.

The following pages outline what has been recently learned about Polynesian canoes and navigation, including the results of the *Hōkūle'a* voyage, and apply the insights gained to the general problem of Polynesian settlement.

Canoes

Ancient Polynesians ventured to sea in both outrigger canoes and double canoes.

Virtually all authorities agree, however, that the Polynesians preferred double canoes for long-range voyaging, particularly migratory voyaging, because of their greater stability and carrying capacity. Furthermore, the broad central platform between the hulls of a double canoe provides a relatively large and dry area to shelter people, plants and animals, and food supplies.

At the time of European contact Polynesians sailed two distinctly different types of double canoes called tacking and shunting canoes, from the way in which they sailed to windward. All vessels move to windward by sailing obliquely, first on one side of the wind, then the other, and so on until the destination is reached. The tacking canoe, like Western sailing vessels, was brought from one side of the wind to the other by swinging the bow across the wind until the sails filled and the canoe could sail off in a new direction. The other type of canoe was shunted, to use Edwin Doran's phrase, from one side of the wind to the other by a unique maneuver in which the sail was shifted from one end of the canoe to the other so that the stern became the bow.

Design followed function. Whereas the hulls of a shunting canoe were equal ended so that either end could serve alternately as bow or stern, those of a tacking canoe had fixed, differently shaped, bows and sterns. And where the hulls of a shunting canoe were unequal in size (the hull always kept to windward being much smaller than the main hull), those of a tacking canoe were roughly of the same size. Finally, whereas shunting canoes were rigged with the Oceanic lateen sail (a full, triangular sail lashed to two yards and rigged with the apex at the bow, well forward of the mast), tacking canoes used the Oceanic sprit sail (a narrow, triangular sail lashed directly to the mast with the apex downward).

The tacking canoe is found throughout Polynesia. The shunting canoe has a more restricted distribution; at the time of European contact it was spreading from Fiji (where the shunting technique had been

14.1 *The* Nālehia, *a 12.9-m reconstruction of a Hawaiian double canoe, under sail off Kualoa, Oahu. (Photo by Inocencio Lapenia, Jr. Reproduced from Finney 1977. Copyright 1977 by the American Association for the Advancement of Science.)*

borrowed from the Micronesians and adapted to double canoes) to Tonga and Samoa, and apparently was influencing canoe design as far east as the Tuamotus. The tacking canoe is therefore almost certainly the type of vessel that carried the first colonists into Polynesia, and hence is our primary interest.

Figures 14.1 and 14.2 show the Hawaiian double canoe I built in 1966, a good example of a tacking type. The *Nālehia*, which literally means "the skilled ones" (referring to the two hulls) is a near replica of a craft once owned by King Kamehameha III of Hawaii. (Because of construction constraints it had to be built to a scale five-

sixths of the original, and with some slightly different proportions.) It is 12.9 m long, has an overall beam of 2.3 m, and displaces some 2,300 kg when fully loaded. It has a single Hawaiian "crab-claw" sail, lashed apex downward to a mast stepped well forward on the central platform. *Nālehia* is a relatively light displacement craft, adapted for coastal and interisland sailing around Hawaii, where strong winds, rough seas, and high surf prevail. Its low freeboard and the wide gaps between the narrow central platform and the hulls facilitate paddling. Its sleek, rugged design and rounded hulls make for easy handling at sea and in the surf.

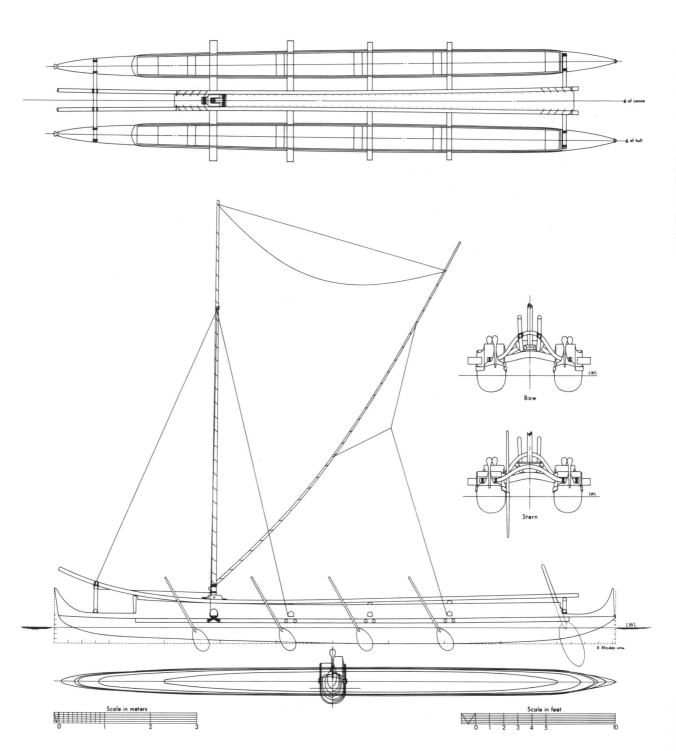

14.2 *Sail and deck plans, end views, and lines of the* Nālehia. *End views omit third through fifth crosspieces.* (*Reproduced from Finney 1977. Copyright 1977 by the American Association for the Advancement of Science.*)

The *Nālehia* is not a long-range voyaging canoe. For the projected round trip between Hawaii and Tahiti we needed a larger craft adapted to deep-sea voyaging. Although there are reports of Polynesian voyaging canoes of up to 37 m in length, we settled for building a medium-sized craft. The design posed a major problem. Our goal was to build a canoe that would represent, as closely as is presently possible, the sort of voyaging canoe used some 800 years ago, the period that legends indicate was marked by long voyages. Yet our earliest plans and drawings date after European contact, by which time canoes from the various islands reflected considerable local development and adaptation. Instead, then, of trying to copy a known canoe type from one island, we analyzed canoes from throughout Polynesia in an attempt to factor out features common to most of them and hence likely to be derived from earlier designs. In so doing we paid particular attention to the best available examples of voyaging canoes, those from Tahiti, Tonga, and the Tuamotus. We cannot, of course, claim that the resultant design exactly duplicates that of ancient Polynesian voyaging canoes. Nonetheless, I should like to stress that, despite numerous suggestions that we "improve" our design by adding sharp keel fins, modern yacht sails, or other innovations, we adhered to a basic principle: all major design features must be based on documented traditional Polynesian design features.

The lines of our canoe, christened *Hōkūle'a* after the Hawaiian name for the star Arcturus, are shown in Fig. 14.3. It is 19 m long, has an overall beam of 5.6 m, and displaces about 11,400 kg when fully loaded. The hull design sets it off from Hawaiian and other types of canoes adapted for coastal use. In cross section the hulls are semi–V-shaped, patterned largely after the deep-sea–adapted *pahi* of Tahiti and *tongiaki* of Tonga. The wedge-shaped bottom gives the canoe some tracking ability and resistance to leeway, and the bulging sides give it considerable carrying capacity—a

combination that seems ideal for a craft required to carry heavy loads over long distances and over routes where the winds may not always be favorable. In contrast to *Nālehia*, *Hōkūle'a* is primarily a sailing canoe. The high freeboard, the lack of space between hulls and central platform, and its weight make paddling difficult.

Hawaiian and other coastal-adapted canoes typically were made from hollowed-out logs to which one or more planks were added to raise the freeboard. For lack of traditional materials and skills *Nālehia*'s hulls were built of modern materials: a fiberglass shell taken from a mold of the hull of a Hawaiian outrigger canoe, with planks added to raise the sides. Voyaging canoes were essentially plank-built craft; a number of planks were fitted edge to edge and sewn together with coconut-fiber line to build the tall, narrow hulls. Again, because we lacked the traditional materials and skills, we turned to modern materials to build *Hōkūle'a*. The hulls were made of cold-molded plywood, covered with a layer of fiberglass and resin, to which was added a single level of side planking. The hulls of both canoes were joined with heavy wooden crosspieces and lashings of synthetic line (in lieu of coconut-fiber sennit, which was not available in the quality and quantity we needed). Despite this use of modern materials, we strove to duplicate the shape and weight of traditional canoes as closely as possible, so that the sailing characteristics of *Nālehia* and *Hōkūle'a* would approximate those of traditional craft.

The chief designer of the *Hōkūle'a* was the Hawaiian artist Herbert Kawainui Kane. For some features of the design, notably the curved form of the crosspieces linking the hulls and the high, curved shape of the bow and stern cutwaters, he followed Hawaiian precedents. In part this was an expression of his Hawaiian bias. But these features also made sense, given the fact that *Hōkūle'a* would be sailed extensively in Hawaiian waters where the winds and seas are generally stronger than

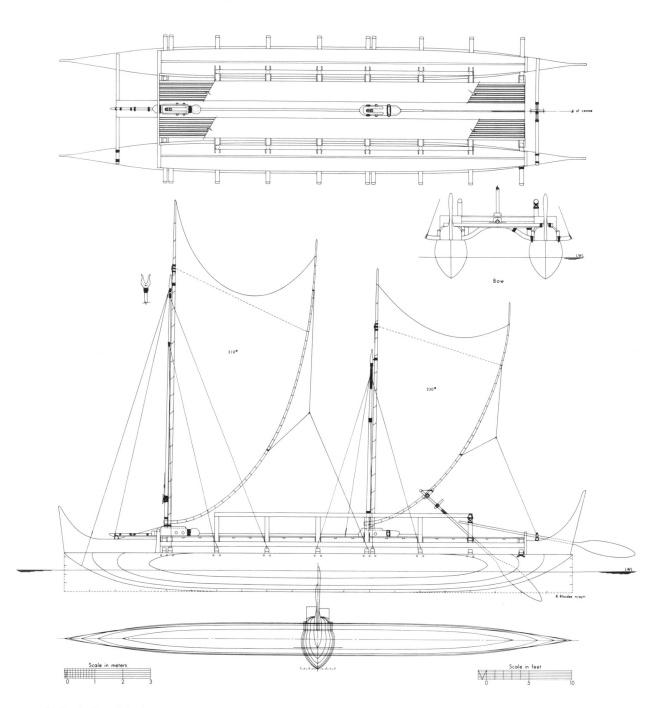

Bow

Scale in meters

0 1 2 3

Scale in feet

0 5 10

14.3 Sail and deck plans, end views, and lines of the Hōkūle'a. Sleeping shelters, animal cages, and stern rails are not shown. (Reproduced from Finney 1977. Copyright 1977 by the American Association for the Advancement of Science.)

BEN R. FINNEY

elsewhere in tropical Polynesia. Curved crosspieces are stronger than straight ones and also serve to elevate the central deck a bit above the swells. The high cutwaters have the all-important function of splitting oncoming or following seas, to keep them from deluging the hulls. The *Hōkūle'a*'s two sails also follow Hawaiian models, in this case the Hawaiian crab-claw sail that is so well adapted to the strong tradewinds of Hawaii. David Lewis has argued that the crab-claw sail had a marginal distribution in Polynesia and Micronesia and is therefore a likely candidate for the sail used by early Polynesian voyagers.

Sailing trials with *Nālehia* and *Hōkūle'a* have convinced us that double canoes are sea-kindly craft. Their slim hulls cut through rough seas with little pitching, and the twin-hulled configuration makes for a stable vessel that hardly rolls. Double canoes are, however, vulnerable to breaking apart and swamping. Each hull tries to work independently, which in heavy seas results in tremendous stresses on the crosspieces and lashings. While both our canoes held up well, another large double canoe of quasi-Polynesian design was lost at sea when its weakened crosspieces snapped in a storm. A month before that occurred, *Hōkūle'a* was almost lost when one hull swamped while crossing the channel between Kauai and Oahu. This sobering experience served to remind us how difficult it is to bail a double canoe at sea: as one hull is emptied of water, its buoyancy submerges the other one further, so that bailing is next to impossible.

Polynesian double canoes sail much like conventional boats, but steer differently. Most boats are steered with a rudder, which is turned right or left to deflect the water so as to turn the bow to one side or the other. Double canoes are steered primarily by paddles, which are raised or lowered to alter the relationship between the center of lateral resistance of the hulls and the center of effort of the sails. By lowering a paddle at the stern, the effective draft aft is increased and the vessel turns

away from the wind; when the paddle is raised, the canoe turns into the wind. Like most vessels, both *Nālehia* and *Hōkūle'a* have a tendency to head into the wind. Sailing to windward then is mostly a matter of adjusting the depth of the steering paddle to compensate for this "weather helm." In addition, by shifting weight aft and trimming the sails, weather helm can be completely counteracted until the canoe will hold a windward course without a steering paddle in the water. Sailing downwind, however, is much more difficult and sometimes requires the undivided attention of a pair of steersmen.

Double canoes sail well running before the wind, but sail fastest on a beam reach (roughly at right angles to the wind). *Hōkūle'a* can make up to about 18.5 km/hr on a beam reach in strong winds, and *Nālehia* about 16 km/hr. These speeds are modest compared to modern racing catamarans. The difference is primarily a function of hull spacing. Whereas the strength limitations of wooden crosspieces and coconut fiber lashings required that the hulls of traditional craft be closely spaced, modern materials and construction techniques allow the hulls of contemporary catamarans to be relatively widely spaced. The traditional configuration reduces speed potential because close spacing between hulls increases wave interference and hence drag, and severely limits the amount of sail that can be carried without danger of capsize.* *Nālehia* and *Hōkūle'a*, for example, carry only 19.5 and 50.2 m² of sail, respectively. Modern catamarans of equal length can carry two to

* The vulnerability of double canoes to capsizing was brought home by the 1978 attempt to sail *Hōkūle'a* to Tahiti. Under new leadership an overconfident but unprepared crew left Honolulu at dusk and despite gale warnings. Four hours later, while driving hard against gale-force winds and heavy channel seas, they allowed the leeward hull to swamp. Before the sails could be cut down, the unbalanced canoe capsized. One man was lost when he tried to paddle a surfboard to the nearest island. The remaining crew members and the canoe might also have been lost had not a passing aircraft spotted them the following day, just as the canoe was drifting out of air and ship lanes.

three times that much in their regular mainsail-jib combination—and much more when a genoa jib or spinnaker is raised.

The central question about the performance of the double canoe is how well it sails to windward. This is crucial when considering the settlement of Polynesia, for the linguistic and archaeological evidence indicates that it was primarily a west-to-east movement in the face of easterly tradewinds and currents. Early observers debated the capacity of Polynesian craft sailing west to east against the tradewinds, and more recent critics like Sharp have flatly denied that Polynesians could have made long windward crossings. How, they ask, could a craft without a deep keel, centerboards, or leeboards resist the tendency to make leeway (move sideways) when pointed to windward? Furthermore, how could the curious "upside-down" sail produce sufficient lift to drive a canoe against the wind? We had our answer one summer day in 1966 when we first raised sail on *Nālehia*. A stiff breeze caught us, and we went sailing downwind out of control because the mast was not properly stayed. Once we had tightened the shrouds, we found ourselves swept a half-mile downwind from our starting point. To our delight, we were able slowly but surely to tack *Nālehia* back against wind and current to where we started.

On the basis of sailing trials later that year, I estimated that a double canoe could "make good" a wind course of 75 degrees. In other words, a double canoe could sail, subtracting leeway from heading, to within 75 degrees of the true wind (not the apparent wind observed from the moving vessel). In 1974, following the technique Doran (1976) had successfully applied to measure outrigger canoe performance, we used a set of instruments to measure the *Nālehia*'s performance and were able to confirm and refine the earlier estimate.

Unfortunately, we could not complete the measurement of *Hōkūle'a*'s performance before she sailed for Tahiti. To judge from incomplete data, *Hōkūle'a* performs similarly to *Nālehia* except that she sails slightly faster, as one would expect of a longer craft, and she points slightly higher into the wind, as one would expect of a semi–V-shaped hull. In tradewinds of 28 to 37 km/hr, for example, *Hōkūle'a* could make good up to about 70 degrees off the wind and still keep sailing 11 km/hr or so. At this point she was sailing "full and by," meaning as close to the wind as possible without forcing her beyond the point where her speed would begin to fall off greatly. She could be pinched closer to the wind, but not without significant loss of speed and a great increase in leeway.

Navigation

Polynesians could not undertake navigated voyages between distant islands, said Sharp and other critics. Their reasoning rested in large part on an ethnocentric logic. Modern sailors can navigate to far-away points because they use instruments —compass, sextant, and chronometer—that enable them to plot their course and position by means of bearings and latitude-longitude coordinates drawn on a map. Polynesians had no instruments or maps. Therefore they could not navigate between distant islands.

We must reject this specious reasoning and examine how the Polynesian navigation system actually worked before making a judgment about its utility and range. All navigators share three basic tasks: (1) to set a course in the direction of their destination; (2) to keep track of their progress en route and make whatever course adjustments are necessary; and (3) to locate and safely reach their destination. The purpose here is to examine briefly how the Polynesian navigator carried out these tasks.

When *Hōkūle'a* arrived in Tahiti after its long journey, we were accused of having used a concealed compass. "We had no need of a compass; we had the stars," replied Rodo Williams, the Tahitian who served as assistant navigator. Stars are the Polynesian navigator's best directional guide for course setting and steering. Stars rise and set at the same points on the eastern and western horizons, although they do so four minutes earlier each night. While they are low on the horizon just after rising and just before setting, they offer directional points like those on a compass. The navigator of long ago steered toward the horizon star that bore in the same direction as his island destination. More accurately, he steered toward the succession of stars that rose out of, or set into, the same "pit," to translate the Polynesian term. He had to use a succession of stars with the same or similar bearings, as any one star is only on the horizon a short time. The navigator thus had to know many stars, their bearings, and the bearings of various islands from one another in order to be able to steer interisland courses.

But the navigator could not rely solely on tunnel-vision observations of a succession of horizon stars. He also had to sail by the "shape of the sky," constantly tracking his course in relation to the bearings of major stars and of the moon to the right or left of his course. When clouds obscured his horizon stars, as frequently happens in tradewind skies, he could switch over to other stars or the moon to keep his course. The navigator also kept track of his course in relation to the dominant swell and the prevailing wind, and had to be prepared to steer by these when heavy cloud cover obscured stars and moon. A practiced navigator could steer by the feel of the long swells. He could also steer by the direction of the prevailing wind, although he had to be alert for wind shifts lest he stray off course by following a wind that had altered direction. The Polynesian navigator was well aware of seasonal variations in the winds, and of the wind changes that accompany passing fronts and storms. We have a number of examples from around Polynesia of elaborate conceptualizations of the bearing of the major winds that amount to detailed wind compasses.

The swells and the wind were also used in steering during the day, as was the sun. Although the Polynesian navigator was well aware of the daily change in the sun's bearing, he did not have to memorize these bearings, as critics have suggested. He had two opportunities, at dawn and at dusk, to compare the sun's bearing with that of his navigation stars.

How did the Polynesian navigator keep his canoe on course? If, upon leaving Hawaii, we had pointed *Hōkūle'a* straight for Tahiti and sailed on that same course setting until we reached Tahiti's latitude, we would have ended up 1,000 km or so west of our target, because the easterly tradewinds and equatorial currents would have pushed *Hōkūle'a* sideways as it moved south. Any navigator must estimate the amount of leeway his vessel makes and the set of the current, then adjust his course accordingly. Estimating leeway is not difficult; the angle made by the wake and an imaginary line sighted down the longitudinal axis of a vessel yields a fairly accurate estimate except in rough seas. Judging the strength and direction of the current is more difficult, however.

Some skeptics maintain that the Polynesian navigator could not have known how far and in what direction his canoe was sent by a current, and that after many days of sailing across a strong current his error would compound and he would be hopelessly lost. But currents were well known to Polynesians. The equatorial current that sweeps west past most Polynesian islands is a fact of life, knowledge of which was essential to coastal fishermen as well as to interisland voyagers. Through experience the Polynesian navigator could discern variation in the current and correct his star course accordingly. He may even have been able to estimate the direction and speed of a current in strange waters by closely observing the interaction between the wind and the surface of the sea. For example, in a flat calm a strong current creates a relative wind that ripples the surface of the water in a way island navigators easily recognize.

How did the Polynesian navigator conceptualize his progress toward his destination? Our knowledge here is poor. The

Caroline Islanders of Micronesia, still vigorous practitioners of traditional navigation, have an ingenious way keeping track of their progress that has been documented by Gladwin (1970). The course is divided into segments marked by successive star bearings of a reference or *etak* island to one side of the course; the navigator mentally calculates when the canoe passes from one segment to the other. This method requires the ability to judge distance covered as well as course made good. Although we have no evidence that the Polynesians used a reference island system like the Carolinians, it does seem that they had a system of dead reckoning, a technique for mentally plotting their progress in terms of course and distance. The Tahitian navigator Tupaia was able to indicate to Captain Cook the location of islands surrounding Tahiti by referring to their bearings from Tahiti and the number of sailing days it would take to reach them. From Tupaia and his own observations, Cook estimated that a Tahitian double canoe could make 222 km or more a day. This is probably a fairly good estimate for an average day's run when sailing on a reach in fair weather, although certainly Polynesian sailors adjusted their estimates according to wind, weather, and current.

Virtually all authorities agree that the Polynesians had no way of astronomically determining their longitude. However, there is some evidence that they may have estimated their latitude by observing the height of Polaris (in the Northern Hemisphere only) above the horizon and the passage of what have become known as "zenith stars."

Finally comes the last test of the navigator's skill: making a landfall. How, critics have asked, could a navigator find a distant island in the immensity of the Pacific when he could not fix his position en route or make the exact course changes necessary to keep him on target? This phrasing obscures the nature of the problem. First, we need not assume, as critics are wont to do, that the inevitable errors in steering and in judging leeway and current accumulate in

one direction so that the farther a canoe travels the farther it will be off course. A steering error of one degree each day does not necessarily mean that a canoe will be 30 degrees off course after 30 days. Unless a navigator is clearly incompetent, his errors are more likely to be randomly distributed, occurring on both sides of the intended course. They would therefore tend to cancel one another, which means that it is not inevitable that a canoe drift farther and farther off course as a trip lengthens. Second, very few Polynesian islands are "lost" in the Pacific. Most of them occur in groups, great chains that stretch for hundreds of kilometers. The initial target of the early navigator thus was the island group, not the individual island. Once any island within the group had been sighted and identified, the navigator could then sail the canoe up or down the chain until his specific island destination was reached.

Despite the large size of many Polynesian archipelagoes, the navigator's task was far from easy. If one relies solely on the visual sighting of an island, it is possible to sail right through an island chain, passing between islands too far separated for ready detection. To forestall such an occurrence, Polynesian navigators used a number of techniques that expanded their radius of detection of an island. They looked for the appearance of land-based birds, which seldom fly more than 75 km or so on their fishing expeditions before returning to their island home at night. They looked for interruptions in the swell pattern, which indicate that a nearby island was blocking the swells or reflecting them back. Floating debris is another sign of land, as are cloud formations. The lagoon of an atoll is sometimes reflected in the clouds, giving the navigator a chance to "see" a low island before the tops of coconut palms rise above the horizon. And where tradewind clouds pile up into a stationary mass, the navigator can with reason suspect that the peaks of a high island are responsible. A successful reading of these signs by the early Polynesian navigator led to a landfall and, perhaps after some island hopping, to a safe arrival at the intended destination.

The Voyage of *Hōkūle'a* to Tahiti

Recent archaeological research indicates that Hawaii was settled by at least A.D. 500, with the Marquesas the most likely source for initial settlement. Except for some late-nineteenth-century fabrications, Hawaiian traditions say little about first settlement. But a number of legends do celebrate the arrival of Tahitian chiefs around A.D. 1100 to 1300, according to estimates based on genealogies. These Tahitians supposedly initiated a brief period of two-way voyaging between Hawaii and Tahiti, after which there is no indication of outside contact until Cook's arrival in 1778.

Our idea was to recreate one of these legendary round-trip voyages. Hawaii and Tahiti are the most widely separated islands in Polynesia for which two-way contact has been claimed. A rhumb-line course between the two is over 4,000 km long. Because of the need to work against winds and currents we estimated that a round trip might take us over some 10,000 km of open ocean. We therefore felt that a successful voyage over this route would go far toward demonstrating that Polynesians could have undertaken two-way voyages between distant islands.

The direction of the prevailing winds and currents in relation to the course is crucial to any sailing voyage. In most of Polynesia easterly tradewinds and currents prevail. If Hawaii and Tahiti were aligned exactly on a north-south axis and the wind blew at right angles to that axis, voyages between the two would be easy. All a vessel would have to do is sail into the wind just enough to overcome leeway and current set. But Tahiti lies significantly to the east of Hawaii, and the tradewinds blow from the northeast above the equator and from the southeast below the equator. Cape Kumukahi, the easternmost point of the island of Hawaii, is at 154°48′ west longitude, while the western coast of Tahiti is 149°37′ west

longitude. A canoe leaving Hawaii must, after clearing Cape Kumukahi, sail at least 576 km to the east against wind and current to reach Tahiti, a task that even worries contemporary yachtsmen with their more weatherly craft. The Hawaii-Tahiti leg of the voyage thus presents a challenge to the windward ability of a double canoe and is the one on which we concentrated our research efforts.

In 1967 I had proposed that this voyage was feasible and hypothesized that if a canoe could consistently make good 75 degrees off the wind it would sail a boomerang-shaped course (curving through the three main wind and current zones) that would bring it to Tahiti with perhaps a few miles to spare. From Hawaii the canoe would sail southeast against the northeast tradewinds and north equatorial current until about 9° north latitude when it would encounter the doldrums, a region of calms and light variable winds at the convergence zone between the northeast and southeast tradewinds. From there southward progress would slow, but the canoe would be pushed farther east by the counterequatorial current—the strong but irregular eastward-flowing current that returns some of the water piled up to the west by the equatorial currents of the Northern and Southern Hemisphere tradewind zones. Upon leaving the doldrums, the canoe would be forced by southeast tradewinds and the south equatorial current onto a course slightly west of south. I argued that if enough easting (progress to the east) could be gained in the northeast tradewinds and the doldrums, and if loss of easting could be held down in the southeast tradewinds, a canoe would make a landfall somewhere in the Tuamotu chain to the northeast of Tahiti. From there it could be sailed with a favorable wind to Tahiti.

Elia Kawika Kapahulehua, a veteran Hawaiian catamaran sailor, captained the *Hōkūle'a*. As we could not find a Polynesian who retained traditional navigational skills, we looked to the Caroline Islands of Mi-

cronesia, where we were fortunate in re-
cruiting Pius Mau Piailug, a master navigator from Satawal Atoll. He was assisted on
our voyage by Rodo Williams, a Tahitian
with many years' experience fishing and
trading in the Tuamotu Islands, and navi-
gator-researcher David Lewis. They helped
Piailug adapt his skills to the eastern Polynesian waters, a region entirely new to
him. First mate David Lyman, a part-Ha-
waiian who is a licensed master, ten others
of us, and two photographers were the remaining members of the total complement
of seventeen.

The primary navigation techniques Piailug used—steering by the stars, sun, and
moon as well as by the wind and swells,
and locating land through observation of
land birds and other cues—were essentially
the same as those a traditional Polynesian
navigator would have used. In addition,
Piailug attempted to apply the Carolinian
etak system of plotting by using the Marshall Islands on the first half of the voyage
and the Marquesas Islands on the second
half as reference islands. Despite the great
distance of these islands from the course
line, and his own lack of first-hand geographic knowledge of the region, Piailug
felt that he was able to keep track of our
progress through mentally breaking the
voyage into segments based on star sight-
ings relative to the bearing of these reference islands.

The Northeast Tradewind Zone (May 1 to 13)

The *Hōkūle'a* left Maui in the Hawaiian Islands on May 1, 1976, tacked northeast to
clear the island of Hawaii before turning
south-southeast for Tahiti. For the next ten
days we sailed as close as we could to the
northeast tradewinds, which blew mainly
in the range of 18 to 28 km/hr. We knew
by checking our course with horizon star
bearings that we were making considerable
easting as we sailed southward, but without instruments aboard we had no way to
determine how much easting. Only after

the voyage were we able to analyze our
daily progress, based on noon positions
taken by the tracking yacht *Meotai*, and estimate our performance by comparing our
course with wind estimates made aboard
Hōkūle'a (Fig. 14.4).

From May 1 to 13 we averaged 196 km a
day, our longest run being 241 km between
the 11th and the 12th. *Hōkūle'a* reached
the latitude of Tahiti on May 10, but she
made less easting than my 1967 estimates—
primarily, it appeared, because the tradewinds were more easterly than usual. Inef-
ficient steering, caused in part by an accumulation of seawater in the bows, probably
also lost us some easting; so did the shov-
ing action of the occasionally heavy seas,
which tended to push the bows to leeward.
Without precise figures on wind direction
and current set we cannot calculate exactly
how close to the wind *Hōkūle'a* was sailing
in this period, although I would estimate
that we averaged at least 75 to 80 degrees
off the wind.

We steered primarily by holding the
canoe as close to the wind as possible,
while Piailug checked our heading by observing where the bow of the canoe was
pointed in relation to horizon stars. Cloudy
conditions, particularly after May 8, made
Piailug's task difficult. At times when the
horizon was completely obscured, he
would have to search the sky for the sight
of other familiar stars on which to orient
himself, or simply use the direction of the
trades and swells.

When Polaris was visible, we estimated
its height above the horizon to gauge our
latitude and hence our southward progress
toward the equator. The angle of Polaris
above the horizon is approximately equal
to the latitude of the observer. Thus when
Lewis estimated that Polaris was 10 degrees
above the horizon, it meant we were 10 degrees north of the equator.

The Doldrums (May 13 to 21)

As *Hōkūle'a* sailed south, hope grew that
we might be able to sail right through the

BEN R. FINNEY

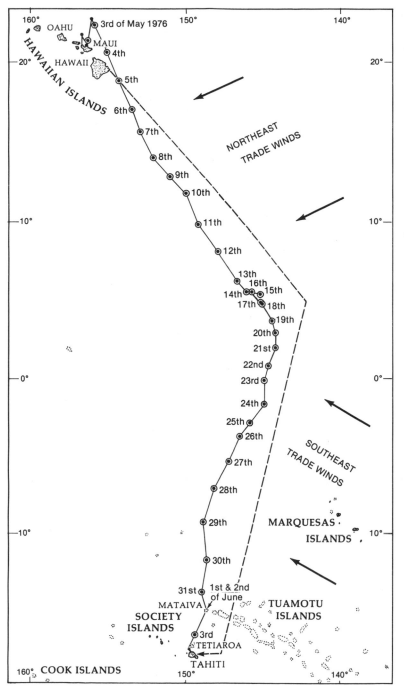

14.4   Projected (----) and actual (——) course of the Hōkūle'a from Honolua Bay, Maui, to Papeete, Tahiti, from May 1 to June 4, 1976. The projected course was derived from sailing experiments conducted with the Nālehia in 1966 (Finney 1967). The actual course is based on noon positions taken by navigator L. Burkhalter aboard the following yacht Meotai, except for May 2, 3, 4, and 14 when dead-reckoning estimates are used. (Reproduced from Finney 1977. Copyright 1977 by the American Association for the Advancement of Science.)

convergence zone of the northeast and southeast tradewinds. Sometimes one wind system shades into the other and allows a boat to sail right through the zone with perhaps only a half-day of slow sailing. Before we left Maui, a yacht that had just arrived from Tahiti reported that it had encountered no doldrums. But on the evening of May 13 we entered a rain squall, and after a night of heavy rain we found ourselves drifting on a calm sea. We remained in the doldrums, sometimes drifting and sometimes slowly sailing in light variable winds, until May 21. Although our southward progress was greatly slowed, the equatorial countercurrent pushed us farther to the east (except on May 15–16 when we seem to have been caught in a back eddy that carried us westward). By May 20 we had made some 1,375 km of easting after leaving Maui and were only 160 km west of the projected course line.

Keeping the canoe on course in the doldrums was difficult at times. The skies were frequently overcast, so that our guiding stars were obscured. When the moon was not visible either, or was too high in the sky to be of directional help, it was easy to become disoriented. The regular tradewind swell had died out, and the light and shifting winds were extremely deceptive. Sometimes we unknowingly followed the wind around the compass as it shifted direction, and a few times we ended up heading north back toward Hawaii. We discovered these short-lived errors when, for example, the moon rose on the "wrong" side of the canoe, or when a just-awakened Piailug (who could always tell direction with a minimum of cues) abruptly corrected us.

The integrity of the navigation experiment was compromised by several incidents during this period in the doldrums. A film of the voyage was being made by the National Geographic Society, with personnel jointly employed by them and television station WQED of the Public Broadcasting Service. In accordance with pleas of the film makers, we had allowed the periodic exchange of fresh and exposed film between the *Meotai* and the *Hōkūle'a* (by quick transfer via an outboard-powered rubber boat). The film team aboard the *Meotai* also recorded on cassettes radio messages to crewmen from family and friends in Honolulu and passed them over to the canoe with the fresh film. Twice, on May 15 and 19, the cassettes included rough position information from Hawaiian newspaper stories read over the radio to the *Meotai* and negligently recorded on message tapes by the film team aboard the yacht. In addition, on the evening of the 19th the film team came over to *Hōkūle'a* in the rubber boat and, against orders, boarded the canoe to fraternize with dissident crewmen. While on board, they gave an obvious hint of our position.

Although to critics these incidents will probably forever serve to detract from Piailug's accomplishments, I believe, as do assistant navigators David Lewis and Rodo Williams, that the episodes were irrelevant to Piailug's navigational decisions. In the first place, I do not think Piailug heard the position information when the tapes were played. In the second place, Piailug was thoroughly immersed in his own method of plotting progress by means of reference islands and star bearings. Position data, already a couple of days old and phrased in terms of miles covered from Hawaii and miles still ahead to Tahiti, were of no interest to him and would not in any case have caused him to alter the basic navigational strategy of sailing as close to the wind as possible to maximize easting.

Neither did Lewis or Williams need outside clues to our position. They had a reasonable idea of where we were from estimating course and distance made good as well as from observing Polaris. For example, early on the morning of May 23 Williams proclaimed that we would cross the equator at 1100 hours. When the canoe finally reached land, we learned that he had been off by only two hours, or about 10 km at the slow rate we were then sailing!

BEN R. FINNEY

The Southeast Tradewinds (May 21 to June 4)

Yachtsmen in Hawaii had warned us that upon leaving the doldrums we were likely to encounter light headwinds that would force us off course. They were right. On May 21 the skies cleared and we encountered light southeast trades that persisted, except for one day, until the 26th and forced us onto a course that threatened to carry us well west of Tahiti. The *Hōkūle'a* sails poorly to windward in light winds, as probably did the heavily laden voyaging canoes of old. Our speed slowed to 5 km/hr or less, and windward performance fell way off. From the 26th to the 28th the wind increased in strength but veered farther south, so that we were unable to correct our course.

During this period a number of rebellious crewmen became disabled by a combination of factors. They sought refuge from the reality of the lengthening voyage by holing up in a hut on the deck. We learned later that while in the hut they clandestinely listened to a small transistor receiver that had also been smuggled aboard and heard alarming reports from Honolulu that *Hōkūle'a* was off course. Their radio listening was doubly unfortunate. Not only did it intensify their fear of being lost on the great ocean, but it was to cast further doubt on Piailug's navigation. Although I do not think any of those who listened to the radio were aware that a transistor can be used to take a navigational bearing, the fact remains that these men used an instrument capable of giving navigational aid.

At times headwinds pushed *Hōkūle'a* so far off course that we were headed directly for the Cook Islands, well to the west of Tahiti. The reaction of some of our supporters in Honolulu to the news of our westward slide bordered on the hysterical. There was even an attempt to radio the *Meotai* to have them break off the navigation experiment by informing us that we were off course and directing us to head the canoe in the right direction. What those who anguished over our predicament did not realize was that we were sailing the best course possible and that we knew where we were going.

After leaving the doldrums, we trimmed the canoe by moving weight aft and adjusting the sails until *Hōkūle'a* would automatically sail to windward without a steering paddle or sweep in the water. When the wind shifted direction, so—automatically— did the canoe, keeping a fixed angle to the wind. From the 24th to the 29th of May the wind kept the canoe's twin bows pointed to the right of the upright Southern Cross, a sure indication that our course was well to the west of south.

Late on the 28th the wind increased to 37 to 46 km/hr and began to back a little to the east. By the 29th it had shifted enough to allow us to sail almost due south, and it had further increased in speed to allow us to cover 267 km, our best day's run of the voyage, between the 29th and the 30th. That gave us hope that we had a good chance to hit Tahiti directly and might even make our first landfall on the Tuamotus.

In the Southern Hemisphere we checked our latitude by the zenith star method. Although the authenticity of this method as an ancient Polynesian technique has not yet been unequivocally established, Lewis used it at this time to monitor our southward progress and to adjust his dead-reckoning estimates.

"*Hōkūle'a*" is the Hawaiian term for Arcturus, a bright star that passes over the island of Hawaii. To an observer there, Arcturus stands directly overhead when it is at its zenith. To a navigator sailing from Tahiti to Hawaii, Arcturus would appear a little over 50 degrees above the horizon when he left Tahitian waters. Its arc would seem to rise higher and higher in the sky until, when the canoe reached the latitude of Hawaii, it would pass directly overhead. What returning Hawaiian navigator would not have been happy to find Arcturus framed in the ellipse inscribed in the night sky by the masthead as it wove round and round to the pitching and rolling of his canoe?

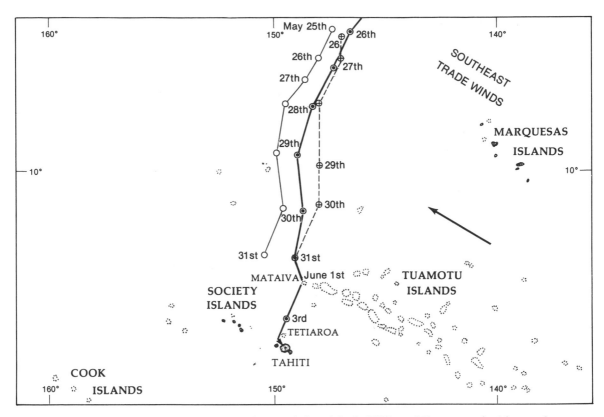

14.5 *Noon dead-reckoning positions of David Lewis (○) and Rodo Williams (⊕) compared with actual noon positions (◉) for the last part of the Hawaii-to-Tahiti voyage of the* Hōkūle'a.

Perhaps this is why Hawaiians called the star *Hōkūle'a*, the Star of Joy. On our voyage we saw the zenith elevation of Arcturus slowly descend in the northern sky as we sailed south, and watched the zenith elevation of Gienah, a star in the constellation Corvus that passes almost directly over Tahiti, slowly rise.

Lewis used zenith star sights plus his estimates of course made good and distance covered to make a daily noon estimate of our position in terms of latitude and longitude. As we began to approach the Tuamotu Islands, Williams also started making noon position estimates. Figure 14.5 shows their noon positions for the last part of the trip, as well as the actual positions determined by the *Meotai*. Their general accuracy is testimony to the fact that we were hardly lost or sailing blind. The last noon posi-

tion calculated by Williams on May 31, the day before we reached land, is especially noteworthy. His estimate of 13°47' south latitude and 149°00' west longitude was off by only one minute, or one nautical mile! (Although Piailug was not keeping track of our position in latitude-longitude coordinates, his own plotting system told him that we were approaching the Tuamotus and would see land the following day.)

At about 1300 on May 31 we entered a squall; upon emerging, we found that the wind had backed markedly to the northeast. *Hōkūle'a*, still trimmed for self-steering, followed the wind around and settled onto a southeast course. At about 1400, terns were sighted, a sure sign that land was nearby. Then at about 1600, the long swell generated by the southeast trade-winds faded out—blocked, we thought, by

BEN R. FINNEY

an island or islands to the southeast of us. That night, at about 0300, we sighted a small atoll and hove to until dawn. Although Williams thought the island was probably Mataiva (the westernmost atoll of the Tuamotu group), we were not absolutely sure of its identity until a boat came out and the people aboard answered my query of "What is the name of your island?" with "*O Mataiva*."

We had reached the Tuamotus after a month at sea. Our route and speed had been much as projected in 1967, except that we were somewhat west of where I had thought a canoe like ours would be (Fig. 14.4). Had *Hōkūle'a* kept on her course and sailed past Mataiva, we would have intercepted the projected route line. Once we met the Mataivans, though, we decided to stay put a while and enjoy Tuamotuan hospitality.

A day and a half later we set sail for Tahiti. The *Hōkūle'a* arrived off Point Venus in the early hours of June 4, having covered some 5,370 km in 32 sailing days. Our feat was particularly appreciated by the 15,000 Tahitians who turned out to welcome us as we entered Papeete Harbor later that morning.

The Return Voyage

We had to abandon the plan to navigate *Hōkūle'a* back to Hawaii by traditional methods because Piailug left the project in Tahiti. He was disgusted with the behavior of the rebellious crew faction, especially their last performance when we were within sight of Tahiti on the afternoon of the 3rd. These crewmen, fortified with champagne that had been tossed over to the canoe when the producer of the National Geographic Society film came out to meet us in a fishing boat, staged an assembly in which those in command of the canoe and in charge of the experimental procedures were denounced, then assaulted. Unfortunately, Lewis also left the project in Tahiti and Williams, the only other person qualified to navigate the canoe without instruments, was unable to sail

back because of an injury sustained just before reaching Mataiva. Leonardo Puputauki, a young professional seaman from Mangareva and Tahiti, was recruited to navigate the canoe home with modern methods.

Still under the command of Captain Kapahulehua, but with an entirely new crew, *Hōkūle'a* left Tahiti on July 4. After an uneventful trip she arrived in Honolulu on July 26. She had averaged 236 km a day, with the longest day's run 343 km. With the wind abeam or abaft abeam, *Hōkūle'a* sailed swiftly and smoothly, in striking contrast to our windward passage. Only mild doldrum conditions were encountered; *Hōkūle'a* sailed from one tradewind zone to the other in a few days. Figure 14.6 shows the return course plotted with the course projected in 1967 for a canoe sailing 95 degrees to the wind.

The Significance of the *Hōkūle'a* Voyage

The concept of an experimental round-trip voyage such as this one evolved twenty years ago, when the notion of two-way voyaging between widely separated islands had fallen into disfavor. The *Hōkūle'a* voyage has demonstrated the worth of the Polynesian double canoe for making long ocean crossings, especially against wind and current. The Tahiti leg of the voyage has also shown how traditional navigation methods can be used to guide a canoe over vast expanses of open ocean—although the interference by the film team and some crewmen will probably allow determined critics to reject this navigational trial as fatally flawed. Finally, while a single experimental voyage does not allow us to speak in terms of "proof," the *Hōkūle'a* venture certainly indicates that two-way communication between ancient Hawaii and Tahiti was possible.

However, the true significance of the *Hōkūle'a* voyage, and of the other recent work on Polynesian canoes and navigation, goes far beyond the debate on two-way

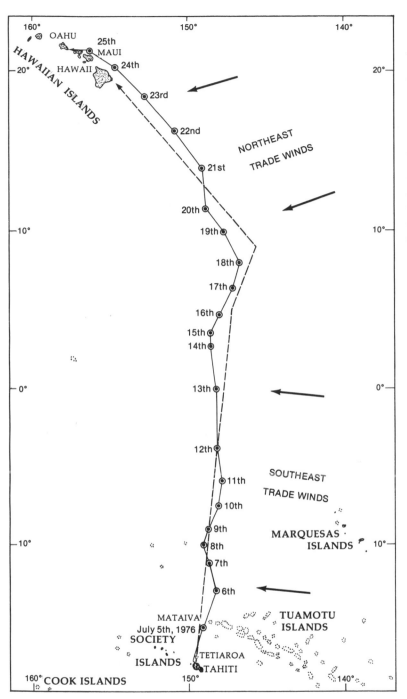

14.6 *Projected (----) and actual (——) course of the* Hōkūle'a *from Papeete, Tahiti, to Honolulu, Oahu, from July 4 to July 26, 1976. The projected course was derived from sailing experiments conducted with the* Nālehia *in 1966 (Finney 1967). The actual course is based on noon positions taken by navigators L. Puputauki and K. Lyman aboard the* Hōkūle'a. *(Reproduced from Finney 1977. Copyright 1977 by the American Association for the Advancement of Science.)*

BEN R. FINNEY

voyaging. With this research in hand, it is now possible to fill in the spare outline of Polynesian settlement offered by linguists and archaeologists with a more detailed scenario of how Stone Age voyagers could have explored and colonized an immense ocean world.

Polynesian Discovery and Settlement

The story begins in Melanesia, in the Bismarck Archipelago and the Solomon Islands that lie north and east of New Guinea. There on a few small islands and on coastal stretches of larger islands archaeologists have found sites of a culture noted for a type of pottery called Lapita. Sites with similar cultural assemblages have been found on Melanesian islands to the east, and on Polynesian islands bordering Melanesia; archaeologists surmise that they testify to the sojourns of a seafaring people ancestral to the Polynesians. They propose that, starting over 3,000 years ago, the Lapita people moved from the Bismarck-Solomons area east to the Santa Cruz Islands, then south to the Banks and New Hebrides groups and to New Caledonia, then east again to Fiji. From Fiji they moved farther east to Tonga and Samoa, arriving there before 1000 B.C. (see Chapter 2).

Green (1974) maintains that these seafarers set up exchange networks in the Melanesian Islands that they colonized, and he cites archaeological evidence of trade in pottery, obsidian, and stone tools. Probably by the time they had reached as far east as Fiji, and certainly by the time they had discovered Tonga and Samoa, these seafarers had passed the frontiers of Melanesian settlement and found themselves alone in the ocean. Then they seem to have paused on these mid-Pacific islands, settled down, and developed in relative if not total isolation the cultural pattern we now recognize as Polynesian.

A thousand years later, give or take a few centuries, the movement eastward began anew. Now we can talk about *Polynesian* voyaging, for the migrants by this time

were full-fledged Polynesians. The archaeological record so far, which may well be grossly incomplete, points to the Marquesas as the first major group in East Polynesia to have been reached. The Marquesas in turn seem to have become a primary center for population dispersal within East Polynesia; later the Society Islands, which may have been settled from the Marquesas or directly from West Polynesia, appear to have become a secondary dispersal center.

From these two primary locations Polynesians spread to nearby groups (where, if we can generalize from some tantalizing evidence from the Cooks, they may have occasionally encountered voyagers coming directly from West Polynesia) and to the islands at the extreme limits of Polynesian settlement: Hawaii, Easter Island, and New Zealand. The first two were reached by A.D. 500; New Zealand was probably reached a few hundred years later. Their settlement marks the apparent end of a migration that had brought voyagers, over a period of several thousand years, from islands off the shore of New Guinea to within a few thousand kilometers of the Americas.

As these voyagers moved east from the closely spaced archipelagoes of western Melanesia, they entered a more oceanic environment. Distances between island groups increase progressively as one moves along the migration route. To sail from the Solomons to the next group eastward, the Santa Cruz Islands, a vessel must traverse some 360 km of open water. To sail farther east, after island-hopping through the Banks and New Hebrides islands, a gap of some 860 km must be crossed. Although distances from Fiji to Tonga and Samoa, via the intervening Lau Archipelago, are no greater than those among Melanesian groups, within Polynesia the gaps between major archipelagoes widen to several times the distances in Melanesia. To cross from the main centers of West Polynesia to those of East Polynesia requires voyages of from 1,900 km (eastern Samoa to the westernmost Societies) to almost 4,000 km (Tonga to the Marquesas). Although the armchair voyager might consult his map and choose routes that hopped from one isolated atoll to another in order to reach these East Polynesian groups without having to make such long voyages, I doubt that the first colonists could have followed such a strategy without prior knowledge of the possible stepping-stone islands.

The other groups in central East Polynesia—the Australs, Cooks, Gambier, and Tuamotu archipelagoes—could have been settled from the Marquesas, or Societies, or both, through a series of medium-length voyages. But to reach the peripheral islands of East Polynesia, canoes had to sail over thousands of kilometers of open ocean. Easter Island lies some 2,500 km from the Gambier group, the closest permanently inhabited islands. New Zealand is some 3,800 km from the Societies (or about 2,800 km from the Cooks, which lie along the route). And Hawaii is some 3,500 km from the Marquesas.

As voyagers sailed farther east, their craft had to be able to stay longer at sea. In addition, the canoes had to be able to carry much heavier loads because of the increased sustenance requirements of the more lengthy voyages, as well as the necessity of transporting domesticated plants and animals needed to recreate the Polynesian horticultural complex on the fertile but biotically impoverished islands of the mid-Pacific. The voyagers needed large, well-constructed craft capable of carrying their pigs, dogs, and chickens, their taro, yams, breadfruit, and other vital plants, as well as the sizable amounts of food and water needed for the long ocean crossings.

The double canoe was the craft that made this long migration possible. It would be difficult to argue that the concept of joining two hulls together was so unusual that it had a single point of origin. But the adaptation of the double canoe for deep-sea voyaging may well have been a unique event that occurred, as Green has posited, early in the history of the Lapita peoples. Green proposes that it was the greater sta-

bility and especially the greater carrying capacity of the double canoe that allowed these seafarers to move eastward from the closely spaced islands of the Bismarcks and Solomons out into the more oceanic environment of eastern Melanesia and then to the western edge of Polynesia.

I would additionally propose that once these voyagers had reached the Fiji-Tonga-Samoa region, the double canoe was further adapted to cover even greater distances and carry even greater loads. Over the centuries that saw the emergence of the Polynesians as a distinct people, this region of many islands spread over archipelagoes a few days' sailing time apart would have provided an ideal voyaging sphere for further development of the double canoe for its ultimate, though perhaps unforeseen, task: the exploration and settlement of the entire Polynesian triangle. Indeed, the time needed to perfect this craft might help to explain why such a long pause followed initial settlement before the movement eastward began again.

We have yet to fully consider those aspects of the oceanic environment most important to sailors: the winds and the currents (Fig. 14.7). At the West Melanesian end of the migration route, westerly winds are common for part of the year. As one moves farther east, the westerlies become less and less frequent, until in Polynesia the easterly tradewinds like those we encountered on the *Hōkūle'a* voyage prevail most of the time. As migrants moved farther east, they therefore found that they were moving against the direction of the prevailing winds and the currents that usually accompany them. This dominance of easterly winds and currents, and their alignment against the direction of human settlement, cannot be ignored. Sharp tried to do so when he postulated that drift voyages could have accounted for much of Polynesian settlement. To be sure, the tradewinds die down periodically and westerly winds spring up. But they do not blow frequently enough, or for sufficiently long periods, to

BEN R. FINNEY

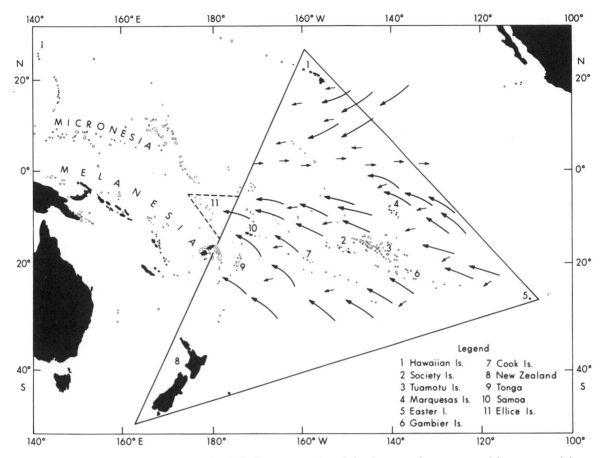

14.7   *Prevailing directions of the tradewinds* (long arrows) *and dominant surface currents* (short arrows) *in the Polynesian triangle. (Reproduced from Finney 1977. Copyright 1977 by the American Association for the Advancement of Science.)*

allow for significant drift movement to the east. Dening (1963) showed this with an analysis of documented drift voyages, almost all of which have been from east to west with the direction of the tradewinds.

More recently, the previously mentioned computer study of drift voyaging by Ward and his colleagues has virtually demolished that hypothesis for the main Polynesian movement. Although the simulation did indicate a high probability for drift voyages between closely spaced islands and archipelagoes in the Tonga-Samoa-Fiji area to the west, and among the central groups of East Polynesia, it also showed that the chances of reaching Fiji or West Polynesia

by drifting from the west were slight, and that the chances of drifting from West Polynesia to East Polynesia were extremely low or nonexistent. The Ward simulation gave no support to the possibility of drifting to the Marquesas and indicated only one chance in seven hundred of drifting from Samoa to the Cooks or Societies. And the authors flatly state (in unpublished results) that for drifting canoes "there is no chance of reaching Hawaii, Easter Island, and New Zealand from other parts of Polynesia."

Thus Polynesia had to be settled by sailing, by trying to push to the east against the direction of the prevailing winds and currents. Paddling would have been of minimal help. Large, heavy canoes with a high freeboard cannot be paddled easily against the wind for long stretches. Even if they could, our paddling experiments with *Nālehia* indicate that the energy costs and water loss would probably have been too high for extended paddling.

Polynesian voyaging legends rarely discuss sailing conditions or problems faced by voyagers (although some information may well be obscured by metaphorical language). But Marquesan legends give us a rare glimpse of how early settlers may have looked at the problem of sailing against wind and current to reach their new home. These legends emphasize over and over again that the first settlers came from "below" (*mei iao mai*) and that they had to sail "up" (*iuna*) to make their landfall. This is the Polynesian way of saying that they came from the west, below the wind, and had to sail east, upwind, to reach the Marquesas.

How did they do it? How did the settlers of the Marquesas and other windward islands sail "up" against the prevailing wind direction? It is unlikely that long migration voyages to windward could have been undertaken by sailing on one long tack close to the wind, as *Hōkūle'a* was sailed from Hawaii to Tahiti and back. Hawaii can be reached by a canoe sailing one long tack from the Marquesas, from Tahiti, and perhaps also from the Cooks, for the courses slant across the tradewinds. Yet most long settlement routes within Polynesia are against the tradewind direction and require a vessel to sail much closer to the wind than a double canoe can. A glance at Fig. 14.7 will show that it is highly unlikely that a double canoe could sail directly from, for example, the New Hebrides to Fiji, from Tonga to the Marquesas, or from the Gambiers to Easter Island, in normal tradewind conditions. A finely tuned racing yacht might be able to make some of these crossings with one long tack, but I doubt many yachtsmen would try it because of the beat-

ing they and their craft would take by forcing their course against wind and sea. Theoretically a double canoe might tack back and forth to cross the windward stretches; still that seems unlikely given the length of time the shallow tacks would take and the suffering they would engender in a crowded canoe.

The early Polynesian sailor probably would have done exactly what observers reported his nineteenth-century descendants did when they wished to make a windward passage. When a Tuamotuan wanted to sail his canoe from Tahiti back to his home island, he waited for a favorable wind. When the wind shifted west, as it occasionally does in the summer months, he set sail and ran before the wind, hoping that it would last the two or three days needed to get him home. Voyagers bound for Tahiti from the leeward Society Islands followed the same strategy—as did voyagers setting out from the Cooks to the Societies. West Polynesian sailors also were observed following this practice. The same strategy of waiting for the west wind probably served exploring canoes well in their search for land to windward.

Westerly winds, however, probably could not have carried exploring canoes all the way across some of the longer crossings, such as the one from Tonga to the Marquesas. In contemporary times at least, westerly winds usually blow for only a few days up to perhaps a week at a time. Here is where the windward capacity of Polynesian craft, however limited in comparison to modern racing yachts, could have made a crucial difference. Let us invent a hypothetical canoe that can sail downwind but cannot point to windward at all, and let us have it sail east from Tonga, pushed by a westerly wind. Once the wind shifts back to the normal southeast tradewind direction, our canoe will be relentlessly forced back to the west. In the same situation a canoe that can make good 75 degrees or so to windward will, by contrast, be able to continue eastward by tacking against the trades. If such a canoe were to run east before a westerly lasting for a week or so and then were to tack northeast with the return of the trades, it would stand a good chance of reaching the Marquesas.

The possibility of sailing to the Marquesas from West Polynesia, and of crossing the other long gaps in the migration trail over which canoes probably could not have drifted, has been confirmed by a series of computer simulations. After Ward and his colleagues found that the drift hypothesis could not explain Polynesian settlement, they reprogrammed to simulate voyages in which canoes were sailed on a predetermined course, as long as that course was not closer than 90 degrees to the wind. They found that on selected courses 7 percent of simulated voyages reached the Marquesas from Samoa, 9 percent reached Hawaii from the Marquesas, 62 percent reached New Zealand from the Cook Islands, and a small but unspecified percentage of voyages reached Easter Island from the Gambiers. It is tempting to assume that the chances for successful voyages over this route might in reality have been higher than these figures indicate. After all, double canoes can sail closer to the wind than 90 degrees, and Polynesian sailors, unlike their computer-simulated counterparts, would certainly have waited for a favorable wind before starting—unless forced by war or famine to embark precipitously.

Even if we were to accept a low probability of success along these routes—lower than the computer simulation suggests—this does not mean that those voyages that did end with an island discovery were accidental.

Much has been written about the situations and motives that led Polynesians to abandon their home islands to search for new land: defeat in war, famine, the ambition of the thwarted younger son of a chief to found a new colony, the search for adventure, and other comparable factors. But little has been written about why Polynesians and their Lapita ancestors moved to

the east, against the direction of the prevailing winds. They did not do so by chance. Intentional voyages of exploration and colonization were surely the main means by which these seafarers migrated halfway across the Pacific. Their historical experience had taught them that the world was an ocean studded with islands, and that more islands—uninhabited and hence inviting to those fleeing war or famine, or simply seeking a new home—always lay to the east, to windward. That thought could have sustained an eastward push for many centuries.

Exploring to windward would also have made good sailing sense. If a craft is sailed far downwind, there is always the problem of the return, either by tacking against the wind or by waiting for a wind shift. This would not have been an enviable prospect for an exploring party low on food and water, and perhaps with a battered canoe. In contrast, if a craft is sailed to windward, it is relatively easy to return home by sailing swiftly downwind. The Polynesian drive to the east was a logical as well as a successful settlement strategy.

The really interesting question is what happened once the Polynesians reached the easternmost groups. Did they realize that they were at the limit of habitable islands and settle there? Or did they keep pushing eastward for a time, to disappear at sea or upon some American shore? Or did they deliberately turn back to the west to explore unknown latitudes—and perhaps find the great islands of New Zealand on an exploratory probe to the southwest?

Did Polynesians reach continental shores beyond Hawaii, Easter Island, and New Zealand? A voyage from Hawaii to North America would have been well within their capabilities; a Tasman Sea crossing to Australia might have been much more challenging. We have no evidence for such voyages, nor has their possibility been greatly discussed. The situation is different with South America, primarily because of the apparently pre-European presence in

Polynesia of a plant of South American origin. Buck (1938) would have us believe that Polynesians fetched the sweet potato from South America. Heyerdahl (1952) proposes that South Americans carried it to Polynesia by raft. Given the difficulty of forcing a canoe, or any other sailing craft, against wind and current all the way to South America, and the subsequent problems of surviving on an alien shore and then of mounting an expedition back to Polynesia, I would lean toward sweet potato introduction by raft to some point in Polynesia (perhaps the Marquesas) and subsequent dispersal within Polynesia by canoe. However, experimental voyaging research the world over teaches us not to underestimate the potential of any craft or, I would add, of any seafaring people. And there still remains the problem of how the coconut, a plant of probable Southeast Asian–West Melanesian origin, reached American shores—particularly since recent research by Ward indicates that viable coconuts probably could not have drifted to South America.

Finally, there is the question of whether any role in Polynesian history was played by two-way voyages in which canoes sailed back and forth between a homeland and a newly colonized island ferrying people, plants, animals, and other supplies. The issue concerns voyages between widely separated islands, not closely spaced ones such as those in the well-documented voyaging spheres that link the Society and Tuamotu groups, and the Tonga-Samoa-Fiji region. Sharp (1956) was adamant on this issue. All long voyages were exile voyages. Once a distant island was reached, there was no possibility of a return home and the establishment of two-way communication. The *Hōkūle'a* voyage and other recent research efforts would seem to show, however, that the Polynesian double canoe and navigation techniques were well adapted for round-trip voyages between distant archipelagoes. Nevertheless, we need to look at each proposed route for two-way com-

munication rather than make a general statement.

Hawaii and Tahiti are almost ideally aligned with respect to the tradewinds for two-way voyaging; Hawaii and the Marquesas are not. Although Hawaii is easy to reach from the Marquesas, it does not seem likely that a canoe could have sailed, directly at least, from Hawaii to the Marquesas, for the Marquesas lie too far to windward. The westerly wind shifts characteristic of the southeast tradewind zone seldom occur around Hawaii, and a canoe would have to make good at least 65 degrees to the tradewinds to reach the Marquesas. While the *Hōkūle'a* was able to hold a course toward the Marquesas in the northeast tradewinds, the southeast tradewinds deflected her far from those islands. The only way that we could conceive to reach the Marquesas would have been to sail to the Tuamotus and then wait for a wind shift that would enable us to sail northeast.

Voyagers who had reached the Societies or the Marquesas from the west probably would not have found it difficult to return home. A competent navigator would have kept track of the course on the outward voyage so that he could calculate the right star bearing to Tonga or Samoa. Or he might have been able to use zenith stars to find the latitude of his home island, and then have sailed downwind along that latitude to reach home. But after arriving, to sail again to windward to reach the Societies or Marquesas would have been, like the initial discovery voyages, a major feat of seamanship.

Round-trip voyages between the Societies (or Cooks) and New Zealand also would have been far from easy. The return from New Zealand would have been the most challenging leg. A navigator might well have been caught between two options: to leave in the fair-weather season, in which case he would have had to battle variable winds around New Zealand and then the trades as the canoe moved north;

BEN R. FINNEY

or to leave in the winter and take advantage of the strong westerlies common then. If crew and canoe survived the cold west winds and rough seas, there would still remain the problem of gaining easting when the canoe entered the tradewind zone. A voyage from New Zealand back to the East Polynesian heartland would have required just the right combination of well-found canoe, skilled crew, and favorable conditions.

Finally, what about the most difficult route, that between the East Polynesian heartland and Easter Island? The initial discovery of Easter Island was a major, and lucky, accomplishment. The island lies far to the southeast, dead into the wind, from the Marquesas, Tuamotu, and Gambier groups. A canoe leaving one of these groups might, with an unusually long spell of westerly winds, gain enough easting to reach the longitude of Easter Island, but I find that a doubtful possibility. I think it more likely that Easter Island was discovered by seafarers who sailed south from the Tuamotu, Gambier, or Austral archipelagoes (or through them, after starting from the Marquesas or Societies) and made it across the tradewind zone into more southerly latitudes where westerly winds are common. Then they might have run before the westerlies until, because of cold and hunger, they turned north toward the trades and chanced upon Easter Island. A return from Easter to the west would have been comparatively simple, as they could have run before the southeast trades. But the possibility of turning around and once more reaching this isolated outpost on the Polynesian frontier would seem most remote because Easter Island is so small, so lacking in surrounding islands that could give a navigator an enlarged target, and so inaccessible with reference to the tradewinds.

These estimates of voyaging patterns and possibilities, as well as the computer simulations of Ward and his colleagues, are based on wind and current data that go back only to the mid-nineteenth century. Yet it may be argued that during the Little Climatic Optimum, a warm period beginning around A.D. 450 and culminating between A.D. 1100 and 1300, conditions more favorable to voyaging might have existed in the tropical Pacific—specifically mild tradewinds with more frequent and enduring westerly wind shifts to allow easier eastward movement and two-way voyaging between distant islands. The coming of the Little Ice Age immediately after this mild period may in turn have ushered in a period of strong trades, more storms, and decreased westerlies—all of which would have made voyaging more difficult. The possibility that these posited climatic changes could have influenced Polynesian voyaging becomes intriguing when we consider that the Polynesians reached the frontiers of their world during the Little Climatic Optimum and, if we can lend credence to oral traditions, seem to have ceased two-way voyaging between distant islands during the Little Ice Age (Finney 1977).

The fit seems good, although caution is warranted. No doubt voyaging had declined by the time of European contact, but that decline may not have been as drastic as supposed. We have eyewitness accounts from the early 1800s of Marquesans setting forth in search of new lands, and well into the European era Tongans were waging a vigorous naval campaign to expand their influence over Fiji. Furthermore, systematic research is needed to see if the legends do indeed chronicle a decline in voyaging activity, and if the wind patterns in Polynesian waters did change as posited.

Even if we accept the supposition that more favorable wind patterns might have made voyaging easier in the past, my belief is that where long-range voyaging occurred it was more a matter of occasional, perhaps semiheroic, voyages rather than regular communication. This view is consonant with the way in which the more plausible of the legends portray voyaging. There are no great fleets sailing back and forth—just a canoe now and then, commanded by a great chief or navigator bent on some important mission.

This examination of Polynesian canoes, navigation methods, patterns of discovery, and two-way voyages has so far ignored the human element that made the great voyages possible. Today when we hesitate to travel without a 99.9-plus percent chance of safe arrival, we find it difficult to imagine how a people could risk their lives to find a new island, or to visit some distant one. Yet from the way voyaging is described in the oral literature, and from the few eyewitness accounts of voyaging activity that survived into the early European era, it is clear that Polynesians went to sea freely, undeterred by obvious dangers.

Still the hazards, the inevitable disasters, and the loss of life cannot be minimized. Many voyages undertaken in thoroughly equipped and manned sailing canoes must have come to grief when canoes broke apart or foundered in heavy seas, or when voyagers died of hunger, thirst, or exposure before land could be found. An even higher mortality rate must have occurred among hastily mounted voyages, such as when a group was forced to flee from famine or following defeat in war.

If, for example, we assume that 10 canoes with 25 persons each were lost every year, and then multiply the product by the last 2,000 years of Polynesian voyaging, we obtain an estimate of a half-million lost souls. And this estimate could be conservative. Nonetheless, despite the hazards of the sea, a migration that began with a small group of seafaring people on the western edge of the Pacific swept eastward until all the major islands of this greatest of world's oceans were settled. The voyaging spirit that sustained this movement must have been tremendous. Without that spirit a whole island world would have remained unknown to mankind until much later in history.

Acknowledgments

Support for measurement of the paddling and sailing performance of the *Nālehia*, and of the sailing performance of the *Hōkūleʻa*, was provided by National Science Foundation grants GS-1244 and SOC 75-13433, by the Bernice Pauahi Bishop Museum, and by the University of California, Santa Barbara. The *Hōkūleʻa*'s voyage was sponsored by the Polynesian Voyaging Society and was made possible by contributions from members of the society including, notably, Penelope Gerbode-Hopper and the Kawananakoa family; the East-West Center; the National Geographic Society; the Tainui Association (of Tahiti); the University of Hawaii; the U.S. Coast Guard; the U.S. Navy; and many other organizations and individuals.

References

Best, Elsdon. 1923. *Polynesian voyagers*. Dominium Museum Monograph no. 5, Wellington.

Buck, P. H. (Te Rangi Hiroa). 1938. *Vikings of the sunrise*. New York: Lippincott.

Dening, G. M. 1963. The geographical knowledge of the Polynesians and the nature of inter-island contact. In *Polynesian navigation*, ed. Jack Golson. Polynesian Society Memoir no. 34, pp. 102–132, Wellington.

Doran, Edwin. 1976. Wa, vinta and trimaran. In *Pacific navigation and voyaging*, ed. B. R. Finney. Polynesian Society Memoir no. 39, pp. 29–45, Wellington.

Finney, B. R. 1967. New perspectives on Polynesian voyaging. In *Polynesian culture history: essays in honor of Kenneth P. Emory*, ed. G. A. Highland et al., pp. 141–166. Bishop Museum Special Publication no. 56, Honolulu.

———. 1977. Voyaging canoes and the settlement of Polynesia. *Science* 196:1277–1285.

Fornander, Abraham. 1878, 1880, 1885. *An account of the Polynesian race, its origins and migration*. London: Trübner.

Gladwin, Thomas. 1970. *East is a big bird*. Cambridge, Massachusetts: Harvard University Press.

Golson, Jack, and P. W. Gathercole. 1962. The last decade in New Zealand archaeology, pt. 1. *Antiquity* 36:168–174.

Green, R. C. 1974. Sites with lapita pottery: importing and voyaging. *Mankind* 9:253–259.

Haddon, A. C., and James Hornell. 1936, 1937,

1938. *Canoes of Oceania.* vol. 1: Polynesia, Fiji and Polynesia; vol. 2: Melanesia, Queensland and New Guinea; vol. 3: Terms and general survey. Bishop Museum Special Publications no. 27, 28, 29, Honolulu.

Heyerdahl, Thor. 1952. *American Indians in the Pacific.* Chicago: Rand McNally.

Levison, Michael, R. G. Ward, and J. W. Webb. 1973. *The settlement of Polynesia: a computer simulation.* Minneapolis: University of Minnesota Press.

Lewis, David. 1972. *We, the navigators.* Honolulu: University Press of Hawaii.

Sharp, Andrew. 1956. *Ancient voyagers in the Pacific.* Polynesian Society Memoir no. 32, Wellington.

Smith, S. P. 1910. *History and traditions of the Maoris of the west coast, North Island, New Zealand.* Polynesian Society Memoir no. 1, Wellington.

Melanesia

CHAPTER 15

J. PETER WHITE

A modern jet airplane that took off from Nandi in Fiji and flew northwest for six hours would fly over or past most of the islands from which the Polynesians came. These include the New Hebrides and Solomon Island groups, the Bismarck Archipelago, and New Guinea—all parts of Melanesia. Our airplane could fly on, over Indonesia to Southeast Asia, and still not have left the area that forms the background to the Polynesian story. To the south of our path for part of this journey would lie Australia, eight times the land area of all the other islands taken together, a basically dry continent whose history is only marginally relevant to Polynesia.

It is the prehistory of these areas—Melanesia, Australia, and Indonesia—that this chapter will outline, for here lie the origins of the phenomenon we know as Polynesia.

Melanesia: The Immediate Homeland

Melanesia, or the "islands of black people," as the early European explorers called them, lies wholly within the tropics, south of the equator. The largest island is New Guinea (780,000 km²), the smallest some tiny coral reef unnamed except by local people. Overall, the size of islands decreases as one moves from west to east and, as a direct consequence, so do the numbers of kinds of native plants and animals.

Geologically, Melanesia lies along the collision and subduction zones between the Indo-Australian and Pacific plates. This

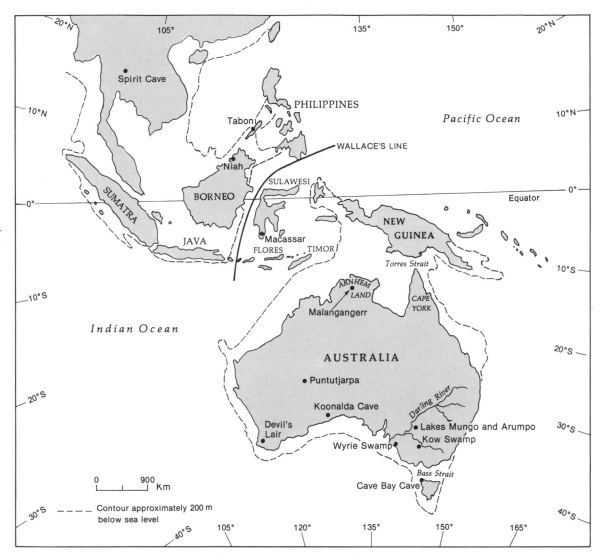

15.1 *The Eastern Hemisphere. Australia and New Guinea have been separated from Southeast Asia by sea barriers since man evolved, as the contour 200 m below present sea level shows. In Australia, more sites are known than are shown here; in Indonesia and on the Asian mainland, few old sites are well known.*

means both that many islands are of continental type (high and geologically complex, with stone sources suitable for human exploitation) and that all are subject to frequent earthquakes and other instabilities. Climatically, the area is always hot, with monsoon and trade winds ensuring high rainfalls sometime during the year in most areas. The plants and animals of the region are Australasian: Wallace's Line (named after the English scientist who first noted

the abrupt floral and faunal change) runs between Borneo and Sulawesi, Bali and Lombok, and divides this area from the Asian realm (Fig. 15.1). The distinction between the two realms is most noticeable in the fauna. Apart from a few native rats and bats, relatively recent migrants, Melanesia contains only primitive mammals (monotremes and marsupials) and highly distinctive birds, reptiles, and insects. Most varieties of fauna and flora are found only on the larger islands, with the consequence that the range of foods available to man, especially in East Melanesia, is quite small. Marine resources, however, are rich. Shellfish and fish can be obtained from various local environments, often without elaborate equipment, and marine protein is an important part of the Melanesian diet.

The Earliest Islanders

Previous chapters of this book have discussed the well-organized and highly developed societies that existed throughout Island Melanesia by 2000 B.C. and from which Polynesian cultures directly evolved. It is now clear that the people of those societies were not the first migrants to enter Melanesia: some parts of it at least had been occupied long before and provided the original setting for the local evolution of Melanesian cultural forms. Nonetheless, the exact nature of these preceramic cultures remains unclear, as does their starting date in various island groups. This is because direct evidence for their existence is scanty, and much of our knowledge inferential. To be precise, there is only the evidence of language type and distribution, plus three pieces of archaeological data, that are relevant. Each of these four data sets has its own problems and makes its own contribution, and it is therefore worth evaluating each independently.

The first indication is the presence of Non-Austronesian (NAN) languages on a number of islands in the Bismarck Archipelago and the Solomons. If, as seems likely, NAN languages are older than Austronesian (AN), and the latter did spread through the area 4,000 to 7,000 years ago, then we may believe that NAN speech communities remain today as indicators of the movement of earlier inhabitants. The model on which this assumption is based is the island of New Guinea, where AN languages are found only along the coasts, while the interior is occupied by NAN speakers, who have been there for 20,000 years at a minimum. But while NAN lan-

guages *may* indicate early occupation of the islands, there is in fact no way of testing when they were spoken in Island Melanesia during prehistoric times, and indeed some linguists now believe that NAN languages may not be the oldest in every area in which they now occur (Green 1976).

The second piece of evidence consists of numerous mounds on New Caledonia and its small outlier, Île des Pins. These earthen mounds are some 2.5 m high, 10 to 15 m across, and contain a core of hard lime mortar that includes shells. Three radiocarbon dates on the shells range from 5000 to 11,000 B.C. (Shutler and Shutler 1975). The problem is the implication of these dates. Are they old because dead coral and fossil shells were used to make the mortar, whereas the mounds were built in much more recent times? And what do the mounds themselves imply, in view of the fact that no other archaeological material has been found in association with them? Without answers to these questions, the dates themselves are not very important.

The third discovery comprises more than 400 flaked stone implements found in streambeds and on hillside paths around Passismanva, 15 to 30 km inland from the southwest coast of New Britain (Fig. 15.2) (Chowning and Goodale 1966). These implements are cores and large flakes of chert that have been worked into a variety of forms, including some with a waist or tang that may have been used for hafting (Fig. 15.3). The range of forms suggests that the tools may have been used for a number of different tasks. They probably were made locally, since similar raw material is still common in the area, but present inhabitants do not recognize these specimens as tools or even as manmade objects. (In the recent past cutting implements have always been made from obsidian imported from the north coast.) The chert tools are heavily patinated to an opaque dark brown color, and they are not found around current villages. These facts—and particularly the presence of tanged forms, which dropped out of use on mainland New Guinea at

J. PETER WHITE

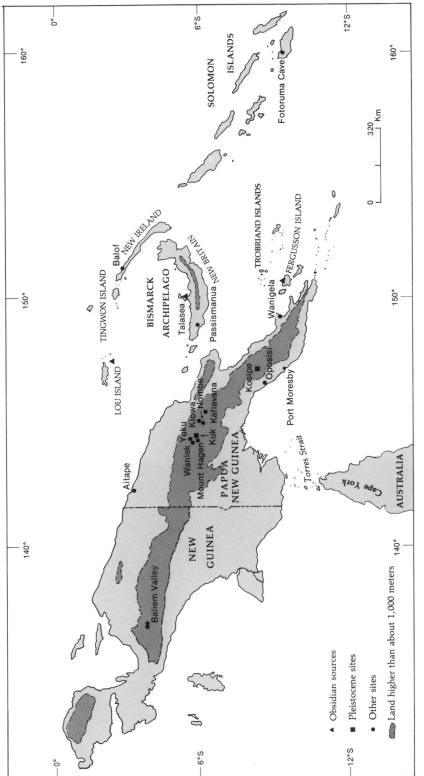

15.2 *Melanesia and New Guinea, showing sites mentioned in the text. The highlands run like a spine down the center of the main island and most sites, including all known Pleistocene ones, occur there. Obsidian from the only three known sources was traded to the highlands, the Papuan south coast, and throughout the Solomons. Modified from Chowning and Goodale (1966) and Mumford (in White 1972).*

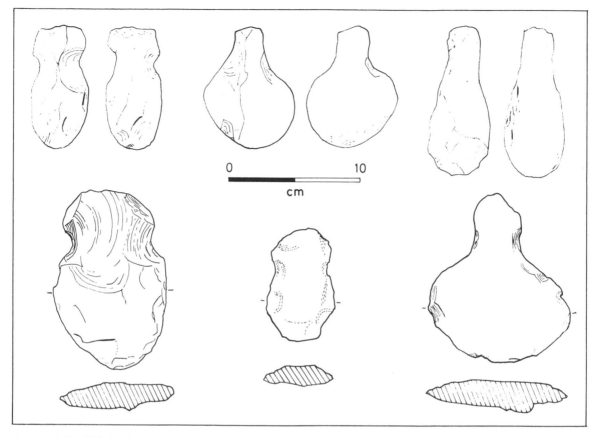

15.3 *Waisted blades from Passismanua, New Britain* (above), *and Kosipe, Papua New Guinea* (below). *The Passismanua blades are generally thicker than the Kosipe specimens and all are made from finer-grained rock. The Kosipe tools date to about 25,000* B.C.; *the others are undated.*

least 4,000 years ago—have led to suggestions that the tools must be at least several thousand years old and thus were made by early settlers on New Britain. As with so many surface finds, the problem is one of testing such a suggestion. Until there is some dated archaeological material to which these tools may be related, they can be no more than suggestive of early settlement.

The final piece of evidence is a definite site with an archaeological deposit dated back to between 4000 and 5000 B.C. This site, Balof rock shelter, is on the northeast coast of New Ireland about 1 km inland (Downie and White 1978). The 6 m² excavated so far reveal a maximum depth of occupation deposit of about 85 cm. The early

users of the shelter were involved primarily in hunting and collecting shellfish from the nearby coast. We do not know if they made gardens, since no plant remains were recovered; but it will be seen later that gardening is likely to have been practiced. A few small pieces of pottery from around 1500 B.C. occur in the site: they are contemporary with other pottery-producing village sites on the coast. It is in these later levels too that pig bones and stone ax fragments first occur, although the numbers of each are so small that their presence there may be very much a matter of chance.

The most significant aspect of the Balof site, however, is the sources from which its inhabitants derived stone to make their flaked tools. Before about 1500 B.C. stone

J. PETER WHITE

was obtained from several locations both on and off the island. Obsidian was obtained from Talasea, 600 km away on the central northern coast of New Britain, while colored and black cherts and chalcedonies may have come from the same island. Other stones probably came from western or southern areas of New Ireland. After 1500 B.C. a much smaller variety of rocks is found, with obsidian predominating. But the obsidian derives from two sources—Talasea and Lou, a small island in the Admiralty group, 500 km away to the northwest.

The change in sources of raw material used at Balof hints at the broad pattern of early settlement in Island Melanesia. By 4000 or 5000 B.C. the Bismarck Archipelago at least had been explored thoroughly enough so that most sources of stone were known. This implies initial settlement of the area at a considerably earlier date, perhaps 7000 to 10,000 B.C. When Balof first came into use, there were enough people in the area for overland and interisland trade to occur, although sea voyages longer than 100 km would not have been required for such commerce. What was traded apart from stone is not known, but perishable goods including pigs, vegetable foods, and items of decoration are reasonable guesses.

The first indication of long sea voyages comes with the presence of Lou Island obsidian. To get from the easternmost small islands in the Admiralties to Tingwon, the nearest small island off New Ireland, requires a direct sea crossing of 180 km, between small, low islands that would not be visible at a great distance. It is probably significant that the evidence for this obsidian trade occurs at about the same time as other changes both in the Balof site and, as Green shows in Chapter 2, elsewhere in Melanesia. The start of this trade and the decline in the use of nonobsidian sources seem to indicate that the region's previously diverse network was being organized and modified into a tighter pattern, probably dominated to a greater extent by long-distance traders. These may have been

the makers and users of Lapita pottery, which has been found on offshore islands to the north and to the south of New Ireland.

The earliest documented settlement in the Solomon Islands is much later than in the Bismarck Archipelago. The oldest site excavated, Fotoruma Cave on Guadalcanal Island, dates back only to 1500 B.C., which is approximately contemporary with the earliest Lapita pottery. It is unlikely, however, that the earliest sites have been discovered by archaeologists. We might also argue that the rapid spread of Lapita pottery makers through the area in the second millennium B.C., and the consistent location of their settlements on offshore islands, implies that the main islands were already occupied by other people. The nature and dating of this inferred early occupation remains to be demonstrated, but 4000 to 6000 B.C. might not be far from the mark.

This section has demonstrated how little is known of the early settlement of Island Melanesia, and also how clear it is that Lapita or other pottery makers do not constitute the whole story. We do not yet know whether the first settlers in the area were agriculturalists, although the data from New Guinea presented below suggest that this is highly likely. It can also be seen that the presence of comprehensive exchange networks are a basic part of the last 6,000 years of the area's prehistory, and that from such a background sprang the settlement of East Melanesia, as well as later developments in the main islands.

New Guinea

Stone tool beginnings. The prehistory of New Guinea involves time and space different by an order of magnitude from those noted in the islands east of it. New Guinea is five times as large as all the rest of Melanesia, and its prehistory stretches back five to ten times the duration of any human history to the east of it. Thus any prehistorian must expect not only to encounter the cultural diversity consequent upon human adaptation to enormous environmental differences—everything from sago swamps at sea level to alpine grasslands at 3,000 m—but also to allow for the effects of climatic changes and economic reorientations upon human lives. Because of this complexity, and the fact that organized research began less than 20 years ago, the prehistory of New Guinea is only sketchily known.

Climate, and climatic change, set the framework of New Guinea prehistory. Fifty thousand years ago, when the first human footprint may have appeared on a western beach, sea level was 40 to 120 m lower than it is now. As a result, Torres Strait, which now separates New Guinea and Australia, did not exist; the Australia–New Guinea continent was 15 percent larger and stretched farther in every direction than it does today (Fig 15.1). The greatest enlargement was between New Guinea and Australia, where a wide plain stretched out toward Timor; the least was on the northeast coast, where the shoreline is steep and the coast uplifting. Nearly all beaches from the Pleistocene period have been drowned by the rising sea levels of the last 15,000 years, so that the remains of the many peoples who probably lived on the coast have been obliterated.

The Pleistocene enlargement of land area affected wind and rainfall patterns, with the result that the southern part of New Guinea was probably somewhat drier than it is at present. This is unlikely to be true of the southeast or northern coasts. In the great highland spine that runs along the center of the island the main effect was increased cold: glaciers formed on a number of mountains, and around them the area of alpine grassland was much greater than it is now (Hope et al. 1976). There is little information about the region between coast and grasslands. We can suggest that some kinds of forest were less or more extensive than is now the case, and that the large highland valleys 1,200 to 2,000 m in altitude were 5° to 8° C colder on the average, but that is all.

The entry of humans into New Guinea by 50,000 years ago can be confidently asserted on the basis of radiocarbon dates from Australia, but the earliest actual records date only to between 30,000 and 25,000 B.C. The earliest settlements presumably were by people who were marine oriented and who had watercraft capable of crossing at least 50 km of open water. They would, on arrival, have colonized first the coasts and major waterways, slowly becoming acquainted with the strange new plants and animals found on the Australasian side of Wallace's Line. By 25,000 B.C. some of them had penetrated inland, to an altitude of 1,800 m. This is shown by a site at Kosipe (Fig. 15.4), which consists of a scatter of stone artifacts and charcoal stratified between a series of volcanic ashes on a slope above a swamp in which many pandanus trees grow (White et al. 1970). The volcanic ashes all come from different eruptions of Mount Lamington, 150 km to the southeast. Each eruption can be identified by its mineral composition, then correlated with a more complete and well-dated series nearer the volcano. The artifacts are what we would expect from the leavings of short-term camps: a few lost flaked axes and some flakes. There are also some "waisted blades" (Fig. 15.3) made, like the axes, of phyllite and shaped like some of the tools from New Britain. Whether these are hatchets or some other kind of multipurpose tool is not known.

Interest in the Kosipe area at this early date was probably concentrated on the swamp, where the pandanus trees provided fruits, leaves, and fibers in season. However, the impact of human activities on the swamp itself is only now being studied. Recently a core 6 m long, with a basal radiocarbon date of 28,000 B.C., was taken from the swamp and its contents of mud, plant pollen, and volcanic ashes are being analyzed. Longer cores, stretching further into the past, may also be obtainable and should provide a complete history of cli-

15.4 *Excavation at Kosipe. In* a, *the Kosipe mission* (center of picture) *sits on a small ridge overlooking a large swamp that seasonally produces prolific pandanus. Pleistocene-age artifacts occurred over the whole hillside but were concentrated near the largest building visible. Modern gardens can be seen in the foreground and background. The excavation is shown in* b. *In the section 1 m deep, composed of a series of volcanic ashes, two buried soils may be seen as darker horizons. Artifacts and carbon were concentrated at the base of the lower soil, about 20 cm above the bottom of the section. Scale in 20 cm.*

matic change and human environmental impact in the area.

The other site of similar age was discovered only in 1976. It consists of 100 m² of burned forest on the edge of a swamp near Mount Hagen. Some unworked but humanly transported rocks were found in the same area, but no tools or other clues to the purpose of this activity have so far been reported.

All other sites that date to Pleistocene times are rock shelters in the central highlands, and complete reports are available for only a few of them (Bulmer 1966; White

1972). There are, however, two significant aspects of the available data. The first is the presence in two sites of ground stone axes dated to around 8000 B.C. At Kafiavana site 54 axes and fragments made of distinctive stone types (hornfels, greywackes, and the like) were found throughout its 4-m depth, and 37 of these pieces bore clear marks of the grinding used to shape them. Similar finds are reported at Nombe, now being excavated, but not at other sites of the same age—although this can easily be caused by the chances of excavation. It is worth noting, however, that some waisted blades from Yuku site are also ground. The importance of these discoveries lies in the links they provide with similar but older evidence from northern Australia (see below) and also Southeast Asia, where ground-edge tools are probably dated to the late Pleistocene in Borneo and in some mainland sites (Hayden 1977). This manufacturing technique is, of course, very economical in its use of raw material, since it allows the same tool to be resharpened many times. The form of the tool, whether ax, adz, or hatchet, is also economical, as it is easily transportable and useful for a wide variety of tasks. The early presence of ground stone tools may thus help to explain the absence in this area—when compared to Europe or Africa—of highly specialized flake tool making.

The second significant aspect of Pleistocene New Guinea sites is related to the first and concerns the flaked stone tools (Fig. 15.5). As has already been implied, these do not come in a highly differentiated range of shapes and sizes that are clearly the product of a series of formal ideas. Rather they appear to be a collection of ad hoc flakes, lumps, and pieces of chert or flint and similar stones that can be held conveniently in the hand and that provide a sharp edge for use in scraping, planing, whittling, and other tasks. When blunted, an edge may be resharpened simply by removing a single flake from it, but there is no shaping of these tools other than the original flaking to create a suitable edge. This method of stone tool manufacture continued in the highlands until stone tools were replaced by steel knives and axes in the twentieth century A.D. (White 1968). More importantly, it seems to have been the basic pattern of tool construction throughout Melanesian (and Polynesian) prehistory, as well as for the earlier periods in Australia and Indonesia. Flaked tools from such sites as Balof, Kafiavana, and Kiowa (New Guinea), Malangangerr, Devil's Lair, and Lake Mungo (Australia), and Spirit Cave (Thailand) all exhibit a similar lack of formal patterning, but are susceptible to a descriptive analysis that concentrates on features of their working edges (see White 1969; Fox 1970). From such studies it should eventually be possible to determine the various tasks for which tools were used, but we expect to find that woodworking, especially to make a variety of hunting equipment (spears, bows and arrows, traps), bindings, and wooden tools, as well as carvings and other decoration, was the most common.

The other way in which these tools are important derives from the kinds of statements about prehistoric societies that have been made on the basis of their lack of formal patterning. To understand the nature of this problem some background information is necessary.

Prehistoric archaeology began in Europe, and prehistorians there were initially faced with the ordering of a very large quantity of stone tools, clearly made in quite regular patterns. They saw in their excavations that, over time, these tools became ever more elaborate and technologically specialized; since other data were rare, they used the changes in stone tools as the primary indicator of technological and social progress. Several decades ago, when European-trained prehistorians started to work in Southeast Asia and the Southwest Pacific and were faced with the almost total absence of specialized forms of flaked tools, they naturally concluded that the makers of

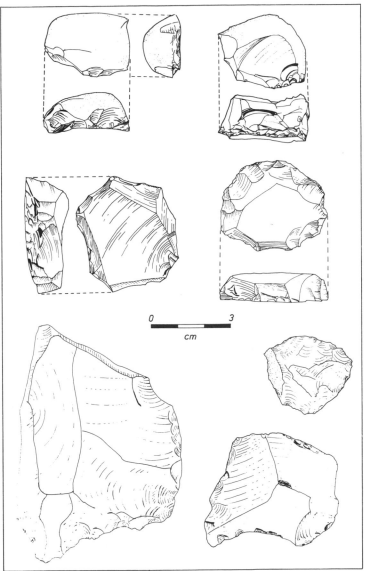
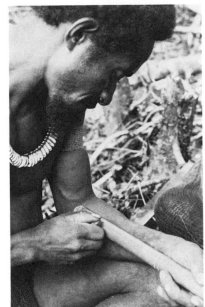

15.5 *Flaked stone tools.* a, *tools from New Guinea (top),* Australia *(center), and Tabon Cave, Philippines (below). The absence of formal shaping and the concentration on useful edges is noticeable. Modified from Mumford (in White 1972), Mulvaney (1975), and Fox (1970). In b, a New Guinea highlander uses a flaked stone tool similar to those shown in* a *to incise decorative lines onto a bamboo tobacco pipe.*

these tools must be technologically and culturally "backward" (White 1977). This view was commonplace until very recently: it may, indeed, still be found in many general textbooks. It is, however, quite untrue.

To take but one modern example, the New Guinea highlanders of the twentieth century used stone tools in very unspecialized forms while simultaneously maintaining an elaborate agricultural system and some of the highest population densities ever recorded among slash-and-burn agriculturalists. Further, as I show below, prehistoric evidence for the development of this economic elaboration does not support any thesis of cultural backwardness. Such an idea depends more on our own viewpoints than on the evidence available.

This discussion of Pleistocene New Guinea has referred primarily to its technology, because little economic evidence has thus far been forthcoming. We believe that the people of this time were plant gatherers and animal hunters, but we do not know, for example, whether their activities were wholly or partially responsible for the extinction or dwarfing of several giant forms of animals that existed in New Guinea. Nor do we know what plants they gathered, though pandanus, sugarcane, and asparagus-like edible grass stems were probably important in the highlands (see Christensen 1975; Paijmans 1976). In lowland areas sago and bananas were probably basic staples (Townsend 1974; Morren 1974).

Plant and water economies. Whereas we have little evidence of Pleistocene economic life, the picture changes dramatically after 9000 B.C. (This date is used worldwide to mark the end of the Pleistocene period and is notable in our part of the world as being approximately when Torres and Bass straits were created as the sea rose.) The economic data come from the central highlands, primarily from a project at Kuk in the Wahgi Valley (Golson and Hughes 1976; Golson 1977).

Although 1,600 m above sea level, the Wahgi River near Mount Hagen lies in a flat 100 × 20 km valley, parts of which are now very swampy. At the time of European arrival (1930) this swamp was not used by New Guineans except for hunting and plant collecting. During the late 1960s parts of the swamp were drained by the Europeans, mostly for tea growing, and their activities produced a number of wooden tools, especially digging sticks and paddle-shaped spades, along with stone axes. Close investigation showed that many prehistoric water-control ditches ("barets") were visible in the walls of modern ditches. These barets seemed to be part of an exten-

sive and long-lasting water-control system, similar in form to that known today in the Baliem Valley in the western New Guinea highlands and therefore almost certainly created for agricultural purposes. Full-scale studies began in 1971 and have revealed a complex picture of agricultural activity at least 9,000 years old (Figs 15.6 and 15.7).

The direct archaeological data have been supplemented by geomorphic studies of the swamp's history and by pollen analysis. The following is the story pieced together so far—and interpretations have changed greatly as the work has proceeded.

Around Kuk the swamp has been built up through the slow washing-in of inorganic sediments from low hills to the south, and also by the local growth of peat. Around 18,000 B.C. the amount of grey clay sediment eroding from the hills increased slightly, and this rate quadrupled (from 0.5 cm to 2.0 cm per 1,000 years) in the period 7000 to 4000 B.C.—apparently because of increased runoff of rain water (which seems best explained as the result of human clearance of vegetation). Pollen analytic studies now in progress will confirm or controvert this interpretation, but the result of the runoff is a visible layer of grey clay that dates from this period. The clay covers and seals both a series of gutters, basins, and hollows that result from human agricultural activity, and a 2-m wide, 1-m deep baret that runs for at least 450 m. That this baret was dug by humans is clear from three things: it cuts through small local rises in ground level; it has sharply angled bends; and it drains away water into a larger, natural channel. Organic material in the bottom of the man-made baret has been dated to about 7000 B.C., and its use for agricultural purposes seems the most reasonable explanation for its existence.

The next evidence of human activity is a series of oval basins, each about 1 × 0.75 × 0.3 m in size, cut into the top of the grey clay and dated to about 4000 B.C. The basins are linked together by small gutters, all of which lead into larger barets,

J. PETER WHITE

15.6 *The Wahgi Valley of New Guinea.* a, *aerial photo of a present-day tea plantation. The modern ditches are parallel to one another; the prehistoric ditches (barets), some of which have been recut, present a more irregular pattern and run at an angle to the modern drainage. (Photo courtesy of QASCO [N.G.] Pty. Ltd.)* b, *aerial photo of a modern garden near the valley. The oldest garden is in the upper left, the most recent is without plants as yet. The distinctive grid pattern of barets is at least 4,000 years old in this area.*

15.7   *The Kuk excavation, Wahgi Valley, New Guinea. Prehistoric barets are visible in the walls of modern drainage ditches. In* a *a small baret about 20 cm wide has been cut into the grey clay and is partially filled with light-colored volcanic ash. The baret is about 5,000 years old.* b, *a baret 50 cm wide cut about 200 years ago.*

J. PETER WHITE

2×2 m, which are clearly, from their shape and direction, man made and which flow into creeks more than 1 km away. No crop remains or tools have been found with these pits and barets, but their similarity to modern agricultural structures makes any other use unlikely. This network lasted for only a short time, probably less than 200 years, before it was silted up and abandoned.

Some 2,000 years later the next set of pits and barets was dug in the area of the Kuk project. Although more complex in pattern, the barets appear to have been used in the same way as the earlier series. This time they remained in use for about 1,500 years, to judge from the stratigraphy and the radiocarbon dates. At about 500 B.C. a significant change occurred. The haphazard network of gutters draining into larger barets was replaced by an organized grid of gutter-like field drains (20 to 30 cm wide and 30 to 40 cm deep), which were set within a grid of larger barets; these in turn were linked to the main creeks. The small basins that formed the core of the earlier system were no longer present, and it seems probable that the plants that used to grow in them were being planted instead on the ground between the ditches, as in many areas of the western highlands nowadays. This change in agricultural practice seems to have been required because of the increasing swampiness of the area (from natural buildup), rather than because of the introduction of any new crop or technology. The system continued in use at Kuk for about 1,200 years, to be abandoned around A.D. 700 or 800. Then, about A.D. 1600 to 1700, very wide barets, dug close together, attempted a more complete drainage than previously. After only 200 years the area again was abandoned.

While few tools have been uncovered at Kuk, the wooden and stone tools mentioned earlier have been found associated with baret grids dated to about 500 B.C. at other sites only a few miles away. All the types of tools used for agriculture in the twentieth century are present, and their close association with the barets (digging sticks and spades lying in them, just as if they had been left there overnight) convinces us that we are dealing with the remains of prehistoric agriculture. The further back in time we go, the less elaborate the baret system is—and the less labor intensive we must suppose the agriculture to have been. The earliest definitely identified basins, at 7000 B.C., were probably used for growing taro. The environments created at Kuk are totally suited to that crop and to little else, other than the water plants sometimes used in making beaten fiber skirts and *pulpuls* (men's aprons), which would hardly have required such a large-scale system. Neither taro (*Calocasia esculenta*) pollen nor remains have been found, but this is hardly surprising for a plant that reproduces vegetatively and has no hard seeds, skins, or woody parts. Any discovery of macrofossil remains would be largely a matter of luck.

It is important to remember that taro is a plant not indigenous to New Guinea but to Southeast Asia. Its inferred presence in the highlands implies an earlier transport from across the sea and perhaps an agricultural use for the plant in Southeast Asia well prior to 7000 B.C., although so far there is no direct evidence on this point (Yen 1973, 1977).

Other evidence of economic change is piecemeal. The most significant material is the probable presence of the pig in two New Guinea highland sites by 8000 B.C. and its definite presence by 4000 B.C. (Bulmer 1975). The natural habitat of pigs is Southeast Asia, and their presence in New Guinea implies that they were brought there by humans—unless we choose to believe that pigs swam across 75 or 100 km of ocean to get there. It seems probable that these pigs would have been domestic, or at least tame.

The increasing numbers of pig bones in more recent levels of archaeological sites confirm the agricultural history documented at Kuk. More intensive agriculture would allow the production of more food, part of which could be fed to pigs, until today's situation is reached in which pigs often outnumber people by two to one. Since each pig is fed as much garden food as a human, the current scene is probably of recent origin, perhaps within the last 300 years (Watson 1977). Earlier gardens would have supported smaller pig (and human) populations. It should also be noted that the presence of pig in the highlands implies its presence on the coasts, where it would have flourished particularly in sago-growing regions.

Other studies show that tree crops, notably pandanus, are likely to have been important prehistoric foods (Christensen 1975) and that houses of a form similar to modern ones have been built in the highlands for at least 3,000 years (Bulmer 1977). Palynological studies document an increasing clearance of forest throughout the main area of highland settlement during the last 5,000 years, with the higher altitudes (up to 2,600 m) being colonized only within recent times. The highest forests and alpine grasslands, on present evidence, were largely unused before 3000 B.C. and are now used for hunting animals and collecting special plants.

To sum up, we now have evidence that the highlands of New Guinea have a history of root crop and tree agriculture and animal husbandry stretching back to 7000 B.C. It is clear that this region at an early date developed economic patterns similar to those found later in the Pacific area, and they were based on the same plants and animals. The existence of this situation in the highlands must imply similar if less elaborate developments elsewhere in the Southwest Pacific, and support the suggestion that the Melanesian and Polynesian islands were settled on similar indigenous economic bases.

Potters on the coasts. The satisfyingly coherent picture from the highlands cannot be duplicated for any area of New Guinea lower than 1,200 m; despite considerable searching, no sites older than 2000 B.C. have been located. The material of that date

consists of some flaked stone tools and bat bones found in a small cave near the coast, 100 km north of Port Moresby, and does little more than indicate the presence of people. All other sites have produced pottery in great quantity and are dated to 500 B.C. or less, but only along the Papuan coast have sufficient excavations and analyses been carried out for a reasonable story to be written (Allen 1977a and b).

There the earliest levels of several sites spread along 700 km of coastline have produced pottery reminiscent in technology and decoration of classic Lapita. At one site, Oposisi, stone adz forms, shell bracelets, and other artifacts are also similar to those found with Lapita ware. Obsidian from a source on Fergusson Island, on the northeast Papuan coast, is found in all sites and is good evidence for a long-distance trade network (Fig. 15.8). There is consistent evidence that the economy relied heavily on marine resources, but gardening and hunting also occurred; one may hypothesize that before the arrival of these people the area was lightly populated. The sites, which continued to be used until around A.D. 1000, seem to result from a migration of people from somewhere farther east in Melanesia, although the precise area has not been located. Their later history is one of increasing economic specialization, including an extensive reciprocal trade in food between coast and inland (what Allen has called "fishing for wallabies" and reciprocally we might call "hunting for fish") as well as along the coast itself, where sago, pottery, shell beads, and armshell rings were exchanged.

On the northeast coast, at Wanigela, and in the Trobriand Islands, ceramic sequences extend back to about A.D. 500 to 800, always in association with villages that show an economic organization similar to the present. Elsewhere along the north coast only occasional finds of pottery and axes are noted, except near Aitape where a human skull, found with organic materials including coconut fronds in river-lain deposits, has been dated to about 3000 B.C.

15.8 An obsidian mine at Voganakai, Talasea, New Britain. This tunnel, hollowed out by fire and water, follows a tube of obsidian into a lava flow. From this and similar sources, obsidian was traded throughout Melanesia and into the New Guinea highlands. (Photo courtesy of J. Specht.)

The absence of long-term coastal evidence for New Guinea is surprising in view of the data from the highlands and New Ireland. It is clear that coastal areas must have been settled, although it is true that most areas now coastal only became so subsequent to 600 B.C. when the sea reached its present level; thus older sites may continue to be scarce. In the absence of these sites, and of studies of the vegetation history (Paijmans 1976), we cannot document the history of agriculture. Shifting cultivation (swidden) is the norm at present, and the basic crop is usually taro, yam, or bananas, or some combination of

these. Sago is exploited in swampy regions. Although not as intensive as the highland (and some Polynesian island) systems, lowland agriculture exhibits many features also found in Island Melanesia and logically should precede it, so that dating its development is of some consequence for Pacific prehistory.

Australia: The Peripheral Continent

The Australian continent lies only 130 km from the southernmost part of New Guinea, across the reef- and island-strewn Torres Strait. In terms of marine travel the trip is of almost no consequence, an easy, line-of-sight sailing in reasonably protected waters for most of the distance. And yet it is Torres Strait that marks the most significant boundary in Oceanic prehistory apart from Wallace's Line. In absolute terms, Torres Strait separates the agriculturalists from the hunter-gatherers, the Australian race from other Pacific inhabitants. The contrast is most striking, of course, when we compare all of Australia with all of the Oceanic world: the more closely we focus upon Torres Strait itself, the more the barrier takes on certain aspects of a bridge between Australia and New Guinea, allowing the transfer of plants, animals, and people from one island to the other (Walker 1972). The bridge, however, was not open to all traffic; it is clear, for example, that agricultural people never crossed it, never established themselves on the Australian mainland. Before about 8000 B.C. the barrier did not exist, and a plain spotted by hills stood in its stead. This was the situation when humans first arrived on the continent.

Pleistocene Australians

The oldest settlement so far recorded in Australia is radiocarbon dated to about 35,000 years ago. This date, and others slightly younger, come from southeastern Australia (Fig. 15.9), where humans camped around inland lake shores and dined on fish, shellfish, emu eggs, small marsupials, and—almost certainly—a range of wild seeds, roots, and fruits (Mulvaney 1975). Older dates than this, some of them back to 70,000 B.C. have been claimed by some workers, but are regarded by others as totally unproven. Given the location of the oldest definite dates and the fact that we would expect early settlers to land in the northern or northwestern part of the country and move only slowly around the coast and inland, it seems likely that people have been in Australia for at least 50,000 years. And if they were in Australia, they were in New Guinea also.

Quite apart from their antiquity, the settlements around Lakes Mungo, Arumpo,

and others on the lower Darling River are remarkable for three reasons: the human types, the stone and wood technology, and the spiritual life found there (Bowler et al. 1970; Jones 1973).

The human remains found at Lake Mungo are all of *Homo sapiens sapiens*—the thoroughly modern human type to which present-day black and white Australians all belong. More than this, the remains are among the oldest of this type in the world. The problem with them arises when they are considered in conjunction with skeletal finds from Kow Swamp, some 300 km to the southwest. The Kow Swamp finds, more than 15,000 years *younger* than those from Mungo, have a number of anatomical facial features that are archaic in form— that is, they are more like earlier forms of man than are the Mungo specimens. The Kow Swamp humans are *not*, let me stress, older forms of human: they simply have some features, especially heavy brow ridges, like earlier man. Three explanations of these features have been advanced, none of them wholly satisfactory, but all of them open to testing.

(1) The first says that they are the evolved relics of a population that arrived in Australia *before* modern *Homo sapiens* evolved in Asia. This would imply that people had been in Australia for 100,000 years or more, which in turn implies that sooner or later we should find much older, more archaic specimens than those we now have.

(2) The next explanation says that ancient Australian populations simply had a greater range of cranial variation than modern Aborigines (who are among the world's most variable people, physically speaking), and that some of that variability has now disappeared. If this is the case, there must be ancient populations whose facial morphology covers the metrical "gap" between the Mungo and Kow Swamp groups.

(3) The third theory sees the Kow Swamp group as a locally adaptive evolution at the end of the Pleistocene, the heavy facial features being selectively advantageous in terms of the climate and diet of that time. Testing of this explanation is possible, but more complex (Wright 1976).

J. PETER WHITE

vive only in very dry or swampy environments, so their discovery is often a matter of luck. By one such chance, a series of wooden returning boomerangs, along with other wooden tools like sharpened digging sticks, were recently found at Wyrie Swamp in southern Australia (Luebbers 1975). Dated to about 8000 B.C., they more than double the known antiquity of boomerangs, and it now seems probable that these were a weapon of Pleistocene Australians (Fig. 15.10).

The range of Australian technology at this early date clearly parallels that of other late Pleistocene hunters and gatherers such as the Upper Palaeolithic people of Europe or the earliest settlers of North America. And in one area of the country it must have gone even further. Along the northern coasts, where the first settlers arrived, people had considerable maritime experience, including the technology that enabled them to cross several score kilometers of open water. This was necessary if they were to arrive in Australia at all!

The first archaeological discovery at Mungo, in 1969, was the skeleton of a female who had been cremated and whose bones had then been smashed and placed in a small pit. This cremation is dated to about 24,000 B.C. Other burials in the Mungo region are of bodies laid out flat and not burned, but all have some kind of grave goods. These include stone tools, ocher, shells, and animal teeth. It is of course impossible now to reconstruct the beliefs of the mourners who made these offerings; what we can do is note that their presence is believed to record a complex set of beliefs about the nonmaterial world. It seems likely that aspects of the "Dreaming," the all-encompassing historical and cosmological structure that is a cornerstone of modern Aboriginal life, were already present 30,000 or more years ago.

Many Pleistocene sites exist, other than those around Lake Mungo. Koonalda Cave in South Australia has rock art that dates back to around 18,000 B.C. (Wright 1971). There is Cave Bay Cave, where Tasmanians hunted, fished, and gathered from 22,000

B.C. until A.D. 1820 (Bowdler 1974). The occupation of Puntutjarpa in the southern Central Desert demonstrates early human use of even this arid environment (Gould 1968). Taken together, the sites show that by late Pleistocene times the greater Australian region was fully occupied by people who were well equipped for survival within their own environment. The evidence from Australia amplifies the New Guinea material outlined above and shows that settlement of the rest of the Pacific proceeded from a wide-ranging and secure technological base.

Aborigines and Plants

It is after 8000 B.C., with the physical separation of New Guinea and Australia, that the prehistories of the two areas really diverge. This is seen most clearly in the economic sphere, for nowhere in Australia did agriculture as we know it develop. Why should this be so? Some scholars have referred to the absence of plants and animals suitable for domestication; others to the intensely conservative Aboriginal religious life, which strongly discountenanced technological change; and still others to the fact that, economically speaking, most Aborigines were affluent and had no motivation to make such a change. None of these explanations is really adequate (White 1971; Allen 1974; Harris 1977). It is not true either that until the arrival of the Europeans, the Aborigines did not know what agriculture was. There is evidence that some Aborigines from the Arnhem Land coast went to Indonesia several hundred years ago (perhaps as much as a thousand), there to live for months in an agricultural community (Schrire 1972). Archaeological evidence from Arnhem Land, in the form of changed economic patterns, demonstrates Aboriginal contact with fishermen from Macassar (and perhaps other parts of Indonesia) for this long period, while Aboriginal oral tradition and Macassan records show that Aborigines were visitors to Indonesia in the recent past at least. It is legitimate to infer

15.9   *Aerial photo of the lunette (dune) around the eastern shore of Lake Mungo, Australia, now extinct. Pre-historic settlement concentrated on the lake side of the lunette (inside the arc) and dates back more than 30,000 years.*

Of the three explanations, the third is the "simplest," in that it requires fewest assumptions about the past; still, none of the three can be preferred at this stage on the basis of the archaeological data. The current situation is a fascinating puzzle.

The only tools recovered at Mungo were made of stone. They include heavy cores and scrapers with robust edges, and lighter convex-edged scraper-knives. The various types belong to the Australian "core-tool-and-scraper" tradition, which is found over the whole continent with only local variations until about 3000 B.C. These tools were used mostly for woodworking, and they are generally ad hoc in shape, like those from New Guinea.

Other tools known to belong to Pleistocene Australians, but not found at Mungo, are the following:

(1) Ground stone hatchet heads. Dated to 20,000 B.C. in northern Australian sites, these are among the oldest examples of ground stone technology in the world.

(2) Small flaked adz blades. Mounted in resin on a shaft handle, these have been used for woodworking (such as hollowing out carrying dishes) in central and southwestern Australia for at least the last 12,000 years.

(3) Bone points and spatulas. These have been found in many Pleistocene sites back to 20,000 B.C. and had a variety of uses, from skin reaming to personal decoration.

(4) Wooden boomerangs. Wooden tools sur-

15.10 *Boomerang-wing fragment from Wyrie Swamp, South Australia. Probably made of* Casuarina *(she-oak) wood, it was found in peat at a level dated to about 8000* B.C. *(Photo courtesy of D. Markovic and R. Luebbers.)*

earlier visits. On Cape York too, Aborigines were in frequent contact with the gardeners of the Torres Strait islands (Golson 1972; Harris 1977). Aborigines in some areas thus had ample opportunity to adopt agriculture, although until the nineteenth-century white colonization they were never forced into doing so. Faced with this apparent paradox, prehistorians are being forced to reconsider the whole problem and inquire whether they are not asking the wrong questions.

If we look carefully at the evidence now accumulating about Aboriginal economic life, it seems this might well be true. The key differences between Australia and New Guinea are that the Aborigines did not make gardens that they fenced, nor did they keep domestic animals that they bred to eat. But in other aspects of human-plant relationships, the two areas are very similar. Consider the following:

(1) Aborigines in the last 20,000 years have greatly altered Australia's floral landscape through their constant use of fire, which clears the land of weeds, provides ready-cooked meat, encourages new plant growth that attracts edible animals, and in some cases assists edible plants to survive and their seeds to germinate. Much of this effect is consciously sought by Aborigines, and it is not unfair to call the process "firestick farming" (Jones 1969). It is paralleled in New Guinea by a combination of fire and ax clearance.

(2) The actual planting of crops is another critical area of similar behavior. In Arnhem Land, for example, yams are not collected simply by digging them out. Rather, the fleshy root is removed while the plant and the upper 10 to 20 cm of root are left in place, so that another crop may grow on the same plant (Jones 1975). Along the Darling River, in a very different environment, Aborigines replanted some of the cereal seeds they had gathered and removed weeds that might otherwise have prevented these plants from growing (Allen 1974). The difference between this and "true" gardening lies not in the actual behavior, but in its location—whether it occurs within a fenced area or not.

(3) The tools used in the two areas did not differ. Both Aborigines and New Guineans relied on wooden digging sticks, spades (though these had a restricted distribution in Australia), and ground stone cutting tools. Carrying vessels were baskets or bags, made of various kinds of fiber.

It is therefore reasonable to say that Aborigines did not just live in and off the land, but managed its production and yield as effectively as many agriculturalists do (see also Harris 1977). The main realm of difference between Aborigines and New Guineans lies in the keeping of domestic animals. Apart from dogs, which seem not to have reached Australia before 2000 B.C., Aborigines kept no domestic animals, whereas nearly all New Guineans owned some pigs over which they exercised at least tenuous control. I have argued elsewhere that it may have been the presence of pigs, with their love of root crops, that encouraged New Guineans to protect with fences the plants they depended on (White 1979). The absence of these animals in prehistoric Australia thus might be causally related to the absence of gardens; but if so, the problem becomes their absence from Australia, given their presence in New Guinea by 8000 B.C. and the lack of water barriers between the two countries at the time. This problem still awaits solution.

What is clear enough is that Aborigines and New Guineans used very similar methods and tools to manipulate the natural environment, but that the spatial ordering and structural organization of these manipulations were significantly different and led to the very dissimilar societies that we know today. We can therefore say that to some extent the question of why Aborigines did not become agriculturalists *is* the wrong question. We should ask rather why they organized their food procurement activities in ways that always allowed them to move their residence around the country at less than yearly intervals (something few New Guinean groups did). This is another question that as yet has no satisfactory answer.

Other aspects of post-Pleistocene Australian prehistory are of less interest to students of Oceania. There is evidence of technological change in stone tool morphology (Mulvaney 1975), of the elaboration of art (Maynard 1976), of economic adaptation to changing climates and environmental situations (C. White 1971; Lampert 1971; Bowdler 1974; Allen 1974; Jones 1977), and of the growth of continent-wide exchange systems (Mulvaney 1976). All of these developments are meaningful, but they occurred primarily in isolation from the rest of the world; for Aborigines had little contact with Melanesians or Polynesians. A few finds of Melanesian and Polynesian stone tools on the east coast could indicate that an occasional lost canoe and its sailors may have made a landfall there rather than

on the north coast, but no settlement has ever been recorded—nor is one likely to have been successful if the fate of isolated white castaways is any guide (Morgan 1852; Moore 1972). Most Aborigines, like most Polynesians, lived in a remote and limited world, into which the entry of Europeans was an unmitigated disaster (see, for example, Rowley 1970).

Islands of the Western Pacific: The Real Homeland?

The northwest monsoon and the southeast trades provided the motive power that allowed Indonesian sailors to cross Wallace's Line and trade with northern Australia and western New Guinea during the past thousand years. Their predecessors in distant antiquity, the first settlers of Oceania, must have used similar winds to assist their moves from island to island. I have said earlier that these migrations must have taken place by 50,000 B.C. But humans and their ancestors had occupied much of the area now called Indonesia long before that.

The oldest hominid material from this region, dated by the potassium-argon method to about 1.5 million years ago, is some skeletal material attributed to *Homo erectus*. These occupants of Java, when it was part of the Asian continent, left only their bones and a few stone tools, sufficient to indicate their presence but little more. Other than these data, originally discovered in 1891 and only now being restudied and amplified, there is no solid evidence more than 100,000 to 200,000 years old. The earlier artifacts, a few rather formless stone tools found in river gravels dated to Middle or Upper Pleistocene in Timor and Flores, are interesting primarily because of their location on two islands which, as far as is known, have never recently been linked by dry land to the Southeast Asian mainland (Glover and Glover 1970). Human ability to make at least small-scale sea crossings must therefore have been present at a date much earlier than people in Europe or Africa are credited with. This ancient utilization of a marine environment was the first step in the conquest of the Pacific.

Subsequent archaeological data are difficult to piece together into a coherent story (Bellwood 1975). Although a number of excavations have been made, most have been of poor standard, with the results published in abbreviated form. Exceptions to this occur in eastern Timor (Glover 1971), southern Sulawesi (Mulvaney and Soejono 1971), and the Sulu Archipelago (Bellwood, personal communication), where a series of excavations are starting to reveal complex local prehistories dating back to the late Pleistocene. Even though we have isolated glimpses into the past, we are very far from knowing about economic or technological organization, or the distribution of raw materials and finished products, in any part of the western Pacific for periods before about A.D. 1000. Yet it is precisely such matters in these earlier periods that must be understood before we can adequately assess the relationship between any part of this area and regions farther to the east, including Polynesia.

The problem we face is a constant one in Pacific prehistory: that of trying to understand how much the culture and people of any area or island derive from migration and diffusion, and how much they are the result of local developments from a similar base. Although we may find similarities between parts of the eastern Melanesian, Polynesian, and western Pacific archaeological records in pottery decoration, in the form of stone adzes, in tropical agriculture and husbandry, in languages and physical anthropology, the real question is, what do these similarities mean? Over the years there have been many attempts at an answer. Two rather extreme alternative replies will give some idea of the range of opinion.

The first view says that Polynesians in Polynesia derive from the makers of Lapita ware. Physically they are Mongoloids, they speak Austronesian languages, and they derive from Neolithic ancestors in the Philippines and eastern Indonesia. In this western Pacific area between 3000 and 2000 B.C. we can find shell adzes, bracelets, beads, and fishhooks—a use of shell similar to that of Lapita ware makers and Polynesians. People in this area also made pottery that was mostly plain ware, but was sometimes cord marked. It was often red slipped. Later pottery (2000 to 500 B.C.) is sometimes decorated with stamped circles, scrolls, and meander patterns and shows formal similarities to Lapita. People making this pottery made their living primarily through agriculture, probably of root and tree crops (although this has not been demonstrated), and pig husbandry.

In the most extreme version of this argument all these aspects of culture were introduced into Melanesia by a direct and fairly rapid series of migrations of peoples who brought new economies, technologies, languages, and racial types into the area (see, for example, Shutler and Marck 1975). In less extreme forms the argument continues to point to the similarities between Indonesia and East Melanesia in physical type, languages, and pottery, but is much less clear about how these features came to be found in Melanesia. Migrations are certainly required, but when and of how many people (compare, for instance, Bellwood 1975)?

The alternative argument agrees that Polynesians in Polynesia derive from the makers of Lapita ware in East Melanesia, but does not accept further migratory arguments. Scholars of this persuasion point to (a) the lack of strong genetic evidence that Polynesians cannot be derived from East Melanesian peoples; (b) the fact that linguists generally date the expansion of Austronesian languages into the Pacific at 4000 to 3000 B.C., which is earlier than the material culture, especially Lapita pottery, they are supposed to be associated with there; and (c) the fact that the major development of the Lapita tradition was in Melanesia itself, so that the interesting similarities to it found in Indonesia (and Micronesia) might be derived as easily *from* Melanesia as the other way round. They draw attention to the facts that, as this chapter has shown, tropical agriculture and pig husbandry have been well established in Melanesia for thousands of years, and that there is also some evidence for long-distance trade systems in the Melanesian islands (as in New Guinea) dating from about 6000 B.C.

In its more extreme form this argument would not accept "migrations" as necessary at all, other than of the most minor and short-distance kind. It would argue that developing trade systems within Melanesia encouraged the indigenous development of oceangoing canoes and voyaging. The people operating these systems were firmly based economically on agriculture and pig husbandry, but did not make pottery. At some time around 2500 to 1500 B.C. the people at the western end of these trading networks came into contact with pottery makers, probably people speaking Austronesian languages. Both the pottery and the languages were taken up for reasons of trade and prestige and spread rapidly eastward through existing trade networks. That neither was "necessary" is shown by their sporadic occurrence in Melanesia; that both could be used in the Melanesian world of 2000 B.C. is shown by their rapid spread.

This, it seems to me, is the most satisfactory of current possible arguments. It derives Polynesians as a people, their language, and their material culture, from East Melanesia. It derives the makers of Lapita ware, Polynesian precursors, from Melanesia also, and makes minimal use of large-scale, long-distance migrations, for which there is currently no archaeological evidence. It allows the derivation of some aspects of prehistoric Melanesian society from eastern Indonesia, but suggests that a two-way interchange is likely. The model is also testable: further archaeological data will show whether it should be supported, modified, or replaced.

The Continuity of Pacific Prehistory

Fifty years ago the question "where did the Polynesians come from?" would have been answered by most scholars in terms of large-scale, long-distance migrations from China, Southeast Asia, India, Egypt, or even more exotic sources. My own feeling is that Polynesian settlement is more easily seen as one of the later chapters in the history of Pacific settlement—and a fairly short chapter at that.

The earliest settlement of the Pacific Ocean occurred on the islands nearest to Asia, within the area stocked with Asian fauna and flora, perhaps 200,000 years ago or more. This chapter of Pacific prehistory at present contains no more than a few randomly collected words.

The second chapter opens about 50,000 years ago, when people crossed the sea barriers between Asia and Australasia and occupied a vast new land with its strange plants and animals. Those in the south, the Australians, continued to develop independently until their hunting and gathering way of life was catastrophically interrupted in 1788. Those to the north, in New Guinea and the Melanesian islands, changed in a different direction. They were part of the world's earliest "experimentation" with plant agriculture and animal husbandry, economic changes that allowed for population growth and cultural diversification. By 6,000 years ago their long-distance trade systems included marine voyaging, and I have suggested that it was the expansion of this trading network that brought them into contact with the eastern fringes of different developments in Indonesia, including pottery making.

The third chapter, the settlement of the smallest and most far-flung Pacific Islands, begins no more than 4,000 years ago. The people who participated came from East Melanesia, but it was their ancestors who had written the earlier chapters of the same book. In this sense the settlement of Polynesia is dramatically a part of Pacific prehistory, one aspect of the human conquest of the world's largest ocean. Polynesians were not strange newcomers to the Pacific: their roots lay in generations of adaptation to this island world.

References

Allen, H. R. 1974. The Bagundji of the Darling basin: cereal gatherers in an uncertain environment. *World Archaeology* 5:309–322.

Allen, Jim. 1977a. Sea traffic, trade and expanding horizons. In *Sunda and Sahul: prehistoric studies in Southeast Asia, Melanesia and Australia,* ed. Jim Allen, Jack Golson, and Rhys Jones, pp. 387–417. London: Academic Press.

———. 1977b. Management of resources in prehistoric coastal Papua. In *The Melanesian environment: change and development,* ed. J. H. Winslow, pp. 35–44. Canberra: Australian National University Press.

Bellwood, P. S. 1975. The prehistory of Oceania. *Current Anthropology* 16:9–28.

Bowdler, Sandra. 1974. Pleistocene date for man in Tasmania. *Nature* 252:697–698.

Bowler, Jim, Rhys Jones, H. R. Allen, and A. G. Thorne. 1970. Pleistocene human remains from Australia: a living site and human cremation from Lake Mungo, western New South Wales. *World Archaeology* 2:39–60.

Bulmer, Susan. 1966. The prehistory of the Australian New Guinea highlands. Master's thesis, University of Auckland. (Available in microfilm as Oceanic Prehistory Records 1, Department of Anthropology, University of Auckland.)

———. 1975. Settlement and economy in prehistoric Papua New Guinea. *Journal de la Société des Océanistes* 31:7–75.

———. 1977. Between the mountain and the plain: prehistoric environment and settlement in the Kaironk Valley. In *The Melanesian environment: change and development,* ed. J. H. Winslow, pp. 61–73. Canberra: Australian National University Press.

Chowning, Ann, and Jane Goodale. 1966. A flint industry from southwest New Britain, Territory of New Guinea. *Asian Perspectives* 9:150–153.

Christensen, O. A. 1975. Hunters and horticulturalists: a preliminary report on the 1972–74 excavations in the Manim Valley, Papua New Guinea. *Mankind* 10:24–37.

Downie, J. E., and J. P. White. 1978. Balof shelter, New Ireland: report on a small excavation. *Records of the Australian Museum:* in press.

Fox, R. B. 1970. *The Tabon caves.* Monograph 1, National Museum of the Philippines, Manila.

Glover, I. C. 1971. Prehistoric research in Timor. In *Aboriginal man and environment in Australia,* ed. D. J. Mulvaney and Jack Golson, pp. 158–181. Canberra: Australian National University Press.

——— and E. A. Glover. 1970. Prehistoric flaked stone tools from Timor and Flores. *Mankind* 7:188–190.

Golson, Jack. 1972. Land connections, sea barriers, and the relationship of Australian and New Guinea prehistory. In *Bridge and barrier: the natural and cultural history of Torres Strait,* ed. Donald Walker, pp. 375–398. Australian National University, Department of Biogeography and Geomorphology, Publication BG/3.

———. 1977. No room at the top: agricultural intensification in the New Guinea Highlands. In *Sunda and Sahul: prehistoric studies in Southeast Asia, Melanesia and Australia,* ed. Jim Allen, Jack Golson, and Rhys Jones, pp. 601–638. London: Academic Press.

——— and P. J. Hughes. 1976. The appearance of plant and animal domestication in New Guinea. In *La Préhistoire océanienne,* ed. José Garanger. IXe Congrès Union International des Sciences Préhistoriques et Protohistoriques, Nice, Colloque 22:88–100. Paris: Centre National de la Recherche Scientifique.

Gould, R. A. 1968. A preliminary report on excavations at Puntutjarpa rockshelter, near the Warburton ranges, Western Australia. *Archaeology and Physical Anthropology in Oceania* 3:161–185.

Green, R. C. 1976. Languages of the southeast Solomons and their historical relationships. In *Southeast Solomon Islands cultural history,* ed. R. C. Green and M. M. Cresswell. *Royal Society of New Zealand Bulletin* 11:47–60.

Harris, D. R. 1977. Subsistence strategies across Torres Strait. In *Sunda and Sahul: prehistoric studies in Southeast Asia, Melanesia and Australia,* ed. Jim Allen, Jack Golson, and Rhys Jones, pp. 421–463. London: Academic Press.

Hayden, Brian. 1977. Sticks and stones and ground edge axes: the Upper Palaeolithic in Southeast Asia? In *Sunda and Sahul: prehistoric studies in Southeast Asia, Melanesia and Australia,* ed. Jim Allen, Jack Golson, and Rhys Jones, pp. 73–109. London: Academic Press.

Hope, G. S., J. A. Peterson, Ian Allison, and Uwe Radok. 1976. *The equatorial glaciers of New Guinea.* Rotterdam: A. A. Balkema.

Jones, Rhys. 1969. Fire-stick farming. *Australian Natural History* 16:224–228.

———. 1973. Emerging picture of Pleistocene Australians. *Nature* 246:278–281.

———. 1975. The Neolithic Palaeolithic and the hunting gardeners: man and land in the Antipodes. In *Quarternary studies,* ed. R. P. Suggate and M. M. Cresswell, pp. 21–34. Wellington: Royal Society of New Zealand.

———. 1977. Man as an element of a continental fauna: the case of the sundering of the Bassian bridge. In *Sunda and Sahul: prehistoric studies in Southeast Asia, Melanesia and Australia,* ed. Jim Allen, Jack Golson, and Rhys Jones, pp. 317–386. London: Academic Press.

Lampert, R. J. 1971. Burrill Lake and Currarong. *Terra Australis* 1.

Luebbers, R. A. 1975. Ancient boomerangs discovered in South Australia. *Nature* 253:39.

Maynard, Lesley. 1976. An archaeological approach to the study of Australian rock art. Master's thesis, University of Sydney.

Moore, D. R. 1972. Cape York Aborigines and islanders of the western Torres Strait. In *Bridge and barrier: the natural and cultural history of Torres Strait,* ed. Donald Walker, pp. 327–344. Australian National University, Department of Biogeography and Geomorphology, Publication BG/3.

Morgan, John. 1852. *The life and adventures of William Buckley.* Hobart, Tasmania: Archibald MacDougall.

Morren, G. B. 1974. Settlement strategies and hunting in a New Guinean society. Ph.D. dissertation, Columbia University.

Mulvaney, D. J. 1975. *The prehistory of Australia.* Melbourne: Penguin Books.

———. 1976. "The chain of connection": the material evidence. In *Tribes and boundaries in Australia,* ed. N. C. Peterson, pp. 72–94. Canberra: Australian Institute of Aboriginal Studies.

——— and R. P. Soejono. 1971. Archaeology in Sulawesi, Indonesia. *Antiquity* 45:26–33.

Paijmans, K., ed. 1976. *New Guinea vegetation.* Canberra: Australian National University Press.

Rowley, C. D. 1970. *The destruction of aboriginal society.* Canberra: Australian National University Press.

Schrire, Carmel. 1972. Ethnoarchaeological models and subsistence behaviour in Arnhem Land. In *Models in archaeology,* ed. D. L. Clarke, pp. 653–670. London: Methuen.

Shutler, Richard, Jr., and J. C. Marck. 1975. On the dispersal of the Austronesian horticulturalists. *Archaeology and Physical Anthropology in Oceania* 10:81–113.

——— and M. E. Shutler. 1975. *Oceanic prehistory.* Menlo Park, California: Cummings Publishing Co.

Townsend, P. K. 1974. Sago production in a New Guinea economy. *Human Ecology* 2:217–236.

Walker, Donald, ed. 1972. *Bridge and barrier: the natural and cultural history of Torres Strait.* Australian National University, Department of Biogeography and Geomorphology, Publication BG/3.

Watson, J. B. 1977. Pigs, fodder and the Jones Effect in postipomoean New Guinea. *Ethnology* 16:57–70.

White, Carmel. 1971. Man and environment in northwest Arnhem Land. In *Aboriginal man and environment in Australia,* ed. D. J. Mulvaney and Jack Golson, pp. 141–157. Canberra: Australian National University Press.

White, J. P. 1968. Ston naip bilong tumbuna: the living stone age in New Guinea. In *La Préhistoire: problèmes et tendances,* ed. Denise de Sonneville-Bordes, pp. 511–516. Paris: Centre National de la Recherche Scientifique.

———. 1969. Typologies for some prehistoric flaked stone artefacts of the Australian New Guinea highlands. *Archaeology and Physical Anthropology in Oceania* 4:18–46.

———. 1971. New Guinea and Australian prehistory: the "Neolithic problem." In *Aboriginal man and environment in Australia,* ed. D. J. Mulvaney and Jack Golson, pp. 182–195. Canberra: Australian National University Press.

———. 1972. Ol Tumbuna. Archaeological excavations in the central highlands, Papua New Guinea. *Terra Australis* 2.

———. 1977. Crude, colourless and uninteresting? Prehistorians and their views on the stone tools of Sunda- and Sahul-lands. In *Sunda and Sahul: prehistoric studies in Southeast Asia, Melanesia and Australia,* ed. Jim Allen, Jack Golson, and Rhys Jones, pp. 13–30. London: Academic Press.

———. 1979. Papua New Guinea: Pleistocene prospects. In a festschrift for H. L. Movius, Jr. (title not yet announced), ed. A. K. Ghosh and W. G. Solheim II. Forthcoming.

———, K. A. W. Cook, and B. P. Ruxton. 1970. Kosipe: a late Pleistocene site in the Papuan highlands. *Proceedings of the Prehistoric Society* 36:152–170.

Wright, R. V. S. 1976. Evolutionary process and semantics: Australian prehistoric tooth size as a local adjustment. In *The origin of the Austra-*

J. PETER WHITE

lians, ed. R. L. Kirk and A. G. Thorne, pp. 265–274. Canberra: Australian Institute of Aboriginal Studies.

———— ed. 1971. *Archaeology of the Gallus site, Koonalda Cave.* Australian Aboriginal Studies 26, Canberra.

Yen, D. E. 1973. The origins of Oceanic agriculture. *Archaeology and Physical Anthropology in Oceania* 8:68–85.

————. 1977. Hoabinhian horticulture? The evidence and questions from northeast Thailand. In *Sunda and Sahul: prehistoric studies in Southeast Asia, Melanesia and Australia,* ed. Jim Allen, Jack Golson, and Rhys Jones, pp. 567–599. London: Academic Press.

Epilogue

JESSE D. JENNINGS

The problem with a book is not the first paragraph, but the last. How can one end gracefully? The summary usually found in works of this kind does not seem quite appropriate here, since each chapter is itself a summary to some degree. I have opted instead for a few short comments and a glimpse into the future.

The first matter that comes to mind is the one mentioned in the opening sentence of the Introduction—the persistent concern with origins, which all observers of the Polynesian world have wrestled with since its discovery. This book documents today's focus on the very same question. But the foregoing pages have also demonstrated the current near certainty of many answers relative to Polynesian beginnings, the time of the dispersal, and some of the mechanisms of the dispersal process.

Other comments are appropriate. Readers will have experienced frustration with the scantiness of our overall knowledge. Time after time authors candidly admit gaps in the information. The record is woefully incomplete. For most of the island groups the sparse archaeological knowledge we do possess has been acquired in less than 20 years, so time itself is one explanation of the spotty nature of the data. Furthermore, archaeologists with interests in the Pacific are rare. Five of the best known are authors here: Davidson, Emory, Green, Howells, and Sinoto. The other contributors are newer scholars—the vanguard, one hopes, of an increasing number of young men and women who will savor the excitement and challenge of study of the prehistoric Pacific. Already data accumulation is accelerating, with many long-range programs in progress but not yet finished. New publication outlets are being developed, so we can expect the volume of research reports to grow and to increase the dissemination of information, terribly restricted until this decade.

Although this book can be taken as the "last" word in late 1978, it appears at the threshold of new ferment in Polynesian and Oceanic studies. Through contact with young scholars (some are authors here) I have come to know of many projected studies that will move beyond the empirical culture history of these chapters into theoretical problems. One is a long-range multivariate analysis of cranial variation, which will result in a confirmation or refutation of Chapter 11 herein. In another case, an individual is embarking on a comparative historical review of the origins of the ubiquitous stratified pyramidal social structure of Polynesia. The thesis he wishes to test is that the Lapita possessed—even developed —the system, and that it survived and was intensified because it exactly fitted the ecological and social needs of Polynesia as populations burgeoned on newly discovered islands. Another scholar wishes to challenge the "complacency" he sees in this book with respect to East Polynesia's origin and dispersal and its development of variant cultures in the open Pacific. In still another vein, I know of a person who recog-

nizes that the Polynesians' dependence on the sea is far too often taken for granted in ecological statements. He proposes to analyze intensively and from every source—archaeology, ethnology, and linguistics—the details of man's symbiosis with marine fauna, including harvesting techniques. That such an obvious topic has been neglected is, of course, a result of the primary necessity for learning the sheer chronology and completing the cultural inventory of each island—a task that is far from finished.

Thus, although one can hope that expansion of raw data collecting in archaeological research will continue unabated, it is evident that topical studies stimulated by theoretical concerns will proliferate. And where better? Given the physical limits, the clearly marked ecological zones, the lack of frequent prehistoric cultural exchange, and the easily detected evidences of trade where contact between island chains has occurred, the islands provide nearly perfect situations for the testing of hypotheses.

As for the book itself, it reflects the seriousness with which the authors took the writing of their contributions. They are—or have reason to be—pleased with their part in fashioning the key needed to understand Polynesia's amazing history. As editor, I am proud of the volume. It is sound, factual, and easily read. It represents fairly the state of knowledge. I hope that each reader, having finished it by now, will have profited from and enjoyed the reading.

Glossary
Contributors
Index

Glossary

Aggraded   Filled and level raised by deposition of sediment.

Agnatic   Related on or descended from the paternal or male side.

Ahu   A stone heap or platform used by the Polynesians as a marker or memorial.

Ahupua'a   A territorial division of an island, the boundaries being usually topographic and the people therein possibly forming a social and/or economic self-sufficient unit.

Andesite line   The boundary dividing the Asiatic continental crust from the Pacific oceanic crust. West of the line are andesitic basalts and other acidic rock. To the east the basalts are olivine and other basic or soda-rich rock. Pacific basalts are usually finer grained than andesitic ones.

Aroid   Any of the plants of the family *Aracea*, including the genus *Arum*. The lily is an example of *Arum*, as is Taro.

Autochthonous   Native to a particular place; aboriginal or indigenous.

Avanga   Cremation pits.

Avifauna   The birds of a given region, considered as a whole.

Baret   A ditch.

Biotope   A limited ecological region or niche in which the environment is suitable for certain forms of life.

Bunded   Embanked or diked.

Canalize   To make a canal or canals through; to divert into channels; to give a certain direction or outlet to.

Cargo cult   A revivalistic or revitalization religious movement in various Melanesian locations. In the face of economic and social changes and deprivation, such cults arise; the cult theme is a return to "the old ways."

Cist   A coffin or grave, often of stone.

Commensality   Eating at the same table, sharing meals; not competing while occupying the same area as another individual or group having independent or different values or customs.

Conical-clan structure   Another term for pyramidal stratified social order, where social power is concentrated in the tip of the pyramid.

Conurbation   A predominantly urban region or metropolis.

Cultigen   A cultivated, fully domesticated plant lacking a wild or uncultivated counterpart.

Cuscus   Phalanger, a genus of arboreal marsupial quadruped found in New Guinea and adjacent islands.

Debitage   Usually applied to the scrap created by the chipping of flint to form stone tools.

Devolution   Passage onward from stage to stage; transmittal of an unexercised right; transfer of power or authority from central to local government. Usually implies degeneration or retrograde evolution.

Diachronic   Relating to changes in a system between successive points in time; a historical concept.

Easting   A navigational term meaning eastward movement.

Edaphic   Of or pertaining to soil, especially as it affects living organisms.

Endemism   Prevalent in or peculiar to a particular locality or people. In ecology, native or confined to a certain region; having a comparatively restricted distribution.

Endogamy   Marriage within a specific tribe or similar social unit.

Esi   A mound or platform used as a resting place for chiefs in Tonga.

Eustacy   World-wide change in sea levels.

Fagaloa volcanics   The term applied to the last major prehistoric lava flows in Western Samoa.

Faitoka   A burial mound of chiefs in Tonga.

Fale   A house.

Fale afolau   A large house of complicated construction in Samoa, said to be originally a Tongan form.

First-order Indicating that evidence is not regional.

Geomorphic Of or pertaining to the form of the earth or the forms of its surface.

Glottochronology A method of calculating the period of separation of two related languages or dialects by formulas derived from observed language change through time.

Hapū A Maori clan or subtribe; section of a large tribe.

Hei tiki A Maori neck ornament of anthropomorphic form.

Holocene Recent (from about 8300 B.C. to the present), or from the end of the Pleistocene Ice Age to the present.

Hominid A member of the *Hominidae* family, comprising man and his ancestors.

Homo erectus An extinct form of *Homo sapiens* that lived about a half-million years ago, prior to Neanderthal man.

Homo sapiens Modern man, who evolved from Neanderthal man 35,000 to 50,000 years ago.

Hydration rind A thin layer that results from the taking up of water from the environment by volcanic glass (obsidian). The rind grows thicker through time.

Hydrology The scientific study of the properties, distribution, and effects of water on the earth's surface, in the soil and underlying rocks, and in the atmosphere.

Hydrophile Something with a strong affinity or requirement for water.

Hydrophyte A plant that grows in, and is adapted to, an aquatic or very wet environment.

Internecine Mutually destructive; of or pertaining to conflict or struggle within a group.

Iwi Maori for tribe or people.

Jabbing fishhooks Hooks having the point or barb at an angle to the stem, in contrast to rotating fishhooks, which are round. These are meaningless descriptive terms, but are retained here because the nomenclature is embedded in Polynesian literature.

Kahawai A Maori fishing lure; a wooden shank with a bone point.

Kōkōwai Maori for red ocher.

Langi A burial mound for members of the Tui Tonga line in Tonga.

Lethrinids Fish that swarm on coral reefs, of the family *Lethrinidae*.

Liku The cliff-bound coast of a Tongan island,

usually composed of raised coral limestone.

Malae (Mala'e) Samoan (Tongan) for meeting ground or village green.

Mana A sacred essence, energy, or power possessed by objects, places, or even people.

Marae The temples of East Polynesia.

Matau A one-piece fishhook, widespread in Polynesia.

Matrilineal Inheriting or determining descent through the female line.

Megafauna The large animals of a region.

Multivallate Surrounded or bordered by many ridges or raised edges.

Pā Maori for fortified place.

Paenga A patrilocal extended family.

Paleosol A buried or fossil soil or soil horizon.

Palynology The science dealing with live and fossil spores, pollen grains, and other microscopic plant structures.

Parthenocarpic Producing fruit without the fertilization of an egg in the ovary.

Patinated Covered with or having a patina (an incrustation produced by oxidation, or a similar film on a substance; a surface calcification of implements usually indicative of great age).

Patrilineal Inheriting or determining descent through the male line.

Patu A short striking or thrusting weapon of the Maori.

Patu ōnewa A short striking weapon of dark grey stone.

Pāua Maori for iridescent shell, *Haliotis* spp.

Peat A highly organic soil, more than 50 percent combustible, composed of partially decayed vegetable matter found in marshy or damp regions.

Pelagic Of or pertaining to the seas or oceans; living or growing at or near the surface of the ocean, far from land (as certain animals and plants).

Phenotype The observable constitution of an organism.

Phenotypic The appearance of an organism as a result of the interaction of the genotype and the environment.

Pii The Polynesian linguistic practice of name avoidance.

Pleistocene Originating one to three million years ago; an era characterized by widespread glacial ice and the appearance of man.

Polity A particular form or system of government; a state or otherwise organized community or body (or a government or administrative regulation).

Pollen analysis An analysis of the fertilizing element of flowering plants.

Potassium-argon dating A method for estimating the age of a mineral by determining the ratio of argon to potassium in the mineral, based on the natural radioactive disintegration of potassium into argon.

Prestation A gift; a levied tax or payment.

Processual In anthropology, concerned with process in culture change.

Proto- Refers to an earlier unobserved or hypothetical form, such as Proto-Polynesian language.

Protohistory The earliest form of history. In anthropology, generally used to mean just prior to recorded history.

Pule Cowrie shell.

Radiocarbon dating Determination of the age of objects of plant or animal origin by measurement of the radioactivity of their radiocarbon content.

Ramage A descent group whose members are descended from one ancestor.

Rei puta A Maori neck ornament made of whale tooth.

Rotating fishhooks Round fishhooks as contrasted to jabbing fishhooks, which have the point or barb at an angle to the stem. These are meaningless descriptive terms, but are retained here because the nomenclature is embedded in Polynesian literature.

Rua Maori for pit or hole, especially a food storage pit.

Scoria A product of vulcanism that resembles coarse pumice, cinder, or slag.

Slash-and-burn A means of clearing ground for planting crops by cutting the ground cover and burning it; the resulting ashes enrich the soil.

Slipped Used to describe a thin wash of mineral pigment on pottery, such as "red-slipped."

Speleotherms Interior deposits in a cave (such as stalactites or stalagmites) carried and deposited by water with minerals in solution.

Star mound A stone structure, often 2 m high by 10 to 15 m or more in total diameter, with several projecting arms, which resembles a cog wheel or starfish. Its aboriginal function is not clear.

Subduction The act of taking away or withdrawing something; the act or process of subduing.

Suids Swine.

Swidden See *Slash-and-burn*.

Tapu The Maori term for being under religious or ceremonial restriction.

Taro A stemless araceous plant (*Colocasia esculenta* or *C. antiquorum*) cultivated for the tuberous starchy, edible root; an Aroid.

Tephra The volcanic material (such as scoria or dust) ejected during an eruption.

Tropophyte A plant adapted to climatic conditions in which periods of heavy rainfall alternate with periods of drought.

Tuff Volcanic ash, sometimes consolidated.

Unitary Of or pertaining to a unit or units; or, of or pertaining to or characterized by unity. Whole, having the indivisible character of a unit. Pertaining to a system of government in which the executive, legislative, and judicial powers of each state in a body of states are vested in a central authority.

Via kana A taro-like vegetable, *Cyrtosperma edule*.

Waka Maori for canoe; a group of tribes claiming descent from the crew of one canoe.

Wallaby Any of several small or medium-sized kangaroos of the genera *Macropus, Thylogale,* or *Petrogale,* some of which are no larger than rabbits; native Australian marsupial.

Wallacea Refers to the territory east of a biogeographic boundary defined by the naturalist A. R. Wallace. Wallace's Line passes between Borneo and the Celebes Islands and marks the eastern edge of the distribution of mammals. East of the line only marsupials and one or two mammals (bats or rats) occur.

Whānau Maori for family group; household.

Whare Maori for house.

Whare puni A substantial rectangular house with an open porch.

Wrasse Reef-dwelling shallow water fish of the family *Labridae,* especially the genus Labrus.

Contributors

Peter S. Bellwood's professional career began at the University of Auckland, New Zealand, in 1967. Currently Senior Lecturer in Prehistory at the Australian National University, he gained his extensive Pacific fieldwork experience in the Marquesas Islands, the Cook Islands, New Zealand, Northern Sulawesi, the Talaud Islands (eastern Indonesia) and Brunei. Although he has written many journal articles, he is best known for his 1975 article on the prehistory of Oceania and his recent books *Man's Conquest of the Pacific* and *The Polynesians*.

Ross Clark received his Ph.D. from the University of California (San Diego) and is now Senior Lecturer in Linguistics, Department of Anthropology, University of Auckland. His main research interests are comparative and historical problems of the Polynesian, pidgin, and creole languages in the Pacific. His publications include *Aspects of Proto-Polynesian Syntax* and various papers.

Janet M. Davidson was educated at Victoria University, Wellington, and the University of Auckland. She has done fieldwork in the Society Islands, Tonga, Samoa, and the Caroline Islands (Micronesia) as well as in New Zealand. Appointed in 1966 as E. Earle Vaile Archaeologist, Auckland Institute and Museum, she continues there. For two years she was Rhodes Visiting Fellow, Lady Margaret Hall, Oxford. Known for a number of provocative and stimulating papers, her major work to date is the definitive two-volume *Archaeology in Western Samoa*, which she edited with Roger Green and to which she was a major contributor.

Kenneth P. Emory completed his graduate work at Harvard and Yale universities. For 50 years he has been Anthropologist and Head of the Department of Anthropology at the Bernice P. Bishop Museum in Honolulu, where he has done research, written scores of definitive articles and publications, and headed a host of research expeditions. He was a pioneer in the study of the monumental religious structures of Hawaii and the Society Islands. Noted for seminal research in archaeology, linguistics, and ethnology, his monographs on Kapingamarangi and the Tuamotus are regarded as classics. He celebrated his eightieth birthday the day he forwarded the manuscript that appears as Chapter 8 herein. He continues to work daily at the Bishop Museum, where he offers stimulus and criticism to his younger colleagues.

Ben R. Finney is Professor of Anthropology at the University of Hawaii. Although trained as a social anthropologist, with a Ph.D. from Harvard University in 1964, he has been intrigued with Polynesian voyaging since 1956, when he sailed on copra schooners through the Society, Tuamotu, and Marquesas archipelagoes. He is the editor of *Pacific Navigation and Voyaging* and most recently directed the *Hōkūle'a* project described in his chapter. *The Way to Tahiti*, a popular account of the voyage, will be published this year.

Everett L. Frost received his doctorate at the University of Oregon in 1970. He has since surveyed and excavated sites in Fiji and Hawaii and assisted his wife, Janet, in American Samoan research. He has served as Visiting Associate Professor of Anthropology at the University of Hawaii and is currently Associate Professor of Anthropology and Assistant Dean, College of Liberal Arts and Sciences, Eastern New Mexico University. His publications include a monograph on Fijian fortified sites and *Cultural and Social Anthropology*, an introductory textbook coauthored with E. Adamson Hoebel.

Roger C. Green holds a chair in prehistory at the Department of Anthropology, University of Auckland. Although an American-trained archaeologist of the southwestern United States, he has long been associated with New Zealand, from which he has worked extensively on the prehistory of a number of Pacific Islands. These include Hawaii, Mangareva, Moorea in the Society Islands, Western Samoa, Tonga, Fiji, and the southeast Solomons. In New Zealand he was for three years the Captain James Cook Fellow of the Royal Society of New Zealand; from a base at the Auckland Institute and Museum he spent three years on the first stage of a cultural history program in the southeast Solomons. This program, under the direction of Green and Douglas E. Yen, is currently concentrating on the Outer Eastern Islands and the Lapita sites referred to in this volume.

William Howells was educated at Harvard University. After being on the staff of the American Museum of Natural History in New York, he taught anthropology at the University of Wisconsin from 1939 to 1954 and at Harvard from 1954 to 1974, when he retired from teaching. He continues at Harvard's Peabody Museum as Honorary Curator of Somatology. His most recent fieldwork was in the Solomon Islands with the Harvard Solomons Project. His books include *Mankind So Far, The Heathens, Mankind in the Making, Evolution of the Genus Homo,* and *The Pacific Islanders.* Multivariate analysis applied to recent and fossil man is a particular field of interest, his principal publication in this area being *Cranial Variation in Man;* he has been continuing such work with special reference to the Pacific.

Although **Jesse D. Jennings** is primarily known as a North Americanist, in the past decade he has developed an interest in Pacific prehistory. He has worked extensively on sites in Western Samoa on the islands of Upolu and Manono, where his work has been directed to extending and expanding the earlier work of Green and Davidson. A major publication resulting from his research is *Excavations on Upolu, Western Samoa.* Since 1948 he has been at the University of Utah, where he is now Distinguished Professor of Anthropology. His publications are chiefly American in content, the most important being *The Prehistory of North America* and *Ancient Native Americans.* He is a recipient of the Viking Fund Medal for Archaeology and has recently been elected to membership in the National Academy of Sciences.

Patrick V. Kirch, anthropologist at the Bernice P. Bishop Museum in Honolulu, received his Ph.D. from Yale University. In addition to directing numerous archaeological surveys and ex-

cavations in the Hawaiian Islands, he has pursued ethnographic and archaeological research in the Solomon Islands, in the West Polynesian islands of Futuna, Uvea, and Tonga, and in western Micronesia (Palau and Yap). His research interests include the reconstruction of settlement-subsistence systems, Oceanic ethnobotany, and ecological approaches to the study of complex societies in the humid tropics.

Patrick C. McCoy received his doctorate from Washington State University, and in 1971 took employment with the Bishop Museum. After research in North America (on plains, plateaus, and the Northwest Coast) his recent work has stressed Oceania. He has had field experience in Polynesia, Australia, and Melanesia and presently has research projects under way in Hawaii and the Solomon Islands.

Yosihiko H. Sinoto received his D.Sc. degree at the University of Hokkaido, Japan. His work in archaeology began late in the 1940s, when he was employed at the Archaeological Institute of Japan in Ichikawa. From there he joined the Bishop Museum, where he is now chairman of the Department of Anthropology. His Polynesian archaeological interests and experience include Hawaii, the Society and Marquesas islands, and other areas in French Polynesia. Best known for the definitive research on the Marquesas that he reviews in this volume, his current research is concentrated on very early sites on Huahine in the Society Islands.

H. David Tuggle received his Ph.D. in 1970 from the University of Arizona. Currently Associate Professor of Anthropology at the University of Hawaii, he taught previously at the State University of New York in Albany. His field experience includes research in Arizona, New York, Mexico, Hawaii, and the Philippines.

J. Peter White is Reader in Prehistory in the Department of Anthropology, University of Sydney, Australia. Educated at Melbourne, Cambridge, and the Australian National University (Ph.D. 1967), he has worked in Papua New Guinea, since 1963 on archaeological and related ethnographic topics. He has done research too in parts of Australia, especially on stone tools. He has written a book on popular misinterpretation of archaeology (*The Past Is Human*), as well as some on more conventional topics.

Index

Bananas, 173, 174, 289, 292, 297
Banks, Joseph, 223, 238
Banks Islands, 15, 38, 45, 343
Barets, 362–365
Bark-cloth manufacture, 9, 44, 68
Barracouta lure, 231
Barrau, Jacques, 289, 291, 297
Barthel, T. S., 158
Basalt, 149, 152, 243, 299
Bats, 223
Bauan Fijian language, 262
Bay of Islands, New Zealand, 223
Bay of Plenty, New Zealand, 234, 243
Bellona, Solomons, 20, 51, 280
Bellows Dune, Oahu, 189, 190, 192–193
Bellwood, Peter S., 2, 6–24, 219, 308–321
Best, Elsdon, 226, 324, 325
Best, Simon, 64, 74, 77
Biggs, B. G., 201, 256, 264, 266, 267
"Big Man" concept, 12
Bird cult, 156–158
Birds, 8, 37, 114, 174, 223, 225, 235, 237, 267
Birks, Helen, 29, 30, 63, 88
Birks, Lawrence, 29, 30, 63, 66, 79, 88
Bishop Museum, Honolulu, 63, 184, 201, 202, 203, 204, 213, 272, 299
Bismarck Archipelago, 352, 354, 357; Lapita sites, 27, 30, 47, 343
Black Rocks, Palliser Bay, 238
Boenechea, Don, 200
Boirra site, New Caledonia, 54
Bone artifacts, 21, 40, 92, 112, 117, 123, 149, 175
Bones, human, 68, 120, 149, 180, 202, 366, 368–369, 370
Boomerangs, 369–370
Borneo, 360
Borrowing, in language, 251, 256, 263–265
Bougainville, Louis de, 83, 200
Bougainville, Solomons, 16
Bracken fern, 235, 288
Breadfruit, 173, 289, 292, 302, 303
Breast ornaments, 127
Buck, Peter H., 49, 86, 225, 324, 325, 348
Buduna, New Britain, 50
Buka, Solomons , 16, 19, 20
Bulrush reed, 143, 144
Burial sites: Carolines, 23; Tonga, 35, 87, 102–107, 310, 313; Samoa, 94, 101; Societies, 113, 121, 122, 219; Easter, 156; Hawaii, 180, 193–194; New Zealand, 202, 219,

240, 242; Australia, 370. *See also* Mounds; Temples
Burrows, E. G., 9, 10, 310
Bush birds, 37, 237

Cannibalism, 94, 95, 101, 120, 142, 159, 225, 242, 243
Canoe petroglyphs, 209
Canoes, 9, 161, 324–332, 338–339, 344, 350; Hawaiian, 171, 175, 329, 331; double, 203, 326, 331, 332, 334, 335, 341, 344, 346–347, 348; Tahitian, 203, 209, 329; Tuamotuan, 203, 329; Maori, 245
Canoes of Oceania (Haddon and Hornell), 324
Cape Kumukahi, Hawaii, 335
Cape York, Australia, 371
Caroline Islands, 7, 9, 12, 18, 22, 23, 335–336
Cassels, R. J. S., 319
Cassis shell, 113, 117, 119
Caucasoids, 11, 272
Cave Bay Cave, Australia, 370
Caves, 160, 161, 180–181, 182
Cellars, 235
Central Eastern languages, 258, 260, 264
Central Pacific languages, 79, 256, 257
Centre National de la Recherche Scientifique (CNRS), 201
Cereals, 12
Ceremonial sites, 23, 75–77, 180, 314–316. *See also* Ahu; Marae; Temples
Chang, K. C., 146
Chariots of the Gods? (Däniken), 136, 281
Chatham Islands, 149, 223
Chert, 38, 39, 77, 92, 299, 354
Chestnut tree, Tahitian, 292
Chickens, 37, 68, 140, 148, 161, 174, 203
Chiefdoms: Polynesian, 11–12, 305, 309, 313, 316–317; Hawaiian, 178, 180, 182, 193–195, 296, 303, 305, 314
Chiefly units, 313, 314
Chisels, 113, 117, 119, 189, 203, 204
Christianity, 83, 136
Clark, Ross, 4–5, 249–268
Classic Maori culture, New Zealand, 225, 227–228, 231, 232, 233–234, 244–245, 319
Clay, 362
Cloak pins, 113, 231
Clustering, 315–317
Coastal settlements, 317; New Guinea, 19, 366–367; Samoa, 93–

94, 96, 98, 99, 101–102; Marquesas, 112
Coconut, 173, 203, 298, 302, 348
Coconut oil processing, 66
Cognates, in languages, 251, 264
Colocasia, 289
Combs, wooden, 232, 234
Commoner units, 313–315
Communication networks, 243–244
Compound-shank hook, 117, 119, 203, 231
Conical-clan structure, 195
Contact. *See* European contact; New World contact; South American contact
Conus shell, 92, 113, 126–127, 204
Cook, James, 83, 105, 111, 152, 182–183, 200, 207, 213, 215, 216, 223, 225, 249, 268, 315, 334, 335
Cooke, G. H., 137
Cooking, 35, 37, 99, 186, 242, 295. *See also* Ovens
Cook Islands, 7, 9, 13, 215, 265, 309, 313, 339; settlements, 316, 318, 343, 344
Cook Strait, New Zealand, 228
Coral, 39, 68, 112, 131
Cordy, R. H., 191, 320
Cores, 149, 354, 369
Coromandel Peninsula, New Zealand, 228, 232, 235, 237, 240, 242, 243
Cowrie (pule) shells, 92, 216
Crania studies, 275–277, 281, 282–283
Cremation pits, 149
Crop rotation, 291
Cultivation techniques, 13, 289–290
Cultural drift, 194–195
Currents. *See* Ocean currents
Cuscus, 37
Cut-away relief, 40

Dalo (taro), 71–72
Damming, 194
Dari bowls, 68, 73, 78
Darling River, Australia, 371
Dating methods, 185–186; glottochronological, 13, 15, 260–266
Daughter languages, 250, 252. *See also* Language
Davidson, Janet M., 4, 23, 82–107, 121, 201, 222–245, 298
Decorative motifs and techniques: dentate stamping, 19, 40, 64; Lapita, 19, 38, 40–44, 64, 86–87, 90, 91; Mangaasi, 20; impressing, 40, 47, 48, 64, 66–68, 72–73; incising, 40, 43, 66, 68–70, 72; modeling, 40; appliqué, 40, 72; relief,

Fornander, Abraham, 323–324, 325
Fortified sites; Fiji, 70–75; in neolithic cultural complexes, 71; distribution, 71–72; chronology, 72, 75; Lau, 74; Samoa, 95, 101, 315; Tonga, 105–107; Hawaii, 180, 315; New Zealand, 223, 226, 239, 240, 242–243, 245, 315, 319; Marquesas, 303, 315; Australs, 315
Forts, 68; ridge, 70, 71, 72, 74, 180, 303, 315; ring-ditch, 71–72, 74; Sigatoka, 72; Wakaya, 72–73; Taveuni, 73–74; pā, 226, 239, 243, 245, 302
Fosberg, F. R., 287
Fotoruma Cave, Guadalcanal, 47, 357
Foué Peninsula, New Caledonia, 27
Foveaux Strait, New Zealand, 237
Freeman, J. D., 86
Friendly Isles. *See* Tonga Islands
Frimigacci, Daniel, 48, 54, 55
Frost, Everett L., 3, 61–80, 64, 73, 74, 77
Frost, J. O., 88
Futuna, New Hebrides, 83, 288, 289; Lapita culture, 20, 38, 44, 78, 91; social structure, 292, 295–296, 303
Futuna-Aniwa (language subgroup), 253, 259

Gambier Islands, 344
Gaming disks, 39
Garanger, José, 47, 53
Garua Island, New Britain, 50
Gathering, 17, 237
Genealogy, 185, 189, 201
Genetic drift, 280, 281, 282
Genetics, 11; language relationships, 15; variations within populations, 272; blood genetic traits, 278–279
Gifford, E. W., 29, 53, 54, 63, 64
Gigantism, 297
Gilbert Islands, 7, 9, 12, 22, 284
Glaciers, 358
Gladwin, Thomas, 334
Glottochronological dating, 13, 15, 260–266
Godwits, 237
Golson, Jack, 29, 30, 55, 64, 86–87, 88, 105, 125, 132, 163, 227, 297
Gorman, C. F., 296
Gourds, 203, 223, 298
Grace, George, 256, 262
Grasslands, 358, 366
Graters, 113, 114, 203
Green, K., 266, 267, 268
Green, Roger C., 2–3, 27–57, 64,

65, 75, 79, 87, 88, 91, 92, 121, 125, 185, 201, 204–205, 207, 215, 218, 227, 230, 256, 260, 265, 283–284, 298, 299, 313, 319, 343, 344
Greenstone, 243
Grinders, 39
Groube, L. M., 30, 32, 37, 43, 47, 78, 79, 88, 89–90, 93, 94, 123, 227, 297–298
Ground-edge tools, 15–16, 360, 369
Guadalcanal, Solomons, 47, 257
Guam, Marianas, 22

Ha'amonga-a-Maui trilithon, Hahahe, 105
Ha'apai, Tonga, 83, 84, 88–89, 90, 105
Ha'ateiho site, Tongatapu, 89
Ha'atuatua site, Nukuhiva, 112, 117, 120, 125, 127, 217
Habitation sites, 70, 107; Easter, 145–146, 148, 160; Hawaii, 179–180, 186, 187–188, 193; Societies, 202, 204–205; New Zealand, 240
Haddon, A. C., 324
Hahahe, Tonga, 105
Hahei, Coromandel Peninsula, 242
Halawa Valley, Molokai, 186, 189, 190, 191, 192–193, 318
Hale, Horatio, 61
Haleakala crater, Maui, 192, 218
Hanatukua site, Hivaoa, 117, 125, 126, 127, 314, 315–316
Hanaui site, Hivaoa, 117, 120
Hand clubs, 130, 202, 203, 217, 233, 243
Hane site, Uahuka, 110, 112, 113, 117, 120, 121, 122, 123, 126, 127, 129, 130, 132, 203, 217, 219, 231
Hapū (clans), 239
Hare moa (stone structures), 146
Hare oka (round houses), 145
Hare paenga (houses), 145
Harpoon heads, 123–125, 203
Hatuatua site. *See* Ha'atuatua site
Havai'i, 217. *See also* Raiatea
Hawaii, island of, 171; agriculture, 173–174, 175, 192, 194, 318–319; society, 178, 193, 194; excavations, 181, 189, 190–191, 193; settlement, 191, 193; volcanic activity, 194; religious structures, 207, 218
Hawaiian Islands: settlement, 2, 107, 131, 132, 143, 172, 181–182, 184, 186, 189, 190–191, 193–195, 219, 265, 318–319, 335, 343, 347, 348; geography, 7, 9, 167, 171, 176, 186, 187, 344; social struc-

ture, 11–12, 178–181, 182, 188, 192–194, 195–196, 296, 303, 305; irrigation, 13, 172–174, 175, 181, 182, 186, 191–192, 194, 195; artifacts, 121–122, 123, 125, 126, 127, 129–130, 149, 175, 182, 184, 192–193, 214, 215, 216, 217, 302; archeological research, 121, 167, 174–175, 182, 184–185, 299–300; religion, 129–130, 178, 184, 189, 207, 218, 313; habitation complexes, 129–130, 178–180, 310, 315; climate, 167, 186, 194, 318–319; agriculture, 171, 172–175, 184, 186, 187, 191–192, 194, 287, 291, 303, 304, 318–319; communications, 171; resource use, 172–178, 191–193; ahupua'a, 176, 178, 181, 182, 186, 187, 193, 195, 309, chiefdoms, 178, 180, 182, 193–195, 296, 303, 305, 314; population, 181, 184, 186, 188, 190–193, 194, 196; resource zones, 181–182, 190–191, 193–194, 195; cultural origins, 185, 188–194, 265, 272, 335; chronology, 185–186; regional studies, 186–188; economy, 186, 191, 193, 195, 302; cultural drift, 194–195; forts, 315; canoes, 171, 175, 329, 331
Hawaiian language, 185, 201, 217, 249, 250, 251, 253, 260
Hawaiians, 176, 277, 281, 282
Hawke's Bay, New Zealand, 235, 243
Hedrick, J. D., 53
Heiau (temples), 313
Henderson Island, 110, 131
Henry, Teuira, 201
Hereditary ranking, 12, 24, 178, 195–196
Heyerdahl, Thor, 4, 137, 138, 141, 143, 144, 152, 153, 158, 160, 162, 272, 324, 325, 348
Hilo site, Hawaii, 191
Hivaoa, Marquesas, 110, 112, 117, 119, 120, 124, 125, 126, 127, 129, 314, 315–316
Hocart, A. M., 63, 78, 80
Hōkūle'a, voyage, 5, 323, 329, 331, 332, 333, 335–341; significance, 326, 341–350
Holmer, R. N., 99
Holmes, C. Thomas, 326
Holocene Period, 10, 16
Hommon, R. J., 191, 194
Homo erectus, 372
Homo sapiens, 10, 368
Homo sapiens sapiens, 368
Honaunau, Hawaii, 288; mausoleum, 180, 194

130°   150°   170°   170°

BONIN ISLANDS

DAITO ISLANDS   VOLCANO
ISLANDS   · Marcus Island

H   A

20°

Philippine   MARIANA   Wake
Island

ISLANDS   Johnston Atoll ·

Sea

PHILIPPINES   M   I   C   R   O   N   E   S   I   A

YAP ISLANDS   MARSHALL
ISLANDS

PALAU
ISLANDS

CAROLINE   ISLANDS   GILBERT
ISLANDS

M   E   L   A   N   · Nukuoro   · Howland Island

0°   · Kapingamarangi   Baker Island

ADMIRALTY
ISLANDS   NEW
IRELAND   · Nuguria Islands   NAURU   PHOENIX
ISLANDS

IRIAN
JAYA   NEW   BISMARCK
ARCHIPELAGO   Mortlock (Takuu) Islands

GUINEA   PAPUA   Ambitle   ├ Nukumanu Islands   TOKELAU
ISLANDS

NEW GUINEA   NEW
BRITAIN   SOLOMON   ├ Ontong Java   ELLICE
ISLANDS

Arafura Sea   BOUGAINVILLE   Stewart Island (Sikaiana)   P

Port   Shortland   ISLANDS   · Duff Islands   ÎLES WALLIS

Torres Strait   Moresby   CHOISEUL   · Santa Cruz Islands   Futuna

Malaita   ├ Nendo   · Anuta   SAMOA
ISLANDS

GUADALCANAL   Uki   Santa   Tikopia   FIJI   Vanua Levu   Alofi   Niuafo'ou

Bellona   Ana Reef Islands   · Banks Islands   ISLANDS   Niuatoputapu

San   Viti Levu   Taveuni

Coral   Rennell Island   Cristobal   NEW   · Emae   Lau Group   Niue

HEBRIDES   Efate   Lakeba

Sea   Aniwa   TONGA

· West Futuna   ISLANDS

Ouvea   LOYALTY ISLANDS

NEW CALEDONIA   Tongatapu

Île des Pins

AUSTRALIA

Brisbane ·

KERMADEC
ISLANDS

Norfolk Island

Sydney ·

Great Australian Bight   Auckland
NORTH
ISLAND

40°

Melbourne ·

TASMANIA   SOUTH   NEW
ISLAND   ZEALAND

Chatham
Island

BOUNTY ISLANDS

Forget   130°   150°   170°   170°